THE
AMERICAN HERITAGE HISTORY OF

AMERICAN
BUSINESS
&
INDUSTRY

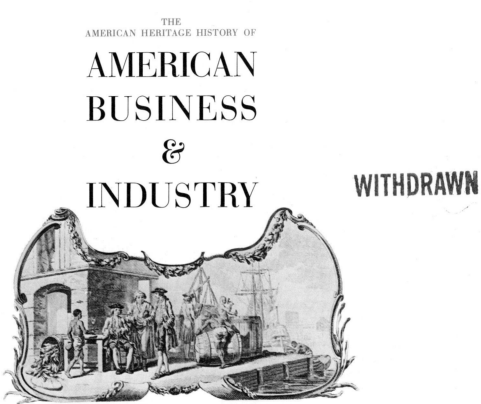

YALE UNIVERSITY ART GALLERY

THE
AMERICAN HERITAGE HISTORY OF

AMERICAN

BUSINESS

&

INDUSTRY

by ALEX GRONER

and the Editors of
AMERICAN HERITAGE
and
BUSINESS WEEK

Introduction by
PAUL A. SAMUELSON
Professor of Economics, M.I.T.

Editor
ALVIN M. JOSEPHY, JR.

Published by
AMERICAN HERITAGE PUBLISHING CO., INC., NEW YORK

D. VALENTINE, *Manual of the Corporations of New York, 1868*

STAFF

ADMINISTRATIVE EDITOR
Mary Elizabeth Wise

ART DIRECTOR
Terrence Gaughan

PICTURE EDITOR
Margaretta Barton

ASSISTANT EDITOR
Peggy Buckwalter

COPY EDITOR
Brenda Niemand

RESEARCHER
Ruth Groner

ADDITIONAL TEXT BY
Jon Borgzinner
and
Alvin M. Josephy, Jr.

AMERICAN HERITAGE PUBLISHING CO., INC.

PRESIDENT AND PUBLISHER
Paul Gottlieb

EDITOR-IN-CHIEF
Joseph J. Thorndike

SENIOR EDITOR, BOOK DIVISION
Alvin M. Josephy, Jr.

EDITORIAL ART DIRECTOR
Murray Belsky

GENERAL MANAGER, BOOK DIVISION
Kenneth W. Leish

Library of Congress Catalog Card Number:
72-80699
I.S.B.N.: Regular Edition 07–001156–7;
De Luxe Edition (slipcased) 07–001157–5

OLD PRINT SHOP

An American market: an 1860 lithograph of the Boston Corn Exchange

Half-Title Page: a scene on a Virginia tobacco wharf, 1775

Title Page: an old print of the Tontine Coffee House, early home of the New York Stock Exchange on Wall Street; opposite page: the twin towers of the World Trade Center, rising over lower Manhattan Island, 1970

CONTENTS

	Introduction		6
Chapter 1	BUSINESS IN THE NEW WORLD	*1607–1783*	9
Chapter 2	THE HOME-GROWN INDUSTRIES	*1783–1820*	47
Chapter 3	A NATION IN MOTION	*1815–1850*	83
Chapter 4	THE BUILDERS	*1840–1865*	117
Chapter 5	UNBRIDLED FREEDOM	*1865–1890*	155
Chapter 6	THE TIME OF THE TITANS	*1890–1918*	193
Chapter 7	GIVING THEM WHAT THEY WANT	*1830–1950*	235
Chapter 8	THE ROLLER COASTER	*1918–1941*	273
Chapter 9	THE AGE OF ORGANIZATION	*1940–1960*	313
Chapter 10	THE NEW AGE OF RESPONSIBILITY	*1960–1972*	351
	INDEX		379

FORCES THAT SHAPED THE AMERICAN BUSINESSMAN

A Series of Picture Portfolios

I	*The Venturesome Spirit*	35
II	*The Inventive Mind*	71
III	*Egalitarianism*	107
IV	*The Wealth of the Land*	143
V	*Opportunity for Enterprise*	183
VI	*The Rage to Learn*	225
VII	*Sense of Community*	263
VIII	*Innovative Knack*	303
IX	*Organizational Genius*	341
X	*Social Conscience*	371

INTRODUCTION

by PAUL A. SAMUELSON

"History is about chaps; geography, about maps." These are not bad for short definitions. But too often the chaps who have dominated our history books were kings, presidents, ambassadors, and generals. These pirouetted at the visible peak of the huge iceberg of existence, while all the time, below, the main business went on unrecorded. Just as many Englishmen went to bed hungry the evening James I became king as had wakened in that condition on good Queen Bess's final day.

Happily, we no longer neglect the history of business and industry. This for several reasons.

Like charity, drama begins at home: there is more romance in the rise — and in the fall — of Henry Ford than in the compromises of Henry Clay. The Model T car, which you could have had in any color provided it was black, remade the face of America. It even remade our morals. Alas, as we gasp for breath in the urban smog, the end of the story is not yet in sight.

The history of America without economic history is *Hamlet* without Hamlet. It is a myth that we were conceived in liberty. America was conceived in the search for a better economic life. For every family coming here seeking religious freedom and respite from despotism, there were a hundred settlers who left the villages of Sussex, the bogs of Ireland, the fishing ports of Norway, the feudal estates of Prussia, the ghettos of Poland, the bleak hills of Sicily, and the sugar fields of Puerto Rico in search of better jobs. Even our black citizens first came to these shores because of some man's lust for the almighty dollar.

Often history is a collection of clichés agreed upon. Frenchmen are gourmets and great lovers; Englishmen, aloof snobs; Germans, schizoid lovers of music and beer who periodically ravage their neighbors. What is the vulgar image of the Yankee? In our pantheon of notables you will not find a Michelangelo, Newton, Louis XIV, or Sir Francis Drake. You will find Eli Whitney, Benjamin Franklin, Alexander Graham Bell, Andrew Carnegie; perhaps also the whitewashed portrait of John D. Rockefeller; maybe even the mugshot of Samuel Insull, who staked all on the Wall Street casino of the 1920's and lost, or of Sewell Avery, who thought that being head of Montgomery Ward & Co. made him bigger than the United States government.

But, you will protest, don't I know that business is today in the doghouse? *Time* magazine no longer names a Walter Chrysler as Man of the Year. Graduating seniors spurn the corporate recruiters who each spring flock to the Ivy League campuses. "Shirtsleeves to shirtsleeves in three generations" must now read: "From farmer, to businessman, to lawyer or doctor, to . . . a pad in Greenwich Village or a social service job grappling with the problems of inner-city clients."

Yes, I do know that the *Saturday Evening Post*, with its weekly panegyrics to self-made tycoons, is now on the nostalgia shelf. No President today would dare utter those smug words of Calvin Coolidge: "The business of America is business." But I also know that along with the "greening" of America (the alleged turning off of youth, their switching from achievement orientation toward fulfillment in communal living, revolt against the establishment, and even various "mind-stretching" drugs) goes the "bluing" of America: if elite college students turn their backs on industry, factories will not thereby rust away or grass grow on Main Street. The Executive Suite will come to be manned by the children of blue-collar workers, by graduates of Iowa State if not of Yale, or by recruits from Brooklyn College, Fisk University, or the Rotterdam School of Economics. Nature does abhor a vacuum.

Charlie Chaplin's movie *Modern Times*, with its unforgettable image of the little man as a mere cog in the works, who spends his whole life turning bolt 999 on the assembly line, tells us more about the "alienation" of the worker than do the books of Herbert Marcuse or the young Karl Marx. Willy Loman, in Arthur Miller's play *Death of a Salesman*, provides a pathetic instance of the hollowness of a life spent in commerce. Still, none of us can escape the tragedy of getting old; and, even among artists and scholars, more of us must be mediocre or outright failures than can climb the greasy pole to success and fame. If we are open-minded, our notions of alienation must perhaps be modified in the face of reports by public opinion polls that show, again and again, that a sizable majority of people say they like their jobs and look with dismay on retirement, even at a good pension.

To know all is not always to forgive all. Sometimes to know all the historical faults of a system is the first step toward correcting those faults. The history of American industry—many times told, and told in this book with a sharp sense of its remarkable energy and its special genius—is more than a rattling good story: it is a cautionary tale that warns us, from the examples of past malfunctionings under laissez faire and rugged individualism, that in the present-day mixed economy and in the good society of the future, business must of necessity be everybody's business.

The wicked flee when no man pursueth. But they flee from their wickedness even faster if pursued by vigilant forces of righteousness. To paraphrase Georges Clemenceau, business is too important to leave to businessmen. President Eisenhower was right, in his valedictory speech, to warn against a "military-industrial complex." The giant corporation is a seat of power, albeit not the absolute monarch that John Kenneth Galbraith makes it out to be. Power needs to be kept in check by the untrammeled competition of rival sellers, by the countervailing powers of labor and consumers, by Ralph Naders and an electorate with heightened consciousness, and of course by all the branches of government. The history of business and industry is still writing itself as an ongoing process.

N° (919) 20ˢ

THIS Indented Bill of Twenty
Shillings due from the Massachusets
Colony to the Possessor shall be in value
equal to money & shall be accordingly
accepted by the Treasurer and Receivers
subordinate to him in all Publick paymᵗˢ;
and for any Stock at any time in the
Treasury. Boston in New England.
February the third 1690 By Order of
the General Court

Elisha Hutchinson

John Phillips

Tim Thornton

Comittee

1

<⟨◉⟩>

BUSINESS IN THE NEW WORLD

1607-1783

Like the voyages of discovery that preceded them, the first colonizing expeditions to America were business ventures. It was with an eye to making a fast peseta, pound, or guilder that companies of investors equipped ships and sent colonists to set up trade that would draw riches from the New World.

Most of the colonists themselves had less grandiose plans. Many were landless farmers or paupers, with no prospect of improving their lot other than migrating to America. Even so, the little band of 105 survivors (out of 144 who began the voyage) who anchored their three small ships in Virginia's James River on May 24, 1607, were possibly less hardy than foolhardy. The middle and northern reaches of North America's East Coast had proved inhospitable to earlier groups of settlers. A colony being established that same year on Maine's Kennebec River was doomed soon to expire. Just twenty years before, Sir Walter Raleigh had established a colony on Roanoke Island, in present-day North Carolina, and the whole party had disappeared mysteriously within three years. Unfriendly Indians, susceptibility to disease, and the settler's own ineptness in the wilderness made colonizing a chancy affair.

Thus the drive to settle in the New World came less from the colonists themselves than from the businessmen backers who envisioned great profits flowing from the newly discovered lands. They had abundant precedent to go on. The East India companies (England, France, Holland, Sweden, Denmark, Prussia, and even Scotland each had one) were reaping a rich harvest from their trading expeditions to the Far East. The Spanish and the Portuguese had already found

enough gold and silver in the New World to change most of Europe's trade from a barter system to a cash economy. And Europe-based voyagers had much earlier discovered the fishing grounds of the Grand Banks and the profitable possibilities of trading in North American furs.

To meet and beat competition, those in the home office knew it was best to have a good base and a strong field force out in the territory. Unlike Europe and Asia, however, the Americas had no coastal cities to gather, process, and display goods from the interior. So permanent trading posts had to be established, and the undeveloped character of the new country dictated that these be colonies of a nearly self-sustaining nature.

But colonies were expensive undertakings. Colonists had to be found and sold on the idea, and expeditions had to be equipped, transported, and supplied for a journey of many months and for an even longer period before they could be productive ashore. Because it was all but impossible to find entrepreneurs with the means for carrying out such schemes, or the willingness to risk those means, special commercial devices had to be created. One of these was the national charter, granting broad commercial, political, and monopolistic powers to those who were willing to put up the cash. Another was the joint-stock company, in which the risk was spread out among a great many shareholders.

Two such companies were chartered by the British government in 1606. The first went to a group of 715 investors—wealthy London merchants, nobles, and citizens, as well as fifty-six lesser companies. They subscribed to a capital of something over £50,000—or about $218,000 in terms of U.S. money when it was

---

An American venture: the note at left predated Bank of England paper money by four years.

9

first issued in the late 1700's. The second charter was issued to a group from England's west country, centering in Plymouth, who could raise far less capital but who felt that their active exploration of the New World entitled them to the same consideration as the wealthier Londoners. The London and Plymouth companies were granted rights to overlapping sections of the North American coast — all of which Raleigh had named Virginia, honoring the virgin Queen Elizabeth.

The London Company was responsible for founding Jamestown, and more than a dozen years later the Plymouth Company settled the Massachusetts town that bears its name. Both colonies were money-losing propositions for their sponsors from the start, and remained so through many reorganizations and recapitalizations of the companies, as good money was poured vainly after bad. Like many another promising investment, these commercial fiascoes stemmed more from timing than from intrinsic worth; considerations of simple survival had to take precedence over those

of profit, and survival in a strange, uncivilized land was a more complex matter than it at first appeared.

THE ECONOMIC WELLSPRINGS

In the fifty thousand or so years since human beings established themselves as the most eating and least eaten of all animal species, men and women have persisted in devising ways of making things a little better or easier for themselves. These improvements are not only something to trade on, but they become embedded in their time and place. Whether they consist of such accouterments as tanned leather to tie to the soles of one's feet or such conveniences as straw beds raised from the damp floor of a cave, the luxuries of one generation tend to become the necessities of the next. Without an understanding of this fundamental economic idea, history is difficult to see whole. Few generations have ever been so poor that they could not look backward in time to find others who lived shorter

A CHARTERED COMPANY

The lure of colonial exploitation was the spur to expanding the corporate form of doing business. The first corporations, called chartered companies, were groups of investors granted special powers by government so that they could serve, in distant lands, what was then deemed a public purpose. The hitch was that the nature of their existence seduced them away from the desires of the state. Sir Edward Coke, an English jurist of the late 1500's, wrote of corporations: "They cannot commit treason, nor be outlawed, nor excommunicated, for they have no souls." Without a soul, divine right, or any endowment other than the search for worldly gain, these protocorporations were immensely appealing.

The Virginia Company of London was such an attraction. Its original charter of 1606 was temporary in nature. Its second, granted on May 23, 1609, created a stronger body, with powers in some ways second only to those of a state. Its name was The Treasurer and Company of Adventurers and Planters of the City of London for the First Colony in Virginia, and it was equipped with a royal seal and a corporate entity. Among its 715 investors

John Smith

J. SMITH, *A Generall Historie of Virginia*, 1632

were 21 peers of the realm, 96 knights, 86 members of the landed gentry, merchants, sea captains, and gentlemen, and 56 London companies representing various professions.

The charter granted to the Virginia Company an immense territory; it opened up land as enormous and ill-defined as it was unknown. Virginia, as the Crown conceived it, was an area that covered eighteen of the nation's present states and parts of fourteen more. Its boundaries ran 400 miles along the Atlantic coast, straight across the continent to the Pacific (then called

the South Sea), and even included a 100-mile limit of ocean at both ends. All told, Virginia was a province of 1,800,000 square miles, with 125,000 square miles more of water.

King James I clearly thought of Virginia as another kingdom. The royal seal bore the motto *En dat Virginia quartam*, "Behold! Virginia gives the fourth" — a bold declaration that the chartered company's holdings in the New World gave the Crown a fourth realm, after England, Scotland, and Ireland. To the investors and their successors, it came to mean something quite different.

The charter turned over to the company "all the soils, grounds, havens and ports, mines, as well royal mines of gold and silver, as other minerals, pearls and precious stones, quarries, woods, rivers, waters, fishings, commodities, jurisdictions, royalties, privileges, franchises and preheminences." All this the company's members and their descendants could exploit and enjoy in perpetuity.

There were certain provisions stemming mainly from the king's inability to bestow money or ships on the company. For seven years the company could export to the colony, without taxes or duties, everything needed to support or defend itself or to trade with the Indians. For twenty years it need

lives and worked longer hours for smaller rewards.

Nevertheless there have been periods of little or no economic progress, and one of them may well have been the centuries before the year 1100 in Europe. Life was a matter of much toil for small recompense. Food was monotonous, often stale or spoiled; clothing was coarse and rough; homes offered minimal protection from the elements. Men deemed themselves fortunate to be able to do precisely what their fathers did before them.

The age that followed brought forth a burst of inventiveness as men sought ways to make science take over some of their burdens. It gave rise to such products as printing presses, gunpowder, clocks, machines that harnessed the energy of flowing water, and in 1492, by a curious coincidence, the construction of a world globe (showing a long stretch of sea from Europe to the Orient) by Martin Behaim, a Nuremberg mapmaker.

It was also a time when men traveled long distances to the Middle East and Far East to bring back the products of richer and older civilizations—pepper, nutmeg, ginger, to season foods; luxurious silks, rugs, and tapestries; pearls and rubies, fine glassware and china; camphor, musk, and opium. First they came by the long land route across central Asia, then by a combination of land and sea from India, China, and the Spice Islands, and finally by the longer but much cheaper water route around Africa.

When the royal houses of Spain and Portugal financed such maritime expeditions, they not only laid the groundwork for their own economic supremacy, but they started to sound the death knell for the system of feudal fiefdoms and baronies on which Europe's economy was based. The trading and merchant class began to be favored over the old ruling nobility class, both by national monarchs and by the new economic order. The Medicis of Florence and the Fuggers of Augsburg were examples of merchants who were so successful that they accumulated funds and became bankers. They helped finance kings in their struggles against the feudal lords for dominance, and the monarchs in turn accorded them privileges that helped their trade to prosper. By the time of Columbus's voyages, the shares of joint-stock companies, as well as commodities, were being traded by Flemish speculators in an exchange at Antwerp. It was the beginning of economic nationalism, in which political and economic interests became closely identified.

PEOPLE, LAND, AND MONEY

The new long reach of trade, the rise of merchant princes, and the discovery of America were all part of what came to be known as the Commercial Revolution. Ships grew stronger and taller for the long ocean voyages. The increase in business brought new trading methods, new industries, more manufacturing, new demands for labor. But perhaps the most significant impetus for change came from two sources: the vast new land areas that became available, and the rapidly growing supply of money.

In the year 1500 there were 100 million people living on Europe's 3.75 million square miles, working out to about twenty-four acres per person—a ratio that was hardly changed for 150 years before and after that date. The discovery of the Americas opened up another 16 million square miles, providing the possibility of a drastic reduction in Europe's population density and introducing to European society a new dimension of virtually limitless land.

The discovery and exploration of America had a similar effect in increasing the supply of capital, principally in the form of the precious metals, gold and silver. The Spaniards, first to arrive, were also the first to find these treasures. Hernando Cortes began

not pay customs on goods imported into Virginia. It would pay only 5 per cent on imports into England—forever. The colony did have to turn over to the royal treasury a fifth of all gold and silver ore that it might find.

There was one stipulation of which Virginians would come to remind the Crown: they and their descendants would enjoy forever the same rights and liberties as native Englishmen. The company had powers to go along with its rights. The charter stated that the company would, "within the said precincts of Virginia or in the way of sea thither and from thence, have full and absolute power and authority to correct, punish, pardon, govern, and rule" all inhabitants of the colony. It would make laws and issue orders, as long as these were not in contradiction to English law. The colony had the right to use military force to protect itself, and its governor might declare martial law just as might the governor of an English home county.

Virginia, in sum, was both a business and a government. In the end, its inhabitants felt that they were its citizens rather than its stockholders and employees. Jealous of external government, they felt best when they could in large measure govern themselves and in that way adapt government to suit their business self-interests.

Buyers and sellers throng the inner court of London's Royal Exchange in this engraving of 1644.

by looting the Aztec gold in Mexico, and then Francisco Pizarro took over the silver of the Incas in Peru. The total amount of gold and silver in 1492 has been estimated at $200 million, a mere $2 per person, which was not nearly enough to carry on trade in a money economy. A century later there was eight times as much, and by 1700 the supply of precious metals was approximately $4 billion, a twentyfold increase in 200 years.

The influx of gold and silver increased the supply of money in relation to goods, so prices rose. This in turn gave a powerful impetus to trade and the production of more goods, which brought huge profits to merchants and to the newly organized joint-stock trading companies that operated around the world. It also encouraged a heavy flow of commodities—cocoa from Africa, coffee from South America, sugar and molasses from the West Indies, and from North America the products of farm, forest, and ocean that came forth in mounting supply.

But the key factor in all the equations was the people supply. As land, money, and commodities be-

came more plentiful, there were fewer people per square mile of land, per dollar of money, per bushel of wheat. The economics of such a situation put a premium on humanity—on human beings, human labor, and human capabilities—that profoundly influenced the social, moral, and philosophic ideas of the New World. In time, it was the individual, rather than people as an abstraction, that became the dominant idea of the emerging era.

WHO THE PEOPLE WERE

The first settlers in that part of North America that is now the United States came for many reasons—religious, political, economic. If one word were to describe their common motivation, it would undoubtedly be "opportunity"—whether it was the debtor who was given a chance to get out of prison, or the ambitious younger son of a wealthy and aristocratic English family, destined under English law to inherit nothing, who saw in America the opportunity to build his own fortune.

12

Quick riches was the lure for many of the original Jamestown Colony, whose talk was of "dig gold, wash gold, refine gold, load gold," as Captain John Smith observed. And, indeed, their sponsors in England looked forward just as eagerly to a fast return on their investment. But as dozens died in the first year, and hundreds more of the new arrivals in the next year or two, if gradually became apparent that there were concerns more important to the settlers than gold and silver. There had to be a reliable source of food, better protection from Indian hostility, and a more healthful location than the swampland on which they had first encamped. There also had to be people who were better equipped to live and build a new society in the wilderness.

On the second voyage to the colony in 1608 the London Company sent along eight Poles and Germans skilled in the arts of making pitch, tar, glass, and soap ashes. Later expeditions brought more carpenters, weavers, and skilled craftsmen of all kinds, as well as farmers who had been crowded off their lands by the British laws that decreed the enclosure of large areas for profitable sheep grazing.

The first returns from the Jamestown Colony were not in gold but in tobacco—the "sotweed"—which Raleigh had first brought back to England and for which a demand quickly developed there and throughout Europe. This market spawned tobacco culture, with its large plantations and its need for large numbers of people to work them.

As profits became available, planters hired all the laborers they could, paying them 30 to 100 per cent more than the going rates in England; when these ran out, the landowners began to buy additional workers. The average English laborer, whose wages amounted to no more than $10 to $15 a year, could not afford the $30 to $50 in transportation costs, much as he might like to come to America to share its opportunities and make a fresh start. So, having no savings, he simply mortgaged his own future. From a shipmaster or emigration broker, he bought his passage in return for three to seven years of work as an indentured servant. Boys and girls as young as ten years or less were placed in bonded apprenticeships, earning only their keep while they learned a trade. Thousands of children and adults were recruited by professional crimps and sold to shipmasters engaged in the people business. Cruel as this system may seem, one indentured servant in Maryland, George Alsop, wrote home: "The servants of this province, which are stigmatiz'd for slaves by the clapper-mouth jaws of the vulgar in England, live more like Freemen than the most Mechanick apprentice in London."

In the hard times that ensued when Britain's continental markets were shut off during the Thirty Years' War, England abounded with vagabonds, beggars, and paupers, and its prisons teemed with debtors and petty thieves. Courts were authorized to have them shipped to the colonies, in return for seven to ten years of their labor. While the colonies protested against becoming a dumping ground for "His Majesty's Seven Year Passengers," many a frontier farmer who could not afford higher-priced help welcomed them. Perhaps half of the white immigrants to the colonies came as indentured servants. By the time of the revolution, it is estimated that 75 per cent of the population of Pennsylvania, Maryland, and Virginia were from this stock.

Another source of cheap labor turned up when a Dutch privateer arrived at Jamestown in 1619 with a cargo of black slaves from Guinea. For those with capital, the economics looked attractive. An indentured servant required an investment of $10 to $20 a year and often earned his freedom at just about the time he was turning most productive. But a slave, for a total investment of $80 to $150, could give a lifetime of work, along with the work his progeny would provide in the future. In a labor-intensive economy, here was an attractive long-term investment.

Whether for moral or other reasons, however, slavery first proved unpopular, and for many years there were relatively few slaves in the colonies. In 1681 Virginia had 6,000 white servants and only 2,000 slaves. When the Dutch slavers' monopoly was broken in 1660, and especially after American traders took over a significant part of the trade, the number of slaves grew rapidly. By the time of the first census in 1790 there were 697,000, making up more than 20 per cent of the nation's total population and about 40 per cent of the population of the South. Indeed, in South Carolina the slaves totaled more than twice the white population.

Another shortage that showed up in the earliest colonial times was that of wives. Officials in London took heed and sent over sixty young women in 1620. These were auctioned off and sold at prices ranging from 120 to 160 pounds of tobacco, which was then selling for about seventy-five cents a pound.

Although the British eventually came to dominate the political and economic life of North America, the earliest settlers in the New World were not the English but the Spanish, who gravitated toward the more languorous tropical regions. Almost fifty years before Plymouth was founded, an estimated 160,000 Spaniards had settled in America, and instead of pushing the natives off the land, had made serfs of an Indian population of some 5,000,000.

The Dutch, who arrived simultaneously with the British, hired the English navigator Henry Hudson to scout the New World for them. His trip up the river that took his name was in search of a shorter water route to the Pacific. Hudson found no northwest passage, but he sent back glowing accounts of the great promise of fur trading. In 1614 an enterprising group of Amsterdam merchants began setting up trading posts in New Netherland. Given a charter to trade and colonize in 1621, the Dutch West India Company brought the first boatload of colonists in 1624. Some of these settled New Amsterdam, at the mouth of the Hudson. Two years later Peter Minuit, the company's director-general, bought the island of Manhattan from the Indians for sixty guilders (about twenty-four dollars) worth of beads and trinkets. Dutch interests then proceeded to take over and settle the entire river region.

Most peripatetic of all those who came to the New World were the French, who explored much but settled little. They traveled far inland in pursuit of the rich fur trade. In 1608 Samuel de Champlain built a trading post at Quebec, and other French pioneers later settled both ends of the Mississippi. But by the middle 1700's there were only some 80,000 French scattered along the continent's rivers and lakes, making up hardly more than 5 per cent of the European population in North America.

English migration to the colonies was almost painfully slow until around 1630, when a combination of economic depression and bad crops brought an unprecedented rush of immigrants. Some 65,000 Englishmen came or were shipped to the colonies and the West Indies in the following decade. A hundred years after the landing at Jamestown there were more than 400,000 in the New World, and just before the Revolution there were 2,500,000 in the British colonies, equal to about a fourth of the population of Great Britain. Most of those who arrived in the 1600's were English, with a handful of others from other parts of Europe. In the next century, however, immigration came mainly from Germany and Ireland, and the new settlements moved inland toward the Appalachian range.

While immigration was substantial during much of the colonial period, most of the population growth

THE ARITHMETIC OF THE SLAVE TRADE

The slave traffic was the leg of the triangular trade that was sailed in chains. To the merchant mariners of New England, the words in their Bibles were tempered by the figures in their ledgers. The account book of the sloop *Adventure*'s voyage in the triangular trade of 1773–74 tells the story vividly.

The vessel was owned by the Champlin family of Newport, Rhode Island. The senior partner was Christopher Champlin, a shopkeeper and importer who ventured into sea commerce as a privateer and an illicit trader with the French West Indies during the Seven Years' War. These businesses helped him accumulate the scarce hard currency needed to restock his shelves with wares from London. Fitting out the sloop took from July until the end of October, 1773, when the *Adventure* set sail on the first leg of her trip.

The master, Captain Samuel Tuell, had a big crew for the long voyage, numbering two mates, a cooper, cook, boy, and five seamen. Along with a pair of swivel guns and grapeshot, his ship's stores included items for use during the so-called "middle passage": many "double warded secret padlocks," "12 pr. Hand Cufs and Shackles," twenty-

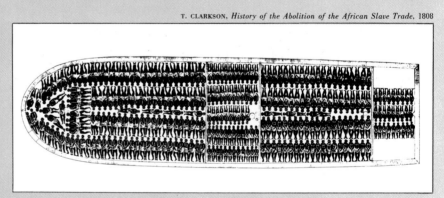

A sectional drawing showed how to pack 400 Africans in a slave ship.

six gallons of vinegar to purify the airless, low-ceilinged slave deck, and plenty of Peruvian bark for dosing sick slaves. Also aboard were 24,380 gallons of Newport-distilled rum, worth £1,500 in sterling.

Christopher had an 11/16 share in the venture, with his younger brother George owning the remainder. To insure his share, Christopher paid some £78 sterling to his London correspondents; it was a low rate to pay for insurance—seven guineas per £100 (the name of the currency was itself derived from the Guinea Coast slave region). The rate was minimal because of the successful voyages in recent years in the "black trade."

The *Adventure* spent five weeks crossing to Sierra Leone on the western coast of Africa. There her master found that the price for slaves had risen since his last voyage in 1772 from an average of 150 gallons of rum each to 190 gallons per female and 220 gallons per male. Seeking better buys, Captain Tuell cruised 1,250 miles along the Gold Coast to Whidah, now Nigeria, and traded rum for sixty-two slaves. Through judicious watering of the rum, he managed to stretch his purchasing power by 500 gallons not on the cargo manifest when the sloop left Newport.

14

in the colonies stemmed from natural increase. The New World's need for people was such that large families were deemed both a social and an economic good, especially in the farming and frontier regions.

FORTUNES IN THE LAND

The new age spawned by the Commercial Revolution did not erase memories of the old. Throughout the feudal era land had been the principal source of economic and political power, and these powers continued to be held by the owners of large estates.

Indeed, land was the most common form of capital. While trade was becoming the quickest road to personal fortunes, there was little flexibility in the form such fortunes could take. The economy of the times lacked both sufficient coin and a reliable system of paper property, so that land remained the most respected and desired symbol of wealth. It was also the best means of passing wealth from one generation to

the next. London merchants had long sought to amass wealth through trade, marry themselves or their children up the social ladder, and then move into the class of gentlemen by means of acquiring landed estates. The early New England merchants, most of whom had been tradesmen in London, pursued upward mobility in the same way, seeking their lands either in the New World or back in the Old.

Generally speaking, the earliest arrivals in the colonies were able to get the best land, especially that along rivers and on shorelines, while those coming later had to take what was picked over or else move on toward the frontier. It was not that simple, of course. The land system in the colonies, beginning with the granting of royal charters for entire colonies, made the development of huge estates all but inevitable. And because the charters included broad powers of self-government, the system favored those with ties to the government, as well as those with capital.

Some individuals claimed title to what later became entire states. Sir Ferdinando Gorges, for example, had roughly what is now the state of Maine, which he passed along to his heirs. Captain John Mason got New Hampshire when the Plymouth Colony apportioned its territory to its directors. William Penn had the Pennsylvania charter, and the absentee Cecilius Calvert, the second Lord Baltimore, had all of Maryland. By the late 1600's or early 1700's most of these claims had been negated by royal decree or overruled by the courts, but this did not mark an end to either huge estates or the hunger for land.

The concentration of wealth represented by large land holdings tended to help create a class system— largely a two-class system—in the early colonial period. This was particularly true in the South, where an aristocracy of landowners sprang up. Almost everywhere the land-rich grew richer. In Virginia it became important to know one's way around the House of Burgesses in order to build up land holdings, and George Washington was one of those who thus enlarged his personal domain.

Nowhere, however, were class distinctions so clearly marked as in the Dutch colony of New Netherland, where the patroon system developed and held sway through much of the colonial period. In an effort to encourage colonization, the powerful Dutch West India Company granted an estate measuring sixteen miles of coastline or shoreline along one river bank (or eight miles along both banks) to anyone who brought fifty settlers to the colony. The grantee, or patroon, was given the manorial rights of a feudal lord to the land and over the people thereon.

Many of the patroons were merchants who were themselves officers and directors of the West India Company, and the prospect of this quick route into

Laden with slaves, a little pepper, palm oil, and some gold dust, the *Adventure* voyaged back across the Atlantic, taking seven weeks to reach the island of Grenada. At auction, the fifty-eight surviving slaves fetched an average of £37 sterling each. Captain Tuell put a third of his slaving proceeds into molasses, taking the rest in bills of exchange upon London—£1,451 sterling against the account of Hayly and Hopkins.

In the accounts, the outfitting, the voyage, and one-third of the original cost of the ship were charged against the gross. Fitting out the *Adventure* ran to £1,310 in the equivalent of sterling, the sloop herself was valued at £250, and wages due on return to Newport in July, 1774, amounted to little more than £45. Other costs were insurance, commissions to factors in the West Indies, and the master's customary "coast commission" of "4 in 104" on the gross sales of the cargo.

How did the Champlins do? The voyage cost a total of £1,743 sterling, but it was paid out in soft Rhode Island currency. The gross revenues were slightly more than £2,145 in sterling exchange. Not including the gain from the returns from the West Indian molasses for rum distilling, the *Adventure*'s venture made £400 sterling—a net profit of 23 per cent.

Johannes Schuyler, New York patroon

the ranks of the landed gentry was enticing. By 1630 five patroonships had been set up. Kiliaen Van Rensselaer, an Amsterdam pearl merchant, had his agents buy still more land from the Indians, and his estate of Rensselaerswyck centered on Albany and covered an estimated 700,000 acres on both sides of the Hudson, extending eastward into Massachusetts.

Patroons usually tried to live up to their lordly station. Many had their own insignia, their own flags and fortifications, and their own paid troops. They sought to increase immigration, in order to have more hands to work their lands and more laborers to do their bidding. The worker had no political powers and few legal rights, but he was free to leave for unclaimed lands, usually in New Jersey or Pennsylvania, if he could manage to assemble the tools of farming or a trade. Otherwise he was confined to the thralldom of his master's duchy, even to the extent of agreeing to trade only at the "company store"—consuming the produce of the manor, grinding his flour at the mill, cutting lumber at its sawmills, and obtaining liquor from its brewery. So the patroon came to dominate not only the land and its produce but also the processes of trade and manufacture in his area.

Between the lordly patroons and lowly laborers was a small middle class of burghers, made up chiefly of small merchants. The burgher right was available by purchase, but at a price far higher than what the average workman could ever hope to accumulate. It conferred a limited voice in public affairs, which was usually exercised according to the wishes of the patroon, on whom the burgher too had a large measure of dependence for his livelihood.

When the British took New Amsterdam from the Dutch in 1664 and renamed it New York, they missed an excellent opportunity to reform the colony's oligopoly of land and political control. Instead, they perpetuated the feudal system and in some ways expanded it. The effect of new, democratizing laws was cancelled out by corruption and favoritism. The peerage that emerged thus included a mixture of Dutch, Scottish, and English names: in addition to the Van Rensselaers, Schuylers, Beekmans, and Van Cortlandts were the Livingstons, the Morrises, the Philipses, and the Heathcotes. The Beekman estate measured 240,000 acres, the Van Cortlandt 140,000, and that of the Scotsman Robert Livingston, the young Secretary of Indian Affairs who married into the Van Rensselaer family, 160,000 acres. What is now New Jersey was divided between John Lord Berkeley and Sir George Carteret.

In this uneven distribution of land, the most important form of capital, lay the seeds not only of some of the great private fortunes but also of what would one day become a rising tide of civil discontent.

FARM AND PLANTATION

From 1600 to 1800 the economy of the New World was overwhelmingly agricultural, with perhaps 95 per cent of the population devoting their efforts to farming in the first century and 90 per cent in the second. But the colonial farmer and his wife also had to be skilled in many other lines of work—building, handcrafting, hunting, and sometimes fishing and woodsmanship. Farmers experimented with their environment in the earliest years and soon learned that most European vegetable products could be grown on the more fertile lands of the colonies.

Because land was plentiful and labor scarce, nobody thought of spending too much time and effort on using land more intensively through fertilization and crop rotation. "They wanted 'labor-saving' devices," the historian Daniel J. Boorstin points out. "And . . . the most obvious labor-saving device happened to be the wasteful use of land."

The colonies also found their land suitable for the same kind of animal husbandry that was practiced in Europe. Sheep and cattle grazing started early in New England, although the price of cattle was almost prohibitively expensive until the number of stock began to increase substantially through successive generations of breeding. The scarcity of clothing led to official encouragement of sheep herding and the increase of flocks. As early as 1640 bounties were paid in Massachusetts for spinning yarn and weaving linen, wool, and cotton cloth. A Stakhanovite-like statute in 1656 not only provided bounty payments for spinning wool but assessed penalties on families whose wool spinners, chiefly women and children, fell below their prescribed quotas.

In 1627 a trade agreement was worked out between the Dutch in Manhattan and the English in Plymouth Colony. But intercolonial commerce remained relatively small for a great many years. Curiously enough, however, a flourishing international trade developed as soon as surpluses began to appear. Exports from the northern colonies were mainly products of the sea and forest; the middle colonies contributed grains, meat, and other farm crops; from the South came tobacco and, later, rice and indigo.

The two major farm staples of the New World were those for which the climate and terrain were well suited—corn, chiefly for domestic use, and tobacco, largely for export. Captain John Smith encouraged the cultivation of both in the earliest years of the Jamestown Colony.

Tobacco took on new importance after John Rolfe (who married Pocahontas) worked out an improved method of curing the leaf, in 1612. As export demand built up, the industry quickly became the most profitable agricultural pursuit in the New World.

The fact that tobacco was raised chiefly for export placed a premium on land located on river banks and other waterways, where wharves could be built. The earliest planters took up the land along Virginia's rivers, then along the many inlets of Chesapeake Bay, and later in North Carolina's Albemarle and Pamlico districts. Later arrivals had to be content with a second tier of farms behind the waterfront, so that they were forced to use their neighbors' docks. A curious link between businessmen of the North and South developed when New England seamen were able to sail their small coastal vessels into the rivers and narrow bays and inlets to pick up the tobacco. As the small planters' chief avenue to the outside world, the New Englanders managed to monopolize the marketing of the crop of Albemarle County, amounting to one million pounds a year.

On the whole, however, the tobacco economy favored the larger planters over the smaller. Those with capital and influence not only got the best grants of land originally but were able to increase them. The high profits helped raise the price of tobacco lands. Then, within a few years, tobacco would exhaust the soil on which it was grown and new lands had to be found for cultivation. This was usually beyond the means of the small farmer with little capital. Raising tobacco also required a high ratio of human labor to crop yield. As the rates for white labor continued to rise, slave labor came to predominate in the tobacco economy—again favoring the wealthier planters, who could best afford the investment required for slaves and for the overseers to supervise them. A great plantation might measure 5,000 acres or more, with 1,000 acres under tobacco cultivation and much of the remainder open to wandering herds of cattle, hogs, and horses—a kind of precursor to the open ranges of the West.

As their capital needs increased, the large planters borrowed heavily in England against the sale of their profitable crops. The first of the restrictive Navigation Acts in 1651 had the effect of limiting their direct marketing efforts, and a long decline in tobacco prices set in. By 1700 many of the planters, unable to switch their large fixed investments to any other purpose, and needing to borrow money for each year's crop, were in a debt cycle that left them largely at the mercy of their creditors abroad. One planter, Thomas Jefferson, complained that the planter himself became a kind of property as these recurring debts passed down from father to son. Even though tobacco cultivation increased, reaching 130 million pounds by 1790, it was no longer a sure and easy road to wealth.

By the late 1600's rice was being grown in the inland swamps of present-day South Carolina, and irrigation methods helped expand rice culture to the point where it was that colony's principal export. Indigo, a plant that yields a bluish dyestuff, later added a second major export crop. Gulian Van Rensselaer had experimented unsuccessfully with indigo seed near Albany as early as 1650. Around 1740 Miss Eliza Lucas succeeded, after two attempts, in cultivating indigo seeds from the West Indies on her father's South Carolina plantation. With profits ranging from 33 to 50 per cent (including a bounty provided by Parliament), indigo cultivation quickly spread to the interior upland regions of the state.

PRODUCTS OF FOREST AND SEA

The earliest commercial products to emanate from the New World were fish and furs—fish not long after the voyages of Columbus, and furs as soon as the earliest explorers arrived on the continent.

Fish were abundant not only in the oceans and bays but in the lakes and streams, so much so that they could be killed with a stick and scooped up with a frying pan. They were useful immediately for food and fertilizer, and very soon as an export commodity. As the demand for fish grew in Europe, especially in Catholic countries, New Englanders moved out after the cod and some 200 other types of available fish. By 1675 more than 600 vessels and 4,000 men were fishing for cod; by 1700 a large proportion of Boston's population of 12,000 linked its livelihood to the sea, and by the end of the colonial period the New England fishing industry brought in $1,125,000 a year compared to $1,000,000 in exports of furs.

English merchants supplied the first capital and sent the first ships to develop the fishing industry in

New England, operating both from their home ports and from coastal fishing settlements in America. But the colonists took control of the industry soon after the Puritans arrived in 1630. Massachusetts became and remained dominant in the fishery, which centered on Gloucester, Salem, Marblehead, and Boston. At first fishing was the province of numerous small enterprisers who owned the vessels and equipment, but within a century there were complaints that a few wealthy capitalists controlled the industry.

The preservation of fish required salt production. The first salt works were authorized by the Council for New England in 1621 and erected two years later. Since no rock salt mines had been found, boiled sea water was the main source of supply.

Whaling, practiced almost from the start, was mentioned as a source of profit in one of the earliest prospectuses for the colonies, George Mourt's *A Relation or Journal of the beginning of the English plantation at Plimoth*, published in London in 1622. Originally, whales would be sighted by a lookout on shore, pursued by a boat, captured, and the carcass brought in. A lucrative haul, the whale was a source of oil for illumination, spermaceti for candles, flexible bone for a variety of uses, and ambergris to fix perfumes, as well as food.

Valuable whale carcasses frequently washed ashore. The town fathers of Orleans on Cape Cod decreed that "every whale that shall come within the bounds of this township . . . shall be disposed of vis: the one half of this town to have one whale and the other half to have the second, and so for the future. . . ." The first sperm whale, with its especially valuable oil, was taken in 1712 by Captain Christopher Hussey of Nantucket when a squall drove his small ship perilously out to sea.

Eventually the whales got smarter and drifted away from the vicinity of Cape Cod. The whalers followed them. By the mid-1700's at least fifty whaling vessels were plying more distant waters, some moving as far off as the Azores and the coasts of Guinea and Brazil.

The forest, like the sea, was another source of wealth, particularly in furs. Some of the English colonies, however, appeared less capable of exploiting the fur trade than the French and the Dutch. Eight of the Pilgrim colonists, for example, agreed in 1630 to take on the colony's debt of $9,000 to the English merchants who had financed them, in exchange for a six-year fur monopoly. Finding that the local Indians were extremely fond of a variety of shell beads called *wampumpeag* ("wampum"), they embarked on a trade for furs with Indians throughout New England. Their enterprise flourished at the start, then dwindled, and came to a halt before 1640. The British furnished new

Steps in the whaling trade, already a big business, were illustrated in this series of engravings, published in 1745.

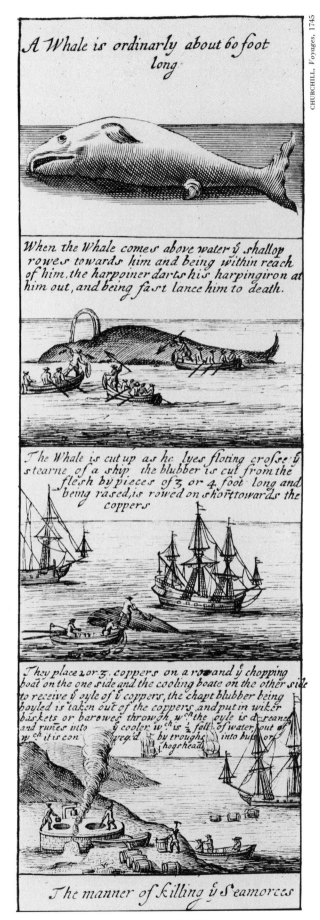

CHURCHILL, *Voyages*, 1745

18

capital to get it started again, but by 1647 it was calculated that the Pilgrims still owed $6,000 of the original $9,000, even though they had produced $50,000 worth of beaver furs alone between 1631 and 1636.

So lucrative was the fur trade to more astute businessmen, however, that there were many efforts to monopolize it. The Dutch West India Company even excluded their patroons from the New Netherland fur traffic. But the wilderness was too vast and there were too many sharp-witted free-lancers engaged in the business; no monoploy could last very long. Among those who did well in fur trading were William Pynchon, who founded Springfield, Massachusetts, the Coopers of Springfield, the Parsons and Wiltons of Northampton, and the Westcarrs of Hadley, many of whom were eventually able to use their profits to acquire that even more valuable commodity—land.

Among the less glamorously profitable products of the New World's abounding forests were pitch, tar, turpentine, and rosin for naval stores; potash, the crude form of potassium carbonate used in textile making; and timber for all kinds of construction.

The endless woodlands provided the settlers with a much-needed building material. At first logs were split and boards hewn with axes and hand tools. But around 1633 the first sawmill was built in Massachusetts, even before there was one in England. The many rivers and streams of the East Coast offered easy transportation for wood products—as they had for furs—and logs, boards, staves, and shingles were floated downstream to the coast, where they could be loaded onto ships for export. Many of the same waterways also provided power for the sawmills that quickly sprang up. Four falls of seventy, twenty, thirty, and forty-two feet on the Saco River in Maine were all used in this way. One stream boasted six sawmills within the space of a quarter of a mile.

Shipbuilding became the point at which the industries of forest and sea were brought together. Small open boats were built from the start, including several by Captain John Smith in Maine. In 1614 the Dutch constructed a sixteen-ton ship in Manhattan, the first large one in the colonies. With raw materials abundant and close at hand, ship construction was 30 to 50 per cent cheaper than it was in Europe. Swedes built ships at their settlement on the Delaware River. A thirty-ton vessel, the *Blessing of the Bay*, was launched at Boston in 1631, marking the start of a major industry there. By 1670 a total of 730 ships had been built in Massachusetts. New York became another center for the industry, and a survey of the city in 1728 showed that the principal occupants of the river front from Beekman Street north were the yards and docks of shipbuilders. By 1760 all the colonies were producing a total of 300 to 400 vessels a year, some 40 per cent of them being turned out for use by

GEORGIA.

SHIPS or VESSELS, of *any* Burthen, may be laden at the *first* Bluff, on the *North* Side of St. *Mary's River*, with LUMBER and SCANTLING for *London*, the *West-Indies* or elsewhere, with Dispatch, at reasonable Rates for Money, or in Exchange for any Kind of Merchandize. For further Particulars enquire at Mr. WRIGHT's Plantation, within a Mile of the said Bluff.

The Inlet lieth between *Cumberland* and *Amelia* Islands, is a safe Navigation, being an easy short Bar to pass over, with sufficient Depth of Water for large Ships; it is about thirty Leagues to the Northward of St. *Augustine* Inlet. The River is bold, the Bluff in sight of *Cumberland Island*, about five Miles up the River, where Ships may in Safety load in all Seasons of the Year.

Land on coastal inlets and rivers was valuable for shipping, as reflected in this Georgia advertisement of the 1700's.

purchasers in Great Britain and the West Indies.

The tall, straight white pines of New England were prized for ship masts, as well as for yards and spars. Late in the 1600's a group of London entrepreneurs and New England merchants organized to monopolize navy contracts for these products. The mast trust operated for a short time, but it could no more be maintained than the earlier abortive fur monopoly. There were just too many trees in the forests, and too many rival groups of merchants.

The occasional monopolies that might be maintained were those that had the official sanction of town fathers, usually granted for a limited time for otherwise excessively risky enterprises. One of such a type was offered in Massachusetts in 1667 to encourage building a dry dock to take a ship of 350 tons. Eventually businessmen grew more confident and moved ahead on their own. By 1725 a "great ship" of 700 tons was built at New London by Captain John Jeffrey, a master shipbuilder who had emigrated from England a few years earlier. And a half century later, on the eve of the Revolution, a submarine that could be raised or lowered at will was built at Essex, Connecticut.

MANUFACTURES

The early 1600's were simple times, when the major sources of energy for men's work were wind, water, and muscle. A great many manufactured products were simply crafted with hand tools, and a farm wife's success rested to a large degree on her dexterity in fashioning products for home and family. She spun the thread from wool or flax, wove it into cloth, and fashioned the cloth into garments; she made soap and candles, preserved meats, fruits, and vegetables, and churned butter and brewed beer. Her husband took timber from his wood lot for building home, barn, and furniture. Leather was tanned and cured on the farm, and fashioned into shoes and clothing.

In the long winter evenings, many a farmer would make barrel staves, casks, or shingles, for which a market could usually be found. Using iron rods furnished by slitting mills, he would make nails at a small furnace in the chimney corner, for his own use or for sale. Eventually some of these home-crafting establishments blossomed into small community shops.

Commercialized industry was slow to develop. If a town were big enough, it would have a scattering of artisans—carpenters, shoemakers, perhaps a smith. And every self-respecting town would want a sawmill, a grist mill, and perhaps a fulling mill for smoothing and dyeing the rough homespun cloth. The first mills for grinding corn and wheat consisted of no more than two smoothly wrought stones, one of which was made to revolve against the other. Records of the Massachu-

setts Bay Colony show that more than fifty dollars was paid for such a pair of millstones sent from England. Corn and flour mills, using both wind and water for power, sprang up wherever grains were grown.

The mills often proved versatile. When they were not processing grain, they might be put to work grinding rags for paper or malt for beer, or saws might be attached to the power wheels. These mills, especially in the middle colonies, expanded into other fields—a cooperage, a bolting mill, a flour packing house, or even a bakery—as their owners prospered. But the ordinary artisan could not open such a business because of the prohibitive capital requirements. These craftsmen could not expect to accumulate more than $500 in a lifetime of work. A sawmill, dam, and water wheel, with a daily capacity of 1,000 board feet, would run from $500 to $1,000. A fully equipped brewery and malt mill cost from $1,000 to $3,000. In 1664 a New York tile kiln cost $25,000. And, much later, an investment of $250,000 went into each of two of the larger

"A KIND OF DRINK CALLED RUM"

Rum was the most beloved liquor of the colonists. It not only warmed bellies—it lined pockets. As a commodity, rum was swapped on the Newfoundland fishing banks for bills of exchange on England. It bought slaves on the African coast. It paid for furs from the Indians. The French had suppressed rum manufacture in their Caribbean sugar islands for fear that it would spoil the market for cognac. This embargo gave the American colonists an advantage they hated to see endangered by the Molasses Act of 1733. So they ignored the tax. By 1763, when Prime Minister George Grenville tried to enforce a new, more lenient molasses duty, 14,500 hogsheads of molasses out of 15,000 brought into Massachusetts for rum distilling were smuggled to save the ninepence a gallon duty.

Rum did not give everybody a rosy glow. "It is an unhappy thing," frowned Increase Mather in 1686, "that in later years a Kind of Drink called Rum has been common among us. They that are poor, and wicked too, can for a penny or twopence make themselves drunk." But strict prohibition had to await a wealthier era. The demand for molasses to distill in Connecticut was so great

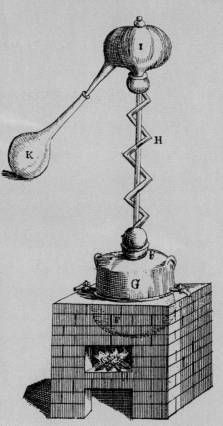

The various parts of a still, depicted in an engraving of the eighteenth century.

in 1727 that prices rose steeply. The government decided to prohibit distilling, pointing out also that rum was "usually unwholesome." But business was hurt so badly that the law was repealed. John Adams commented dryly: "You may as well preach to the Indians against rum as to our people."

Though rum originated in the West Indies, where it was called rumbullion, it was popular under many names, including Stinkebuss, throughout the American colonies. There, rum was blended into such questionable quaffs as Calibogus or Bogus (cold rum and beer), Blackstrap (a blend of rum and molasses), Bombo (a weak cooler contrived of rum, sugar, water, and grated nutmeg), and even a fearsome potion called Whistle Belly Vengeance. This terrible tipple was sour beer cooked in a kettle, sweetened with molasses and rum, filled with brown bread crumbs, and then somehow drunk hot. A tastier concoction called a Stone Fence was simply cider laced with rum. Ben Franklin had his own recipe for a Shrub: rum allowed to sit with orange juice for three or four weeks, then passed through a filtered funnel to Franklin's parsimonious advice "that not a drop may be lost." Shrubs and Bounces, mostly fruity rum drinks, abounded in the South. Where it was colder, there was hot buttered rum. Another New Eng-

steel mills—the Peter Hasenclever works in New Jersey and the Principio establishment in Maryland.

Breweries appeared early on the colonial scene. The Dutch West India Company built one in 1633 that extended from the present Wall Street to Hudson Street. Four years later the General Court in Boston ordered the licensing of all brewers. Philadelphia brewers produced ale that brought a higher price in Barbados than the British product, and Connecticut was esteemed for the quality of its porter and cider. Drunkenness became so prevalent in New Amsterdam that authorities in 1641 prohibited "the tapping of Beer during divine service, or after ten o'clock at night."

The Dutch began distilling brandy as early as 1640. The alcoholic beverage that took on the greatest importance to trade, however, was rum, made from West Indian molasses. Distilleries sprang up all through New England, especially in the coast towns, and at one point there were twenty in Newport alone. Rum found

land favorite was the hot Flip. Served by the bowl, it was prepared by sticking a loggerhead (also called a flip dog— an iron rod used for stirring the liquid), red-hot from the fireplace, into it to raise a froth. The expression "to be at loggerheads" with someone stemmed from hearthside arguments which, with the influence of a little rum, might be settled with the long iron mulling rods. One kind of hot Flip, picturesquely called a Yard of Flannel, consisted of a quart of ale brought just to a boil, then blended slowly into four beaten eggs with four tablespoons of sugar, some grated nutmeg or ginger, and inspired with a half cup of dark rum.

A very civilized form of rum consumption was the Fish House Punch, the traditional welcoming cup of Philadelphia's famed club, the State, founded in 1732 by sociable anglers and businessmen. The recipe for this punch called for a heady blend of two quarts of Jamaican rum, one quart of cognac, a half cup of peach brandy, and a quart of lemon juice—all sweetened to taste. Even the Indians had a rum drink, called Coow Woow, presumably for the whoops they felt obliged to utter after drinking enough of it. In short, rum found its way into just about everything in one form or another, and the per capita intake in colonial America got as high as eighty quarts a year.

a ready market in the slave trade, in supplying fishing vessels, and in trading for furs; home consumption was also substantial.

Some families sold homespun cloth, but only to local markets. Beaver hats, on the other hand, went into the export trade almost as early as they were produced. Early efforts were made to turn out silk in the southern colonies, but most of these failed. Swiss who settled in South Carolina in 1733 produced some silk there, and one shipment of eight pounds of raw silk went to England the following year. Cotton manufacture was even slower in developing; a joint-stock company was formed in Philadelphia in 1775 for what is thought to be the first enterprise for manufacturing cotton goods in America.

When cattle prices dropped in New England's early years, the colonies became beef exporters, a circumstance that probably influenced the development of leather and shoe manufacturing. In 1630 a Mr. Higginson of Salem mentioned the extraordinary increase of cattle and "store of sumacke trees, good for dying and tanning of Leather." The colony's first tannery was built at Swampscott. Shoemakers settled at Salem and Lynn in 1635. By 1648 there were so many coopers and shoemakers in Boston that both crafts petitioned the legislature for powers to regulate their trade. In New York, Coenraet Ten Eyck was prospering from his tannery and shoe business by the mid-1600's. The Virginia legislature encouraged the leather industry (and prohibited the export of hides) in 1662. New Jersey got its first shoemaker in 1676 and tannery in 1698. Georgia became the largest supplier of deerskin, mainly for the military.

The first glasshouse was built in 1609, in the forest about a mile from the fledgling Jamestown settlement. The wood fuel and alkaline salts needed for glass production were plentiful, but labor was scarce and hard to come by. Nevertheless, glass production grew, partly because breakage made the price of imports high and partly because of the desirability of beads and other trinkets for trading with the Indians. In New Amsterdam a glassmaker, Jan Smeedes, was among the first to receive allotments of land, just north of Hanover Square. Until another century had passed, however, glass for windows was deemed an unnecessary luxury, and a member of the Plymouth Colony counseled his friends in England to "bring paper and linseed oil for your windows."

Bricks were made in Virginia as early as 1612. The first record of a brick kiln in New England goes back to 1629, when one was built in Salem. Around the middle of the century the trades of lime, brick, and tile making were pursued as independent callings, but most houses continued to be built of wood, in spite of the ravages of fires, until around 1700.

The colonists wanted iron for a great variety of

purposes—among them pots, kettles, nails, wagon wheels, sleigh runners, chains, anvils, anchors, guns, and cannon. Because of the complexities of extracting, forging, and shaping the metal, these products came primarily from England, but some iron production began early in the New World. Iron ores were found on the surface of the ground in Virginia in 1610, and bog iron was fairly common in Massachusetts. Reduced by charcoal, the ores were found to produce good iron.

The London Company sent 150 emigrants skilled in iron manufacture to Virginia in 1619, and a smelting works was built on Falling Creek, a branch of the James River. This enterprise came to a sudden end when an Indian attack killed all but two workers and demolished the plant.

Iron works were set up in New England at Concord, Taunton, Pawtucket, and Rowley, but none of these fared well. The most ambitious of all was at Hammersmith, close to sizable supplies of bog iron. Representing a group of merchants organized as the Company of Undertakers for the Iron Works in New England, John Winthrop, Jr., left for England in 1642 to raise money for the project. The enterprise was capitalized at $60,000, and control went to a group of British business leaders headed by John Becx, who owned furnaces and forges in Gloucestershire. Massachusetts granted a twenty-one-year monopoly and other special privileges to the business. Within a few years the furnaces were producing a ton of iron a day, much to the satisfaction of the colonial government, but no profit, much to the displeasure of the investors in London. Debts piled up, managers were replaced, bills were protested, and lawsuits were filed. Litigation dragged on for more than twenty years. Major creditors took control and then lost possession by foreclosure in 1676, by which time the physical enterprise was abandoned and in total disrepair.

It was many decades before any significant amount of iron was produced in the colonies. Iron manufacture began in Pennsylvania, with its rich resources of

CALVINISM AND BUSINESS

Americans were the children of the Reformation. Many came to the colonies to escape persecution for their religious faiths. But whether they were Puritans in Massachusetts or Quakers in Pennsylvania and Nantucket, French Huguenots in New Rochelle, Reformed Dutch in New York, Methodists, Moravians, or Mennonites, they were all spiritual descendants—if not followers —of the teachings of the revolutionary theologian John Calvin.

This great reformer of the 1500's preached the gloomy conclusion that mankind had been predestined by Adam's original sin, and only a so-called "elect" few had heaven as their final destination. Prayer, alms-giving, vows of poverty, contemplation, or cultural pursuits—none of these could buy one's way to salvation.

The only way to bring the kingdom of heaven to earth was through the glorification of God by action. To do that required sacrifice, labor, discipline, and hard work by the individual. These virtues—clearly the same ones that enhance the doing of business—would prove that man was worthy of God. Doing good was a way of giving proof— both to oneself and to others—that a

ROSENBACH COLLECTION, FREE LIBRARY OF PHILADELPHIA

"The idle Fool is Whipt at School," warned the New-England Primer *in 1769.*

man had earned divine approval. And, in Calvin's view, doing well was evidence of doing good. Hard work that yielded riches could provide visible testimony to all men that one was elect.

Thrift, sobriety, and industriousness thus became the greatest of Protestant virtues. By the same token, indolence, sloth, and poverty (as debtors discovered) were sure indications that eventually there would be hell to face.

The true Calvinist was a driven man. Since luck and circumstance had no bearing on his fate, a person could achieve the personal satisfaction that he was one of the elect only by his own actions. The late British economist R. H. Tawney described him this way: "Tempered by self-examination, self-discipline, self-control, he is the practical ascetic, whose victories are won not in the cloister, but on the battlefield, in the counting-house, and in the market."

Calvinism dovetailed into a society that was moving into a money economy. Calvin's elite were not the rich, land-owning aristocracy nor those who inherited nobility. He was addressing the emerging middle class, and the American colonies provided a uniquely fertile ground from which it could spring. "What reason is there," wrote Calvin, "why the income from business should not be larger than from land-owning? Whence do the merchant's profits come, except from his own diligence and industry?"

While Calvinism did not discourage the accumulation of money, it took a dim view of wearing wealth on one's sleeve. The sober black garb of the Puritans, and even of many American businessmen today, attests to that conservatism. One Nantucket Quaker of the 1800's warned that if his son built his home two stories high, the father would never set foot in it. The son did; the father did not.

In sum, *laborare est orare*—"to work is to pray." Calvin even referred to God as "the great Taskmaster" and looked around for tasks man should undertake. In time, the harsh ethics of the Puritans were tempered by utili-

ore and coal, about 1720 in the Coventry forge on French Creek. By 1728 there were four blast furnaces operating in Pennsylvania, and Lancaster gradually became a major center for the industry. But the earliest iron exports of any consequence appear to have been produced at works in Virginia and Maryland, and the two middle colonies shipped most of the bar and pig iron that was sent to England between 1728 and 1755. British policy, however, saw to it that most of the finished iron products went in the opposite direction, from England to the colonies.

MERCANTILISM AND THE MERCHANTS

In Europe the expanding trade of the Commercial Revolution hastened the decline of feudalism. Former serfs became yeomen, hired laborers, or rent-paying tenants. The power of the craft guilds to distribute work to skilled laborers was undermined by the growth of larger manufacturing establishments. The decen-

tralized power of the nobility and the trade primacy of the towns were replaced by national power and a growing spirit of nationalism.

In the new order, a nation had to mobilize all its strengths and resources to compete with other nations. The commercial goal, not much different from today's, was to achieve a favorable balance of international payments by exporting goods that had a greater total value than those imported, so that a treasury of gold and silver would be built. To do this, home industry was encouraged through protective tariffs, through bounties for production of certain goods, and through actual restriction of imports. Such measures were part of what came to be known as mercantilism, a system that closely identified the interests of the merchants and manufacturers with those of the nation itself. Under mercantilism it was felt that commercial power could be translated directly into national wealth and political and military power.

Colonization also fitted neatly into mercantilistic thinking. By supplying raw materials, colonies could lessen the dependence of the mother country on outside sources of supplies. In return for these raw materials, the older nation could supply a wide variety of finished goods and in this way build up its own more profitable manufacturing industries.

Britain's colonies in the New World exemplified the scheme, producing the raw materials that otherwise would have to be purchased outside the empire, and providing a market for finished goods. To maintain this condition, manufacturing had to be discouraged in the colonies, and this occasionally required specific prohibitive legislation passed by Parliament. But the colonies derived benefits from mercantilism, too, especially in the early years. For one thing, they were part of the system and therefore stood to participate in its rewards, as long as it continued to work. For another, the easiest industries to start in a new country are those that seek to extract the natural wealth of soil, sea, and forest; the system of bounties paid for the most desired products made such industries profitable. Finally, whenever the system became too oppressive, it could be evaded through smuggling and the corruption of petty officials, both relatively easy in a land separated from England by 3,000 miles of difficult navigation.

Much as the mercantile system might subordinate colonial interests to those of England, the merchants in the New World were happy to work within it, as long as they were able to turn a profit. Even the Puritan merchants, whose disaffection from the mother country was on other than commercial grounds, believed in the principle of the "just price"—one by which the buyer might meet his needs and the seller would be rewarded for his industry. There was nothing in the rigid Calvinism of the Puritans that conflicted with

tarian thinkers. A notable example was Benjamin Franklin, who, though he counted himself a freethinker, was brought up in a strict Calvinist household. His father drilled into him the exhortation from Proverbs: "Seest thou a man diligent in his business. He shall stand before kings." And Franklin penned his aphorisms as if he were shaking his finger at his readers. Thus, in his *Advice to a Young Tradesman* of 1748:

Remember that *time* is money. He that can earn ten shillings a day by his labour, and goes abroad, or sits idle, one half of that day, though he spends but sixpence during his diversion of idleness, ought not to reckon *that* his only expense; he has really spent, or rather thrown away, five shillings besides.

Idleness led to doing the devil's work, rather than God's, and debtors' prisons were an invention of the 1600's.

The religious justification that Calvinism gave to doing business diligently has been diluted over the years. But the concept has lingered on with particular strength in the United States. Horatio Alger stories of self-made men still fill the press. Several American Presidents were born in log cabins. One who came from modest surroundings was aptly named Calvin Coolidge, and he told the American people: "America recognizes no aristocracy save those who work."

the idea of venturing for possible gain, which was one of the essentially capitalistic ideas built into mercantilism, as was the practice of lending money for whatever interest the traffic would bear.

It was a system that attracted the shrewd and unprincipled as well as the hard-working and the experienced. As the joint-stock companies disintegrated around the 1630's, control of New World commerce was taken over by a few leading colonists, as well as by a new breed of adventurers who left England, often under a cloud, to make their killings in America. Among the first to arrive were Thomas Weston, a refugee from a charge of arms smuggling; John Oldham, who was evicted from Plymouth Colony for his behavior; and Thomas Morton and Edward Astley, who sold arms and liquor illegally to the Indians—all of them looked on by the Puritans as religious and social outcasts. But this hardly impaired their capacity to make a good trade and draw a fast profit.

One source of such profit lay in selling manufactured goods—a skillet, a yard of woven cloth, a pound of nails. As population increased in the 1630's, such products became exceedingly scarce and prices inflated wildly. The merchant who was first at the docks and fastest with a deal for fresh cargo could expect rich gains, whether he was an established tradesman or a fly-by-night. At one point the Puritans granted to nine men from as many towns the exclusive right to board incoming ships in their own areas. But this monopoly, like so many others, was unenforceable, and the law was quickly repealed.

The success of most colonial industries depended largely on the merchants and their astuteness. The merchants needed to be skilled and knowledgeable in all matters pertaining to trade—buying, selling, shipping, currencies, tariffs, and all the news they could gather of new laws, treaties, wars, and political upheavals. It was they who organized, shipped, and marketed the hauls from the fishery, tying into the capital and the market connections of other merchants in England. Or a merchant might himself go into the business of providing fishing vessels or of processing timber. Two members of the Hutchinson family, for example, bought out nineteen sawmills on New Hampshire's Great Works River in order to assure themselves of all the timber products they needed.

International commerce was frequently more than just a two-way transaction. A Massachusetts Bay merchant, Samuel Maverick, who exhibited all the free-wheeling independence of his later Texas namesake, set up in 1641 what may well have been the first "triangular" trade. He bought goods shipped from Bristol, paying for them by sending back whale oil and by shipping clapboards to Málaga in Spain, from whence Spanish money and fruit were sent to the Bristol agent and credited to Maverick's account. Much of what came to be called triangular trading actually amounted to polygons of more complex structure. They might have involved fish and tobacco from the colonies, molasses and sugar from the West Indies, wine from Madeira, slaves from Africa, and a variety of manufactured products from England and other European ports. While many of these trades were organized in London, American merchants soon managed to take over two or three legs of such a journey, or even to initiate the voyages themselves.

Links of kinship or acquaintance with London merchants were especially valuable to those engaged in trade in the colonies. One of the leading Boston merchants, Valentine Hill, had dealings with his brother in London. Robert Keayne and Thomas Savage began their careers in the tailoring trade in London, then used their British connections after they emigrated to Massachusetts. The same method was used to develop reliable agents and correspondents for international commerce. Keayne's son, Benjamin, moved back to London to become his father's agent there; merchants William Vassal and Richard Vines left the colonies for the West Indies, where they represented some of their old business associates.

Around 1660 many of the first generation of leading merchants—Keayne, Hill, William Tyng, Henry Shrimpton, and others—died off. Some of their sons had returned to England, while others took their father's place in the mercantile world. But still other merchants came from England or emerged from the background of colonial affairs to take on new prominence—Colonel Thomas Temple, who controlled the trade of Nova Scotia; Thomas Breedon, Temple's Boston agent and banker; and Richard Wharton. To the already settled members of the Puritan establishment, this was an upstart breed. Not only were they single-minded merchant adventurers, but their sights and their allegiance were pointed primarily toward England, to which many hoped to return and whose interests they defended over those of the colonies. Maverick testified before government councils in London as to the excessive spirit of independence of the Puritan colonists, and Shrimpton's son, Samuel, thought of himself as more Englishman than New Englander.

Although the differences were sharp, many of them were eventually dissipated by intermarriage and by remarriages among widows and widowers, and these unions virtually created many-tentacled merchant clans in each community. By 1700 the Pepperrells, Frosts, and Brays, leading merchants of Kittery, Maine, were all intermarried. In the course of his thirty-year business career, Richard Wharton married, successivly, daughters of the Tyng, Higginson, and Winthrop families. And the ten children of William and Edward Tyng also married into the Bradstreet, Savage, Usher,

The South East Prospect of the City of Philadelphia B: Peter Cooper Painter

Philadelphia on the Delaware River was a thriving mercantile city when this view was painted by a signboard artist in 1720.

Gibbons, Brattle, Searle, and Dudley families.

It was people like these who were forming the nucleus of a colonial upper class in the northern cities — merchants who had accumulated extensive holdings of property, owned their own wharves and warehouses, operated shops as well as counting houses, and who often had their own ships or shares in shipping ventures. Among the best known were Andrew Belcher, Samuel Lillie, William Clarke, and Andrew Faneuil in Boston; Samuel Carpenter, Edward Shippen, and Isaac Norris in Philadelphia; and Caleb Heathcote, Benjamin Faneuil, Abraham De Peyster, Rip Van Dam, and the Van Horns in New York.

How rich were they? In 1670 some thirty Massachusetts merchants had estates valued from $50,000 to $150,000 each. Samuel Shrimpton, who had inherited almost $60,000 from his father, parlayed this into a much larger fortune through land investments and became the richest man in Boston, in 1687 paying the largest tax in that city on his mercantile property. But even an accumulation of $15,000 or $20,000 was then regarded as substantial wealth. Cornelius Steenwyck, a liquor dealer thought to be New York's richest merchant, left an estate of something under $25,000 when he died in 1686.

In the colonies, unlike England, the way of trade was regarded not so much the symbol of a discrete social stratum as it was an open road to wealth and position. But even in the New World the concentration of economic and political power among the merchant groups was hardening into set patterns, so that the ladder was becoming more difficult to climb in the 1700's.

THE NAVIGATION ACTS

The late 1600's and the 1700's were years of capital accumulation and growing capitalism in the colonies. In the South were the plantation lords, with their slaves and servants; in New York were the landgraves, with their tenant farmers and paid workers; in the towns, and especially in New England, were the merchants, who not only carried on trade but organized it — buying from the backland farmers, processing goods or having them processed, transporting them overland and overseas, finding markets, and wheeling and dealing.

This capacity for organizing the many processes of business was making the merchant the dominant class throughout the colonies — and with this leadership came social and economic tensions. Even though the wealthy landowners were the ostensible targets of such uprisings as Bacon's Rebellion in Virginia and other popular outbursts in New York and Georgia, the essential class division that was forming was between the laborers and back-country farmers, on the one hand, and the powerful merchants of the coastal cities, on the other. The very real gulf between them was probably wider than the developing rift between the colonies and the mother country. Indeed, the clash of interests between America and England was not so

25

much one between the two peoples as a whole as it was between the merchants of the New World and the Old, and it was these tradesmen who felt the effects first and hardest when the British applied restrictive measures to colonial commerce.

Colonial merchants managed to achieve a degree of commercial independence by setting up manufacturing facilities in the New World, by organizing their own trading voyages in the world, by letting the Dutch handle their shipping, and by going to sea in their own bottoms. The reactions of the British merchants were those of a parent to a thankless child. They turned to their government and, under the prevailing mercantilistic notions, succeeded in having laws passed to curtail such initiative on the part of the colonists.

These came to be known as the Navigation Acts, the first of which were enacted in the 1650's and 1660's. The Act of 1651 required that any goods imported into England, Ireland, or the colonies be in ships owned and manned primarily by British subjects. When the colonies bridled at this restriction and sought to evade it by continuing to trade with Dutch middlemen, Parliament in 1661 passed an act "enumerating" articles that could be shipped only to England from the colonies — sugar, tobacco, wool, and indigo, all of them important to the American export trade.

While some merchants felt their effects more than others, the Navigation Acts were not very damaging to the fundamental economy of the colonies. They did not, for example, prohibit the export of fish, lumber, and naval stores to Europe and the Atlantic islands off the European coast. They helped eliminate the competition of foreign merchants who were engaged in colonial trade. And they exempted imports of such items as wines from Madeira and the Azores, and salt needed by the fisheries. Yet their intent appeared to be discriminatory. The acts emphasized that the colonists existed for the mother country, without providing the corollary that England sought the greatest good for her colonies as well.

A great many factors contributed to this sense of colonial subordination, not the least of which was a chronic money shortage in the New World. Although great stocks of gold and silver had come originally from America, the precious metals moved swiftly toward European treasuries, and inadequate supplies of hard money and credit had long been an impediment to colonial merchants. Although most business was transacted in pounds, shillings, and pence, these coins were rarely seen in the colonies, since any currency that reached the New World was quickly drained away to pay debts and dividends in England.

In these circumstances the colonies did what they could. Barter, of course, was the earliest and easiest solution. Eventually this gave way to a somewhat more sophisticated form of trading — commodity money.

The Custom House Quay on London's Thames River was pictured in this 1757 painting by Samuel Scott.

Tobacco warehouse receipts were popular forms of credit in Virginia and Maryland. Other makeshift forms of staple currencies at various times included lumber in New Hampshire and wheat, beef, pork, cattle, Indian corn, and barley in most of the middle colonies and New England. Beaver furs and wampum beads also figured in trade at times. In virtually all cases, colonial laws provided that these commodities be legal tender for all public and private debts, unless otherwise provided by contract.

So short was the supply of hard money that any means would be employed to obtain it. Piracy and privateering were probably the major sources of currency for the colonies, and it has been estimated that $500,000 of such treasure annually found its way to New York alone. Some charity money was raised by British sympathizers with the Puritan cause, and merchants sought to use such funds, on deposit in London, as credits to pay off British debts, on which interest rates of 20 to 25 per cent were common.

Duties imposed on imports by the colonies, for both foreign and intercolonial trade, were small, usually under 5 per cent. They were primarily for the purpose of raising revenues rather than for the protection of local industries. Indeed, a number of colonies sometimes practiced a reverse protectionism by banning the *export* of much-needed goods.

Although the Navigation Acts were quite well enforced, there were merchants willing to take great risks by smuggling and engaging in illegal trade with

France and the Spanish West Indies, which paid in cash. In the 1660's, Philip English (who had changed his name from Philippe L'Anglois after he moved from the island of Jersey to Salem, Massachusetts) was carrying on extensive trade with merchant connections from Spain to Sweden. And in 1675 a temporary glut of French merchandise was reported in the Boston market, the result in part of the activities of a Frenchman, Andrew Faneuil, precursor of one of New England's major commercial dynasties.

This illegal trade did not sit well with the London merchants, twenty-four of whom signed a petition of protest that was presented in 1686 to the Lords of Trade, the committee of the Privy Council that looked after colonial affairs. The Lords estimated that the smuggling trade cost the British $300,000 a year in lost duties. In 1696 the responsibility for overseeing the colonies and their commercial life was given to the newly created Board of Trade, whose eight active members were representative of the English merchants and

were confirmed mercantilists. A glaring weakness of this arrangement was that none of the eight had ever lived in the colonies, and consequently they had little feel for the mood or outlook of the colonists.

By the early 1700's many forces seemed to be conspiring to drive wider the wedge between the merchant classes of England and those of her American colonies. One English economist estimated that the domestic commerce carried on among the northern colonies was almost equal to that with Britain, and that their trade with the West Indies and southern Europe was greater than either. Intercolonial trade kept increasing, as the older settlements tended to supply provisions to the newer. New York exchanged flour for New England rum, which in turn was distributed inland and to the south; Pennsylvania sold beer to Canada, and Massachusetts cider was sent to Maryland; a young Benedict Arnold made good profits selling Connecticut cheese in Canada; and soap was traded from Massachusetts to Virginia. These activities helped give the business-

The Way to Wealth
MOSES BROWN

Moses Brown (1738–1836) was the most eccentric of the premier family of Rhode Island business. He converted from a Baptist to an ardent Quaker at the age of thirty-five, but his spiritual fervor seemed only to inflame and give added inspiration to his inventive business sense.

The Browns had arrived in Providence in 1638; their ledger books date from 1732 and have not yet been closed. Moses was one of four brothers who inherited their father's wealth and commercial energy. He learned the art of double-entry bookkeeping, new in the colonies, from his Uncle Obadiah's 1729 edition of *A Guide to Book Keepers According to the Italian Manner*. Soon he and his brothers, under the firm name of Nicholas Brown & Co., cornered the spermaceti candle trade. They even tried to control prices by setting up an early form of trust called the United Company of Spermaceti Chandlers.

As an agent for his brothers, Moses frequently traveled to Nantucket to secure supplies of whale spermaceti and to Newport to underwrite voyages in the triangular trade. His exposure to the inhumanities of the slave trade

Moses Brown

turned him into an early abolitionist (he freed his few slaves in 1774) and led to his becoming a Quaker.

Moses came from an adventuresome family. Uncle Obadiah built a mill to grind "chocklit," and brother John led the capture and burning of the British schooner *Gaspee* after it pursued smugglers too zealously into the Narragansett shoals. Moses even tried to introduce silkworms into the colonies in

1764, but failed when the worms found no vegetation amenable to their tastes. In 1770 he took a lead in bringing Rhode Island College to Providence where it became Brown University thirty-four years later, and in 1791 he was instrumental in founding the Providence Bank, the fifth commercial bank in the United States at the time.

Most of all, Moses realized early that commerce alone could not support the new republic and that domestic manufacturers were essential to combat trade imbalances and the resultant debt to Britain. He welcomed the young English spinning mechanic, Samuel Slater, to Providence to start what became the great textile industry of New England. The first piece of "double Jane back" twilled cotton cloth was spun on June 6, 1789, in the factory owned by Moses and his son-in-law, William Almy.

Moses was all for the exchange of business information to further national industry. He wrote: "I think it will be for the advantage of the manufactory to hold an open correspondence and communicate freely what may tend to perfect the business and promote it in our country."

men of the colonies a stronger sense of identity and interdependence than they had ever had before.

THE ACTS OF TRADE

The 1700's were a period of vexation and counter-vexation between the colonies and the center of empire. Stubbornness, thoughtlessness, and selfishness on both sides played a large role in these misunderstandings and mounting antagonisms. But mainly at fault were the inherent weaknesses of the mercantilist system, which had served well in drawing the curtains of feudalism but which was ill-fitted to usher in yet a new economic era.

As manufactures developed in the colonies, British tradesmen objected to the competition. Parliament in 1699 forbade the export of wool yarn or cloth from the colonies. The paper industry was similarly restricted. With increasing iron production in America, the British ordained that the colonies could send pig and bar iron to England, for further processing there, but could operate no slitting or rolling mills. When colonial hat-makers began to reach out to markets in Spain, Portugal, Ireland, and the West Indies, the London Company of Feltmakers had an act passed that prohibited both export and intercolonial commerce in hats.

The mercantilist doctrine that made the home country the purveyor of expensive finished goods and relegated the colonies to supplying inexpensive raw materials was bound to leave the New World with an unfavorable trade balance. In 1700 the colonies imported about $250,000 more in goods from England than they sent back. By the 1760's this imbalance had reached an average of $5 million a year, most of it applicable to the colonies north of Maryland. The difference was made up largely by profits from the extensive molasses trade with the West Indies. Only about a fifth of the molasses used by New England's distilleries was provided by the British sugar islands, the remainder coming from the more efficient and pro-

The Way to Wealth
WILLIAM BYRD II

William Byrd II

William Byrd II (1674–1744) knew Eden when he saw it, and during his lifetime he bought 180,000 acres of it. As a result, he left a name that continues to spell wealth and prerogative in Virginia. Born in that colony, Byrd was sent to Europe for his education. It included studying trade with the Dutch when he was fifteen, and then law at London's Middle Temple. At age thirty-one, upon news of his father's death, he returned to Virginia and succeeded to an inheritance of 26,000 acres.

Byrd approached colonial life with the lofty philosophy of an Enlightenment man; the day-to-day exigencies of his widespread interests in Virginia demanded encyclopedic knowledge. His botanical pursuits won him election to the Royal Society. He wrote a medical "Discourse Concerning the Plague," which, naturally, recommended tobacco as a curative. He planted tobacco, traded furs and slaves, raised fruits and vegetables, mined coal and iron, tanned hides, and manufactured home-spun. At thirty-two he was appointed Receiver-General of Her Majesty's revenues in Virginia from quitrents—rents paid in lieu of other services owed the Crown—and later he also became a councilor in the House of Burgesses.

And Byrd bought land. "I must needs be of your opinion," he wrote a friend in 1736, "to convert as much of your income as possible into ground rents, which will withstand every calamity but an earthquake."

At fifty-three Byrd was appointed one of three Virginia commissioners to conduct a survey of the boundary be-tween his colony and North Carolina. With a party of forty laborers, six other commissioners, four surveyors, and a chaplain to convert the Indians, he laid a line 241 miles long, stretching inland to the foothills of the Appalachians. En route, through questionable preference, he acquired from the North Carolina commissioners some 20,000 acres of land for himself for £200. He termed it the "land of Eden," after Governor Charles Eden of North Carolina.

Byrd built a lordly Georgian house, which he called Westover, on the James River. Its enormous library of 3,675 volumes and an Italian marble mantel in one of its rooms were considered wonders of the colonies, but its basement was nevertheless burrowed with secret tunnels to provide escape from Indian raids.

Byrd was the archetype of the southern tobacco squirearchs who dominated the tidewater and thrust the boundaries of the coastal states inland in latitudinal lines toward the Mississippi River. Land was wealth to these men. But they had a further motive: tobacco burned up the unfertilized soil of the South, and new lands to the west were a necessity for their annual income.

ductive sugar industry in the French islands.

In 1733 Parliament imposed a tax of twelve cents a gallon on all molasses coming into the colonies from non-British sources. Such a tax, of course, was ruinous to the distilling industry, but by the same token it threatened all industries involved in the triangular trade—in rum to Africa, slaves from Africa to the colonies, and fish, produce, and slaves to the West Indies. The tax was so prohibitive as to be unenforceable, since it occasioned the most extensive smuggling trade the colonies had seen up to that time.

But this situation could not last, because sugar was too important to British capitalists. British investors had sunk $300 million in Jamaica, Barbados, and the other sugar islands by the 1760's, six times as large as their total investments in the colonies of the American mainland. Protecting these interests were seventy "sugar lords" in Parliament. So while many in England were inclined to overlook the smuggling trade that was so vital to the colonial economy, the sugar interests were unhappy—and were particularly incensed that French smuggling had continued through the French and Indian War.

Though that war had won Canada and the Mississippi Valley for England, it had been costly in both men and money. Britain's national debt had risen from $360 million in 1755 to almost $650 million in 1764. While this represented an investment that might eventually pay off when the prolific British colonists (they doubled their population every twenty-five years) exceeded the number of French and Indians in these territories, there was still a burdensome short-term expense. The British had to maintain an army of 10,000 troops, at an annual cost of more than $1 million, in the colonies—a force whose need was demonstrated when Pontiac led a major Indian uprising in 1763.

The British quite logically felt that it was only fair for the colonists to share in these costs. When the war ended, George Grenville, brother-in-law of William Pitt, became Prime Minister of England and undertook the job of balancing the budget. He and Charles Townshend, who was named president of the Board of Trade, decided that the period of "salutary neglect" of the colonies had to come to an end.

When he took office in 1763, Grenville found laws on the books that should have been providing a sizable income from the colonies, but the actual collections amounted to a paltry $9,000 a year. Some new approaches appeared to be needed. The first law passed by the new regime was the Sugar Act—which, oddly enough, *cut* the molasses tax in half. The intention was to discourage evasion of the tax. Although colonial administrators cautioned that the lower duty of seventy-five cents a gallon was still more than twice the cost of smuggling, the British this time intended to enforce the tax. They assigned the job to the Navy, which was

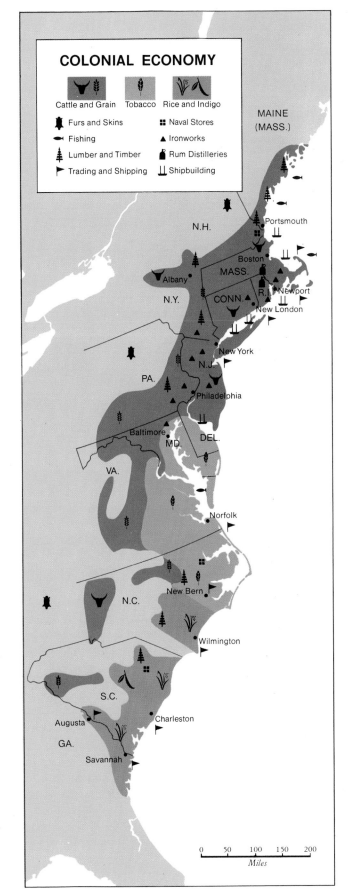

COLONIAL ECONOMY

Cattle and Grain   Tobacco   Rice and Indigo

Furs and Skins   Naval Stores
Fishing   Ironworks
Lumber and Timber   Rum Distilleries
Trading and Shipping   Shipbuilding

The repeal of the Stamp Act produced this British print, showing Grenville carrying his dead "child" in a funeral procession.

too inflexible and unimaginative to understand the practical need for smuggling, and the prosecution of violators was turned over to the admiralty courts.

Although the molasses tax was the most burdensome, other restrictive measures contributed to the heavy yoke on colonial businessmen. Duties were also placed on coffee, wines, foreign indigo, silks, and calicoes. The first duty on Madeira wines—thirty-five dollars a ton—was bound to hurt the trade with the wine islands. A sizable commerce in lumber had been built up with Europe, and new restrictions forbade the shipment of lumber to any place in Europe except Great Britain, so that reshipment costs would necessitate raising prices. The immediate consequence of these Acts of Trade was an economic depression in the middle and northern colonies, felt first by the merchants and soon afterward by the small tradesmen, workers, and farmers.

With every new effort the colonies made to operate under the mercantilist system, things seemed to fall apart. When they tried to increase manufactures to make up the trade deficit, their British competitors were quick to have restraining laws passed; their efforts to develop greater external trade were frustrated and banned; increased smuggling brought more stringent enforcement; even when colonists sought to expand the base of their domestic economy by building new enterprises, these were discouraged by British investors who had a large stake in colonial businesses and who feared added competition.

Even the last—and worst—resort, that of issuing paper money to facilitate commerce, was prohibited. Massachusetts had issued bills of credit as early as 1690 to pay soldiers who had been sent on an expedition to Canada. Other colonies found this a means of filling the commercial need that grew out of the shortage of hard money. Paper money worked at first, but when too much was issued it weakened in value and finally collapsed. Parliament in 1751 forbade the issuance of bills of credit as legal tender in New England, and in 1764 the Board of Trade banned paper money in the colonies—a prohibition that would have hamstrung trade, had it been effective.

In these circumstances, a stamp tax on all legal and official documents, as well as on newspapers, dice, and playing cards, became the indignity heaped on injury. Grenville had first thought of such a tax, which had long been in force in England, in 1763. The act became law in 1765 and aroused an immediate and loud storm of protest, far out of proportion to the minor hardship the taxes caused. Resentment at first took only the form of grumbling, and one colonial official pointed out that "the Merchants talk much, but cannot bring them to Act." But a Stamp Act Congress, the first such joint action undertaken on the colonists' own initiative, met in the New York City Hall in October, 1765. Public clamor mounted. Officials pretended not to know how to distribute the stamped documents, and stamp collectors, often fearful for their persons, turned in their resignations. The stamp tax also came under pressure from British merchants, whose trade was being hurt by recession and by boycotts in the colonies, and it was repealed in 1766.

The following year, however, the British came back with new taxes — a series of measures known as the Townshend Acts, which imposed duties on colonial imports of glass, lead, painters' colors, paper, and tea. Customs commissioners were named and sent to the colonies and, not loath to call for the support of British troops, they actually collected the duties, which was a somewhat novel experience for the times.

Although colonial merchants were traditionally competitive, they started to sense the advantages of organizing to protect their commonality of interests. Throughout the colonies the upper classes objected to Grenville's measures, and this helped bring to a focus all their resentments, old and new, against Great Britain. Southern planters — including George Washington, Thomas Jefferson, and James Madison — voiced their protests against the low prices paid for their crops by British merchants, who were also their creditors. Colonial merchants — such as John Hancock, Elbridge Gerry, and Robert Morris — complained of heavy taxes and the reduction of their profits. The New York aristocrats — typified by Philip Livingston, Stephen van Rensselaer, and Gouverneur Morris — felt the pinch in their interests in land, commerce, and the fur trade.

The first answer to the Townshend Acts was a boycott against British goods, initiated by merchants of the northern colonies. At the instigation of Captain Daniel Malcolm, widely known as a smuggler, a group of Boston merchants met in March, 1768, to discuss boycott plans. After several meetings, a nonimportation agreement was drawn up, its adoption depending on a similar agreement by the other major northern ports, New York and Philadelphia. The New York merchants proposed to halt imports until the duties were repealed, provided the other ports concurred. But the Philadelphians felt their interests were not as much affected, and the entire project fell through.

The Boston merchants then decided to go it alone, and early in 1769 agreed to stop all but a few exempted imports from Britain for a year. Merchants of the other two ports joined in, and they put pressure on Newport to do the same. Expressing his approval of such a plan for Virginia, George Washington told his neighbor George Mason that it might be even better to urge the people not to buy British imports. By that autumn all the colonies but New Hampshire had adopted nonimportation agreements. Boston merchants even went so far as to refuse to deal with any vessel that had loaded any of the forbidden goods at a British port.

A British customhouse officer, tarred and feathered, is threatened with a dousing of tea by colonials in Boston.

So popular were these measures that many colonists were encouraged to play an activist role in helping to enforce them. A Boston informer was tarred, feathered, and paraded through the streets. Three others in New York suffered similar indignities. The revenue sloop *Liberty* was dismantled and burnt when it brought two suspected smuggling vessels into Newport harbor. And no one tried to collect a reward of fifty pounds sterling offered to apprehend the perpetrators of a tarring and feathering.

On top of these pressures from the colonies, London merchants, hurting from the slowdown in colonial trade, expressed their displeasure at the offending acts, and a group of twenty-eight organized a committee to get other merchants to swamp Parliament with their objections. In 1770 most of the duties were withdrawn, and only a nominal tax on tea was left.

In the three years from 1770 to 1773 political tempers cooled, and business flourished in the colonies. European floods created a great demand for corn. In the wake of nonimportation, the favorable trade balance shifted for the first time toward the colonies, and there was even a net flow of gold and sterling from London. But this did not last long, as colonial merchants went on a buying spree and overstocked their shelves.

The political climate soon warmed up as well. The colonists' response to the remaining tax was to boycott British tea and smuggle in Dutch tea instead. Then, in 1773, Parliament decided to come to the rescue of the faltering East India Company, near bankruptcy as

31

great stores of unsold goods lay in its warehouses. They permitted the company to sell the tea directly to the colonies, free of all taxes except the threepence Townshend duty. The effect would be to cut the price of tea to the colonies to half of what the Dutch product cost, and to less than what the English themselves had to pay.

The tea bargain appeared to be a great parliamentary ploy, bracing up the foundering company, offering the colonists a price they could not resist, and reasserting the principle of the right of Parliament to levy taxes on the colonies. But the wary colonial merchants were not taken in by any of this. Such a special monopoly privilege for the East India Company might be followed by having it distribute tea through its own agents in the New World, the merchants feared. Similar monopolies on other products might then squeeze local merchants out of business.

On December 16 the citizens and merchants of Boston met at Faneuil Hall. That night three companies of fifty men each, masquerading as Mohawk Indians, left the meeting to board three tea ships in the harbor, under the guns of the British Navy. With considerable help from the crews, they dumped all the tea overboard but carefully avoided damage to the ships or other cargo. The Boston Tea Party was followed by others over the course of the next year: tea was thrown into the Cooper River at Charleston, South Carolina; burned by "Indians" at Greenwich, New Jersey; dumped and burned in New York and Annapolis.

But except for its symbolism, tea was no longer the issue. The lines had been drawn, and the colonists were not about to retreat. Their opposition now centered firmly on the principle of taxation without their consent and participation. In England too there was a back-stiffening. For more than a century Parliament had been imposing duties on the colonies, even in times of penury and deprivation. So how could the colonists, many of them now men of great substance

TWO DOCUMENTS OF 1776

By a coincidence of history rather than of forethought, two documents made their appearance in 1776. Which one had more enduring significance remains moot—the Declaration of Independence, published July 4 in the American colonies, or Adam Smith's *An Inquiry Into the Nature and Causes of the Wealth of Nations*, published in the spring of that year of ferment.

Both tolled the knell of the mercantile system, of which the colonies were legitimate offspring. As a political paper, the Declaration of Independence, drafted by the thirty-three-year-old Virginia lawyer Thomas Jefferson and tempered by the seventy-year-old master of many trades Benjamin Franklin, ignored the divine right of kings and assumed that the mercantile system was a dead letter. Adam Smith's *Wealth of Nations* presumed the same and, at much greater length, set out to prove it. Smith believed that economic health arose from free trade, little government intervention, and the exercise of self-interest by reasonable men engaged in the profitable use of capital. The Declaration asserted the right of the American colonists to live by those principles; in subsequent years the new American states gave Adam Smith's ideas their first great test.

A fifty-three-year-old retired professor of moral philosophy at Glasgow University in Scotland when his *Wealth of Nations* appeared, Smith endeavored to produce the first lucid, detailed review of international economic principles. In his work is a condemnation of mercantilism as a wasteful illusion. He itemized the vast expense of defending the British colonies in North America, an outlay which the colonists refused to repay even in part.

The mercantile system of colonial monopolies seemed to work well when the mother country traded with a distant population, different in kind and character from that of the motherland. But prior to the 1640's the British colonies in North America were colonized with British people. They carried overseas a sense more of British liberties than of British identity, and when the time came, they behaved too much like the British.

The population of these colonies by 1776 was fully a fourth that of the British Isles. These people were imbued with a high degree of self-interest and small concern for a mother country from which most were removed by generations. Edmund Burke, hardly a revolutionist himself, analyzed the colonial spirit in his famous speech on "Conciliation With the Colonies," on March 22, 1775. It was immediately reprinted in New York. Said Burke:

England, Sirs, is a nation which still I hope respects, and formerly adored her freedom. The colonists emigrated from you, when this part of your character was most predominant; and they took this bias and direction the moment they parted from your hands. They are therefore not only devoted to liberty, but liberty according to English ideas, and on English principles.

In view of such Anglo-Saxon attitudes, Smith opted for the pragmatic course in colonial relationships. Though he was aware that nationalistic pride would dictate an attempt by the Crown to hold on to its colonies, he deplored it. In the closing paragraph of his book, he said:

The rulers of Great Britain have, for more than a century past, amused the people with the imagination that they possessed a great empire on the west side of the Atlantic. . . . the effects of the monopoly of the colony trade, it has been shown, are, to the great body of the people, mere loss instead of profit. . . . If any of the provinces of the British empire cannot be made to contribute towards the support of the whole empire, it is surely time that Great Britain should free

and prosperity, object to a small tax whose proceeds were meant for their own defense and expansion?

BUSINESSMEN AND THE WAR

Late in 1774 the colonial legislature and the Continental Congress encouraged the start of a new boycott. A number of merchants, remembering their earlier losses, were reluctant to go through the same thing again, but they could not hold back a tide that they themselves had helped unleash.

Colonial merchants, like businessmen throughout history, were people of a decidedly practical turn of mind. Yet many of the wealthier colonists were also among the best educated and most politically sophisticated people of their time. They tended to be avid readers, and much of the reading then available dealt with the law and political philosophy. The Founding Fathers, who included a large number of merchants, wealthy planters, and landed aristocrats, had an aware-

ness of their own philosophical background that was rare for businessmen of any era.

Not too far back in the history of the time was the great British struggle against the arbitrary or divinely bestowed power of the kings, which climaxed in England's bloodless Revolution of 1688. The man who best articulated the meaning of that contest was John Locke, whose treatise *Of Civil Government* helped shape the rationale of the American revolutionary leaders.

Locke wrote of man's natural rights within the natural law. It was the duty of civil government, he said, to preserve these natural rights, and the responsibility of men to choose new leaders or a new form of government if they failed in this responsibility. Some of Locke's language found its way into the Declaration of Independence. "We hold these truths to be self-evident" may very well have had its source in Locke's discussion of "self-evidence"; "life, liberty, and the pursuit of happiness" may have had some roots in Locke's declaration that "happiness, and that alone"

herself from the expense of defending those provinces in time of war, and of supporting any part of their civil or military establishments in time of peace, and endeavour to accommodate her future views and designs to the real mediocrity of her circumstances.

Only months after he wrote those words, the colonists themselves acted on them.

Their Declaration explained, rather than declared, the compulsion toward American independence. The Continental Congress had already accepted a resolution of independence, submitted weeks before the Declaration was drafted. From the day the Congress opened colonial ports to the trade of the world, April 6, 1776, John Adams felt that the Declaration was inevitable. "As to declarations of independency," he wrote, "read our privateering laws and our commercial laws. What signifies a word?" The act had indeed foreshadowed the word. The Congress had already legislated independence for the colonies when it ended the mercantile dependence on Great Britain. What remained of the Navigation Acts was scuttled.

In the bill of indictments set forth in the Declaration, the colonials complained about Crown control of colonial economies, the use of the royal veto to curb liberal trade and finance laws

passed by colonial legislatures, and acts intended to prevent land settlement westward. The Declaration accused the king of "cutting off our trade with all parts of the world"—a resounding indictment. True, the Boston Tea Party had been an irresponsible act of vandalism that irked many a conservative New Englander—but it did not justify shutting down Boston Harbor. This heavy-handed response by Parliament to the destruction of 342 chests of tea hurt the very merchants who loathed the Sons of Liberty.

Despite the political cartoons of the time, in which the colonies were often personified as a red-skinned daughter in a feather bonnet altercating with her wise mother country, the child had grown up. Burke knew the American character was more than adolescent. Smith had learned it from his meeting in Paris with Franklin, and he predicted that the colonies were a nation "which, indeed, seems very likely to become one of the greatest and most formidable that ever was in the world."

In his *Wealth of Nations*, Smith had warned: "To prohibit a great people, however, from making all that they can of every part of their own produce, or from employing their stock and industry in the way that they judge most advantageous to themselves, is a manifest violation of the most sacred rights

of mankind."

Worse, it violated their sense of self-interest. In Smith's view, economics had to dispense with the notion that its proper end was fattening the national treasury. "It is not from the benevolence of the butcher, the brewer, or the baker that we expect our dinner," he stated, "but from their regard of their own self-interest. We address ourselves not to their humanity, but to their self-love, and never talk to them of our own necessities, but of their advantage." In postulating an economy motivated by the fulfilling of one's own self-interests, Smith was advocating laissez faire—hands-off by government. It was a worldly philosophy that was virtually embodied in the notions of New England's merchants and Virginia's planters.

This sense of self-interest loomed large in the eyes of the fifty-five signers of the Declaration. John Hancock, who penned his name so big that the king could read it without his spectacles, was then under some 500 indictments for smuggling. When the signatories pledged "our lives, our fortunes, and our sacred honor," the order of their pledging had significance. Among them were many wealthy men for whom independence—from the Crown or from any other form of government restraint—made sound business sense.

is what "moves desire"; and, possibly more in the spirit of the businessman's thinking, Locke joined "lives, liberties, and possessions" as being in the province of government to protect for the law-abiding or to take from the disobedient.

The fact that there was available a philosophy to fit the times did not mean that all men, or indeed all those of any single class, subscribed to it. Indeed, there were a great many in all classes of society whose sentiments were markedly loyal to Britain and British authority. Their numbers, if not the decibel count of their assertions, may have been as great as those of the patriots and radical revolutionaries.

A leading symbol of the loyalist cause was Thomas Hutchinson, heir to a huge merchant fortune and the royal governor of Massachusetts. Among the loyal merchant families in New York were the Van Cortlandt, Smith, De Lancey, and Bayard families. Landed families who enjoyed special advantages under the British system included Sir William Pepperrell, with an estate reaching thirty miles along the Maine coast; the Philipse family in New York, with three hundred square miles of land; Lord Granville, who owned a third of North Carolina; and Sir John Johnson, with 50,000 acres in the Mohawk Valley. Also loyalist were the Penn family, whose lands were worth $5 million, and the Calvert family of Maryland.

Supporting the Revolution and seeking independence from Great Britain were families of equal stature and reputation, if not wealth. These included merchants who expected the cancellation of their debts to the British if the colonies won the war.

Members of both groups took up arms and offered some of their resources for the causes they espoused. Of the two, the resources of the revolutionaries proved decidedly slimmer. Indeed, in terms of what was available to get the job done, the American patriots had no business winning the war at all, or even being in it.

Using the fixed standard of the value of gold, the war cost the colonies $104 million—a trifling amount for so vast an enterprise. But it was raised with the greatest of difficulty. Most of it took the form of paper money (continentals), of which Congress had issued almost $250 million by 1780, when they had dropped to a fortieth of their face value. At that level, Congress offered to accept them in payments due from the states. The states themselves had issued about the same amount in paper money, and this too diminished in value. France and Spain helped support the colonies' efforts with loans and gifts, but the total amounted to less than 10 per cent of the costs of the war, while taxes, in the form of requisitions on the states, contributed only about 5 per cent.

To keep war costs down, both Congress and the states made efforts to hold prices in line, particularly on imported goods. The New England states undertook jointly to set wage and price ceilings but were unable to do so without the co-operation of other sections. Eventually, neither the states nor Congress proved up to the job, so that prices soared, profiteers and speculators had a heyday, and debtors paid off their loans in virtually worthless money. Robert Morris, the man whom Washington called "the financier of the Revolution," was named Superintendent of Finance in 1781, and he tried to make better sense of both government financing and spending. But the monetary system remained chaotic and the union's financial state precarious throughout the war.

For most forms of enterprise, however, business went on as usual, or somewhat better than usual. Farmers were happy to sell their products at the price the market would bear—whether the market consisted of local merchants, blockade runners, or Howe's troops. Flour, tobacco, and rice were the chief items of export. Meanwhile, Dutch, French, and Spanish merchants, encountering little trouble in sending their ships through to colonial ports, were delighted to have new markets.

Privateers—who might in other times be deemed pirates—did almost as much business in raiding British shipping abroad as the merchants did in more legitimate commerce. An estimated two thousand privateers, hailing mainly from Massachusetts, sailed in and out of American ports, in almost total disregard of British warships. Cargoes they captured were valued at $18 million. So lucrative was this business that many an ordinary ship was fitted out for these new duties. Before the war, Salem was a fishing community; in wartime its privateering fleet, numbering perhaps as many as 180 vessels, brought in almost 450 prizes; the town's chief shipowner, Elias Hasket Derby, left about one million dollars, mostly in privateering profits, when he died in 1799.

But the most important and longest-lasting business consequences of war were those felt by manufacturing industries. Freed from the confinement of British restrictions, new iron works were started, and paper mills sprang up to feed the needs of newspapers, grown from thirty-seven to more than a hundred during the war. Skilled locksmiths expanded into gun manufacture and collected bounties from the states for the arms they produced. The accurate long rifles of Pennsylvania were in great demand. Congress opened a national armory in Springfield for casting cannon. And businessmen and artisans sought to fill the demands for a great many products in which shortages had developed.

By the time a disorganized and exhausted United States was ready to emerge into the society of nations in 1783, these manufacturing skills and activities carried some of the new nation's brightest hopes for the future.

I The Venturesome Spirit

There were no Indians at Plymouth, but this nineteenth-century version of the 1620 landing pictures the adventurous roots of America. Like all immigrants after them, the Pilgrims risked everything to start anew in an alien world.

"America had to be made before it could be lived in, and that making took centuries, took extraordinary energies and bred an attitude to life that is peculiarly American. It bred the temper of the pioneer, the temper of the gambler, the temper of the booster, the temper of the discounter of the future who is to some extent bound to be a disparager of the past. It took optimism to cross the Atlantic, optimism or despair and anger at the old world from which the reluctant pioneer had come . . . there was always tempting the adventurous or the unlucky the dream of a new chance a little farther on. Movement became a virtue, stability a rather contemptible attitude of mind . . . ."

D. W. Brogan, *The American Character*, 1944

35

The restless tradition of Americans uprooting themselves for new starts and new opportunities has never halted. At left: the chaos of moving day in New York City, pictured about 1840. Above: the opening of a new housing development in Los Angeles in 1953

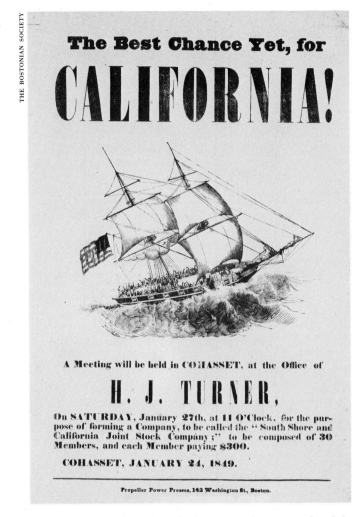

The Best Chance Yet, for
CALIFORNIA!

A Meeting will be held in COHASSET, at the Office of

H. J. TURNER,

On SATURDAY, January 27th, at 11 O'Clock, for the purpose of forming a Company, to be called the "South Shore and California Joint Stock Company;" to be composed of 30 Members, and each Member paying $300.

COHASSET, JANUARY 24, 1849.

Propeller Power Presses, 142 Washington St, Boston.

The California gold rush and other mining booms populated the American West with fortune seekers. Above: a ship card of 1849

Above: on the road to developing the Fordson tractor, Henry Ford in 1908 sits at the controls of what he called an "automobile plow." One of the greatest American venturers, he failed in business twice, finally won a mass market for his low-priced cars. Below: tireless movement—workers going west on the new transcontinental railroad in 1869

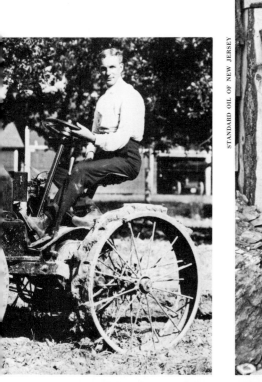

HARDLY ABLE MINE

Modern times have continued to provide adventurers with frontiers to open and worlds to explore. A new generation of miners braved perils searching for uranium in Utah's waterless canyonlands after World War II (left). On the moon Americans opened a new chapter in mankind's history (below).

The oil industry, providing the possibility of fast fortunes, was built by speculators and has had a continuing appeal for Americans. The 1865 song sheet, above, was commissioned by an oil firm to help advertise the company. Below: spectators view an oil pool at a new field in California early in the 1900's.

*Finance and business have offered
unending temptations to optimists
and gamblers. Among them (left, top
and bottom): the stock market, and an
"absolutely safe" western development scheme of the nineteenth century*

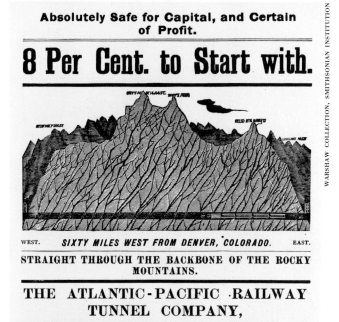

Absolutely Safe for Capital, and Certain of Profit.

8 Per Cent. to Start with.

WEST. SIXTY MILES WEST FROM DENVER, COLORADO. **EAST.**

STRAIGHT THROUGH THE BACKBONE OF THE ROCKY MOUNTAINS.

THE ATLANTIC-PACIFIC RAILWAY TUNNEL COMPANY,

Incorporated in 1884, under the laws of Colorado, to buy land, mines, mill sites, water powers, etc., in Colorado; to drive a gateway or Tunnel straight through the Continental Divide, at a depth exceeding 4,000 feet below the surface, and to operate the same for mining and railway use perpetually.

☞ This Tunnel will be 25,200 feet long, 40 feet wide and 20 feet high, to allow a double track standard gauge railway service straight through the centre, and on each side of these, a track for running cars into and out of the veins of gold, silver and lead ore it has already crossed and will cross, that the mineral contents of the mountains may be brought all the way out on wheels. Exceeding 3,600 feet east end, and 1,700 feet west end, already driven, and more than thirty mineral veins already opened, the ore ranging in value from $60 to $1,500 per ton.

700,000 SHARES, PAR VALUE $10 EACH.

The Tunnel, and other immensely valuable properties, all belong to those who own shares as issued by the Company, which consists only of those owning shares as already sold, and now being sold, from shares in its treasury not yet disposed of.

Shares full-paid and cannot be assessed or jeopardized for any purpose. More than 5,000 men and women jointly interested as share-owners, and, therefore, members of the Atlantic-Pacific Railway Tunnel Company, which is steadily driving a tunnel through the great mineral belt of Colorado, and straight through more than 250 veins of gold, silver and lead ore. The primary object of the work is to reach all these veins and open them at great depths for extensive mining to great profit, and the secondary object, to use the Tunnel, when completed, for railway purposes, thus shortening the distance between Denver and Salt Lake City more than 230 miles.

☞ **The Company has more than four millions of dollars worth of property all fully paid for.**
☞ **All its interest obligations are met promptly as they mature.**

8 Per Cent. Bonds.

Work is carried on steadily, both ends of the tunnel, day and night, advancing about five feet per day. When the new Thomson-Houston Co. electric plant is in operation to operate all required machinery and to light the Tunnel and mines by electricity, the total progress of the Tunnel will be 20 to 30 feet per day. This work is paid for from the proceeds arising to the Company from the sale of EIGHT PER CENT. FIRST MORTGAGE COUPON BONDS, of which $500,000 of its only issue of $2,000,000, are now offered at par, interest accruing from date of investment. Bonds $250 and $1,000 each. Interest payable in cash March 1st and September 1st each year till 1907, when the principal will be paid. Interest on bonds paid by sale of gold, silver and lead

*Charles Ponzi, exploiting the lure of "get rich quick" deals,
promised 50 per cent profits in ninety days, bilked gullible Boston investors of millions in 1919, before he was imprisoned.*

41

Shrewd, aggressive, and daring, John D. Rockefeller (right), son of a patent medicine salesman, made his own rules in a ruthless attempt to achieve monopoly in the oil business. Setting his own standards also was Howard Hughes, who pursued a variety of interests, including a 1947 try at marketing a mammoth flying boat of plywood (below).

Moved, stone by stone, from England's Thames River to Havasu Lake, Arizona, London Bridge (above) helped Robert P. McCulloch, oil executive and manufacturer of motors and chain saws, promote a town he conceived and built from scratch in the desert.

Ruler of a massive conglomerate, Harold S. Geneen, a British-born American, built the International Telephone and Telegraph Corporation into an international corporate empire and his own salary (with bonus) to $812,494, the largest in the nation.

An enterprising U.S. merchant and his family, painted by an artist in Japan soon after Perry opened that country in 1853

This nineteenth-century ad reflected an American company's vision of the whole earth as a marketplace for its product.

Aged sixty-six and almost broke, Colonel Harlan T. Sanders peddled his chicken recipes into the start of a huge franchise business.

96   THE NEW YORK TIMES, WEDNESDAY, OCTOBER 27, 1971

One problem with 96% of American manufacturers is that they only sell to 5% of the world.

■ This is where they're selling.
☐ This is where we can help.

Economic conditions in the U.S. over the past couple of years have certainly proven the need for American companies to diversify their marketing efforts and their markets.

And whether your company is one of the 96% who don't do business internationally or one of the 4% who do, there are a great many international business opportunities open to you. With export being just one of them.

You might find that in certain markets your company might be more competitive by opening a plant and manufacturing locally. Or you might find it advisable to go the acquisition route.

Our world-wide people.

But no matter what sort of international operation your company is undertaking, or should be considering, Chemical Bank can provide all the international banking and financial support and advice you need.

Everything from routine banking and financial services like: foreign exchange and letters of credit; to financing exports, plant acquisitions and expansions; to sophisticated international financial concepts.

Our world-wide services.

Chemical Bank has been providing services like these for over 140 years.

And the way we provide you with all these services today is through a U.S. international officer who is responsible for your relationship worldwide.

You get him in addition to the account service officer other banks offer.

The international officer calls upon the knowledge and experience of our foreign country specialists and coordinates their efforts in your behalf.

And that saves your having to deal with one man for your business in the Far East, another for your business in Europe, and others for other areas.

Further, we back our people up with people and branches in Brussels, Frankfurt, London, Paris,

Zurich, Nassau and representative offices throughout the world.

So maybe you ought to stop poring over those profit and loss statements long enough to pore over a map of the world and telephone your Chemical Bank representative. Or write to: Mr. Chandler Mahnken, 20 Pine Street, New York, N.Y. 10015. Telephone (212) 770-1848. And take advantage of the 11 billion dollars we have invested in the world.

It just might be more profitable for your company in the long run.

Our world-wide offices.

Main Office: New York. Branch Offices: Brussels, Frankfurt, London, Paris, Zurich, and Nassau. Representative Offices in Beirut, Madrid, Bogotá, Buenos Aires, Caracas, Rio de Janeiro, São Paulo, Mexico City, Hong Kong, Manila, and Tokyo. Correspondent banks in over 185 nations.

CHEMICAL BANK
We do more for your money.

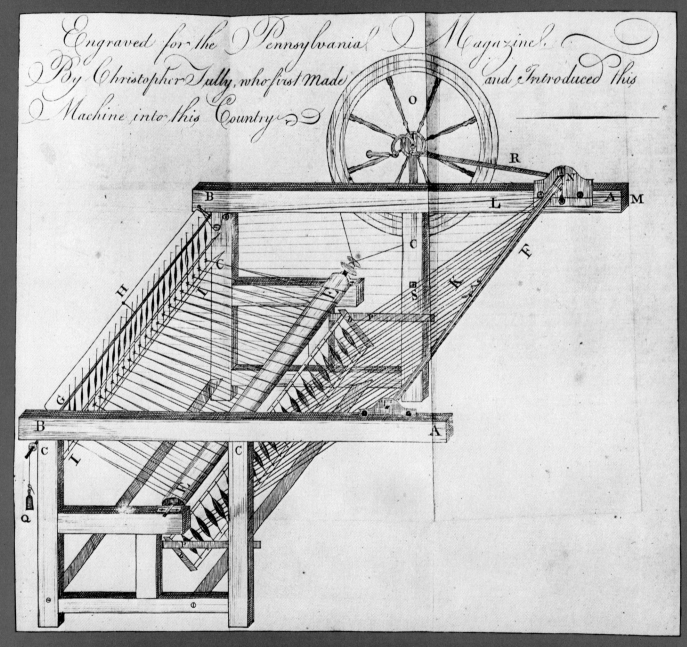

Interest in American manufactures was nourished by designs of new machines, like this one published in Philadelphia in 1775. The plan shows the first American-made spinning jenny, an adaptation of the one that James Hargreaves had recently invented in England.

2

THE HOME-GROWN INDUSTRIES

1783-1820

What emerged from the Revolutionary War was hardly a nation. There were some four million people living in thirteen states, joined in a loose federation and strung out along the Atlantic seaboard. They—both the people and the states—had varying interests, were suspicious of each other, and clung jealously to what they saw as their own rights and prerogatives. With the war over, they were no longer held together by the bond of a common enemy and a common cause.

It seemed altogether unlikely that such a nation could one day fashion its destiny around a few pieces of paper. Disunities of every variety threatened to pull the country apart almost from the start. The interests of the North were distinct from those of the South, or even of the middle states. There were wide gulfs between debtors and creditors, farmers and tradesmen, merchants and manufacturers, frontiersmen and townsmen rooted in the coastal cities, and between war veterans and war profiteers.

These dichotomies were soon reflected in national politics. The Revolution had strengthened the already powerful American penchant for individual liberty, which translated further into local home rule and the vesting of broad sovereignty in the states. But war had also had the opposite effect of promoting national unity through the economics of a growing foreign trade and commerce that was increasingly centralized in the cities. Mercantilist thinking was deeply embedded in the ways of commerce, even though Adam Smith's monumental treatise on the new economics of freedom in the marketplace had been in print since 1776. And so it was that the most powerful drive for national unity came from businessmen and from those politicians who identified the nation's welfare with business and commercial interests.

Peace swiftly brought problems, most of them economic. The burned and battered cities—New York, Charleston, Norfolk, New London, and others—needed rebuilding. Hard money was difficult to come by, and much of the paper money—$438 million worth issued by Congress and the states during the war—was worth less than the cost of printing it, so barter again became common. There was a short-lived business boom when the war ended, but this soon turned into a deep and prolonged depression. Dumping by European merchants quickly sated the stored-up appetite for goods that had been in short supply or unavailable during the hostilities. During the war, many workers and much investment money had drifted into privateering and infant manufacturing industries, and now both were virtually out of business.

The British, smarting from the indignity of military defeat, were not inclined to be helpful. Wartime Navigation Acts, still in effect, banned American ships from West Indian ports, and this once-thriving trade dwindled. New acts aimed at American shipping were passed in 1786 and 1787. Safeguarding the secrets that were bringing her increasing industrial prowess, Britain forbade the export of textile machines, as well as the emigration of skilled workers who could build or tend such equipment.

These acts aimed at the United States were not wholly without provocation. The peace treaty had provided that Tories be permitted to keep their property and that private debts of Americans to British subjects be paid. In these and other respects the treaty had been unpopular in this country, and many states took it upon themselves to decide which provisions they would honor. Those Tories who remained in the states were often lynched or beaten, and their property seized. Debtors, particularly in the tobacco regions, would have been loath to pay their British debts even if they had had the money. When Virginia finally passed a bill recognizing those claims, it was conditioned on payment for slaves taken away by the British during the war and on the evacuation of British troops from outposts on the frontier.

If the national government had wished to keep the states in line, it had only the weakest tools to do so. Its very imperfect instrument was the Continental Congress and the piece of paper behind it was that product of cautious compromise, the toothless Articles of Confederation. These now exhibited, even as they had in wartime, their glaring weakness: the absence of power either to raise money or to regulate commerce.

Well aware of the impotence of Congress to control even its own shipping, navigation, and commerce, the British felt no reluctance about imposing their own conditions on American trade. The individual states, too, moved into this vacuum, and Pennsylvania, New York, and New Jersey enacted their own tariffs and fees on goods imported from abroad by way of other states. The need for imposing some sort of order on such chaos became ever more apparent.

THE HAMILTON YEARS

When Washington resigned his commission after the war, the country had no single person who could be deemed a leader. Perhaps the most influential man in government at this time was Robert Morris, head of the Finance Office. A bold and confident man, with a fondness for good living and entertaining, Morris was a wheeler-dealer who might one day arrange a loan for a congressman, the next give a job to one of Washing-

SHAYS'S REBELLION

Like the nation itself, almost everybody in it was broke after the winning of the War of Independence. In Concord, Massachusetts, the scene of one of the first battles of the Revolution, there were three times as many people in jail for debt in 1786 as for all other crimes combined. In Worcester county the ratio was twenty to one.

Most of the prisoners were small farmers whose freeholdings and livestock had been sold off by constables at vendues for fractions of their worth, and who had then been jailed because they still could not pay all that they owed. Their appeals to the distant legislature in Boston brought no satisfaction. Only property holders could vote, and the merchant aristocrats of Boston paid little heed to the cries for relief from the backwoods.

What came to be called Shays's Rebellion began in August, 1786, when mobs of musket-bearing farmers seized county courthouses to prevent the trials of debtors. The state legislators reacted angrily against the farmers, dubbing them "stubborn Jonathans," but took no action to ameliorate their plight. As the unrest spread, the rebels recruited Daniel Shays, a Continental Army cap-

Benjamin Lincoln

tain and veteran of Lexington, Bunker Hill, and Saratoga, to lead them. Wearing sprigs of hemlock in their hats, Shays's men attacked the federal arsenal at Springfield but were repulsed by a blast of grapeshot.

The rebellion continued on into the winter, causing dismay to the new nation, whose leaders heard exaggerated reports of the uprising and feared that the British might take advantage of it. Wrote George Washington to a friend:

For God's sake, tell me what is the cause of these commotions? Do they proceed from

licentiousness, British influence disseminated by the Tories, or real grievances which admit of redress? If the latter, why were they delayed until the public mind had become so agitated? If the former, why are not the powers of government tried at once?

The difficulty was that the Massachusetts government had neither the sense to act in behalf of the farmers nor the funds with which to raise a militia to quash the rebellion. In the end, a former general, Benjamin Lincoln, borrowed enough capital from nervous merchants to enlist a force of light horse cavalry and artillery and go after Shays's bands.

The farmers surrendered quickly. But their action had philosophical support from Thomas Jefferson, who, representing the United States in far-off Paris, wrote with the defiant air of a man of the soil: "I hold it that a little rebellion now and then is a good thing, and as necessary in the political world as storms in the physical. . . . The tree of liberty must be refreshed from time to time with the blood of patriots and tyrants. It is its natural manure."

The rebellion ended without bitterness. There was little bloodshed; the fourteen leaders, including Shays—though sentenced to be hanged—were pardoned swiftly; and a new legislature in Boston eased debt regulations.

ton's nephews, and then talk young Alexander Hamilton into taking a job as tax collector so that he could get experience as a fiscal administrator. Few could fathom from his maneuvering just which of his transactions were on behalf of the state of Pennsylvania, which for the benefit of the Continental Congress, and which for the account of Robert Morris. Of Morris and his mysterious transactions, Washington once wrote, "I do not suppose that by art magick, he can do more than recover us, by degrees, from the labyrinth in which our finance is plunged." But Washington did understand and agree with his finance officer's unflinching belief in a strong national government. As early as 1782 Morris had urged, in his Report on Public Credit, the enactment of taxes adequate for "supporting Government and defending the State."

During the heated debates on such issues at the Constitutional Convention, Morris preferred to make his views known at quiet dinner parties. His only contribution on the convention floor was to nominate his friend, George Washington, as president of the convention. When Washington subsequently, as the nation's first President, offered him the post of Secretary of the Treasury, he chose to go to the Senate, but suggested that Hamilton be named, instead.

Hamilton was born in 1755 on the island of Nevis in the British West Indies. He demonstrated his business acumen very early, when he was apprenticed to a merchant in a trading house at St. Croix. When the owner became ill, the young Hamilton, not yet fifteen, took full control of the establishment and ran it very well. At the urging of a teacher, Hamilton sailed for the colonies and enrolled at Princeton University at the age of sixteen. But when he insisted on entering an advanced class, with the right to proceed at his own fast pace, he was disenrolled. He matriculated, instead, at King's College (now Columbia) in New York, which was willing to go along with his stipulations.

Heir to West Indian resentment of Britain's restrictive policies, he quickly absorbed the seething excitement of the city around him. He began a career of pamphleteering: what Tom Paine so passionately expressed in eloquent prose, Hamilton complemented with relentless logic. Early in 1776 he managed to get himself commissioned by the New York Provincial Congress as captain of an artillery company. His cool efficiency in action brought him to Washington's attention. The general made him his aide-de-camp, with the rank of lieutenant colonel, and Hamilton spent most of the war years as Washington's secretary.

Hamilton married into the wealthy Schuyler family and pursued his natural bent into politics, with the support and assistance of his influential father-in-law. Appointed a Receiver of Continental Taxes for New York, he took on the job of lobbying for revenue measures in the state legislature. He persuaded that assem-

Alexander Hamilton

INDEPENDENCE NATIONAL HISTORICAL PARK COLLECTION

bly as early as 1781 to pass a bill recommending a convention to revise the Articles of Confederation. It was 1787 before such a convention was called, and Hamilton, by then a member of the state assembly, was named one of New York's three delegates.

When the delegates gathered in Philadelphia in May, much of the nation pinned its hopes on their meeting. Mired in depression, disillusioned with cheap money, frustrated by conflicting state laws, all were certain that the convention could bring forth a better system of government.

How to bring this about was something else. The cleavages were broad. The principal differences soon became personified by Hamilton and Thomas Jefferson. Jefferson leaned toward the small states and the preservation of states' rights. He favored the farmers and planters and felt that they made up a kind of natural aristocracy. He welcomed commerce, and indeed recognized its importance in distributing the products of the soil. Because he looked on governmental activity in the economic area as official sanction of the transfer of wealth from "the plundered ploughman" to the merchant, he sought a greater diffusion, rather than a concentration, of power.

Hamilton, too, believed in an aristocracy but felt that a kind of natural selection had already chosen the rich—the bankers and traders—for that lot. He favored a strong central government with power to tax, to regulate shipping and trade, to deal with other nations, to assure the sanctity of contracts, to establish a uniform currency, and to pay its debts. He believed that not only investment activities but even a certain amount of speculation could be made to serve a useful purpose for the economy. Hamilton nurtured a vision of his country as a great industrial power, and indeed he was one of the few men of his time to grasp the implications of the Industrial Revolution that was just taking hold in England. But to bring all this about, he believed, it was vital to have a government that would encourage the formation and flow of capital through sound fiscal and monetary policies.

When concession and compromise had finally hammered out the shape of the new government, businessmen seemed happier than most citizens at what had been wrought. The new Constitution appeared to promise the kind of economic stability that only a strong central government could provide. The states in due course ratified the document, and Washington's Federalist government took office.

The administration faced monumental tasks, not the least of which were those that fell Hamilton's way. Just ten days after he became Secretary of the Treas-

ury in September, 1789, Hamilton was called on by the House of Representatives to draw up a plan for meeting the nation's debts. He went to work on what was to be known as his First Report on the Public Credit.

First he had to define just what was involved. There was no question about foreign debts, which with interest now amounted to almost $12 million owed to France, Holland, and Spain. The domestic debt of the national government had consisted originally of loan-office certificates, the interest-bearing "war bonds of the Revolution." But Congress had also assumed responsibility for money owed to veterans and merchants, for which the government had issued certificates promising to pay in the future; in fairness, interest charges were added to these debts too. The various forms of domestic indebtedness amounted to about $40 million. In addition, there were some $25 million in state debts. All this totaled more than $77 million.

Hamilton proposed that the new government take on the obligation of the entire debt, refunded at a lower

A HAMILTONIAN SAMPLER

As Secretary of the Treasury, Alexander Hamilton, at the age of thirty-four, wielded power in the nation second only to that of the President. Among his responsibilities were not only the collection and disbursement of federal funds, but also public land surveys, the coast guard, the customs, and even, until 1792, the post office department. By the end of the century the Treasury Department had nearly 1,700 people working for it, double the number of employees of the newly established post office.

It was an awesome domain, but Hamilton brought to it a firm economic philosophy, which was reflected in his series of reports to Congress, as well as in his letters and in the earlier papers he had written for *The Federalist*.

Following are excerpts from some of Hamilton's writings, expressing sentiments that he translated into action as he sought to create a viable economy for the new republic.

On the blessings of commerce:

The spirit of commerce has a tendency to soften the manners of men.
—*The Federalist*, No. 6

On money:

Money is, with propriety, considered as the vital principle of the body politic; as that which sustains its life and motion, and enables it to perform its most essential functions.
—*The Federalist*, No. 30

On the benefits of a national debt:

A national debt, if it is not excessive, will be to us a national blessing. It will be a powerful cement of our Union. It will also create a necessity for keeping up taxation to a degree which, without being oppressive, will be a spur to industry, remote as we are from Europe, and shall be from danger. It were otherwise to be feared our popular maxim would incline us to too great parsimony and indulgence. We labor less now than any civilized nation of Europe; and a habit of labor is as essential to the health and vigor of . . . minds and bodies, as it is conducive to the welfare of the state.
—*Letter to Robert Morris*, 1781

On the stimulation of the economy by a national bank:

This, I regard, in some shape or other, as an expedient essential to our safety and success. . . . There is no other that can give to government that extensive and systematic

credit which the defect of our revenues makes indispensably necessary to its operations. . . . The tendency of a national bank is to increase public and private credit. The former [public credit] gives power to the State, for the protection of its rights and interests; and the latter [private credit] facilitates and extends the operations of commerce among individuals. Industry is increased, commodities are multiplied, agriculture and manufactures flourish, and herein consists the true wealth and prosperity of a state.
—*Letter to Robert Morris*, 1781

On the purpose of a national bank:

Public utility is more truly the object of public banks than private profit. And it is the business of government to constitute them on such principles that, while the latter will result in a sufficient degree to afford competent motives to engage in them, the former be not made subservient to it.
—*Report on a National Bank*, 1790

On the need for manufactures in a young nation:

It seems not always to be recollected that nations who have neither mines nor manufactures can only obtain the manufactured articles of which they stand in need, by an

rate than the 6 per cent interest on most of the obligations. His plan ran into immediate, and sometimes impassioned, opposition, for both good reasons and bad.

For one thing, there was already a national tradition of nonpayment of taxes, starting with the unpopular British levies and continuing with the assessments by the Continental Congress. From 1783 to 1789 the states had paid only $2 million in specie, which was about one fourth of the total levied. In 1786, the historian Curtis Nettels has noted, the total income of the central government was less than a third of just the interest charges on the national debt.

For a second thing, repaying the debt would be rewarding speculators who had bought up various forms of certificates for as little as twelve cents on the dollar. Businessmen and the landed gentry were among the heaviest speculators, buying seemingly worthless paper from hard-hit farmers and veterans. But this was no underhanded trade carried on furtively in dark cor-

ners. There was a lively market in this scrip in a new trading center in New York, eventually to become the New York Stock Exchange. It was bought up by all sorts of people—merchants, lawyers, landholders. It has been estimated that at least forty out of the fifty members of the Constitutional Convention, whose work was to help determine the fate of these obligations, were holders of the securities. Prices rose sharply from 1789 to 1791, as the new government's plans took form. There was a drop in the summer of 1791, but the securities started moving up again, and speculative fever early in 1792 helped precipitate the nation's first panic.

Finally, the opposition to Hamilton's proposal had a sectional cast. Most of the state debts were owed in the North, and assumption of these obligations would penalize the states with little or no debt. Hamilton struck a bargain with Jefferson to get the two southern votes he needed in Congress. The final bill provided subsidies for the states that had paid their debts, and enough northern votes were swung to locate the new national capital on the banks of the Potomac. In time, with the Jay Treaty of 1794, the national government also assumed many of the private debts owed to British citizens.

During the twelve years of the Washington and John Adams administrations, the public debt accounted for about 30 per cent of the cost of government, while 50 per cent went to the Army and Navy and 20 per cent to other government expenses. The effects of assumption of the debt were a testimony to Hamilton's financial astuteness. Money began to flow into the United States from abroad, and foreign holdings of the domestic debt of the United States rose from $2.7 million in 1788 to $20 million in 1795 and $33 million in 1801, much of it purchased at or above par.

In addition to carrying out the many routine duties of his office, Hamilton issued a number of other special reports, which became economic landmarks for the new nation. A Report on a National Bank was issued in December, 1790, a Report on Manufactures a year later, and a Second Report on the Public Credit in 1795.

He urged extension of import duties and the first internal revenues. Both met resistance at the start. After several months most of his recommended tariff changes became law. When the first tariffs failed to bring in the desired revenues, rates were increased in 1790, 1792, and 1794. An excise tax on distilled spirits drew defiance from farmers, to whom whiskey represented an economical way to transport grain, but the new central government demonstrated its strength in putting down the Whiskey Rebellion of 1794 in Pennsylvania.

For his Report on Manufactures, Hamilton worked hard and long. He wrote scores of letters by hand, send-

exchange of the products of their soils; and that if those who can best furnish them with such articles are unwilling to give a due course to this exchange, they must, of necessity, make every possible effort to manufacture for themselves; the effect of which is, that the manufacturing nations abridge the natural advantages of their situation, through an unwillingness to permit the agricultural countries to enjoy the advantages of theirs, and sacrifice the interests of a mutually beneficial intercourse to the vain project of selling every thing and buying nothing.

—*Report on Manufactures*, 1791

On the advantages of manufactures:

To affirm that the labor of the manufacturer is unproductive, because he consumes as much of the produce of the land as he adds value to the raw material which he manufactures, is not better founded than it would be to affirm that the labor of the farmer, which furnishes materials to the manufacturer, is unproductive, because he consumes an equal value of manufactured articles. Each furnishes a certain portion of the produce of his labor to the other, and each destroys a correspondent portion of the produce of the labor of the other. In the meantime, the maintenance of two citizens, instead of one, is going on; the State has two members instead of one; and they together consume twice the value of what is produced from the land.

—*Report on Manufactures*, 1791

ing his inquiries all over the country and to many other parts of the world. The answers were painstakingly read and filed. Most of them told of what American businessmen needed and wanted—capital, workers, greater know-how, bounties, and protection through tariffs. Hamilton's report, aimed at making the United States independent in manufactures, especially of military equipment and supplies, reflected the spirit of these letters. It called for protective duties, import restrictions, bounties, encouraging the import and prohibiting the export of raw materials needed in manufacture, stimulating inventions, and easing the movement of cash payments around the country—all the things that could help fulfill his vision of the manufacturing giant that America might become. As an added sign of the times, Hamilton saw a special virtue in that "children are rendered . . . more early useful by manufacturing establishments than they would otherwise be."

LAND FEVER

While industry's potential fired Hamilton's imagination, it was still agriculture that gave employment to most Americans and supplied the bulk of the nation's export commodities. Land, the great capital item of agriculture, remained the keystone of every freeman's desire.

Washington epitomized the strong attachment to land. He owned thousands of acres in Virginia, Pennsylvania, Maryland, and other states. His fortune, valued at $530,000 at his death, consisted mainly of his estates and farms. An earnest student of scientific farming, he fertilized his fields with river-bottom mud, kept detailed records of plantings and harvests, invented an automatic seeder, and exchanged notes on his experiments with his political foe, Jefferson. Both were interested in the newest developments in the plow, the key implement of early agriculture. Improvements in plow design by Charles Newbold of Burlington, New Jersey, Robert and Joseph Smith of Bucks County, Pennsylvania, and Jethro Wood of Cayuga County, New York, all contributed importantly to increases in agricultural productivity in the late 1700's and early 1800's.

But old patterns were changing, both in land ownership and in the produce that the soil brought forth. Tobacco still headed the export list in 1791, when $4.5 million worth was sent abroad, and through 1800, but thereafter it dropped off in importance. Rice increased in value as a crop, as did hemp in the South. Louisiana became the center for expanding sugar production; sugar imports from the West Indies were cut back after a refining industry was established in that state around 1800. But after the invention of the cotton gin in 1793, cotton became the nation's fastest-growing farm product and export.

As for ownership of land, the first major changes took place when Tories fled the country and the states took over their landholdings, broke them up, and sold them to help pay war expenses. In New York State, where most of Westchester County consisted of manor lands as late as 1769, the 300 square miles of the Philipse manor and the 50,000 acres of the Johnston estate were among those seized and sold, largely in 500-acre parcels. Massachusetts confiscated the Pepperrell estate, with its thirty miles of coastline, and Pennsylvania expropriated the $5 million Penn estate.

But the tendency to create great new estates seemed irresistible. During the war many of the western lands that had once belonged to the French and had later been termed the Indians' country and barred to settlement by the British were turned over to the states. Large tracts were acquired by individuals and companies. In western New York, Oliver Phelps and Nathaniel Gorham bought 6 million acres; Georgia transferred huge territories to private companies, and the Ohio Company of Associates acquired a vast tract north of the Ohio River from the federal government. Some states gave land to their soldiers as bounties, and many of these parcels were bought up by speculators and brought together into major holdings. European money, as well as American, went into these ventures. Their original charters had given some of the states title to lands stretching far to the West. But the six states with no such claims—Maryland, Pennsylvania, Delaware, New Jersey, New Hampshire, and Rhode Island—insisted, as early as 1779, that these lands be turned over to the central government. One by one, the other states relinquished their rights.

The nation's public land system began with the Land Ordinance of 1785, which provided for cutting up the western territories into neat squares. Starting with what is now the Ohio-Indiana border as a "prime meridian" and an intersecting east-west line, the area was surveyed and divided into square townships running six miles on each side. Each square mile thus surveyed became a "section" of 640 acres and was put up for public sale by the federal government at $1 an acre, except that one section out of the thirty-six in a township was reserved for the support of common schools. In 1796 the minimum price went up to $2 an acre. With the passage of the Harrison Land Act in 1800, the size of the smallest parcel that might be sold was cut from 640 to 320 acres, and in 1804 to 160 acres, or a quarter of a section, which was about as much as the average farmer could manage. In 1820 the minimum became 80 acres, and the price was reduced to $1.25 an acre.

While much of this land was settled and worked, a good deal was bought with the hope that prices would rise, even among the farmers themselves. The government contributed to the speculative fever by opening more than thirty land offices in the newly opened areas, then known as the Northwest and Southwest. The terms required payment of one fourth of the purchase price, or $80 on a quarter section of 160 acres, within forty days, the rest to come from working the soil. Some years later an Englishman, D. W. Mitchell, wrote of the land fever: "Speculation in real estate has for many years been the ruling idea and occupation of the Western mind. Clerks, labourers, farmers, storekeepers, merely followed their callings for a living, while they were speculating for their fortunes." Far from being a simple pioneer, the frontiersman chose his site principally on the basis of how much the value of the land might rise. He built a cabin and worked the land only to enforce his claim, and was ready to sell out as soon as the price was right.

Excessive land speculation contributed to a panic in 1819, and Congress abolished the credit payment system. By 1820 almost 20 million acres had been sold, but some 6 million could not be paid for and were turned back to the federal government for resale.

The larger economic consequences of opening the West were a redistribution of population and the presentation of opportunities that tended toward a spreading and leveling of American wealth. Only a few hundred British colonial settlers had crossed the Alleghenies by 1776. When the Revolution ended, about 25,000 had moved west, some as far as the Mississippi, but mostly to the Cumberland and Kentucky river regions. By 1790 more than 94 per cent of America's 3.2 million people still clung to the eastern side of the mountain divide, but close to 250,000 had crossed the barrier. Kentucky was admitted as a state in 1792, and Tennessee in 1796. At the turn of the century, the number who had moved to the West still amounted to fewer than 10 per cent of the 5.3 million population of the United States, and the center of population lay within eighteen miles of Baltimore. But in Kentucky there was a population of respectable size, some 220,000 freemen and slaves, while Tennessee had

"HOW DOES YOUR CHICORIUM PROSPER?"

In the years following the Revolution, the American economy was still based primarily on agriculture. Despite the young republic's pressing concerns with problems of self-government, the daily livelihood of nine out of ten of its citizens demanded their close attention to matters of the land and its produce. Even two Founding Fathers, George Washington and Thomas Jefferson, often reflected this interest in their letters to each other.

On June 19, 1796, Jefferson wrote President Washington from Monticello:

I put away this disgusting dish of old fragments, and talk to you of my peas and clover. As to the latter article, I have great encouragement from the friendly nature of our soil. I think I have had, both the last and present year, as good clover from common grounds, which had brought several crops of wheat and corn without ever having been manured, as I ever saw on the lots around Philadelphia. I verily believe that a yield of thirty-four acres, sowed on wheat April was twelvemonth, has given me a ton to the acre at its first cutting this spring. The stalks extended, measured three and a half feet long very commonly. Another field, a year older, and which yielded as well the last year, has sensibly fallen off this year. . . . I am trying the white boiling pea of Europe (the Albany pea) this year, till I can get the hog pea of England, which is the most productive of all. But the true winter vetch is what we want extremely. I have tried this year the Carolina drill. It is absolutely perfect. Nothing can be more simple, nor perform its office more perfectly for a single row. . . . I have one of the Scotch threshing machines nearly finished . . . Our wheat and rye are generally fine, and the prices talked of bid fair to indemnify us for the poor crops of the last two years. . . . With very affectionate compliments to Mrs. Washington, I have the honor to be, with great and sincere esteem and respect, dear Sir, your most obedient, and most humble servant.

The reply from the President was sent from Mount Vernon July 6, 1796, and included these agronomical observations:

It must be pleasing to a cultivator to possess land which will yield Clover kindly, for it is certainly a great desideratum in husbandry. My soil, without very good dressings, does not produce it well, owing, I believe, to its stiffness, hardness at bottom, and retention of water.

Washington informed Jefferson that he had his hands on field peas from England and winter vetch. He had received eight bushels of each, but they came in late April instead of early March, when they should have been sown, so they were a loss. He was unfamiliar with the Carolina drill, a device to plant deeply, but he evinced considerable interest in such labor-saving machinery.

How does your Chicorium [chicory] prosper? Four years since I exterminated all the plants raised from seed sent me by Mr. Young, and to get into it again, the seed I purchased in Philada. last winter and what has been sent me by Mr. Maury this spring has cost upwards of twelve pounds sterling. This, it may be observed, is a left handed way to make money; but the first was occasioned by the Manager I then had, who pretended to know it well in England and pronounced it a noxious weed. The restoration of it, is indebted to Mr. Strickland, and others (besides Mr. Young) who speak of it in exalted terms. I sowed mine broad cast; some with and some without grain. It has come up well; but there seems to be a serious struggle between it and the grass and weeds; the issue of which (as I can afford no relief to the former) is doubtful at present, and may be useful to know. If you can bring a moveable threshing machine, constructed upon simple principles to perfection, it will be among the most valuable institutions in this country, for nothing is more wanting and to be wished for on our farm. Mrs. Washington begs you to accept her best wishes, and with very great esteem and regard, I am, dear Sir, yours, &c.

Cincinnati, founded by land speculators soon after the Revolution, was building fast when this scene was drawn in 1816.

more than 100,000, and Ohio, admitted to the Union in 1803, 45,000. The city of Pittsburgh had an "old" society of around 75,000. What became known as "the Great Migration" followed the War of 1812, when thousands moved west, and five states—Indiana, Mississippi, Illinois, Alabama, and Missouri—were admitted in rapid succession. By 1820 the U.S. Census showed a population of 7.9 million, with fully 27 per cent living west of the Alleghenies.

While there were a few great fortunes—and $250,000 was deemed a measure of vast wealth in 1800, when America had fewer than a half dozen millionaires—the great bulk of American families could claim about the same level of resources. Henry Adams estimates that the nation's total wealth as the 1800's began was $1.8 billion, equal to $418 for each free white. Almost every white family, averaging five persons, was likely to have $2,000 worth of property—land, house, furniture, utensils, and livestock. Unskilled laborers earned about fifty cents a day at the time of the Revolution, about ninety cents a day in 1800, and one dollar in 1825; skilled workmen might expect about twice as much, while farm hands received seven to fifteen dollars a month, plus board.

Although the great fortunes remained in the East, important opportunities for creating new wealth emerged in the West. Food production, naturally, was of paramount importance at first. Western New York and northern Ohio became dairy and fruit growing areas. Animal husbandry increased throughout the north-central states. At first the easiest way to ship meat was on the hoof, but around 1818 a sizable meat-packing industry grew up in Cincinnati. Among those who had joined the westward migration were a number of skilled workers and mechanics, and a variety of industries sprang up, mainly along the Ohio River, in Pittsburgh, Lexington, and Cincinnati.

THE MERCHANT CAPITALISTS

American wealth came mainly from the soil, but money moved most readily into the hands of the merchants. As had been true in colonial days, the merchant remained the dominant figure of the capitalistic economy. He acquired goods, put them up for sale in his shops, sent them abroad, and brought other goods back from overseas. Buying at the lowest price, he increased the competition among manufacturers, thereby putting pressure on the wages paid to the growing class of factory workers. Or he might go into manufacturing himself.

Wartime privateering fortunes frequently formed the base for new merchant enterprises. Asa Clapp, who had been a privateering officer, went into shipping and banking and eventually became the richest man in Maine. Joseph Peabody of Massachusetts built up a fleet of eighty ships. Boston's Joseph Cabot used the proceeds from his fleet of twenty privateering ships to set up his brother and himself as merchants.

While many leading merchants had inherited their wealth or their enterprises, there was always room for an ambitious young man to move up or even rise to the top. Thomas P. Cope, for example, a Quaker from Pennsylvania's Lancaster County, finished the education needed for a mercantile career in 1786 and went to get experience in a Philadelphia counting house. He advanced to positions of larger responsibility. In 1790 he went into the importing business for himself and opened a store at Second Street and Pewter-Platter Alley. He built his first ship in 1807 and several years later was operating the first line of packet ships between Philadelphia and Liverpool.

Overseas trade became the focus of the new nation's business hopes as soon as the Revolution was over. A major obstacle to even more extensive commerce was the havoc that had been wreaked on the American shipping fleet during the war. This was overcome in part by the gradual resumption of shipbuilding and in good measure by the venturesomeness and industry of its sea captains.

From the great Oriental trading center of Canton, the *Empress of China* came to New York harbor in 1785, and the *Grand Turk* sailed into Salem in 1787, opening up vistas of great new trading possibilities. American ships began to sail to China, to Baltic ports, and to the Near East. Captain Robert Gray set sail from Boston in 1787, made his way to the northwest coast of America, picked up furs for China, and returned by way of the Cape of Good Hope, in the first American voyage around the world. A new three-cornered trade opened up between New England, the fur regions of the northwest coast, and the mercantile offices of China. More than one third of the forty-six foreign vessels sailing into Canton Harbor in 1789 were American.

The first measure passed by the new United States Congress, aside from formal organization bills, was the tariff act of July 4, 1789. Although nominally for the purpose of protecting manufacturers, it was equally helpful to shippers, allowing them a 10 per cent reduction in duties of imports carried by American-built and -owned ships.

American shipping was also given powerful impetus by the war that broke out between France and Austria in 1792, which involved most of Europe for a period of more than twenty years. Yankee merchants made big profits from trading with the belligerents and carrying the products of their colonies under the only neutral flag of any major ocean fleet. The average earnings of the American merchant marine from 1795 to 1801 were estimated at more than $32 million a year.

Many a private fortune was built in these years. The Baltimore trading firm of Robert Oliver & Brothers cleared $775,000 in just eighteen months in the early 1800's. The China trade was particularly lucrative. Ebenezer Townsend, Jr., kept a journal of the voyage of his father's ship, the *Neptune*, of New Haven, Connecticut in 1796–99. "The voyage . . . produced 80,000 seal skins which sold in Canton at $3.50 each, or a total of $280,000," reported Frances Robotti in *Whaling and Old Salem*. "In exchange . . . the *Neptune* imported from China a fabulous, assorted cargo of teas, silks, jades, teakwood, etc., for both American and European markets. The custom duties paid by the *Neptune* on this voyage . . . came to $75,000 which exceeded the Civil List Tax of the entire state of Connecticut."

The effects of shipping prosperity spread throughout the American economy, which flourished from 1792 to 1807. Much in demand were the raw materials that the United States produced—grain, meat, cotton, leather, and wool. With prices rising, farmers did well. Foreign sailors became American citizens in order to share the high wages, which had risen from eight dollars a month to thirty dollars.

Shipyards were busy supplying the craft for this trade, raising their output from 200,000 tons in 1789 to 1,400,000 in 1810. In the same period there was an eightfold increase in the registry for foreign trade, from 124,000 tons to 981,000. American ships, which had carried only 17.5 per cent of the nation's imports and 30 per cent of her exports in 1789, hauled 90 per cent or more of both imports and exports two decades later.

As an indication of the importance of foreign trade in the postwar years, the value of exports in 1790 was $20 million and of imports $23 million—more than triple that of the 1760's. In another thirty years they had more than tripled again, exports climbing to $70 million and imports to $74 million. Re-exports of goods that had originated abroad accounted for more than half of the export total during some of these years, as American merchants took advantage of the foreign wars to gain experience as middlemen in world trade.

THE BANK OF THE UNITED STATES

Banking is often thought of as a kind of black art, not only by politicians unable to fathom its mysteries but by a great many other people. This may stem from natural suspicion of an industry that deals with money as though it were a commodity. The basic ingredient of the banking business, however, is not money but confidence—not just in the bank itself but in the willingness and ability of the entire business community to meet its obligations.

Thus the merchant who sells his goods on credit, taking a note from his customer, places his trust in the customer to make future payments. A bank that then buys the note from the merchant is demonstrating confidence in both the merchant and the customer. The net result of this transaction is to substitute a piece of paper for metallic coin, and thus create money that did not previously exist.

The moneylending craft is almost as old as human society. But the traditional moneylender could put out only what he had. Banks added the extra dimension of credit by using paper to help finance business transactions. Through much of American history, many banks were empowered to issue paper on their own credit, and to put this paper in circulation as money. Two things helped give this paper its value for the early banks. The first was the reserve of specie, or metallic currency, prudently ranging from a fifth to a third of the total amount of paper issued by the bank. Second was the confidence that businessmen and the public placed in the bank and its ability to operate on a sound basis. The effect of all this was to multiply the supply of money available for a currency-hungry world of commerce.

The American colonists, long hampered by currency shortages and wide fluctuations in the value of paper money, had talked about banking for a century. When the Revolution freed them from British limitations, the first banks were started, usually by groups of merchants—the Bank of North America in Philadelphia in 1781, the Bank of New York and the Massachusetts Bank in 1784. In addition to these legally chartered institutions there were some informal banks that existed purely on the confidence in the men who backed them. A remarkable example of the strength of such confidence appeared when Robert Morris printed notes that were supported only by his own name, and these notes were deemed of more value than the continental currency.

The early banks served their local purpose well. Conservative and sound, they provided a market for short-term commercial paper—the thirty-, sixty-, and ninety-day notes so essential to merchant trade. Directors of the Massachusetts Bank voted on all loans by dropping white or black balls into a box; one black ball, and no loan was made. In its first seven years, the bank actually charged depositors a fee for keeping their money. Because of the shortage of change, the bank issued notes in denominations up to $100, including those of $1.50, $2.50, $3.50, and $4.50. The state eventually made notes for less than $5 illegal.

To help provide an adequate supply of money (which the states were no longer permitted to issue, under the new Constitution), to stabilize the currency, and to provide the federal government with a reliable place to deposit and borrow money, the infant nation needed a national bank. This Hamilton recognized and recommended in his third report. Jefferson saw in such a bank merely a device for transferring more money to the capitalists of the Northeast. But Hamilton was able to marshal the votes that were needed, and

in 1791 the First Bank of the United States was chartered for twenty years.

Modeled on the Bank of England, the Bank was to be a mixture of public and private elements. The federal government was permitted to subscribe to a fifth of its $10 million capital, and government officials were to make up a fifth of the board. It was designed not only to be the intermediary between public and private financial interests, but to act as the banker for both.

In the tasks assigned to it, the Bank was remarkably successful. During its twenty years it loaned the federal government $13.5 million, and the government made a $700,000 profit when it sold its stock interest. The Bank also acted as an important stimulus to merchants and manufacturers, and the nation's economy prospered throughout the Bank's tenure. It gave the nation a sound dollar, helping drive out unbacked fiat money by refusing to take the notes of banks that would not pay in specie. The Bank opened eight branches in major coastal cities, and other banks continued to be chartered at a moderate rate to meet various needs—a total of twenty-six by 1800 and eighty-eight when the Bank's charter expired in 1811.

The Bank's major difficulty lay in the varying economic needs of the different sections of the country. If it was to serve the commercial interests of the Northeast well, it had to meet the needs of the expanding frontier poorly. Crops do not grow at the rate that merchants turn over their inventory. Farmers opening up new lands had little use for money loaned on thirty-day notes. They needed mortgages that would run long enough for them to earn the money back from the soil—three, five, or seven years.

The many small banks that sprang up in the frontier regions between 1803 and 1811 were meant to meet local needs, and they were subject to local pressures. Once they overextended themselves with long-term loans, however, they could no longer count on the Bank of the United States to back them up. When price fluctuations or nature's vagaries brought hard times to an area and loan payments were not met, the small banks were caught in an economic-political vise. If they started foreclosure proceedings, they might trigger a local panic or arouse the enmity of the community; if they did not, they were certain to get into trouble themselves.

As the West grew, and as local pressures were transmitted to the national level, many of the Jeffersonian Republicans tended to fix the Bank of the United States with the blame for these troubles. When the original charter expired they refused to renew it, although the vote in Congress was so close that Vice President George Clinton cast the tie-breaking vote against it.

Released from the chafing restrictions, the state-

The Bank of the United States, in Philadelphia, was chartered in 1791 and ended in 1811.

chartered banks boomed, increasing in number from 88 to 246 in five years. Speculators and charlatans swarmed into the business, issuing so many of their own notes that the amount of currency in circulation more than doubled in that short period, reaching $100 million, which was more than the nation's commerce required. As a result, prices inflated. The notes gyrated in value, sometimes selling at discounts of as much as 50 per cent. These difficulties were compounded by the War of 1812, financed with treasury notes of almost $37 million and $80 million in loans. Unable to raise all the money it needed for the war loans, the government was bailed out by the large bond purchases by such wealthy men as John Jacob Astor and Stephen Girard.

With inflation, unstable currency, and the problems of war finances fresh in their minds, the Republicans chartered the Second Bank of the United States in 1816, again for a twenty-year period, the government once more subscribing to a fifth of the capital (now $35 million) and naming a fifth of the twenty-five directors. The new central Bank immediately opened sixteen branches, of which eleven were to the west and south of the main office at Philadelphia. Throughout its term, the Second Bank tended to neglect the needs of New England. In its earliest years it was managed almost as irresponsibly as the local banks whose excesses it should have curtailed.

When land speculation helped set off the panic of 1819, and state banks suspended specie payment, a sterner management was put in charge of the bank. Its rigorous measures tended to multiply the nation's economic troubles, putting many of the smaller banks and weaker merchants out of business. The Bank, however, managed to save itself and in time put the nation on a sounder financial footing. But it also helped harden a growing notion that banks were arrayed on one side of an uneven economic equation, with the common people on the other.

THE REPUBLICAN YEARS

Jefferson's public actions did not always match his private views. As Secretary of State in Washington's administration, he favored strong protectionist action and showed great concern for the country's economic development. He favored internal improvements, as did his Republican successors—James Madison, James Monroe, and John Quincy Adams. Unable to understand banking, he feared that the country would be flooded with paper by note-issuing banks, even though Swiss-born Albert Gallatin, who served the country with distinction as Secretary of the Treasury from 1801 to 1814, understood and recognized the need for sound banking practices. Gallatin waged an unsuccessful campaign in his party to have the charter of the First Bank renewed.

It was President Jefferson who more than doubled the land area of the United States by purchasing the Louisiana Territory for a trifling $15 million, when Napoleon gave up his dream of a new colonial empire. He then planned the exploration of this region by the expedition led by Captain Meriwether Lewis and Lieutenant William Clark in 1804–6. Taking the

57

difficult and hazardous overland route, they reached the Columbia River and the Oregon coast that Captain Gray had visited by sea some fifteen years before. Lewis and Clark demonstrated the immensity of the still untouched continental expanse of open land.

Jefferson inherited the prosperity that blossomed from foreign trade during the Napoleonic wars, as well as the nettlesome problems. As war dragged on, Britain became less tolerant of America's trade with her enemies and their colonies. Her men-of-war seized American ships and their cargoes. Under the pretext of seeking British nationals who had signed on as crewmen of American merchantmen, an estimated 6,000 American seamen were impressed into service in the British Navy. France, too, made free with American shipping, and the two belligerents seized about 1,500 American ships in a space of less than ten years. But Britain's provocations were more demeaning. With lofty arrogance her ships stood outside American harbors in full view of the shore to await their prey. American anger rose to a fever point in June, 1807, when a British frigate stopped a United States warship, the *Chesapeake*, to take suspected deserters from its crew.

Staving off the pressures for war, Jefferson instead called for an embargo. That America might succeed in starving Britain into submission — or at least into a more conciliatory attitude — was an intriguing notion and not altogether out of the realm of possibility. The trouble was that the United States itself soon started hurting much more than England or France did. From 1807 to 1808, exports dropped from $108 million to $22 million, and imports from $139 million to $57 million. Idle ships lay in the harbors, and unsold goods piled up in warehouses. Thousands of sailors, laborers, and mechanics were thrown out of work. Although a few shippers resorted to the familiar practice of smuggling, most took heavy losses and applied relentless pressure on Congress to end the embargo.

After fourteen months the Embargo Act was repealed. In its place went the Nonintercourse Act, prohibiting trade with Britain, France, and their possessions. This too was repealed, but a new bill provided that the restrictions of the Nonintercourse Act should be applied to either France or England, as soon as the other withdrew orders against American shipping. The British minister gave assurances that his country's decrees would be cancelled, but he was recalled and new orders were proclaimed. The French proved no more dependable. Napoleon announced a repeal of the interdiction, but his navy continued to

An 1827 water color by D. J. Kennedy depicts the works of the Union Glass Company at Kensington on the Delaware River.

seize American ships.

Even so, America's foreign trade increased after repeal of the embargo, and shippers were far from unhappy. But in the West and South the Republican "war hawks," led by Henry Clay, hungry for more land annexation in Canada and Florida and eager to end British flirtations with the Indians, called for war. Because national honor had been under such flagrant attack, they were able to prevail.

The war continued until nearly the end of 1814. Militarily it ended in a stalemate. Economically it was disastrous for most of the country—but less so for the New Englanders, who traded with the enemy in Canada and Maine and got special dispensation from the British to carry on their seagoing trade. But nationally, exports dropped from $61 million in 1811 to just $7 million in 1814, while imports slipped from $53 million to $13 million. The British effectively blockaded coastwise trade as well. A barrel of flour, which was worth $4.50 in Richmond in 1813, brought $11.87 in Boston. Prices of groceries and iron products rose, while such native staples as wheat, tobacco, and cotton had no export market, so the prices paid to farmers dropped.

With peace, these situations reversed. Flour went up by 50 per cent, while the price of sugar was cut in half. Shipbuilding, depressed during the war, revived and a new record number of 1,314 vessels was built in one year. Exports climbed to $93 million by 1818; imports rose even more dramatically, to $147 million by 1816. Again, the flood of postwar imports glutted the American market and hit hard at some of the newer manufacturing firms. Sending over far more goods than the United States could absorb also meant losses for some British shippers, but one member of Parliament philosophized: "It was even worth while to incur a loss upon the first exportations, in order by the glut to stifle in the cradle these rising manufactures in the United States, which the war had forced into existence, contrary to the natural course of things."

For a time it appeared that the Republicans were becoming the party of commerce and protectionism. One of their first postwar acts was a bill repealing discriminating duties against the shipping of any country that ended discrimination against American shipping. The first of a series of reciprocal trade treaties was signed with Great Britain. As far back as 1801 Jefferson had sent warships to the Mediterranean to end Barbary Coast piracy against American ships, but to little effect. Finally, in May, 1815, Captain Stephen Decatur sailed into the harbor of Algiers and forced the ruling dey to renounce the old practice of exacting an annual tribute, to release all American prisoners without ransom, and to guarantee the freedom of U.S. commerce. Similar guarantees were exacted from Tunis and Tripoli.

The first clearly protectionist tariff act was passed in 1816, providing duties of 7.5 to 30 per cent on the value of imports and giving special consideration to cottons, woolens, and iron, as well as various manufactures that had developed during the war. Two years later the duties on many of these items were increased and extended.

THE LOWLY MANUFACTURER

The fabled ingenuity of the Yankee tinkerer probably sprang more from necessity than native skill. Smiths, shipbuilders, tanners, and tailors had to learn to make do with what was available in the New World and to advance their arts in spite of official discouragement by Britain. A class of mechanics developed, mainly in the North.

As these makers of things underwent the transition from artisan to manufacturer, however, they were able to advance little in social esteem. Gouverneur Morris, who eventually went off to live in Europe, felt that merchants and landowners should present a common front against the dangers of political control by greasy mechanics.

On the other hand, there was official encouragement. Hamilton urged not merely protection; he strongly recommended bounties for manufacturers. "The complete success which has rewarded manufacturing enterprise in some valuable branches," said his 1790 Report on Manufactures, justified "a hope that the obstacles to the growth of . . . industry are less formidable than they were apprehended to be."

Even before Congress had time to act on his report, Hamilton helped organize the Society for Establishing Useful Manufactures, a private organization designed to manufacture cotton, linen goods, and paper, to engage in printing, and to build various public works. An initial $100,000 was quickly subscribed, and another $150,000 was paid or pledged in a few months. Under the leadership of William Duer, the society sought a charter from New Jersey. It proposed exemption from real-estate taxes for ten years and from personal property taxes forever, exemption from military service for all workers, the right to conduct lotteries and charge tolls for the canals and roads it built, and the right of eminent domain in its own thirty-six-square-mile municipality, to be known as the Town of Paterson. All of this was granted by the state legislature.

Before long the society was in deep trouble. The personal failure of Duer, who had tried to corner the market in the government's 6 per cent notes, was a factor in precipitating the panic of 1792. Duer himself went to jail. The society had actually built a mill, but most of the grand plans never materialized, and the investors were soon discouraged about their prospects. Dissolution was proposed, but, fortunately for the in-

EVANS'S AUTOMATIC FLOUR MILL

American inventiveness produced many innovations of profound, and sometimes dramatic, importance—from the sewing machine to the six-shooter. One invention, almost forgotten today, played a significant role in helping to turn the American land into a horn of plenty. It was a machine-driven wonder, devised in 1790 by the Delaware-born mechanical visionary Oliver Evans, which eliminated human labor from the process of turning grain into flour.

At the close of the 1700's grain mills, powered by water wheels or wind, were small affairs, usually comprising a single pair of millstones. Men still had to perform the backbreaking chores of hoisting the grain to the top of the gravity system that fed it down between the turning stones, then hauling it up again to feed it into storage silos.

Evans had already invented a machine to make carders, or combs, to clean wool and cotton; it was, in effect, a machine tool. Turning to the milling process, he registered dismay at the amount of work it required, as well as at the dirt that workmen at the mills inevitably trampled into the meal. "People," he said later, "did not even then like to eat dirt if they could see it."

In time Evans designed, patented, and sold a series of interconnected machines that supplanted man in the milling process. His apparatus, he wrote, was able "to receive the grain from the waggon, or ship, etc., and to elevate and convey it, until it should be placed over the millstones to be ground, and then to elevate the meal as ground to fall on the meal loft, there to spread, stir and cool it, and attend the bolting [or sifting] hoppers; in short, to perform the whole operations, until it be completely manufactured into superfine flour ready for packing."

His mechanism had a hoist with an endless belt and buckets that could lift 300 bushels of grain an hour, endless screw conveyors, a "hopper boy," or rotating rake that dispensed with a boy to spread the meal to cool, and a device that separated bran from the flour. With his automatic flour mill, six men, employed mainly to close the barrels, could turn 100,000 bushels of grain into flour

Oliver Evans

in a year.

His invention was greeted at first with skepticism but soon won enthusiastic acceptance. The machine appeared everywhere, but despite a fourteen-year patent that Evans held on it, he had great difficulty collecting royalties.

His technical manual, *The Young Mill-Wright and Miller's Guide*, was published in fifteen editions from 1795 to 1860. By 1837 there were 1,200 mills in five western states alone, using Evans's elevators and producing 2 million barrels of flour a year. It was a triumph of mass production that eventually benefited not only the United States but the people of all the world.

The use of steam for machinery also fascinated Evans, who recognized that subjecting steam to high pressure would improve on Newcomen's atmospheric steam engine. In 1817 Evans's own foundry and engineering plant, called the Mars Works, built a 100-horsepower engine capable of pumping three million gallons of water in twenty-four hours, for Philadelphia's Fairmount Waterworks, the first municipal water system of its kind in the United States.

Earlier—in 1805—Evans's steam-driven dredge, the *Orukter Amphibolos*, an exercise in Greek for "amphibious digger," had chuffed through Philadelphia streets, amusing onlookers who expected to see it blow up. But the 15½-ton vehicle worked; equipped also with paddlewheels, it steamed down the Schuylkill River to prove that it could dredge the harbor. And in 1813, sixteen years before the first railway locomotive engine was imported to run successfully in the United States, Evans foresaw that "the time will come when people will travel in stages moved by steam engines from one city to another, almost as fast as birds fly, fifteen or twenty miles per hour."

Evans's greatest contribution, however, was his flour mill, which liberated the American economy from subsistence agriculture and paved the way for numerous other advances that brought technology and science to the service of the farmer. Another American innovation—the grain elevator that stores wheat against seasonal price changes—was patented by Joseph Dart in 1842. But it was based on Evans's principles.

O. EVANS, *The Young Mill-Wright and Miller's Guide*, 1795

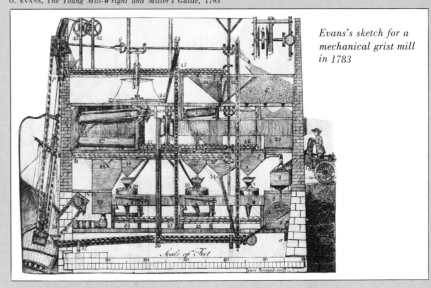

Evans's sketch for a mechanical grist mill in 1783

vestors, it was never carried out. When Paterson later developed, the real-estate holdings and water rights turned out to be very valuable; as late as 1937 the New Jersey Supreme Court refused to revoke the old charter to end the tax exemption. Finally, some 150 years after the society was formed, the city of Paterson acquired all the stock and dissolved the corporation.

Similar societies for the encouragement of manufacturing sprang up over the next twenty-five years in New York City, Providence, Philadelphia, Wilmington, and elsewhere, and President Monroe frequently spoke of the government's role in fostering domestic manufactures. But most of these had indifferent success, especially in comparison with the manufacturing plants that were started as the outgrowth of specific technologies or to meet an expressed popular need.

It was during this same period that the remarkable metamorphosis of the American corporation began to take shape. Corporations were initially chartered, like the joint-stock companies of the mercantile era, to enable groups of private people to achieve what was recognized as a public purpose. During the colonial period the corporate device was commonly used to establish towns or educational and eleemosynary organizations, and only rarely to set up a business.

Between 1783 and 1801, however, more than 300 business corporations were chartered by the states. The great majority were for purposes that might classify the corporations as public utilities—such as roads, bridges, canals, and water systems. But an increasing number were incorporated for other purposes.

There were thirty-two, for example, chartered to write insurance policies. Insurance underwriting of ships and their cargoes had begun well back in the colonial period, and the business got a boost from rising postwar commerce and the uncertainties that accompanied shipping during the European wars. Especially in Philadelphia, insurance brokers and underwriters multiplied to the point where a former privateersman, Captain John Macpherson, began publishing a semimonthly paper listing the current rates.

The Philadelphia Contributorship, for which Benjamin Franklin and Samuel Morris were among the original signers of the deed of settlement, began insuring its members against fire hazards back in 1752. They offered rewards to organizations that put out fires on their insured properties. Competition became so keen that the contributorship felt constrained to issue notices that no more gratuities would be given out unless the fire fighters started paying less attention to fighting with each other and more to putting out the fires. Fire losses actually proved to be less than the organization's income from investments, so that by 1810 the policies were recognized as perpetual, without further payments.

The fact that corporate charters were given freely to manufacturing companies was testimony to the general feeling that industry had a semipublic, rather than private, character. In one brief period, from 1808 to 1815, New York State issued 175 charters to manufacturing companies, which exceeded the 164 granted to various public utilities, a significant reversal of the proportions common both before and after that time.

Manufacturing nevertheless merited the description of "infant industry" during the nation's early years. Most of the goods made in this country were crude and the processes unsophisticated. Finer products were imported mainly from England, from which American manufacturers tried to steal both trade secrets and skilled artisans whenever they could. Almost until the Revolution there was so little understanding of the principle of transmitting power that separate wheels were used for each machine to be activated.

The factory system, as such, began very hesitantly, and most factories were augmented by networks of home workshops. Although Boston had few manufacturing plants of its own, it was the commercial hub around which were clustered the textile centers of Fall River and Lowell, and the shoemaking towns of Lynn, Brockton, and Haverhill. The availability of cheap water power, as often as not, determined the site for a New England factory. This was less true of the quieter waters of the Ohio Valley, where steam power came into its first extensive use.

An atmospheric steam engine was first built in England in the early 1700's by Thomas Newcomen. The Scottish engineer James Watt developed a low-pressure engine with a separate condenser in 1765, and the Boulton-Watt Company began producing these commercially. Oliver Evans, one of America's first mechanical geniuses, developed his high-pressure, reciprocating steam engine in 1804, and put that on the market.

Steam engines were probably first used in this country for pumping mines. One of Evans's early engines, shipped to New Orleans in 1802 to propel a small boat, was stranded by heavy floods a halfmile from the water. It was put to work running a sawmill instead, and a demand developed quickly for more steam-driven saws. Steam power became popular in industries that used heat, such as glass and iron manufacture.

Evans also pioneered in building grist mills that were the closest thing to automation in his day. His first mills, using water power, carried the grain on a kind of endless chain from the farmer's wagon to finished flour, foreshadowing the modern assembly line. In 1808 Evans constructed a steam flour mill in Pittsburgh, where nine bushels of wheat or ten of rye could be ground in an hour. Evans later built more powerful steam engines, one of which was used to operate printing presses in New York City by 1815.

The period's other major contribution to modern manufacturing methods was that of interchangeable parts, developed by Jethro Wood for his plow and later refined to an industrial art by Eli Whitney in gun-making. But more significant for his own era was another of Whitney's contributions to the economy.

ELI WHITNEY'S REVOLUTION

Until 1793 cotton had been of small importance to the South. The green seeds of the short-staple variety clung to the boll, so that a slave could produce no more than a pound of cotton a day, and even that was indifferently cleaned.

Long-staple Sea Island cotton, with black seeds that could be removed easily with rollers, was introduced from the Bahamas in 1785, but it could grow well only along the coast. Imported long-staple cotton carried an impost of three cents a pound. Said the Rhode Island merchant and manufacturer Moses Brown of the home-grown short-staple variety: "The unripe, short, and dusty part . . . so spoils the whole as to discourage the use of it in the machines, and obliges the manufacturer to have his supply from the West Indies under the discouragement of the impost."

Eli Whitney was a young Yale graduate who had taught school and who went south to take a job as a private tutor. He had been engaged by Phineas Miller, who managed a Georgia estate owned by the widow of General Nathanael Greene and who subsequently married Mrs. Greene. From the moment he arrived at the estate, Whitney kept hearing about the need for an efficient method of removing seeds from the short-staple cotton. He wrote his father at the time, "There were a number of very respectable Gentlemen at Mrs. Greene's who all agreed that if a machine could be invented . . . , it would be a great thing both to the Country and the inventor."

Whitney himself had an ideal temperament for invention—a mechanical bent, a logical mind, imagination, and persistence. Within ten days he had built a model of the machine that was needed—a cylinder barely two feet long and six inches in diameter, with rows of teeth to comb out the troublesome seeds and brushes and a fan to move away the cleaned cotton. The model was fifty times as efficient as hand labor and could separate ten times as much cotton as more primitive machines—and clean it much better.

The machine occasioned great excitement in the household. In her enthusiasm, Mrs. Greene invited friends from all over the state to come and marvel at its accomplishments. Word of the contrivance got around fast. Some local people, denied the privilege of seeing the model, broke into the building where it was kept and carried it off. Simple in its principle and con-

Eli Whitney, from a painting by Samuel F. B. Morse in 1822

struction, the cotton gin was copied with slight variations before Whitney was able to obtain a patent. Whitney did get a patent, however, and formed a partnership with Miller, who was to supply the capital for the new enterprise. A yellow fever epidemic and a fire caused delays and troubles. But the worst was still to come.

In those days, business was thought of primarily in terms of commerce and trade, rather than manufacture. So instead of building and selling the machines outright, they decided to erect cotton gins throughout the South and collect a fee on all cotton processed. An operation of this kind, however, proved too extensive and cumbersome for their limited capital, and it was also unsatisfactory to the planters; all of which acted as a stimulant to infringements of the patent.

By 1796, three years after the gin was invented, the firm was unable to raise enough money to pay expenses. At one point Miller offered 30 per cent interest to borrow $1,000 and was turned down. They filed suit for damages on the patent infringement. So certain were they of winning in court that Miller mortgaged Mrs.

Greene's properties. At the close of the trial the judge gave his charge in their favor, but the jury nevertheless ruled against them. Broke and despondent, the firm of Whitney and Miller gave up the cotton gin business.

None of this deterred the spectacular growth of cotton planting and its spread to the upland regions, now that the short-staple plant could be processed efficiently. Once a luxury fabric, cotton became the cheapest and most commonly used cloth. Virtually every southern planter went into cotton cultivation, and production rose from 2 million pounds in 1790 to an average of 60 million between 1801 and 1805, and 80 million ten years later. Except for the years of embargo and war, exports climbed steadily and steeply, from just 200,000 pounds in 1790 to around 40 million pounds, valued at almost $67 million, by 1810.

Land once deemed all but worthless became valuable again. Those who could afford it bought slaves. The trend toward abolition, spurred when men like Washington and Jefferson provided in their wills for their own slaves to be set free, was reversed. Because virtually entire families could be put to work in the fields for most of the year, the slave economy proved ideal for cotton culture. The price of a good field hand, about $300 before Whitney's invention, doubled in twenty years. Poor whites, who could afford neither slaves nor land at the higher prices, moved west in mounting numbers and soon dominated the Southwest. President Madison issued orders to the military to take possession of the Gulf Coast region known as West Florida. By 1819 Spain was ready to give up East Florida; in exchange the United States assumed claims against Spain amounting to $5 million.

Eventually Miller and Whitney were able to have a small share of all the new cotton wealth. Largely through their efforts, the nation's patent law was amended in 1800 to remove earlier ambiguities. Miller started a series of lawsuits, and Whitney went to South Carolina to appear before the legislature. A number of southern states voted that payments would have to be made for the patent rights.

But Whitney had not been idle in the intervening years. Thoroughly disheartened by the legal debacle over the cotton gin, he had nevertheless shown enough resilience to go after government contracts to make other products. Even in defeat, Whitney retained confidence in his knowledge and abilities. Cocksure to the point of audacity, he got in touch with Treasury Secretary Oliver Wolcott in 1798, saying that he had noted that Congress was discussing appropriations for arms. "I have a number of workmen & apprentices," he wrote; ". . . I should like to undertake to Manufacture Ten or Fifteen Thousand Stand of Arms."

It was all but unthinkable that a man who had never made a single gun should propose to build thousands. But with war threats looming, and with Whitney's reputation for mechanical competence firmly established, he was awarded a contract to produce 10,000 muskets at $13.40 each and was advanced $5,000 to start on the work. At the same time, twenty-six others were granted contracts to make arms, but these averaged fewer than 1,000 muskets apiece. What had obviously impressed Secretary Wolcott was Whitney's proposal to improve the machinery and techniques for arms manufacture in the United States—improvements that could well be the only means of supplying the nation with arms in the desired numbers. "One of my primary objects," Whitney had written, "is to form the tools so the tools themselves shall fashion the work and give to every part its just proportion—which when once accomplished, will give expedition, uniformity, and exactness to the whole. . . . The tools which I contemplate are similar to an engraving on a cooper plate."

By making a metal mold, or "jig," for each part of the gun, Whitney was able to use ordinary metalworkers, rather than skilled gunsmiths, to hand-tool the mechanisms. Thus the parts in each of his guns would be exact duplicates of the parts in every other gun. Precision gauges were made to assure exact measurements.

Whitney's plans went forward with less precision. First there was a second scourge of yellow fever in Philadelphia. Then he had difficulty in securing the mill site he had decided on in New Haven. Snowstorms delayed construction of the factory. And because industrial enterprises were not deemed proper businesses, he had trouble getting credit. As a consequence of these troubles, the first 500 muskets were delivered in September, 1801, later than had been promised. They were inspected and proved satisfactory, however, and he proceeded to execute the remainder of the contract. By the time it was completed in 1809, his establishment was deemed a model of efficiency and was

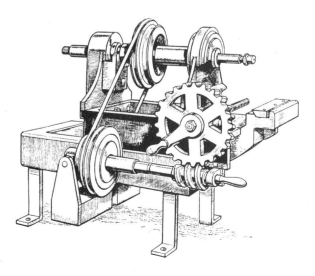

Machine used by Whitney for milling interchangeable parts

widely imitated. The census of 1810 showed that more than 40,000 firearms were being turned out by 140 plants.

Whitney later used his system of interchangeable parts for clockmaking, so that large numbers of clocks became available at lower cost. In these enterprises, he had laid the seeds for an even greater revolution in industry and the American economy than the one started with the invention of the cotton gin.

SLATER AND THE FACTORY SYSTEM

The most important developments in England's Industrial Revolution came in the field of textiles—in carding, which prepares the fiber; in spinning, which produces the thread; and in weaving, which converts the thread into cloth. In 1733 John Kay developed the "flying shuttle," a simple string-pulling device that enabled the weaver to work on a wider section of cloth. In 1769 Richard Arkwright, a barber, perfected a water frame, a series of rollers that turned out stronger cotton thread. In 1770 James Hargreaves improved the spinning wheel by inventing the "spinning jenny," which hooked up a number of spindles to be operated simultaneously. In 1779 Samuel Crompton combined the water frame and jenny into a "mule," thus producing stronger thread at higher speed. And in 1785 Edmund Cartwright, a clergyman, built a power loom for weaving, using horse power at first, and then steam.

In the forefront of technology, Britain was not about to share her knowledge with others and kept it closely guarded. But a few of the simpler devices were easily understood and copied. Factories using jennies were established in 1787 at Philadelphia, at Beverly, Massachusetts, and elsewhere, but none proved successful. Americans in even the highest circles of officialdom were not above encouraging efforts to steal the secrets of others. Washington, wearing a full suit of broadcloth ordered from a New Haven woolen factory, said in his first message to Congress in January, 1790: "I cannot forbear intimating to you the expediency of giving effectual encouragement to the introduction of new and useful inventions from abroad, and to the exertions of skill and genius in producing them at home."

At that very moment a young immigrant was preparing to exercise such skills and genius. Samuel Slater had been a bright young apprentice in Belper, England, working for Jedediah Strutt, a partner of Arkwright and the inventor of a machine for making ribbed stockings. Starting to work at the age of fourteen, Slater had shown great aptitude for the business and was soon an overseer.

But the young man felt that prospects for the textile business were much better in America, where the industry was still backward and bounties were being offered for its development. Because Parliament had prohibited both the exportation of the machines and the migration of skilled mechanics, he laid his plans stealthily. Possessed of a good memory and a fine flair for mathematics, he memorized the equipment and worked out its method of operation. Disguised as a farm boy, he sailed for New York.

The ship's captain advised him to seek out Moses Brown, who had a spinning mill in Rhode Island. He first went to work for the New York Manufacturing Company, but found their equipment inferior. Early in 1790 he went off to Providence to see Brown. In short order he had made an agreement with the firm of William Almy and Smith Brown to reproduce Arkwright's machinery in a new mill, with Moses Brown supplying most of the financing. Slater was to get half the profits of the enterprise, out of which he would repay his 50 per cent share of the costs of new equipment and expenses.

Behind drawn blinds in a fulling mill owned by Ezekiel Carpenter, Slater went to work building carding machines, water frames, and the other equipment needed, relying on his own memory and ingenuity and working with his own hands. Within a year he had constructed three carding machines, a spinning frame with 72 spindles, and other needed equipment. When the dramatic moment arrived to set it all in motion, however, it failed to work properly. Slater thought about the problem constantly, trying to determine what had gone wrong. Finally, in a dream, he saw an adjustment that would overcome the trouble. Applying it the next day, he found that it worked. Four days before Christmas, 1790, the machines started to spin, with power supplied by the arm of an elderly Negro, Samuel Brunius Jenks. Later, water power was applied from the falls of the Blackstone River. Poorly constructed, the water wheel froze nightly at first, and Slater often spent as much as two or three hours before breakfast freeing the wheel, a practice that subsequently affected his health.

Slater disdained the use of the poorly cleaned American cotton and chose to pay the duty on imported products, instead. Even so, buyers were skeptical of the quality of American-made cotton yarn. In time, however, the mercantile firm of Almy & Brown established and broadened its market. The first lot of 116 pounds of machine-spun yarn was sold for around $175 in June, 1791. By the following February the charges against Slater for his share of machinery and stock amounted to almost $2,500. But later that year another entry in the books showed nearly $5,000 credited to his account.

Wool manufacturing had a similar genesis in America. Woolens were largely a product of home industry, and only coarse materials could be produced from the quality of fleece available. Other countries banned the export of better grades of sheep for breeding. In

1793 a young Bostonian, William Foster, smuggled two Merino ewes and a ram out of Spain and gave them to his friend, Andrew Craigie, of Cambridge. Several years later Foster met his friend at a sale, where Craigie was paying $1,000 for a Merino ram. He had either been unaware of the value of the earlier stock or unable to sell their wool. Asked what had become of them, he replied simply, "I ate them."

Improved breeds were brought in from Spain, Ireland, and England, in time, and crossbred with American stock, just as factory production of woolens had its beginnings. Paul and Arthur Scholfield, brothers engaged in wool manufacture in Yorkshire, emigrated to America and set up a factory at Byfield, Massachusetts, using improved machinery. Other mills were established, using the same equipment, and the industry grew rapidly. The 1810 census enumerated 1,776 wool-carding machines. By the end of the War of 1812 it was estimated that $12 million had been invested in woolen mills that had an annual output of $19 million and employed 40,000 people. By then factory production exceeded the homespun product.

Cotton factories had a similar growth, many of them started by men who had learned the business through Slater, directly or indirectly. By 1804 a Pittsburgh factory was selling carding machines, drawing frames, spinning mules with up to 200 spindles, and twisting frames for yarn stockings. Cotton mills sprang up throughout southern New England, encouraged by the embargo and then the war. In 1807 there were fifteen or twenty mills, with about 8,000 spindles. By 1810 there were some ninety firms with perhaps 80,000 spindles, according to Gallatin's report to Congress. Ten years later the number of spindles in use had climbed to 191,000.

Francis Cabot Lowell spent two years in England, from 1810 to 1812, and carefully observed the textile machinery there. On his return he had spinning machines and power looms built, which he too designed from memory, and to which he added his own improvements, at a Waltham plant in 1814. This may well have been the first time anywhere that all the spinning and weaving processes came together under one roof. Patterns of the Scotch loom were brought to this country, improved, and built for as little as $70 per machine by David Wilkinson, brother-in-law of Slater's wife and operator of a machine shop where most of the nation's textile-machinery makers got their training.

Samuel Slater's textile mill, the first successful one in the U.S., was on the Blackstone River at Pawtucket, Rhode Island.

Slater himself built additional mills, the first in partnership with his father-in-law and brothers-in-law in 1800. He sent for his brother, John, who presumably came armed with the latest secrets of the British industry, and began a new project with him, Almy, and Brown. Slater continued to branch out into new enterprises, and at one time or another he was involved with at least seventeen different people in eight different partnerships, only two of which were dissolved. When he purchased an interest in a store in Providence, he reversed what had become the traditional procedure of the merchant branching out into manufacture.

Although he built a fortune of about $500,000, Slater remained a frugal man, describing his habit of self-denial as "a duty in me to set an example of prudence to others, and especially to my children."

He frequently expressed opinions quaintly and forcefully. When Vice President Andrew Jackson visited Slater in Pawtucket during a tour of manufactures, he told the industrialist, "I understand you taught us how to spin, so as to rival Great Britain in her manufactures."

"Yes, sir," replied Slater. "I suppose that I gave out the Psalm, and they have been singing to the tune ever since."

"We are glad to hear also that you have realized something for yourself and family," said Jackson.

To which Slater observed, "So am I glad to know it, for I should not like to be a pauper in this country, where they are put up to auction to the lowest bidder."

THE RICHEST MAN IN AMERICA

America had always been a place of high hope for most of those who came to her shores. For quite a number, who saw some of these hopes realized, it became a land of rising expectations. And for a very few, the realization must have surpassed their own wildest dreams.

Among those who managed to build on their family fortunes or create new fortunes after the Revolution

---

The Way to Wealth

PIERRE LORILLARD

A Huguenot immigrant to America, Pierre Lorillard (1742–76) learned how to make a profit by adding value to the vast American crop of tobacco. And his sons and their descendants thrived by adding to the same crop the value of advertising.

The French-born Lorillard set up his tobacco "manufactory," the first in America, at No. 4 Chatham Street in New York City in 1760. There he made pipe and snuff tobacco from "puddings" —wrapped-up, loglike sticks of tobacco leaves from Virginia. Snuff buyers were particular in their tastes, and Lorillard was successful in catering to their scents as well as their dollars.

His recipe for Paris rappee snuff showed how he sweetened the "pudding." He used strong virgin tobacco, trimmed off its stems, and soaked it in rum. Then, he prescribed, "set it in sweet room at 100 degrees for 12 days. Make into powder, letting stand three to four months, adding 1½ pounds salmoniac, 2 pounds tamarind, 2 oz. vanilla bean, 1 oz. tonka bean, 1 oz. camomile flowers." Other additives included lavender oil, gentian root, licorice, and other exotic oils.

Pierre was killed by Hessian mer-

Tobacco & Snuff of the best quality & flavor,
At the Manufactory, No. 4, Chatham street, near the Gaol
By Peter and George Lorillard,
Where may be had as follows :

Cut tobacco,	Prig or carrot do.
Common kitefoot do.	Maccuba snuff,
Common smoaking do.	Rappee do.
Segars do.	Strasburgh do.
Ladies twift do.	Common rappee do.
Pigtail do. in small rolls,	Scented rappee do. of different kinds,
Plug do.	
Hogtail do.	Scotch do.

The above Tobacco and Snuff will be sold reasonable, and warranted as good as any on the continent. If not found to prove good, any part of it may be returned, if not damaged.
N. B. Proper allowance will be made to those that purchase a quantity.   May 27—1m.

The first Lorillard advertisement, May 27, 1789, featured snuff and pipe tobacco.

cenaries during the Revolution, but his sons, Peter and George, carried on the business vigorously. Their first advertisement appeared in the New York *Daily Advertiser* on May 27, 1789. It promoted "cut tobacco, common kitefoot, segars, ladies twist, pigtail, hogtail, plug, prig or carrot" and the following varieties of snuff: "Maccuba, Rappee and Strasburgh." Their trademark, which was to endure for many generations, was an Indian puffing on a clay pipe and leaning on a hogshead labeled "best Virginia." The Lorillards helped to start the American tradition of putting a carved wooden Indian in front of every tobacconist's store.

In 1792 the sons moved the factory to the banks of the Bronx River north of New York City, using the stream's ample water supply to provide power. Their "Acre of Roses," used to flavor the snuff, eventually became part of the New York Botanical Garden. The stone-walled mill operated until around 1835. In the 1830's the company pushed for national distribution, signing up United States postmasters to stock and sell Lorillard tobacco products by mail order.

In time, Lorillard brands proliferated. Their chewing tobacco, Beech-Nut, was emblazoned on barn walls all over America. Private brands, labeled expressly for individual dealers, included Sweet Conqueror, Sweet Cob, Yellow Jacket, and Featherbed. The Lorillards introduced trade cards in their packaging, some engraved, some on multicolored enameled board, and

were the Rhinelander brothers, the Lorillards, John Jacob Astor, and the Schermerhorns. Eleuthère Irénée Du Pont, son of a well-to-do French government official and landowner, set up a gunpowder plant to help prosecute the war. Peter Goelet's sizable fortune came from a mixture of commerce, land, and banking.

Perhaps the first to earn the title of "richest man in America" was Stephen Girard, a one-eyed ship agent from Bordeaux who got into the wine business and shipping after the Revolution. When a partnership with his brother was dissolved in 1790, he took out his profits of $30,000, a very respectable fortune. By hard, shrewd dealings he made one killing after another with the voyages of his ships around the world. By 1810 he was able to ask the merchant banking house of Baring in London to invest $500,000 of his money in stock of the First Bank of the United States. When the Bank's charter expired he was the largest creditor, and he bought the bank building and cashier's house for $120,000. The following year he opened the Girard bank, capitalized at $1,200,000.

Girard made money fast and hung on to it. He lived alone in a four-story house on Water Street in Philadelphia, a miserly old Scrooge who was disliked and feared by his neighbors. His conversion did not come on a Christmas Eve but became evident after his death in 1831 at the age of eighty-one, when his largesse poured forth to his relatives, his servants, his apprentices, hospitals, and charities. Philadelphia got $500,000 for civic improvement. Pennsylvania received $300,000 for canals; the remainder, about $6 million, went to found a college for orphans, which he stipulated that no man of the cloth might ever visit. His estate amounted to $10 million, the largest in America at the time.

But the title of richest man was soon to be transferred to Astor, who outlived Girard by seventeen years and outdid him by $10 million. Also an immigrant, Astor was born in Waldorf, in the German Rhine country. At seventeen he set off for London, where his brother made musical instruments. In 1784, at the age of twenty, he arrived in Baltimore with seven flutes and $25. He went to New York, where another brother, Henry, was a butcher, and he put his flutes out for sale.

Having learned something about the fur trade from passengers on the voyage across the Atlantic, he went to work for a furrier, and did some trading on his own account. Within a year he was back in London, selling furs and buying merchandise to bring back.

In 1785 he married Sarah Todd, a sea captain's daughter, and opened a shop in his mother-in-law's home. Helped by his business-minded wife, he dealt in furs as well as musical instruments and supplies. By 1788 furs were his principal stock, and he was making annual buying trips to Montreal, the center of the North American fur trade.

Business had its ups and downs, and the story is told that Astor would occasionally go to his brother for a loan or to have a note endorsed. Tiring of this, Henry is said to have told him, "John, I will give you $100 if you will agree never to ask me to loan you any money, endorse a note, or sign a bond for you." Astor weighed the proposition, decided $100 in the hand was worth more than the prospect of future loans, accepted the offer, and thereafter lived strictly up to its terms.

In the early 1790's he had agents make the fur-buying trips, and he was branching out into other businesses. He held shares in New York's first bank in 1791 and in an insurance company in 1792. He was an importer and dealer in pianos and musical supplies, then in materials to be traded to the Indians for furs and in supplies for his trading posts. By 1800, when he was worth around $250,000, he owned one ship and his principal imports were arms, ammunition, and wool. He soon got into New York real estate, buying up a long-term lease from Trinity Church for valuable land in what is now Greenwich Village. Astor, who then

used premiums to sell their products. Silk stockings, lamps, and shoelaces were among the items offered in return for coupons; the company even packaged $100 bills at random in a brand of cigarette tobacco named Century, for its one hundredth anniversary in 1860.

The money that the Lorillards made, they spent lavishly. Pierre IV, born in 1833, helped make Newport, Rhode Island, a yachting center, bred trotters at his vast stables in Rancocas, New Jersey, and watched his colt Iroquois carry his cherry-and-black colors to win the English Derby in 1881. He owned 7,000 acres in Orange County, New York, turned it into a shooting, fishing, and residential club called Tuxedo Park, and for one of its functions designed and wore the first dinner jacket, a tail-less coat—which brought the club's name into the language.

At the turn of the century the Lorillard firm became part of a giant trust, the American Tobacco Company, but the U. S. Supreme Court in 1911 broke it into American Tobacco, Liggett & Myers, and, of course, P. Lorillard. Now part of Loew's Corporation, the company has provided many contributions to America's panoply of trademarks—Old Gold, Murad, Between the Acts, Kent—as well as compelling proof that marketing in America possesses enormous powers.

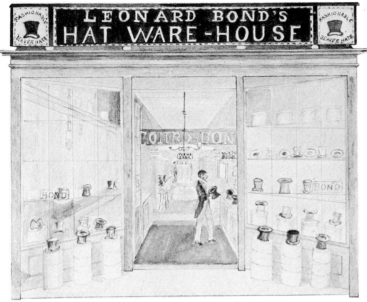

LEONARD BOND'S HAT WARE-HOUSE

This early nineteenth-century store featured beaver hats.

lived at 221 Broadway, acquired the lease from his next-door neighbor, Aaron Burr, when Burr had to flee after he shot Hamilton in a duel in 1804.

The fur business made for a natural entry into the China trade, and Astor was soon having ships built to carry furs to Canton, Oriental goods back to New York, and New England and European wares to the Northwest and China. He was one of the few who managed to circumvent government shipping restrictions. During the embargo Jefferson got a request to permit "a Chinese mandarin" to return home for family reasons after the death of his grandfather, a favor the President granted with courtesy and dispatch. The mandarin, if there indeed was one, sailed on Astor's *Beaver*, along with an outbound cargo of otter skins and cochineal. Later, during the War of 1812, the British permitted Astor's *Hannibal* to transport an anti-Napoleonic general back to France—along with a $60,000 cargo. This voyage also put an Astor ship in Europe, ready for the peace.

With commerce languishing during the war, Astor bought more than $2 million in bonds the government was unable to sell, at 88. The bonds did well for a time, but when they slipped to 75 he bought more on the open market. He later pointed out how he had fared in all this: "My losses by Sea are made up in the peace by the rise on my Stocks of which I have something more than 800m$ [$800,000]."

During the years of war and embargo, Astor chafed at the dominance of the continent's fur trade by two Canadian companies—the Canadian North West and the Michilimackinac. He started the American Fur Co., capitalized at $1,000,000, and concluded a trading alliance with the Russian American Co. He also set up the Pacific Fur Co., whose agents established the

post of Astoria at the mouth of the Columbia River. But those proved to be ill-starred ventures when war interrupted his operations. His Pacific Fur properties were sold to the Canadian North West Co., and Astor retired to other battlegrounds of trade by setting up better connections in the Missouri region.

After the war, Astor was ready to take on the Canadian interests. With nine ships, a sizable capital, and an organization of ruthless agents in a traditionally lawless industry, he set out to monopolize the fur business. He drew great help from an 1816 act that required licensing of foreign companies operating on American soil. When Astor did finally subdue his rivals, he either tired of the game or felt that the fur business had a limited future. In any event, he virtually abandoned it, turning his attention primarily toward New York City real estate, the spring that fed the greater part of his fortune.

A lover of music and literature, Astor patronized writers and artists, including Washington Irving, who wrote *Astoria*, the tale of the fur magnate's dream of building a trading empire in the American Far West. But Astor's consuming passion was business, his relentless goal, profits.

He also had an overpowering sense of the value of money in hand. He is said to have subscribed to John James Audubon's *Birds of America*, priced at $1,000. When the artist asked him to pay, he complained, "Money is very scarce. I have nothing in bank. I have invested all my funds." Similar requests drew similar replies. On Audubon's sixth visit to seek payment, Astor pleaded his cash pinch, and turned to his son to ask whether they had any money in the bank. The son, who had not been listening, started to enumerate the deposits—$120,000 in one bank, $220,000 in another. Astor interrupted at this point to ask his son to make out a check for $1,000.

TOWARD SELF-SUFFICIENCY

Hamilton's very comprehensive report on the nation's manufactures in 1791 was tinged by his personal enthusiasm for the subject and was perhaps a touch more sanguine than actual conditions warranted. He found that a great many areas of manufacturing had grown up rapidly and were flourishing—among them leather products, iron and iron implements and utensils, woodworking, spirits and malt liquors, papermaking, sugar refining, animal and vegetable oil processing, copper and brass works, tinware, carriages of all kinds, painters' colors, and gunpowder. To provide the raw materials from which these products could be made, he urged protective tariffs on imports of iron, copper, lead, fossil coal, wood, skins, grain, cloth staples, glass, and paper.

In 1812 Tench Coxe, who had held the office of Purveyor of Public Supplies, reported to Secretary of the Treasury Gallatin that manufacturers had outstripped native sources of raw material supply in a great many products. From 40 to 50 million pounds each of wool, flax, hemp, hides, and domestic animal skins had been imported annually for a number of years to meet manufacturing requirements. Pig iron and brass were also in short supply, he found. Of 110 listed items of export, about 70 were manufactured in the country.

Although the great advances in iron and steel production were still far in the future, iron nonetheless dominated the metalworking industries. Just before the Revolution there had been iron forges in virtually all the colonies, and 30,000 tons were produced in 1775. When the war started, iron manufacturers received contracts for large quantities of military supplies. In Pennsylvania, many a gun barrel was machined in the secluded boring mills of Lancaster County, and cannon were cast at the Durham Iron Works. When the war ended, Congress and local assemblies hastened to en-

courage the industry by offering bounties for iron and steel products. The first tariff in 1789 laid duties of 10 to 15 per cent on iron, steel, and hardware, higher than on most products.

Gradually the bog iron that had been widely used was supplemented and then replaced by the richer magnetic ores found first in southern New York and New Jersey, and later in Pennsylvania, Kentucky, and Tennessee. The census of 1810 reported that 54,000 tons of iron were produced by 153 furnaces.

Other metalworking industries and sources were developed to meet demands. Copper was found in Ohio, and there were numerous coppersmiths and brass-founders. A West Virginia mine produced abundant supplies of lead, which went largely for military uses during the war and for a greater variety of purposes afterward. Production of a few chemicals was started—epsom salts from mineral springs in Vermont and sal ammoniac and Glauber's salts in Pennsylvania.

Glassmaking made substantial progress in a num-

The Way to Wealth

ELEUTHERE IRENEE DU PONT

Among the first businessmen to sense the importance of manufactures in invigorating the young republic's economy, Eleuthère Irénée Du Pont (1771–1834) made his name synonymous with gunpowder.

A member of the French aristocracy and the son of an inspector general of commerce in the royal cabinet before the French Revolution, Du Pont came to the New World in 1800 after an unsatisfying venture in publishing. He tried to set up a utopia, a French émigré colony in Virginia, but like most such ventures it failed through undercapitalization. So Du Pont turned to something that he knew well. As a former apprentice to a great French chemist, Antoine Lavoisier, he could tell good gunpowder when he fired it — and he was appalled at the lack of it in the United States.

Du Pont established a powder factory, called the Eleutherian Mills (after his own name, from the Greek for "freedom"), alongside the Brandywine Creek near Wilmington, Delaware. President Thomas Jefferson met him and in 1801 gave him his first business order — refining some saltpeter. By 1804 Du Pont was selling fine grade gunpowder.

The business was financially strapped for many years. Against Du Pont's urgings, the original investors refused to plow profits back into expansion and better-quality production. Du Pont began buying up his investors' holdings on credit and rapidly sank $60,000 into debt. "I have spent my life here building up a very difficult industry," he wrote at one point to a friend in France, "and the disappointments I have had to bear have given me an habitual dullness and melancholy."

In 1809 his total operating investment amounted to $109,000. But by 1811 his mills had become the largest of any industry in America and turned a profit of $45,000. When he died in 1834 the value of cash on hand, accounts and notes receivable, plants and properties, inventories, and securities had risen to $317,124, and his mills in Delaware were producing more than a million pounds of explosives a year. "Manufacturing is a true creation of wealth," Du Pont had once written. "It is taking cotton which costs 20 cents per pound and making it *worth* several dollars."

The man who had failed to establish

a utopia, moreover, had continued to think like a utopian. When an explosion in 1818 killed forty of his men, he provided pensions, education, housing, and medical care for the victims' families, although neither law nor custom at the time required it.

A century later, during the pacifistic mood of the nation in the 1930's, the company that Du Pont had established was assailed as a "merchant of death" by some members of Congress — although the country had many times relied on its products during years of war. It is still an important producer of munitions, but its slogan, "Better things for better living — through chemistry," adopted in 1935, helped change its public image. The company has lived up to the slogan, becoming the world's largest producer of synthetic products for the consumer. One of its best known "better things" is nylon, which was first marketed by Du Pont in 1938, and many of the company's familiar trademarks — Dacron, Duco, Mylar, and Lucite — have almost become generic, too. By 1951 Du Pont's average operating investment was over $1,500,000,000 — nearly 5,000 times as much as in 1834.

ber of states immediately after the war, mainly for windows, bottles, and glassware. Henry William Stiegel, a German emigrant who settled in eastern Pennsylvania, became a pioneer iron manufacturer in colonial days, then switched to glassmaking after visiting British plants and bringing back skilled European workers. In Lancaster County he built the town of Manheim and erected the largest glasshouse in existence. Starting with flint glass tableware, he moved toward colored glass in rich blues, greens, and violets that were later to become collectors' items.

Special privileges were granted glassmaking establishments after the Revolution. A Boston company received a charter in 1787 as the state's exclusive glass manufacturer for fifteen years. They began operations in 1792, and their production reached $76,000 a year before the turn of the century. Ten miles west of Albany, the village of Hamilton was laid out as the home of the Hamilton Manufacturing Company, which was given a five-year tax exemption. The company built a sawmill and two glasshouses, making an average of 20,000 feet of glass per month, in addition to flint glass and bottles. The first glassworks west of the Alleghenies was the Craig and O'Hara plant at Pittsburgh, opened in 1797.

The substitution of soda for potash in glass manufacture cut costs and increased consumption. The embargo and war period also did more for domestic glassmaking than for most industries. The census of 1810 listed twenty-two glassmaking companies, with a total output of $62,000, of which four fifths was in window glass. By 1815 the industry's production had almost quadrupled, to $235,000.

The Hamilton report noted that the manufacture of brick, tile, and potters' ware in the United States had grown to keep pace with demand and even permit small exports by 1790, mainly to the West Indies. A number of manufacturing improvements were patented after that year, and George Hadfield built the first brickmaking machine in 1800.

As late as 1812 the value of anthracite coal had not yet been recognized, and the soft, smoky bituminous was the only fossil fuel in use. As Virginia coal became scarcer, experiments were conducted with the harder variety. But when it was suggested that the deposits at the headwaters of the Schuylkill River be developed, the state senator from the area declared there was no coal there, only a "black stone" that was called coal but would not burn.

People of widely separate positions and disparate skills developed new products or made improvements in old ones. These ranged from the skilled clockmaker Eli Terry, who made the first mantel clock in 1814, to Miss Betsy Metcalf, who at the age of twelve succeeded in taking oat straw and fashioning a very creditable imitation of the English straw bonnet, thus starting a new industry in New England.

By a substantial margin, most of the nation's manufactured products still came out of the homes and workshops of skilled craftsmen. But slowly, inexorably, changes were taking place. All along the Appalachian fall line, rivers were being harnessed for their power. Factory chimneys that belched the black smoke of their coal furnaces punctuated the New England landscape.

The factories, with their high wages and their special challenges to ingenuity, became magnets that attracted people of mechanical bent. Where once there were few who understood more than the simplest principles of power transmission, now there were scores of mechanics familiar with the use of gears, belts, chains, cams, pistons, joints, and friction wheels. Having constructed many of these parts of wood to meet their own needs, they were easily able to translate the principles involved in using the more precise and durable metal elements of machinery. Francis Lowell found many able craftsmen with "the training of many generations of farmer-mechanics."

But subtle changes took place when artisans became wage-earners. Because they required large numbers of workers, and because travels of more than a few miles were often difficult and time-consuming, particularly since working hours stretched from dawn to dark, the mills became the focal points around which towns quickly developed, sometimes expanding into cities. The skilled journeyman had formerly lived where he pleased, owned his own tools, and crafted and sold his products in his own small market. Lured into the factory, he found himself living the cramped life of the mill town, working impersonally at machines, and losing touch with the buyers of his products. In time, as the number of employees increased and as managers moved in, the worker would also lose contact with the owners. When business fell off, or as skilled workers became more plentiful, his once good wages would be cut.

As the gulf widened between workers and owners, conflict was inevitable. The first unions came into being before 1790, and indeed there had been a printers' strike in Philadelphia as early as 1766. But most early labor organizations were more concerned with regulating the conduct and improving the industry of their members than in commencing adversary representation against the employers. But in Philadelphia the shoemakers organized in 1792, and in New York the printers formed the Typographical Society in 1794, both concerned with raising wages, shortening hours, and improving working conditions. These were clouds no larger than a man's thumb, but they adumbrated the gradual closing of the homespun era, as well as profound changes in the social and economic fabric of American life.

70

II *The Inventive Mind*

Franklin's electrical experiment, an 1830 painting from a fire wagon panel

INSURANCE COMPANY OF NORTH AMERICA

"Intellectual freedom and curiosity about the new, the instinct of the American mind to look into, examine, and experiment—this led to, among other things, a willingness to 'scrap' not only old machinery but old formulas, old ideas; and brought about, among other results, the condition expressed in the saying that 'American mechanical progress could be measured by the size of its scrap-heaps.'"

Mark Sullivan, *Our Times*, Vol. I, 1926

Rube Goldberg's cartoons of torturous "time-saving" inventions touched the funny bone of a deep-lying national trait. As tinkerers and amateur inventors, Americans have forever sought short cuts and ways to do things easier, faster, and better.

Meeting the needs and pressures of the wilderness and frontier, where a person had to "make do," bred a tradition of improvisation and invention that resulted in a host of ingenious products and methods. Among them: the famed Kentucky long rifle; a pioneer ferry across Arizona's Little Colorado River (opposite, top); the useful can opener (1874) and safety pin (1849), below; and homemade motorized devices like the Rube Goldberg-ish engine-driven washing machine pictured opposite.

U.S. PATENT OFFICE

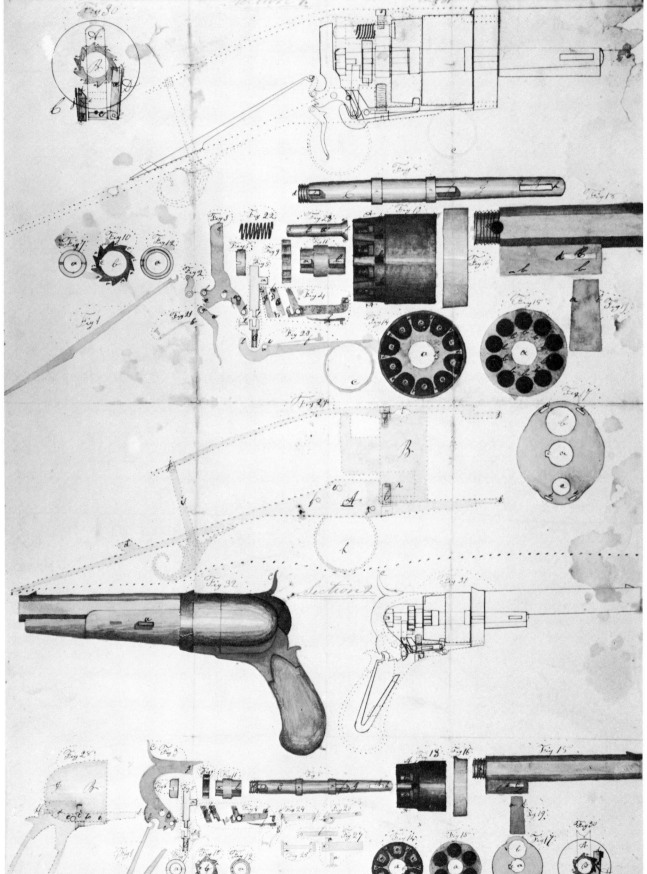

Two revolutionary inventions: above is Samuel Colt's 1835 patent drawing for a repeating pistol. Modified, it became standard equipment in the Mexican War. At right is a detail of the 1901 model of the Huber steam tractor, a replacement for horses.

SMITHSONIAN INSTITUTION

SMITHSONIAN INSTITUTION; ARNOLD NEWMAN

Many men received patents for sewing machines. Elias Howe's model of 1845, above, was the best and won final acceptance.

Printer Christopher Sholes, aided by Carlos Glidden and Samuel Soulé, produced this first practical typewriter in 1867.

GEORGE EASTMAN HOUSE

No. 1.	No. 2.
PRIX FR. **6.50**	PRIX FR. **12.50**
Donnant des Clichés 6 x 6 c/m.	Donnant des Clichés 6 x 9 c/m.
Bobines de 6 Poses 75 Centimes.	Bobines de 6 poses 1 Franc.

LES "BROWNIE" KODAKS

Fonctionnement Demontre en Quelques Minutes. GRATUITEMENT.

SE CHARGENT EN PLEIN JOUR.

Un Enfant peut faire des Jolies Photographies avec un Brownie

Kodak's box Brownie simplified picture-taking for amateurs throughout the world. This ad sold the camera in France about 1900.

READY-MADE HOUSES.

COL. DERROM'S PATENT.

The Great Want of our Day is CHEAP HOMES for the People.

Cottages, Villas, and other Constructions.

Contracts taken to Erect Buildings of Any Style or Size.

DOLLARS CAN BE SAVED BY CALLING ON US.

Ahead of their time: prefabricated homes, advertised in a builders' periodical, 1871

The early days of a new industry: frozen food products displayed in a market in the 1930's

The inventors of the airplane, Wilbur (seated) and Orville Wright, demonstrate one to King Alphonso of Spain in 1909.

The wizard of American science, Thomas Edison (above, right, with Henry Ford) changed civilization with his inventions.

Charles P. Steinmetz (below), mathematical genius at General Electric, provided the basis for modern electrical engineering.

The "father of rocketry," Robert H. Goddard (above) is seen in 1926 prepared to launch the first liquid-fueled rocket.

Science and technology, still resting on inventiveness, have continued to open new vistas for industry. Left: a "horn" antenna in Maine, one of the links of the Communications Satellite Corporation's space-age communications system. Above: Monsanto's AstroTurf (synthetic sod) in use at St. Louis. Below: J. P. Stevens & Company's stockings for pantyhose

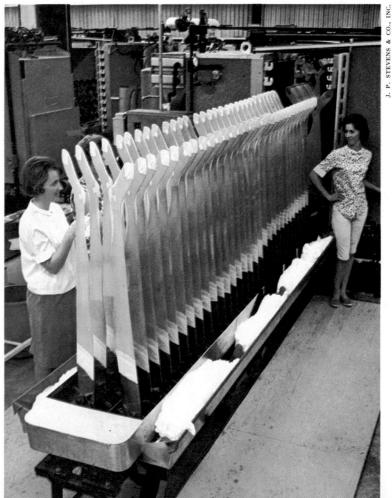

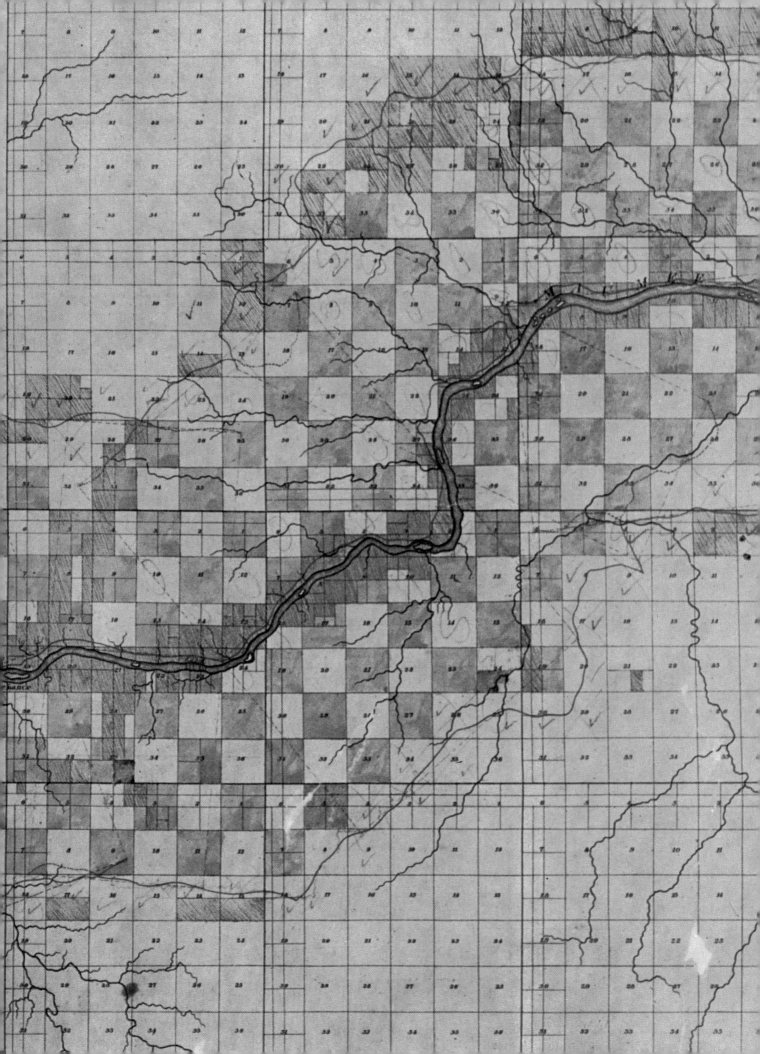

3

A NATION IN
MOTION

1815-1850

The Industrial Revolution had been under way in England for perhaps fifty years before it was exported to America, Switzerland, Belgium, and other countries sufficiently advanced in science, technology, and education to participate in it.

The United States might have begun to industrialize sooner if it had felt the need. But the nation's limited supply of human resources was taken up in other, more urgent pursuits, and manufactured goods were readily available from England during most of the country's formative years. Furthermore, America was far from ready to challenge British superiority in the quality and craftsmanship of industrial products.

When the Industrial Revolution did come to America, it was welcomed. Unlike the deep suspicion and antagonism that greeted steam power and machines in England, there was widespread interest and approval in the United States for any device that could augment labor and diminish the human work requirement. Accustomed to having change often work against their interests, British workingmen clung to the known, for whatever measure of security it afforded, and rejected the unknown as a threat; in some cases they physically attacked and demolished the new machines. But Americans were used to having change bring betterment, and they reached for it with curiosity and eagerness. For the workers, machines could lighten the drudgery of a great many tasks that had formerly called for muscle power. For consumers, machines brought more goods, usually at lower prices. And for employers they meant lower unit labor costs at a time when the cost of labor was a more important factor in the New

World than it was in the Old.

Even without major opposition, industrialization developed slowly. The United States remained predominantly a farming nation through most of the 1800's. In 1820 just under 72 per cent of all workers were engaged in agriculture; by 1840 the ratio had barely changed, with almost 69 per cent of the work force on farms. Possibly more significant, however, is the fact that, although agricultural labor increased 79 per cent over the two decades, the number of manufacturing and construction workers more than doubled, from 350,000 to 790,000.

The look of New England belied these statistics, for it was in the Northeast that most of the industrialization took place, and there was bustling activity everywhere in that part of the nation. But the South was more than ever a land of plantations, and the westward-moving migrants took their much-needed home crafts with them to the frontier. Although household manufacture, other than the preparation of food, started to decline in 1815, it was not until almost 1840 that more goods were produced in the mills than in the homes and shops of America.

The glut of British merchandise, the panic of 1819, and the ensuing depression brought ruin to many an American enterpriser who had staked all he had on one of the new mills. One after another shut down, and workers turned to public charity in the cities or went back to the farms. Henry Clay told Congress in 1820 of seeing "large . . . buildings, with the glass broken out of the windows, . . . enveloped in solitary gloom. Upon inquiry . . . you are almost always informed that they were some cotton or other factory."

A section of an 1836 map of Ohio's Maumee River valley, left, shows checkerboard
pattern of public lands available for grant by the government to finance a canal.

But with a resiliency born of renewed hope, these and other businessmen returned to start over again, moving into the shuttered buildings and putting up new ones, often mechanizing more and more of their output. A fast-growing population meant greater markets; the new opportunities for profit proved an irresistible lure for capital. While the population nearly doubled between 1820 and 1840, capital invested in the nation's factories quintupled, from $50 million to $250 million, in the same period.

Still attuned to the hand-to-mouth regimen of an undeveloped nation, the United States did not have enough money left, after meeting its immediate needs for consumption, to supply the capital it required. Perhaps New England after 1830 might be said to have entered the "take-off" stage of industrial development, in which the earnings generated by industry were great enough to make continuing growth automatic. But most of the investment money was actually furnished by foreign sources, and particularly by the London capital market. Up to 1839 the British had invested more than $170 million in American enterprises, and the United States remained an importer of capital, on balance, throughout the 1800's and beyond. Where overseas and private sources did not suffice, substantial amounts of capital were also furnished by local, state, and federal governments—in bounties, tax exemptions, special franchise and monopoly privileges, as well as in direct investment.

In the sense that it was short of capital, young America might have been regarded as an underdeveloped nation. But in most other ways—the educational level of its people, their background and interest in technology, their push toward new lands, their eagerness to find and exploit natural resources, a flourishing ocean commerce—it was one of the more developed and modern nations of its time.

ROADS, RIVERS, AND CANALS

Ordinarily the earliest projects undertaken in the development of newly emerging industrial countries are those making up the "infrastructure"—a word adapted from the military that has come to represent the web of transportation, communication, and basic industries that are essential to advanced forms of industry and trade. The United States managed to create its own infrastructure, keeping pace with—or occasionally outrunning—the needs of the moment. This was especially true of transportation, so vital to the movement of goods if there was to be any commerce.

America was blessed with an abundance of navigable rivers—the Hudson, the Connecticut, the Raritan, the Delaware, the James, the Potomac, the Susquehanna, and others, including the Mississippi and its tributaries. These simplified the early penetration of inland areas and the transport of produce back to the coastal settlements.

But the rivers failed to link region with region. The coastal sailing route was the best connection between New England and New York and Philadelphia, or between those cities and the Carolinas. Inland communities, except those on the river banks, were far more difficult to reach. As for the lands farther west, these were insulated from the East by a hundred miles of difficult mountain country. Overland routes became an early necessity, and the first of these followed time-worn paths. "The buffalo trail became the Indian trail," said frontier historian Frederick Jackson Turner, "and this became the trader's 'trace'; the trails widened into roads, and the roads into turnpikes, and these in turn were transformed into railroads."

Some of the earliest American capital turned toward the building of hard-surface roads. From New York and Philadelphia roads ran to Albany, and from there to Fort Schuyler, New York, opening up the fertile Mohawk Valley to both cities. Roads ran west from Baltimore to the Monongahela River and from Philadelphia to Pittsburgh, giving the coastal cities access to the Ohio and Mississippi rivers. Philadelphia and Baltimore also had roads to Winchester, Virginia, and thence through the Cumberland Gap to Lexington, Kentucky. A north-south road, better in the North than in the South, connected Savannah, Charleston, Richmond, Baltimore, New York, and Boston.

Horse-drawn wagons hauled freight, and stagecoaches carried passengers, at a cost of about six cents a mile. The thrice-weekly journey from Boston to New York required three days, and the daily New York-to-Philadelphia stage took two. The first shots of the Revolution fired at Lexington and Concord may have been heard 'round the world, but the echoes were a long time in transit; a swift messenger dispatched with the news reached New York City in four days and brought the word to Charleston, South Carolina, eleven days after that.

Turnpikes, which took their name from England's spiked poles—or pikes—that were turned aside when a highway toll was paid, were among the new nation's first improved roads. An early success was the Philadelphia–Lancaster turnpike, built in 1792 at a cost of $465,000 by a private company chartered by the Pennsylvania legislature. Paved with stones and surfaced with screened, crushed rock, the road ran for sixty-six miles, measuring from sixteen to twenty feet in width and sloping to the sides from an eighteen-inch crown in the center. The company was able to pay dividends as high as 15 per cent, and the road set off a flurry of turnpike construction that continued well into the 1820's. With high costs of maintenance and toll collection, not all turnpikes were profitable, and the rush for

THE NEW YORK STOCK EXCHANGE

The new United States in 1789 was desperately short of money in any reliable or secured form. Accounts were still kept in pounds, shillings, and pence. But the creation of the national debt led to a money market. When Congress authorized the issue of $80 million worth of government bonds to fund that debt, those securities established a market.

In the beginning it was a haphazard one. Brokers, or stockjobbers as they were first called, did their business out on the street, retiring to nearby coffee houses when the weather turned bad. They bid for and sold United States government bonds and the stocks offered by the new Bank of the United States. Speculation was feverish, and the marketability of securities was always questionable.

"In fact, stock jobbing drowns every other subject," wrote James Madison to Thomas Jefferson on July 10, 1791. "The coffee house is an eternal buzz with the gamblers." Gamblers they must have seemed, but there were some who felt that taking a risk on the nation's future was prudent—a risk born of necessity and nurtured with trust.

On May 17, 1792, a band of twenty-four merchants and brokers met to bring some order into the market. They gathered under a buttonwood tree at a curbstone on Wall Street in New York City and signed a simple agreement written out on both sides of a single sheet of paper. It read: "We, the Subscribers, Brokers for the Purchase and Sale of Public Stocks, do hereby solemnly promise and pledge ourselves to each other that we will not buy or sell, from this day, for any person whatsoever, any kind of Public Stock at a less rate than one-quarter per cent Commission on the Special value, and that we will give preference to each other in our negotiations." It was negative and tentative in tone, but the "buttonwood compact" changed the securities market from a catch-as-catch-can auction, where real values were all but impossible to ascertain, into a nearly viable exchange.

The following year, the buttonwood signers moved indoors in the newly built Tontine Coffee House. Business did not increase for years. There was little flow of capital, the banking system was feeble, and the Jeffersonian government was suspicious of what it regarded as an oligarchy of rich, powerful merchants.

In 1817 the market became formalized with a constitution and the name "New York Stock & Exchange Board." There was an initiation fee of $25 and a penalty of expulsion for selling fictitious securities. Following the English practice, stocks were called out for trading at closed sessions, with the names of the buyers and sellers undisclosed.

As the national debt kept shrinking, paid off by parsimonious government leaders, so did the securities market. There was some slight expansion in the number of listed securities, if not of their value. By 1827 the stocks of twelve banks, nineteen insurance companies, the Delaware & Hudson Canal Co., the Merchants' Exchange, and the nation's first utility, the New York Gas Light Co., had joined the board. The dullest day in the history of the exchange occurred on March 16, 1830, when only thirty-one shares were traded for a total of $3,470.25.

Fortunately, 1830 also marked the introduction of railroad issues, with the appearance of Mohawk & Hudson Railroad shares. Soon railroads and canals became the stock-in-trade of the exchange, and they helped to attract foreign investors. By 1856 English investment alone in American railroad issues amounted to 80 million pounds sterling.

Making the market more available became a prime concern of the New York Stock Exchange (which adopted that name in 1863) during the 1860's. Prices were first posted in London via transatlantic cable in 1866 and at the Paris Bourse in 1869; telegraphic tickers were installed in 1867 and telephones in 1879. The first day of million-share trading took place in 1886. The Stock Exchange moved in 1865 to new quarters at No. 11 Wall Street, only a few steps from where the buttonwood agreement had been signed, and completed its present Roman Renaissance building at the same location in 1903. In 1901, the first billion-dollar corporation in the United States was underwritten, its designation for trading appearing on a numerical call board that back in 1871 had replaced the vocal announcements and created a continuous market for stocks. The company's name: the United States Steel Corporation; its Stock Exchange symbol: X.

A view down Wall Street from Broadway in 1834

charters subsided—at least in the East. In the West, turnpikes and post roads continued to be built, bringing Kansas, Minnesota, and Oklahoma into contact with the East long before they became states.

The building of the National Road, which was to stretch from Baltimore more than 800 miles into Illinois, was authorized by Congress in 1806, but the first contracts were not signed until 1811. It reached Wheeling, Virginia, in 1818, Columbus, Ohio, in 1833, and Vandalia, Illinois, in 1852, and was for many years a major artery to the West. The leisurely pace of construction might be explained in part by such diversions as the request by a certain John Eoff that the road run by his farm—"a leetle out of the way"—so that Eoff's son-in-law, a civil engineer on the road, might get to see his wife more often. When Senator Henry Clay was asked what he thought of the request, he replied, "As a Kentuckian, I endorse romance."

Wagons to travel these highways were turned out by hand until around 1830, then by various mass-production techniques. Philadelphia's Wilson & Childs put a farm wagon into volume production in 1829 and were mass producing a standardized army wagon twenty years later. A wagon designed as early as 1750 in the Conestoga River valley in Pennsylvania, boat-shaped to keep loads from shifting on hills, proved for over a century the most versatile means of carrying

household goods for families moving westward. The Studebaker Company, after its founding in 1852, was among the firms that turned out thousands of Conestoga wagons.

But while wagons and roads served a vital purpose, they were an expensive way to carry merchandise, especially bulk freight. Transporting goods one hundred miles in the United States averaged ten dollars per ton, not much different from the cost of shipping merchandise from America to Europe. The overland freight charges from Philadelphia to Pittsburgh around 1800 were $125 per ton, which was higher than sending it by water between the same cities—down the Atlantic coast, across the Gulf of Mexico, up the Mississippi, and up the Ohio. River transportation made much more sense economically than shipping by roads, and it was river traffic that turned St. Louis, Cincinnati, Louisville, and Pittsburgh into busy ports by 1830, while New Orleans became a river-and-ocean crossroads, the third largest trading center after New York and Philadelphia.

But the trouble with rivers was that traffic had to go where the rivers went, which was not necessarily where people wanted their goods to go. One solution to this, of course, was to build canals. Small canals were built very early in some of the eastern states, with the twenty-seven-mile Middlesex Canal from the

A waterside warehouse on the Erie Canal, painted in 1865 in Schenectady by J. N. Barhydt, handled cargoes shipped by barge.

Charles River to the Merrimac in Massachusetts being the most successful. Through the still canal waters a horse could drag a load fifty times as heavy as on land.

An important impediment to longer canals was the difference in the water level of the bodies of water they connected, which required locks that were expensive to build and that slowed traffic en route. But it became evident that these costs were not too great if new water routes could be created to tie together the commerce of different regions. Perhaps the most obvious route for a major canal enterprise was one linking the Northeast to the Northwest. New York's Governor DeWitt Clinton was among the early advocates of a canal from the Hudson River to Lake Erie, where there would be a rise of only 630 feet. On April 15, 1817, his state legislature set up a fund to build the Erie, Champlain, and Hudson Canal, at a cost estimated to be $5,752,738. Ground was broken less than three months later, on July 4, and "Clinton's ditch" was finally completed in October, 1825, at an actual cost of $8,401,394. Crowds gathered at the banks, bands played, flags fluttered, and, as the first boats began the 363-mile journey from Albany to Buffalo, the booming of cannon placed at intervals along the entire length relayed the announcement.

Even before the canal was completed, and while only sections of it were in use, the tolls exceeded the interest charges on the debt. Tolls reached $8,500,000, more than the project's cost, in the first nine years.

More impressive was the Erie Canal's effect on the movement of goods. The produce of the tier of states on the southern border of the Great Lakes—Illinois, Indiana, Ohio, and northern New York—now had easy access to the Atlantic coast. Freight rates from Buffalo to New York dropped 85 per cent, and the time of shipment was cut to eight days, less than half of what it had been. In 1827 the governor of Georgia complained that wheat from central New York carried a lower price tag in Savannah than wheat from central Georgia. Freight carried on the Erie reached almost $10 million in value by 1836, and peaked at $94 million in 1853.

New York City, which had passed Philadelphia in population in 1810, was well on its way to becoming the nation's center of trade. By 1830, its population doubled in ten years, New York had surpassed Philadelphia as a seaport. Land values rose around the Great Lakes, and towns along the canal—Rochester, Syracuse, Utica—blossomed into cities.

Other sections followed the leader. Another water loop was closed with the completion of a canal from Lake Erie at Cleveland to the Ohio River at Portsmouth in 1832. Panic and depression in the late 1830's temporarily slowed canal building, but it was soon resumed. The Toledo–Cincinnati Canal provided a second link between Lake Erie and the Ohio River in 1845, and the Illinois Canal joined Lake Michigan at Chicago with the Mississippi in 1848, making possible a trip by inland waters from New York to New Orleans. Coal and iron moved east and manufactured goods west in the Pennsylvania Canal System that joined Pittsburgh with Philadelphia; Easton, Pennsylvania, had an outlet to the sea by way of the Morris Canal to Jersey City.

Today most of the canals are only muddy memories of past glory. But in their time they did more to cut freight costs and knit the country's regions than any other aid to transport before or since.

STEAM LOCOMOTION

After James Watt made major improvements in 1769 on the steam engine patented more than sixty years earlier by Thomas Newcomen, it was only a matter of time before someone would adapt the new power package to the job of moving men and materials. Water transport, especially on rivers, was an obvious target. Farm products could be floated downstream easily enough, if slowly, on flatboats and keelboats. But the return trip ranged from difficult to impossible, depending on the speed of the current.

James Rumsey of Virginia built a small jet-action boat, powered by a steam pump, back in 1784, and it reached a speed of four miles an hour in a test on London's Thames River. Two years later John Fitch built a small steam-propelled boat, following this with a sixty-passenger craft and then the *Thornton*, a steamboat whose three stern paddles pushed her along the Delaware River at eight miles per hour. Fitch took a number of delegates to the Constitutional Convention for a ride up the river in 1787, possibly helping convince them that the federal government should be empowered to control interstate commerce.

None of these vessels proved commercially successful, possibly because their boilers could not take the strain of continued use. Colonel John Stevens used some British parts to build a steam craft in 1804 that incorporated some highly advanced elements—a high-pressure boiler and twin-screw propellers. He and his gifted sons began building the *Phoenix*, a 100-foot steamboat, in 1806, and it became the first seagoing steamboat when it traveled from New York to Philadelphia. In England, William Symmington had demonstrated the practical use of a steamboat on the Clyde back in 1803.

In 1806 Robert Fulton returned from Europe, where he had spent twenty years painting and tinkering. He had obtained some British patents on devices related to water transportation and had tried vainly to get Napoleon to use the *Nautilus*, a submarine he had developed. Fulton had managed to take a Boulton & Watt engine out of England and bring it home with him, and he enlisted the aid of Charles Brown, a shipbuilder,

Fulton's drawing of the Clermont's *paddle wheel and engine*

in building the *Clermont*. Robert R. Livingston, who had helped negotiate the Louisiana Purchase, shortly became his partner, and their ship made a successful voyage up the Hudson to Albany in August, 1807, traveling the 150 miles in thirty-two hours.

Not one to rest on such laurels, Fulton virtually exploded with new ventures, schemes, and dreams. With Livingston, he succeeded in obtaining a twenty-year steamboat monopoly of New York State waters, and not long afterward another franchise for the lower Mississippi. They soon had several boats on the Hudson. Fulton wrote to President Jefferson that within a few years he would have a line of steamboats operating on the Hudson, the Mississippi, the Delaware, the Ohio, and the St. Lawrence. He sought exclusive rights from the czar of Russia to operate his ships between St. Petersburg and Kronstadt, and made an agreement with an English friend to bring steam travel to India's Ganges River.

More realistically, he and Livingston, together with Nicholas Roosevelt, built the *New Orleans* at Pittsburgh, launching it on the Ohio River in 1811. She went down the Ohio and Mississippi in the winter of 1812, but could not manage the full return voyage. Even so, the *New Orleans* repaid her owners half the full $40,000 cost in the first year, plying between Natchez and New Orleans, negotiating the round trip in seventeen days. Not until after the War of 1812 were steamboats powerful enough to fight the swift river currents; the first ascent from New Orleans to Louisville required twenty-five days.

This was good enough, however, to launch a two-way river trade that quickly grew in volume. The downstream trip that had taken months in the flatboats could now be accomplished in a few days. By 1820 there were sixty steamboats on western rivers. As ships and engines improved, and as Americans followed the British lead in using screw propellers, the upstream voyage to Louisville was eventually reduced

to less than five days. Even though passenger and freight rates were cut sharply, profits remained high. Freight tonnage carried by steamboats on the western rivers in the late 1840's was believed to be greater than that of the entire British Empire. Steamboats were largely responsible for the growth of Mississippi Valley commerce, estimated at more than $650 million by 1852.

On the eastern rivers, passenger traffic was more important, and it was fought over strenuously. In 1818 Thomas Gibbons, a southern planter, set up a steamboat service between New York City and Elizabethport, New Jersey, and hired a young Staten Island ferryboat operator, Cornelius Van Derbilt (a name that subsequently came to be spelled *Vanderbilt*) as a skipper. Gibbons took his battle with the Livingston-Fulton monopoly to the courts, while the combative young Vanderbilt kept his craft running in the forbidden waters. Daniel Webster, representing Gibbons, argued the case to the Supreme Court. In what became the landmark case of Gibbons v. Ogden (the latter being the holder of a license from Fulton), Justice John Marshall held in 1824 that no state could monopolize river traffic.

Vanderbilt started building his own steamboats in 1829, having earlier sold his interest in sailing schooners, convinced that the future lay with steam travel. By 1836, having built a fortune of $500,000 at the age of forty-two, he had steamboats operating all along the coast. Before his mind turned to railroads, he had become one of the largest steamboat builders in the country.

But long before Vanderbilt was ready for the railroads, they had established themselves as a vital part of the nation's commerce. Unlike rivers, railroads could be routed almost anywhere at will; unlike canals, they could not be stopped by winter freezes; unlike roads, they provided their own motive power. Railroads, moreover, were cheaper to build than canals, more durable than most highways, and faster than either. From the time it was first shown to be practical, the railroad was obviously an important element of the United States transportation network.

But railroads got a much later start than steamboats, partly because of the large capital expense required and partly because of lagging technology. The latter problem was deemed solved in 1829 when George Stephenson's "Rocket" hauled a thirteen-ton train between Liverpool and Manchester, averaging fifteen miles per hour.

In that same year the "Stourbridge Lion" was brought from England to pull a train on the Carbondale and Honesdale Railroad (later part of the Delaware and Hudson), but the road's rails and trestles were not strong enough for the heavy British locomotive. Two years earlier a charter had been granted for the Baltimore & Ohio, which was to become the country's first successful railroad. By 1830 the B. & O. opened its first thirteen miles of track, designed primarily for use by horse-drawn cars. Peter Cooper, a New York merchant, was permitted to use the B. & O. shops to build his steam engine, the "Tom Thumb," mainly from scrap materials. Cooper raced his engine against a horse for the thirteen-mile trip from Baltimore to Ellicott's Mills—and would have won, if a pulley belt had not begun to slip near the end of the race. But the demonstration was enough to convince the railroad's management to switch to steam locomotion.

Other railroads that opened in 1830 were the Charleston & Hamburg and the Mohawk & Hudson, soon to be followed by the New York and Erie in New York, the Western in Massachusetts, and many more small lines. The Mohawk & Hudson, chartered in 1826, was the earliest forebear of the New York Central. Completed in 1834 was a line between Philadelphia and the Susquehanna, the first in the Pennsylvania Rail-

road system. The first locomotive built in the United States for regular use was the "Best Friend of Charleston." In 1830 it pulled four loaded cars at speeds of sixteen to twenty-one miles an hour on six miles of Charleston & Hamburg tract; when this road's 136 miles of track were completed in 1833, it became the longest railroad in the world. The "Best Friend" had been built at the West Point Foundry in New York, as were a number of other early steam locomotives, including the "Phoenix" and the "West Point." The first locomotive made by the Baldwin Locomotive Works in Philadelphia was "Old Ironsides" in 1832.

With longer distances to traverse and bulkier commodities to be carried, steam railroads developed far more rapidly in the United States than in Britain, where they had got their start. By 1840 more than 400 companies were operating almost 3,000 miles of track, more than the total mileage in Europe. Most of the lines were local, built around cities to bring in the neighboring produce and to reach nearby markets. But these small

The Way to Wealth

PETER COOPER

Many businessmen, throughout the nation's history, have been firm believers in the value of a good education. For example, Ezra Cornell, one of the pioneers in the telegraph industry, who made millions as a director of Western Union, helped to found the university named for him.

Peter Cooper (1791–1883) was another industrialist supporter of sound schooling. His own youthful experience left him with a craving for education. At the age of eight he began working for his father, making hats at Newburgh-on-Hudson. At seventeen, after his father had also tried brickmaking and brewing, Peter left him for the larger promise of New York City.

There he apprenticed to a coachmaker for four years before helping to design a cloth-shearing machine. He secured New York State rights for it and sold one of the first to an ambitious Poughkeepsie brewer, Matthew Vassar—who eventually endowed a college for women—and with the proceeds bought real estate and a glue factory. Parlaying his earnings into the purchase of more land, Cooper in 1828 bought 3,000 acres in the city of Baltimore for $105,000.

COOPER UNION

An unfinished portrait of Peter Cooper

When he built the "Tom Thumb," a successful steam locomotive engine able to negotiate the curves and steep grades on the Baltimore & Ohio's right of way in 1830, it was to help save the railroad from bankruptcy. In the process, scrounging in scrap piles for iron tubes and other parts, he recognized an opportunity for a plant that would turn out fabricated iron. Soon he had built the Canton Iron Company on his Maryland property. The venture was close to iron and coal deposits and showed good profits. Cooper sold it to a group

of Boston investors for $90,000, much of which he took in stock at $45 a share, the par then being $100. When the stock jumped above $225 a share, Cooper sold it.

In 1854 he became president of the New York, Newfoundland & London Electric Telegraph Company, which was trying to lay a cable across the Atlantic Ocean to Great Britain. Regular service began in 1866.

An honored man in his time, Cooper refused to run for the Presidency in 1876, although he was nominated on a platform calling for the issuance of federal paper money. He simply thought he was too old.

As early as 1856 Cooper reckoned his net worth at more than a million dollars, but he nonetheless felt handicapped by his lack of formal education. His eagerness to provide others with what he had missed enriched the nation: he funded and built Cooper Union, principally an educational institution for workingmen, and presented it to the people of New York City in 1859. It has continued ever since to provide schooling in the arts and sciences for men and women in all trades and professions.

roads eventually became parts of the trunk lines that were to connect the major cities and sections of the country.

The cities en route became terminals, thus being able to share in a much larger market. Rivalries among these cities often became intense. The Boston and Albany Railroad in 1842 helped Boston renew its contest with New York as a seaport. Philadelphia got a firmer grip on the commerce of the Ohio Valley when it had an all-rail connection with Pittsburgh to supplement its all-canal route. Wheeling carried on a long-drawn competition with Pittsburgh to become the western terminal of the Baltimore & Ohio, and Wheeling hired the B. & O.'s longtime chief engineer as a consultant

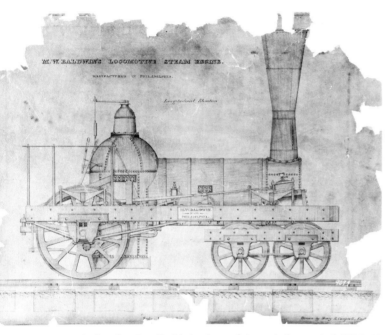

A sketch of a Baldwin locomotive of the period 1834–42

to help find a better rail route.

Local businessmen, who looked not only for dividends but hoped to gain from better transportation facilities to their cities, were frequently among the backers of the railroads. Even though near-term dividend prospects were not very bright, the railroads soon became the major users of capital in the United States, absorbing some $1.25 billion between 1830 and 1860. A substantial portion came from abroad, but government investment—city, county, state, and federal—was also heavy. Maryland bought $3 million in B. & O. stock, and New York loaned $6 million to the New York and Erie. An estimated $90 million was put into railroading by the states up to 1840, and city and county contributions were probably even higher. Wheeling offered to subscribe $1,000,000 to the Baltimore & Ohio. By 1853 the city's per capita railroad debt was $55 and Baltimore's was $43.

It was hardly reasonable to expect that such enthusiasm would not be accompanied by some chicanery and fraud. Some of this involved "banking privileges," by which railroads were permitted to issue notes on no security other than their own plans. Promoters found it far easier to dispose of the notes than to lay rails; they concentrated so heavily on the former that the state of Mississippi, for example, became crisscrossed with imaginary railroads. Most states eventually banned railroad banking privileges.

Railroad technologies advanced rapidly, if unevenly. The Eastwick & Harrison firm of Philadelphia developed locomotives that were able to burn anthracite coal as early as 1835. They also developed the eight-wheel engine, with four driving wheels, and the company's talented Joseph Harrison, Jr., patented a method of equalizing the weight on the driving wheels in 1839. One bottleneck to railroad expansion was in the spikes that held the rails to the ties. In 1839 the Burden railroad spike machine was developed to form the spikes in one operation, producing fifty a minute, or more than could be forged by fifty blacksmiths and their helpers.

American railroad equipment and know-how was soon in demand overseas. The Baldwin Locomotive Works was shipping engines abroad by 1838, and in 1840 the Norris Company sent a locomotive to the Birmingham and Gloucester Railroad in the center of England's own locomotive-building region. That year Russia sent two of its engineers to study American railroads, and Colonel George W. Whistler was hired to take charge of building the $40 million Moscow–St. Petersburg Railway, more than 400 miles long. Colonel Whistler took with him a team of experienced engineers, and in 1842 they started to lay out the roadbed in a 400-foot right of way. The following year Eastwick & Harrison won a $3 million contract to build, in Russia and using Russian labor, 160 locomotives, 2,500 freight cars, and more than 170 passenger cars. In spite of language barriers and inexperienced workmen, the work was completed a year ahead of schedule.

Railroad building in the United States picked up a big head of steam after 1840, absorbing so much capital that the development of some other industries was probably slowed down. But, like the canals and steamboats, railroads cut inland freight rates still further and brought a mobility that was vital to the nation's internal commerce.

JACKSON AND BUSINESS

By the time Andrew Jackson was elected President in 1828, American businessmen came in many varieties. Still dominant were the merchants and traders, although their center of gravity had shifted away from New England and toward New York, Philadelphia, and

Baltimore. Closely allied with them were the money specialists—bankers, brokers, and insurance men—in Philadelphia, New York, and Boston; and smaller banks were opening everywhere. Still secondary in importance, but growing in number and in the size of their operations, were the manufacturers, also concentrated in the Northeast. Some individuals and companies of businessmen specialized in land—buying, selling, and trading; still others did business in internal improvements—setting up roads, bridges, canals, and public utilities. Among all of these there was considerable crossing of lines—people who moved from one field to another or the very wealthy, who might be active in all of them. In addition, there were small shopkeepers and tradesmen scattered through the length and breadth of the country. The farmer too was a man of business, producing and marketing his crops, whether he was a large plantation owner in the South or a settler working his quarter section in the Northwest.

The most immediately evident characteristic of such a group was its diversity, both in occupation and interest. On any given issue there might well be as many opinions as there were groups. Certainly there was no longer the kind of business community that had once united behind Hamilton's mercantilist notion that what was good for business was good for the country. Under Jefferson it became evident to many a businessman that government was not working primarily in his interest, and even that some businessmen could be hurt more than they were helped by government. Jackson made this even more clear.

Jackson was a man of the West, and he shared its sense of individualism and opportunity. With this, most businessmen could be temperamentally in accord. But Jackson also believed that it was the role of government to represent the people and their ultimate power in an *adversary* relationship to businessmen, bankers, and those concentrations of money power and wealth that smelled to him of monopoly. At this point he parted company with most businessmen, who much preferred Hamilton's *co-operative* relationship, as well as a free rein to move as fast and grow as big as they were able.

When Chief Justice John Marshall died in the summer of 1835, Jackson appointed as his successor Roger B. Taney, a Maryland lawyer who had been a leader of the radical Democrats and Attorney General and then Secretary of the Treasury in Jackson's Cabinet. Taney proceeded to emulate his predecessor in interpreting the Constitution to fit his own convictions—but these were much different from Marshall's. In the Dartmouth College case, for example, Marshall had held in 1819 that a corporate charter issued by the state was a contract, the obligations of which could not subsequently be impaired by the state itself. Taney virtually reversed the impact of this decision in 1837 in

the Charles River Bridge case, in which a company that had been given a franchise to operate a toll bridge over the river complained about the state's authorization of funds for a competing free bridge. Taney ruled against the company, holding that the granting of a corporate charter was for a public purpose, so that any rights conferred under such a charter must always be subservient to the broad public interest.

This was a blow to those businessmen who had come to expect that a certain sanctity attached to all contracts, including those with the state. But it also turned out to be a blow in favor of free enterprise, as first Connecticut and then other states passed general corporation laws, making the corporate form equally available to all rather than a granting of monopoly privileges. In this sense, the doctrine of wide-open competition that had been set forth by Adam Smith

U.S. SUPREME COURT

Chief Justice Roger B. Taney

was closer to Jackson's policy than to the desires of the tight-knit community of financiers of his day.

In the matter of the tariff, Jackson's views were more ambivalent, as were those of the different business communities, or even of the same people at different times. New England's Daniel Webster opposed the tariff of 1816, which raised duties on iron, cotton, and woolen goods, while South Carolina's John Calhoun favored it. By 1828 Calhoun was the leader of the opposition to a new tariff bill, which Webster strongly supported.

These men mirrored the changing moods that predominated in their regions, just as Jackson tended to reflect those of the West. New England's businessmen split between the shipping group, who favored freer trade, and the growing ranks of manufacturers, who sought protection. The farming belts of the central and western states at first found their major markets in the antitariff South, and identified with southern interests; later, as improved transportation built up their trade with the Northeast, they tended to favor higher tariffs. The South, meanwhile, after a short-lived try at developing new industries after 1816 to balance its economy, turned more and more toward cotton and against tariffs. As an exporter of raw materials and an importer of finished goods, the South logically blamed tariff laws for the high prices it had to pay and the low prices it received.

From 1816 on, the protectionist movement attracted more and more adherents, as new industries sprang up. Associations of industry formed, and these in turn banded together in the National Institution for the Promotion of Industry, among whose members were E. I. Du Pont and Mathew Carey, an outspoken Philadelphia publisher. Henry Clay, whose neo-Federalist "American system" held brief sway under the Presidency of John Quincy Adams, helped devise a tariff bill in 1824 that combined the interests of the manufacturers with those of the hemp-growing and wool-raising western states.

The wool interests continued to agitate for even higher tariffs. In his campaign for the Presidency, Jackson gave tacit support to a tariff bill far more protectionist than any the nation had ever known. His campaign supporters tried to spread the impression in the North that he was protectionist, and in the South that a bill with higher duties on raw materials than on manu-

facturers would be defeated by New England's congressmen. To everyone's surprise, the measure passed and quickly became known as the Tariff of Abominations.

The South rose up in anger. South Carolina, suffering mainly from the uneven competition between its own depleted soils and the new cotton-growing states to the west, made the tariff the scapegoat for its troubles. The situation was aggravated by a decline in cotton prices—from about eight and one-half cents a pound in Georgia in the fall of 1830 to about six and one-half cents the following June. A new tariff bill was enacted in 1832, leaving high duties on iron and textiles but removing most of the worst features of the Tariff of Abominations. South Carolina was no longer to be appeased. The legislature, taking its lead from Calhoun's philosophy of states' rights, nullified the tariff acts of both 1828 and 1832, prohibiting collection of duties within the state. The immediate effect was a sharp cleavage between Jackson and the antitariff South; in a longer perspective, this was the first in a chain of events, most of them with economic underpinnings, that culminated in the Civil War.

The following year Clay, Calhoun, and Webster worked out a compromise by which duties would be reduced gradually over a ten-year period. The new low level reached in 1842 lasted only a few weeks, when a somewhat more protectionist tariff bill was again passed, under pressure from Pennsylvania's iron-

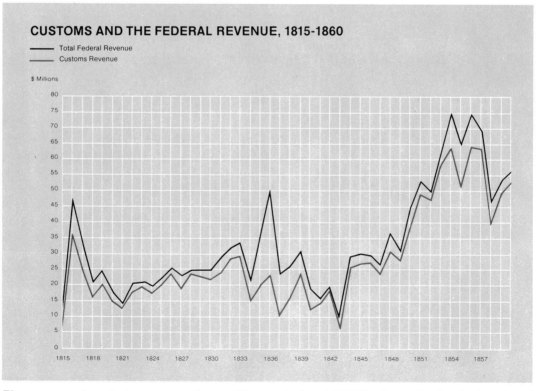

The government's main income came from tariffs, save in the mid-1830's when public land sales jumped.

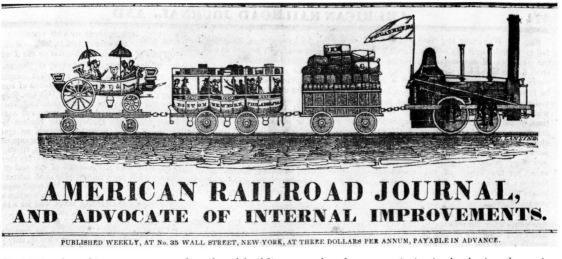

AMERICAN RAILROAD JOURNAL, AND ADVOCATE OF INTERNAL IMPROVEMENTS.

PUBLISHED WEEKLY, AT No. 35 WALL STREET, NEW-YORK, AT THREE DOLLARS PER ANNUM, PAYABLE IN ADVANCE.

By 1834, when this paper appeared, railroad building was already a top priority in developing the nation.

masters and various other manufacturers. Thereafter, tariffs generally tended lower. In the Walker tariff of 1846, imports classified as luxuries carried duties of 100 per cent; semiluxuries were taxed at 40 per cent; and various commercial products had duties ranging from 5 to 30 per cent.

Throughout this period, tariff receipts constituted the basic support for the government, and they were higher than all other sources of federal income combined in every year except 1836.

FILLING UP THE WEST

Between 1820 and 1850 the population of the United States grew from 7.9 million to 19.6 million. In the same period the proportion living west of the Alleghenies rose from 27 to 45 per cent.

The historian Frederick Jackson Turner has characterized the frontier as the safety valve—the available alternative to people in the East and South for whom social or economic conditions became intolerable. Others have argued that this was not so, that the West was populated largely by migrants from neighboring states and by those newly arrived immigrants in the country who did not stop at the seaboard but continued on to find their place of settlement. The truth probably partook of both, with personal temperament having more to do with the willingness to move west than the goad of social and economic circumstance. Those restless souls who looked for new beginnings and fresh opportunities could more readily be beckoned to the West than the settled citizens who were reluctant to give up the comforts and the relative certainties of the homes and jobs they had. This was probably equally true of both immigrants and native Americans, although the immigrant had already displayed an adventurous character by coming to America in the first place.

Sales of government land dwarfed those of the earlier push to the West, rising from its previous peak of 3.5 million acres in 1818 to 20 million in 1836. While speculation motivated a substantial portion of these purchases, many of the buyers stayed to farm; some settlers simply moved onto the land without paying for it. Much of the farming was for subsistence or for supplying local needs, but gradually more distant markets were developed. From the Ohio and Mississippi river valleys, farm produce was shipped on the river routes to the South.

Eastern manufacturers at first resented the West as a drain on their labor supply. But as the canals and railroads began to open up viable channels of commerce, they welcomed this vast new market for their goods, as well as the rich new source of food commodities. The opening of the Erie Canal turned the Lake Erie ports at Buffalo, Cleveland, and Toledo into cities almost overnight. With a population of more than 1,000,000 by 1830, Ohio had more people than Massachusetts and Connecticut combined. The population of Illinois tripled between 1830 and 1840, from 157,000 to 476,000, and that of Chicago had an eightfold increase, but from a base of only 500. Chicago land sold at the going rate for all western acres— $1.25—in the 1820's, but this leaped to $100 in 1832 and $3,500 by 1834. When the canal to the Mississippi was approved in 1836, one lot along the route sold for more than $21,000.

While much of the land speculation concentrated on rural areas, there were fortunes to be made in city real estate. Nicholas Longworth, born in Newark, New Jersey, moved to Cincinnati in 1803 at the age of twenty-one and studied law. One of his clients, charged with horse theft, had only two used stills with which to pay his fee. Longworth traded these for thirty-three acres of outlying land, then continued to buy more. As Cincinnati grew from 800 inhabitants when Long-

93

A state bank of the mid-1800's in Conway, Massachusetts

worth arrived to 25,000 in 1830 and almost 120,000 by 1850, his property kept going up in value. Before 1820 he had given up his law practice to concentrate on his land business and cultivate wine grapes. When he died at the age of eighty-one he had become the largest landowner in Cincinnati and was worth $15 million.

As it became evident how much could be done for their economies by improved transport, the western states poured millions of dollars into internal improvements—mainly turnpikes, railroads, and canals, but also into banks that could, in turn, finance the land sales. In less than twenty years after 1820, credit advances of more than $150 million for these purposes had been authorized by eighteen states. Western and southwestern states issued more than $165 million in bonds for banking capital between 1824 and 1840. With an average annual income of just $250,000, Illinois underwrote almost $12 million in bonds. Pennsylvania, largest borrower of all, wrote into its charters for new banks the requirements that they give financial help to transportation companies.

With such encouragement the number of banks grew rather spectacularly, from just two in 1791 to 246 in 1816 to 502 in 1834. In the same period, their capital rose from $2 million to $169 million, in addition to the $35 million capital of the Second Bank of the United States. Many of the state-chartered institutions were banks of issue, authorized to print their own notes. The constitutionality of this practice was called into question, and in 1837 the Supreme Court ruled that such bills might be issued by a bank in which the state was the only stockholder.

The expansive policies followed by states, banks, and some private companies made the spirit of speculation more contagious than ever. By the nature of such things in the American business system, the nation—and especially the West—was building up for a crashing fall.

JACKSON AND THE SECOND BANK

When the Second Bank of the United States was chartered in 1816, it had some inherent problems. Everyone agreed that it should stabilize the nation's currency, and most people felt that it should bring about a resumption of payments in specie on demand. Beyond that, however, its mission was difficult. It needed to serve the short-term needs of eastern commercial interests, along with the long-term financial requirements of the farmers and speculators of the West. It was also charged with the collection and disbursement of the funds of the federal government, which it could hold without paying interest.

Under its first president, William Jones, who had been an acting Secretary of the Treasury, the Bank followed the expansive policies favored by the government. As capital was drained from the East to the debtor sections of the West and Southwest, the Bank soon ran into liquidity troubles. Jones resigned and was succeeded by Langdon Cheves of South Carolina. Cheves took strong corrective measures and brought the bank back to an extremely sound position, but in doing so he almost eliminated its business.

Cheves was succeeded in 1823 by Nicholas Biddle—brilliant, debonair, versatile. Descended from a distinguished Philadelphia family, Biddle by the age of thirty-seven had already been a child prodigy, a lawyer, a writer, editor of the journal of the Lewis and Clark expedition, a state senator, and a diplomat. Along with his unquestioned intelligence, Biddle also tended to be prideful and uncompromising.

These qualities served him well for a time. He used the Bank's reserves to help tide the country over one period of financial strain in 1825 and, to a lesser extent, another in 1828. Following a generally conservative banking policy, he had shown that he could discipline any bank by forcing it to pay debts to the Bank of the United States and its branches in specie. It was sound banking, and an impressive demonstration of the Bank's great powers, but it did not win Biddle many friends in the newer sections or in the South.

Biddle's cavalier posture was especially unfortunate, because he was faced with a master political tactician as his opponent. Jackson had never liked the national bank, thinking of it as a monopoly that used public funds to enrich a few wealthy men and thus to impoverish further the common people. He had thought about getting rid of the Bank before he took office, but he did not make it an issue until his hand was forced.

Egged on by Webster and Clay, who felt that a fight over the Bank would give them a presidential campaign issue in 1832, Biddle sought a renewal of the Bank's charter that year, four years before the original charter was to expire. It was a major error. The recharter issue was passed by both houses of Congress but was angrily vetoed by Jackson, who gladly carried the question to the people. The President proceeded to win re-election by a wider margin than he had in 1828.

But Biddle was far from out of the fight. Possibly because the election put a cloud over the Bank's future, or perhaps simply to demonstrate the Bank's power over the economy, he began to contract loans. Jackson decided to halt government deposits in the Bank, but he had to fire two Treasury Secretaries before he could find one to do his bidding. Large drafts were given to state banks, empowering them to withdraw government funds from the Bank without notice. With government money being disbursed and not collected, the Bank decided to make loans still tighter, creating a credit crunch that came to be known as Biddle's Panic.

The move boomeranged. Many who had not yet taken sides began to agree with Jackson that the Bank's powers were too great. The Bank's loans decreased $17 million, or 27 per cent, in little over a year. This strengthened the Bank's position but weakened the nation's. Money rates climbed, business houses started to fail, wages dropped, and unemployment rose. Even conservative businessmen were unhappy about the Bank's actions. Boston's merchants met in Faneuil Hall and named a committee, headed by Nathan Appleton, to go to Washington. "The Statement of the Bank," Appleton wrote back to its Boston branch, ". . . shows a degree of strength wholly unprecedented. . . and its ability . . . to make discounts far beyond the

A contemporary cartoon depicted Jackson (left) attacking the Bank (Biddle in top hat) and its branches with his veto stick.

present actual wants of the community."

In July, 1834, the Bank finally began to relax its loan policy and, even without government deposits, loans climbed back to their former level by the middle of 1835. The battle was over. From 1834 to 1836 the Bank concentrated on preparing for liquidation, and this meant moving its capital to the East. But late in 1835 it was decided to continue the Bank under a state charter, so the moves toward liquidation were halted. Biddle subsequently turned his attention to pegging the world price of cotton, because this was so crucial to American credit abroad. Biddle's plans worked, and his cotton pool earned $800,000. A second pool, however, failed, to the tune of $900,000, and this led to the end of the Second Bank of the United States, which closed its doors in 1841.

Jackson's moves against the Bank had been largely under the supervision of Roger B. Taney, his Secretary of the Treasury. Taney and Senator Thomas Hart Benton of Missouri were the principal architects of a hard-money policy. They favored letting banks conduct a commercial credit system, accepting deposits and discounting business paper, but were opposed to their issuance of notes on their own credit—that is, to letting them issue currency. In order to increase the circulation of metallic currency, Benton introduced a measure to raise the value of gold, then undervalued at fifteen times the value of silver, to a 16:1 ratio. After its passage in 1834, the quantity of specie in the country rose sharply. The rest of the Taney-Benton program was not put into effect. Banks continued to issue paper in quantities that helped fuel one of the biggest speculative orgies of the 1800's.

PANIC AND DEPRESSION

The first disturbing event had been a crop failure in 1835, when farmers, unable to pay their debts, passed along their distress to the merchants and speculators, who in turn defaulted with their banks. The chain reaction then extended to foreign credits, as requests increased for payment in specie abroad.

None of these portents was enough to dampen the fever of speculation, however. Public land sales had climbed from less than $2 million in 1830 to over $20 million in 1836. Alarmed at its extent, Jackson issued a Specie Circular in July, 1836, requiring all payments for land to be made in gold and silver. While this slowed down land purchases, it also undermined confidence in the bank notes that had been used for this purpose. In 1837 there was a distribution to the states of the government surplus of about $28 million, which counteracted the effects of the specie directive and again fanned the flames of speculation. One indication of the extent of investments in internal improvements was the increase in state debts from $13 million in 1820

to $200 million in 1840. The roads, canals, railroads, banks, and new markets gave the nation an intoxicating sense of its own potential, but it was all happening too fast for the economy to absorb.

Almost predictably, these events culminated, in 1837, in the worst panic the United States had experienced up to that time. By May every bank in the country had suspended specie payments, even including the staid and solid Bank of Massachusetts. Millions of dollars in "shinplasters," small notes that ranged in denomination from five cents to five dollars, circulated through the country, and almost nobody could say what they were worth. Many of them, badly printed, were easy to counterfeit, but there was sometimes little difference in real value between a phony bill and the genuine article. The circulation of bank notes dropped from $149 million in 1837 to $58 million in 1843. Sales of public land plummeted to $1,000,000 by 1841, scarcely one twentieth of what they had been. Cotton prices slumped. By the summer of 1837 most of the factories in the East had shut down. As states were unable to finance their internal improvements, these projects were abandoned or sold out to private companies. Most states were unable to pay interest charges on their debts.

The effect on foreign credit sources was catastrophic. A worldwide depression in the 1840's dried up much of the money that might have been available for major capital investments, but America deservedly got less than its share from abroad. Of $200 million in United States securities owned by British investors, about three fifths were of questionable value by 1841. The crowning blow was the repudiation of their debts by Indiana, Michigan, Mississippi—and even by Maryland and reliable old Pennsylvania.

Widespread depression in the United States did not become severe until 1839, when the full effects of the boom had worn off and the contraction in capital goods orders had taken effect. Those businesses that were foresighted enough to trim their sails helped intensify the drop, while those that expected the boom to start again any day helped prolong it.

The depression remained severe for four or five years, and while any political blame would have to be laid at Jackson's doorstep, it was Martin Van Buren who inherited the problems. He did his best to lock the barn, and he tried to ameliorate the depression's worst effects.

For the first time, for example, some protection was given the squatters, who moved onto public lands, cleared the wilderness, built homes, and worked the farms, then found that the land would be put up for public sale and sold out from under them. They had long sought the right to buy such land at the minimum price—and sometimes managed to enforce that right through "protective associations" that persuaded

This satiric bank note, a jibe at Jackson's money policies, appeared in New York in 1837 when specie payments were suspended.

outsiders not to bid at the public sales. In 1841 a general pre-emption law gave the squatter the right to buy his land at $1.25 an acre before it was placed on public sale. What actually happened in many cases was that speculators then offered the settlers prices they could not resist; the squatter would sell out and move on, having thus, in a sense, become a speculator himself.

Van Buren's substitute for the Bank was a national treasury system, with a network of subtreasuries to collect revenues and disburse funds. Established in 1840, discontinued in 1841, and re-established in 1846, the independent treasury system was able to handle government funds, promote specie circulation, and prevent excessive bank note issuance for many years. It was eventually made a part of the Federal Reserve System in 1913.

"REPOSITORIES OF POSSIBLE THINGS"

To be inventive was a major virtue in the folklore of early America, and Eli Whitney was a heroic figure to his own generation and those that followed. As a consequence, those who could invent, did. They turned out so many new ideas and products that Americans were not above a degree of self-congratulation on that score. Wrote Simeon DeWitt, of Albany, in 1813:

The Americans are an inventive people; perhaps more so than any other existing. Without arrogating to ourselves any superiority of intellect, the cause may be traced . . . to the facility with which a respectable education and comfortable subsistence may be procured, and which leaves leisure to the mind to wander through the mysterious, unfathomable repositories of possible things . . .

The tinkerers, the inventors, and the "breathless generation" of the second quarter of the century did provide a remarkable outpouring of gadgets and devices, many devised to cut the human work requirement in producing goods. The average number of patents recorded by the Patent Office between 1790 and 1811 was seventy-seven per year. From 1820 to 1830 it had climbed to 535 a year—compared to only 145 for Great Britain, then the world's most industrialized country. The yearly average rose to 646 in the 1840's and skyrocketed to 2,525 in the 1850's.

Not all of the earliest patents represented real inventions. Until 1836 the applicant needed only to show that his product was not harmful, not that it was new or original. Inevitably, there were sharpies who got patents on things already in use and then blackmailed their users—who might be the real inventors—with demands for royalty payments. Patent infringement suits were backlogged in the courts.

All this was changed with an 1836 patent law that required that all patent applications be examined for originality. The act was sponsored by Maine's Senator John Ruggles, who was issued Patent No. 1 for his own invention of an engine for locomotives, "designed to . . . prevent the evil of the sliding of the wheel."

Senator Orville Platt of Connecticut was moved to observe that the new law came "when the American brain evolved and the American hand fashioned labor saving machines that made this nation throb with new energy and new life." Ralph Waldo Emerson was so taken by what was going on about him that he pitied "our fathers for dying before steam and galvanism . . . and before we borrowed the might of the elements."

New products were triumphantly displayed at trade fairs, among which were the annual spectacles of the American Institute of New York, held at Niblo's Gardens. At such shows most people got their first glimpse of Samuel Morse's telegraph, Samuel Colt's revolver, Charles Goodyear's vulcanizing process, Elias Howe's sewing machine, and Cyrus McCormick's reaper. Another display point was the country fair, which usually had exhibits of the latest labor-saving machines and improvements designed for farm use.

Although they were impressed by what the new tools could do, most farmers lacked the capital to give them more than a passing thought. In the early 1800's the farmer still fashioned many of his own tools, and the use of farm labor still made better economic sense than large investments in equipment. By the 1830's, however, there was the start of a revolution in agricultural technology that was to bring about undreamed miracles of farm productivity within a few decades.

Jethro Wood's cast-iron plow, made with three replaceable parts, was developed in 1819 and began to move into general use in 1825. John Lane's plows, their shares made from saw blade steel, proved even better for scouring through the matted roots of tough prairie grasses. Improved by John Deere, a blacksmith, the plows sold in the 1840's as fast as the proper steel could be obtained; Deere's output reached 10,000 a year by 1857.

Meanwhile, others were working on the problem of bringing in the wheat harvest when the grain became ripe but before it was overripe. The grain cradle had been introduced about 1800, allowing a mower to cut two to three acres a day, about four times the output of a man with a sickle. By the early 1820's the British were experimenting with mechanical mower-reapers. In the following decade two Americans, Obed Hussey in Cincinnati and Cyrus McCormick in Virginia's Rockbridge County, worked simultaneously on per-

THE SUBTREASURY SYSTEM

After the demise of the Second Bank of the United States, Andrew Jackson retired to his mansion, The Hermitage, in Tennessee, leaving the shambles of the nation's monetary system in the lap of his successor, Martin Van Buren.

The diminutive New Yorker—known as the Little Magician for his ability to profit from opportunities—faced a serious situation. He had inherited the country's first real depression, which followed the panic of 1837.

By mid-April after his inauguration, 128 brokerage houses in New York City had shut their doors. By May 10 every bank in the city had stopped making payments in hard money, and across the country other banks had followed suit. The flow of money in the nation was at a standstill.

To cope with the crisis, Van Buren proposed a bill separating the public and private purses. He wanted an independent treasury, which would build its own vaults, collect all federal receipts, and make all payments in bullion. Furthermore, he wanted the specie located in a number of regional subtreasuries that could support the banking and commercial needs of the dif-

Martin Van Buren

ferent sections of the country.

Largely for Jacksonian reasons, Van Buren opposed setting up a new national bank. It would, he pronounced, "impair the rightful supremacy of the popular will, injure the character and diminish the influence of our political system; and bring once more into existence . . . a concentrated money power, hostile to the spirit, and threatening the permanency of our republican institutions."

The argument against his subtreasury system was slender—principally that it would lead to the use of an exclusively metallic currency, a weighty inconvenience that might handicap the conduct of business. The press bemoaned the dwindling of paper bank notes, whether adequately backed or not, and called the reliance on silver and gold coins a threat to commerce.

In the Senate, Henry Clay decried the new system for much the same reasons. "It was paper money that carried us through the Revolution, established our liberties and made us a free and independent people," he said. He had a point: the paper issued by the revolutionary government had proved valuable in keeping business active. But its own value was questionable until the government redeemed it in hard currency.

The real danger in the subtreasury system lay in the possibility that the gold and silver of the general population might gravitate to the treasuries, building a large government surplus, instead of flowing into bank reserves where it could be used to back paper money. But

fecting a reaping machine. Hussey got his patent in 1833 and McCormick, using different principles, obtained his in 1834. Sweeping the grain against the cutting surfaces of blades and then gathering the cut stalks on receiving tables, the reaper enabled one man to cut ten to twelve acres a day.

Hussey inexplicably moved his plant east to Baltimore, while McCormick in 1844 moved his to Chicago, close to the grain country. McCormick pioneered by making installment sales, geared to the farmer's own seasons, and made it a practice never to sue for payments in arrears. As farmers began to realize that the reaper would enable them to plant more acres and raise production, McCormick's output rose to 1,000 a year, and his name became all but synonymous with the product.

Hiram and John Pitt of Maine produced the first practical thresher in 1836. This machine performed three processes—threshing, separating, and winnowing—and could turn out from 200 to 250 bushels of wheat a day, which was about twenty times the production of a man with a hand flail. Since threshing required a large piece of equipment that the average farmer could use for only a short time, the task was eventually taken over by itinerant operators using improved machines.

Also contributing to farm mechanization were such machines as mechanical harrows, seed drills, and corn planters. Most farmers had developed their mechanical abilities well enough to keep their own equipment in repair.

In 1842 Joseph Dart patented a granary that could be filled directly from the hold of a docked ship and that kept the grain insulated from heat and moisture. The first grain elevator, which could empty its grain at the bottom through a hopper, was built in Buffalo. As the railroad network spread westward, however, making Chicago a great national crossroads, the western city became the focal point for grain shipments and for elevator construction. Elevator design continued to advance, but many of the improvements had been foreshadowed in ideas pioneered by Oliver Evans many decades before.

COTTON AND TEXTILES

It was not only the plantations of the South but also the factories, shipping merchants, and banks of the North whose economies became tied more and more closely to cotton. But even though both were links in the same chain of cotton commerce, their interests came sharply into conflict.

The tariff was one case in point. It was commerce and industry that required protection from foreign competition, not agriculture. So tariffs, which did not affect the prices of farm products for home consumption, helped keep up the domestic prices of manufactured goods, to the vexation of the South.

Land policy was another area of difference. The South had committed itself not merely to agriculture but to intense cultivation of the soil. Just as had been true earlier in the case of tobacco, intensive farming of cotton depleted the soil. Looking ahead to the time when their soil would be less productive, plantation owners sent slaves who were not otherwise occupied out to the "new grounds" to cut down and burn trees, with no thought of the wasted resources. The South thus favored more expansive policies with regard to public lands, urging the sale of larger tracts at lower prices. Northern manufacturers, meanwhile, were opposed to the encouragement of western migration, because this would cut into their potential work force and therefore keep wages up.

There was also marked southern resentment about the division of cotton profits. Northern shippers, having developed a sizable merchant fleet, needed cargo for

the times worked for the system.

Advances in wheat production led to big exports of the grain in 1847, paid for by gold from abroad. Investments in the rapidly growing network of railroads within the United States were also largely supported by gold from Great Britain. Then, in 1848, came the discovery of gold in California. And the supply of gold in circulation expanded faster than it accumulated in the subtreasury vaults.

By 1851 the annual coinage of gold had reached $63.5 million, almost ten times the $6.6 million coined only five years before, in 1846. As it was, the storing of gold by the subtreasuries stemmed inflation. In the decade from 1846 to 1856, the wholesale price index rose only some 6 per cent.

The government also hit upon a device that, in effect, permitted limited adjustments of the quantity of money in circulation. It was simply the purchase of government bonds in the open market by the Treasury. Under this system the Treasury behaved much like a central bank. But the free-swinging, note-printing bank of Nicholas Biddle was never revived, and Van Buren's device adequately served the nation's basic currency needs until the Federal Reserve System was created in 1913 to meet the requirements of a greatly expanded and more complex economy.

their outbound trading voyages. The North also had banks to finance this trade, and warehouses to store the commodities. As the cotton crop grew in size and importance, it was only natural for the North to engage in a commercial invasion of the South, and for the South to co-operate by offering its products to this ready-made world marketing system. As a result, northern middlemen took a sizable bite out of the proceeds of the cotton crop—an estimated forty cents out of every dollar went into freight charges, insurance, commissions, and interest. (South Carolina Congressman George McDuffie characterized it as the plunder of forty bales of cotton out of every hundred.)

Each section tended to develop its own business morality, but because most businessmen are essentially pragmatists, these were moralities that were best suited to their own business needs. Those in the North professed to despise slavery, and the South reviled northern manufacturers for their exploitation of workers. But these attitudes did not keep individuals from crossing the lines. Enterprising people from all sections and classes came to the new lands opening up in the southwestern states of Tennessee, Alabama, Mississippi, and Louisiana, from 1820 to 1850. For farms near navigable waters, cotton crops offered large returns in a single year and real opportunities for growth. Some northerners also took to the South their knack for organizing manufactures. Daniel Bratt of New Hampshire began manufacturing cotton gins in Autauga County, Alabama, in 1834, and soon added a sawmill, a planing mill, and the state's first flour and grist mill. By 1846 he had added a cotton factory, iron foundry, and other works.

What North and South had in common was the prosperity resulting from the growth of cotton production. The size of the crop climbed steadily, from 80 million pounds in 1815 to 460 million, or more than half the world's output, by 1834, and to more than a billion pounds by 1850. The value of the crop in 1834 worked out to some $75 million, and exports of 384 million pounds were worth about $49 million. From 1830 until the Civil War, cotton provided approximately half of the nation's total value of exports.

Cotton for domestic use kept the North's mills busy. The number of cotton spindles in United States factories had a tenfold increase, to 2,250,000, between 1820 and 1840. While some cotton manufacture was taking place in most of the older sections of the country, New England continued its dominance of the industry, with 69 per cent of the 1840 production.

Textile manufacturers continued to improve their technology. The Slater mills in Rhode Island imported the English power loom, and they switched from water power to steam as soon as the railroads had been well enough developed to haul coal inexpensively. Spindles that once ran no faster than 50 revolutions per minute were speeded up to 7,000 r.p.m.'s by Charles Danforth's "cup spinner" and to 11,000 by John Thorpe's

Long chutes were used to carry cotton bales down tall bluffs to the decks of waiting steamboats on the Alabama River.

"ring spinner." Iron replaced wood in the carding drums, and leather belts came into use to drive the spindles. Power looms were improved for steadier operation and greater output per worker, to enable the American mills to compete against lower European wages. Chemists were called on to devise methods of speeding up the bleaching and dyeing processes, in order to match the faster spinning and weaving.

At Waltham, Massachusetts, the nation got an early taste of large business organization. There the Boston Manufacturing Company was set up by Francis Lowell, Patrick Jackson, and Paul Moody, with Nathan Appleton as the major financial backer. The Waltham group then organized the Merrimack Manufacturing Company, capitalized at $600,000, in Lowell, a town that soon evolved into the Manchester of America. Lowell had twenty-five factories by 1827 and was producing 40 million yards of cloth annually by 1835. It had also pioneered another innovation—good employee relations. Charles Dickens, whose novels depicted the penury and squalor among Britain's factory workers, said after a visit to Lowell that "no face there bore an unhealthy or an unhappy look."

The technology of wool manufactures, which were slower to move out of the home workshop, began to improve markedly in the 1830's, when cleaning, spinning, weaving, and finishing were brought together as a single industry. Advances included a condenser, combining a group of carding machines, in 1826; a burr-picking machine to clean the wool, in 1834; and a card-making machine that Daniel Webster deemed "more nearly endowed with human intelligence than any machine ever invented."

A British industrialist warned in 1835 that England's supremacy in textile making was jeopardized by America, "where ingenuity and enterprise mark the national character."

THE RISE OF MANUFACTURES

During the first half of the century manufacturing clearly outgrew its infancy. Between 1819 and 1849, private production income from manufacturing increased from $64 million to $291 million. While this latter figure amounted to only about an eighth of total national income from private sources, manufacturing was the fastest growing segment of the economy in this period.

Inevitably destined for growth was the iron industry, in part because the raw materials, iron ore and coal, were found in abundance, and partly because iron was in demand for so many consumer and industrial products, from bathtubs to kitchen utensils, from printing presses to sugar mills. Pig iron output expanded from just over 50,000 gross tons in 1810 to 600,000 by 1850. Gradually production moved out of

the blacksmith shops to forges and mills; instead of meeting increased demands simply by opening more shops, as had been true until about 1830, existing establishments were expanded and new technologies were developed.

Some of the major advances involved fuels for the iron furnaces. As eastern forests started to be thinned down, increasing amounts of anthracite, and later bituminous, coal were used in the blast furnaces. A Lutheran clergyman, Dr. Frederick Geissenhainer, obtained a patent in 1833 for burning anthracite by means of a strong blast of hot air. Another who experimented with using anthracite, rather than charcoal, was Peter Cooper, who built an iron foundry in New York City after he had encountered a shortage of the iron parts he needed to build the "Tom Thumb" locomotive. A Welsh immigrant, David Thomas, successfully used a hot blast to burn anthracite at the Lehigh Crane Company furnace in Pennsylvania in 1840. Although it was found that coke made from bituminous coal was an even better fuel, it was not extensively used until much later, when an efficient method was found for producing the coke.

The use of anthracite had wide-ranging consequences. One was the rapid growth of the cooking range industry, because coal proved so popular for iron stoves. Stove production grew to 300,000 units, valued at $6 million by 1850.

Coal, and the increased railroad network that could transport it, also helped the iron industry (which had begun to shift westward) come back to the East, as well as to spread farther west. Pittsburgh already had its first foundry and rolling mills by 1820. In 1824 Peter Schoenberger built the Juniata Iron Works there, and he later came down the Ohio to found another ironworks and to help Wheeling become the "Nail City." Pittsburgh had eight rolling mills and nine foundries by 1829. In eastern Pennsylvania, New York, and New Jersey, iron smelting was revived along the routes of canals and railroads. George Price Whitaker and his brother Joseph bought the Principio Iron Works in Maryland, famous from colonial and Revolutionary days, and rebuilt and operated them. They also bought the Durham furnace in Pennsylvania, almost as old, and made iron there. Peter Cooper helped establish the Trenton Iron Co. in New Jersey, to which bridge-building pioneer John A. Roebling turned for iron cable for hauling canal boats over the Alleghenies. Roebling used Trenton wire to build a suspension bridge in 1846 at Pittsburgh, across the Monongahela, and to complete the 800-foot bridge crossing the Niagara Gorge in 1850.

Tooling and production of smaller metal products was centered in New England, where craftsmen had developed mass-production techniques for turning out clocks, axes, springs, cutlery, and firearms. Samuel

Colt, the boy whittler who had first fashioned in wood a model of his pistol with a revolving cylinder for the cartridges, got an American patent in 1836 and shortly afterward started the Patent Arms Manufacturing Co. in Paterson, New Jersey. But when orders, as well as some of the capital he had been promised, were not forthcoming, his enterprise went bankrupt.

The start of the Mexican War in 1846 created a surge of orders for the Colt "six-shooters," and Colt was soon back in business, this time with Eli Whitney, Jr., in Whitneyville, Connecticut. In a few years Colt had learned enough about production methods to go out on his own to build the world's biggest arms plant at Hartford, Connecticut, and to perfect the mass-production techniques that the senior Whitney had originated.

All sorts of metal products became objects of increasing specialization. Fine cast-iron hardware was produced in Albany by Bartlett Bent & Co. and by Maury & Ward. Heavy casting became a branch of engineering, since this industry was often called on to supply parts of heavy machinery and equipment. Some foundries along the Ohio River concentrated on the production of steam engines. Hollow ironware with enamel or tin finishes was being produced in quantity by 1845, with automatic and semiautomatic machinery, by Stuart & Company of Philadelphia. Robert Eastman of Brunswick, Maine, patented the first circular saw in 1820, and many saw-making plants were established, most notably the Disston Company of Philadelphia. Straight pins, which had sold for as much as thirty cents apiece in colonial days, were produced at the rate of fifty a minute by a machine patented by John Howe of North Salem, New York, when the Howe Company went into mass production in 1835. Chauncey Jerome, a onetime apprentice of famed clockmaker Eli Terry, revolutionized the clock industry by substituting brass for the old wooden wheels, and with mass production he was able to cut the cost of a clock movement; by 1853 he was producing 444,000 clocks

THE GIRLS OF LOWELL

The British novelist Charles Dickens had inveighed against the plight of the working class in England. But during his visit to the United States in 1842, he lavished praise on the working conditions of the girls who labored in the textile mills at Lowell, Massachusetts.

At that time, they lived in boarding houses, owned and run by their employers, and were paid from $2.50 to $3.00 a week, from which their room and board—amounting to about $1.25 a week—were deducted. Their working day varied with the length of sunlight, from eleven hours and twenty-four minutes in December to twelve hours and thirty-one minutes in other months.

Dickens reacted glowingly to the scene in which they worked. In his *American Notes* he wrote: "Lowell is a large, populous, thriving place. . . . The very river that moves the machinery in the mills (for they are all worked by water power), seems to acquire a new character from the fresh buildings of bright red brick and painted wood among which it takes its course. . . . One would swear that every 'Bakery,' 'Grocery,' and 'Bookbindery,' and other kind of store, took its shutters down for

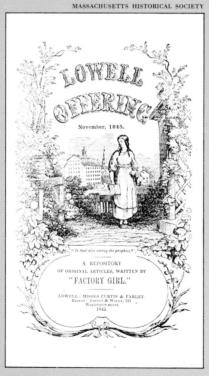

The title page of one of the issues of the Lowell mill girls' own publication

the first time, and started in business yesterday. The golden pestles and mortars fixed as signs upon the sun-blind frames outside the Druggists', appear to have been just turned out of the United States' Mint; and when I saw a baby of some week or ten days old in a woman's arms at a street corner, I found myself unconsciously wondering where it came from: never supposing for an instant that it could have been born in such a young town as that."

The marks of egalitarianism were noted everywhere by the visiting English author. "There are several factories in Lowell," Dickens observed, "each of which belongs to what we should term a Company of Proprietors, but what they call in America a Corporation. . . . I happened to arrive at the first factory just as the dinner hour was over, and the girls were returning to their work. . . . They were all well dressed, but not to my thinking above their condition. . . . They had serviceable bonnets, good warm cloaks, and shawls; and were not above clogs and pattens. . . . They were healthy in appearance, many of them remarkably so, and had the manners and deportment of young women: not of degraded brutes of burden."

Next, Dickens turned to one of his favorite subjects—the plight of working children. With approval, he noted that, "there are a few children employed in these factories, but not many. The laws of the State forbid their working

a year, and the price was down to $1.25 each.

The period saw the beginning of many a great new industry and enterprise. The Brandywine Powder Works, founded by French immigrant Eleuthère Irénée Du Pont of Wilmington, Delaware, had become the most extensive of its kind in the country when it was taken over by his sons at his death in 1834. In 1839 Charles Goodyear discovered a method for vulcanizing rubber with sulfur to keep it from becoming too hard in winter, too soft in summer. Shortly after he patented the process in 1844, new industries sprang up to use the product for footwear, rubber bands, inflatable beds, and fire hoses. William Colgate, who had founded a soap business in 1806, went into mass production. William Procter and James Gamble went into partnership to make soap and candles in 1837 and peddled their wares from door to door in Cincinnati.

Inventions that developed new techniques, rather than new things, were most significant in revolutionizing old industries. As new methods were developed for

splitting and coloring leather and new machines were invented for shoe manufacture, the boot and shoe business expanded from $1,000,000 in 1830 to more than $60 million just thirty years later. "Crooked" shoes, i.e., shoes cut differently for left and right feet, did not become common until 1850, although diagram patterns for cutting uppers had been introduced as early as 1832.

When the Frenchman Louis J. M. Daguerre developed a method of using silver salts and light to fix an image on a metal plate, Americans were quick to use his process and develop it further. John William Draper, a British-born scientist and photographer who came to the United States in 1831, used a mixture of bromine and iodine fumes to speed the exposure process. The Scovill Manufacturing Co. went into the production of metal daguerreotype plates, and many firms, including the Lambert Company of St. Louis, later began to manufacture glass plates.

The harpsichord, clavichord, and spinet, once made painstakingly by hand, moved out of the luxury class when some fifty plants went into mass production of the instruments after 1840.

Confronted with such an array of products to choose from, most Americans decided they wanted as many of them as they could possibly afford. And manufacturers were discovering a secret that older European economies were not to learn until many decades later—that mass production and low prices could lead to mass markets, and that these in turn could provide profits undreamed of in low-production societies.

A PREOCCUPATION WITH THINGS

From its Puritan beginnings, America had always been materialist in outlook. There had long been a sense that much of the nation's wealth was up for grabs for those who were both venturesome and lucky enough to start the right business at the right time, or to strike oil, iron, coal, or copper at a time and place that fitted the current transportation and marketing equations. But most Americans simply wanted things—things they needed to survive, or had once had in Europe, or had never had but could now acquire. When the Monroe Doctrine was first set forth, European diplomats dismissed it lightly on the ground that Americans were too much concerned with making money to be willing to fight for hemispheric integrity.

This spirit of materialism was nevertheless attractive enough to bring Europeans to American shores in mounting numbers. Immigration, almost all of it from northwestern Europe and Germany, increased exponentially, from 8,000 in 1820 to 23,000 in 1830 to 84,000 in 1840 to 370,000 in 1850. Most looked for the familiar surroundings of farms, but growing numbers came to the cities, as did an increasing proportion of

more than nine months of the year, and require that they be educated during the other three. For this purpose there are schools in Lowell; and there are churches and chapels of various persuasions, in which the young women may observe that form of worship in which they have been educated."

Dickens was amazed at the frugality of the Lowell girls: ". . . in July, 1841, no fewer than nine hundred and seventy-eight of these girls were depositors in the Lowell Savings Bank: the amount of whose joint savings was estimated at one hundred thousand dollars, or twenty thousand English pounds." He noted also that the girls had a jointly owned piano in each boarding house, that they subscribed to circulating libraries, and that they published their own periodical called the Lowell *Offering*.

"It is their station to work. And they *do* work. They labour in these mills, upon an average, twelve hours a day, which is unquestionably work, and pretty tight work too. Perhaps it is above their station to indulge in such amusements, on any terms. Are we quite sure that we in England have not formed our ideas of the 'station' of working people, from accustoming ourselves to the contemplation of that class as they are, and not as they might be?"

native citizens. In the same time span, the number of people living in cities of 2,500 or more rose from around 700,000 to more than 3.5 million; this fivefold increase was twice as great as the growth of population as a whole.

It was in the cities that new products were introduced first, that new comforts and conveniences multiplied most readily, and that luxuries quickly became necessities in an ambiance of rising expectations. Middle-class people in the seaboard towns and cities owned such amenities as linens, glassware, porcelain, colored paper hangings, clothing made of finished cloth, as well as tools and utensils. They could never again be satisfied with the crude life the colonies had once known or that even then characterized the new frontier regions.

In the 1820's most homes were lighted by candles, made of spermaceti for those who could afford the best. In the following decade these were gradually replaced by oil lamps, and by gas in some large cities. Boston

and New York got street lighting in the early 1820's, much improved when a limestone gas mantle was introduced in 1835, and Philadelphia's streets were lighted in 1837. One small section of Philadelphia had water distributed from the Schuylkill River through log pipes as early as 1799, and this was expanded in 1822 to provide water for the whole city, piped with cast iron. New Yorkers in the Wall Street area got their water through wooden pipes until 1842, when the Croton Reservoir system was completed to supply the entire city. Most of the nation, however, still got its water from wells and cisterns.

A Philadelphia hotel installed a bathroom as early as 1820, and indoor plumbing was a proud boast of the Tremont House in Boston in 1828 and the Astor House in New York in 1832. The first home bathrooms, looking like small Greek temples, were produced around 1840, and some had hot running water ten years later.

Stoves increasingly replaced open fireplaces and were in turn augmented by central heating. The first

---

The Way to Wealth

WILLIAM COLGATE

"Cleanliness is next to godliness," preached the Methodist John Wesley. It was the sort of lesson that the young religious nonconformist, William Colgate (1783–1857), took to heart as well as to mind. He was only twelve years old when his father, Robert, fled with him from England to Maryland in 1795, after heading a list of dangerous Anabaptists destined for prison, or a worse fate.

William's father did poorly at farming and in 1830 moved to Baltimore to make soap and candles. When he took up farming again, he left William to run the business. The youth had little success, however, and in 1803 moved to New York City. He became an apprentice in a soap factory, and after three years struck off on his own.

To the business he established, he brought a concept of uniform quality that won a market for his products. He added a scent to his soap and cut the cakes into equal-sized bars of one-pound weight. The popularity of his pale soap and pearl starch, along with the fact that he delivered his products to people's homes, earned him a fast-growing clientele.

In 1807 Colgate took in a partner,

COLGATE-PALMOLIVE CO.

William Colgate

who provided him with $700 of new capital. After six years he bought him out for $1,000. In 1817 he ran his first public ad: "Have for sale on best terms a constant supply of Soap, Mould, and Dipt Candles of the first quality." He even bid for sales abroad in his advertisements — a step that eventually paid off handsomely.

The completion of the Erie Canal in 1825 opened a new sales territory in the West. Colgate's sons and nephews

joined him in the thriving business. By 1835 exports of soap and candles from the United States totalled $534,476, and the American industry was on its way to becoming soap sellers to the world.

In 1872 the company that Colgate had founded introduced the brand-name soap Cashmere Bouquet, and the following year it brought out the first flavored toothpaste. By 1906 the firm was making 160 different kinds of toilet soaps, laundry soap, and 625 varieties of perfume. In toiletries, multiplicity spelled additional success.

When in 1928 Colgate merged with the Palmolive-Peet Company, which had learned the virtues of combining palm and olive oils in soap, the new firm had assets of $63 million.

The religious bent of the Colgates never vanished. From the early days, when William was supplied with potash from the New York State farm on which his father had finally settled, the family remained associated with the Baptist Education Society of New York. The Society had started a school in 1820 near Hamilton, New York. Although William made no direct gift to the school when he died in 1857, the family gave so much money to the college that, by 1890, half its endowment stemmed from Colgate fortunes. Quite naturally, the college changed its name to Colgate.

warm-air furnaces were no more than large stoves encased in brick. Anthracite coal had been used for home heating as early as 1815, but wood was the chief fuel until the railroads made coal more widely available.

The growth of the cities also brought greater diversity—in tastes, in backgrounds, in capabilities, in earning power. The jacks-of-all-trades were giving way to the specialists—millhands, machinists, carpenters, metalworkers, engineers, men who tended spinning mules in the textile plants, and men who drove teams of mules along the towpaths of canals.

Building and earth-moving projects required large amounts of unskilled labor, and many immigrants were attracted by American wages, a third to a half higher than those prevailing abroad. In the Massachusetts factories, where the pay was highest, men earned $5.00 a week, children from $1.00 to $2.00, and women from $1.75 to $2.50, but some women worked in the shoe factories for as little as sixty cents a week. Most unskilled laborers worked for seventy-five cents to $1.25 a day around 1820, but even as late as 1846 some received as little as sixty-five cents a day on construction projects in Brooklyn and iron works in Baltimore. The pay for agricultural labor, about fifty cents a day in 1800, rose gradually to about $1.50. More highly skilled workers, both in factories and on the farm, could earn from $1.00 to $2.00 a day.

Most of the women working in the Massachusetts textile mills were young girls recruited from nearby farms. Since the factory sites were chosen for water power, and often lacked housing, shops, schools, and churches, these were frequently built by the mill owners, who put up such company towns as Waltham, Lowell, and Chicopee. In the honest Puritan belief that it was their duty, the Cabots, Lowells, Appletons, and Jacksons provided their charges with religious, educational, and moral guidance. Each working girl was given a free bed, but about half her salary was deducted for board. From what was left, the girls could buy their needs at the company store, and were often able to put some money aside to help their families or for their dowries.

The company town system around the iron mills of New Jersey and Pennsylvania was more feudal. Entire families worked in the mines and factories, bought their needs at company stores, and, perpetually in debt to their employers, never saw cash wages. Conditions improved when corporations started to replace the baronial fiefdoms of individual owners in the 1830's.

Working shifts, ordinarily from dusk to dawn, ranged from $11\frac{1}{2}$ to $13\frac{1}{2}$ or more hours a day, depending on the season. A movement to cut back to a ten-hour work day started in the 1830's and took firm hold among the textile workers. Feeling betrayed, the mill owners gradually reduced their paternalism. In an executive order in 1840, Van Buren approved the move-

Samuel F. B. Morse, artist, inventor, and businessman

ment to shorten hours. But one bill after another was killed by the Massachusetts legislature, with the explanation that a short work day would "waste life."

Labor societies and organizations began to spring up. The carpenters of Philadelphia struck for a ten-hour day in 1827 and were joined by the bricklayers, painters, and glaziers. A Union of Trade Organizations was formed to include fifteen unions there, and they sponsored an American Working Men's political party. A number of unions organized on a national basis, and a national labor convention was held in 1834. From 1834 to 1837 union membership swelled from 26,000 to hundreds of thousands. One claim, probably much exaggerated, placed the total at 300,000, which represented about half the skilled workers in American cities.

For all this militant organization, strikes were few and rarely successful. For the most part they were waged as protests against pay cuts, rather than in an effort to raise wages and improve working conditions. But the allied craft organization in Philadelphia did win a ten-hour day by means of a general strike in 1835.

THE NEW ERA OF COMMUNICATIONS

Bit by bit, the mysteries of electricity, which had so fascinated Benjamin Franklin, were being unraveled—static charges, Allesandro Volta's voltaic pile con-

105

denser, André Ampère's work on electrical currents, Hans Oersted's discovery of electromagnetism. Joseph Henry, in the United States, showed how the power of an electromagnet could be intensified by increasing the windings of wire around the magnet, and sent a current from a battery through a mile of wire to ring a bell.

One of those who envisioned an important practical use for this new knowledge was a prominent artist, Samuel F. B. Morse, son of a geographer and grandson of a former president of Princeton University. On a long sea voyage from Europe in 1832, he devised a method of sending coded letters over such an electrical system. With the help of Joseph Henry and Alfred Vail and working with the crude materials of the time, he developed a working model and demonstrated it before a group of scientists at New York University in 1837. That year Sir William Fothergill Cooke patented an electromagnetic telegraph in England, and Carl August von Steinheil put a recording telegraph into operation in Germany.

Unable to find investors imaginative enough to provide funds for the development of his telegraph, Morse sought help from Congress for six years, and finally won a $30,000 appropriation to build a demonstration line from Baltimore to Washington. On May 24, 1844, Morse, hunched over the key in the U.S. Supreme Court chambers, sent the first message, "What hath God wrought!" The following day, news from the Democratic convention, meeting in Baltimore, was flashed over the wire to Washington, and the wire later carried word from the Whig convention, which was also held in Baltimore.

The telegraph occasioned much excitement, but, when a private company was formed, investment funds were still hard to come by. In 1846 a line was opened from Philadelphia to Newark, and later extended to Jersey City, with messages then ferried by boat to New York. Demand for more telegraph lines developed swiftly, chiefly from newspapers and from brokers eager to get or send market quotations. Ezra Cornell, who had advocated overhead wires and had helped plan the original Baltimore–Washington link, organized the rapid growth of the telegraph system. Within a year or two, New York had lines to Albany, Buffalo, Boston, Cleveland, Detroit, and Chicago. Wires stretched to Louisville and Cincinnati, and President James Polk's message to Congress in December, 1848, was telegraphed to St. Louis, where it was printed in newspapers the following day.

Newspapers had already become major instruments for the communication of ideas, and the telegraph increased their impact and importance. The number of newspapers grew with the country, from 150 in 1800 to 863 in 1830 and about 2,800 in 1850. At the start they were mostly small, four-page sheets, printed badly on a poor quality of paper. Editors kept asking for rags with which to make paper by the slow processes then in use.

Then technology moved in. Thomas Gilpin of Delaware produced machine-made paper in 1817, using a cylinder of wires and felt that picked up the pulp and passed it along to rolls for flattening. His machine was improved by John and David Ames of Springfield, Massachusetts, in 1822; by 1830 machines could produce paper in a continuous train at a speed of forty-five feet per minute, and the United States had become the world's chief producer and consumer of paper. Straw was first used to make paper in 1829.

At that time most printing presses were still being cranked by hand, rolling a sheet of paper over a flat bed of type. Robert Hoe, a press repairman and carpenter who had emigrated from England, built a cylinder press adapted from a British model, and he and his son continued to improve their press. By 1847 R. Hoe & Co. had developed the new principle of placing type on a revolving cylinder that pressed against a roll of paper moving around other impression cylinders, making possible high-speed printing of large newspaper runs. It was installed by the Philadelphia *Ledger*, and before long most major city newspapers boasted Hoe Lightning rotary presses.

News coverage and news gathering also improved. From the first publication of the *Freeman's Oath* in Cambridge, Massachusetts, in 1639, publishing had been more a political tool than a news-dispensing service. Usually tinged with special interest, sometimes tainted with venality, the early newspapers were devoted more to polemics than to reporting facts.

Book publishing often provided more solid fare. Corey and Webster of Cincinnati published 200,000 copies of *Webster's Spelling Book* in 1833. *Godey's Lady's Book* was printing patterns with which middle-class wives could dress themselves as fashionably as the wealthy. In 1835 the Cincinnati *Gazette* began publishing *Price Current*, the first commercial paper in the Northwest.

Printed materials were still a luxury, however. Newspapers generally sold for six cents, much more than the workingman could afford. Then the "penny press" emerged to add a new dimension to city living. By 1838 Benjamin Henry Day's New York *Sun* had the world's largest newspaper circulation of 38,000 copies a day, and James Gordon Bennett's New York *Herald* was not far behind. Just about everyone could buy a penny paper. Literacy spread, local consciousness increased, and the city dweller was brought infinitely closer to the political, economic, and philosophical mainstream of his day. If nothing more, the penny press made newspaper reading a daily habit for thousands of families, and it laid the foundation for a larger revolution in communication.

III Egalitarianism

The democratic base of American society, exemplified on election day: George Caleb Bingham's The Verdict of the People

66 . . . the sense of equality permeated the American's life and thought, his conduct, work, and play, his language and literature, his religion and his politics, and it conditioned all the relationships of his life. . . . where so few started with anything but their strength and character and where success was so easy, artificial advantages counted for little. Where all men were equal in the sight of God, it was difficult not to admit equality in the eyes of men. . . ."

Henry Steele Commager, *The American Mind*, 1950

107

In "the land of the free and the home of the brave," humble birth has carried no stigma. Many a famous man was born in a log cabin and made capital of it in later life. Above: an 1840 song sheet for Whig presidential candidate William Henry Harrison

The "common man" image of the every-day American was idealized by William Jennings Bryan and erstwhile haber-dasher Harry Truman (right).

Norman Rockwell's painting "Freedom of Speech" reflects the traditional town-meeting right of citizens to participate equally in affairs that affect the community.

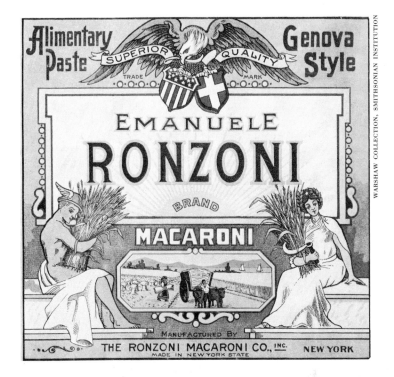

Though a person's antecedents have meant less than the measure of his or her own character and abilities, the diverse origins of Americans have enriched the nation. At left: immigrant children at Ellis Island waiting entry to the U.S. in the early 1900's. At right: one of numerous foreign-derived food products. Below: a Russian-born American citizen converts her A.T.&T. debentures into stock in 1956.

In 119 books that sold more than 200 million copies, Horatio Alger nourished the "rags to riches" dream. Alger himself demonstrated that the ease of mobility led in both directions. He made a fortune, squandered it, and died poor.

Unimpeded by a class system, many persons soared like Alger's heroes. David Sarnoff (above, as a young wireless oper-

At twenty John Jacob Astor came to America with seven flutes to sell. Furs and real estate made him a $20 million fortune.

Born to slave parents, agricultural scientist George Washington Carver aided the South's economy with his research.

ator) thought Alger stressed luck rather than hard work, the
key to his own rise from poor immigrant to R.C.A. chairman.

Andrew Carnegie's saga inspired generations of schoolboys.
An immigrant, he became the greatest of the steel barons.

This statue outside the mansion of U.S. Steel head Charles
Schwab reminded him of his start as a dollar-a-day worker.

In a land of equal opportunity, aids to "get-*ting ahead" like this journal have thrived.*

The talent and abilities of advertising executive Mary Wells, above, helped erode discrimination that denied equality to women in business.

The "town meeting" of business: a stockholder questions management at the Bulova Watch Co.'s annual meeting in New York.

Opposite: the face of American egalitarianism—lignite miners of different back-grounds photographed early in the 1900's at Rockdale, Texas

Shrewd, merciless Cornelius Vanderbilt (1794–1877) left $100,000,000, made in steamboats and railroads.

4

THE
BUILDERS

1840-1865

By the mid-point of the 1800's the United States was on the threshold of becoming one of the great economic powers of the world. Agriculturally self-sufficient, she was Europe's standby granary, ready to export at the smallest sign of strength in prices. Her carrying trade on the seas remained substantial. Immigration and natural population growth provided an ever-increasing labor pool. The government's remarkable fiscal strength helped lure capital from abroad. Rising prices and general prosperity bred still more optimism. The nation had quickly built the world's largest railroad network and was expanding it even more swiftly. The manufacturing and industrial complex, while still smaller than England's, was becoming more innovative and led Britain in both worker productivity and wage levels. Business leaders, slowly and subtly, were assuming a more important role in helping to steer the nation's course.

Agriculture was still the country's economic mainstay. Even into the 1860's, 80 per cent of the people lived on farms, which made up half of the nation's wealth. The opening of vast new lands and the substantial strides in bringing mechanization to farms lifted American farm production to unprecedented heights—more than doubling its value in ten years, from $900 million to $1.9 billion. Wheat output rose from 44 million bushels in 1840 to almost 200 million bushels by 1860. In the decade of the 1850's, the cotton crop more than doubled, barley production tripled, corn output rose 40 per cent, and rye 50 per cent. Tobacco production, which had been slipping, soared. In what was at once the most thorough and the most

literate census report the nation had yet known, Joseph C. Kennedy, who supervised the 1860 census, pointed out:

The tobacco crop, in 1849, amounted to 199,752,655 pounds, being a decrease of more than 19 million pounds . . .; in 1859 it reached 429,390,771 pounds. . . . It would seem surprising that a crop which is said to impoverish the soil more than any other, and to injure to some extent every one who uses it, should be found so desirable as to increase 106 percent in ten years; but such is the effect of a ready market with remunerative prices.

In the same decade, the value of farm machinery increased from $7 million to more than $20 million. Factory plows almost completely replaced the blacksmith's product, and John Deere's factory alone turned out 13,000 plows for the western prairies in just one year—1858. Cyrus McCormick had become a millionaire by 1860. But farm machinery sales were yet to get their biggest push from the Civil War, which cut into farm manpower by taking the young men off to fight. "Without McCormick's invention," said Edwin M. Stanton, Lincoln's Secretary of War, in 1861, "I feel the North could not win."

One mid-century agricultural offshoot was the dairy industry. New York's city dwellers, who had grown accustomed to getting their milk from cows that roamed the streets and were fed on discarded brewery mash, were dismayed by the "yellow scum"—cream—on top of their milk when the first large shipment of country milk was made in 1842. But the industry developed quickly, bringing to the cities and towns not only the familiar milk cans but also butter and cheese. Jacob Russell opened the first commercial ice cream plant in Baltimore in 1851. By 1860 increasing quantities of Cheddar cheese were being exported, and the nation's dairy industry was the largest in the world.

Slower to develop, but even more significant, were the first important studies in soil science. Justus von Liebig, a German chemist, wrote *Chemistry and Its Application to Agriculture*, which had an important impact when it was published in the United States in 1841. Liebig showed that plants are nourished not mainly from the air, as many had thought, but from the soil, and that fertilizers replenish the soil with the same chemicals that plants use up. A number of important papers on soils, planting, and fertilizer were filed with the U.S. Commissioner of Patents in the 1850's.

Food processing followed food production. Cincinnati, the leading packing center in 1850, soon felt Chicago, St. Louis, and Louisville hard on its heels. The packing industry turned out a long list of by-products—glue, oils, soaps, candles, fertilizers, and brush bristles. The meat, once preserved mainly by salting, was now sterilized by heat and packed in airtight containers. Chicago was becoming the leading grain center, increasing its shipments of wheat from 6 million bushels in 1853 to 50 million by 1861. All this brought a wave of prosperity to the West.

In the sense of newness, enterprise, and opportunity, the West was vital and growing. For the nation as a whole, population had increased more than 35 per cent, to more than 31 million, during the 1850's. In the same period Illinois showed a gain of more than 100 per cent, to 1.7 million people. Railroad and telegraph lines stretched inexorably toward Chicago and the Mississippi River. Public lands enjoyed a lively sale, as speculators bought up land warrants issued to veterans of the Mexican War, and 50 million additional acres were brought under cultivation during the decade. Statehood had been granted to all the land east of the Mississippi, as well as to Louisiana, Texas, Arkansas, Missouri, Iowa, Minnesota, California, and Oregon. The Midwest had copper, lead, iron ore, and vast untapped forests. The value of individual property in the United States grew more than 125 per cent in the 1850's, to $16 billion, and the rate of increase in the West "has been immense," said Census Director Kennedy, "while the absolute gain in the older States has been no less remarkable."

America's promise brought not only immigrants from abroad but foreign investment funds seeking to share in the nation's growth. What helped make these investments attractive was the nation's sound fiscal condition. The national debt, which had reached $128 million, or $15 per capita, in 1815, was completely eliminated in 1835, as the United States became the only modern nation ever to pay off its debt. The debt

Beyond the opened Michigan Avenue bridge, grain carriers and other merchant ships crowd the Chicago River in the mid-1800's.

then rose to $63 million by 1850, dropped again to $10 million by 1857, and shot up during the Civil War to $2.7 billion by 1865. According to Treasury estimates, foreign capital invested in the United States grew from $222 million in 1853 to $400 million by 1860, and then diminished to half that amount during the war.

Capital from abroad, however, was becoming relatively less important to American industry, since business was increasingly able to generate its own funds for reinvestment. In the early days, the major source of domestic capital in the United States had been, as it had been in England, the profits of mercantile enterprises, mainly from those engaged in world trade. Gradually an increasing proportion of these profits was transferred toward manufacturing enterprises — first the textile mills of New England and then a variety of other industries. For example, John Perkins Cushing, a Boston merchant active in the China trade, began to shift his investments to domestic enterprises around 1828. By 1832 more than half of his funds were still committed to foreign trade, but just seven years later his total shipping investments had dwindled to less than $10,000, while he had put more than $1,000,000 to work at home.

In time, some manufacturers no longer needed to rely on outside sources of capital but developed their own funds out of profits. Peter Cooper built his Trenton iron mills largely from the earnings of his glue and gelatin company. The Fall River Iron Works, which started out with capital of $24,000 in 1821, was worth $500,000 by 1845, even though no additional funds had been invested and substantial dividends had been paid out.

It was not easy, however, for an industrial firm to supply all its own capital needs, even if operations were profitable. Manufacturers usually had to pay cash for their raw materials, but they often put out their finished goods to dealers on consignment or commission. They then had to wait until their wares were sold before getting paid, and in some cases this took years. To carry such remote inventories, a business had to be well supplied with working capital. To solve problems like these required not just a good plant manager or mechanical genius, but a competent businessman.

Subtly, but perhaps inevitably, American business was undergoing a major change, one that was accompanied by a corresponding change in the character of business leadership. In the long term, the processes of business are dominated not so much by those in possession of capital and resources as by those who can most successfully put capital and resources to work. In different terms, it is the organizers of the systems of finance, production, and distribution who are mainly instrumental in determining the course of business, and thereby of national economies.

First it had been the landowners — the royal grantees and the patroons — who had been the chief organizers of the colonial economy. Then came the merchants and traders, the shippers who skillfully played their games of cargo-swapping in distant ports and who sought to use the long travel times to their own advantage.

But now other economic factors favored a new breed of business leadership. Common carriers began to take over the transportation role once dominated by the merchant-owned ships. The telegraph carried word of changes in prices or business conditions almost instantaneously. As household manufacture virtually disappeared and large factories produced much more sophisticated goods, there was a significant increase in the value added to raw materials by manufacture. Price trends also played a major role. The period from 1815 to 1843 was one of generally declining prices; under those circumstances it took adept and facile merchants to deal with the problems of organizing business operations, especially those involving distribution. But from 1843 to 1866 prices were generally rising; this meant that unsold inventories would increase in value, so that there was small risk of loss during the time it took for goods to go through the distribution pipeline. Finally, the spirit of egalitarianism that pervaded American life made it easier for capable people from almost any station in life to rise to commanding positions of economic power.

Among those who came to prominence were industrialists, i.e., businessmen who keyed their organizing abilities to manufacturing processes. Others were finance capitalists — the wheeler-dealers of New York's Wall Street, Philadelphia's Broad Street, and Boston's State Street — who used money power to buy, sell, and control enterprises, but who were usually smart enough to let good managers run their businesses. The given factors in the equation of the times were abundant material resources, a growing supply of labor, a large and expanding market, a lively technology, and the means for moving goods over long distances. How all these might be juggled in terms of plant location, factory organization, marketing practices, shipping terms and methods, pricing, and capital flows — in short, how good the manager was — would determine whether and to what extent a business might succeed.

It was no longer enough merely to be a millionaire. At some time between 1845 and 1850, New York, Boston, and Philadelphia could each boast about twenty of those. To reach the top now required broad vision, a relentless competitive urge, and a driving desire to be first and best. Most of those who rose to greatest prominence had unfamiliar names: Andrew Carnegie, a Scottish immigrant boy; Cyrus McCormick, a blacksmith's son; Cornelius Vanderbilt, son of a Staten Island farmer; John D. Rockefeller, son of a patent medicine salesman from western New York;

market operators Jacob Little and Daniel Drew.

Some of them were helping shape their times, and others would have even greater impact on the times to come. But the nation first had to undergo some growing pains, as well as the huge and illogical convulsion of fratricidal war. The century's middle years were at once a heady and a trying time, in which Americans savored the sense of their own strengths and awesome potential, but in which they set themselves on a collision course with their own destiny.

RICHES FROM THE SEAS

Spawned of the efforts to create new ocean commerce, the United States itself had always looked abroad to buy the things it needed and to find markets for its own products. While territorial expansion and the Industrial Revolution had helped create vast new internal commerce, overseas trade had never lagged far behind. From the five-year period ending in 1820 to that

ending in 1860, foreign trade had more than tripled, from an average of $186 million to $616 million a year. This was an even faster growth rate for that period than that of the United Kingdom, the world's foremost trading power.

During part of this span, notably the late 1830's and the 1840's, the nation had reversed its traditional position as a net importer and had sold more to other countries than it bought. Much of this favorable trade balance was due to cotton sales, which made up more than half of all exports — and, along with such other southern products as rice, tobacco, and sugar, accounted for 75 per cent of all overseas shipments. Total exports in the 1850's were double those of the 1840's, which in turn were twice as high as in the 1820's.

The markets for about half of these products were in Great Britain, with the rest of Europe taking another 20 to 25 per cent. The chief markets for manufactured goods, which made up only 12 per cent of all exports even as late as 1860, were Mexico, the West

---

The Way to Wealth
JOHN DEERE

THE GENUINE MOLINE PLOW.
John Deere's product, advertised in 1868
DEERE & CO.

In the 1840's a farmer who plowed an acre by sundown reckoned it a good day's work. But as they moved westward with the opening of new lands, farmers found a problem in the heavy loam of the prairie. Their iron plows, forged by the best blacksmiths, had difficulty breaking through the wiry prairie grass and scouring clean as they struggled to turn the earth. The problem was solved by John Deere (1804–86), founder of the agricultural machinery company that bears his name.

Deere was a Vermont-born blacksmith who traveled west along the Erie Canal and through the Great Lakes states, reaching Illinois in 1836. There he observed the farmers' difficulties with the prairie and reasoned that a steel plow, sharper and more durable than one of iron, might be the answer. He fashioned his first plow from a circular saw blade of Sheffield steel. The tough prairie soil not only scoured with less effort from the steel plowshare and moldboard, but actually polished the plow's surface so that it furrowed more easily.

Deere made three steel plows in 1838 and by 1842 was turning out twenty-five a week. His need for steel

soared, but English steel, with its high shipping charges, cost him $300 a ton and often arrived pitted from the salty sea air. So Deere went to Pittsburgh for American-made steel. He moved his factory across Illinois from Grand Detour to Moline on the Mississippi, where coal, transported by water, was more accessible. Soon he was employing blacksmiths for ten-hour-a-day stints in his factory at $20 to $30 a month, including board.

Deere's son Charles came into the business in 1853, after acquiring some knowledge of management at Bell's Business College in Chicago. By 1869 the plant's office, equipped with gas chandeliers, central heating, and silver-plated locks and doorknobs, and ornamented with a frescoed ceiling, was a showplace of the Midwest. By the time of his death in 1886, Deere had seen

his catalogue expand to include subsoil, root-ground, and listing plows, a "bluebeard steel plow," a "New Deal gang," a "Gopher cultivator," a "Gilpin sulky," scarifiers, harrows, and potato diggers.

It was probably a Deere salesman whom Mark Twain quoted in *Life on the Mississippi* in 1883: "You show me any country under the sun where they really know *how* to plow, and if I don't show you our mark on the plow they use, I'll eat that plow, and I won't ask for any Woostershyre sauce to flavor it up with, either."

Today more than a billion dollars' worth of Deere agricultural machinery, painted a distinctive green, is sold each year. And the company that a blacksmith began in the West ranks among America's 200 largest industrial firms, with its headquarters still at Moline.

Indies, and China. The three-cornered Far Eastern trade in ginseng, Oregon furs, tea, silks, and the cotton fabric known as nankeen had flourished briefly, then fallen off sharply after 1830, even though American shippers competed for the opium trade with the British and the Indian Parsees into the 1850's. On a trip to England in 1829, John Cushing observed that it hardly paid to ship textiles from China to the West, since they could be "made cheaper in this country and France." By 1830 John Jacob Astor was virtually out of foreign trading altogether. The once substantial trade in re-exports, which had been carried on with ports all around the world, had dwindled to relative unimportance by the 1850's and was then directed primarily at Great Britain and British North America.

In both the 1840's and 1850's the United States was able to maintain a favorable balance of international payments. In the earlier decade, exports and imports were nearly in balance, but the drying up of foreign investment after a number of states repudiated their bonds in the early 1840's resulted in a net outflow of about $100 million in capital and interest. In the next decade, imports were $385 million higher than exports, but there were substantial European investments and a heavy outflow of newly discovered gold from America. What made a substantial difference in both periods were sizable credit balances earned from carrying freight in American bottoms and from the sale of ships.

As international commerce flourished, shipbuilding and shipping became lucrative businesses. The average shipping tonnage built in the United States in the 1840's was almost 200,000 tons a year, which was more than double that of the 1820's. By the 1850's the annual average was over 350,000 tons. The tonnage registered for foreign commerce rose just about as rapidly, from an average of 635,000 tons in the 1820's to 2,300,000 in the two years just before the Civil War. Because the ships were progressively bigger and faster, the tonnage entering and clearing American ports showed an even greater proportionate increase, from 1.6 million tons in 1820 to 12 million in 1860.

In the early years, American shipping was carried on at the whim and in the interests of the shipowner. The voyage was his voyage, the cargo what he chose to carry, the ports of call where he chose to go. Tramp ships roamed the seas, seeking out the most profitable deals and trades. There were also regular traders, journeying to fixed ports but following their own time schedules and occasionally leaving their predetermined courses to pick up some profitable cargo elsewhere. The merchant whose goods were being carried for hire was often at the mercy of the shipmaster or his supercargo, and his merchandise sometimes reached its intended port after a disastrous drop in prices.

Inevitably, something had to give. When packets began to travel between fixed ports on a regular schedule, their carrying business grew quickly. The first sailing packets across the Atlantic started before 1820. The Black Ball Line from New York to Liverpool was started in 1816, and other lines were soon organized to ply between New York and London, Le Havre, and Bremen. They were reliable, accommodating, and fast, making the voyages in as little as eighteen or twenty days. By 1845 there were regular sailings by fifty-two transatlantic packets. They carried sizable cargoes; in the 1850's merchant ships were typically three times the size of those built thirty years earlier.

The value of these shipping enterprises was quickly recognized by nations and cities. The British encouraged regular packet service on the Atlantic and Indian oceans with subsidies, and Britain's Cunard Line prospered under such encouragement. The United States finally awoke to the advantages of the practice, and it began subsidizing mail on a small scale in 1845, and ship construction the following year. But American subsidies were under constant jeopardy from political pulling and hauling, and they soon disappeared altogether.

New York and Boston were for many years keen rivals for port leadership in foreign commerce. When Boston's harbor froze in 1844, the businessmen went out to help break up the ice so that the Cunard Line's *Britannia* could sail on schedule. But New York moved inexorably to the forefront, and by 1860 the port was handling a third of the country's exports and two thirds of the imports.

Where speed in transit was of the essence, American shipbuilding seemed to have the edge. Generations of Yankee shipbuilders had learned how to design ships with fast, clean lines, as well as maximum utilization of sail. The culmination of their art came in the fabled clipper ships, which were a logical outgrowth of the packet era. Scientifically designed, with a long, sleek hull, a deeply arched bow, and sheets of canvas billowing almost 200 feet above the smooth lines of the deck, the clipper was the fastest thing afloat.

A predecessor, the *Ann McKim*, had been ordered built as early as 1832 by the Baltimore merchant Isaac McKim. But the first real clipper was the 750-ton *Rainbow*, designed by naval architect John Griffiths and launched in January, 1845. Bigger and faster clippers soon followed—the 900-ton *Sea Witch*, the 1,800-ton *Flying Cloud*, the 2,400-ton *Sovereign of the Seas*, and, greatest of all, the 4,000-ton *Great Republic*, spreading 15,000 yards of sail to the breeze. The *Lightning*, which sailed to Liverpool in thirteen and a half days, logged 436 miles in one twenty-four hour period. Eighteen different ships sailed from New York around Cape Horn to San Francisco in less than 100 days, and the *Flying Cloud* set the record for this course of eighty-nine days and eight hours. During the height of the clipper era, records were set of eighty-six days from Singapore to New York and eighty-four days from Canton to New York. Also contributing to the high-speed voyages were the charts and maps developed by Matthew Maury, superintendent of the U.S. Naval Observatory. These helped trim many days off the longest sea journeys.

The clippers were in demand not only to haul cargo but to carry passengers, particularly after gold was discovered, first in California and then in Australia. Where speed was required, particularly for long ocean hauls, the business went to the clipper ships. For a time, they could not be built rapidly enough. Donald McKay, builder of the biggest and fastest clippers, turned out 160 ships in his Newburyport, Massachusetts, yards in just four years. A clipper being built by McKay for the Boston shipowner Enoch Train was sold by Train for $90,000—about twice what he was paying—before it was completed.

But the bubble burst very soon thereafter. By 1855 some of the clippers had proved to be losing propositions, and the demand quickly slacked off. A few years later it was virtually nonexistent. Shipbuilding, which had averaged 400,000 tons a year in the decade before 1858, slipped to 244,000 tons that year and 156,000 in 1859.

The plain fact was that the clipper ships were truly marvels of their kind, but they came about a generation too late. For the amount of freight that the narrow-beamed vessels could carry, they were simply too expensive. So they ignominiously gave way to the more pedestrian half-clipper and to the snub-nosed steam freighters. With the clipper went any hopes the United States might have had of dominating the merchant sea-lanes.

The very skill and artistry that Americans had developed in building and designing wooden sailing ships helped put them behind in the development of steamships, on which the more practical British ship-

---

THE RISE AND FALL OF A CLIPPER SHIP

In its heyday, the Yankee clipper—combining speed with economy—was a dramatic answer to the needs of America's increasing merchant trade. No one designed these tall, graceful ships better than Donald McKay (1810–80) of Boston.

McKay's last famous clipper was the *Glory of the Seas*, launched in 1869. By then a new age of shipbuilding had arrived: iron hulls were a better insurance risk than the wooden hulls of the clippers, and steam was more reliable than sails. McKay himself was already working on locomotive engines, but there was still a market for clippers. The *Glory*, afloat for fifty-four years, became a long-enduring image of the romantic era of sails dominated by McKay's ships.

The *Glory* was 250 feet long, 44 feet wide at her beam, and had a roomy hold 28½ feet deep. Her mainmast towered 188 feet from the keel, and her burden was 2,102 tons register. Although she was a sensation at her launching in East Boston, she attracted no buyers at McKay's asking price of $190,000. To prove that she was a worthwhile investment, he sailed her around Cape Horn to San Francisco in 120 days—not a record but still an impressive passage.

Donald McKay

On his arrival, however, he found that bankruptcy proceedings had begun against him in the East; *Glory* wound up in the hands of Boston's J. Henry Sears & Co.

The square-rigger was entered in the grain trade between San Francisco and London, a 14,000-mile voyage in which cargo rates were as high as $20 per long ton. *Glory* once carried a $242,665 manifest to England. By the age of thirteen she had sailed 350,000 nautical miles, but the era of committing perishable merchandise to wooden hulls was over.

In 1886 the clipper was chartered in the Pacific Coast coal trade. Running between San Francisco and British Columbia, she grossed $12,000 a voyage. In 1892 she was servicing the Pacific steam whaling fleet, hauling fuel as far north as the Aleutians. Six years later she was the only McKay merchantman still sailing.

She was lying on a mudbank at San Francisco when the earthquake struck that city in 1906. In the months that followed, she carried lumber for the rebuilding of the city. In 1911 she was sold to the Alaska Fish Company for $4,050. Her new owners fitted her with gasoline engines and electricity, dismantled her masts, and used her as a floating cannery. Her first year's output of 40,000 cases of tinned "Glory of the Seas Alaska Brand Salmon"—with a picture of her on the labels of the cans—netted a $40,000 profit. Her next owner, the Glacier Fish Company, bought her for $23,500 in 1913, converted her into a floating refrigerated factory, and packed 1,800,000 pounds of fish in a year. Her sails were used as awnings.

In 1923 her end finally came. She was too old to be moved, and her owners burned her. James Farrell, the president of U.S. Steel, bought her figurehead, a bare-bosomed Greek goddess, and presented it to New York City's India House, a businessman's dining club, where it is still displayed.

builders were placing their bets. When the Cunard Company started in business in 1840 with four side-wheel wooden steamships, it had a large subsidy from the British government. Scottish manufacturers started early to build their ships of iron. By 1853 fully a fourth of British ships were built for steam, which was slightly higher than the U.S. proportion, but a fourth were also made of iron, compared to almost none in the United States, where iron hulls were more costly.

In neglecting steam for ocean travel, the Americans gave up the leadership they had begun to take long before. The first steamship to cross the Atlantic was the 300-ton *Savannah*, built in New York; in 1819 it crossed from Savannah to Liverpool, using steam power for only eighty hours of the twenty-seven-day voyage. The British experimented with steam packets for shorter voyages to European ports. In April, 1838, two British steamers, the *Sirius* and the *Great Western*, arrived in New York on the same day. Steam voyages across the Atlantic increased gradually over the next ten years, but the ships, beset with mechanical troubles, offered little competition to the sailing craft.

But then technology took over. The first important development was the screw propeller, first made practical by John Ericsson, a Swede who had emigrated to the United States. But screw propulsion did not work too well on the large wooden ships favored by American shipbuilders. The *Great Britain*, which crossed from Liverpool to New York in 1845, was the first large ship to combine the principles of the iron hull and the screw, but with indifferent success at the start. In time, however, four technical advances—steam, iron, screw propulsion, and boilers fired by anthracite coal—came to dominate the economics of ocean navigation.

There was a marked increase in steam travel across the Atlantic from 1848 to 1860; registered steamship tonnage in the United States climbed from just 5,600 in 1847 to 97,000 in 1860. But most of the American ships were still wooden, many with paddle-wheel propulsion, and iron steamship construction in the United States in the 1850's totaled only about 15,000 gross tons. Boilermakers and machinists, rather than shipbuilders, built most of the iron ships. American steamers were built to carry auxiliary sails; it was not until 1899 that the White Star Line ventured to put a ship with no canvas on the Atlantic. Still, the need for refueling made steam travel impractical from New York around Cape Horn to California and the Far East.

A steam packet service between Liverpool and New York was started by Cunard in 1848, and the Ocean Steam Navigation Co. of New York began a scheduled service to Bremen, Germany, with a stop at Southampton, England. But a federal subsidy was withdrawn after some years, and the line stopped operating.

The first real challenge to the very successful Cunard operation was posed by the United States Mail Steamship Company, with an annual subsidy of $385,000 from Congress. Starting with four ships and strong financial backing, Edward K. Collins, a New York merchant, set out to give Cunard a run for its money on the Atlantic. His ships were faster than the Cunarders (Collins's *Baltic* made the westward voyage in less than ten days in 1851), offered fine appointments and good service, and they soon cut into Cunard's business. By 1852 the subsidy was raised to $858,000. But the Collins line lost money, while Cunard was making a profit with its smaller subsidy. And eventually the tortoise outraced the hare. While Cunard operated conservatively, emphasizing good business practices and safety at sea, the Collins line fell victim to two catastrophic sinkings, from which it never recovered.

The only one able to give Cunard real competition was Commodore Vanderbilt. With no subsidy, he cut rates and kept fast steamships operating to Le Havre and Bremen, but his sailings were irregular and he often withdrew his ships in the more treacherous winter months. Vanderbilt also had ten ships in the California passage; Pacific Steamship had thirteen, the New York–San Francisco Line four, and the Empire State Line three. But by 1860 the American merchant marine was in a declining phase from which it would not recover for another fifty years.

American whaling ships brought back another kind of wealth from the sea. Whaling tonnage increased steadily from 35,000 in 1820 to 190,000 in 1858. The industry's best years were in the quarter-century span from 1835 to 1860, when the value of its products averaged $8 million a year and in some years exceeded that of all the rest of the fishing industry. Most whalers sailed out of a few ports, with New Bedford, Massachusetts, in the lead, followed closely by Nantucket and at a greater distance by New London, Connecticut, Salem, Massachusetts, and Sag Harbor, New York.

The chief commercial products were whalebone, whale oil, and sperm oil, some of it for export, but most for domestic use. Average annual production for the twenty-five year period was 2.3 million pounds of whalebone, 216,000 barrels of whale oil, and 118,000 barrels of sperm oil. The flexible whalebone had dozens of uses where both strength and springiness were desired, most notably for buggy whips and in women's clothing. The ability to withstand temperature extremes made sperm oil especially useful as a lubricant for machinery. Whale oil was used primarily as an illuminant, lighting European and American streets, serving in lighthouse beacons and in locomotive headlights. Writes Salem historian Frances Robotti: "Many a beautifully attired woman danced in gay ballrooms lighted by sperm candles in gowns which patient seamstresses had supported with whalebone. Beneath the outer glory was the reliable and supple whalebone corset."

In 1846, the peak year for whaling, there were 736

Barrels of whale oil unloaded from whalers at New Bedford

American vessels in the industry, which employed an estimated 70,000 people and represented an investment of $70 million. As the big herds began to diminish, new whaling grounds were sought. The whaler *Superior*, out of Sag Harbor, sailed through the fog-shrouded Bering Straits to find the bowhead whales of the Arctic Ocean. The best whaling grounds were in the Pacific, and a small fleet sailed out of San Francisco in the 1850's. But the industry was soon to enter its long decline, in which most of its products would be replaced by others from more readily available sources—chiefly petroleum oil and springy steel.

RICHES FROM THE EARTH

Migration across the Mississippi amounted to hardly more than a trickle before 1840. The westward trek picked up in 1846, when an agreement was reached with England to extend the forty-ninth parallel to the Pacific as a boundary, and when the Mexican War began. But 1848 turned out to be a far more significant

turning point.

Some forty miles from present-day Sacramento, California, on a millrace channel he was building from the American River for a Swiss settler named Johann Augustus Sutter, a young hydraulic carpenter from New Jersey named James W. Marshall spotted some shiny yellow flecks. Sutter himself tried to keep the discovery quiet, because news of a gold find would upset the development of New Helvetia, the colony he had founded on his semifeudal estate. But the news would not stay down. Nor would people give credence to the many periodicals that sought to restore calm by belittling the gold strike.

Instead, the gold-seekers came by the thousands, armed with picks, shovels, knapsacks, tin pans, and hope. Most were Americans, but they came from abroad as well. California, with only a sprinkling of American farmers before 1848 (when Mexico ceded it to the United States), had an influx of 6,000 newcomers by the end of the year. In 1849 some 35,000 came by sea and perhaps 45,000 more by the overland route, many in covered wagons. By 1850 California's population was 96,000, larger than Delaware's.

Sutter's estate was overrun and his Mexican land grants challenged. Intruders camped on other farms and estates, with small regard for ownership or titles. Sacramento grew from just four houses on Sutter's land to a bustling community of almost 10,000 people within a few months in 1849. San Francisco was converted from a quiet port town to a roaring metropolis. Men left farms and industries to seek gold; abandoned ships, some converted to hostelries, dotted the bay. Those familiar with the ways of the sea signed on to whaling crews in the East, then deserted when the ships arrived at Pacific ports for refitting. Eventually entire crews, including the officers, left the whalers to join the gold rush.

Anyone with anything to sell could usually do better than most of the miners. Coffee went for $4 a pound, flour for $400 a barrel, old New York newspapers for $1 a copy. A lawyer was offered a cave dug into a hillside as an office for $250 a month, and a large canvas tent rented for $40,000 a year.

Before the clipper ships arrived, the sea voyage from the East around the Horn took as long as eight months, while those willing to take their chances crossing the pest-ridden Isthmus of Panama could make it in two months. Most of the sea trade was monopolized by the Pacific Mail Steamship Co., which ran ships to Panama along both coasts and charged $600 for the full trip. Vanderbilt decided to cut the price in half, and trimmed 600 miles from the journey by crossing at Lake Nicaragua. He put four steamers on the Atlantic side, with one leaving New York every two weeks, five on the Pacific side, and had smaller side-wheelers on Lake Nicaragua and the San Juan River. This trade netted him more than $1,000,000 a year, and when he sold the route to the Transit Line in 1853, he told a friend that he had invested $11 million in a way that would bring him a risk-free return of 23 per cent.

More than half a billion dollars in gold was taken out of California in the first five years after the discovery, and the West Coast was transformed—more by the new industry and agriculture that developed than by the quick wealth from the yellow metal. Other effects were more far-reaching. Gold bullion and coin became more common, and many who were never before able to fathom banking and credit gained a new understanding through this tangible symbol of wealth. The silver dollar, worth close to $1.01 in gold with the change in the mint ratio to 16:1, became even more valuable as gold streamed in from the West. The Subsidiary Coinage Act of 1853 lowered the silver content of the half dollar, quarter, dime, and half dime, so that they were worth more as coins than as metal, and for a short period these coins became more plentiful than they had ever been.

Not many forty-niners hit it rich, or even remained miners, but the strike fired the imagination of many people, and prospecting parties roamed the West. Carson City, Nevada, was founded in 1858, when gold deposits were found there, and a rush developed to Colorado when gold was discovered near Pikes Peak. But the Colorado gold, embedded in quartz, had to be worked with heavy machinery, requiring sizable capital. More than $300 million in gold came out of Cripple Creek. Gold was discovered on the Nez Perce Indian reservation in Idaho in 1860, and other gold finds led to the founding in Montana of Alder Gulch, Virginia City (where 10,000 came in 1864), and Helena, the last boom town of the period. Silver discoveries were similarly rewarding. More than $300 million worth came out of the Leadville, Colorado, mines, while the Comstock Lode, near Lake Tahoe, led to the formation of the Nevada Territory and eventually yielded $340 million in silver.

Less glamorous minerals were obtained largely in the East and Midwest in this period. The Galena district of Illinois and Wisconsin produced considerable quantities of lead in the last half of the decade of the 1840's. Copper had been found in scattered locations, including the Ducktown area of Tennessee and Georgia, but the richest copper deposits were in Michigan's Upper Peninsula, which was producing three fourths of the national output by 1860. The rich iron ores of Minnesota, which were one day to become the backbone of the nation's production, were exploited with the opening of the St. Mary's Canal in 1855, but by 1860 they still provided less than a tenth of the national pig iron output.

Coal, perhaps the least romantic of all the minerals, continued to grow in its importance to the economy.

It had become, by the 1850's, the chief cargo for coastwise sloops on the Atlantic, for Ohio River flatboats, and for boats on all the ocean-bound canals south of the Erie. It accounted for more than 40 per cent of the Pennsylvania Railroad's tonnage in 1856. Bulk cargo for lake, river, and canal craft was also provided by stone, lime, sand, and gravel, most of it destined for nearby markets, while marble and granite were quarried in Vermont and brownstone in Connecticut.

Corporations moved into many of the extractive industries. Most of these corporate enterprises were organized during the years of the Civil War to mine coal, iron, and metals, although the Delaware, Lackawanna & Western Railroad began to mine coal for sale as early as 1851.

Liquid wealth from the earth first turned up in appreciable quantities in Pennsylvania. Petroleum oil had been known for centuries but was not deemed a very useful commodity. Indians daubed themselves with it where it seeped to the surface in Venango County, along Oil Creek, a branch of the Allegheny. Early settlers used it as medicine, as a lubricant, and for illumination. But the raw product, when burned, gave off more smoke than light and more foul odors than heat.

Oil was often found during drilling for salt wells. When David Beatty drilled a 170-foot well for salt in eastern Kentucky in 1818, he abandoned it after it brought a flow of petroleum—the first flowing oil well. In 1845 oil was struck in a salt drilling near Tarentum on the Allegheny River thirty-five miles above Pittsburgh. Samuel M. Kier, a successful Pittsburgh businessman, believed it had medicinal properties, and began to sell the bottled product, first from wagons, later from drugstores, as "rock oil."

The oil was studied by a number of doctors, who thought it might have medical possibilities, and by chemists in this country and abroad, who saw in it other uses. In 1855 a Yale chemistry professor, Benjamin Silliman, Jr., reported in a study of petroleum that it was a good lubricant and could provide a better and cheaper illuminant than any product on the market. Later that year Silliman was made president of the Pennsylvania Rock Oil Company, with a stock authorization of $300,000. Nothing much happened until one of the key stockholders got Edwin L. Drake, a former New Haven Railroad conductor, to look over the company's properties near Titusville, Pennsylvania, and to commence drilling operations there.

Drake went to work. When water began percolating from the nearby river through the porous soil, he got the idea of using an iron tube to encase his well. Boring and drilling went on slowly, and the directors of the company, as well as of a successor company, got tired of sinking capital into it and gave up the venture. Drake managed to get financial help through friends in Titusville. On Saturday, August 27, 1859, drilling was halted at sixty-nine feet, for the customary observation of the Sabbath. On Sunday afternoon someone noticed a dark fluid in the tubing, tied a string to a tin water spout, let it down the well, and brought it up filled with petroleum.

The well was soon producing 1,000 gallons a day. But there were immediate problems of marketing, transportation, and refining. As fast as these were solved, new difficulties appeared, and finally a disastrous explosion destroyed virtually all the installations above ground. By the time these were replaced the following spring, rival companies were in high gear and producing so much oil that the price collapsed. By the end of 1860 there were an estimated 2,000 wells and borings in Pennsylvania, with a daily production of 1,165 barrels of crude oil.

In a few years the marketing and distribution systems had developed to the point where they could absorb all the oil that was produced. Additional strikes were made all through the adjoining country, and the flourishing new industry became the subject of a giant wave of speculation. The thirty-eight-acre Egbert and Hyde farm along Oil Creek, purchased in 1859 for oil exploration, was not developed until 1864, and the output turned out to be fabulous. It soon had flowing wells that brought an estimated $6 million to the owners within a year. A one-twelfth interest in the Coquette, a 600-barrel-a-day producer, went for $200,000. People lined up in Philadelphia to buy some of the 50,000 shares, offered at $10 each, in the Maple Shade well, producing 1,200 barrels a day. Before long, the shares sold for $44 each.

Yet all this was no more than a microcosm of what the American petroleum industry would one day become.

INTERNAL TRANSPORTATION

At one time or another, Americans tried virtually every known device to make transport smoother, quicker, and cheaper. Plank roads, an idea imported from Russia by way of Canada, had a surge of popularity from 1845 to 1855. Inexpensive to build ($1,000 to $1,800 per mile) and easy to travel (a horse "seemed more in a gay frolic than at labour" on one of the roads, wrote a Canadian editor), the plank roads enjoyed a heyday in which some 7,000 miles were built as toll roads by private companies. But when the wood tended to rot and maintenance costs proved too high, the roads gradually disappeared.

A fast parcel-delivery service, first set up between Boston and New York in 1838, was extended westward, city by city, until it reached the Pacific Coast by 1858. Owned by the William F. Harnden organization, it was merged into Adams Express Company in 1854. Monthly stagecoach service between Independence, Missouri, and Salt Lake City, Utah, started in 1850, followed by a more erratic service from Salt Lake to Sacramento. In 1858 the government awarded a contract to John Butterfield to carry mail to California from Memphis and St. Louis. William H. Russell, of the freighting firm of Russell, Majors and Waddell, organized the Pony Express in 1860 to carry mail by relays of horseback riders from St. Joseph, Missouri, to Sacramento in ten or twelve days, compared to sixty days by stagecoach. It proved to be a

A consignment of stagecoaches leaves the factory of Abbott, Downing Company in Concord, New Hampshire, in 1868, bound on

money-loser, however, and the company, which had once operated some 6,000 wagons, went into bankruptcy and was sold to Wells, Fargo & Company.

But the important contributions to national commerce were those made first by canals and later by railways. By 1840, with the great era of canal-building virtually ended, there were 3,326 miles of canals in the United States. While no new major canals were built thereafter, large amounts of money went into improving and enlarging those in use. The reconstruction of the Erie Canal in 1853–54 cost $44.5 million, more than five times its initial cost. By 1850, however, more miles of canals were being abandoned than were being built.

Canals nevertheless continued to carry large quantities of bulk freight, and as late as 1860 their total volume was about equal to that of the railroads. And even while rail freight rates dropped steadily, haulage costs on the canals were lower still. In the 1850's, rates on the Ohio and Illinois canals ranged from 1 to 1.4 cents per ton-mile, while the Chesapeake and Ohio Canal charged as little as .25 cent for coal and as much as 2 cents for more costly goods. Railroad rates varied widely by district and by commodity, but their trend was steadily downward. Average rates for New York State railroads ranged from 5 to 9 cents a ton-mile in 1848, but were down to 4 cents by 1851 and 2.2 cents by 1860.

In the 1840's and 1850's the railroads came to be recognized not just as a means of serving business and commerce generally, but as important enterprises on their own. When soundly operated, they could be made to yield good profits to the owners of securities in their rather imposing capital structures.

The railroads, moreover, provided the sole or major support for a number of other businesses, and spurred the development of technology in many areas. Quite a few shops went into locomotive building, but in time they tended to concentrate at Paterson, New Jersey, and in Philadelphia, where the Baldwin and Norris plants, two of the earliest, were located. Onetime watchmaker Matthias W. Baldwin made higher steam pressures possible, devised the sand box for better braking, put cabs on locomotives, and helped eliminate the look of "a cook-stove on wheels." Geared to complete an engine a week, his plant had turned out 1,500 locomotives for American and foreign railroads by the time he died in 1866.

The early rails were made of wood covered with iron straps. Under the weight of trains, the straps tended to come loose, curl up, and break through the floor of cars as "snake-heads," presenting a major hazard to passengers. On a locomotive buying trip to England, Robert L. Stevens, president of the Camden and Amboy Railroad and son of steam pioneer John Stevens, whittled out a T-shaped rail cross-section; he ordered iron rails made to this design in England and installed them on his line. The Savage Iron Works in Maryland began making these iron rails in 1844, and fifteen U.S. mills were producing 45,000 tons of them by 1850. The T-rails became standard for American railroads, and they were required in New York State as early as 1847.

Engineering for railroad construction itself was of a high caliber, and many of the basic principles developed in this period are deemed valid today. Peter Cooper's "Tom Thumb" had set out to demonstrate that a locomotive could handle curves. Others later

flatcars for Omaha and Salt Lake City, where Wells, Fargo put them into use between populated centers in the West.

showed that it could haul a train up steep grades without slipping. Negotiating rough terrain, spanning valleys and waterways, and tunneling through mountains became the work of many outstanding engineers—Moncure Robinson, who pioneered route locations; Benjamin H. Latrobe, Jr.; George Washington Whistler; William Gibbs McNeill; and bridge-builder John A. Roebling.

The 3,328 miles of railroad in the United States in 1840 grew to 8,879 during the depressed 1840's and to 30,600 during the more prosperous 1850's, more than any other country in the world. Serving mainly as feeder lines for canals and natural waterways before 1840, the railroad network soon began to develop an independent identity. Briefly, Boston was the leading rail center of the country, with connections to New York, Albany, Montreal, and Portland, Maine. But New York State, with 1,300 miles, had the most track by 1850, as well as the first line linking tidewater with the Great Lakes and thus the water basins of the West. But it had its shortcomings. Although continuous, it was made up of the trackage of sixteen different companies, requiring the payment of separate freight tolls and transfer when the gauge of the tracks changed.

In 1851 the first trunk line to the West was opened when the Erie completed its line through southern New York to Dunkirk on Lake Erie. In a burst of expansion over the next few years, the Pennsylvania was completed to Pittsburgh; the Baltimore & Ohio to Wheeling; the Illinois Central was built from Chicago to Cairo, Illinois; and the New York Central was organized into a single system running to Buffalo. Railroads crossed the Mississippi into Texas, Arkansas, and to St. Joseph on the Missouri River, and southern lines reached up from Atlanta and Mobile to join the transportation systems of the Northwest. By 1860 the railroads stretched to St. Louis, New Orleans, Memphis, and Milwaukee. Chicago, junction point for about a dozen lines, had become the hub of the nation's rail traffic.

All this cost far more money than any single industry had ever required in America. The investment totaled almost $300 million in the 1840's, another $840 million in the 1850's. It was a time for testing the abilities and the nerve of large-scale financiers, as well as speculators, promoters, and market manipulators. Not often heard or widely heeded was such counsel as that offered by William Sturgis, former China merchant turned railroad director, who advised his road to avoid debt, to buy no property it could not use, and to use profits for price cutting rather than large dividends.

Because a railroad needed great amounts of capital—the Baltimore & Ohio cost around $15 million, the Erie $25 million, and the New York Central $30 million—most railroads were organized as corporations, in order to provide the broadest possible base for financing. Cities, counties, and states contributed an important share of the total investment, principally to underwrite the development of local lines, especially where the risks were high. Once the memory of panic, repudiation, and bankruptcies had died away, the financial and banking communities were able to sell sizable quantities of railroad securities in the East and abroad. Fully 26 per cent of all oustanding American railroad bonds, but only 3 per cent of their stocks, were held in foreign hands by 1853, and by 1857 there was perhaps $300 million in foreign money invested in American railroads.

Railroad stock in many cases was widely held. The New York Central had almost 2,500 stockholders in 1853, and the Pennsylvania, largely financed through door-to-door sales, had even more. Stock was often issued in payment to construction companies, and it was not too difficult for an astute speculator or manipulator to gain control of a railroad by acquiring its voting shares. In and on the fringes of the financial community there developed a coterie of specialists in corners, pools, bear raids, and similar tactics.

Cornelius Vanderbilt displayed a special knack for these activities. When he pulled out of shipping at the start of the Civil War, he was prepared to sink into railroading the $3 million for which he had sold his fleet, but backing this up was the rest of his $20 million fortune.

Urged to become a director of the Harlem Railroad by Charles W. Sanford, its counsel, Vanderbilt consented to buy into it if Daniel Drew would join him. He began buying its stock when it was selling at less than 10 in the winter of 1862–63. When the New York Common Council authorized the line to build a street railway down Broadway, the stock shot up to 75 and then to 100. Vanderbilt was elected president of the road. Then he got wind of the fact that some of the council members who had passed the ordinance were selling the stock short. The more they sold, the more he bought. The ordinance was rescinded, and the stock plunged to 72. But when the short sellers tried to cover their commitments by buying the stock, the price zoomed right back up again. It turned out that more stock had been sold than the 110,000 shares in existence, and Vanderbilt and his cronies, who had been doing all the buying, had it cornered. They settled at $179 a share, ruining the councilmen and netting millions for Vanderbilt and his associates.

No one knew better than Vanderbilt and his fellow operators that no special virtue attached to the mantle of public office, and that it was not uncommon for elected officials to enrich themselves from their positions. Senators Thomas Hart Benton of Missouri and Stephen A. Douglas of Illinois, even while they were helping to give 25 million acres of public lands to the railroads, were themselves speculating in both

The Baltimore & Ohio Railroad spanning the junction of the Potomac River (left) and the Chesapeake & Ohio Canal on a combined highway and railroad covered bridge at Harpers Ferry, Virginia, in 1857

railroad securities and western lands. The La Crosse & Milwaukee Railroad was given 1,000,000 acres after it had handed out to a long list of Wisconsin state officials, including the governor, $900,000 in its securities—which became worthless when the road went bankrupt two years later.

Vanderbilt's next venture was in the Hudson River Railroad, which he wanted to merge with the Harlem. He began buying the stock at 25. When he got the legislature to authorize the consolidation, the stock went up to 150. Some of the legislators, like the councilmen scenting a fast profit, began to sell the stock short. As they sold, Vanderbilt bought. When authorization of the merger was repealed, the stock dropped to 90. The lawmakers decided to hold out for 50, but the stock went down no further. Vanderbilt and the members of his pool kept on buying and, because of the short interest, were able to buy up 27,000 more shares than the road had outstanding. The Vanderbilt group, deciding finally on a price of 285, again made a killing.

As long as their adversaries were financially unsophisticated and the prizes were relatively small, the operators could feel as though they were matched against sitting ducks. Eventually, however, they would be pitted against each other, and the consequences would rock the financial world.

Another factor that would separate the big boys from the little ones were the great consolidations that would bring the small lines together into sprawling systems that represented huge capital investments. Just before and during the Civil War, such major lines as the Pennsylvania, the Lehigh, and the Erie were buying up smaller roads. During the decade of the 1850's, there were twenty railroad combinations in Ohio alone. The first line to join Lake Michigan with the East Coast was the Pennsylvania, when it acquired the Pittsburgh, Fort Wayne & Chicago Railroad. A single system finally linked New York and Chicago by 1860, but Boston and Albany were not similarly connected until after the war.

Construction, limited during the war, included the Philadelphia and Erie, between Philadelphia and the new oil fields, and the Atlantic and Great Western, which stretched the Erie system to Dayton, Ohio, and, with the Ohio and Mississippi, connected St. Louis and New York with tracks of uniform gauge. All this activity notwithstanding, there were still hundreds of small, independent lines, still a variety of different gauges of track, and vital links missing from the overall network.

Railroads also found a new kind of market as city populations expanded. By 1860, New York had more than 1,000,000 people, and eight cities had more than 100,000. Carrying passengers on their streets were horse-drawn carriages and omnibuses, charging fares that ranged generally from 6 to $12\frac{1}{2}$ cents. In New York, some of these coaches moved on steel rails,

129

growing from one line in 1832 to five in the 1850's. But perhaps the most significant move was that of the Boston and Worcester Railroad in 1838, when it sold an annual ticket to a commuter. By 1843 the line was operating a commuters' train, and in 1857 it was carrying almost 500,000 passengers a year to Boston from within ten miles of the city.

VALUE ADDED

Only 4 per cent of the nation's people were engaged in manufacturing just before the Civil War, but they were responsible for an impressive amount of production. The value of manufactured products crossed the $1 billion mark in 1850. By 1860, while prices had climbed about 11 per cent, manufactures increased about 86 per cent, to $1.886 billion. The amount of capital employed had similar growth, from $533 million in 1850 to over $1 billion in 1860, while the number of establishments was up to only 140,000 from 123,000,

indicating that the individual firms were getting bigger.

The leading manufacturing industries, in terms of the value of product, were flour and meal, $249 million; cotton goods, $107 million; lumber, $105 million; boots and shoes, $92 million; men's clothing, $81 million; iron, $73 million; and smaller amounts for leather, woolen goods, machines, and carriages and wagons. Perhaps more significant than product value, however, was the total value added by the manufacturer, since that reflected his contribution and was therefore more pertinent to his profit. On the value-added scale, cotton goods ranked first, at $55 million, followed closely by lumber, $54 million. Then came boots and shoes, $49 million; flour and meal, $40 million; men's clothing, $37 million; iron, $36 million, and the others.

For those businesses that managed to survive, profits were generally high, although differences in accounting procedures make them difficult to compare with later periods. Iron manufacturing was a feast-or-

WALT WHITMAN'S AMERICA

In 1844 Ralph Waldo Emerson called for a poet of the people—a poet who would sing America's praises. He received his response five years later when an obscure political writer named Walter Whitman was fired by the Brooklyn *Eagle* for supporting Martin Van Buren's comeback bid as President on the Free Soil ticket.

Whitman shortened his name to Walt, opened the collar of his blouse to show his red flannel undershirt, and donned a floppy felt hat. It was a robust image, and it was borne out in the exuberance of the blank verse that he began publishing under the title *Leaves of Grass.*

Whitman's poetry reflected the America of his day. In the decade of the 1850's, the population grew from 23 million to 31½ million. Farm production more than doubled, the value of manufactures increased almost as much, and railroad trackage tripled. In 1856 Whitman wrote that the number of inventions listed by the U.S. Patent Office in one week "illustrates America and American character as much as anything I know." There was an ebullient mood to the land, and Whitman strove not only to express it but also

Whitman of the Brooklyn Eagle, *1846*

to embody it.

In his "Song of the Broad-Axe" (1856), he exulted in the spirit of an America that was creating and building:

The shapes arise!
Shapes of factories, arsenals, foundries, markets,
Shapes of the two-threaded tracks of railroads,
Shapes of the sleepers of bridges, vast frameworks, girders, arches,

Shapes of the fleets of barges, tows, lake and canal craft, river craft. . . .
The tools lying around, the great auger and little auger, the adze, bolt, line, square, gouge, and bead-plane. . . .

Whitman rhapsodized also about the rich resources of the nation and about the inventiveness and creativity of Americans who used them productively:

Interlink'd, food-yielding lands!
Land of coal and iron! land of gold! land of cotton, sugar, rice!
Land of wheat, beef, pork! land of wool and hemp! land of the apple and the grape!
See, in my poems, cities, solid, vast, inland, with paved streets, with iron and stone edifices, ceaseless vehicles, and commerce.
See, the many-cylinder'd steam printing press—see, the electric telegraph stretching across the continent,
See, through Atlantica's depths pulses American Europe reaching, pulses of Europe duly return'd,
See, the strong and quick locomotive as it departs, panting, blowing the steam-whistle,

famine business, with earnings ranging from 10 to 25 per cent of invested capital in many years and as high as 40 to 60 per cent during the boom years of the 1850's, while failures were common during depression periods. Textile profits were more stable. The Appleton Company, which started in 1829, paid an average of 8 per cent in dividends over the next fifty years; dividends of the Merrimack Company averaged 12 per cent from 1822 to 1850, and Lowell's Middlesex Mills paid dividends averaging 12 per cent from 1830 to 1860.

While the gains in manufacturing output were impressive, some much more significant events were taking shape on the industrial landscape. Industry was just beginning to work out the new processes, the techniques, and the methods that would change not only its scope but its very character, mainly by adding more value to the product. There were a number of contributing forces.

For one thing, invention became a kind of national passion. When the Commissioner of Patents reported in 1850 that more than 17,000 models had piled up, Congress voted funds to add two wings to the Patent Office. No less imposing a figure than Abraham Lincoln received a patent for "a device for buoying vessels over shoals and sand bars."

For another, the use of interchangeable parts and a continuous flow of production, pioneered by Eli Whitney and Oliver Evans, continued to gain in favor, abetted by the development of precision machinery and finer measurements. Machine shops became adept at making taps, dies, and gauges. In 1851 J. R. Brown of Providence introduced the vernier caliper, which made possible measurements to a thousandth of an inch by an ordinary workman. The manufacture of locks adopted interchangeable elements and precision tools, and Linus Yale brought out the Yale Infallible Bank Lock in the early 1850's. Clocks and watches were made by similar principles; the first mass-produced American watch was being made by the Waltham Watch Company by 1850, and the National Watch Company of Elgin, Illinois, was organized in 1860. Fine firearms were such an advanced art in the United States that two of Britain's most vaunted weapons, the Enfield rifle and the Armstrong gun, were developed by Americans.

Yet another factor was the development of improved industrial machinery. The textile industry was generally using metal machines after 1835. George Henry Corliss brought out a steam engine with rotary valves in 1849, leading to the reciprocating engine that was widely copied in this country and in Europe. The manufacture of machine tools—machines to make machines—became a separate industry. Stephen Fitch built a turret lathe in 1845, and within ten years it was being produced commercially by Robbins and Lawrence of Windsor, Vermont. About the same period, Niles Brothers of Cincinnati was producing machine tools, as well as locomotives and steam engines. Pratt & Whitney, the precision machinery firm, was organized in 1860 by Francis A. Pratt and Amos Whitney, who met when both were working at the Phoenix Iron Works in Hartford, Connecticut.

The period before the Civil War was notable for a number of discoveries and developments that achieved a new level of sophistication—vulcanized rubber, vacuum food canning, the Kelly-Bessemer steel process, the sewing machine—but whose chief industrial consequences would not appear until years afterward.

Charles Goodyear was hopelessly insolvent when he became interested in rubber in 1834, and soon afterward he was put in the Philadelphia Debtor's Prison. But with the help of friends, tolerant prison officials, and his wife's rolling pin, he continued his experiments there. Five years later, in a "hot stove" accident in his wife's kitchen, he discovered that rubber heated with sulfur would hold its elastic character through

---

*See, the ploughmen ploughing farms—
    see, miners digging mines—see,
    the numberless factories,
See, mechanics busy at their benches
    with tools—see from among them
    superior judges, philosophs, Presidents, emerge, drest in working
    dresses . . . .*

"Whitman," wrote Henry David Thoreau, "is apparently the greatest democrat the world has seen." Yet he was never as popular with the people as Longfellow. Whitman wrote on more themes than invention and industry, but his profound appreciation of human enterprise echoed an American credo: work is creative.

During the Civil War he served as a volunteer hospital aide, but even that tragic struggle did not dampen his enthusiasm for the achievements of his fellow countrymen. In his 1865 poem "Years of the Modern," he wrote:

*Never was average man, his soul, energetic, more like a God,
Lo, how he urges and urges, leaving the masses no rest!
His daring foot is on land and sea everywhere, he colonizes the Pacific, the archipelagoes,
With the steamship, the electric telegraph, the newspaper, the wholesale engines of war,
With these and the world-spreading factories, he interlinks all geography, all lands . . . .*

wide ranges of temperature. But friends and former investors had turned skeptical; he moved from town to town in New England, barely scratching out a living, accepting the charity of friends, developing his process, and seeking financial backing. He did not even patent his discovery until 1844. He next mixed the gum with cloth fiber to make India rubber cloth. In all, Goodyear took out sixty patents related to rubber and saw his inventions applied in an industry that turned out $8 million worth of products, including $5.8 million in India rubber goods. But the rewards eluded him, and he died a poor man in 1860.

The preservation of meat and other foods by sterilization and packing in airtight glass and tin cans went all the way back to the 1820's, but later technologies began to make foods easier to keep and transport. A can-making machine was invented in 1847. In the 1850's Gail Borden perfected a process of preserving milk through evaporation in a vacuum; during the Civil War, the government took over all canned milk supplies. The glass industry was given a considerable boost in 1858, when a patent was obtained on John L. Mason's screw-top jar, a major contribution to home canning of fruits and vegetables.

By 1860, consumption of iron in the United States had increased fivefold over a fifty-year period to approach 120 pounds per person per year. Mineral fuels had virtually replaced all bog ores, and nearly all smelting was done in coal furnaces that used a hot air blast. But perhaps the industry's most important development—using a blast of cold air to remove carbon from the iron—was not in use at all in this country, even though it was first discovered here.

William Kelly was a metallurgical tinkerer who built his own furnace when he found rich hematite ores on the ground near his home in Eddyville, Kentucky. Acting on the suspicion that pig iron contained its own fuel, he blew cold air through the molten metal and saw it become hotter as the oxidizing carbon flew off in a shower of sparks. When he announced his discovery that cold air could heat iron, his wife naturally sent for the doctor. The doctor, of scientific bent, thought Kelly had a good point. But most people, siding with Mrs. Kelly, thought him mad, and he withdrew into the forest to continue his experiments in secret.

That was in 1846. He made small headway over the next decade. In England, meanwhile, Henry Bessemer made the same discovery, independently, in 1854, and he patented both the process and the large tilting ladle, known as a converter, in which it could be carried on efficiently. In 1856 Bessemer sought an American patent, but Kelly proved that he had got there first and was awarded the patent. That same year Robert Mushet in England further developed the process by "recarbonizing" the iron through the subse-

J. PARTON, *History of the Sewing Machine, 1867*

Five seamstresses (rear) race Howe's sewing machine in 1845.

quent addition of spiegeleisen—pig iron that contains carbon and manganese, giving it a near mirror shine.

England was soon producing fine Bessemer steel, the superiority of which was demonstrated for railroads with the sale of rails to the Midland Railway in 1857. But American manufacturers were embroiled in quarrels over the patents. Alexander Holley bought the exclusive American rights to the Bessemer process and converter. But American rights to the Kelly and Mushet processes were held by Captain Eber B. Ward, who made the first commercial Bessemer steel in America at his Detroit plant in 1864, and the first steel rails at his Chicago rolling mill in 1865. In an eventual settlement with the Holley interests, Ward and his associates got only a 30 per cent interest in the consolidation. Meanwhile, the Civil War was fought without the benefit of Bessemer steel.

Another man with an inventive obsession was Elias Howe, who put his mind to the problem of building a practical sewing machine. An Englishman named Thomas Saint had patented one fifty years earlier, and a Frenchman, Barthélemy Thimonnier, had eighty machines working on army uniforms until the needle workers of Paris destroyed them. The principle of the lock stitch had been discovered by an American, Walter Hunt, who built a machine and then unaccountably abandoned the project. There is no reason to believe that Howe had ever heard of any of these when he, too, got the idea of a machine that could make a lock stitch—a kind of weaving stitch. Financed by an old schoolmate, George Fisher, Howe built first one model, then another, and patented his machine in 1846.

After investing $2,000, Fisher gave up on the

machine when no buyers for it could be found, and Howe went off to England to follow some promising avenues. When one venture there fell through, Howe got some money from an acquaintance, Charles Inglis. He sent his family back to America and booked passage in steerage to follow them in 1848. Back home, he discovered that a number of people were making and selling sewing machines, infringing on his patent. Far from becoming his undoing, these transgressions proved the key to his success. Much better businessmen than he, they had improved on his machine and were building flourishing enterprises around it.

The best of these businessmen was Isaac Merrit Singer, who built a sturdier machine, operated by a foot treadle, and was promoting and marketing it aggressively. Howe filed suit against the infringements, and Singer fought back by joining forces with Hunt and claiming prior development of the lock-stitch machine. Howe won the suit in 1854 and began collecting royalties from Singer and the other firms that had entered the field, most notably Wheeler & Wilson and Grover & Baker. Two years later, after much squabbling about patents, these manufacturers and Howe formed a patent pool known as the "Combination," which received royalties.

Howe eventually became a wealthy man, getting as much as $4,000 a week in royalty fees. But it was Singer who built the business to major proportions, bringing the machine within reach of the poor by means of installment sales, and pushing his itinerant sales force toward the realization of his slogan, "A machine in every home."

Unlike most other producing machinery, the sewing machine tended to decentralize industry by lending itself to home manufacture and thus promoting the putting-out system for ready-made clothing, which increased in overall value from $40 million in 1850 to more than $70 million ten years later. Shoemakers also used the sturdily built Singer machine to sew leather. Rapid expansion of the boot and shoe industry was helped by the high-speed McKay machine for sewing uppers to soles.

By 1860 the sewing machine industry had a capital of about $2.5 million, and the year's production amounted to 116,000 machines, valued at $5.6 million. There were 3,000 salesmen selling the machines at home, and many others, notably Singer's, hawking them around the world; more American machines were being sold in Europe than in the United States.

The Singer sewing machine and the McCormick reaper had much to do with drawing attention abroad to American industrial products. But other manufacturers were also eager to display their wares at international fairs and expositions. At London's great Crystal Palace Exhibition in 1851 top awards and medals were given to Charles Goodyear for India rubber products, to Gail Borden for a special meat biscuit, to Blodgett and Lerow of Boston for their sewing machine, and to Colt, to Palmer, and to Robbins and Lawrence for their firearms. The McCormick reaper, after a spectacular demonstration at a nearby farm, drew more visitors than the Kohinoor diamond. American businessmen were not slow in turning these plaudits into overseas sales.

SPINNING THE WIRE WEB

The telegraph moved quickly from scientific phenomenon to novelty to profitable business. Pioneer Samuel Morse brought in Amos Kendall, a former U.S. Postmaster General, as president of his Magnetic Telegraph Company. The Magnetic's first line was between New York and Philadelphia. In 1846 this was tied in to the original Baltimore–Washington wire with a new Philadelphia–Baltimore link. Eventually a lease arrangement extended the wire system as far as New Orleans.

Competition appeared very early. Because the capital requirement was small, and financing—including door-to-door stock sales—was easy to obtain, new lines began to spring up everywhere. By the early 1850's the growing Morse system was being challenged by rivals everywhere, and by 1854 two other major systems were vying for industry leadership. One was Cyrus Field's American Telegraph Company, which fought some pitched battles with Magnetic in its effort to take over the East Coast network of lines. The other was Hiram Sibley's Western Union (known earlier by the unwieldy name of New York & Mississippi Valley Printing & Telegraph Company), which started as a small line in 1851 but soon began to expand by taking over other lines in the Midwest and drawing up exclusive contracts with railroads.

Field, a successful New York merchant who had retired at the age of thirty-five, got into overland telegraphy by a back door. His brother, Matthew, an engineer, had met Frederick N. Gisborne, who wanted to extend the existing telegraph system, which then reached to Halifax, Nova Scotia, by laying an underwater cable across the Gulf of St. Lawrence from New Brunswick to St. John's, Newfoundland. Matthew Field brought in his brother Cyrus, who looked at a map, decided that the project was too unambitious and that he would be interested only if the cable were laid across the Atlantic to Ireland. With a group of business associates, Field organized the New York, Newfoundland & London Electric Telegraph Company, capitalized at $1.5 million, with Peter Cooper as president. Field brought together a group of technical experts that included Naval Observatory chief Matthew Maury in oceanography and the Scottish professor William Thomson in instruments, and he flattered Morse into giving up his patent rights by naming him honorary electrician.

To make their project a business success, the Field group knew they needed telegraphic access to New York and other American business centers. So they organized the American Telegraph Company to bring into their system, principally by lease, key lines from Newfoundland to New Orleans. Both Morse and Kendall were eager to bring their lines into the American Telegraph system, and terms for leasing Magnetic Telegraph were negotiated in 1857, but American then mysteriously withdrew. It turned out subsequently that Sibley had undermined the negotiations by planting seeds of suspicion about Magnetic's good faith. Magnetic fought back by leasing other lines, including the Western Telegraph Co., to compete with Western Union, and supported a rival underseas cable project to Europe, via Greenland. Finally, late in 1859, a settlement was reached that tied together the leading telegraph interests of the nation.

Meanwhile, after several unsuccessful attempts,

Field's ocean cable had been laid, and a signal had been flashed from Valentia, Ireland, to Trinity Bay, Newfoundland, but the cable was not yet reliable enough for commercial use. In what had been perhaps the most conciliatory gesture yet made to its former colonies, the British government in 1856 had offered a subsidy of $70,000 a year to the cable project, and had given its blessing to the Atlantic Cable Co., which was co-operating with American Telegraph. The goodwill gesture came full circle when the U.S. Congress matched the subsidy, and both governments offered ships from their naval fleets. The transatlantic cable did not start successful operations, however, until 1866.

More than any other single factor, the telegraph gave the nation a sense of its wholeness and extent, and began to inject a hint of national interest where local and regional concerns had long predominated. Of more than 4,000 publications in the United States, including more than 3,000 newspapers, the 1860 census noted that over 80 per cent were "political in their character."

"YANKEE, SIR—YANKEE"

The year 1851 focused international attention in England on products made in different countries; it turned out to be a triumphal year for the American inventor and producer.

The full salvo of triumphs came at the "Great Industrial Exhibition," held that year at London's Crystal Palace. In what was proclaimed as "a tournament of industry," American participants got off to an unhappy start. Because of a scarcity of funds, many of the spaces allocated to American exhibitors stood unused. Those who did exhibit found themselves the butt of early ridicule because of an unfortunate cardboard eagle that hung over their displays. There was, moreover, a plethora of worthy native produce on exhibition—Indian corn, cotton, preserved peaches, tobacco, and maple sugar—but fewer manufactured products than most of the other participating countries displayed, and the United States won only a modest share of the top awards.

But if the judges applied one set of standards—based more on aesthetic than pragmatic considerations—the fair-goers used another. It was soon

evident that the crowds were fascinated with the mechanical ingenuity demonstrated by the American products. They pored over things they had never seen before—a solar compass, an alarm barometer, a bell telegraph, a hot-air furnace, an artificial leg, waterproof India rubber clothing, and various machines to press, lathe, sew, bind books, and plane wood. The clicks of Colt's revolving pistols were a constant sound as thousands examined the American firearms. It moved *Punch* to comment:

Oh! Colonel Colt
A Thunderbolt
I'd buy—for no small trifle;
But that can't be,
And so let me
Get your revolving rifle!

As the exhibition continued, American products received more and more attention. "Formerly," wrote the London *Daily News*, "the crowds used to cluster most in the French and Austrian section, while the region of the stars and stripes was almost deserted —now the domain of Brother Jonathan is daily filled with crowds of visitors." The interest in the American displays was finally noted, too, by the influential London *Times*, which declared in

M'CORMICK'S REAPING AND MOWING MACHINE,
(OF WHICH 50,000 HAVE NOW BEEN MADE IN THE UNITED STATES) WITH HIS NEW
PATENT AUTOMATIC SHEAF DELIVERY ATTACHMENT.

INTERNATIONAL HARVESTER CO.

Advertisement in England for the American hit of the Crystal Palace exhibition

A total annual circulation of 928 million copies, more than double that of ten years earlier, testified to their widespread readership. The formation of the Associated Press in 1848, and the subsequent increasing use of the telegraph, helped bring to these readers important world and national news not long after it happened.

Both railroads and the telegraph had reached St. Joseph, Missouri, on the Missouri River, by 1859, and Hiram Sibley was pushing the idea of extending Western Union the remaining 2,000 miles to the West Coast. By 1862 the wires were up all the way to San Francisco.

During the Civil War, the two major telegraph companies, Western Union and the American Telegraph Company, were challenged by a newcomer, the United States Telegraph Company, which was responsible for the construction of 13,000 miles of line between 1861 and 1865. But by the end of the war Western Union controlled twice as many miles of wire as the other two companies put together, and a few years

later it had acquired 66,000 miles of the nation's 73,000-mile web of telegraph lines.

ON BORROWED TIME

With only the briefest of interruptions, the period from 1843 to 1857 was the most prosperous the nation had known up to that time. Flushed with high profits and the expectation of even greater gains, businessmen—and much of the rest of the nation—momentarily pushed political differences aside, and the election of 1852 was dominated by a spirit of don't-rock-the-boat.

As wages and prices kept rising, people grew accustomed to the jingle of money. The nation took on the look of affluence; construction projects transformed the raw earth; old buildings came down in the cities to make way for newer and grander ones; New York got the world's most expensive hotel when the St. Nicholas was rebuilt at a cost of $2 million.

As in most times of rising expectations, a lively and healthy spirit of discontent seethed in some quarters. There was a revival of trade unionism and flurries of strikes. National unions were formed, and the strongest were able to survive the economic setback of 1857. The ten-hour-day movement made some headway, especially among the scarcer skilled workmen. Workers in some Massachusetts mills managed to get an eleven-hour day, and the women cotton mill operators in western Pennsylvania got a ten-hour day, but only at the cost of a 16 per cent cut in pay. Horace Greeley's *Tribune* in 1851 printed a $10.37 weekly budget for a family of five, and two years later the *Times* followed with a $12 budget, but both figures were out of the reach of all but the most skilled and sought-after workingmen. Co-operative societies of both producers and consumers enjoyed a boom from 1845 to 1860, after which the movement subsided. But German immigrant Joseph Weydemeyer, chief spokesman for Karl Marx in the United States, was able to drum up little response from workers in the 1850's.

One obstacle to collectivist ideas was that there were too many capitalists around. The number of corporations in the country doubled in the decade, and trading in stocks and bonds was more widespread than ever. Owner-managers who had to pay close attention to their own businesses expanded into other fields, such as railroads, by the simple expedient of putting some surplus profits into securities. Many men of lesser means—farmers, tradesmen, and professionals—were lured into the market by rising prices, and a few mill workers put their little hoarded savings into the stocks of their employers' enterprises.

Even those who had no desire to participate in the speculative binge had their savings channeled into the securities market through savings banks and insurance

September: "It is beyond all denial that every practical success of the season belongs to the Americans. Their consignments showed poorly at first, but came out well upon trial. Their reaping machine has carried conviction to the heart of the British agriculturist."

This reference was to a demonstration of McCormick's reaper, which had cleared a field at Tip-Tree Farm in Essex, gathering grain from seventy-four yards in seventy seconds, a rate that would reap twenty acres a day.

The Crystal Palace exhibition gave a historic boost to American exporters. Nine years later, the English author Charles Reade echoed the opinion of many persons outside the United States when he remarked that "American genius is at this moment ahead of all nations in mechanical invention." Americans, he noted, patented new products at a faster rate than the British and were selling abroad many of the products of their inventiveness. Indeed, he pointed out, his own shirt was sewn on a Singer machine, most of his newspapers were printed on American Hoe presses, and when he walked on the Liverpool docks and inquired about the nationality of the smartest-appearing ships, the reply always came back, "Yankee, sir—Yankee."

companies. Savings banks, originally a device to help the poor stay off relief during bad times, were gradually taken over by business managers; their total deposits rose from $7 million in 1835 to $43 million in 1850 and $150 million in 1860. Insurance had an even more spectacular growth. Life insurance, totaling less than $10 million in 1840, reached a coverage of $180 million, with $7 million in annual premiums, by 1860. Fire and marine risks, reflecting the rising tempo of business, reached almost $3 billion.

Within their limitations, commercial banks, too, oiled the flow of money into securities. To encourage banking competition, New York State passed a Free Banking Act in 1838, under which banks were granted charters without special legislation, and note issues were protected by having the bank deposit securities with a public group. It was so successful that other states tried to copy it, and it became a model for the National Banking Act of 1862. But similar laws in Michigan, Indiana, and Wisconsin seemed only to encourage unsound and dishonest "wildcat" banking, while state-owned banks in Alabama, Mississippi, Kentucky, and Illinois were just as unsatisfactory. An 1842 law requiring reserves of specie and short-term paper helped the Louisiana banks weather the financial storm of 1857. The following year a Massachusetts law was passed requiring a 15 per cent reserve against all notes and deposits, and this also became part of the National Banking System established in 1862. New York became the only central reserve city under that act, thus giving official recognition to a financial leadership that was already a fact.

But the chartered corporate banks neither could nor would meet all the demands for funds generated by the wave of speculation. So private banks, with virtually no legal or operating restrictions, moved into the void. Private banking grew rapidly, especially in the investment field, in the 1850's. As brokerage houses, private banks took over much of the trading in securities already on the market; as commission dealers and invest-

AN 1851 BUDGET FOR FIVE PEOPLE

YALE UNIVERSITY PRESS

Horace Greeley

As one of America's most influential newspaper editors, Horace Greeley of the New York *Tribune* was full of advice, and he imparted it to the nation at every opportunity. "Go to the West," was perhaps his most famous injunction. But he also had plenty to say about business and economics.

In a lecture to students at Cooper Union, he defined success in business. He singled out the wealthiest men of his day and, reminding his audience that in America status and education were not prerequisites for success, pointed out that John Jacob Astor was an orphan and Cornelius Vanderbilt had started his career with a single sailboat.

Broad education ("many-sidedness," he termed it) was an advantage. But he particularly urged persistence, frugality, and the recognition of the value in money of one's time. Like Benjamin Franklin and Walt Whitman, he believed that it was good business to provide the greatest good for the greatest number. He counseled the students "to satisfy some decided want in a more convenient and economical manner than it has been hitherto subserved." Implicit in his advice was the belief that business had a philosophical justification: it helped mankind. He ended with a criticism that underscored his message. "We are energetic," he said about the American people. "We are audacious; we are confident in our capacities and in our national destiny; but we are not a systematic, a frugal, economical people."

On that point he had more to say in the columns of his newspaper. In 1851 he estimated the needs of the average skilled workman and four dependents and proposed this weekly budget for them:

Barrel of flour, $5, which will last eight weeks . . .	$ .62
Sugar, 4 lbs. @ 8¢	.32
Butter, 2 lbs. @ 31½¢	.63
Milk	.14
Butcher's meat, 2 lbs. beef a day	1.40
Potatoes, ½ bushel	.50
Coffee and tea	.25
Candle light	.14
Fuel, 3 tons of coal per year, $15; matches, etc.	.40
Salt, pepper, vinegar, starch, soap, soda, yeast, cheese, eggs	.40
Household articles, wear and tear	.25
Rent	3.00
Bedclothes	.20
Clothing	2.00

Greeley, quite naturally, added twelve cents a week for newspapers and came up with a total of $10.37 a week for a family of five. It was high for most workers, since only blacksmiths, machinists, engineers, and skilled building tradesmen earned as much as $12 a week at that time. But Greeley felt that by following his budget, every workingman could eventually make his way upward on the economic ladder.

ment bankers, they handled a large share of the issuance of new government and corporate securities. Early leaders in the field included Brown Brothers & Co., E. W. Clark & Co., Astor & Sons, and Nevins, Townsend & Co., followed later by Drexel & Co., Jay Cooke & Co., and the wartime influx of banking houses with English and German connections—J. P. Morgan, Jacob Schiff, the Seligmans, and L. P. Morton.

The rapid increase in securities trading spurred the development of stock exchanges as central market places. The New York Stock Exchange had been organized by a meeting of brokers in the old Tontine Coffee House back in 1817, but trading at first averaged no more than 100 shares a day, and the first 1,000-share days did not come until the 1830's. Transactions were handled by members of the Exchange board, which met behind locked doors from 10:30 A.M. to 3 P.M. Outside on the street, however, there was another market for securities. When the Exchange board was not in session, the members, along with other brokers and traders, would assemble conspicuously at fixed locations in the financial district. An early location for this "curb" market, which eventually became the New York Curb Exchange and then the American Stock Exchange, was at the corner of Wall and Hanover streets; later it moved to William Street.

The board of the old Exchange operated almost like an exclusive club, admitting new members on payment of a $400 fee if they had been in business in Wall Street for at least a year, were "at peace with all the world, or . . . have satisfactorily settled all just obligations," and had fewer than three black balls cast into a box in the balloting. The curb market was organized as a rival institution in the mid-1830's by a small group of outsiders, most of whose members were admitted to the New York Stock Exchange board in 1848.

Listings on the New York Stock Exchange consisted mainly of railroad securities, along with a few mining and gas lighting companies. Until the Civil War, the stocks of industrial companies were important only on the Boston Stock Exchange. Grain dealings centered in the West, where the Chicago Board of Trade was organized in 1848. Trading in wheat "futures" began in 1855, making it possible for farmers to shift the risk of future price changes to specialized dealers.

Fueled by the great expansion of money and credit, much of it channeled toward New York, the fires of speculation burned brightly. The supply of hard money climbed from $90 million in 1843 to $186 million in 1851 and to $283 million in 1862. Bank notes rose even more rapidly, from $59 million in 1843 to $155 million in 1851 and $301 million in 1866. Total money in circulation, which had averaged $7.87 per person in 1843, was up to $31.18 in 1865.

All that loose money, coupled with an almost complete absence of regulation or controls, made fraudulent operations irresistible to some. Stocks were watered, forged, and sold without authorization. The Harlem Railroad's secretary, Alexander Kyle, enriched himself by selling $300,000 worth of forged stock, and the New Haven's president, Robert Schuyler, took the $2 million proceeds from sales of stock in his railroad. There was a short-lived financial panic in 1854, when the discovery of these and other frauds frightened money out of the market, but the ebullient spirit of speculation soon returned.

Manipulators busied themselves even in the hallowed confines of the New York Stock Exchange. John Ward, along with Jacob Little and Daniel Drew, cornered the stock of the Morris Canal & Banking Co. as early as 1835, the first indication that the Exchange could not always guarantee a free market. Gold was a favorite target of the larger operators during the war years, and gold exchanges were organized when banks and the federal government suspended specie payments. Petroleum and mining shares also came in for much speculative activity, and forty-one brokers organized the Mining Board of New York in 1864. There were a few fly-by-night exchanges: the Coal Hole, with low membership fees, was set up in a dark basement in 1862; Goodwin's Room based its operations on stock quotations relayed from a keyhole watcher at the New York Stock Exchange.

A new type of credit instrument, the call loan, was developed especially to facilitate trading in securities. With New York the great center of trade and liquid capital, small banks all over the United States and Canada found it useful to leave demand deposits, against which they could draw drafts at any time, in New York. They were encouraged by a number of New York banks that paid interest on deposits by other banks. To keep these funds busy, banks and brokers lent them out to stock traders, holding the purchased stocks as security. This created a "margin" purchase, with the bank advancing most of the money for the transaction, and the stock buyer putting up the rest, an amount that could be regarded as the lender's margin of safety.

The call-loan market became extremely active as stock speculation increased, and rates for the loans were quoted in newspapers. Banks found them attractive because, backed by securities, they constituted a kind of reserve, so they felt they did not need to hold specie. Moreover, the securities tended to grow more valuable in the rising market. Call-loan rates were generally lower than those for time loans, and call loans could usually be obtained at a price when money was tight and other loans were unavailable. It was a brand new way of doing business, feeding on itself by encouraging even more stock trading.

The national mood of optimism was in good part sustained by the visible signs of growth and progress.

137

Factories were being built and expanded, minerals were coming out of the earth, telegraph lines were going up, railroads were being constructed, and vast quantities of goods were being moved by railroads, canals, and ships at sea. But many of the new projects were premature in time or place, and when they failed to show the expected profits, confidence waned. By the summer of 1857 railroad stocks were 45 per cent below their 1853 peak, and banks that had loaned funds on such collateral were growing nervous. The sources of capital began to dry up.

On August 24, 1857, the New York branch of Ohio's leading bank, the Ohio Life Insurance and Trust Company, shut down. News soon followed of a huge embezzlement by the bank's cashier, and the parent bank closed, triggering a panic in the nation's financial

Harper's Weekly, 1857

The 1857 panic in Wall Street, depicted in Harper's Weekly

markets. Western banks began to demand their deposited funds, and there were runs on the New York banks. Stock prices dropped, and banks began to call in their collateral loans. When stocks could not be sold fast enough to protect the margins, the weakness of the call-loan system became apparent. The entire economy was vulnerable to a crisis in the market for securities. Themselves the center of the banking system, the New York banks had nowhere else to turn.

The easiest way to bring about a temporary increase in credit was to suspend specie payments, which most banks had done by October. Industrial plants closed, and wages stopped. Much of the nation's business was paralyzed. The Erie, Illinois Central, Michigan Central, and Reading railroads failed. More than 5,000 other business failures involved total liabil-

ities of almost $300 million.

James Buchanan, who had taken office as President just a few months earlier, reaped the unhappy harvest of bad times. Hundreds of thousands of unemployed, with no resources, were given poor relief. Tens of thousands rallied at protest meetings, or roamed the streets calling for "bread or blood."

The depression was probably as deep as any the nation had suffered, but, possibly because the panic was more one of timing than of underlying substance, it did not last long. Most banks had resumed specie payments by early 1858. The wheels of commerce and industry soon began turning again. Before Lincoln came to the White House in March, 1861, the nation was in the midst of a new wave of prosperity and indulging in a resurgence of speculation.

THE OTHER ECONOMY

Buoyed by growing demand and generally good prices for cotton, the South had a prosperity of its own. It also had an economy of its own, so different from that of the North and West as to make it seem almost another nation.

Grown to an area that may have measured as much as 400,000 square miles, the cotton kingdom imposed on the South a near feudal economic and social system, much more akin to the agrarian life of colonial times than to contemporary life elsewhere in the United States. The great argument in cotton's favor was an imposing one—it was the keystone of the nation's foreign commerce. Cotton shipments abroad in the year ended June 30, 1850, totaled $72 million, just under half of the nation's export dollars; by 1860, cotton accounted for $192 million in exports, or considerably more than half of the total of $334 million.

But cotton hurt hardest those who loved it most— the people of the South. Years of high prices brought good profits that were soon reinvested in more land and more slaves. Low prices—and anything under eight cents a pound often resulted in losses—meant that cotton farmers and planters had to borrow to carry themselves into the next season. In either case, there was little of the liquid capital that gave northern businessmen their maneuverability.

What capital there was in the South went largely into local improvements, and about $237 million had gone into building 9,500 miles of southern railroads, just under a third of the nation's total. There were some major lines that tied in with the rest of the national transportation system, but for the most part the South's railroads were built simply to haul plantation produce to tidewater, and lines were often not connected with each other.

In spite of the impassioned pleas by those who sought to reform the economy of the South, manufacturing was slow to develop. Manufacturing capital in the southern states amounted to $96 million in 1860, out of the national total of $1 billion, while the South's industrial product was valued at $156 million, which was less than 8 per cent of the whole nation's output. Lumber, tobacco, flour, and meal were the region's chief manufactured products, and some beginnings had been made in producing iron, machinery, and cotton goods. William Gregg had demonstrated that slave labor could be used economically in cotton manufacture, and eastern capital was showing some interest in Virginia and Carolina cotton and woolen mills. Transplanted New Englander Daniel Pratt exhorted his fellow Alabamians to turn their attention from talk of secession to action in building commerce and industry. But not much came from either the pleas or

the 1840's. The thorough records of Farish Carter, also of Georgia, showed that his $150,000 investment yielded no more than 1.25 per cent in 1851.

The underlying reason may well have been that the slave economy itself had built-in inefficiencies. It was still true in America, as it had been since the earliest colonial days, that a higher premium was placed on human labor here than elsewhere. With these high labor costs, the escape valve for most producers was better production methods—improved machinery and more efficient techniques—to make their businesses less dependent on human work, i.e., to make them capital intensive rather than labor intensive.

But the plantation economy could not do this, because the slaves were a form of capital, rather than labor. The price of slaves was controlled largely by

At a Providence, Rhode Island, wharf, cotton from the South is transferred from ship to rail for transport to mills in New England.

the example of these and men like them. Many in the South made much of the fact that the cotton economy had come through the 1857 panic unscathed.

In the sense that they were large and complex producing units, the big plantations were the South's factories. The hundreds of slaves included large numbers of production workers—the field hands—as well as such specialists and skilled artisans as carpenters, drovers, watchmen, coopers, tailors, millers, butchers, shipwrights, engineers, dentists, and nurses. The owner not only had to deal with production and marketing, but also had to provide the living necessities for all these people, and this involved quantity purchasing.

For the most part, the plantation factories were not very efficient. Profits of the well-run Hopeton plantation in Georgia were under 4 per cent during most of

the cost of free labor, and rose from an average of $250 in 1815 to $700 in 1860, and from $500 for "prime field hands" in 1800 to as much as $2,000 in 1860. It was all but impossible to get from them the greater productivity that would justify the higher costs of these "capital goods."

Aside from the outrage to basic humanity, slavery was also an affront to the nation's fundamental economic beliefs. It was already an article of faith in America that progress grew out of opportunity and incentive, that people would be most productive if their thought and labor would be of value to themselves—in short, if they owned their own human capital. That this had nothing to do with skin color was clearly evident from such examples as William T. Johnson, a free mulatto of Mississippi who opened a barber shop and

139

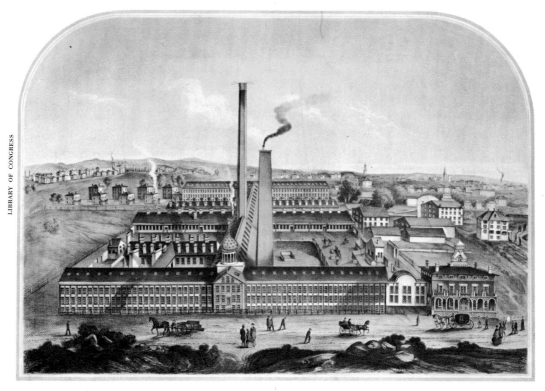

The Colt Patent Arms plant at Hartford, Connecticut, on the eve of the Civil War

soon had two more, along with a bathhouse, a plantation, and other real estate, and who conducted a profitable business lending money to whites.

Because of the high costs of slave capital, the value of land—the other major form of southern capital—was low, even though southern crops were worth more than $20 an acre and those of the North less than $10. Agricultural land in the South had an average value of $5.34 an acre in 1850, compared to $6.26 in the Southwest and $11.39 in the Northwest.

The extent of the problem was coequal to the extent of slavery. There were 3.2 million slaves, making up about a third of the South's population, in 1850. Of the 2.5 million engaged in agriculture, almost three fourths worked on cotton plantations. Although all the numbers increased by 1860, the proportions changed little.

But very few whites, even in the South, actually owned slaves. The 1860 census showed that 384,000 southern whites, fewer than 5 per cent, held slaves, and almost three fourths of these had fewer than ten. Fifty or more slaves were owned by 10,781, and 100 or more by 1,733—the large-plantation elite. But while millions of poor whites had no direct economic interest in slavery, the tenant farmers and back country "rednecks" felt threatened by abolition, both socially and in the possible economic competition that would ensue. Even resenting the power and privilege of the handful of wealthy landowners, the impoverished hill dwellers were ready to defend their system fiercely. For support

they could point to such respected names as Calhoun, Professor Thomas R. Dew of William and Mary College, and Thomas Carlyle, who asked rhetorically, "Would you turn out slaves, like horses, to graze? . . . Every man is created to work, some at menial tasks, some at higher callings." Carlyle disregarded the fact that Britain had freed all her slaves in 1834.

Like feudal barons, the leading businessmen controlled both the economic and political life of the South. Of $110 million in personal income for the section, $50 million, or almost half, went to just 1,000 families, while the remaining $60 million was spread thinly among 666,000 families. The Hairstons had 1,700 slaves on plantations in three states, and Georgia's Howell Cobb had 1,000. Joseph Davis, brother of Jefferson, and the Aikens of South Carolina were millionaires. The ruling cliques could hand-pick men for political office, they dominated the churches, and they applied the brakes to forces of social change. Fully aware of the extent to which their economy rested on slavery, they were determined to keep that unconscionable institution in their social structure.

Among the strongest supporters of this southern aristocracy were the businessmen of the North and West. Although many among them were strongly abolitionist in sentiment, most were more inclined to keep the peace and maintain the status quo—that is, the level of the nation's and their own prosperity. They strongly endorsed political compromise. New York merchants set up a Union Safety Committee to propagandize on behalf of the South. The Boston *Courier* suggested a boycott of those who sought to violate the Fugitive Slave Act, and in April, 1861, on the eve of war, the New York *Journal of Commerce* was calling for peace.

In some cases there were more than just business ties, since many wealthy families tended to intermarry without regard to sectional boundaries. Jefferson Davis married the daughter of a former New Jersey governor. The Roosevelts were related to the Barnwells of Charleston, South Carolina. Even Illinois Senator Stephen Douglas was married to an heiress who owned a Mississippi plantation with 100 slaves.

THE BUSINESS OF WAR

As far as most businessmen were concerned, the start of the Civil War meant the same thing to them as had the wars of the past: they lost money. The $300 million that was owed by southerners to northern merchants was chalked up as a total loss. Cotton factories and ships were idled. The needs for cash squeezed the banks, and this meant a repetition of the now-familiar pattern of panic and depression. The Dun reports recorded almost 6,000 business failures involving $500 or more in 1861, more than in the still vividly remembered 1857–58 collapse. Except in New Orleans, southern banks suspended specie payments for the duration. Northern banks did not suspend until December, 1861, and the government soon did the same. Metal currency went into collectors' hoards. Economic ties with the South affected many of the western wildcat banks, and more than 80 per cent of the 110 banks in Illinois failed.

But better times were soon on their way for northern businessmen. Their interests well represented in Congress and the national administration, they were awarded lucrative contracts for war materials and supplies. In March, 1861, the Senate passed J. S. Morrill's tariff act, designed to restore rates to the 25 per cent average of the Walker Tariff of 1846; by 1864 duties were averaging 47 per cent. Even with the new agricultural machinery, western farmers could scarcely meet the demands for their grain, particularly when European harvests were disappointing in the early 1860's. The West got its matching prizes with the Homestead Act, which gave 160 acres of public land to anyone who would work it for five years, with a potential 70 million acres for the western railroads, and with the Morrill Act, giving the states thousands of land-grant acres for colleges "in agriculture and the mechanic arts." By 1863 a war boom enveloped almost all types of enterprise in the North.

Wars change their faces with the cosmetic of new technologies. And technology had made unprecedented advances in the fifty years since America had last fought a major war. The Civil War was destined to be the first whose outcome would hinge largely on metals, machines, chemistry, and the logistics of procurement and supply. In most or all of these respects, the North had unassailable superiority.

To start with, the North had 22 million people, against only 9 million in the eleven seceding states, and a great many more northerners were equipped with technical and mechanical abilities. The South produced only about a fourth of the nation's wealth, concentrated in products that were useful chiefly as exports. The pig iron output of the nation in 1860 totaled around 860,000 tons, of which the South produced only 26,000. Virginia provided a microcosm of the warring forces. When the predominantly secessionist General Assembly at Richmond voted to join the Confederacy in May, 1861, a convention of northwestern Virginians at Wheeling voted to secede from the secession, and formed the new state of West Virginia. The chief products of the old state were tobacco and slaves, both raised for sale to other states. But the area of the new state produced iron, coal, oil, and machinery, and the businessmen of West Virginia were soon prospering with wartime orders for their goods.

While northern generals were displaying their ineptness on the battlefronts during the early years of the war, industrialists showed adeptness on the home front. The cities undertook their production tasks with vigor. Philadelphia, the largest manufacturing center, built fifty-eight new plants in 1862, fifty-seven the following year, and sixty-five in 1864. The North had three cannon factories in 1861 and built four more in the next two years. The small-arms production of the government armory at Springfield, Massachusetts, was augmented by that of private firms, including the highly automated and efficient Colt Patent Arms plant at Hartford, Connecticut. When England balked briefly at shipping Indian saltpeter that Lammot Du Pont had purchased, he developed a method for using sodium nitrate in its place to make gunpowder.

The South, meanwhile, scratched and scraped for its needs. Lead pipes were melted down for cartridges, and brandy stills became copper percussion caps. Where northern mills went to work making shoes with new machinery and set looms and sewing machines humming on army uniforms manufactured from smuggled cotton and vastly increased wool supplies, the South pulled out its hand looms and spinning wheels in a backward technological march toward home industry. Belatedly the South set out to create industry under the capable leadership of Josiah Gorgas. The government awarded contracts to the large Tredegar Iron Works in Richmond, subsidized the construction of new plants, and set up its own arms and munition factories. But so laggard was their production of rifles and ammunition that thousands of pikes were ordered, to be used if other weapons were unavailable.

Both sides misjudged the course the war would take at the start. The North underrated the determination and fighting spirit of the southerners. And the South counted heavily on help from Europe, which they felt was heavily dependent on their cotton. It turned out that cotton managed to get through the embargo in some quantity, and that Europe was just as eager to get northern grain; wheat exports climbed from 20 million bushels in 1860 to 60 million in 1862.

The South was also hard put when it came to financing its side of the war. The Confederacy sold bonds and issued notes, as did many of its states, cities, and even private businesses. In 1863 the southern congress voted internal taxation, but no significant amounts were ever raised from this source. As more notes were printed, backed only by a government in rebellion, they dropped in value. Early in 1864 a new Confederate act called for either exchanging the old notes for new ones on a basis of $300 worth of old for $200 of the new or turning them in for 4 per cent bonds. This served to undermine the credit of the government even further. By the end of the war the South had issued $2 billion worth of paper, all of which became worthless.

With most of the nation's wealth, the North had a clear advantage in financing its part in the war. The tariff had traditionally been the source of funds for government operations, and the Morrill tariff did provide some additional revenues. A 3 per cent income tax, the first in the country's history, was passed in 1861, and was gradually increased until it reached 10 per cent on incomes of more than $5,000 in 1865, when internal revenues provided the government with twice as much income as the tariff.

But like the South, the North generally shunned taxation as a means of raising funds, mainly on the theory of Treasury Secretary Salmon P. Chase that wars should be financed on borrowed funds and that taxes should be increased only to cover service on the new debt. Most of the needed money was borrowed. In February, 1862, Congress authorized a new kind of note to be issued against the general credit of the United States; unlike previous government notes, these would be issued in small denominations, would bear no interest, and would be legal tender — that is, they would have to be accepted in payment of debts, and would thus circulate as currency. The original authorization was for $150 million, and the eventual total of "greenbacks" — so named because of the characteristic green ink used to print the back side — reached $450 million.

The great bulk of the war's costs, however, was raised through the sale of bonds, and the great government bond salesman of the period was Jay Cooke. Affable, outgoing, optimistic, Cooke had served a mixed apprenticeship with a St. Louis merchant, as an advertising writer and salesman for a packet company, and as a clerk with the domestic exchange house of E. W. Clark & Co. He grew with the firm, becoming its leading partner before leaving to start his own private bank, Jay Cooke & Co. The successful sale of a $3 million Pennsylvania loan brought him to the attention of the national government.

Cooke was twice asked to act as agent for the sale of government loans after banking syndicates had failed to dispose of them — the "five-twenties" of 1862 (so named for the years until redemption) and the "seven-thirties" (for the 7.3 per cent interest rate) of 1865. Instead of simply seeking out big investors, as other banks did, Cooke set up a national organization of banks, insurance companies, and individuals as agents and subagents for the sale. Backing them with newspaper advertising, posters, handbills, and publicity, Cooke combined the appeals of economics with patriotism. In this way he managed the successful sale of more than $1 billion worth of bonds, earning for himself only a small commission that barely covered his expenses. But his real gain came in the growth of his reputation and in the widespread banking connections he made.

In all, the war was estimated to have cost the North more than $4 billion, and the direct and indirect costs to both North and South probably amounted to $9 billion. This was three times as much as the slave property of the nation had ever been worth, it was pointed out by Special Revenue Commissioner David A. Wells, and the value of slave output in its best years was less than half of the interest this sum would yield "to the end of time."

A less visible cost of war was the price inflation that came in the wake of rising government debt and printing-press money. Labor, which had been doing pretty well before the war, soon began to feel the pinch and, encouraged by the manpower shortage, called a number of successful strikes. On the army's insistence, a government order forbidding strikes was issued in 1864. Although wage rates had risen by an average of about 60 per cent during the war, prices were up even more, and many a salaried white-collar worker experienced drastically reduced living standards.

Northern businessmen, meanwhile, suffered under no such handicap. Output had risen in virtually every industry, and so had profits. With more liquid capital, greater production capabilities, and a reopened southern market for its products, industry looked to a future brimming with promise. Perhaps most important of all was the fact that business, united in purpose and direction, had at long last broken the agrarian stranglehold over politics and now had its own strong voice in the halls of government.

IV   *The Wealth of the Land*

A new frontier is opened: John Steuart Curry's version of settlers rushing to stake land claims in Oklahoma Territory, 1889

"America is a wonderful country, endowed by the Omnipotent with natural advantages which no other can boast of. . . . The wide expanse of territory already occupied—the vast and magnificent rivers—the boundless regions, yet remaining to be peopled—the rapidity of communication—the dispatch with which every thing is effected, are evident almost to the child. . . . We must always bear in mind the peculiar and wonderful advantages of *country*, when we examine America. . . . it is the *country*, and not the government, which has been productive of such rapid strides as have been made by America. . . . There is room for all, and millions more."

Captain Frederick Marryat, *Diary in America*, 1839

Since colonial days the rivers and falls of the United States have inspired Americans by their beauty and power. Also since the time of the first settlements men have been harnessing them productively with water wheels, dams, levees, and other structures—and, sadly, polluting their waters. The spectacular waterpower of Niagara Falls, depicted awesomely by an unknown artist of an earlier century (left) was first utilized (by a ditch that diverted some of the water) in 1757 for a sawmill. Kentucky Dam (above) is one of the many electricity-producing components of the vast T.V.A. project.

Open-pit mines have provided the nation with many of the basic resources for industrial growth. With little concern for reclamation, however, they have despoiled large areas of the land and have challenged a more socially conscious industry of the 1970's to eradicate the scars they create. Left: nineteenth-century coke ovens at Henry Clay Frick's Pennsylvania coal mines. Below: Kennecott Copper's mine at Bingham, Utah

The great mines of Minnesota's Mesabi Range have been the main source of iron for America's huge steel industry since the 1890's. Above: the Mesabi mine of a U.S. Steel subsidiary in the 1930's. Below: after the California gold rush, more substantially capitalized (and destructive) hydraulic mining replaced the slower methods of the small prospector. The scene is at Nevada City in the 1870's.

147

The lure of land that was free, or almost so, drew waves of settlers westward from one frontier to another, dispossessing the Indians and creating "breadbaskets" that fed the world. Above: hillside combines on a northwestern wheat farm in 1908

At Hutchinson, Kansas, above, grain elevators (an American innovation) have a combined storage capacity of 27 million bushels. Below: a pioneer turning the sod for the first time on a homestead on the Great Plains near Sun River, Montana, in 1908

Dry, barren lands and lush, verdant forests alike have contributed to America's production. Above: the huge Columbia Basin irrigation project in Washington State. Right: oxen in an earlier day haul logs from the California woods on a corduroy road.

Many businesses were built on the products of America's seemingly inexhaustible wildlife. Beaver pelts supplied world fur markets, and buffalo robes, meat, and bones found many commercial uses. By the 1880's the animals were almost gone, and the industries they had supplied were history. On the plains, cattle, seen below in the Chicago stockyards, had replaced the buffalo. Still to come were the oil booms, like that in 1918 near Wichita Falls, Texas (opposite), where buffalo had also roamed.

"WHAT A FALL WAS THERE, MY COUNTRYMEN!"

5

UNBRIDLED
FREEDOM

1865-1890

North and South, torn apart by war, were not brought much closer together by the silencing of the guns. What separated them, as it had before, was perhaps fifty years of industrial progress.

The northern soldiers streamed back to their humming cities, villages, and farms. Nearly a million of them were absorbed into the economy with scarcely a ripple of disruption. But the cream of southern manhood slogged back on foot to stricken cities and devastated plantations, finding present prospects dim and future hopes not much brighter.

The North was making sure that the South should savor fully the bitter dregs of defeat. Savings that had been patriotically invested in Confederate and state bonds and notes were wiped out. Some $2 billion in the human capital of slavery had to be written off the books. The South's small prewar banking capital, about $85 million, was gone. A punitive federal cotton tax drained $68 million of the region's slim resources.

High postwar cotton prices offered hope of revived fortunes to a few. But where there was once slave labor, there now had to be cash for wages. Marketing crops was often prohibitively difficult in the disorganized region, with many railroads virtually stripped of their rolling stock. The tax of three cents a pound was another crippling barrier. Small wonder that many a former plantation owner gave up his almost worthless land to seek out the better prospects of the cities.

With the surrender at Appomattox Courthouse in April, 1865, and the end of organized resistance the following month, all restrictions on trade with and within the South were removed by a series of executive orders. The Mississippi River was reopened to traffic, and all southern ports to trade, by mid-year. Business relations were resumed, and people moved freely in both directions. Some southerners came North to find better opportunities; even more northerners moved South to buy plantation land at bargain rates. But when they tried to cash in by raising cotton, they were defeated by the difficulties of producing and marketing the crop.

Where capitalism could not work, there was a return to a feudal economic system—sharecropping. The planter rented out parts of his land to those who would farm it—both poor whites and former slaves—getting a third to a half of the crop in return. The owner would furnish tools and seed, borrowing against his part of the crop from a merchant or banker. And the tenant would borrow for living needs, giving a lien against his share to the local storekeeper. A poor crop or low prices could then ruin everyone—landlord, sharecroppers, and merchants. Those who sought to diversify their plantings and escape from the one-crop economy were frustrated by the lenders, who knew there would always be some kind of market for cotton and were reluctant to advance funds against other crops.

Even so, the South managed to make a recovery, in part by producing more cotton than ever and in part by branching out in other directions. The cotton crop equaled its prewar peak in 1877 and continued to grow thereafter. Tobacco, too, was soon setting new production records; other familiar crops—sugar cane, rice, and corn—contributed to the recovery. There were major advances in southern pine lumbering and

Thomas Nast's cartoon for Harper's Weekly *on* Wall Street's Black Friday crash in *1869, which followed the attempt of Jay Gould and Jim Fisk to corner the nation's gold*

in the production of turpentine. Railroads were rebuilt and new lines laid, but not as rapidly as in the rest of the country.

By the 1880's enough local capital had been accumulated to finance manufacturing enterprises. With the power of the Piedmont rivers harnessed and with labor plentiful, a major textile industry grew up in the Carolinas and Georgia. So fast were new machines installed that southern cotton manufacturing rose from scarcely 5 per cent of the nation's total in 1880 to more than half by 1910. As mill towns sprang up, parts of the South began to look like New England. In Tennessee and Alabama, plentiful coal and iron ore led to the establishment of iron and steel plants. And Birmingham, which did not even exist when its site was designated as a proposed railroad terminus in 1871, was soon the roaring Pittsburgh of the South.

Yet America's great postwar outpouring of energy and enterprise came not in the South but in the North and West. The war itself had helped lay the pattern.

The closing of the Mississippi had meant that more western farm produce had to go by rail. The unslakable demands of armies for supplies and of farms for machines had led to expanded factories and to ever greater production capacity. There had been a high tariff and a new national banking system, and the massive issues of government bonds and greenbacks had helped create liquid capital that gravitated to the large pools in New York and Philadelphia.

The war's end proved no interruption, but a spur, to the expansive thoughts of American businessmen. Having demonstrated their productive prowess, they were ready to move on to greater things. The war had spawned dozens of millionaires, and many were eager to add to their fortunes by tapping the great resources and markets of the nation. It was a time for builders and doers and pragmatists. In a kind of call for relevance in education, Harvard professor Jacob Bigelow in 1867 saw less need for teaching dead languages and more for such fields as science; he urged colleges to

DARWINISM IN BUSINESS

In the years after the Civil War, the freebooting nature of much of American business and industry lacked nothing but moral justification. It was an age of uninhibited exploitation and cutthroat competition, and Calvinist attitudes no longer sufficed to explain and excuse what was happening. The English philosopher Herbert Spencer filled the gap with writings that won ardent acceptance in the United States.

Spencer had speculated on the evolution of the human race before Darwin published his *Origin of Species* in 1859. But where Darwin limited his investigations to biology, Spencer applied the fundamental principles of evolution to society. His was a thesis of "social Darwinism," which stated that, in the struggle for existence among men, survival went to the fittest.

Applied to economics and business, the message was clear: the fittest had to become the wealthiest. The less interference in an individual's affairs, the lesson also stated, the less interference with the operation of nature's laws. It was an argument for laissez-faire government, since, according to Spencer, free competition was not only desirable, as Adam Smith had contended, but was a requirement of nature that would

tolerate no obstruction.

Industrialist Andrew Carnegie claimed that Spencer was his only idol, explaining that when he read Spencer's *First Principles*, published in 1862, "light came as in a flood and all was clear." Spencer himself might have replied, "Why not?" All was simple and obvious to him. "I am never puzzled," he once announced. He was an engineer who had designed railroads and bridges, and he appealed to practical men. Cool and self-taught, he had read almost no philosophy before he turned philosopher at the age of thirty. His cosmos was mechanical, deterministic, and inevitable—a mechanism of matter and motion, no more metaphysical than the 2,500-horsepower Corliss steam engine that was the wonder of the 1876 Centennial Exposition in Philadelphia.

Many a businessman used Spencer as an argument against governmental regulation and the rise of unions. Tinkering with the workings of nature was bad. Besides, if survival of the fittest was the law, what survived must be inherently good. And if the elite through free competition created combines, trusts, and monopolies, so be it for the progress of America.

The irony of this "law of the jungle"

was that it was used to justify the conduct of American economic life just when big business, with considerable help from the government, was most active in throttling free competition. If its processes had been carried to their logical limits, it would have meant the survival of the most ruthless businessmen and of virtually no one else.

Spencer's philosophy nevertheless bolstered the freedom of businessmen on many fronts. They used his arguments about the uselessness of strikes, pointing out that if workers constantly won increases in pay, the rise in prices would eliminate their gains. His thesis on the survival of the fittest also supported the businessmen's stands against such impositions as the graduated income tax. "There shall not be a *forcible* burdening of the superior for the support of the inferior," he ordered in 1867. He was not against charity, however, since it would improve the morals of the fittest.

As a philosopher for business, Spencer fell into disrepute even before his death in 1903. Excesses brought on demands for reform, and a new generation finally perceived that the nation's well-being could not stand the social injustices that resulted from a jungle concept of business. But Spencer's credo never wholly died and continued, even through the New Deal era, to have influence in American business life.

"adapt themselves to the wants of the place and time in which they exist."

The demographic ground swells that the nation had known from its start were accelerated. More people were moving from farms to towns and cities, from agriculture to industry, from East to West. In 1860 there were 6 million working on farms, 4 million in other occupations. By 1880 there were fewer farm workers than nonfarm workers, and by 1900 the pre-Civil War proportions had been more than reversed. The mobility of people was matched by that of industry. The center of manufacturing moved 225 miles westward between 1850 and 1890, from a spot near the center of Pennsylvania to one southwest of Canton, near the center of Ohio. The 1890 census showed that industry had replaced agriculture as the chief source of wealth.

Markets for goods, which had been predominantly local or provincial before the war, were now becoming regional and even national. The railroads had much to do with this, as they reached across the continent. From 1867 to 1873 about 33,000 miles of track were laid, more than the total trackage in 1860. By 1880 railroads totaled 93,261 miles, and 167,191 by 1890. Much of the capital—probably more than half—for this unprecedented expansion came from abroad, and more than $1 billion from public funds. By 1900 rail investments reached nearly $10 billion. Railroad issues dominated the securities markets, representing the bulk of the New York Stock Exchange's listings right up to the end of the century.

Stock trading, which reflected the exuberance and optimism of the times, was given greater immediacy by technology. In 1867 the Gold and Stock Telegraph Co. built a workable stock ticker and installed it in a broker's office. More than 100 subscribers signed up for the service within a few days, and other ticker companies soon offered competing products. The successful completion of the transatlantic cable in 1866 added an international dimension to daily stock transactions, giving rise to the arbitrage business, in which profits could be made from price differentials between countries by simultaneously buying at the lower quotation and selling at the higher.

Interest in industrial stocks developed as expanding industries required more capital and got much of it through stock issues. Between 1860 and 1900 there was a tenfold increase, to $10 billion, in the amount invested in manufacturing. Largely because of stepped-up trading in industrial shares, the New York Stock Exchange had to add more space in 1887. Industrials proved less stable than the rails, with wider price fluctuations, and banks were slow in accepting industrial stocks as loan collateral.

While some traders thought of stocks as investments, the stock market for a great many persons represented out-and-out gambling. With almost no restraints or controls, the times were made to order for the shrewd and the scheming, for ploys and stratagems and the matching of wits.

Perhaps at no other period in the nation's history were businessmen left so throughly to their own devices, so free to move in their own ways. Indeed, business appeared to have taken charge of the country in the years after the Civil War. The nation's vast resources were waiting to be exploited, and technology was helping to show the way. There were coal and oil and metal and ores to be drawn or torn from the earth. There were millions of acres of mountain and prairie and plain to be used for man's interests. Few questioned whether a society dominated by business could or should function well, and fewer still would listen to such questions.

The men in public office, for the most part, were either complacent or amenable or both. Almost all of them believed in business, and a great many saw no harm in swapping their own favors for those that businessmen offered them in return. The apologists for the times, if there were need for any, could cite Englishman Herbert Spencer, more than 300,000 of whose books were sold in the postwar United States. Spencer held that the "survival of the fittest" was just as valid a doctrine for economic systems as Darwin had shown it to be for biological systems.

In a sense, business was on trial, although few businessmen thought of it in that way. Given freer rein than ever before, could business really provide for the greatest good of the greatest number? In one way it did, as the nation underwent a period of spectacular material gains. The value of American manufactures, which was less than that of Germany, France, or the United Kingdom in 1860, came very close to equaling the total for all three in the early 1890's. But in another sense, business failed its test. The period produced a number of business leaders so rapacious, greedy, grasping, and corrupt as to make it obvious that they were guided by no moral sense higher than pure self-interest.

Charles Francis Adams, who spent a twenty-five-year business career in the company of many of these men, said in his autobiography: "I have known . . . tolerably well a great many 'successful' men . . . . Not one that I have ever known would I care to meet again either in this world or the next . . . . A set of mere money-getters and traders, they are essentially unattractive."

TAKE THE MONEY AND RUN

The four great eastern railroad systems—the Pennsylvania, the Baltimore & Ohio, the New York Central, and the Erie—were all busy in the postwar years buying small lines, laying track, and generally making their way toward Chicago. Not one to be left out of such plans, Cornelius Vanderbilt, who already controlled lines running from New York City to Albany, began buying up New York Central stock in 1865.

Within a year he had accumulated $2.5 million in Central shares and was able to get his son-in-law elected to the board. Unhappy over the fact that his Hudson River line transferred much of its westbound freight to the Central, but got little freight in return, he managed to work out an agreement by which the Central gave his line a prorated share of its long-distance freight charges and a bonus of $100,000 a year. When the powerful group of "old money" families and politicians who controlled the Central heard of this, they were incensed. Vanderbilt's man was thrown off the board, and a new president, who canceled the bonus, was elected.

Now it was Vanderbilt's turn to hit back. In January, 1867, when boats could not travel the frozen Hudson, his Hudson River line informed the New York Central it would no longer accept Central freight. The

Hudson's trains began stopping short of a bridge at Albany, forcing the Central's passengers to cross by themselves to make the connection. With no means of sending goods to New York City, the Central's stock dropped from $130 to $95. Vanderbilt began to buy shares and soon had $6 million of the line's $23 million capital. The Central capitulated. When its major stockholders, including John Jacob Astor II, later asked Vanderbilt to become its president, he accepted grandly.

He combined the Central with his Hudson line and, on the theory that the road's value was enhanced by the combination, declared an 80 per cent stock dividend, giving himself and his friends millions more in par value of the stock.

Vanderbilt ran the Central well, but freight rates continued in a long-term decline, a situation not much to his liking. He tried to get the Pennsylvania and the Erie to agree to higher rates, but the Erie would not listen. When his Central raised rates, the Erie was as

"THE PUBLIC BE DAMNED"

When old Commodore Vanderbilt died in 1877, the scepter of his empire passed to his eldest son, fifty-six-year-old William Henry Vanderbilt. Until he was forty-three, the latter had lived as a modest farmer on Staten Island; only then had Cornelius taken him into the railroad business and taught him how to make big money.

Two years after the Commodore's death, the government began to investigate ways to regulate the railroads, and William Henry decided to lower his profile as the one-man owner of the New York Central. He turned over 250,000 shares—more than half of his New York Central holdings—to Drexel, Morgan and Company at $120 a share. Such a huge offering could have triggered a panic in the United States, so Morgan wisely sold most of the shares to British buyers. So well did he handle the offering that the stock climbed to $130, and Morgan cleared $2,500,000.

William Henry used his proceeds to buy bonds, eventually increasing his investments to a total of $70 million in U.S. government bonds, $22 million in railroad bonds, $3.2 million in state and municipal bonds, and several million more in mortgages and stocks. "I

wouldn't walk across the street to make a million dollars," he once said. He did not have to. His income from his holdings was $10,350,000 a year, or $1,200 an hour.

With taxpayers providing him with a good part of his wealth, he was hardly in the best position to have made the remark that gave him his greatest fame —or notoriety. A newspaper reporter was questioning him about why the Chicago Limited, a fast, extra-fare mail train, was being eliminated. "Don't you run it for the public benefit?" he was asked. "The public be damned," Vanderbilt answered. What was widely ignored was the rest of his reply: "I am working for my stockholders. If the public want the train, why don't they pay for it?"

In cultural matters, William had little more taste than his father. His Fifth Avenue mansion was an elegant showplace for such objects as a life-sized gilt and bronze statue of a female slave crowned with a tiara studded with electric light bulbs. Regarding one of his possessions, a Rosa Bonheur painting of oxen pulling a plow, William, the onetime farmer, said, "I don't know whether it's art, but those oxen are

An 1885 Judge *cartoon depicts W. H. Vanderbilt riding ruthlessly over the U.S. public.*

right."

On his death in 1885, he left $67 million and $65 million, respectively, to his sons Cornelius II and William Kissam. The other children received $10 million —as much as the budget of New York State that year. (In the same year President Cleveland vetoed a bill to give disabled Union veterans $12 a month.)

likely as not to cut its own. The Erie was a "guerrilla," he said, waiting in ambush to block him. Moreover, he was seeking to establish through connections to Chicago, and the Erie seemed to be engaged in a similar objective. For Vanderbilt, the solution was an old, tested one: buy the Erie.

He began buying shares on the open market, accumulating some 20,000 and getting himself elected a director. But the Erie was not to be so easily bought. At its helm was old Daniel Drew, a man Vanderbilt had dealt with before, as both an ally and an adversary. A hard-bitten and hard-dealing market operator, Drew had as many tricks in his bag as Vanderbilt, and no scruples about using any of them. A former cattle drover, he was reputed to have salted his cattle and kept them thirsty en route to market, then let them drink their fill before being weighed; "watering" later came to mean the creation of worthless corporate stock. Allied with him in the Erie were two younger but equally sinister characters, flamboyant Jim Fisk

The sons lived lavishly. William Kissam spent $500,000 on a 285-foot, steel-hulled, three-masted schooner, which had a crew of 53 and cost $5,000 a month to run. When the crew struck for higher wages during a cruise to Greece, Vanderbilt threw them off. In 1892 the ship sank after a collision, and William simply built a bigger yacht. His daughter, Consuelo, married the Duke of Marlborough in 1895, acquiring a British title and providing the duke with a dowry of $2,500,000. Cornelius made his mark in Newport, Rhode Island, where he built The Breakers, a $5-million •mansion modeled after a North Italian villa. Its elegantly fitted bathrooms had hot and cold salt water, as well as fresh.

The Commodore's descendants gradually lost their grip on the family railroads, retaining board chairmanships but relinquishing active roles in management. In 1928 Harold Vanderbilt, the Commodore's great-grandson, still owned 173,000 shares of New York Central stock. By 1953 his holdings were down to 10,000 shares. The next year Robert Young, with the help of two Texas oil men, Clint Murchison and Sid Richardson, won full control of the Central. The Vanderbilt name remained a household word, but America's first great transportation fortune no longer had a roadbed.

and taciturn Jay Gould. Treachery was their common denominator, but Vanderbilt considered himself a match for all of them.

The Erie was then a trunk line of almost 500 miles, running from New York to the Great Lakes. Originally capitalized at $15 million, its stock had been watered to a value of $26 million. In 1854 Drew had loaned it $1.5 million in exchange for a chattel mortgage on its cars and locomotives. He advanced it $3.5 million in 1860, taking $3 million in convertible bonds and 28,000 shares of unissued stock. At the same time, he was selling the stock short, and he made another fortune when he unloaded his holdings and it plummeted from 95 to 50. He was named a director, then treasurer, and under his management the Erie came to be known as the "scarlet woman of Wall Street."

As Vanderbilt kept buying Erie stock, Drew and his cohorts sold it. They converted Erie bonds to new stock, sometimes legally, sometimes with questionable legality. Fisk and Gould found a printing press in the cellars of the Erie offices, and there they churned out stock certifications, dumping 100,000 shares on an already dropping market. "If this printing press don't break down," said Fisk, "I'll be damned if I don't give the old hog all he wants of Erie."

Vanderbilt got his own Tweed Ring judge, George C. Barnard, to enjoin the conversion of Erie bonds and the issuance of more securities. Gould found another state supreme court judge to issue counterinjunctions. Vanderbilt then got Judge Barnard to order the arrest of Gould, Fisk, and Drew. The trio hastily packed into suitcases some $6 million they had netted, mainly from Vanderbilt purchases of stock, along with securities and documents, and fled to New Jersey, out of reach of New York State contempt orders. In Jersey City, with fifteen policemen on guard duty and three twelve-pound pieces furnished by the Hudson Court Artillery company to stave off any amphibious assault across the river, the three holed up at Taylor's Hotel, which they promptly renamed "Fort Taylor."

Gould now took charge, with Fisk as his front man issuing bulletins to the eager members of the press. When Vanderbilt had a receiver appointed for the Erie, Gould incorporated under New Jersey laws. He started a small rate war cutting passenger fares. He conducted long-distance bear raids on Vanderbilt's Central stock, helping drive it down from 132 to 109. And the picture the Erie group helped paint for the public was that of a small band of refugees fighting the Vanderbilt colossus.

Eventually Gould came to Albany, and Vanderbilt had him arrested. Gould was able to post the $500,000 bail, but this was money he needed to bribe state legislators, so he called on his colleagues for more. The Vanderbilt forces were also busy buying legislators, but Drew won this battle when the legislature retroactively legalized all his actions.

Weary and disgusted with the battle, Vanderbilt sent Drew a cryptic note—"Drew: I'm sick of the whole damned business. Come and see me. Van Derbilt." The warring forces made peace, with the Erie gang restoring all but about $1,000,000 of his losses to Vanderbilt, who thereafter steered clear of the Erie. But he was to be bested yet once more by Fisk in a rate war, when he cut the price for shipping cattle from Buffalo to New York City to $1 a carload. Fisk promptly bought some 5,000 head of cattle and shipped them on the Central at the bargain rates. Fumed the Commodore, "From now on, I'll leave them blowers alone."

Gould and Fisk continued to make the Erie their plaything, until a group of insurgent stockholders managed to steal incriminating records in 1872 and confronted Gould with them. He offered to restore $6 million in real estate and securities, in exchange for 200,000 Erie shares, then selling for 30, after which they could all be enriched by the rising market. They agreed. When the bargain was made public, Erie's stock shot up. Gould unloaded his holdings at a good profit. But the assets he had surrendered turned out to be worth only $200,000. It was Gould's farewell gesture to the Erie as he went on to other pastures. Fisk was shot and killed in 1872 by a man who had earlier taken from him his favorite mistress, Josie Mansfield. And Drew went bankrupt a few years later, then died in 1879.

Commodore Vanderbilt continued to build his railroad empire—occasionally milking it by watering the stock. But he contended, as modern analysts would agree, that earnings, rather than initial capitalization, determined the real value of a business and its securities. To help assure those earnings, he improved the line. He replaced the old iron rails with steel, at first importing from England, and wooden and iron bridges with steel ones; he built New York City's Grand Central Terminal in the heart of the city; he built new passenger and freight stations and increased the number of tracks; he introduced efficiencies and economies and cut the time required for a trip from New York to Chicago from fifty hours to twenty-four, and the number of train changes from seventeen to none. And the road managed to pay dividends of 8 per cent or more throughout his lifetime.

Together with his son, William Henry, he acquired the Lake Shore, the Michigan Southern, the Canada Southern, and the Michigan Central railroads. It gave him a continuous line of 978 miles, in addition to side lines, and he owned half of the $150 million in capitalization. He continued to run them all with the same irascible independence he had displayed when an associate complained he was violating the New York statutes. "My God," said Vanderbilt, "you don't suppose you can run a railroad in accordance with the statutes of New York, do you?" In his last years, he consulted spirit mediums, played whist, switched from gin to beer, chased the female servants in his home, and married a twenty-nine-year-old distant cousin. He died in 1877 at the age of eighty-three, leaving a fortune of $104 million, about 90 per cent of it accumulated since the end of the Civil War. It was almost the exact amount in the federal government's treasury at the time.

The bulk of the estate, about $94 million, was left to his son, in order to keep the properties intact. Far more timid and eager to avoid pitched battles, William gave way under threats, compromised much too readily, and made some serious blunders. Even so, in the space of just eight years he managed to double the family fortune.

RAILROADS TO THE WEST

As early as 1845, China merchant Asa Whitney proposed that Congress undertake to back a railroad line to the West Coast, thinking of it primarily as a means to facilitate trade with the Far East. The clamor for such a line grew louder and more insistent after the territorial acquisitions from the Mexican War and the Oregon boundary treaty, and after the California gold rush. To shorten the westward journey, engineers planned a railroad across the Isthmus of Panama in 1849, and it was completed five years later after great hardship. But it was still far from being the transcontinental route across the United States that was needed.

North and South at first vied to have the line built in their own latitudes, both to promote trade and to encourage the westward spread of their own social systems. In the South, leading businessmen discussed proposals for a southern route at conventions held at Charleston, Montgomery, and other cities. The Northeast supported Whitney's proposed northern route to Oregon, but a convention held in St. Louis late in 1849 besought the government to help establish a central trunk line from the Mississippi Valley to the West Coast, with branch lines to Chicago, St. Louis, and Memphis.

The business-dominated wartime Congress first passed a bill in 1862 authorizing the construction of a railroad from Omaha, Nebraska, to Sacramento, California, the central route that the South had opposed. Business dragged its feet for a time, and the law liberalized benefits to the private companies in 1864. The new act gave federal charters to the Union Pacific Railroad Company, which was to start building from Nebraska, and to the Central Pacific Railroad Company, which was to lay track from the West Coast and meet the Union Pacific line. They were to get federal subsidies of $48,000 per mile for each mile that they built in the mountains, $32,000 for the areas between mountain ranges, and $16,000 in level country. In addition, the Central Pacific was granted 12 million acres of federal land along its right of way and a $27 million mortgage loan in government bonds, and the Union Pacific was given 9 million acres and a $24 million loan in government bonds.

In the West, the Central Pacific was the instrument of the Pacific Associates, three merchants and a former gold miner who had joined together to move into bigger things. The leader of the group was Collis Huntington, the partner of a second member, Mark Hopkins, in a large Sacramento hardware store. The other two were Leland Stanford, a mining supplies merchant, who in 1861 was elected governor of California, and Charles Crocker, a onetime prospector and ironworker.

Looking about for new ventures for their little pool, in 1860 they attended one of a series of meetings held by Theodore Judah, an engineer who had explored and surveyed the region through which an eastward-bound railroad might go. The four Associates questioned Judah closely, went out with him to explore the ground on horseback, and decided to put all their energies behind the railroad scheme. By the time Congress was ready to act on the road, they were easily the leading candidates for the western section. When the plum fell to them, Huntington enthusiastically sent Stanford the news in a five-word message: "We have drawn the elephant."

At about the same time, Congress took up the question of standardizing railroad gauges, of which there were almost a dozen in use on the nation's lines, varying from 56 to 60 inches. President Lincoln took the matter into his own hands, decided that the width between rails should be $56\frac{1}{2}$ inches, and this eventually became the uniform gauge for the nation.

The building of the new transcontinental railroad got off to a slow start at both ends. The Central Pacific began to move eastward in 1864 but had built only fifty-six miles by the beginning of 1866, and the Union

The Way to Wealth

LELAND STANFORD

In 1878 Amasa Leland Stanford (1824–93) wrote the following in the Central Pacific Railroad's annual report to its stockholders: "There is no foundation in good reason for the attempts by the General Government and by the State to especially control your affairs. It is a question of might, and it is to your interest to have it determined where the power resides."

Stanford believed he knew where power resided: business should have the upper hand over government, and not vice versa. He used government to help his own interests, but when it got in his way, he fought it bitterly.

Born in Watervliet, New York, the son of an innkeeper, he headed first for law, opening a practice in Wisconsin but giving it up when his law books were destroyed in a fire. In 1852 he moved to California, where he joined his four brothers in a mercantile business that sold supplies to miners, and made $400,000 from a lucky mine interest.

A politician at heart, he was elected a justice of the peace, but he was later beaten in races for state treasurer and governor. Finally, in 1861, he won the gubernatorial election. In the mean-

Leland Stanford, governor of California

time, with Mark Hopkins, Charles Crocker, and Collis Huntington, he became interested in building a railroad to link California with the East. They organized the Central Pacific Railroad, and, as governor, Stanford pushed through bond issues to help finance the venture and signed acts that granted railroad warrants of $10,000 for each mile that it built.

Stanford was president of the Central Pacific from 1863 until his death

and was also a director of the Southern Pacific Railroad. At the same time he was involved with, and made profits from, the construction companies that received government funds to build the roads. It was an association termed "indefensible" by the U.S. Pacific Railroad Commission.

After driving the golden spike that completed the first transcontinental railroad in 1869, Stanford went on to purchase competing California railroads and to build the Southern Pacific into a system that reached to New Orleans. With the money he made, he bought vineyards, established a horse ranch called Palo Alto, and founded Stanford University.

In 1885 he defeated George Hearst for the U.S. Senate and went to Washington, where he fought government attempts to regulate business. When the bill to create the Interstate Commerce Commission seemed certain to pass, he refused to appear for the vote.

Time eventually proved that ultimate might resided in the government, which could, and would, stand in the way of business when the public good demanded it. But Stanford did not live to see that day. So many wealthy men sat with him in the Senate that it was known as the "Millionaires' Club," and they saw to it that, more often than not, business had its way.

A railroad car conference of Union Pacific officials, complete with spittoons and firearms, at Echo City, Utah, 1868

Pacific had managed to complete only forty miles. But soon the two companies, competing for the federal payments for the track that was laid, were racing against each other. Judah at first supervised construction for the Central Pacific, but he died and Crocker replaced him. When large numbers of laborers on the western road drifted off to try their luck on the new-found Comstock Lode in Nevada, Crocker looked appraisingly at his Chinese servant, Ah Ling, and was soon scouring San Francisco and Sacramento to hire thousands of slightly built but untiring coolies, who won the lasting gratitude of the four partners because they toiled for just $1 a day, about half the wages of white workers.

Working in mountain blizzard and desert sun, Crocker's army of 10,000 Chinese cut the Summit Tunnel in the Sierra Nevada by hand and laid 689 miles of track. In the East, the Union Pacific's General Grenville Dodge, a former army engineer, pushed thousands of Irish immigrants across 1,086 miles of the plains country, even laying temporary tracks on snow.

The crews met at Promontory, Utah, about fifty miles west of Ogden, on May 10, 1869. The last tie was of laurel wood from California; Nevada gave a silver spike, Arizona one of iron, silver, and gold, and Stanford himself drove home the last spike of Cali-

fornia gold with a silver-plated hammer; a telegraph conveyed the message of each hammer blow, to be matched by the tolling of bells in all the nation's major cities. An iron road joined the coasts at last.

Up to this point all the profits growing out of the transcontinental road were those of the construction companies that had built it. But the construction companies turned out to be owned by the same people who owned the railroad companies — and the profits were enormous.

The building contracts for the Union Pacific had been sublet by its owners to themselves through the Crédit Mobilier, their own creation. Through Massachusetts Congressman Oakes Ames they had discreetly distributed 343 shares of Crédit Mobilier where they would "do the most good" — that is, to key members of the House and Senate, to former Vice President Schuyler Colfax, to Vice President Henry Wilson, and to future President James A. Garfield. Thus fortified with friends in high places, the group owning Crédit Mobilier had made direct profits put at more than $33 million by a House investigating committee and estimated by others at up to $50 million. No slackers at this game, the Pacific Associates had set up dummy construction companies that lubricated the movement of public subsidy funds toward their own pockets. The construction company for the Central Pacific was paid $120 million to build a railroad that cost around $58 million.

With a huge potential for carrying cattle, ores, and other products of the West, trans-Mississippi railroad earnings' prospects were bright, so it was not long before competitors entered the picture. By 1870 the Kansas Pacific was completed to Denver. Cyrus K. Holliday, a Pennsylvania lawyer who moved to Kansas, planned to build a railroad to replace the old Santa Fe trail, reaching Colorado by 1872 and finally getting to Santa Fe by 1880. The Chicago, Burlington & Quincy reached Denver by 1882, the same year that Thomas Scott's Texas Pacific joined the Southern Pacific at El Paso, thus linking New Orleans with the West Coast by rail. The following year the Southern Pacific also met the Santa Fe. In all, the government gave the railroads 242,000 square miles of land, or more than the total area of France, plus mortgage loans of some $65 million.

Even before their Central Pacific was completed, the West's "Big Four" reached out for other lines, secretly acquiring the California charter of the Southern Pacific in 1868 and eventually gaining control of that road. They set up the Western Development Co., a holding company to carry on their building and other operations in southern California. They gathered other California railroads into their empire, along with coal and iron mines, and in the East, Huntington built the Chesapeake & Ohio Railroad. When Hopkins and Crocker died, their estates were valued at around $20 million. Stanford left $30 million to found Leland Stanford Junior University, in his son's memory, and Huntington's fortune was considerably larger.

GOULD AND THE CORNER IN GOLD

With the Civil War issuance of greenbacks, which could not be redeemed in specie, speculation in precious metals, particularly in gold, was encouraged. Indeed, traders in the Gold Room of the New York Stock Exchange had run up the price during the war as high as $241 in paper for $100 in gold. But postwar prosperity and the growth of confidence in the government sent gold back down again.

By the spring of 1869 the price of gold came to the bottom of a long slide at 131. Jay Gould, with the profits of assorted larcenous enterprises and with the Erie treasury at his command, decided to buy, and, picking up $7 million worth, sent the price back up to 140. With the entire floating gold supply amounting to no more than $15 or $20 million, however, he owned a respectable portion of the available total. He may have set out with the intention of cornering gold, or it may only have occurred to him and Jim Fisk at about this time. Nevertheless, they started to use their funds, as well as the funds of the Tammany Hall bank they controlled, the Tenth National, to buy all the gold there was—and more, since some traders sold it short.

The hitch was the U.S. Treasury's gold supply, some $75 or $80 million, which might at any time be thrown on the market. To insure against such a calamity, Gould befriended Abel R. Corbin, a speculator and lobbyist who the year before, at age sixty-four, had married President Ulysses Grant's middle-aged sister. Gould first sought to convince Corbin that a price rise in gold would mean high farm prices, good railroad profits, and national prosperity, whereas government gold dumping would bring depression and war. He then sweetened the argument by purchasing for Corbin's account, on margin, $2 million in gold bonds, from which Corbin could reap the profits of a gold price rise without putting up a cent.

Within a short time the message was getting through to the President, and Treasury Secretary George S. Boutwell began to feel pressure from the White House to keep gold off the market. Throughout the summer of 1869 the plotters bought gold. Major General Dan Butterfield was named Assistant U.S. Treasurer at New York, and he too suddenly became the owner of $1.5 million in gold bonds, purchased by Gould on margin.

By the end of August, Fisk and Gould owned twice the floating supply of gold. As they kept buying, Gould sat in his office at the Grand Opera House in New York, nervously tearing paper into tiny bits until the floor was littered with the scraps. Fisk poured another $8 million into the market on September 13. By September 22 the price was up to 141. But that night Gould was called to the Corbin house. President Grant was obviously displeased with what was going on; Mrs. Corbin had a letter from her sister-in-law, the President's wife, warning her to stop speculating in gold. Gould persuaded the Corbins to keep the letter secret. The next day, outwardly acting like a bull, Gould started quietly unloading his holdings. The price reached 144, closing at $144\frac{1}{4}$. The following day, September 24—"Black Friday"—the market opened wildly at 150, shot up to 160. General Butterfield, who had already sold out, wired the Secretary of the Treasury: "Gold is 150. Much feeling and accusations of government complicity." At 11:25, after gold had peaked at 164, a messenger brought the news that the President had ordered the Treasury to sell $5 million in gold immediately, an order Boutwell followed "as publicly as possible."

The market broke more than 25 points in fifteen minutes, as the bulls who had followed what they thought was Gould's lead fell over themselves to get out. A crowd of furious traders went to the brokerage rooms of Heath & Co., looking for Fisk and Gould. But the two were already at the Opera House, guarded by police and their own thugs, preparing to have Tammany judges issue injunctions against anyone trying to collect on Fisk's repudiated contracts to buy gold. Gould, $11 million the richer, announced his regret over the Black Friday panic, and General Butterfield sanctimoniously pointed out that only the gamblers had lost.

Gould went back to his favorite pastime of taking over plundered railroads and demonstrating how much more could be wrung out of them. Leaving the Erie in 1872, he moved his sights toward the greater opportunities across the Mississippi. Together with Russell Sage, he got control of the Union Pacific, which, although bent under a load of debt its builders had left behind, still had great potential as a profitable carrier. The one railroad that Gould tried to develop was the Missouri Pacific, for control of which he paid $3.8 million—after the state of Missouri alone had given it subsidies of $25 million. He built up its traffic, added connecting lines, and boasted a twentyfold increase in its revenues. Even so, Gould could not resist an occasional foray into the market, manipulating the road's stock. The ultimate judgment of railroad historian R. E. Riegel was: "The roads that he touched never quite recovered from his lack of knowledge and interest in sound railroading."

Partly as an outgrowth of his interest in the Union Pacific, Gould in 1875 got control of the Atlantic & Pacific telegraph line, some of whose coast-to-coast wires ran along the railroad's right of way. He had a warm feeling for the telegraph, since some of his

Jay Gould, slick master of an age of financial buccaneering

earliest investment successes had resulted from the advance word of Union victories he received from well-placed informants in the War Department through a private wire service he had once owned. In two years Gould built the Atlantic & Pacific into a major system, with 18,000 miles of wire. Its president was General Thomas Eckert, who had been head of the Military Telegraph Bureau during the war and may well have been Gould's principal informant at that time.

In 1877, along with Sage and a group of speculators, Gould began buying into Western Union, which still monopolized most of the nation's telegraph traffic. To maintain its monopoly, Western Union absorbed Atlantic & Pacific in an income-pooling arrangement, giving the smaller system an eighth share of the total income.

Gould asked for a place on the Western Union board, but the Vanderbilts and Astors, then in control, would not hear of it. So he began to form another telegraph company, American Union, capitalized at $10 million. Seizing wires along the rights of way of railroads in which he had an interest, building and acquiring other lines, and opening 2,000 branch offices, he soon had assembled a 50,000-mile telegraph system. Then with a bear pool he began to drive the Western Union stock down, first to 90, then as low as 78. William Vanderbilt asked Gould to come and see him, and they talked in Vanderbilt's library. In a few days, Western Union stock was over 100, then up to 114½.

Gould, Sage, Eckert, and another Gould man went onto the board, and Gould, as controlling shareholder, moved his offices to the Western Union Building.

At his death in 1892, Gould had a fortune estimated at $77 million.

BUILDING UP THE NORTHWEST

When in 1864 Josiah Perham of Boston said he was ready to build a railroad along the Canadian border to the Pacific, he was given a charter by the federal government for the Northern Pacific Railroad. He was also given a strip of land grants, contingent on actual construction, of 47 million acres, totaling more than the area of all of New England.

To raise capital for construction, Perham and his associates went in 1865, 1866, and again in 1867 to Jay Cooke & Co., which had become the nation's largest investment firm as a result of successful wartime financing for the government. Each time they were turned down. Jay Cooke & Co. had become expert in the sale of government obligations, then the safest and most profitable area in investment banking, but was not much interested in railroad financing.

But when the Northern Pacific's promoters came knocking at the door again in 1869, Cooke had changed his mind. He had been trying since the war, without success, to get the government to undertake a general refunding of its long-term bonds at lower interest. Other investment firms had already tied up the financ-

Gould's flamboyant sidekick, Jim Fisk, drawn by Thomas Nast

164

ing operations of the better-established railroads. Now Cooke decided it was a field he should get into.

What made the Northern Pacific especially attractive was its huge land grant. If the sale of bonds could handle construction of the road, he surmised, land sales would then take care of themselves. So he made a preliminary deal to serve as the Northern Pacific's banker and to try to sell $100 million of its 7.3 per cent bonds.

Members of his firm were by no means unanimous about this decision. They went to Europe but found little enthusiasm in capital markets there. Jay Gould's Black Friday had brought on a recession and a cooling of speculative fever in the United States. Nevertheless, on January 1, 1870, Cooke decided to move ahead with modified plans — that is, to build only to the Red River on Minnesota's western border and then seek government aid.

He organized a pool into which subscribers would pay $5.6 million over a fifteen-month period. In return, the subscribers would receive $5 million in bonds and twelve shares of stock of which the total par value would be $41 million, as well as a half interest in the Northern Pacific's land affiliate. In spite of a stringent money market, the whole $5.6 million was sold, but Jay Cooke & Co. had to make large advances to carry the subscriptions.

While work began on the road, renewed efforts were made to sell the $100 million bond issue. The response was very poor, both in this country and in Germany, where the Franco-Prussian War had drawn off much of the free capital. Construction made insistent demands on the limited funds, and Jay Cooke continued to make advances. Meanwhile, money grew ever tighter, and in September, 1872, the *Commercial & Financial Chronicle* reported "the most protracted monetary pinch" in twenty-five years. At one point some money rates reached as high as 160 per cent.

Construction continued to go well, reaching the Missouri River from the east and through the interior of Washington Territory from the west, for a total of some 500 miles. But the economic situation did not improve, and receipts lagged far behind expenses. For months, laborers were paid in scrip. Then, on the morning of September 18, 1873, a $1,000,000 note came due and could not be paid. Jay Cooke & Co.'s New York office closed its doors just before 11 A.M., followed in short order by the Philadelphia and Washington offices and the First National Bank of Washington, D.C.

The failure set off a panic in New York. Stocks broke, and for the first time in its history the New York Stock Exchange suspended trading, not to be resumed for ten days. Numerous banks failed; a depression set in that was to last five years. Back of it lay not only excessive speculation and overbuilding,

as had been true in the past, but also a loss of confidence engendered by the excesses of business plunderers and the corruption in high political places. Even before the panic, western railroads had been scratching out a minimal return on their invested capital. Cornelius Vanderbilt went to Washington and offered to put up $10 million in railroad securities to save the failing Union Trust Company if the Treasury would lift a freeze on $30 million in gold. President Grant refused. There were some who blamed the powerful Vanderbilt for failing to forestall the crash, but he could no more have done that than he could have halted the tides. The causes were deep and beyond his curative powers. Indeed, it was Vanderbilt himself who had once warned: "Building railroads from nowhere to nowhere at public expense is not a legitimate business."

By-products of the depressed times were the bargains that became available to anyone with some money put aside and enough nerve to run counter to the prevailing mood. One such person was James J. Hill, who had moved to St. Paul, Minnesota, from Canada in 1856 at the age of eighteen, worked as a transportation clerk and as an agent for the St. Paul and Pacific Railroad, centered in Minnesota, got into the transportation business on the Red River, and managed to accumulate $100,000 in about twenty years. Along with a group of Canadian and American associates, he saw latent possibilities in the bankrupt St. Paul & Pacific, then chiefly the property of a group of bondholders in the Netherlands. The 200-mile road was one of those commonly described as "a streak of rust running through a desert" and was saddled with a capitalization of $28 million, but it had both federal and state charters as well as 5 million acres of Minnesota land grants, the retention of which required the continued building of the railroad.

Members of Hill's group picked up the road's bonds wherever they could at six to eight cents on the dollar. Then, without necessarily telling all they knew or suspected about the growth of population and trade in the area, they entered into negotiations with the Dutch bondholders. An agreement was reached whereby Hill's group assumed the bonded debt at a fifth of its face value, giving as evidence of good faith their promissory note for $1,000,000, and pledging to extend the line to the Canadian border at St. Vincent, Minnesota. By borrowing on all their own property and by selling land at $2.50 to $5 an acre, mainly to immigrants, they managed to rush construction toward a junction with a branch of the Canadian Pacific, which was then being built farther north. Thus Winnipeg gained a rail link to the Mississippi.

The St. Paul & Pacific was reorganized as the St. Paul, Minneapolis & Manitoba, and Hill sold his Red River transportation interests to devote full time to

About to start for the Northern Pacific's "golden spike" ceremony, Henry Villard posed hatless (center) at St. Paul in 1883.

railroading. As the region began producing more and more wheat, the rail line prospered, and new construction kept extending it westward in spurts, across Dakota, to Great Falls in Montana Territory, to Helena and Butte. Finally, as the Great Northern, it reached Puget Sound in 1893, a soundly built system with almost 4,000 miles of track running from St. Paul to Seattle.

The uncompleted Northern Pacific, meanwhile, was not going to rust. German-born (as Heinrich Hilgard) Henry Villard had started a newspaper career as a youth, gone west for Horace Greeley's *Tribune*, and worked for Jay Cooke's immigration service. When he learned that the Columbia River Line of the Oregon Steam Navigation Company could be bought for much less than its real value, he got an option on it and managed to raise funds for its purchase in New York. He then bought into other steamship and railway companies and soon had a small but prospering transportation empire in the Northwest. By 1880 he had an agreement prorating traffic with the Northern Pacific and was inconspicuously buying its stock.

The following year Villard managed to get control of the Northern Pacific and began pushing it through to completion. Thousands of laborers went to work on the main line, which was finished in 1883, with Villard

at the center of the customary "golden spike" ceremonies. These were auspicious enough for the Crow Indian tribe generously, if symbolically, to sell some of their Montana hunting grounds to him. But the ceremony also marked another, sadder termination for the ambitious young man from Bavaria. The road had a deficit of $5.5 million, and construction had exceeded estimates by $14 million. Villard, no railroad builder, was broke. Within a few months, he stepped down from his office, and his company quietly went bankrupt.

What Hill and Villard, good railroad builder and bad, had in common was their accomplishment in helping to populate the Northwest. With flyers, advertisements, and circulars, both in this country and abroad, they attracted thousands of migrants and immigrants, both to buy their land and to build up the commerce of the region to feed traffic and freight to their lines.

THE STEELMAKERS

In the Pittsburgh *Dispatch* of November 2, 1849, the following item appeared: "A messenger boy of the name of Andrew Carnegie, employed by the O'Reily Telegraph Company, yesterday found a draft for the amount of $500. Like an honest little fellow, he

166

promptly made known the facts, and deposited the paper in good hands where it awaits identification."

At the time, the sum in question represented almost ten years' wages for the honest little fellow. But in due course Carnegie would be getting that much income during every ten minutes of his waking and sleeping hours.

The son of a Scottish weaver, Andrew was brought to America at the age of twelve and began to live out his Horatio Alger life. He worked first in a cotton mill for $1.20 a week, became interested in telegraphy, and got a job with the Pennsylvania Railroad. One day word came of an accident that was tying up traffic. With no one in authority available, Carnegie took it on himself to telegraph orders that would get the trains moving, signing them with the name of the head of the road, Colonel Thomas A. Scott. When Scott later heard of this, he made Carnegie his private secretary.

It was the perfect spot for an ambitious young man who was inclined to save money for the right opportunity. He was at the locus of much inside information, some passed along by the avuncular colonel, some coming from other good sources. Carnegie gave his note for stock in a small Pennsylvania oil company, repaid it out of earnings in a year when a gusher was struck. A borrowed investment of $217.50 in the Woodruff Palace Car, a sleeping car company, was soon paying him dividends of $5,000 a year.

When a railroad engineer named J. H. Linville showed Carnegie the iron railroad bridges being fabricated in Pennsylvania shops to replace the old wooden ones, it sounded like an attractive business to get into. While still with the Pennsylvania, he organized his own company to build railroad bridges, and his employers became both investors in and customers of his new company. With his brother and two friends, Carnegie bought into the iron foundry of a German named Andrew Kloman, who made railroad car axles and had more business than he could handle. That was in 1863. In 1864 he put some of his capital into a company making iron rails. And in 1865, with all these enterprises humming, he finally left his job with the Pennsylvania.

More than 250 firms were producing almost 1,000,000 tons of iron in 1860, but this was not enough to satisfy the demand. Among the larger enterprises were the Cambria Iron Works in Johnstown, Pennsylvania, opened in 1853; the Jones and Laughlin Mill, opened the same year in Pittsburgh; the Cooper & Hewitt Works at Phillipsburg, successor to the mills started in the 1830's at Trenton by Peter Cooper; the Bethlehem Iron Company at Bethlehem, Pennsylvania; the Pencroyd Iron Works, opened in 1853 near Philadelphia; and, in the Midwest, the Illinois Steel Company, which grew out of a mill started in 1857. What Carnegie brought to the industry was aggressive sales-

manship and a relentless demand for more and more production from his plants.

But he was no iron man in the sense of feeling kinship with the fiery furnaces and the rolling and shaping mills that could turn the product out. Indeed, he was a come-lately to the age of steel. Alexander Holley of Troy, New York, used the Bessemer process to make an experimental batch of steel in 1865, and subsequently became the genius who planned and improved steelmaking works from Bethlehem to St. Louis. When the Cambria Iron Works rolled two and a half tons of steel rails in 1867, the Pittsburgh *Chronicle* hailed the achievement, declaring that the steel would last twenty years in contrast to the three-year life of the iron rails it replaced. William Coleman, along with other Carnegie partners, suggested that they branch out into Bessemer steel. Carnegie would not hear of it. But after visiting England in the early 1870's, watching the Bessemer process, and talking to steel men there, he returned a thorough convert to steel, insisting that a plant be opened immediately. He subscribed most of the $700,000 capital used to form Carnegie, Mc-Candless and Company, which built a steel plant near Pittsburgh, shrewdly named the J. Edgar Thomson Works, for the president of the Pennsylvania Railroad.

Carnegie was also slow in moving toward the "open hearth" process, a new steelmaking method that was called "the scavenger of the steel industry," because it could use large amounts of steel scrap, and that turned out a product at once tougher and softer than Bessemer steel. The Siemens brothers had introduced the process in England in 1858, and the Cooper, Hewitt & Company built an open-hearth furnace in this country ten years later. Bethlehem Steel began building open-hearth furnaces in the 1880's, in order to meet the Navy's quality standards for armor plate and heavy forgings. The open hearth was introduced at the Carnegie-Phipps works at Homestead, Pennsylvania, in 1888. Scarcely more than a decade later, more than half the nation's steel tonnage was turned out by open hearths.

The Cambria firm developed a reputation for producing not only fine steel but great steel men as well. John Fritz had come from Cambria to head Bethlehem in 1860. One of the greatest steel men was Captain William R. "Billy" Jones, a popular, lighthearted boss who might stop work to take his men to the ball game. But Jones resigned when the works manager died in 1873 and he was passed over in the succession in favor of Daniel N. Jones. When Carnegie heard of this, he lost no time in hiring Captain Billy Jones as superintendent of his new Braddock works, near Pittsburgh— and with the same gesture he drew to the plant dozens of hard-to-find skilled steelworkers.

Jones immediately began giving Carnegie the kind of production he liked to see, doubling and redoubling output until it reached 3,300 tons a week. His targets were the Cambria production records of his old Johnstown chums, Jack Frey, Bob Hunt, and Dan Jones, as well as British supremacy in steel output. He achieved one goal when his former employer at Cambria admitted "I hired the wrong Jones," and another when he was able to present a paper at a British Iron and Steel Institute meeting in 1881 pointing out that the United States had passed Britain both in total production and in steelmaking methods. Among the reasons he cited for this were the employment of men of mixed nationalities and the eight-hour day. He spurned a proffered stock interest in the company, which would have made him enormously wealthy, and settled instead for a salary equal to that of the President of the United States—$25,000 a year. When Billy Jones was killed in a fiery furnace accident in 1889, Carnegie was brought to tears and thousands of grieving workers marched in the funeral procession.

The nation's steel output climbed rapidly. For rails alone it rose from just over 30,000 tons in 1870 to 850,000 tons in 1880 and almost 1,900,000 tons by 1890. In 1880 nearly half of the rails built were still made of iron, but just five years later almost 99 per cent were fashioned from steel. And in 1900 the United

States *exported* more than 6 million tons of steel rails. Carnegie sought to supply an ever larger share. Once, when a superintendent wired him about a new weekly production record, he shot back: "Congratulations! Why not do it every week?"

The key to Carnegie's—and the nation's—success in steelmaking was an unceasing effort to produce a better product at a lower cost. The country that produced the cheapest steel, he said, would "have all other nations at its feet." He was willing to go to great lengths to become the low-cost producer. Once, being shown around a new installation that would cut steel costs by fifty cents a ton, he noted that his bright young assistant, Charles M. Schwab, looked unhappy. When Carnegie asked what was wrong, Schwab admitted that he had since thought of how he might have saved another fifty cents a ton, but now it would mean tearing down the new mill. "Then go ahead," said Carnegie, "tear it down."

At the same time, he hired topnotch metallurgists and chemists to improve the quality of his steel. In his *Autobiography* he wrote: "If faced with the loss of buildings and plants, or the services of scientists, I would prefer to lose the former. Plants would be less difficult to replace." For his own epitaph he once sug-

Above: late-nineteenth-century view of the National Tube Co. plant at Pittsburgh, which in 1901 became part of U.S. Steel. Right: Pennsylvania coke king and steelmaster Henry Clay Frick was a top Carnegie executive and a bitter foe of union labor.

gested, "Here lies the man who was able to surround himself with men far cleverer than himself." The men he had primarily in mind were his long-time associates and friends—Henry Phipps, Schwab, and Henry C. Frick. Phipps, a boyhood playmate, was his detail man, his bookkeeper, his economizer, a man who a Pittsburgh banker once said "could keep a check in the air for three or four days." Schwab was the warm-hearted and affable production man who was liked and admired by the brawny steelworkers. But Frick was another breed—unyielding, cold, efficient.

When he joined Carnegie in 1882, Frick had already made his fortune as the coke king of Pennsylvania. As a youth, Frick roomed in a miner's house and worked as a bookkeeper for a few dollars a week in the Connellsville district of Pennsylvania. The area was rich in a bituminous coal especially suited for coking—heating in a beehivelike brick oven to produce coke, a porous fuel especially desirable for steelmaking because of its high heat yield. In 1871 Frick went to Pittsburgh to see Thomas Mellon, a retired judge who had a year earlier opened the T. Mellon & Sons Bank. The twenty-one-year-old Frick asked for $10,000 to build fifty coke ovens to help meet the increasing demand from the steel industry in the area. Impressed by

the young man's earnestness and intelligence, the banker made the loan. At the same time, Frick entered into a lifelong association with Mellon's son, Andrew, then a student at Western University.

Frick was soon making profits many times greater than the loan, and pouring the earnings back into the business to build more coke ovens and buy more coal lands. In the panic of 1873 he borrowed money to buy mines at bargain rates. To avoid threatening labor problems, he imported hard-working Hungarians and Slavs. By 1882, in control of 80 per cent of coke production, the H. C. Frick Coke Company was bought out by Carnegie, and Frick himself joined the steel master as one of his top executives.

BEEF AND FLOUR

The development of industries that could serve national markets was accompanied by an increasing number of large farms, ranches, and food processing industries. In California, for example, farms of 10,000 acres or more were common by 1873 and occupied more than twice as much land as the thousands of subsistence farms of 500 acres or less.

Improved agricultural machinery, some with steam power, gave added impetus to large-scale farming. McCormick, already dominant in the industry, increased his advantage in 1874 when Charles B. Withington of Janesville, Wisconsin, brought him a device for his reaper that would bundle the wheat into sheaves, tie them with wire, and leave them on the ground. Then a former dry goods retailer from Maine, William Deering, came along with an improved knotter that was faster and safer for man and beast because it used twine instead of wire. When McCormick died in 1884, his sons took over, retaining leadership in their industry, but Deering was in second place by the turn of the century. For the larger farms, the combine—a combined harvester and thresher drawn by steam power or teams of up to thirty mules—would cut, thresh, clean, and bag up to thirty acres of grain in a day.

The developing cattle industry of the Southwest had much of its market cut off by the Civil War, so that the Texas range developed a surplus of stock. With the end of the war came the major problem of sending the steers northward to the packing centers—as historian Walter Prescott Webb has said, "to connect the $4 cow with a $40 market." The common method was by long cattle drives to such points as Sedalia, Missouri, from where they could be shipped by rail to St. Louis. But en route were such hazards as settlers who did not appreciate having their lands crossed or rustlers who might stampede a herd at night or beat or murder the drovers.

The man who did most to make the drives safe was J. G. McCoy, who ran a livestock shipping business in

169

Illinois. In 1867 he approached the Missouri Pacific Railroad with a plan to intercept the livestock route with a shipping center along the railroad. The railroad's president took him for a fast-talking promoter and ordered him out of the office. But within a few hours the general freight agent of the Hannibal and St. Joe line had signed a contract giving McCoy favorable rates for shipping beeves from the Missouri River to Chicago. This incident, McCoy always felt, was what made Chicago, rather than St. Louis, the country's chief packing center.

After looking around, he chose Abilene, Kansas, which he described as "a very small, dead place . . . of about one dozen log huts." He brought in timber and built chutes and pens for 3,000 head, then sent scouts out to meet the herds. The first drover, a man named Thompson, found it incredible that a Texan would be greeted by "any other reception than outrage and robbery," McCoy related. More than 1,000,000 head of cattle moved through Abilene within the space of three years. Other cow towns grew up at Wichita, Ellsworth, and Dodge City, Kansas, and, as the herds moved north as far as the Canadian border, at Ogallala, Nebraska, and Miles City, Montana. The ranges were hard hit by the panic of 1873 but were recovering in a few years and getting ready for a major boom in the 1880's. By then corporations and syndicates had begun taking over much of the industry, staking out land holdings that ran into the hundreds of thousands of acres. Even so, the states and territories west of the Mississippi in 1880 had only about a third of the cattle in the United States.

Farmers who moved into the wide-open prairie spaces encountered two major shortages: water and fencing materials. The answer to the first was to pump water from wells by means of small metal windmills, which soon dotted the plains. The second was solved by the development of barbed wire, patented by two Illinois farmers. Barbed wire sales zoomed from just 10,000 pounds in 1874 to more than 80 million pounds by 1880. A leading salesman was John W. "Bet-a-Million" Gates, who sealed a plaza in San Antonio, Texas, with the wire and kept thirty fierce and unwilling steers caged for an afternoon. This started a whirlwind of sales that ended with Gates as head of the American Steel and Wire Company.

The firms destined to become America's packing giants dated mostly from the years during or just after the war. Nelson Morris as a young man of twenty-two went into the business in Chicago at the start of the war and soon had big contracts to supply the Union Army. Philip D. Armour was a partner in the Milwaukee packing house of Jacob Plankinton when he took heed of Grant's march toward Richmond in 1865. Armour hurried to New York, sold pork short at $40 a barrel. With the end of the war, pork prices collapsed to less than half of what they had been, and Armour, $2 million richer, started his own business in Chicago.

Gustavus F. Swift began his career with a $20 loan from his father when he was sixteen; he bought a fat heifer and dressed and sold it to neighborhood women in Sagamore, Massachusetts, on Cape Cod. He kept expanding his meat business and moving farther west until he reached Chicago in 1875, at the age of thirty-five. His major innovation was to send dressed meat by refrigerated railroad cars, thus saving half the shipping weight of live cattle. To do this he had to overcome the stubborn opposition of the rail lines and of some local butchers, finally winning out through determination and the fact that the consumers of the nation wanted his products.

The flour milling industry became centered in Minneapolis after 1870, when a way was found to process the region's hard spring wheat into a white flour rather than into coarse, dark meal. This was the work first of Cadwallader C. Washburn, a flour maker who had been governor of Wisconsin, and his partners, George H. Smith, an expert miller, and George H. Christian, a southerner who had come north after the war to become a flour broker. They hired Edmond La Croix to build a device known as a middlings purifier, which helped keep the gluten while removing the bran. Charles A. Pillsbury and others went to visit European flour mills and brought back from Hungary the method of passing wheat slowly through a series of chilled rollers to produce a fine, white flour. Similar systems were adopted by both the Washburn and Pillsbury mills in 1874. More mills sprang up, and in the decade of the 1870's the value of northwestern flour grew from $7.5 million to more than $41 million.

A number of technical improvements sped the growth of many other processed and canned foods. The Howe floater, which rolled cans in a solder bath, did away with individual soldering. This was improved with progressive steps leading to faster and more automated production. Eventually, solder was eliminated entirely, with the invention of a machine that crimped the top over the flanged edge of the can.

Other food processing devices included corn cutters, pea shellers, and viners. The latter had to wait until horticulturists developed a pea of which the entire crop matured at about the same time, so that it could be picked mechanically. Tomatoes did not become a member of the "big three" of canned vegetables until the 1870's, after the superstition that they were poisonous had begun to dissipate. So rapidly did canning techniques advance in the space of about fifteen years that Missouri Senator George Vest pointed out in 1890 that canned foods were no longer luxuries but "the poor man's food, being cheaper . . . than the green articles."

SILVER AND GOLD

From the outset there had always been a kind of American who was steeped in protest against the established order. And from the earliest colonial times there developed his counterfoil, who believed in the status quo and the sanctity of established institutions.

The dissident prototype immigrated to escape religious tyranny, became the Puritan farmer, then the backwoodsman, the frontiersman, and the westerner. He took many forms — Chartist, Marxist, Abolitionist, Granger, Prohibitionist, Mormon, Mennonite, Greenbacker, Antimason — and in his more activist aspects he was the engineer of strikes, demonstrations, Bacon's Rebellion, Shays's Rebellion, the Whiskey Rebellion, and the Civil War. The articles of his faith were the democratic spirit, land for homesteading, internal improvements, cheap and plentiful currency, and limitless opportunity to better his lot — presumably to the point where he too would come to favor the preservation of established institutions.

Arrayed against the protesters was the ruling coalition of wealth and power, the broad lines of whose evolution went from land grantee to merchant to industrialist to financier. This breed paid its homage to the principles of the high protective tariff, a plentiful supply of labor, controlled national development, and a sound and stable currency, preferably one backed by a gradually increasing supply of gold.

The lines between these two groups were not always hard and fast; in socially and economically mobile America, people might cross back and forth between them, and adherents to either might be betrayed by the unpredictable course of events. One such event was the Civil War. Because the farmer-frontiersman had always felt a strong sense of identity with the agrarian, debtor South, he could not wholeheartedly oppose the principles for which the South was willing to fight. But the northern businessman could resist the southern institution of slavery, untroubled by any division of loyalty, and feeling almost no kinship to the southern variety of capitalist. As a result, business was able to seize control of the Republican party and, fortified by the conservatism of a growing middle class, maintain control of the party and the nation's political institutions for a number of decades after the war. There were plenty of forces opposed to the businessman's government, but this opposition was fragmented until the late 1870's and largely ineffective until near the end of the century, when the closing of the frontier eliminated an important alternative for the laboring man.

The wartime greenback currency, not redeemable in gold or silver, was a thorn in the side of the sound money men. The Treasury began to retire the greenbacks shortly after the war. But so strident were the cries of anguish from the debtor groups, mainly farmers, that the action was stopped before it had proceeded far. Large amounts of unbacked currency meant inflation, higher prices for land and commodities, and cheaper money with which to repay debts.

The agrarian debtor groups even wanted the amount of greenbacks increased. They proposed that the wartime bonds not specifically redeemable in gold be repaid with additional greenbacks. This was known as the Ohio idea, and although it was actually included in the Democratic platform of 1868, presidential candidate Horatio Seymour refused to endorse the plan. Thwarted in their efforts to retire the greenbacks, the Republicans turned toward a resumption of specie payments. When they lost the congressional elections of 1874, the Republicans passed a lame duck measure to resume specie payments on January 1, 1879. When that day arrived, there was only $140 million in gold in the Treasury, but so strong was the government's credit that $400,000 in gold was actually turned in for paper, while only $125,000 in paper was presented for payment in gold.

Impelled by the resumption act, as well as by the continuing long-term decline in prices, the agrarian groups formed the Independent National party, soon to be known as the Greenback party. Joined by labor, the Greenbackers polled 1,000,000 votes in the 1878 elections and put up presidential candidates in 1880 and 1884 before disappearing as a party.

But the Greenback spirit did not disappear. It was picked up by the Union Labor party in 1888, and then by the Populist party, which drew more than 1,000,000 votes in the presidential election of 1892. The spirit of the Greenbackers also stayed alive in the long-drawn controversy between silver and gold.

Another way of keeping the money supply plentiful and prices high was to permit free coinage of silver at a fixed ratio to gold, particularly when the supply of silver was increasing so rapidly that it almost lost its status as a precious metal. The world's supply of gold had quadrupled by 1852, after the California discovery. But America's industry thereafter grew faster than its supply of gold, which made the bankers happy but failed to supply the processes of trade with the money lubrication they needed. Silver, meanwhile, had a major spurt in production after the Comstock Lode was found in Nevada, and American production of silver increased from an average of 503,000 fine ounces in the decade of the 1850's to almost 3 million in the next ten years, and it kept right on growing.

In 1873, however, the silver dollar was still worth $1.02 in gold, and Congress stopped its coinage. But the discovery of new deposits and the adoption of the gold standard by a number of European countries unloosed more silver on the market, so that the silver dollar was worth only ninety cents by 1876. Southern debtors, western farmers, and silver states demanded

Above: a contemporary view of a clash between troops, called out by President Hayes, and striking railroad workers in Baltimore, Maryland, 1877. Right: Samuel Gompers during an A.F.L. organizational drive among striking West Virginia coal miners

that the government "do something for silver." Congress did, passing the Bland-Allison Act, which called for monthly purchases by the government of $2 to $4 million in silver, to be coined into dollars weighing 412.5 grains of pure silver (compared to 371.25 grains in the older silver dollars). President Hayes vetoed the measure as inflationary, but it was passed over his veto in 1878.

Ironically, the silver purchases seemed to help business more than it did the farmers. Prices of commodities, including silver, kept dropping. The $378 million in silver bought during the twelve years of the Bland-Allison Act was readily absorbed by the increasing needs of railroad and industrial expansion. The value of the silver in the dollar dropped to seventy-two cents in 1889, and the following year Congress passed the Sherman Silver Purchase Act, requiring the Treasury to buy 4.5 million ounces of silver per month, virtually the total output of American mines. This requirement to buy by weight, rather than value, meant that less had to be spent for the purchases as silver declined further to sixty cents by 1893. But the continued buying did eventually put pressure on the gold standard.

When cheap money advocates sought to close ranks

politically, they discovered that both major parties had fallen under the influence of their adversaries. Democrat Grover Cleveland, sent to the White House in 1884, followed the business party line almost as faithfully as his predecessors. So farmers and workers gave themselves a voice by forming organizations of their own.

In 1867 farmers formed the National Grange of the Patrons of Husbandry, initially to promote co-operative buying of farm machinery. The Grange came to speak for the farmer in such matters as the inadequacy of the national banking system in serving small communities, the monopolistic practices of business, the government's deflationary policies, and such abuses as railroad rebates and rate discrimination. In the 1870's they helped push regulatory acts, known as "Granger laws," through state legislatures to prohibit these and other acts by railroads. The Supreme Court initially upheld these statutes but subsequently ruled that states could not regulate the rates of interstate carriers. Before that decision, however, the Interstate Commerce Act was passed in 1887, providing for a five-man commission to supervise railroad rates and practices.

For their part, industrial workers organized into

172

unions, and perhaps 250,000 were enrolled in thirty-two national unions by the early 1870's. The Brotherhood of the Footboard, later to become the Brotherhood of Locomotive Engineers, was formed in Detroit in 1863, followed in 1869 by the Brotherhood of Locomotive Firemen. Ironworkers called themselves the Sons of Vulcan, and shoemakers the Knights of Saint Crispin. Uriah Stephens, a Philadelphia garment worker, in 1869 became head of the Noble and Holy Order of the Knights of Labor, an organization that protected its members by maintaining strict secrecy in its activities.

Part of the impetus for union organization was the heavy influx of immigrants, often brought in as contract labor gangs. Willing to toil long hours uncomplainingly, they were resented by native workers. But a more compelling influence was wage cutting, usually done at the first sign of hard times and progressively increased during depressions.

Railroad workers, who felt they possessed skills vital to their industry, had built strong organizations. After two 10 per cent pay cuts in 1877 were followed by the use of "double-headers"—trains of twice the normal length but with a single crew—workers on the Baltimore & Ohio walked off their jobs, followed by

those on the Pennsylvania. As the strike spread and rail traffic ground to a halt, the governor of Maryland called out the National Guard to protect railroad property. A mob formed, stones were thrown, shots rang out, and ten workers lay dead. In Pittsburgh, units of the Pennsylvania militia were besieged in a roundhouse, and scores of workers and soldiers were shot before the troops broke free. Violence spread throughout Pennsylvania and to Chicago and St. Louis. At the request of several governors, President Rutherford Hayes called out the army. With troops protecting strikebreakers, the strike collapsed. Because employers thereafter continued to seek the help of troops in labor strife, armories were built in major cities to make the soldiers more readily available.

But out of labor's defeat rose a stronger national organization, as the Knights of Labor drew up a constitution, found a leader in Terence V. Powderly, and brought their activities into the open. The membership rolls climbed dramatically from 100,000 to 700,000 in a single year after a strike threat won concessions from Jay Gould's Missouri Pacific.

Meanwhile, another labor organization was forming in Pittsburgh under the leadership of Samuel Gompers. First called the Federation of Organized Trades and Labor Unions and reorganized in 1886 as the American Federation of Labor, it clung more strictly to trade union objectives than did the Knights of Labor. There followed a series of miscalculations by the Knights, along with some bad luck. When Powderly refused to go along with the Federation's idea for a walkout in support of the eight-hour day, the Knights lost some of their appeal to workers. A new strike against Gould's railroad system was defeated. And one of seven anarchists, condemned to die for the mysterious Haymarket bombing during a strike against McCormick Harvester, was suspected of having been a member of the Knights of Labor. While there was no clear evidence as to the identity of the bombers, seven policemen had died and there was a wave of public revulsion against the violence.

As the star of the Knights waned, that of the Federation rose, and Gompers's organization easily took over leadership of the American labor movement.

MAKING THE WHEELS SPIN

In spite of wage cuts and high immigration rates, the condition of the American worker underwent solid improvement in the generally prosperous years from 1865 to 1890. The long-term trend of wages was upward and that of prices downward, so that the real wages of those in industry actually doubled in the period.

Beyond this measurable improvement, there were a number of new inventions and discoveries which made both work and life easier and which introduced

173

The towering, 2,500-horsepower Corliss steam engine, a wonder of American industry at the Centennial Exposition, 1876

new dimensions of leisure and activity into the lives of people. There were ready-made clothes, the phonograph, the camera, trolley cars, elevators, gaslight, electricity, and the ubiquitous bicycle, among a great many other things. Housewives had sewing machines, carpet sweepers with revolving brushes, and geared egg beaters. A magic lantern with kerosene light could be bought for $12 to project pictures against a wall or a sheet. Working hours had dropped from around eleven a day in 1865 to an average of ten in 1890. Heavy work in factories was being done by steam power, which passed water power in use during the 1880's and supplied 75 per cent of all manufacturing power by 1900.

Led by such industries as steel, railroads, and petroleum, the value of all manufactures rose from $1.9 billion in 1860 to $9.4 billion in 1890. The wages of industrial workers climbed from $379 million to $1.89 billion.

The nation could not resist showing off this outpouring of goods, as well as its progress in the arts. In 1876 the government sponsored a Centennial Exposition in a fourteen-acre structure in Philadelphia. Here was a huge Corliss steam engine, standing forty feet high, weighing 700 tons, and developing 2,500 horsepower to send its energy along 11,000 feet of shaft-

ing to 8,000 machines scattered through the hall. A Worthington pump powered the water supply, including a cascade of fountains. "Here," announced the *Atlantic Monthly* that July, "is Prometheus unbound."

The look of the land reflected man's newfound prowess. John Roebling's great Brooklyn Bridge, using pneumatic caissons and wire suspension, was deemed one of the wonders of the modern world when it was completed in 1883. Skyscrapers lifted their steel skeletons to support the weight of curtain walls and floors, first in Chicago and later, when building laws permitted, in New York. Elevators made the high-rise buildings possible. The first practical elevator, with a safety stopping mechanism, was devised by Elisha Graves Otis to move furniture in his New York bed factory. This was progressively improved until Cyrus W. Baldwin built a hydraulic elevator that could travel 600 feet a minute. An electric elevator went into a Baltimore office building in 1884.

After undergoing the tortures of an overnight trip in an early railroad "sleeping car" in 1853, George Pullman took two old day coaches and built his own sleepers. The first was used to carry Lincoln's body from Washington to Springfield, Illinois, in 1865. Within two years forty-seven more were constructed. Pullman next built a "hotel car," which was soon replaced by the Pullman diner. Pullman cars were on coast-to-coast trains as early as 1870.

The typewriter, credited with doing more toward emancipating women than Susan B. Anthony, was first built and patented as a practical machine in 1868. The inventor, Christopher Latham Sholes, had started out to make a numbering machine for tickets, when a friend, Carlos Glidden, suggested adding letters. James Densmore, an oil man from Meadville, Pennsylvania, bought a share in the machine and spent a fortune making one improvement after another until, after some thirty models had been built, he was satisfied. The machine was sold to Eliphalet Remington and Sons, firearms makers in Ilion, New York. Densmore elected to take his payment in royalties, rather than in cash, and he eventually pocketed $1,500,000 on the arrangement. One of the machine's earliest users was Mark Twain, who sent a typescript of his *Adventures of Tom Sawyer* to the printer.

Photography, first confined to professionals, began to catch on in the United States after George Eastman read in an English almanac about a means of cutting the size and weight of camera equipment. He patented a paper-backed film in 1884 and started manufacturing a hand-held camera—after concocting a distinctive name for it, the Kodak. He sold the camera with enough film for 100 exposures, after which camera and film were returned to the factory for developing, printing, and reloading. "You press the button—we do the rest," Eastman advertised.

Printing underwent a number of major improvements. Stereotype plates, cast from impressions on papier-mâché matrices, were developed in the early 1860's by Charles Craske to replace the more awkward method of wedging type into place on the curved cylinders of Hoe presses. The halftone photoengraving plate was first used by the New York *Daily Graphic* in 1880. When a U.S. Patent Office employee, Ottmar Mergenthaler, developed a machine that could set type in hot metal from a keyboard, the New York *Tribune*'s Whitelaw Reid began using the Linotype as soon as he could get one, in 1886.

Ready-made clothing enjoyed a major boom, with an estimated sevenfold increase to $250 million between 1870 and 1890. Virtually all men's clothing and perhaps half of that worn by women and children were being produced in this way in factories and shops.

In this period the purchase of life insurance became an option of the workingman. John F. Dryden had noted that the Prudential Assurance Company of London was selling industrial insurance in England for as little as three cents a week and was enormously successful. He tried to sell the idea of a similar business in Newark, New Jersey, in depressed 1874. He pointed out that Newark workers earned an average of $513 a year and spent $521, that their death rate was 29.9 per thousand annually, and that one of their most pressing needs was for burial expenses. He set out to raise starting capital of $30,000, selling his first $1,000 share to Dr. Leslie D. Ward, a young Newark physician. In 1875 the Widows and Orphans Friendly Society changed its name to the Prudential Friendly Society, got its full capital subscribed, and started in business.

Dryden spent his lunch hours addressing meetings of workers but managed to make only a trickle of sales, mostly in the evening. But claims were paid, even though expenses far outran receipts. When, on one occasion, the company learned that the holder of a $500 policy had pneumonia and would probably not

---

The Way to Wealth

W. R. GRACE

W. R. GRACE & CO.

International trader W. R. Grace

Running away to sea, Americans often said, would make a man out of a boy. In the case of William Russell Grace (1832–1904), it created a mercantile genius of vision and drive. After roving the oceans for two years, Grace left his Irish homeland, which was beset by a potato famine, and settled in Peru, where he found work with ship chandlers in the port of Callao. The marine outfitters catered to vessels engaged in the trade in guano, bird droppings valued as fertilizer. Recognizing and making use of opportunities, Grace opened trade with Americans, exchanging guano for U.S. products to sell in Peru. He married a Yankee skipper's daughter, and at the close of the Civil War established himself at New York City's India House as a commercial correspondent in the South American trade.

His firm, W. R. Grace & Co., became influential in Peru, serving as confidential adviser to the government and supplying the country with arms that it used in a war against Chile. When Peru lost the war and was saddled with a $250 million debt—owed mostly to British bondholders—Grace reorganized the country's finances. He set up the Peruvian Corporation, Ltd., with a British peer at its head and his own firm as adviser, and assumed Peru's bonds. In return, he acquired the silver and copper mines of Cerro de Pasco, 5 million acres of oil- and mineral-rich lands, sixty-six-year leases on two railroads, the rights in perpetuity to build and own another railroad, together with its substantial land grants, and all the country's supply of guano.

Grace also moved into Chile to develop the trade in nitrates, build cotton and sugar mills, and form traction, light, and power companies. All the while, he continued to expand his export trade of U.S. manufactures that ranged from pins to locomotives, and by 1891 his mercantile house had its own steamship line.

In the meantime, Grace found time to be elected New York City's first Roman Catholic mayor, in 1880. He opposed Tammany Hall, reformed the police, curbed vice, and reduced taxes—and was re-elected in 1884.

After his death, his firm began to manufacture goods in Peru and Chile, largely to circumvent those nations' new tariffs that were designed to protect native industries. In 1928 the company went into an equal partnership with the fledgling Pan American to form the airline Panagra.

The stately old pioneer firm of international trade still possesses the rolltop desks of an earlier age in its New York offices and is still run by a member of the Grace family. Its annual sales of $2 billion rank it among the nation's fifty largest industrial corporations.

last the night, Dr. Ward rushed to her bedside and spent the night nursing both the patient and the coal stove, saving both the policyholder and the company.

The Prudential kept growing stronger, catching the attention in 1879 of the old-line Metropolitan Life Insurance Company, headed by Joseph Knapp. He had watched his own company flounder during the depression, while the Prudential's business expanded, and he decided to put Metropolitan's much larger organization to work selling industrial insurance too. In 1885 Prudential had assets of more than $1,000,000, and wrote its millionth policy. By the following year it decided it was big enough to invade Metropolitan's field, and it began selling ordinary life insurance, writing more than $4,000,000 in ordinary policies by the end of 1890.

ALADDIN OF BIG BUSINESS

John Davison Rockefeller, son of a western New York patent medicine salesman, was brought to Ohio at the age of fourteen, in 1853. He boarded in Cleveland, where he went to high school and attended the Erie Street Baptist Church regularly. In 1855 he got a job with the commission merchant firm of Hewitt and Tuttle, and there he decided that he liked the world of business with all its trappings. With a partner, Maurice Clark, he went into the produce business on his own.

Sent by some Cleveland businessmen to look over the booming oil fields of Pennsylvania, he concluded that he did not care for the wildcat, feast-or-famine production part of the petroleum industry, with its roller-coaster prices, but that the refining end had much promise. In 1862, he took his small savings and persuaded Clark and a chemist, Samuel Andrews, to join him in refining petroleum, a business that was just getting under way in Cleveland.

The refining process consisted simply of heating the crude oil in retorts, passing the vapor through a condensing worm, and separating the distillate in tanks. The first product, naphtha, was thrown out, and the final one, a heavy oil laced with paraffin, was hardly more useful. But in between came the valuable kerosene, the illuminating oil that was then lighting the lamps of the world. Rockefeller noted that while 75 to 80 per cent of the crude oil became illuminating oil, a single gallon of kerosene sold for twice as much as a barrel of crude.

Rockefeller dominated the partnership, insisting that all profits be left in the business. "Take out what you've got to live on," he advised his associates, "but leave the rest in. Don't buy new clothes and fast horses; let your wife wear her last year's bonnet. You can't find any place where money will earn what it does here." He saw that cash was vital to a business that

bankers believed untested and speculative; money would be difficult to come by when hard times arrived.

In 1865 Rockefeller bought out Clark's share. Two years later he brought together the interests of his own firm, Rockefeller and Andrews, with those of his brother William; of Henry M. Flagler, the son-in-law of a wealthy whiskey distiller; and of S. V. Harkness, who put $70,000 into the business. The new firm, under the name of Rockefeller, Andrews & Flagler, bought a second refinery. The company was soon the largest of some thirty refineries in Cleveland, a city that had natural advantages for oil refining because it possessed alternative rail and water transportation facilities.

In 1870 the firm was reorganized as the Standard Oil Company of Ohio, with $1,000,000 in capital and with warehouses, tank cars, a barrel-making plant, and two refineries producing 1,500 barrels of oil a day —the world's largest oil manufacturing concern. Standard's aggressive expansion policies soon made Rockefeller widely known, but his name became a household word with the public disclosure of his role in a rebate contract between the South Improvement Company and the railroads.

The rebating of freight charges to large shippers was a common, if somewhat disreputable, practice among railroads in those days. The South Improvement Company was a defunct Pennsylvania corporation whose charter, authorizing it to engage in virtually any kind of business, had been bought up by new owners; Rockefeller and his close associates owned 900 of the 2,000 South Improvement Company shares. South Improvement contracted with the Pennsylvania, New York Central, and Erie to prorate the oil traffic of a pool of independent refiners, headed by Standard. In return, South Improvement was to get a rebate of about half the freight charges, while other refiners would pay full rates. In addition, South Improvement would be paid a "drawback," which amounted to a rebate on freight paid by competing oil companies, as well as full information on the *competitors'* shipments. It turned out that the contract had probably been the idea of the railroads, rather than of the refiners. William H. Vanderbilt, asked some years later why the rebates had been granted, said of the Standard Oil group, "They are mighty smart men. I guess if you ever had to deal with them you would find that out."

The public outcry led to abandonment of the whole scheme and the cancellation of the South Improvement charter. But within the quiet confines of the oil industry, the point had been made: Standard Oil had the inside track with the railroad companies, and that would make them even tougher competitors than they already were. Rockefeller men began making offers to the smaller companies. In the spring of 1872 about 80 per cent of the other Cleveland refiners sold out— mostly for cash, although a choice of stock was offered.

Standard Oil's capacity increased eightfold, to 12,000 barrels a day, or about a third of the U.S. oil business.

The Cleveland acquisitions proved an opening wedge, driven further by the depression of the 1870's, for buying up Pittsburgh's thirty refineries, as well as the largest firms in New York, Philadelphia, and Baltimore. John D. Archbold, a brilliant young refiner and an outwardly bitter foe of the Standard octopus, began bringing independent refiners in the oil-producing regions into his own Acme Oil Company, and managed to absorb most of them. Then it turned out that Acme was a Standard Oil subsidiary. Rockefeller had obviously set out years before to monopolize the oil business; it was equally obvious that he was about to succeed. The smartest policy for the other refiners, hindsight showed, would simply have been to take Standard Oil stock rather than cash.

One obstacle to full domination of the industry lay in the imperative need to transport its products. Standard held the whip hand over the railroads but did not own them. Furthermore, there appeared to be a better method of transporting oil on its own slippery way. General S. D. Karns in 1860 first suggested a pipeline for moving oil downhill. Five years later Samuel Van Syckel of Titusville, Pennsylvania, built a four-mile oil pipeline, equipped with a pump, so that it could be sent along level ground. Other pipelines soon cut the price of carrying crude oil to the Allegheny River from as much as three dollars a barrel to as little as fifty cents.

As pipelines and pipeline companies grew bigger, Standard began to buy them up. It acquired a one-third interest in one of the largest, the American Transfer Company, and then got control of the United Pipe Line Company. The Pennsylvania Railroad started its own pipeline and oil refining subsidiary, the Empire Transportation Company, but Standard bought it out in 1877. The Tidewater Pipe Company was organized in 1878 to lay a line from the Bradford, Pennsylvania, field across the Alleghenies to the seacoast, and engineers agreed that the oil could be made to flow uphill. With Hoosac Tunnel builder General Herman Haupt in charge, the company set out against its adversaries—nature, finances, and competitors. The following May the oil was flowing 109 miles to a meeting with the Reading Railroad. After four years the line had been completed to Baltimore, and in 1886 it reached New York City. But Tidewater had meanwhile concluded an agreement giving Standard 88.5 per cent of the business and keeping the rest for itself.

By 1880, its coffers swollen with more than $40 million in cash, Standard Oil had virtually eliminated competition and controlled 90 per cent or more of the nation's oil business. By then it had absorbed the Vacuum Oil Company, which had developed a method of deriving a superior lubricating oil from petroleum. And Rockefeller, turning pennies into dollars, was still keeping the same watchful eye on the business that had once induced him to write to his barrel factory: "Last month you reported on hand 1,119 bungs. 10,000 were sent you beginning this month. You have used 9,527 this month. You report 1,092 on hand. What has become of the other 500?"

Like a great cartel, Standard Oil divided the country into districts, with an agent in charge of each and subagents in charge of smaller divisions. The instruction given to each was, "Sell all the oil that is to be sold in your district." It did not matter whether this meant spying on competitors or bribing railroad freight agents. Results were all that counted.

The twelve original stockholders of the Standard Oil Company had grown by 1881 to no more than forty-one. As additional properties were brought into the organization, these interests were held by trustees for the benefit of all the stockholders. In 1882 a Standard Oil lawyer set up a simple, yet ingenious, instrument for maintaining a centralized administration of the entire organization, including the many companies that had been absorbed. This was a trust, in which nine trustees were to hold all the stock in Standard and the subsidiary companies for the benefit of all the stockholders. The stockholders were given $70 million in trust certificates, as evidence of their participation.

Other businessmen admired and copied the device, but even though the trust merely formalized the already-existing near monopoly in the petroleum industry, there was a public outcry against it. With the passage of antimonopoly legislation, the Ohio courts in 1890 broke up the Standard Oil Trust into twenty companies, ordering that proportionate shares of stock in each one be issued to the individual trust certificate holders. The trust was then replaced with an even more flexible—and legal—device, when the Standard Oil Company of New Jersey was formed as a holding company to own and control the various Standard subsidiaries.

THE GREAT SILENT SERVANT

The harnessing of electricity for communication by Samuel F. B. Morse was only a beginning, and his work was carried on in the postwar years by two worthy successors—Thomas Alva Edison and Alexander Graham Bell.

Thomas Edison was born in Milan, Ohio, in 1847, and his family moved to Port Huron, Michigan, seven years later. There he went to school for three months until he overheard the headmaster call him "addled." He stalked out, not to return. Immensely curious, he made the whole world his school. He set a fire in his father's barn "just to see what it would do"; what his father did was whip him in the village square. He wanted to know why a goose squatted on eggs, and was soon found curled up over a nest of goose and chicken eggs. He played with chemicals, built his own telegraph set, and, when he started selling newspapers on a train, a sudden lurch upset a jar holding some sticks of phosphorous and set fire to his "laboratory"—a little-used mail and baggage car.

He learned telegraph dispatching and spent five years as an itinerant operator, once devising a clockwork mechanism that would automatically report in with a "sixing" signal while he catnapped. He arrived in Boston in 1868, got work as a night operator, and spent much of his daylight hours studying. He purchased a used two-volume set of Michael Faraday's *Experimental Researches in Electricity* and considered it a major turning point in his life.

After getting his first patent, on an automatic vote recorder, he came to New York in 1869, arriving at the office of the Gold Indicator Company just as their central transmitting instrument broke down. In the excitement, neither Franklin L. Pope, the electrical engineer, nor a Dr. Laws, the inventor, could find the trouble. Edison looked it over, located the problem, and had it repaired within two hours. He was hired to assist the engineer and later replaced him at a salary of $300 a month when Pope left to become a consulting engineer.

Edison's inventions netted him considerable sums of money, which he never quite learned how to manage. He improved the Laws printer and later, with Pope, developed a new type of printing telegraph, for which he received $5,000. For a unison-stop device that kept stock tickers from printing wildly he got $30,000. But so untrained was he in business matters that he did not know how to cash the check; then, when he did so, he spent a sleepless night guarding the money until friends told him he could redeposit the cash in the bank.

He invented a device called a mimeograph in 1875

THE "WAR OF THE CURRENTS"

Those who sought wealth in the California gold rush, suggested Thomas Ewbank, U.S. Commissioner of Patents, "should seek placers inexpressibly more precious than any to be found on the Sacramento by digging in the mines of the motors."

Thomas Alva Edison did so, inventing the light bulb and the dynamo, and building the first electrical generating station. Edison's system of power transmission was based on the use of direct current, a one-way flow of electricity that required wires as thick as a man's arm to carry power within New York City.

George Westinghouse, a New York engineer who had become wealthy developing a railroad air brake that reliably stopped what steam set in motion, inspected Edison's system in 1880. He was disappointed to discover that the generating plant could not illuminate lamps more than a few miles away.

Westinghouse made an analogy with his air brake system. "In our gas system," he told a colleague, "we took gas at high pressures and delivered them at a low pressure wherever it was needed. Why can't we do the same thing with electricity?" He found his answer in the inventions of an English engineer and a French electrician. It was called a "secondary generator"—or transformer—that could step current up or down.

WESTINGHOUSE, INC.

George Westinghouse

He bought the patent rights for $50,000 and was able to pump high-voltage current for long distances, then reduce it to the lower power needed to illuminate lamps. Fewer generating plants meant greater efficiency and lower costs.

The device required a pulsating current, known as alternating current, that kept reversing its direction of flow. Edison was stubbornly opposed to its use. The outcome was a so-called "war of the currents," a contest of opposing technologies carried on in public view.

Using advertisements, Edison claimed that alternating current was unsafe and deadly, and legislators in some states responded by trying to outlaw a.c. In the *North American Review* in 1889, Edison wrote that the "high tension alternating-current system" was a purveyor of death and cited the recent adoption of electrocution, using a standard Westinghouse alternator, for capital punishment in New York. "I have never killed anybody," he announced.

In the same magazine, Westinghouse retorted, "The alternating current can kill people, of course. So will gunpowder, and dynamite, and whiskey, and lots of other things; but we have a system whereby the deadly electricity of the alternating current can do no harm unless a man is fool enough to swallow a whole dynamo."

and sold it to A. B. Dick of Chicago. Much of his time he worked for Western Union, except for a year of estrangement when he got most of his income from Jay Gould's Automatic Telegraph Company; he was paid $30,000 for work on developing a system of quadruplex telegraphy, in which four messages could be sent on a single wire. For a period, when Western Union had him work on a "speaking telegraph," Edison and Bell were crossing wires in their inventive efforts. In 1877 Edison built his first primitive phonograph.

But the inventor's greatest concentration was on the incandescent lamp, at his laboratories in Menlo Park, New Jersey. Charles F. Brush of Cleveland had produced a usable carbon arc lamp, a generator to supply current, and a shunt coil to let the current bypass a burned-out unit. The lamps were used to light Cleveland streets, and night window shopping became fashionable after John Wanamaker first installed arc lights in his Philadelphia store in 1878.

Scores of people were working on an incandescent lamp, after the invention of a mercury vacuum pump made it possible to protect the filament by sealing it in a vacuum. But the problems remained of finding a substance for a filament that would glow for a sufficiently long time, and devising a means of "subdividing the current" among many lamps. After trying thousands of vegetable and nonvegetable substances, including hairs from the beards of his associates, Edison finally settled on a carbonized strip of Japanese bamboo, which provided the first filaments for a half dozen years. Edison's basic patent on the lamp was dated January 27, 1880. His backing in this work came from a group of capitalists, including J. P. Morgan, who subscribed $50,000 for 500 shares in the Edison Electric Light Company, with Edison getting 2,500 shares. The problem of "subdividing" electric current was solved almost simultaneously by Richard Werdermann in London and by Moses G. Farmer of the U.S. Naval Station at Newport, Rhode Island, both of whom devised "ladders" of parallel circuits. Edison later invented a three-wire system and adopted the 110-volt potential, which became standard in the United States.

The early users of electric lights had power units chugging in their basements, but Edison realized that a central power station was essential to an electric lighting business—and he actually had one worked out on paper before the electric light was perfected. Into the Pearl Street central power station in New York he had poured $600,000 for boilers, steam engines, dynamos, and switches by the time it opened in 1882. His first customers were downtown stores. He was supplying current for 5,000 lamps within four months and for 20,000 by 1890.

Power stations were soon sought by other cities, including even isolated little Sheridan, Wyoming, with its 600 people. George Westinghouse, who had made a fortune from his air brake, also got into the business of supplying dynamos to produce electric power. Westinghouse got the jump on Edison by adopting alternating current, fed to users by step-down transformers, much more practical than sending electricity over long distances by direct current. Alternating current quickly won "the war of the currents" waged with Edison, and became the power used to light 25 million incandescent lamps in the U.S. by 1900.

Frank J. Sprague, who had worked with Edison, designed motors to use his current. Smoothly and noiselessly, the low-power motors ran coffee grinders, fans, and printing presses, and 10,000 were being turned out by a number of manufacturers by 1890. In 1887 Sprague also built the first complete electric railway system in Richmond, Virginia.

The Pearl Street station in New York City became the main unit of the Edison Illuminating Co., which eventually became the Consolidated Edison Company.

In time, technology made its own case. An a.c.-driven motor supplied twenty times more power than Edison's motors, a convincing point to industry. Westinghouse won out, his alternating current making possible the electrification of railroads and traction trolleys. In 1895 he received the contract to harness the flow at Niagara Falls for the long-distance transmission of electric power.

By 1900 some $1 billion was invested in the business of electric lighting. The nation had 15,000 miles of electrified railroads, compared to a total of 1,000 in Canada, England, France, and Russia combined. In that same year, Henry Adams wrote that he felt "the forty-foot dynamos as a moral force, much as the early Christians felt the Cross. . . . Among the thousand symbols of ultimate energy the dynamo was not so human as some, but it was the most expressive."

American electrical equipment makers, in that year of 1900, sold more than $5 million worth of their products abroad. It was mostly a.c., rather than d.c. And in its competition with Westinghouse Electric, General Electric—the industrial giant that grew out of Edison's pioneering work—was also soon making most of its products to generate or be powered by alternating current.

The various Edison equipment and lamp makers were brought together into the Edison General Electric Co., of which Henry Villard became the first president after he helped market the stock in Germany. A merger in 1892 of this company with the Thomson-Houston Electric Co., founded by Elihu Thomson of Philadelphia, formed the General Electric Company.

Bell, the other major inventor of the period, was born in Edinburgh in 1847, came first to Canada and then to Boston in 1871. His father and grandfather had done acoustics research and had taught the deaf and dumb, and he had intimate knowledge of their work. It chanced that two wealthy Bostonians, Gardiner G. Hubbard and Thomas Sanders, had daughters who were deaf-mutes, and Bell was hired to teach the girls.

When Hubbard and Sanders learned of Bell's familiarity with acoustics, they decided to back him in experiments aimed at developing a harmonic telegraph, which could send different messages over a wire by tuning the receivers to different pitches of

sound. Unknown to Bell, Western Union's Elisha Gray was working on the use of the same principle. To the considerable dismay of his backers, Bell abandoned this project for the more exciting one of trying to send the human voice over an electric wire.

Their support withdrawn, Bell and his assistant, Thomas A. Watson, carried on alone. One day Watson accidentally plucked a piece of clock wire, and Bell, in another room, heard the distinct twang, carried to him over a telegraph line. They worked for forty weeks on their new device. Finally, on March 10, 1876, Bell picked up his instrument and said "Mr. Watson, come here, I want you," and Watson, holding a receiver in a distant room, heard the message. Bell had filed his patent application almost a month earlier, on February 14, just two hours before Elisha Gray filed the description of an electric telephone that would work on the same principles.

Hubbard and his deaf daughter, Mabel, who had become Bell's fiancée, urged that the telephone be

FINANCE CAPITALISTS: THE MIDWIVES OF BUSINESS

Before the Civil War, labor and natural resources were the principal contributions of the United States to its own economic growth. Capital — the vital ingredient for stimulating that growth — was largely imported. The industrialization and accumulation of wealth during the war, however, created a money market within the country and provided a heady stimulus to men who made the finding of capital their sole business.

They were a new breed in America. Their forerunners were men like Stephen Girard, John Jacob Astor, and William Wilson Corcoran, a banker who left a great art gallery in Washington, D.C. But in their day there were relatively few areas where money was required in advance. One of them was in the merchandising of dry goods and textiles, and as a result many of the men who emerged as the most prominent investment bankers in the post-Civil War era of industrialization came from the mercantile trade. It was where Junius S. Morgan, George Peabody, and Jay Cooke started; it was the genesis of Brown Brothers & Co., J. & W. Seligman, and Kuhn, Loeb & Co. They financed imports of copper and exports

KUHN, LOEB & CO.

Jacob H. Schiff

of cotton, transactions in which credit was essential. In Europe and England they were known as "merchant bankers," inheritors of a tradition as old as the East India Company.

Investment bankers engaged in the business of finance capitalism — channeling funds from where they had ac-

cumulated to where they could be put to work at a profit. By the time of J. Pierpont Morgan, the son of Junius, bankers had become the midwives of business, giving birth to new enterprise by securing the capital it needed. From 1890 to 1915, the capitalization in stocks and bonds — which reflected the faith of investors in future earnings — of such public-service corporations as railroads, street railways, and utilities alone swelled from less than $20 million to nearly $20 billion. Mindful of the stakes of those who bought the securities, investment bankers watched carefully over the enterprises they helped to create, sometimes insisting on a considerable measure of control of their affairs.

One of the earliest investment banking houses was Kuhn, Loeb & Co. It was started by two German-born brothers-in-law, Abraham Kuhn and Solomon Loeb, who had built up a merchandising business in Cincinnati. In 1867 they opened a banking house in New York. Not until Loeb's son-in-law, Jacob H. Schiff, joined the firm did it begin to play a major role in American finance capitalism. Brought up in the German financial capital of Frankfurt am Main,

put on display at the Philadelphia Centennial. It was placed in an obscure corner, but there Brazil's young emperor, Dom Pedro, who was visiting the United States, put it to his ear while Bell spoke at the other end. "My God! It talks!" he exclaimed.

The Bell Telephone Association was formed in 1877 by Bell, Watson, and their backers, once more including Hubbard and Sanders, but the business had hard sailing. And small wonder. The same funnel-shaped device was used for both talking and listening, and it was necessary to "shout like a Gloucester sea-captain at the height of a storm" to be heard, according to writer Burton Hendrick. At the telephone exchange, boys ran around with wires, trying to make the right connections, cursing volubly all the while.

Hubbard had been impressed with a young man named Theodore N. Vail, working in Washington as general superintendent of the Railway Mail Service, and he lured him into the enterprise with glowing promises of a $3,500 annual salary. Vail saw none of it for ten years, but he measured up to all of Hubbard's expectations. The vision he pursued relentlessly was one in which anyone in the United States could pick up a phone and talk to anyone else. This meant standardized equipment, which in turn meant leasing the instruments, rather than selling them. Vail also insisted on good engineering and on courteous treatment of the public.

Vail pressed a seemingly hopeless infringement suit against the giant Western Union in 1878. After about a year, Western Union settled, agreeing to get out of the telephone business and sell its interests to Bell Telephone, which was then able to take over the Western Union system of 56,000 phone subscribers in fifty-five communities. Bell also acquired Western Electric Manufacturing Company, which made telephone equipment.

The American Bell Telephone Company was organized by Vail in 1881. Six years later the company had 170,000 subscribers in the United States, each

---

Schiff had come to New York at the end of the Civil War, become a licensed broker in 1866, and worked with a firm called Budge, Schiff & Co. until its dissolution in 1872. He returned to Germany until summoned by Kuhn, Loeb & Co. two years later.

Schiff brought valuable contacts— London financier Sir Ernest Cassel, the Banque de Paris in France, Hamburg's M. M. Warburg, Copenhagen's Henriques, Amsterdam's Hope & Co., Tokyo's Baron Takahashi, and the Rothschilds throughout Europe. He built up, as well, connections with Americans upon whose funds he could call, including Edward H. Harriman, George Westinghouse, and members of James Stillman's National City Bank.

Railroads attracted Schiff. In 1877 Kuhn, Loeb raised the money needed for the Chicago and North Western, and in 1881 for the Pennsylvania and the Chicago, Milwaukee & St. Paul. By 1885, when he was thirty-eight, Schiff had become head of the firm. He helped capitalize more than twelve other railroads, then reorganized the Union Pacific—in 1897 a "ribbon of rust," deeply in debt.

By 1900 Kuhn, Loeb & Co. was engaged in capitalizing almost all types of American industry, from smelting, leather, and locomotives to rubber, telegraph, and electrical equipment.

The firm helped to open the iron ore deposits of Minnesota's Mesabi Range, the basic source of supply for the United States Steel Corporation. Schiff, known as a hoarder of writing paper and string, had been reluctant to invest in industrials even up to the turn of the century. But when he did become involved, he followed through meticulously, usually securing a seat on the new venture's board of directors.

When he considered the time was ripe, Schiff looked overseas. His firm led the underwriting of $200 million for Imperial Japanese government loans during the Russo-Japanese War that are largely credited with moving that country into its industrial age. And he sought funds for China's acquisition of the Manchurian railroad system; American money in that railroad, it was thought, would prevent future wars between Russia and Japan.

By 1902 investment bankers had helped put together more than 200 industrial enterprises, capitalized at $10 billion. Eleven years later, while the number of rails listed on the Stock Exchange had only doubled, to 147, since the Civil War, the number of industrials had increased more than twelvefold, to 191.

Securities were the daily bread of the investment bankers. They sold foreign government and corporation bonds, the bonds of U.S. railroads, industrials, and utilities, and preferred and common stocks. The securities could be their cake, too. In 1929 one major corporation, Pennroad, considered too high the request of Kuhn, Loeb & Co. for $250,000 to service and market their securities and offered, instead, shares of their stock. The investment firm agreed and in a six-month period made $5,800,000 total in profits, fees, and commissions in the deal.

Income was derived not only from purchasing issues from a corporation and selling them to the public at a few points' increase in price, or for a cash commission, but also from payments in kind. When United States Steel was launched, the syndicate put together by Morgan was paid 1,300,000 shares of stock, rather than cash, for its services. When the issue was distributed on the open market, the syndicate made a clear profit of $62,500,000; Morgan's share was $12,500,000.

With the middleman function of the investment banker went risk and possible loss of reputation. The risk was that of making an investment in a bad business; the loss of reputation would come from selling it to others. As Schiff said of reputation: "If that is gone, our business is gone, however attractive our show window might be."

paying $240 a year. By 1900, after the American Telephone and Telegraph Company had taken over the business, there were more than 600,000 subscribers, and the company was growing faster than ever.

COMBINATIONS AND REORGANIZATIONS

With government giving at least the appearance of tacit approval, monopolistic practices took on many forms in the decades after the Civil War.

Six corporations had come to own most of Pennsylvania's anthracite coal and transportation facilities by 1873, and they subsequently gathered in the bituminous supplies as well. In Michigan the salt producers formed the Michigan Salt Association in 1876, a pool in the form of a stock company in which the members received one share of stock for each barrel of their own company's average daily capacity. Each member had to turn over either his plant or his production to the association, which could then set both quality standards and prices. The agreement was to last for just five years, but it was continued for two more five-year periods. Following the Rockefeller example, James Buchanan Duke of North Carolina brought together the country's five leading cigarette makers into a $25 million trust in 1890, and Henry O. Havemeyer helped organize a group of sugar refineries into a price-fixing trade association in 1887. The American Cottonseed Oil Trust was formed in 1884, the National Linseed Oil Trust the following year, and the National Lead Trust in 1887.

Specialists developed in the business of pooling, combining, and reorganizing. A Chicago lawyer, W. H. Moore, headed a firm that reorganized the Diamond Match Company by increasing its capital and bringing in the sawmills, factories, and box makers that supplied the match trade. Charles R. Flint, Jr., a merchant known as the "father of trusts," helped organize combinations of companies making starch, rubber, and other products. But the greatest combiner and reorganizer of them all was a quiet, dignified New England banker named John Pierpont Morgan.

Morgan was born in Hartford, Connecticut, in 1837, and was virtually brought up in the international banking business. His father was Junius S. Morgan, an expatriate American who had moved to London in 1837 to be the representative of America in British capital markets and who worked for the merchant banking house of George Peabody & Co. The firm became J. S. Morgan and Company after Peabody, noted for his widespread philanthropy and his refusal of a title from Queen Victoria, retired in 1864.

John Pierpont worked in the London office but was sent to New York when the American correspondent firm ran into difficulty in the 1857 panic. Young Morgan

formed a partnership with the firm's accountant, and they took over the J. S. Morgan correspondency. When his partner later retired, J. P. Morgan joined forces with the Philadelphia Drexels. Senior partner Anthony J. Drexel bought the southeastern corner of Broad and Wall streets in New York, put up the Drexel Building, and Drexel, Morgan and Company opened its offices.

The firm challenged Jay Cooke & Co. in an effort to get contracts for government financing, but lost out. Drexel, Morgan persisted, however, and finally was given half of the sale of $300 million in bonds in a huge government refunding in 1873. After Jay Cooke & Co. failed, the Drexel, Morgan interests, with their excellent connections overseas, and in combination with banker Levi P. Morton, moved into the vacuum.

William H. Vanderbilt, owning 87 per cent of the New York Central's stock and feeling numerous pressures to dispose of it, turned to Morgan for advice. Through the London house, Morgan formed a syndicate in November, 1879, to sell 250,000 shares to scattered, but long-term, investors abroad. The whole transaction was conducted quietly, and Drexel, Morgan cleared about $2.5 million in a rising market for the shares. Morgan himself went onto the Central's board.

By the early 1880's the country had developed more railroads than it could profitably utilize; rate-cutting wars set in, and Wall Street had a panic in 1884, driving down the prices of railroad securities. Between Chicago and the East Coast there were five squabbling railroads, one bankrupt, three others nearly so, and the New York Central getting ready to cut its dividends. Morgan invited the top executives of the roads to a meeting on his yacht, where there would be no telephone calls, no interruptions, and no opportunity to walk away in anger. Before the day ended, the rate war was over.

Morgan's reputation as a doctor of sick railroads grew. Robert Garrett, in trouble with the Baltimore & Ohio, came to him for help. Morgan began the slow process of reorganization, making sure that the line would be able to tie in with the Vanderbilt roads on the west bank of the Hudson River. Morgan reorganized the Southern system, then the Erie, in each case seeking to get enough control to see his plans through, and in that way protect the interests of investors to whom he sold new issues of the railroads' securities. He was instrumental in reorganizations of the Hocking Valley, the Northern Pacific, and the Atchison, Topeka, and Santa Fe, among others.

As a consequence of these activities, he emerged as the most powerful man in American railroading, with voting control over a number of systems and a dominant voice in others. But the great era when railroads epitomized America's amazing expansion was drawing to a close. The time of great industrial consolidations was about to begin. And J. P. Morgan was ready.

V Opportunity for Enterprise

The pinnacle of American power: John D. Rockefeller (left), builder of an industrial and financial empire, out for a stroll

66 The desire of the individual to be let alone, to do as he pleases, indulge his impulses, follow out his projects . . . has been extremely strong in America, being rooted in the character and habits of the race. . . . the circumstances of colonial life, the process of settling the western wilderness, the feelings evoked by the struggle against George III, all went to intensify individualism, the love of enterprise, and the pride in personal freedom. And from that day to this. . . [they] have been deemed by Americans not only their choicest, but their peculiar and exclusive possessions."

James Bryce, *The American Commonwealth*, 1888

Opportunity for Enterprise

Many merchandisers got their start as peddlers (right), sharpening their skill at selling and, like traveling salesmen, valuing the freedom of their occupation.

The springing into existence of brand new towns (still an American phenomenon) provided opportunities for enterprising pioneers. Below: the birth of Guthrie in Oklahoma's land rush, 1889

Admiration of rugged individualism made folk heroes even of daring outlaws like Jesse James, a U.S. celebrity at his death in 1882 (left).

"I go my own way," said Hetty Green (right), an eccentric miser who managed her own money and ran $1 million up to $100 million.

A musing Uncle Sam (below) ponders overseas sales opportunities in an 1877 drawing: "The world is my market. My customers are all Mankind."

Enterprise in the field of transportation took many directions. Above: putting final touches on George M. Pullman's cars, which brought comfort to railroad travel. Right: workers on John A. Roebling's Brooklyn Bridge during construction in 1872

Gail Borden EAGLE BRAND CONDENSED MILK

Best Food FOR INFANTS AND CHILDREN

IVORY IT FLOATS 99 44/100 Per Cent PURE

Achieving the mass production of goods was one thing; getting masses of people to buy them was another. And persuading purchasers to buy a particular product rather than one that competed with it was perhaps the most difficult task of all. The challenges of the expanding marketplace gave rise to the enterprise and art of advertising. The ads shown here, some of the most famous of the past, made their products household names and enormously profitable.

The sweetheart of the corn

Kellogg's
TOASTED CORN FLAKES
The package of the genuine bears this signature
W. K. Kellogg
Toasted Corn Flake Co., Battle Creek, Mich.
Canadian Trade Supplied by the Battle Creek Toasted Corn Flake Co., Ltd. London, Ontario

Kellogg's
TOASTED CORN FLAKES
W. K. Kellogg
TOASTED CORN FLAKE CO.
BATTLE CREEK, MICH.

H. J. HEINZ CO.

ARROW
COLLARS

WHEN you buy an Arrow you get the best that there is at the price you are asked to pay. That is the one big fundamental reason for the preference shown for Arrows.

Cluett, Peabody & Co., Inc., Troy, N. Y.
Makers of Arrow Shirts and Gotham Underwear

"I'D WALK A MILE FOR A CAMEL"

—but a "MISS" is as Good as a MILE

'Ever-Ready'
12 Bladed
Safety
Razor $1.00
Complete

WARSHAW COLLECTION, SMITHSONIAN INSTITUTION

Henry J. Kaiser's enthusiasm and initiative made him a giant in a variety of industries. From paving and building (above: at Hoover Dam, which he helped raise), he went on to cement, steel, aluminum, shipbuilding, and automobile manufacturing.

190

Authentic originals like Hugh Heffner (above) and R. Buckminster Fuller (below) have continued to intrigue the world with new ideas. From Playboy *magazine Heffner built a sex-oriented empire of clubs and resorts, staffed by scantily clad "bunnies." Technologist Fuller, designer of the geodesic dome, grapples inspiringly with the compelling problems of mankind's survival.*

6

THE TIME OF THE
TITANS

1890-1918

Toward the close of the century, two forces acted to curb the business buccaneering that had characterized the post-Civil War era. The first was a wave of reform that welled up as a reaction to the more flamboyant excesses of the time and which began to permeate political institutions, locally as well as nationally. The second was the ascendance of a group of more responsible business leaders, motivated both by their desire to forestall government regulation and by their sense that business and industry had larger purposes than simply accumulating wealth.

Typical of these men was John Pierpont Morgan, a hulking bear of a man who dominated American finance throughout the turn-of-the-century era. Morgan had as little patience with government efforts to intrude into what he regarded as his private business domain as he had with the manipulators and speculators who brought disrepute to finance. "Send your man to my man," he once suggested to President Theodore Roosevelt, in order to dispose of the annoyance of a threatened antitrust action.

More and more, real businessmen were taking charge of business. Edward Harriman and James J. Hill, although not above a little financial legerdemain, were both devoted to building and running good railroad systems. The Rockefellers were builders, producers, and sound businessmen. James Stillman and George F. Baker were careful and prudent bankers. Meyer Guggenheim rose to industrial power because he insisted on learning everything there was to be known about a business. Andrew Carnegie and Charles Schwab were hard-nosed producers and sellers of

steel. Henry Ford was a mechanic who built new ideas not only into his cars but also into his manner of running a business.

Whereas the nation had been able up to this time to achieve great feats of production *in spite of* some of its business leaders, these new giants of the production line and finance were energetically pushing America to new heights of industrial power. In one category after another, the United States moved from the position of trying harder to that of being No. 1 in the world. By 1900 the nation was producing approximately a third of the world's coal, iron, and steel, having just passed England in all three products. That same year America overtook Germany, her nearest rival, in machine-tool output.

The nation's productive power grew even faster after 1900. Its real wealth, placed at $65 billion in 1890 and $88.5 billion by the census of 1900, more than doubled in the next fourteen years. The value of manufactured products soared from around $11 billion to $60 billion by the end of World War I. But farming remained the largest single industry as the new century began and as the value of farm crops rose from just under $3 billion in 1899 to almost $5.5 billion ten years later. Meanwhile, the value of all farm property had doubled, to more than $41 billion, and the average value of farm land more than doubled, from $15.57 an acre in 1900 to $32.40 in 1910.

Another hoary tradition was shaken when the United States in 1901 passed Great Britain in the value of her export trade. The American frontier, as historian Frederick Jackson Turner noted, was virtually closed by 1890. Businessmen had to start to

Looking J. Pierpont Morgan in the eye was like facing the headlights of an onrushing express train, said Edward Steichen, who took this memorable photograph in 1903.

look elsewhere for markets for this great outpouring of goods. At the same time came America's first stirrings of colonial expansionism, starting with the Spanish-American War in 1898, the conquest of the Philippines, the interference in Mexican affairs, and the treating of much of Central America as a protectorate.

More than simply encouraging foreign trade, these adventures spurred American overseas investments, which in time became a kind of colonialism by other means. But the United States remained a net importer of capital until 1914, at which time some $7 billion in European funds, more than half of it British, was invested in America. Still, the tide was beginning to turn. America was financing more and more of its own business expansion and putting some money to work overseas, both by purchasing securities and by placing funds directly into business ventures. These investments grew from $658 million in 1897, just before the Cuban war, to $2.5 billion by 1914. Europe, Mexico, Canada—these were the places where Americans felt most secure about investing their money. Mexico led all other countries, with $200 million in U.S. investments in 1897; in 1910 Americans controlled 80 per cent of the investment in Mexican railroads and 70 per cent of her oil output. But Canada moved up rapidly and by 1908 had taken the lead from Mexico as the chief target of U.S. capital.

While most Americans enjoyed the identification with all this burgeoning growth, they nevertheless tended to vote their pocketbooks. Grover Cleveland, who rode a tide of reform into the White House in 1884, carefully avoided antagonizing the business community. But Benjamin Harrison defeated him in 1888, when for the first time in the country's history the tariff was made the major issue of the campaign. The McKinley tariff, passed in 1890, raised the average level of import duties to almost 50 per cent. When these rates were quickly reflected in higher living costs, Cleveland was brought back to office in 1892, sweeping other Democrats along with him. Even though some of the Democrats knuckled under to the tariff lobby, duties were trimmed back to an average of about 40 per cent by the Wilson-Gorman Act of 1894. William McKinley had hardly got settled into the Presidency in 1897 when he called a special session of Congress, which increased average tariff rates to a whopping 57 per cent by the Dingley Act.

The McKinley years were mainly a time of prosperity and growth, bulwarked by a succession of good harvests and lubricated by new discoveries of gold. Business and government frequently worked hand in hand, and the voters tended to endorse the consequences. On the Hill in Washington, House Speaker Joseph "Uncle Joe" Cannon and Senator Nelson Aldrich became leading voices in behalf of business

interests. They were able to stave off strong railroad legislation until 1910, tariff cuts until 1913, and an effective antitrust law until 1914. The Aldrich-Vreeland Act of 1908, which empowered banks to issue currency backed by either corporate or government bonds, operated as a stopgap to fend off more radical banking laws until a commission headed by Aldrich had made a world banking study, which set much of the groundwork for the Federal Reserve Act of 1913.

The courts were, if anything, even more probusiness. A tax of 2 per cent on personal incomes over $4,000 was declared unconstitutional in 1895. While a few business combinations were ordered dissolved under state laws, federal courts were quick to label unions "in restraint of trade" under the Sherman Antitrust Act, but slow to apply similar strictures against business monopolies.

On the whole, government followed a hands-off policy, and business was glad of it. A remarkable transformation had taken place in business-government relationships in the course of a century. The Hamiltonian notion had been that government needed to protect and nurture the nation's commerce and industry, while the Jeffersonians, attuned to the freedoms of an agrarian age and an open and unlimited continent, extolled "that government which governs least." Now the tables had turned, and it was business that wanted less government and a freer hand. But the land was no longer open, and the choices that most men could make had narrowed drastically, so a great many people looked to government to regulate and control—or even to conduct—business, thus helping the workers in their unequal struggle against corporations and financiers and the immense power these represented.

THE MORGAN GOLD RESCUE

President Cleveland started his second term at an inauspicious moment. For a number of years the railroads had been overbuilt, overexploited, and undermanaged. In late February, 1893, ten days before the inauguration, the Philadelphia and Reading Railroad went bankrupt. This set off a wave of selling on the stock market, and then more railroads, banks, and other businesses came tumbling down. The box score for business failures during 1893 tallied 74 railroad companies that held 30,000 miles of track, more than 600 banks and banking institutions, and over 15,000 commercial firms with liabilities of $346 million.

Adding to the pessimistic mood of the times was the lack of liquidity occasioned by the virtual disappearance of gold from circulation. On top of heavy spending by the Harrison administration, the large silver purchases authorized by Congress had caused a severe drain on gold supplies. The Secretary of the Treasury was authorized by an 1882 enactment to suspend issuance of gold certificates whenever the reserve of gold bullion or coin slipped below $100 million. It had been successfully kept above that point. But when Cleveland took office the government's supply was at $100,982,410, dangerously close to that mark. In less than two months it fell below $100 million, and it dropped rapidly thereafter.

In August, Cleveland called Congress into special session to repeal the Sherman Silver Purchase Act. The Senate delayed passage until the end of October. By November the reserve had slipped to $59 million. The Treasury in January sold $50 million in ten-year, 5 per cent bonds to replenish its gold supply, and made another $50 million loan in November. The trouble was that the bond buyers could demand their gold back at any time, and many did. By February, 1895, the Treasury's gold reserve was down to $41 million and diminishing at the rate of $2 million a day. Not only was the gold reserve in serious danger, but the entire structure of the government's credit was imperiled at

home and abroad. The Treasury's failure to meet its obligations would endanger banks, trust companies, and any businesses that had contracted to meet their obligations in gold.

Some who had seen the trouble coming had hoarded gold or had shipped it abroad to be held by associates overseas. Virtually every ship coming from Europe had on board some American securities to be turned in for gold. With these clouds hanging over the government's credit standing, it was all but impossible to sell more bonds for gold abroad.

President Cleveland, firmly committed to maintaining the gold standard, was nevertheless reluctant to ask for help from Republican financiers. Late in January he sent a special message to Congress on the gold crisis and asked the legislators to authorize the sale of fifty-year bonds. Two days later William E. Curtis, Assistant Secretary of the Treasury, came to New York to sound out August Belmont, the American agent for the Rothschilds, on what the bankers might be able to

---

The Way to Wealth

JAMES B. DUKE

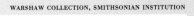

WARSHAW COLLECTION, SMITHSONIAN INSTITUTION

A Duke advertisement

From the time of Jamestown, tobacco earned fortunes for many Americans, but none was larger than that built by a poor North Carolina farm boy, James Buchanan Duke (1856–1925). His father had returned from the Civil War with little save two blind mules and an instinct for profits to be made from the light, Bright leaf tobacco that grew on his farm.

Duke and his sons labeled their tobacco brand Pro Bono Publico and marketed it in pocket-sized bags for rolled smokes, in competition with Bull Durham. In 1872 W. Duke, Sons & Co. sold 125,000 pounds of their product.

Young "Buck" Duke was sent to a Quaker academy, but when his teachers plied him with Latin he announced, "I ain't going to be a preacher or a lawyer. I am going to be a businessman and make my pile." With that goal in mind, he went on to the Eastman Business College at Poughkeepsie, New York, and sharpened his talents in arithmetic.

Duke recognized early that rolling one's own smokes was not the way to a tobacco merchant's prosperity. In 1881 he improved on a design for a cigarette-making machine that could turn out 200 cigarettes a minute. With his eye

on vastly increased sales, he gave his products brand names and put 20 per cent of his gross revenues into promoting the brands. By 1889 he was selling more than 800 million cigarettes annually and had captured 38 per cent of the market.

In 1890 the five principal cigarette manufacturers joined in a combine called the American Tobacco Company, with $25 million in capital and Duke as president. Eight years later the manu-

facturers of plug tobacco combined in a $75 million company, Continental Tobacco, also with Duke as president. American Snuff was formed in 1900, American Cigar in 1901, then American Stogie, and finally Duke entered retailing by acquiring a partial interest in the United Cigar Stores Company.

At the same time, Duke tried to take over the market in the United Kingdom by buying up Ogden's tobacconists. The British countered him by forming Imperial Tobacco; rather than do battle, the two agreed not to infringe on each other's territory. Duke and the British then joined hands in the British-American Company—with Duke getting two-thirds of the stock—and started selling to the rest of the world. At that point, Duke's holdings included 150 factories capitalized at $502 million.

American Tobacco was ordered dissolved by the Supreme Court in 1911, but it hardly put a crimp in Duke's style. He had already gotten into the development of water power in the Carolinas, built hospitals, and established a trust fund of $100 million that helped create Trinity College (later Duke University) at Durham, North Carolina. The company he built bought out its rival, Bull Durham, early in the 1900's, and, despite the growth of all its other products, it still puts out that brand of roll-your-owns in bags.

An attack on Bryan's use of sacred symbols in his 1896 oration, "You shall not crucify mankind upon a cross of gold"

do to help the government. With no financial training of his own, Curtis was nonetheless a capable lawyer who proved more adept at handling the situation than his superior, Treasury Secretary John G. Carlisle.

Belmont sent cables to his connections abroad but was offered small comfort from those sources. Curtis, Belmont, and Conrad Jordan, the nation's assistant treasurer, met to discuss the problem. Whichever way they seemed to turn, the compass needle always pointed in one direction—toward J. P. Morgan.

On January 31 Curtis went to see Morgan, explaining in some embarrassment that he had already begun to negotiate with Belmont. "Don't let that stand in your way," said Morgan. "I will aid Mr. Belmont in any way you desire." Then Morgan, Belmont, Curtis, and Jordan huddled further—while gold kept flowing out of the Subtreasury Building at the corner of Wall and Nassau streets, across from the offices of J. P. Morgan & Co.

With the newspapers following the crisis, moment by moment, as it developed, Morgan knew that it would be impossible to obtain the gold by public subscription to government bonds. But he was in contact with J. S. Morgan and Company in London, and they in turn were in touch with the Rothschilds. On the basis of information from them, Morgan decided to go out on a limb and give his assurance that the gold could be

obtained. So an agreement was worked out with Curtis, by which the Morgan-Belmont syndicate would underwrite an issue of $50 million in thirty-year bonds, with an option for another $50 million; half the gold needed to pay for the bonds would come from abroad. These were to be 4 per cent bonds, a somewhat higher rate than the government was then paying, but Morgan set a premium price on the issue, so that the annual cost to the government would be no more than $3\frac{3}{4}$ per cent. All the parties felt that the matter was settled, and Curtis returned to Washington. When the newspapers surmised that a solution had been found, the gold drain stopped temporarily.

Morgan and Belmont then spent thirty-six sleepless hours sending dozens of cables to their overseas connections, making commitments on their part to deliver the bonds and receiving commitments for gold in return. They were finally assured of a market for all $50 million of the bonds, to be sold at a yield of no less than $3\frac{1}{2}$ per cent.

But it turned out that their agreement with the U.S. Treasury was anything but firm. Curtis reported back by phone that the President and Secretary Carlisle considered the interest rate too high, and that they were leaning toward issuing the bonds for public subscription. Morgan pleaded for a day's delay in publishing the government's advertisement for the bonds, and was given it.

Morgan and Belmont sped to Washington to put their case before the President. They were met, however, by Daniel Lamont, Secretary of War, who told them that the President was set against a private sale of the bonds, and that he would not see the bankers. Said Morgan: "I have come down to Washington to see the President, and I am going to stay here until I see him." Morgan was willing to brush aside the personal affront; not only the nation's credit but his own credibility was at stake. On the strength of his agreement with Curtis, he had left himself vulnerable by making commitments abroad without qualification.

The following day a meeting was arranged with Cleveland. The President announced that the decision had been made in favor of public subscription. Morgan, knowing that the gold drain on the Treasury was continuing, had to follow the protocol of waiting until he was asked for an opinion. At one point Cleveland left the room for more than an hour, while the others continued discussion. Later, with the President back in the room, a bulletin was read with the report that just $9 million in gold was left in the Subtreasury. Morgan reported that he had heard that a draft for $10 million would be presented for payment in gold that day.

Cleveland finally turned to Morgan for his suggestions. The banker lost no time in outlining the situation. He recalled that Lincoln had been faced with a similar problem and had had a wartime measure passed authorizing the Secretary of the Treasury to buy gold with bonds or any other government obligations. The appropriate statute was found. It was then agreed that the Morgan-Belmont syndicate would be authorized to take not the $100 million in bonds agreed upon earlier, but $60 million. The crisis was over.

Morgan offered participation in the offering to every banking house and firm with European connections, turning them all into backers of the undertaking. The gold drain stopped, and by midsummer the Treasury had more than the required minimum reserve of $100 million in gold. A $100 million bond issue a year later, following a renewed run on the Treasury's gold supply, was substantially oversubscribed by the public.

But gold remained a major political issue. Farmers were suffering as the long-term decline in crop prices continued into the 1890's. Wheat slipped to forty-nine cents a bushel in 1894 and corn as low as twenty-one cents in 1896. In some places prices were so low that it was more economical to burn crops for fuel. To make their protest more effective, the Populists joined the Democrats in nominating William Jennings Bryan for the Presidency in 1896. The stirring orator made free and unlimited coinage of silver the principal campaign issue. When he was defeated by William McKinley, silver became virtually a dead issue, and the nation's leading capitalists had a sympathetic ear in the White House.

TRUST AND ANTITRUST

Despite their protestations, most businessmen dislike competition—or, at least, they like it best when they are beating the tar out of their competitors or are eliminating them entirely. Thus it is not just excessively restrictive government that stifles free enterprise but often business itself, or even business acting in concert with government.

The turn of the century was a heyday for business monopolists, and giant combinations were turning up in virtually every major industry. Greater efficiency, economies of scale, the predictability of sources of supply and of intermediate markets in integrated industries, the elimination of destructive and cutthroat competition—these were the justifications that business monopolies appeared to offer, and they were all the justifications that were needed for the merger-minded.

Most of the business combinations sought no more than to become the leaders in their fields, but some came completely to dominate their industries. The American Sugar Refining Company at one point controlled most of the sugar refining business in the country. The Pullman Palace Car Company took an 85

per cent cut of its industry's pie. More than one hundred plants were brought into the American Smelting and Refining Company; the major railroad car builders merged into the American Car and Foundry Company, and more than twenty manufacturers of leather for shoe uppers were consolidated into the American Hide and Leather Company. James Buchanan Duke was one of the earliest to see the possibilities in cigarettes and cigarette-making machinery; he merged with four rival cigarette manufacturers in 1890 and became president of the new American Tobacco Company, which for a period controlled 80 per cent of the nation's tobacco production and grew into a $500 million giant by 1907.

As early as 1893 there were already a dozen large combines, but their capital aggregated less than $1 billion. This, however, was just a beginning. Hard times cooled off the ardor for corporate marriages for a few years, but it returned with a consuming passion when reviving prosperity coincided with the return of the Republicans to power in 1897. The years from 1897 to 1904 witnessed the greatest surge of business combinations in the nation's history up to that time. According to the financial analyst John Moody, there were 318 industrial combinations that included almost 5,300 plants and had a combined capitalization of more than $7 billion. In addition, more than 1,000 railroad lines had been consolidated into six major systems that controlled almost $10 billion in capital, and there were 111 public utility companies, capitalized at almost $4 billion, controlling 1,300-odd plants.

Where voting trusts had once been the chief instrument for centralized control, the new device was the holding company. Chartered under the friendly statutes of a few states—New Jersey, Delaware, Maine, and West Virginia—holding companies exercised control by trading their own stock for the stock of companies that joined in the new combinations. The holding company would usually be capitalized for more than the total of its constituent units, the added value representing "goodwill" or the special value that any monopoly might represent for its owners. The organizers or promoters often retained a controlling interest in the holding company itself.

The American Bell Telephone Company and the Pennsylvania Company had already used this device for their own ends, but the Standard Oil Company now led the way, as it had with the trust, in using holding companies to bring about industrial consolidation. Following the dissolution order of the Ohio courts, Standard Oil formed twenty holding companies, which held the stock of smaller firms and which were themselves linked through common officers, directors, and major stockholders. These companies became known as the "Standard Oil interests." In 1899 the Standard Oil Company of New Jersey, with John D.

Rockefeller as president, became the central holding company for a combination of some seventy companies. Jersey Standard was also an operating company, carrying on oil refining and marketing activities. By 1904 it controlled 85 per cent of the domestic trade and 90 per cent of the nation's petroleum exports; its earnings in 1905 amounted to $54 million.

As active as any in the field of consolidation was the giant of Wall Street, J. P. Morgan & Co. Beginning with the joining of railroad lines into larger systems, Morgan soon branched out toward industrial mergers. He and Charles Coster, the Morgan partner who had proved to be expert in railroad reorganization, combined a number of smaller concerns into the General Electric Company in 1892, and competition in the electrical equipment industry was curtailed further when General Electric and Westinghouse entered into a patent pool in 1896. Some years later General Electric absorbed its other major competitor, the Stanley Electric Company. General Electric also got into the business of selling electric power, mainly through the North American Company, which had once been Henry Villard's private holding corporation. North American got control of the Detroit Edison Company, Milwaukee's public utilities, and the lighting and street railway companies of St. Louis.

Morgan was the key figure in financing the start of the Federal Steel Company, and he brought a number of transatlantic shipping companies, including the White Star, the Red Star, and the Leyland lines, into the International Mercantile Marine Company, which nearly became one of his few disastrous ventures. Unlike railroads, with their prized rights of way, ocean shippers use the free channels of the ocean sea lanes. No amount of merging and combining can offer them any assurance against wide open and sometimes cutthroat competition. The immense demand for ocean shipping in World War I eventually provided a boon for International Mercantile Marine, but the company never became a diadem in the Morgan crown.

The Morgan firm was more successful in bringing together all the major manufacturers of farm machinery in the United States and abroad, a coup for which a young Morgan partner, George W. Perkins, was chiefly responsible. The leading figures in the industry—McCormick, Deering, J. J. Glessner, and W. H. Jones—were hard-bitten individualists and fierce competitors who had made careers of trying to best each other in the marketplace. After convincing each of the value of joining forces, Perkins had to bring them together to work out the final details—but he did not dare to have them meet face to face. So they were put into four separate rooms, with Perkins bobbing from one room to another to carry the terms and details of the negotiations. The outcome was the highly successful International Harvester Company which turned out 85 per cent of the machinery used by America's 10 million farmers. Whereas the capital of the individual companies had totaled only $10.5 million, the new combination was capitalized at $120 million. But the revenues and earnings of the combination easily justified the new capitalization, since sales of the McCormick firm alone had reached $75 million by 1902, the year of the merger.

In time, the public began to feel uneasy about these vast concentrations of wealth and power. Journalists found a ready market for their stories about the "trusts" and the wealthy and powerful men behind them. Indeed, even some of the newspapers themselves were following the current fashion of combination, and chains of papers were being formed by William Randolph Hearst, Frank A. Munsey, and Edward W. Scripps; Scripps's growing journalistic empire numbered nine newspapers in 1900 and twenty-two just ten years later.

The Sherman Antitrust Act, on the books since 1890, proved notably ineffective in curbing business mergers and monopolies. In 1895 the Supreme Court ruled that the American Sugar Refining Company, in control of 95 per cent of its industry, was not a monopoly in restraint of trade and was therefore not in violation of the act. Just a year earlier, however, the courts had issued an injunction against the union in the Pullman strike on the basis that it was a conspiracy in restraint of interstate commerce. In the Danbury Hatters case of 1908, furthermore, the striking union was declared financially liable for damages resulting from a boycott.

When President William McKinley was assassinated in 1901, Theodore Roosevelt succeeded to the office. He sensed the restiveness in the public mood toward business combinations and soon pledged a "square deal" to industry and labor. But in contrast to his announced public posture, Roosevelt tended to speak harshly and carry a small stick. His Attorney General, Philander Knox, started antitrust prosecutions against two of the more brazen combinations—the Northern Securities Company and the meat packers' trust—but Roosevelt then called off his Justice Department, lest business become overly concerned. In his seven years in office, the "great trustbuster" carried forward scarcely forty antitrust actions against business, considerably fewer than his successors of both parties.

In other respects as well, Roosevelt tended to mollify business. His legislation forbidding railroad rebates was not rigidly enforced, and his newly organized Department of Commerce and Labor, which included a Bureau of Corporations that could investigate interstate businesses, was no major threat to private enterprise. What Roosevelt did seek to do was to increase the size and the power of the federal govern-

The greedy image of monopoly, demanding more profits from farmers, workers, and merchants: an antitrust cartoon of 1890

ment to match that of business, so that government might be able to exercise a greater degree of control and regulation over the huge and growing elements of the business and industrial communities. In these efforts he received public support from some unexpected quarters—from George Perkins, the Morgan partner, for example, and from the conservative journalist Herbert Croly, who believed that a certain amount of monopoly was inevitable and that only tighter regulation was needed.

William Howard Taft, Roosevelt's successor, proved a far more determined trustbuster, even to the point of creating a rift between himself and Roosevelt. His administration brought a series of forceful antitrust court actions against International Harvester, American Sugar Refining, General Electric, U.S. Steel, and National Cash Register. But the most spectacular suit of all was the case brought against Standard Oil. In its 1911 ruling that Standard Oil would have to be broken up, the Supreme Court set forth its famous "rule of reason," to the effect that only an "unreasonable" restraint of trade could be considered a violation of the Sherman Act; the court all but pledged greater leniency in the future.

Even this action did not really "break up" Standard Oil. The twenty-nine pieces into which the company

was split continued to operate like the parts of a well-oiled machine. Standard Oil's major stockholders still numbered fewer than a dozen men, and these were able to keep the entire complex of producers, refiners, marketers, pipelines, and other units working smoothly and in unison.

But Standard Oil was unable to hold on to its monopoly position for very long. Unintimidated by the giant, Lewis Emery, Jr., fought off Standard competition, built pipelines to carry crude and refined petroleum to the East Coast, and made a success of his Pure Oil Company. Near Texas' Gulf Coast, Anthony Lucas had sent his rotary drill spinning through the sandy soil under a salt dome in 1901 and struck the spectacular gusher known as Spindletop. Lucas was backed by Colonel J. M. Guffey and John H. Galey of Pittsburgh. When more capital was needed, it was obtained from the Mellons, the wealthy Pittsburgh bankers. In return for their investment, the Mellons took 40 per cent of the J. M. Guffey Petroleum Co., later to become Gulf Oil.

Standard moved into the Texas area too, but so did such robust new competitors as the Texas Company and Shell. While Standard concentrated on protecting its technological edge in producing kerosene for lighting, the newer companies showed greater alacrity in going after the developing market for gasoline to power the new motor cars. So whereas the coercive efforts of government failed to curb the Standard Oil monopoly, the forces of the marketplace were remarkably successful in cutting it down.

RAILROADERS HILL AND HARRIMAN

The nation's railroads, pawns in many a financial power struggle, had nevertheless been the key to filling and developing the West. Dominating the investment world for half a century, the railroads continued to expand until 1916, after which track mileage started to decline. But even in the period of their greatest growth, there were setbacks and skirmishes that shook the financial community.

Major realignments of ownership and control had begun when Morgan marketed a large block of Vanderbilt's stock and then insisted on a place on the Central board as the representative of his British investors. Moving rapidly thereafter into the railroad reorganization field, the House of Morgan insisted on retaining a measure of control over the lines whose capital structures they were reshaping. In the depression of 1893–96, no fewer than 156 railroads collapsed, and dozens of others hovered at the edge of bankruptcy. Morgan put a number of them back on their feet—the Erie, the

group of roads that became the Southern system, the Lehigh, the Norfolk & Western, the Hocking Valley—placing his people on their boards or setting up voting trusts to protect the interests of those to whom he sold the new bond issues.

Consolidation moved into the railroad field just as it had for large industries. By 1906 about 150,000 miles of the country's 228,000 miles of track were combined into seven great systems—the 22,500-mile Vanderbilt roads from New York to Chicago, the Pennsylvania's 20,000 miles, the 18,000 miles of Morgan roads in the Southeast, the Mississippi Valley's 17,000 miles of Gould roads and the 15,000-mile Rock Island system, James J. Hill's 21,000 miles of lines in the Northwest, and Edward Harriman's 21,000 miles covering the central and southern trans-Mississippi routes. With just two thirds of the trackage, these seven accounted for about 85 per cent of railroad earnings. Moreover, interlocking ties of various kinds gave to the same groups major interests in two or more systems—and, indeed, it was already clear that much of the railroad mileage was polarizing around even fewer groupings.

Jim Hill, for example, had moved into the Morgan orbit. The one-eyed, heavy-set, hustling Canadian had built up his Great Northern by helping develop the territory it covered—bringing in settlers, promoting

In the proud days of railroads, when passenger traffic mattered: a promotional drawing of a Pennsylvania Railroad facility

200

industries, draining the land, pushing crop diversification, and improving the strain of cattle. When hard times sent other roads into bankruptcy, his remained solvent.

When the Northern Pacific went under in 1894, Hill unsurprisingly set out to gain control of the rival line. The Supreme Court overruled his own plan of having the Great Northern take over half of the $100 million in new stock of the reorganized railroad. So Hill allied himself with Morgan, who managed the reorganization, and they jointly bought enough common stock on the open market to gain control. The two railroads were then joined in a "community of interest," a favorite Morgan phrase to indicate the consolidation of businesses competing for the same markets.

The other up-and-coming railroader in the West was Edward H. Harriman, a slight, shy, quiet man who looked like a bookkeeper and operated like a tycoon. The son of a minister, he first found work as a quotation boy, or "pad shover," on Wall Street. By selling short during Jay Gould's Black Friday raid in 1869, he had made $3,000 and was able to buy a seat on the Stock Exchange when he was just twenty-one. He was soon serving such clients as August Belmont, the Vanderbilts, and, on occasion, Gould himself.

In 1879 Harriman married the daughter of William J. Averell, part owner of a small railroad in Ogdensburg, New York. Harriman bought out the other stockholders, then got both the Central and the Pennsylvania to bid for his little line, finally selling out to the Pennsylvania. He next went in league with Stuyvesant Fish, who had been a fellow director of the Ogdensburg and Lake Champlain Railroad, and in time the two of them came into control of the Illinois Central, which had fallen on bad days.

They bought more railroads, eventually controlling a 5,000-mile system. But it was Harriman who insisted on good management, efficient operations, and maintaining the physical property. As a result, he turned the Illinois Central into a moneymaker and was able to sell bonds at a mere 3½ per cent rate, while other roads with good credit had to pay 5 or 6 per cent for their borrowings.

In pursuit of his objectives, Harriman was willing to take on anyone, even the great J. P. Morgan. In 1887 he clashed with Morgan over the Dubuque and Sioux City Railroad, which he wished to bring into his Illinois Central system, and he defeated the great financier. Some years later, as an Erie bondholder, he brought suit over the treatment of his securities in the road's reorganization, and won concessions from Morgan. This did nothing to build warmth between the two men, but it taught Morgan to respect Harriman's abilities.

When the time came for the Union Pacific to be reorganized in 1895, the road was in an almost hopeless state, and Morgan disdained to take on the job. This left an opening for Kuhn, Loeb & Co.'s Jacob Schiff, who sought help from the Vanderbilts. When Schiff and his associates tried to move, however, they were aware that some other force was working against them. Schiff went to Morgan, who told him that Harriman was the man in his way.

For a while Schiff ignored Harriman, but finally a meeting had to be arranged. Harriman admitted freely that it was he who was blocking Schiff's plans, and that he planned to bring the Union Pacific into his own system. To finance the reorganization, Harriman said, he planned to issue $100 million worth of bonds at 3 to 4 per cent against the credit of his Illinois Central. Schiff could not hope to get the needed capital for under 4½ per cent and would probably have to set his bond interest rate up to 5 or 6 per cent. Unable to beat Harriman, Schiff joined him, and Kuhn, Loeb reorganized the railroad, but Harriman became first its board chairman, then its president. To get cash to repay $45 million in federal government loans, Schiff and Harriman turned to James Stillman of the City Bank (soon to become the National City), which had by then become a major repository for Rockefeller money, and Stillman was made a member of the reorganization committee. Ownership of the country's major rail lines was becoming concentrated in the nation's two great centers of money power, Rockefeller and Morgan; Hill had cast his lot with Morgan, and Rockefeller served as the anchor of the Harriman-Schiff-Stillman axis.

Almost predictably, with Harriman at the controls and this great power behind him, the Union Pacific turned into a moneymaking machine. Harriman sold off excess properties and obtained more cash to handle the increased business of the boom he correctly forecast. In 1898 he made an inspection tour of his new line and examined minutely every detail. When Collis P. Huntington died, Harriman quickly raised more than $50 million to buy up the Southern Pacific rail empire. On a similar tour of that railroad, he recommended such changes as shorter bolts that did not protrude beyond the nuts, thus saving an ounce of steel per bolt, or 50 million ounces for the whole line. Within a period of eight years, the value of the Rockefeller-Harriman railroad investments grew 1,400 per cent.

With the nation's rail power increasingly clustered around its two chief poles of finance, a clash between them was almost inevitable. It came in 1901. That year the Chicago, Burlington & Quincy Railroad, a line that drew freight from the rich producing centers of Denver and Minnesota to Chicago, came onto the market. Harriman wanted it as a feeder route into Chicago. So did Hill, but for his Great Northern and Northern Pacific. Both bid for it, and Hill won.

But Harriman was not willing to admit defeat so readily. Quietly his group began to buy stock, not in the Burlington but in the Northern Pacific, which now controlled the Burlington. Picking up shares as they became available, including some from the Morgan interests, Harriman and Schiff accumulated more than half the preferred, nearly half of the common, and more than half of the two classes combined—a total of $78 million worth. Morgan was vacationing in France, at Aix-les-Bains, but Hill began to grow suspicious. He fired off a cable to Morgan, who immediately ordered massive purchases of the stock. Harriman needed only 40,000 more shares of common for full control, but he was unable to get his purchase orders executed. The Morgan forces, in part because Jacob Schiff would not forgo his Saturday worship at the synagogue and in part because of a provision empowering the Northern Pacific directors to retire the preferred stock, were able to maintain control of the road.

Chief among the victims of this huge struggle were the brokerage houses and speculators who had watched Northern Pacific's stock rise without apparent reason and, hoping for quick profits, had sold it short. When the time came to cover, the stock kept climbing, pushing up from 110 to reach as high as 1,000 at one point. To avoid disaster, Morgan arranged for them to pay just $150 a share, administering severe losses but saving them from utter ruin.

To forestall further depredations against the vulnerable segments of the western rail kingdom, Morgan formed the Northern Securities Company to hold the controlling stock interest in the Northern Pacific, the Great Northern, and the Burlington. Always the realist, and never one to harbor a grudge if it interfered with his business objectives, Morgan welcomed the Harriman-Schiff group, as holders of about half the stock of Northern Pacific, into the inner councils of the Northern Securities. This was one of the earliest of what was to become a number of close links between the Rockefeller and the Morgan interests.

With authorized capital of $400 million, Northern

SPINDLETOP

At the turn of the century, petroleum was still to play a dominant role in America's economy. The entire oil production of the United States was only 64 million barrels a year—11 million less than Russia's output—and it was used mainly for lamps.

Almost all the oil came from eastern states, where a well that produced 4,000 barrels a day was considered spectacular. A Standard Oil Company executive remarked that he could drink all the oil found west of the Mississippi. He would soon, instead, be swallowing the words. On January 10, 1901, on a mound known as Spindletop, on the coastal prairie of east Texas, a black geyser of oil shot 200 feet into the air to signal the birth of a vast new oil-producing area. The gusher blew out the equivalent of 100,000 barrels of oil a day for ten days before drillers could cap the bonanza.

Spindletop rewarded the determination of a Texan named Pattillo Higgins, whose picnics on the mound had been disturbed by the smell of gas seeping from the ground. For years he suspected that the fifteen-foot-high rise was not a freak of geology but a bulge that covered a "salt dome" filled with oil under tremendous pressure. In 1892 he formed a syndicate, the Gladys City Oil, Gas and Manufacturing Company, to buy up and lease acreage around the mound. He even designed a letterhead for the company with an illustration of what Gladys City would look like as a boom town built by oil money.

The town remained in imagination until an Austrian-born mining engineer, Anthony Francis Lucas, arrived. He had a knowledge of "salt dome" geology and the conviction that a rotary drill would be needed to dig deeply in Texas' sandy soil. At 1,020 feet Lucas struck oil on that January, 1901, day, his well producing as much in a year as did 37,000 wells in the East.

Money poured into the area, financing the purchasing or leasing of land for thirty miles around Spindletop. Tellers in banks at nearby Beaumont used shovels to move silver dollars. Millionaires were made in minutes. Within the year, Texas had chartered 491 oil companies, authorizing them to issue nearly $240 million in capital stock. By the fall of 1902, a forest of derricks had brought in 440 gushers on Spindletop.

Men made money in a variety of ways. One company bought the nonexistent streets and alleys of Gladys City from Higgins's firm for $90,000. It was a clever purchase; the crosshatch of thoroughfares covered most of Spindletop, and the company could simply wait for someone else to make a strike and then drill next to it. The firm, headed by Colonel Edward M. House, who later became an adviser to President Woodrow Wilson, was capitalized for one million dollars and sold out its stock in thirty-six hours.

At the start of the boom no one had figured out what to do with all the oil (17 million barrels were produced the first year). It sold in Texas at three cents a barrel, $2 below the wellhead price in Pennsylvania. Even water in that arid part of Texas cost $6 a barrel. But the nation soon found use for the new oil supply. In 1901 there was only one oil-burning locomotive in the country; by 1905 there were 227. Oil was so much cheaper than coal that the Southern Pacific saved $5 million in a year after switching to oil-fired engines. A man named Joseph S. Cullinan was the first to fuel a locomotive with oil. He also started Spindletop's greatest success story.

A Pennsylvanian-turned-Texan, Cullinan was a veteran of thirteen years at Standard Oil. He knew that the only way to prosper in the business was to get the oil from the wellhead to the market, and in 1897 he had built the first oil refinery west of the Mississippi, in northwest Texas. When he heard of the gusher at Spindletop, he hurried to the scene, arriving before the discovery well was brought under control.

Securities stock was exchanged for 76 per cent of the Great Northern and 96 per cent of the Northern Pacific. The holding company was empowered to issue dividends on the pooled earnings of the two systems and to name the officers and directors of both railroads. It seemed the perfect arrangement for government officials looking for a likely antitrust test case, and President Roosevelt moved against Northern Securities in February, 1902. Surprised by this move, Morgan went to see the President and told him, "If we have done anything wrong, send your man to my man and they can fix it up." Morgan was also concerned about similar attacks on some of his industrial combinations, but Roosevelt, while not giving him complete assurance, was already inclining toward conciliation of business.

In a major turnaround from previous rulings, the Supreme Court held that Northern Securities was an illegal holding company, since its intent was to monopolize railroad traffic in a vast region of the country, and it was ordered dissolved. Thereupon Harriman, always more inclined toward rugged individualism than toward business combination and Morgan's brand of harmonious co-operation, again tried to get control of the Northern Pacific. But the Supreme Court held in favor of Northern Securities and its plan to distribute its securities in a way that gave Hill and Morgan continued control.

Harriman, still the competitor, kept trying to build a banking power to rival that of Morgan. From the Mutual Life Insurance Company, he bought an interest that represented half the control of the Guaranty Trust Company in 1908. The next year he bought an option for acquiring a similar degree of control over the Equitable Life Assurance Society. In railroading, his vision extended beyond the nation's borders. He obtained an option on China's South Manchurian Railway and appeared to be preparing to link Siberia with European capitals. How far he might have carried his plan will never be known, because Harriman became

---

He formed the Texas Fuel Company on paper and found willing partners in the Hogg-Swayne syndicate, headed by former Texas Governor James Stephen Hogg. The syndicate had bought a piece of Spindletop land for $105,000 from a man who had paid only $450 for it the year before. Its members had also bought land for a refinery and storage farm at Port Arthur on the Gulf Coast, but they realized that their expertise was limited. Cullinan got part of the Hogg-Swayne holdings for $25,000 worth of stock in his company.

Another $25,000 in stock was sold to Arnold Schlaet, a New Yorker who managed the eastern oil investments of two wealthy leather merchants, John J. and Lewis H. Lapham. Cullinan bought a refinery site of his own at Port Arthur and, in a year, had thirty-six storage tanks and a twenty-mile pipeline. Against Schlaet's advice he also organized an oil-producing affiliate with funds from Chicago financier John W. ("Bet-a-Million") Gates, who received a part interest in the fuel company.

Cullinan's enterprise continued to thirst for new capital. In 1902 his company was rechartered as The Texas Co. and capitalized at $3 million. It was a sound gamble. Cullinan had learned that Louisiana sugar planters used 450,000 tons of coal a year to stoke their boilers. Replacing coal with oil would provide a market for 1,350,000

The Spindletop gusher, January 10, 1901

barrels. Even at $1 a barrel, the sugar planters would make a considerable saving; meanwhile, Cullinan could buy Spindletop oil at an average of twenty-one cents a barrel.

The whole deal depended on a cheap and plentiful supply of oil, but suddenly Spindletop's flow dropped as the natural pressure beneath its salt dome was drawn off. Fortunately, Cullinan's insistence on getting the oil he needed led to a new strike in 1903 twenty miles from Spindletop. As the years passed, the company kept finding oil in other parts of Texas. By 1910 Texaco—as it became known from its cable address—owned 1,010 tank cars, nineteen barges, and five ocean-going tankers. Cullinan was too much of an individualist for a company grown so large, and in 1913 he resigned. But the enterprise he had started continued to grow until it was among the nation's ten largest industrial corporations.

The little mound that Lucas had first tapped was siphoned dry by 1925 after having produced 60 million barrels of oil. But prospectors drilled farther out on the flanks of the original field, taking out more oil by 1933 than Spindletop itself had produced. By then the giant, forty-mile-long East Texas oil field had been discovered, and the old cattle kingdom of Texas was lubricating its economy with another source of fabulous wealth.

ill and died in 1909. The Morgan group lost little time in acquiring his interests in Guaranty Trust and Mutual Life.

THE BIRTH OF BIG STEEL

Perhaps the commonest measures of modern man's industrial progress — i.e., his ability to transform the earth to serve his own ends — have been the production and consumption of steel. Here the United States moved swiftly, first toward leadership, then toward dominance. In 1880 American steel output was 1.4 million ingot tons, in 1890 it was 4.8 million, and by 1900 it had reached 11.4 million. Alabama's Congressman Joseph Wheeler said in 1897 that his own state produced as much steel as France or Russia.

Production then grew even faster. By 1910 it had reached 29 million tons, and by 1918 it was 45 million, compared with Germany's 14 million, 9 million for England, and 2 million for France. Consumption rose similarly, from 500 pounds per person in 1900 to 1,200 pounds twenty years later. Prices moved the other way. Rail steel, the industry's largest single product, dropped from $93 a ton in 1870 to $24, about a fourth of what it had been, by 1900. As the price dropped to around a penny and a half a pound, steel came into more common everyday use. The demand for canned food, and thus for tin plate, increased rapidly. Under lobbying pressure, Congress gave protection to the tin plate industry in the McKinley tariff of 1890 — even though there was not a single tin mill in the country at the time! Skilled workers were brought from Wales, and by early 1892 there were nineteen tin plate producers in operation.

Consolidation came early to the steel industry. The 1880 census showed there were then 1,005 plants, but there was soon a rush by the bigger plants to absorb the smaller ones. Carnegie led the movement, forming the giant Carnegie Steel Company in 1892. But there were a number of other big companies as well, most of them at least partially integrated — the Illinois Steel Company, the Tennessee Coal, Iron and Railway Company, and, in the West, the Colorado Fuel and Iron Company.

Around 1897 J. P. Morgan began looking at the steel industry, still largely fragmented and highly competitive, as a likely candidate for his own talents of effecting business combinations. What he needed was someone who knew the steel industry as thoroughly as Coster knew the railroads. Morgan found his man in Judge Elbert H. Gary, a sagacious Chicago corporation lawyer who was general counsel for Illinois Steel. With Gary's help, Morgan in 1898 organized the Federal Steel Company, bringing into one firm with a capital of $200 million the Illinois Steel Company, the Lorain Steel Company, the Minnesota Iron Com-

pany, and the Elgin, Joliet and Eastern Railway. Gary became the first president. Morgan also brought about two other consolidations in the steel industry, organizing the National Tube Company and the American Bridge Company.

Others were also active in merging steel plants. John W. Gates, who played a part in the Federal Steel combine, himself organized a number of western plants, specializing mainly in nails, barbed wire, and wire fencing, into the $90 million American Steel and Wire Company of New Jersey. The Moore brothers, William and James, who promoted combinations in the biscuit, match, and chewing gum fields, were active in the organization of four other steel industry consolidations — the American Tin Plate Company, the American Steel Hoop Company, the National Steel Company, and the American Sheet Steel Company. Within about two years these eight new consolidations took in a large part of the scattered elements of the steel industry that were not already in Carnegie's hands.

But Carnegie was still the key to any truly major steel combination in the United States. William Moore, on the heels of his other successful promotions, offered Carnegie $1 million for a ninety-day option to buy his stock in Carnegie Steel for $157,950,000, more than a third to be in cash. Carnegie's condition was that Frick and Phipps be part of the purchasing team. But the death of a leading market operator, Roswell P. Flower, caused a temporary tightening in the money supply. The ninety days passed, and Carnegie kept the $1,000,000. When Rockefeller next bid for the Carnegie interests, the price quoted to him was $250 million, and the negotiations failed.

Now Wall Street set out after Carnegie. Many of the smaller companies had traditionally bought their raw materials from the Carnegie mills, which had most of their own sources of supply and produced a fourth of the nation's Bessemer steel output. Now joined into more fully integrated organizations, they informed the affable Charlie Schwab, who had been president of the Carnegie Steel Company since 1897, that they would no longer need his steel. This was a declaration of war.

Carnegie, who had all but retired from business, took up the gauntlet. From his vacation home in Scotland's Skibo Castle in the summer of 1900, he sent off his marching orders to Schwab: "A struggle is inevitable and it is a question of the survival of the fittest. . . . Our safety lies in being independent." Carnegie laid plans to move into steel finishing himself. He bought 5,000 acres at Conneaut, Ohio, for a new tube mill to compete with National Tube; he had surveyors lay out a rail route from Pittsburgh to the East Coast to compete with the Pennsylvania; he ordered a new fleet of Great Lakes ore carriers built; and he announced plans for a huge new rod mill at

Pittsburgh to rival American Steel and Wire. Nobody knew whether he meant to carry out these plans, but everyone knew that he could.

On December 12, 1900, Schwab was invited to speak at an imposing dinner party at New York's University Club, at which Morgan and many of his associates were present. Schwab, scarcely twenty years removed from his first steel industry job as a dollar-a-day stake driver, spoke on what he said was the only subject he knew—steel. He painted a glowing picture of the industry that would bring his company net profits of $40 million that year, including $25 million to Carnegie himself, and of the even brighter future.

These numbers were Morgan's language. The banker took the steel man aside and plied him with questions. Schwab replied with assurance and optimism. Some weeks later, Schwab was back to see Morgan again. Morgan had more questions, mostly about the prospects of a huge steel combine, whose facilities might range from ore and coal mines to plants that turned out finished steel products. When his curiosity was sated, Morgan wanted one more answer from Schwab: "Go and ask him his price."

Schwab went back to Carnegie, and the two worked out their figure—$303,450,000 in 5 per cent gold bonds, $98,277,000 in preferred stock, $90,279,000 in common, for a total of $492 million. Morgan, never one to haggle, glanced at the price on the scrap of paper Schwab presented, and simply accepted the offer. Carnegie had won his war. In January, 1901, Carnegie and Morgan met for a cool fifteen-minute exchange that "made Carnegie the richest man in the world," according to Morgan. Carnegie, who had once said it was a disgrace to die rich, spent the rest of his life giving his money away.

For Morgan himself, this was simply one more transaction in a very busy year, and he promptly moved to the next stage of building the huge steel combination he had in mind. Judge Gary, Percival Roberts, and other Morgan partners began their labors of going after all the lesser barons of steel and hammering out the trades that would bring them in. Toughest of all was Gates, the gambler who was reputed to have just lost $1,000,000 on a single turn of the cards. Morgan wanted to buy American Steel and Wire, but did not want Gates in the management of the new company; Gates wanted every dollar he could wring from the deal. While Gary and Gates negotiated, Morgan waited outside. Finally, his patience exhausted, Morgan stormed into the room and announced: "I am going to leave this building in ten minutes. If by that time you have not accepted our offer, we will build our own wire plant." After he had left the room, Gates wondered whether "the old man" was bluffing or serious, finally decided that Morgan held the high hand, and accepted the offer.

On March 3, 1901, newspapers carried an ad advising the stockholders of Federal Steel, National Tube, National Steel, American Steel and Wire, American Tin Plate, American Sheet Steel, and American Steel Hoop of the formation under New Jersey laws of the United States Steel Corporation. Also into the company came the Mesabi Range in Minnesota, then the world's richest iron ore mine. Discovered many years before by Lewis H. Merritt, the Mesabi had eventually been turned over to John D. Rockefeller for a sum reputed to be only $420,000. Now Rockefeller received $80 million in U.S. Steel stock for his ore, and was joined with Morgan in yet another alliance.

The vast new holding corporation, with some 170 subsidiaries, had tangible assets valued by the Commissioner of Corporations at $682 million. But U.S. Steel's capitalization amounted to $1.4 billion, including $510 million in preferred stock, $508 million in common, and $303 million in mortgage bonds. Thus was formed the world's first billion-dollar corporation, almost ten years before annual appropriations of the U.S. government reached $1 billion. For the first year of its operations, the net earnings of U.S. Steel amounted to $90 million, indicating that the new giant had not been overcapitalized on an earnings basis.

U.S. Steel brought together thousands of acres of lands for producing ore, limestone, and coal; furnaces, mills, and plants; 1,000 miles of railroad; and more than 100 steamships. Supplying half the nation's requirements for steel rails and most of its nails and wire, its annual capacity was about 8 million tons of finished steel.

Schwab was named president of the new corporation, and Gary headed an executive committee created by the bylaws "to direct the affairs of the corporation." After losing out in a corporate power play, Schwab resigned in 1903 to consolidate interests he had acquired in Bethlehem Steel two years earlier. Gary continued to move up in the power hierarchy until, as chairman of the board in 1910, his role was declared to be that of "the chief executive officer . . . and . . . in general charge of the affairs of the corporation."

The corporation did not long remain immune from the guns of antitrust. President Roosevelt's Bureau of Corporations busied itself examining U.S. Steel's books from 1905 on, and the company once needed thirty auditors to supply the investigators with the information they sought. Gary tempted the fates even further by inviting rival steelmen to a series of "Gary dinners," at which they were urged to keep prices "reasonable" so that all could show acceptable returns. Kentucky Congressman Augustus Stanley introduced a resolution in 1911 that resulted in an investigation of U.S. Steel, which showed that the men who controlled the company were also directors of scores of steel-using companies. And later the same year the Justice Department instituted an action requesting the dissolution of the corporation and eight of its subsidiaries as unlawful monopolies. Roosevelt himself was one of the 400-odd witnesses who testified over a two-year period. In June, 1915, the federal district court ruled in the company's favor, and the judgment was affirmed by the Supreme Court in 1920, after the war.

Again, market forces accomplished what the courts demurred to do. At its formation, U.S. Steel controlled nearly 60 per cent of national steel production and enjoyed about 65 per cent of the market. This market share dwindled to around 45 per cent when World War I broke out, and eventually came down to about 25 per cent. Newer companies, less weighed down with expensive fixed plant, could more easily adopt such new techniques as electric furnaces, or exploit new metallurgical advances, and thus become powers in the industry themselves.

SOUND AND LIGHT

A limitation of $10 million by the Massachusetts legislature on the capitalization of the American Bell Telephone Company proved a severe restriction on the company's growth. So, to construct the long lines linking the exchanges of different cities, a new corporation, the American Telephone and Telegraph Company, was chartered under New York laws. Commonly called the Long Distance Company, this subsidiary was made the parent in 1899.

Around this time the House of Morgan moved into a controlling position of the company's finances, increasing its resources through the sale of stocks and bonds. A major part of the expansion cost was in the copper for long-distance lines, which needed to be about an eighth of an inch in thickness. In 1893, the New York–Chicago lines required more than 400 tons of copper wire. Only about 100 copper wires could be squeezed into a cable, until research by Columbia

2,811 LIBRARIES AND 7,689 ORGANS

Many of the men who amassed fortunes in American business life hoarded their money, frittered it away, or passed it on intact to their descendants. But others used their great wealth in philanthropic ways to enrich society. The Boston Symphony Orchestra was founded and financed in 1881 by investment banker Henry Lee Higginson. George Peabody, a financier who profited by selling American securities in London, established natural history museums at several colleges. And scores of universities, research institutions, hospitals, and foundations today bear the names of businessmen who were their benefactors. No one, however, not even John D. Rockefeller, ever succeeded as admirably as Andrew Carnegie (1835–1919) at giving away his wealth in style. He laid down a pattern for philanthropy that many businessmen have followed ever since.

The Scottish-born steel mogul grew up with a respect for learning. Although he never had a college education, he studied a little Latin as a child. At fourteen, while a messenger boy for a Pittsburgh telegraph office, he rushed congratulatory telegrams to the theater just after the curtain went up so

A 1903 commentary in Judge *on Andrew Carnegie's philanthropic activities*

he could stay in the wings to watch Shakespeare's plays. In 1868 he wrote a memo to himself:

"Thirty-three and an income of $50,000 per annum! Beyond this never earn—make no effort to increase fortune, but spend the surplus each year for benevolent purposes. Cast aside

business for ever, except for others."

He failed to follow this advice himself until he was sixty-six, but his openhandedness was foreshadowed in his essay "The Gospel of Wealth," which was published in the *North American Review* in 1889. In it he urged that the later portion of a rich man's life be spent in giving away his surplus wealth. He spelled out the duty of the rich man as "becoming the mere trustee and agent for his poorer brethren, bringing to their service his superior wisdom, experience, and ability to administer, doing for them better than they would or could for themselves." If his attitude had an undertone of social Darwinism, it was natural, since Herbert Spencer was his philosophical mentor. Still, Carnegie had a strong personal sense of social conscience; he concluded that "the man who dies thus rich, dies disgraced."

Carnegie listed projects for philanthropy in the order in which he ranked their worthiness:

1. universities
2. free libraries
3. hospitals
4. parks
5. concert and meeting halls
6. swimming baths
7. churches

It resulted in a howl of protest from clergymen, and although Carnegie's

University's Dr. Michael I. Pupin around 1900 developed the "Pupin coil," which permitted the use of thinner wire, so that as many as 1,800 strands could go into a cable.

Half the people of the country were close enough to telephones to talk to each other by 1900, when 1,000,000 miles of wire had been strung. McKinley used the telephone during the 1896 campaign, and President Taft had an instrument installed in the White House. By 1910, less than thirty-five years after the telephone had been shown as a curiosity at the Centennial Exposition, there were 5 million phones in the United States, or one for every eighteen persons.

From 1906 to 1912 the Morgan group sold approximately $300 million in A.T.&T. bonds, some of the proceeds being used to finance expansion but a good deal going into the development of a more complete monopoly—a more logical development for this business than for most. A.T.&T., however, not only bought up small independent and semi-independent telephone companies but also acquired a controlling interest in the Western Union Telegraph Company, in a move aimed at monopolizing all wire transmission of messages.

One trouble with monopoly is that it is vulnerable to attack from many directions—one of the most potent being the birth of new technologies. Major competition came into the field of communications as the result of an international chain of technological events and discoveries that enabled signals to be sent without wires.

Joseph Henry had found that discharges from an electrical machine could put a charge on a needle across the room. It was phenomena like this that British physicist James Clerk Maxwell covered in his theory of electromagnetic waves. In Germany, Heinrich Hertz showed that a system of wires, known as a Hertzian loop, could intercept these waves as they traveled at the nearly instantaneous speed of light. Frenchman Edouard Branly then devised a coherer, a tube with metal filings that clung together when struck by

own preference was free libraries, he did give 7,689 organs to churches at a cost of more than $6 million.

The sharpest criticism of "The Gospel of Wealth" came from William Jewett Tucker, a liberal theologian who became president of Dartmouth College. "That wealth is the inevitable possession of the few, and is best administered by them for the money," he said, "begs the whole question of economic justice now before society, and relegates it to the field of charity, leaving the question of the original distribution of wealth unsettled, or settled only to the satisfaction of the few. . . . The ethical question of today centres, I am sure, in the distribution rather than the redistribution of wealth."

Carnegie retired after receiving $250 million from the sale of his steel company to the new United States Steel combine in 1901. On parting, he left a $5 million pension and benefit fund for his employees, and then he kept right on giving. More than $60 million of his money went into the building of 2,811 free public libraries around the world, 1,946 of them in the United States.

At first no specifications for architecture accompanied the gifts, but after a few botched buildings, a set of plans was included, and "Carnegie Classical" libraries became easily identifiable across the country. The size of Carnegie's gift depended on a town's population and averaged some $2 per person; many small towns found their library uneconomical to run, and no one thought of pooling the funds for regional libraries.

The aging steelman found that giving was an exhausting activity. "Pity the poor millionaire, for the way of the philanthropist is hard," he wrote to a newspaper in 1913. Worse, he was under constant attack. One commentator wrote of him: "He would have given millions to Greece had she labeled the Parthenon Carnegopolis."

Although he claimed he was engaged in "scientific philanthropy," he could not resist calling his benefactions "sweetness and light," borrowing a phrase from his late friend, the poet Matthew Arnold. Among the thousands of requests for money that came to him daily, the most numerous were from universities. Carnegie turned down most of them, save for Berea in the Kentucky hills and the southern black college, Tuskegee. Woodrow Wilson, then president of Princeton, finally managed to get Carnegie to visit the campus in 1906. Proudly, Wilson showed him the playing fields, but what he did not know was that Carnegie detested football as a dangerous, stupid sport. As the philanthropist took his leave, he told Wilson he knew precisely what Princeton needed. "What?" asked Wilson. "A lake!" replied Carnegie. "That will take the young men's minds off football." And so, Princeton got a $400,000, 3½-mile-long lake.

Carnegie worked for ten years at giving away more than $350 million. Finally he realized that the job was too big for one man to handle. He set up the Carnegie Corporation in New York with an endowment of $125 million. It was the first modern philanthropic foundation administered by skilled trustees. Wisely, he shunned so-called experts in the arts, sciences, and education in favor of trustees who were good businessmen.

In the years before World War I, Carnegie turned to the promotion of world peace. His manner was somewhat quixotic, but he did push for a league of nations among the United States, Great Britain, France, Germany, and Russia. He built a Palace of Peace at The Hague in Holland, as well as a library and an edifice for a world court. He lived long enough to see the great war end and his personal pledge to give everything away fulfilled. But the trustees of his foundation shepherded his endowment so carefully that within a few decades they again had as much to give away as he had personally distributed in his lifetime.

207

Boys as well as girls were hired to run the switchboards at the Bell central telephone exchange in New York in 1879.

electromagnetic waves, thus closing an electrical circuit; the filings fell apart to break the circuit when tapped.

All these developments were brought together and put to practical purpose by the Italian Guglielmo Marconi. Working on his father's farm, Marconi made a better coherer and built a device that could send signals for two miles. In 1897 he obtained a British patent and organized the Wireless Telegraph Company. In 1899 the Marconi Wireless Telegraph Company of America was organized, and in that year Marconi was sending messages across the English Channel. A signal sent from Poldhu Station, Cornwall, was picked up across the Atlantic at St. John's, Newfoundland, in 1901.

Since wireless messages could carry more readily over unobstructed stretches of water, the first real use was made in seagoing vessels. A young Yale graduate, Lee De Forest, developed superior wireless equipment, which was installed on a number of U.S. Navy ships. Sending and receiving stations were set up at Coney Island, New York, and at Block Island and Point Judith, Rhode Island, by 1904, and four years later the public could have "Marconigrams" sent across the Atlantic. Congress in 1910 made it mandatory for large passenger ships to carry wireless, and this had become standard shipboard equipment by 1914.

A number of Americans made wireless improvements that helped lead to the establishment of a major new industry—notably De Forest's vacuum tube, an improved receiving device developed by Reginald Fessenden, and Edwin Armstrong's superheterodyne system. Mainly for its novelty value, the John Wanamaker Company set up a wireless system between its

New York and Philadelphia stores, under the charge of a young operator named David Sarnoff, who was eventually to head the Radio Corporation of America. De Forest early sensed the entertainment potential of wireless. In 1910 he got the great Enrico Caruso to broadcast an opera, and in 1916 he started broadcasting from the Columbia Phonographic Laboratories.

Another new technological device was seen as having important entertainment value. When Eastman replaced bulky photographic plates with roller film, Edison quickly saw that a pictorial record of motion might be achieved by putting sequential pictures on a roll, and by taking advantage of the eye's natural retention of images. He thought of this as an addition to his phonograph, and developed a companion "Kinetograph" camera.

In 1893 Edison had his young assistant, William Dickson, build "Black Maria," a black shed that revolved, concentrating light on his subjects by following the sun. One of the earliest films was *The Sneeze,* which was accompanied by recorded sound. In 1896 there was a public presentation of films at a New York variety theater, where Edison projected on a white screen films of dancing ladies, comedians, and breaking waves.

The "world's first all-moving-picture theater" was the Nickelodeon, opened in Pittsburgh by J. P. Harris in June, 1905. People paid five cents to sit in an old storeroom and see a reel or two of film. With continuous day and evenings showings, as many as 5,000 might come in one day. Attracted by all those nickels, impresarios opened thousands of nickelodeons across the nation. By 1910 there were 10,000 movie houses in the U.S., and by 1920 there were 17,000. With an estimated weekly audience of 10 million, movies had become the nation's major form of commercial entertainment.

Cinderella, the first feature-length film, was produced by director Georges Méliès, and this was followed by Edwin Porter's *The Great Train Robbery.* In 1912 Sarah Bernhardt appeared in *Queen Elizabeth,* which was followed by such classics as *Tess of the d'Urbervilles, The Prisoner of Zenda,* and the two-and-a-half-hour *Quo Vadis* in 1913. The early films were produced mainly in New York City, but southern California's climate of more reliable days of sunshine attracted producers, who established Hollywood as the industry's center.

The business was not a difficult one to enter. In 1918, when Signal Corps cameramen were discharged from the Army, a projection booth and its equipment could be obtained for several hundred dollars. But more lavish elements had already come on the scene. In *The Birth of a Nation* in 1915, David W. Griffith had introduced mob scenes and spectacular fires and battles. But with close-ups, long shots, fades, and other dramatic devices, Griffith was also helping to make the film a major new art medium on its own, as well as a big new business.

BUILDING AN ELECTRIC ERA

Electricity had enormous implications for a business society. In new ways, it took over many of men's more burdensome tasks. It meant new equipment and devices for comfort, convenience, and pleasure, and these in turn led to new or expanded businesses. It made practical the massive production of some metals and materials, and it introduced a new scale to the consumption of others. And, not least important, the production of electricity itself became a vast new industry.

Both the generation of electrical energy and one form of its consumption, electric street railways, lent themselves to public franchising, because they required the use of public lands and rights of way. Not unnaturally, these industries tended to become intertwined with politics, chiefly local.

The franchising power became the source of huge new fortunes as cities developed public transport, starting in the mid-1880's, first with overhead trolleys, then on elevated tracks, and subsequently in underground subway systems. Almost 50,000 miles of track were built in the cities by 1920. In New York, William C. Whitney and Thomas Fortune Ryan, powers in Tammany Hall, got control of the Metropolitan Traction Company, the Brooklyn Railroad, and other properties and placed them in a holding company, building small stakes into immense fortunes in a short time. Charles T. Yerkes was a political force in Chicago, where he bought the street railways and had them rebuilt by his own construction companies, milked them, unloaded them on Whitney and Ryan, and took off for London. Ohio's political boss, Mark Hanna, was active in the Cleveland street railway system; Peter Widener and William Elkins in Philadelphia used their political power to help build a public utility empire; and Roswell Flower, who had been governor of New York, was a leading figure behind Brooklyn Rapid Transit.

The control of electric utility companies moved into more varied hands. Some were political figures. A few were business individualists like Samuel Insull, who had emigrated from London, become an executive associated with Edison, then moved to Chicago to build a billion-dollar utility empire, but who always remained adamant against dealing with any New York banker. And still others, like the men behind Electric Bond & Share Company, were closely tied to Wall Street traditions. Electric Bond & Share was organized in 1905 to take over General Electric's weaker utility companies, build them up, and sell them to the public; instead, it became a holding company for a widespread group of utility firms. The industry had fantastic growth: the capitalization of U.S. public service companies ballooned from $200 million in 1890 to almost $20 billion by 1915.

Electricity powered not only the street railways but thousands of elevators in office buildings, along with many of the early automobiles and buses. Factory consumption in 1900 amounted to almost 200,000 electrical horsepower. About this time the much more compact and lighter-weight steam turbine began to replace the less efficient reciprocating engine as the prime mover for dynamos, and it no longer made economic sense for a manufacturer to produce his own electrical power. More and more homes were wired for current that could turn on incandescent lights and power electric fans, flatirons, grills, and toasters.

When a 5,000-horsepower turbo-generator driven by power from Niagara Falls went into operation in April, 1895, there was an immediate demand for two more. Among the industries that moved into the locality was the Pittsburgh Reduction Company, which eventually became the Aluminum Company of America — the outgrowth of an efficient new method of extracting aluminum from its ores devised by Charles M. Hall, who had gone to the Mellons for capital. Andrew Mellon, who then headed the T. Mellon & Sons Bank, advanced $250,000 in exchange for a controlling interest in the company. The Mellons also got major interests in Pittsburgh Glass and other glassworks, the Pennsylvania and other railroads, Westinghouse, Equitable and other insurance companies, and, as noted earlier, in Gulf Oil. Aluminum was unique as an industry that needed large amounts of electrical power to fuel its spring toward giantism.

Another metal whose destiny was tied closely to electricity was copper, highly desirable as a conductor to transmit current. The use of copper was restricted largely to roofing, ship sheathing, cooking utensils, and brass and bronze hardware at the time former Union soldier Michael Hickey staked a claim on a hill overlooking Butte, Montana, in 1875. Intent on finding gold and silver, he picked up some copper carbonate and discarded it. Some $90 million in gold had come out of the Montana region in just six years during the 1860's, and no one then dreamed that this was just a small fraction of the value of the copper that would one day be mined there. Hickey named his claim Anaconda, from a line in a Horace Greeley editorial that had once appealed to him: "Grant will encircle Lee's forces and crush them like a giant anaconda."

Hickey had staked out twenty-five claims in the region by 1880, and he gave Charles Larabie a half interest in the mine in exchange for sinking a deeper shaft. Marcus Daly, an experienced mine operator, came along in 1881, recognized the promising mineral deposit, bought a third interest for $15,000, and got

209

an option on the remaining interest for another $30,000. Then he set off for Salt Lake City to see the lawyer for the highly successful mining syndicate of James Ben Ali Haggin, Lloyd Tevis, and George Hearst (father of publisher William Randolph). Daly persuaded them to buy into the mine, and he thereafter became a member of their team, which eventually owned or controlled 100 North American mines, including the Homestake and the Anaconda, the greatest gold and copper mines, respectively. Daly took over the Anaconda in 1882, the same year that Edison's Pearl Street generating station, using almost sixty-five tons of copper, opened in New York.

With the capital from his new associates, Daly developed the mine, built the town of Anaconda, and engaged in rugged competition with Montana's other leading copper producer, William A. Clark. Anaconda was incorporated in 1895 with a capital of $30 million, and it produced zinc, lead, silver, and gold, as well as copper.

Another mining power developing concurrently in the West was that of the Guggenheims. Meyer Guggenheim, a Swiss immigrant, was eking out a living as a peddler when he learned that while he made just a penny on a ten-cent sale of shoe polish, the maker earned seven cents on the same can. He consulted a chemist and soon put members of his family to work making polish, thus getting both the manufacturer's and the marketer's profits. He did the same thing with a popular household lye for soap making, from which he made a modest fortune. He then took a flyer in Hannibal & St. Joseph stock, timing his purchases and sales accurately to correspond with Jay Gould's maneuvering in the issue, and ended up more than $300,000 to the good.

Eventually, Guggenheim owned a couple of Colorado silver mines. He had to put money into them to pump water out, but he hit it lucky when a rich lode of silver and lead was struck. As with the shoe polish and lye, he was more concerned with the larger smelting and marketing profits made by the smelter. He sent one of his seven sons to the Columbia School of Mines, another to study metallurgy and finance at the University of Pennsylvania, and groomed the others in his business. In 1889 they built their own smelter at Philadelphia, capitalized at $1.5 million without banker help. When an embargo was placed on Mexican silver, Guggenheim set up a plant in Mexico, and by 1895 the family holdings were producing profits of about $1,000,000 a year.

In this period Henry H. Rogers, backed by Rockefeller money, was putting together a copper trust, the Amalgamated Copper Company, and he decided in 1896 to add a smelter trust. The investment firm of Moore & Schley sent its agents to the West to bring in the smelter people and to sell $65 million in American Smelting and Refining Company stock. All were willing to sell except the Guggenheims, who held out even when the ante was raised. Finally, in 1900, the Guggenheims agreed to sell out all their smelting interests and most of their other properties for $42.5 million in stock — which was enough for them to control American Smelting. Subsequently, some Guggenheim interests in Alaska became the basis for a new copper mining and smelting combination, organized by Morgan as the Kennecott Copper Corporation.

Daly sold out his Anaconda mining interests to Rogers's Amalgamated, which then took over a running feud with one of the shiftier operators in the copper industry, Frederick A. Heinze. Heinze was a part Irish, part German-Jewish Brooklyn youth who had attended the Columbia School of Mines, then gone out West to seek his fortune by the shortest and quickest route. He milked one mining lease and went on to bigger things, deciding to take on the major producers.

One Heinze mine, the Rarus, adjoined the copper-rich holding of the Boston & Montana, which became part of Amalgamated. Heinze cut underground to the B.&M. ore beds. In court he cited the "apex" theory, enacted into federal law in 1872, which held that the owner of land that held an ore vein where it came to an apex could follow the vein even into adjacent property.

Heinze used every weapon he could in the battle — his personal good looks and charm, his crew of thirty-seven lawyers, the antagonism between Clark and Daly, the truculence of the mineworkers, and, certainly not least, William Clancy, a judge whom he and Clark had in their pockets. The judge dutifully ordered the B.&M. mine closed, as well as three Anaconda mines whose veins were claimed to apex in a tiny Heinze plot. He then declared Amalgamated an illegal combine and enjoined its subsidiaries from paying it dividends. Eventually all of Amalgamated was shut down.

Amalgamated finally got the state to pass a "fair trial" bill, which permitted the removal from a case of a judge charged with prejudice by one of the parties. Even so, Heinze was able through a little more financial sleight of hand to get $10.5 million for his properties. He retired from the scene and returned to New York to become a bank president, which was bad news for the banking business in New York

FIGHTING OFF THE PANIC

In 1906 the economy had been strong and buoyant for perhaps ten years. Harriman's railroads were paying top prices for other rail stocks. Schwab went into large-scale mining. And Heinze, with the help of the Mercantile National Bank, of which he had bought control, was promoting something called the United Copper Company. He was associated in this enterprise with Charles W. Morse, a former ice merchant and promoter who had discovered that he could own a string of banks by the simple expedient of borrowing from those he already controlled to gain control of others.

The first trouble signals came in March, 1907, when prices dipped sharply on the Stock Exchange, and new issues of securities became difficult to sell. Morgan and three other financiers called on the President in Washington and came away satisfied. In August there was another stock price break, and the Treasury put $28 million in banks in smaller cities to promote liquidity. In October, with other copper stocks sliding, United Copper stood firm, then broke sharply on a Saturday. But on Monday the price shot up from 37¼ to 60, as short sellers covered their commitments.

At this point Heinze and his crew felt that they had the stock cornered, and they called for delivery of short sales the following afternoon. But there was no corner, and plenty of stockholders thought this was a

good time to unload. With their money running out, the Heinze crowd sold their shares in a desperate effort to raise funds. The stock slipped to 36 that day and plummeted to 10 the following day. Otto Heinze & Co., a brokerage house in which two of Heinze's brothers were involved, failed.

Depositors, alarmed, started a run on Heinze's Mercantile National, and other banks came to the rescue, on condition that Heinze and the directors resign. They did, but it was too late. Soon the Morse banking chain began to go down, then the Knickerbocker Trust Company, whose president committed suicide, the National Bank of America, and a number of trust companies.

Word of the crisis was sent to Morgan, who was attending an Episcopal Church convention in the South. When the meeting was over, he hurried back to New York to assess the situation. J. P. Morgan & Co. itself, its affairs highly liquid, was in excellent condition, and George F. Baker's First National and James

The Way to Wealth

GEORGE HEARST

Indians called him "Boy That the Earth Talks To." In a way, George Hearst (1820–91) lived up to the name; he became one of the richest men in the history of American mining.

As a Missouri farm boy, he loved to explore nearby caves. When he was twenty-two, he opened a small merchandise store, but his father's death left him a legacy of debts. His discovery of rich lead ore in nearby mines bailed him out.

He was twenty-eight when gold was discovered in California, and in 1850 he set off for the mines. He panned gold in camps with such names as Hangtown and Jackass Gulch, but when his one good prospect petered out, he started selling merchandise again, in Sacramento. His competitors were tough businessmen—Charles Crocker, Mark Hopkins, and Collis P. Huntington—who made fortunes building the first transcontinental railroad. Hearst's wealth ultimately came to him in another way.

He heard that some dull blue sand that had annoyed prospectors in Nevada was found by assayers to contain $3,196 to the ton in silver and $1,595 in gold. He rushed to the Nevada strike and acquired a half interest in the Ophir mine for $10,000. It was the best

NEVADA HISTORICAL SOCIETY

The father of William Randolph

part of the fabulous Comstock Lode.

Hearst stayed in mining. With two Californians, James Ben Ali Haggin and Lloyd Tevis, he bought the Ontario silver mine in Utah for $33,000. In 1876 he acquired a gold mine property in South Dakota's Black Hills for $80,000 and, remembering his wife's request, "George, if you find a good mine, let us have a home stake," named it the Homestake. It became the mainstay of his fortune and to date has paid more than $160 million in dividends.

Hearst also bought up large land properties. At one time he owned a Mexican ranch of 1,000,000 acres, for which he paid forty cents an acre. The absentee owner, fearful of Apache raids, was glad to sell it, but Hearst knew when he made his offer that the Apaches had been rounded up. In California he paid seventy cents an acre for a 40,000-acre ranch that ran from the mountains to the ocean.

Like Leland Stanford, he served in the U.S. Senate and, about that body, remarked: "I do not know much about books; I have not read very much; but I have traveled a good deal and observed men and things and I have made up my mind after all my experiences that the members of the Senate are the survivors of the fittest."

In 1880 he bought the San Francisco *Daily Examiner*, but he is barely remembered as a publisher. It was his son, William Randolph, who, asking for and getting the *Examiner* in 1887, used it to embark on his own career as the builder of a great newspaper and magazine empire. But the riches that bankrolled young Hearst's early days came from the "Boy That the Earth Talks To." When George Hearst got his syndicate into Anaconda in Montana, it could truly be said that his miner's instincts had led him to the greatest gold, the greatest silver, and the greatest copper mines in the world.

The financial crisis of October, 1907, saw thousands of investors thronging the Wall Street area, above, gathered worriedly "as if to watch a fire." At right is Morgan's guarantee, penned on his library stationery, to support the credit of New York.

Stillman's National City could be counted on to stand by with their immense resources.

If there was a major financial weakness about, it lay with the trust companies. Until 1893 they had confined their activities largely to acting as trustees and financial agents for corporations and individuals. But then they began to represent security holders' committees and reorganization committees, and, finally, to handle corporate financing and reorganizations directly themselves. There were many banking functions that trust companies could not perform, but they were also free of bank restrictions. They could buy real estate or stocks, they could underwrite financing, and they were not required to keep a cash reserve. As a result, their earnings rose and their deposits increased from under $200 million in 1898 to $800 million in 1906.

Now the trust companies were in trouble, and Morgan, although the Treasury had placed $42 million of interest-free deposits in banks he controlled, was not much inclined to give them a hand. It was Stillman who, with gentle prodding, finally convinced Morgan to help them out.

Morgan had put experts to work assessing the condition of the banks that were in the most danger. One of these was the Trust Company of America, whose president kept appealing to Morgan for funds to satisfy depositors. One day, on which $13.5 million was withdrawn, a $1,000,000 loan from First National, National City, and the House of Morgan arrived just in time to enable the bank to hold out until the three o'clock clos-

ing time. Then Morgan got a report that the bank was solvent, and he announced, "This is the place to stop this trouble."

And stop it he did. What was especially significant was not that the other men of wealth and power turned to Morgan in this crisis, but that the federal government itself relied on him. Treasury Secretary George B. Cortelyou had hurried to New York to confer with the bankers, looking chiefly to the seventy-year-old Morgan for direction. There was no central banking system, either government or privately controlled, and Morgan himself offered the closest approximation to such a central authority. It was Morgan who decided where the panic should stop, who got bankers to put up millions of dollars to keep stocks from collapsing, and who turned thumbs down one day when the president of the Stock Exchange wanted to move up the closing hour.

Things were beginning to look better, when Morgan got word that the brokerage firm of Moore & Schley was in danger of bankruptcy. Involved in a speculative pool in Tennessee Coal, Iron and Railway Company stock, the brokerage house had pledged $6 million of the stock for bank loans. The banks were calling the loans, and Moore & Schley could not pay. The firm's failure might well set off many others on Wall Street.

Frick and Gary urged Morgan to lend the brokers $5 million. But Morgan wanted U.S. Steel to buy the Tennessee Coal stock outright, substituting its own more negotiable bonds. First, however, a delegation

212

was sent to Washington to seek assurance there would be no antitrust prosecution. President Roosevelt gave his word, and the deal went through. U.S. Steel paid $30 million in its bonds for control of the major element of the southern steel industry.

Before the end of the year, security prices started to come back. The recession that followed was extremely mild. Industrial output dropped in 1908 and commercial failures were up, but most of the nation hardly felt the effects of the downturn.

The House of Morgan continued to strengthen its position. First the Trust Company of America and later the Mercantile Trust were absorbed by Morgan's Bankers Trust Company. Six more trust companies were absorbed by the Guaranty Trust. "Community of interest" was brought into the electrical equipment industry, as the Morgans, long dominant in General Electric, reorganized the Westinghouse Electric Company and placed one of their partners on the board.

From 1902 to 1912 the Morgan firm took charge of marketing some $2 billion in various security issues and also carried on a substantial business in commercial banking. On November 1, 1912, J. P. Morgan & Co. had more than $160 million in deposits and held the accounts of some 100 large corporations.

Morgan was never without a sense of his own immense power, but he felt that it had come to him by legitimate means and that he retained it by dint of responsible economic behavior. As a kind of unelected economic president of his country, he felt that he could shrink neither from making decisions nor from accepting their consequences, and time and again he demonstrated unlimited faith in his beliefs, as well as great courage. When he died in Rome early in 1913, he had already begun to sense that important changes were on the way and that his own era was ending. Not long before he died he said philosophically, "American business must henceforth be done in glass pockets."

THE MONEY TRUST

In the freewheeling business climate of the late 1800's and early 1900's, the rich got richer and money gravitated to money. The Rockefellers earned more than their growing oil business could hope to absorb. Even though Standard Oil paid out $118 million in dividends between 1882 and 1895, the company's assets increased from $55 million to $150 million. And to the Rockefellers, idle money, like idle hands, represented a waste of God's benefactions.

Expansion into railroading was almost an adjunct to their own business, because they initiated so much freight themselves. But they also moved into businesses with little or no relation to their own. A small loan to the sons of Lewis Merritt became the basis for vast Rockefeller iron ore holdings in the Mesabi Range; they

built a fleet to carry the ore down the lakes; they acquired the Colorado Fuel and Iron Company; they were behind the formation of Amalgamated Copper and of American Smelting & Refining; and their share of the Union Pacific brought them into that railroad's widespread holdings. Most of these investments simply became new and greater sources of wealth.

While John D. Rockefeller had long ago laid down the policy of steering clear of loans from bankers, some Standard Oil money began to trickle into New York, where it could help finance other businesses. The chief conduit for this money movement became the National City Bank. The National City had formerly been simply the City Bank, for long years one of the soundest and strongest banks in New York. Largely the creation of Moses Taylor, an old-style merchant who had become its president in 1855, the City had become first the bank of the sugar traders and the raw-materials merchants, then of the Cuban planters, the cotton traders, the metals importers, and finally of the coal and metal merchants.

To the presidency of the City Bank in 1891 came Texas-born James Stillman, who had been a fellow director with William Rockefeller on the boards of the Chicago, Milwaukee & St. Paul Railroad and then of the Hanover Bank. Equally taciturn, the two men admired and respected one another, and Stillman said he liked Rockefeller because the two could sit together for fifteen minutes in total silence. But the Rockefeller cash spoke volumes; the bank's deposits swelled from $12 million in 1891 to $31 million in just two years, when it was the biggest bank in New York. Not long afterward, as the National City, its deposits rose to $100 million, and the Rockefellers joined William Whitney in the control of the Consolidated Gas Company of New York, which in 1899 merged with the Edison Illuminating Company of New York as Consolidated Edison.

While the Rockefellers were building up the National City, Morgan worked through other banks, mainly the First National and Bankers Trust. But Morgan was genuinely far more interested in controlling enterprises than in owning them, and in directing the use of other people's money than in making it all his own.

So Morgan's interests turned naturally to the places where money accumulated—banks and trust companies, insurance companies, and the industrial and railroad companies that could be organized, reorganized, and combined into good profit producers. In some cases he owned stock or other interests in these enterprises, but his tools were more commonly voting trusts and directorships, or even an active role in management. George Baker's First National Bank was by itself probably wealthier than the House of Morgan, but the self-effacing Baker was usually content to follow Morgan's lead. Somewhat more independent, but ordinarily unwilling to cross Morgan, was Jacob Schiff, whose Kuhn, Loeb & Co. was the second largest factor in corporate financing.

After John D. Rockefeller went into semiretirement in the 1890's, the Standard Oil group appeared more fearful of government restraints and more willing to co-operate with other financial leaders—which usually meant Morgan. The consequence was a concentration of money power that amounted to nothing less than a money trust. Into its orbit were drawn the banks and bankers of other cities—Chicago's First National Bank, Illinois Trust and Savings Bank, and Continental & Commercial National Bank; Boston's National Shawmut Bank, First National Bank of Boston, and Old Colony Trust Company, and the investment banking houses of Lee, Higginson & Company and Kidder, Peabody & Company.

Insurance funds tended to move toward the lucrative trust companies in the 1890's, but by 1900 insurance company assets were large enough to attract Wall Street attention directly. The House of Morgan began to develop ties to the New York Life, and John A. McCall, its president, got to be known as a Morgan man. The Mutual Life Insurance Company was closely linked with the Guaranty Trust Company, which it once controlled. And in 1910 Morgan paid $3 million to obtain just $51,000 in par value of stock in the Equitable Life Assurance Society, the other member of the Big Three in insurance, an investment that paid small returns but gave Morgan working control of the Equitable's half billion dollars in assets.

All this and more was brought out by an investigation conducted by Louisiana Congressman Arsène Pujo in 1912, which set out to discover whether a "money trust" indeed existed. The congressional Committee on Banking and Currency found that J. P. Morgan & Co. dominated or controlled three national banks, three trust companies, three life insurance companies, ten railroad systems, and five industrial giants,

A BRIDLE ON FREEDOM

In the free enterprise system, American business has sought to grow stronger and more profitable by serving the market better. Yet one measure of the success of a business has been its ability to stifle competition, thus weakening one of the essential freedoms of the system—the free market.

American political figures who were deemed most antibusiness—Jefferson, Jackson, Wilson, and Franklin D. Roosevelt—were actually devout believers in the business system as it was constituted in their times. What they tried to curb was the concentration of business power that would have meant less, rather than more, competition.

Jefferson knew that merchants and traders were essential, but he sought to balance their power with that of the major producers of his age—the planters and small farmers. Jackson believed in the sanctity of contractual pledges, but he sought to eliminate the monopolistic powers inherent in state-granted exclusive charters. As the nation grew bigger and wealthier, so did many industries. The era of trusts created monopolies or near-monopolies without the help, or, indeed, the hindrance, of the state.

These large combinations, whether viewed as a product of the American spirit or as plain greed, enabled industries to produce more, cut prices, and, in time, pay higher wages, as well as compete abroad. But what was more visible to the public was the vast concentration of power and wealth that the trusts represented. To the average man at the turn of the century, when the trusts were in their heyday, they seemed to be a dangerous revival of an aristocracy of wealth.

The industrial magnates, in turn, cited the Fourteenth Amendment as an injunction against government interference in their affairs: "No state shall make or enforce any law which shall abridge the privileges or immunities of citizens of the United States; nor shall any state deprive any person of life, liberty, or property, without due process of law, nor deny to any person within its jurisdiction the equal protection of the laws."

Eventually those phrases would be emphasized in behalf of human and civil rights, but until well into the twentieth century the majority of the members of the Supreme Court interpreted them as affording protection to big business. In 1905 Justice Oliver Wendell Holmes felt constrained to tell his colleagues that "the Fourteenth Amendment does not embody Mr. Herbert Spencer's Social Statics." He was referring, in a dissenting opinion, to the Court's consistent refusal to rule favorably for the Interstate Commerce Commission in cases brought against railroads. The Interstate Commerce Act of 1887 had set down rules to prevent railroad rate manipulation, but the Court simply muzzled the watchdog.

The Sherman Antitrust Act of 1890 suffered nearly the same fate. The Justice Department lost seven of the first eight cases it brought before the courts under the act. Ironically, the case that it did win resulted in breaking the Pullman strike of 1894, when judges held that the strikers were conspiring to restrain interstate commerce. In 1911, in the Standard Oil case, the Court finally broke up a trust, but muddled the issue by finding it engaged in "unreasonable" restraint of trade.

The biggest trust to come under scrutiny was the so-called money trust. In 1912 Representative Arsène Pujo's congressional committee began an investigation to unravel the business ties among investment bankers, big corporations, commercial banks, and insurance companies. By the time the committee had untied all the knots, it reported that, "If, therefore, by a 'money trust' . . . an established and

in addition to possessing affiliations with other railroads and corporations. Morgan partners held a total of seventy-two directorships in forty-seven corporations whose capital or resources totaled $10 billion. Key figures in the First National Bank, in which Morgan owned a large block of stock and which, with Morgan, controlled the Guaranty Trust, were also directors of a number of Morgan-dominated railroads and industrial companies. Next in line came the National City, five of whose officers held thirty-two directorships in twenty-six corporations, some of them crisscrossing with the Morgan and First National interests.

The committee's summing up, which presented a factual but probably not totally true picture of the state of affairs, showed that the Morgan-Baker-Stillman-Rockefeller interests held 341 directorships in 112 banking, insurance, transportation, industrial, and utility corporations with total resources or capitalization of $22.25 billion. Morgan, in hours of mostly glowering but occasionally jovial testimony, contended

that these men did not act in concert and that many of them did not even know each other. Asked whether he favored competition or combination, he replied, "I would rather have combination." But he subsequently showed evenhandedness when he conceded, "I do not object to competition either. I like a little competition." But always he contended that it was a man's character—something he himself could obviously judge well—that counted, rather than his position or wealth.

But what could not be denied, in the face of overwhelming evidence, was that there was such a thing as a money trust in the United States. A small group had it in their power to bestow or withhold capital as they saw fit, to have a powerful influence on the prices of securities, and, in the final analysis, to exercise inordinate control over the national economy.

The Pujo committee recommended closer supervision over the Stock Exchange, the breaking up of financial concentration, competitive bidding among investment bankers for the securities of railroad cor-

well-defined community of interest between a few leaders of finance which has been created and is held together through stock holdings, interlocking directorates, and other forms of dominion over banks, trust companies, railroads, public-service and industrial corporations, and which has resulted in a vast and growing concentration of control of money and credit in the hands of a comparatively few men . . . the condition thus described exists in this country today."

The implication was that men like J. P. Morgan, James Stillman, George Baker, and the Rockefellers, and the men who represented them, all acted in concert. The actual testimony revealed something else—they had acted similarly because they thought similarly and followed the same ethical standards. They thought that they were the best men for the job, and they thought that they were acting in the best interests of the nation.

J. P. Morgan himself steadfastly denied that he possessed any excessive power. In one of the hearings, the committee counsel inquired of him: "Well, assuming that you had [the power], your idea is that when a man abuses it, he loses it?"

MORGAN: Yes, and he never gets it back again, either. . . . The question of control, in this country at least, is personal; that is, in money.

COUNSEL: How about credit?
MORGAN: In credit, too.
COUNSEL: Personal to whom? To the man who controls?
MORGAN: No, no, he never has it. He cannot buy it.
COUNSEL: No, but he gets—
MORGAN: All the money in Christendom and all the banks in Christendom cannot control it.
COUNSEL: Is not commercial credit based primarily upon money or property?
MORGAN: No, sir; the first thing is character.
COUNSEL: Before money or property?
MORGAN: Before money or anything else. Money cannot buy it.
George F. Baker of New York's First National Bank was a little more candid about how perilous the so-called money trust was. But he, too, held to the view that money power could not fall into bad hands.
COUNSEL: I am not speaking of incompetent hands. We are speaking of this concentration which has come about and the power it brings with it, getting into the hands of very ambitious men, perhaps not overscrupulous. You see a peril in that, do you not?
BAKER: Yes.
COUNSEL: So that the safety, if you think there is safety in the situation, really lies in the . . . men?

BAKER: Very much.
Woodrow Wilson followed up the Pujo hearings with pressure for legislation to clarify the Sherman Antitrust Act. The result, the Clayton Antitrust Act of 1914, barred interlocking directorates, price discrimination among buyers where it lessened competition, and the binding of a dealer by a manufacturer to prevent his selling competitive products.

Another consequence of the Pujo investigation was the Federal Reserve Act of 1913, which, in an attempt to remove the ultimate control of money, and its availability, from private hands, set up a new central banking system. It required a number of years for the system to take its final form, but it removed many of the previous laissez-faire attitudes from banking.

They were only the first of many steps intended to balance the freedom of business to grow big against its freedom to stay competitive. The contest has never stilled, and to many businessmen, words written by Woodrow Wilson in *The New Freedom* in 1913 still have validity: "American industry is not free, as it once was free. . . . the man with only a little capital is finding it harder to get into the field, more and more impossible to compete with the big fellow. Why? Because the laws of this country do not prevent the strong from crushing the weak."

215

porations, and improved banking laws. In time, most of these recommendations were followed, some by voluntary action, some through natural shifts in financial power, and almost all by government fiat.

One of the earliest changes was in the provision for greater and more centralized government control over the nation's banking resources. Once he had got tariff reduction under way, President Woodrow Wilson called for a new banking system that might avert the kind of chaos that had occurred in 1907. Bankers wanted a system that was privately controlled, while political progressives called for complete government control.

The system that emerged in the Federal Reserve Act of December, 1913, was a compromise between the two. There would be twelve reserve banks, each for a different section of the country. These would be bankers' banks, their stock owned by national and other banks in their districts, to which special banking functions were offered. By issuing notes against short-term paper, there would be a kind of automatic provision for matching the amount of currency in circulation with the current volume of business.

Directing the entire system and determining broad monetary policies for the nation would be a Federal Reserve Board, its members named by the President. More than just a reform measure, the act gave tacit recognition to the fact that these responsibilities were now too large for one man or one small group of private citizens. The nation had outgrown its Morgans.

THE WORKERS' WELFARE MOVEMENT

"I feel fit as a bull moose," proclaimed the newly elected Vice President, Theodore Roosevelt, as the second term of McKinley prosperity began in 1901. Hope and optimism were in the air as the century opened with the consciousness that the United States was the world's richest and greatest industrial power.

But did everyone really share in the prosperity of those years? The evidence indicates that most people did not. Between 1860 and 1890 the wage level increased by two thirds, and real wages went up even faster, because prices had a general decline. But between 1890 and the start of the First World War, wages had a hard time keeping up with rising prices, and any upturn in living standards was more the result of technological improvements than of higher earnings for working men and women. An 1890 study showed that more than half the nation's wealth was held by one per cent of its families, a situation that was little changed by 1914.

The rising sentiment for progressive reform was something that Presidents Taft and Wilson had both sensed, as receptive ears were turned to Robert La Follette's "Wisconsin Idea" that government could and should serve the people more directly and better.

Tom L. Johnson, who had espoused Henry George's theory of a "single tax" on land use, was named mayor of Cleveland in 1899. Back in 1897 Toledo, Ohio, elected as its mayor Samuel M. Jones, an enlightened businessman who had exemplified the Golden Rule by giving workers in his factory the eight-hour day, high wages, paid vacations, and a share of profits. As mayor he took away the policemen's nightsticks, put city employees on an eight-hour day, and started free kindergartens, public playgrounds, and park concerts. This was too much for the leaders of his party, who dropped him, but he won re-election as an independent three times.

Progressivism was not merely the flag of the disgruntled and impoverished but the faith of a large segment of the growing middle class. This included, as it always had, the small businessmen who struggled for survival against the giants of monopoly. But they had only doubled in number between 1870 and 1910, expanding not even as fast as the general population. The real middle-class growth was among the white-collar workers—salespeople, teachers, clerks, technicians, and so forth—whose numbers increased almost eightfold, from 750,000 to 5.6 million, over the same forty years.

It was in this group that Wilson found much of his support, and he responded by instituting major reforms in his first term. The Underwood-Simmons Tariff Act retained a protectionist flavor, but it added a large number of items to the free list and cut duties on others. The Sixteenth Amendment to the Constitution made it possible to pass an income tax law that would stick, and the Seventeenth Amendment provided for the direct election of senators. Antitrust legislation was made more meaningful by the Clayton Antitrust Act of 1914. The Federal Trade Commission was formed to keep a watchful eye on business. But by Wilson's second term, progressivism was overwhelmed by appeals to patriotism in the nation's increasing involvement with producing materials for the European war, and then in fighting in the war itself.

But the progressive idea had another dimension that proved equally rewarding to many workers. Big business, which had traditionally regarded labor as an impersonal element of the supply-demand equation, began to look at workers as people, much as most American employers did 100 years earlier. This could serve both a practical and an altruistic end for the employer. Under the right conditions, a workman might turn out more in nine hours than in ten; rest periods might increase production by reducing fatigue, and lower labor turnover could cut costs.

As early as the 1890's a few employers started pension, profit-sharing, and other welfare plans for their employees. The Du Pont Company instituted pension insurance and savings plans in 1904, A.T.&T. in 1913,

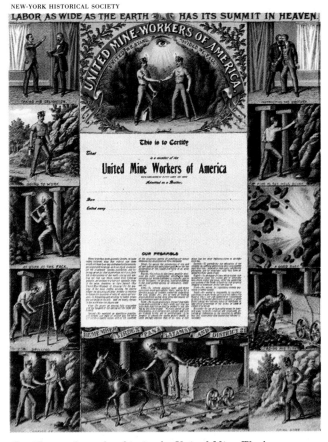

LABOR AS WIDE AS THE EARTH HAS ITS SUMMIT IN HEAVEN

Certificate of membership in the United Mine Workers, organized in 1890 for men who worked in or around the coal mines

and Sears, Roebuck in 1916. Equitable Life in 1912 wrote a group life insurance policy to cover the employees of Montgomery Ward and Company. Egged on to some extent by state commissions studying compensation laws, U.S. Steel began paying six months' to three years' wages to the families of deceased workers. The U.S. Rubber Company, one of the earlier business combinations, began in 1912 to sell its stock to key employees (those earning $1,300 or more a year) and in 1917 instituted a pension plan for aged and infirm workers. A dozen or more companies adopted the Scanlon Plan (named for its originator, Joseph Norbert Scanlon), which called for employees to help make business decisions. Edward A. Filene of Boston had his employees help make management decisions for a period of twenty years, during which sales had a thirty-fold increase. The Dennison Manufacturing Company tried to level off seasonal business fluctuations, and a guaranteed annual wage plan was inaugurated first by Jay Hormel in the highly seasonal packing business and then by Procter & Gamble.

Managers who had scoffed at efficiency experts and careful job measurements took another look when they found themselves outdone by efficient European managements. Scores of business management books were published in the first decade of the century. The

ideas of Frederick W. Taylor, who had started making detailed analyses of factory tasks in the Midvale Steel Company as early as 1882, began to catch on in the United States as they had long before in Europe. Personnel management came under study, and personnel departments were set up by the hundreds, particularly during World War I, when labor was short.

Another aspect of middle-class growth was the increasing number of people who owned corporate stocks. Jay Cooke had probably started it all by trying to sell government bonds to everyone who might conceivably buy, and by teaching that investments could grow in value. The number of shareholders in U.S. corporations, estimated at 4.4 million by 1900, had almost doubled, to 8.6 million, by 1917. Per capita life insurance rose from $41 in 1885 to $179 in 1910.

At the laboring level, American workers did not fare so well. The great trusts and combinations were dedicated in their opposition to unionized labor. John Gates once simply shut his big Chicago plant, explaining that business was bad, something nobody else had noticed. After a while, he reopened at full blast. But occasionally a smart labor leader took advantage of a consolidation to win some points. T. J. Shaffer, head of the Amalgamated Association of Iron, Steel, and Tin Workers, judged that the period of floating new securities to form U.S. Steel would be a good time to negotiate hard for worker gains. He turned out to be right; the New York financiers insisted that the individual plant managers bend a little in their bargaining, rather than invite strikes. When Shaffer later tried to carry his advantage too far, Morgan resisted, and the union lost some of its gains.

The American Federation of Labor continued to gain ground rapidly, increasing its membership rolls from about 100,000 in 1890 to more than 500,000 in 1900 and 2,000,000 by 1914. Some of the A.F.L.'s best years came in the prosperous period from 1897 to 1904, when many unions and employers got along so well that it was known as the "honeymoon period of capital and labor." But in many communities the battle lines were being drawn, as smaller employers stiffened their backs against union organization and formed "citizens alliances." These were brought together in a nationwide Citizens Industrial Association by David M. Parry, president of the National Association of Manufacturers, and the A.F.L. actually lost ground in many places.

Still, as unions went, the A.F.L. was already becoming the conservative old guard. Far more militant and subject to more general disapproval was a group of labor leaders whose aims ranged from broad-gauge industrial unionism to the use of organized labor as a spearhead for revolution. These included Eugene V. Debs, who had led the American Railway Union and was now head of the Socialist party; other Socialists,

217

such as Morris Hillquit, a lawyer, and Kate Richards O'Hare, a Kansas firebrand; Daniel De Leon, who started the Socialist Labor party, and William D. Haywood, head of the violence-prone Western Federation of Miners and a founder of the Industrial Workers of the World.

Organized in 1905, the I.W.W., known as the Wobblies, brought an aggressive spirit to the labor movement, particularly in the Northwest. The union managed to get more than its share of public attention, although the membership probably never exceeded 60,000 or 70,000. Although some of its strikes were successful, much of the public was repelled by its advocacy of sabotage and revolution and subsequently by its opposition to the war. After the war, many I.W.W. leaders and members transferred their allegiance to the American Communist party.

While the existence of the I.W.W. probably helped rather than hurt the A.F.L., the older labor organization managed to make some mistakes on its own. When the government demanded that war industries engage in collective bargaining with their workers, a great many large companies quickly formed their own unions. One of the first company unions was set up as the result of a Rockefeller Foundation study, following a bloody strike at the Rockefeller-owned Colorado Fuel and Iron Company. A.F.L. chief Samuel Gompers at first welcomed these unions as a chance to introduce more workers to labor organization, but after the war he realized that company unions were actually harmful to labor's cause.

Perhaps a more important failing was one inherent in craft unionism. It was almost solely the skilled workers who were organized, while unskilled laborers were not eligible for union membership in most cases. This division also took another form, between newly arrived immigrants and Negroes on the one hand, and native-born whites on the other. Immigration was extremely heavy between 1890 and 1917 and some two thirds or more of the 18 million new Americans were from eastern and southern Europe, by contrast with the earlier preponderance of immigrants from northwestern Europe. The result was a racial and ethnic bias in the unions that performed a disservice to the labor movement for many years afterward.

THE AUTOMOBILE INDUSTRY

Experiments with powered carriages began almost as soon as there were mechanical sources of power. A Frenchman, Nicholas Cugnot, put a steam engine into a three-wheeled carriage back in 1769. In Brandon, Vermont, an electrically powered car was built and driven by Thomas Davenport, a blacksmith. Etienne J. J. Lenoir used a one-cylinder internal combustion engine to propel a carriage in France in 1863. It was fourteen years later that George B. Selden of Rochester built a vehicle powered with a gasoline engine, but he was not granted a patent on it until 1895.

Much of the early experimentation with automobiles was carried on in Europe. Germany's Gottlieb Daimler designed a lightweight, high-speed engine in the 1880's, while Karl Benz developed an electrical spark system and the differential drive. Inspired by these and other developments, U.S. tinkerers finally got into the act in the early 1890's.

It was not, as might be expected, the Brewsters, the producers of prize-winning carriages, or the major manufacturers who built 12 million bicycles in the 1880's and 1890's who made the first cars, but all manner of machinists and craftsmen. Mechanics Charles E. and J. Frank Duryea put America's first gasoline-driven car on the streets of Springfield, Massachusetts, in 1893. The following year Elwood Haynes, a Kokomo, Indiana, metallurgist and petroleum engineer, built a car, and by 1896 Henry Ford and Ransom E. Olds had built automobiles with internal combustion engines. Alexander Winton, who pioneered the ideas of spare parts and of service stations for repairs, was building bigger cars in his bicycle repair shop in Cleveland in 1897. Duryea, driving his two-cylinder "buggy-aut," won a fifty-two-mile automobile race sponsored by the Chicago *Times-Herald* on Thanksgiving Day, 1895.

The Hartford Rubber Works, which eventually became a part of U.S. Rubber, began making pneumatic tires for automobiles in 1895. But not until around 1900 did the commercial prospects seem bright enough for a number of small firms to go into auto manufacture. That year the first automobile show was held in New York's Madison Square Garden, and many listened with disbelief when Winton arrived in an auto which he announced had been driven under its own power from Cleveland. The 1900 census reported the production of 4,192 cars: 1,681 steam-powered, 1,575 electric, and 936 propelled by "hydrocarbon."

Olds was producing and selling his two-passenger runabouts for $650 each in 1901. William Crapo Durant was still confining himself to horse-drawn carriages, his Durant-Dort Carriage Company selling as many as 50,000 a year, all produced by W. A. Patterson's factory in Flint, Michigan. But the Studebakers, long famed as the builders of chuck wagons, Conestoga wagons, and Civil War artillery wagons, began building electric cars in 1902 and five-passenger, sixteen-horsepower Studebaker-Garford gasoline "buggies" in 1904.

Also struggling to get started at this time was the young Detroit mechanic Henry Ford. Born on a Michigan farm in 1863, Ford was interested only in machinery, and he ran off to work in a machine shop at the age of sixteen. He built himself a steam car, which he discarded as unsafe, then a small gasoline engine. By

The first Model T: Saturday Evening Post, *October 3, 1908*

the early 1890's he was at work in earnest trying to build an automobile. By day he was a $45-a-month mechanic, by evening a dedicated worker in his shed. When he finally came out for a midnight meal at a quick-lunch wagon, it was to the proprietor that he let out his hopes and frustrations, and "Coffee Jim" was the man who had enough faith in Ford to advance money for his project. After building his first working models, Ford started the Detroit Automobile Co. in 1899 and the Henry Ford Automobile Co. in 1901, backed in both ventures by William H. Murphy, a lumber dealer. He failed both times, and Murphy turned to Henry M. Leland and with him started the Cadillac Automobile Co.

Racing was then the showcase for automobiles, and in 1901 Ford managed to drive one of his own models to victory in the Grosse Point, Michigan, races. Barney Oldfield next won a race with a Ford "999" model, and a new group of backers, headed by Detroit coal dealer Alexander Malcomson, raised $28,000 to get Ford started in business for a third try in 1903. This time there was an uninterrupted upward climb. Taking for himself the titles of designer, master mechanic, superintendent, vice president, and general manager, Ford set out to build a simple, standard model that large numbers of people could afford.

His first cars sold for $825 to $850, below the aver-

age for those days, but not low enough for Ford. His vision was like that of Vail with the telephone, McCormick with the harvester, and Singer with the sewing machine: the lower the price, the larger the sales —and the larger the sales, the greater the overall prosperity. There is no evidence that Ford foresaw that the automobile would power the same kind of industrial growth that the railroads had created in the preceding half century, but he showed consistent and ample faith in his own vision. The price of a Ford reached $950 in 1909, but by 1913 there were models selling for as little as $550, in 1914 for $490, and eventually some for $260.

Meanwhile, production and sales climbed. In 1909, the first year of the selling of his Model T, the company marketed just over 10,000 vehicles. Four years later output reached 168,000, more than a third of the American market; the next year sales rose to 248,000, or 45 per cent of the market. Mass production, interchangeable parts, and central assembly were not especially new ideas in manufacturing, or even in auto making. What Ford did was to bring them all together with great effectiveness and to add the concept of keeping costs low enough to price his product for the largest possible mass market.

Automobile manufacture in those days was largely a matter of having parts made separately, usually by outside suppliers, and then bringing them together at a central assembly point. In 1908 Walter Flanders rearranged some of the machinery at a Ford plant to have the assembly line itself move, making the work more efficient by dividing it into smaller, if highly repetitive, operations. This was done only for small parts at first, but was soon expanded to larger ones, and finally to the whole automobile. In 1914 Ford startled the industrial world by cutting the hours of work from nine to eight and raising the minimum wage for most production tasks to five dollars a day. In his view this was not humanitarianism but good business. If higher pay could give him more production and better workmanship, not only were the benefits worth the costs, but he was helping set a standard whereby more Americans would be able to afford his products.

Not everyone saw it quite that way. In 1916, after Ford had announced a price cut from $440 to $360, stockholders brought suit, claiming that he was unjustified in thus giving away their money. Said Ford: "We could easily have maintained our prices for this year and cleaned up . . . but I do not think it would be right . . . . We . . . are now clearing $2 million to $2.5 million a month, which is all any firm ought to make." But the court held for the stockholders, ruling, "It is not within the lawful powers of a corporation to . . . conduct a company's affairs for the merely incidental benefit of shareholders and for the primary purpose of benefitting others."

What the court failed to recognize was the part played by Ford's pricing policies in boosting his firm to industry leadership by 1911 or, perhaps more important, in putting 4 million cars, a sixth of them Fords, on the road by 1916. And what Ford himself did not fully realize was the contribution others had made to his huge enterprise. His distrust of bankers was an understandable outgrowth of his agrarian wellsprings. But he also insisted on buying out backers and partners as he became the increasingly crusty autocrat of his growing industrial empire.

An auto-making firm more in the tradition of its times was that started by William Durant, a salesman-promoter who made his first easy million selling carriages but knew nothing about automobiles. When the auto company started by his Flint neighbor, David Buick, ran into money problems, however, Durant took over. He put in $75,000 of new money, quickly raised $1.5 million more, and introduced assembly line techniques that had the plant producing 8,000 cars a year by 1908. Durant induced Charles Mott to bring his axle plant to Flint, and got French racing driver Albert Champion to make his porcelain AC spark plugs for the Buick.

Also in the fashion of his day, Durant in 1908 incorporated a New Jersey holding company, named General Motors, with a capitalization of $12 million. He brought into his new auto combine Cadillac, Oakland, Weston, and Oldsmobile. To add Ford and Maxwell to the combination, he went to J. P. Morgan & Co. for capital, claiming expansively that automobile sales would soon climb to 500,000 a year. "If he has any sense he'll keep such notions to himself if he ever tries to borrow money," said Morgan partner George W. Perkins, and Durant was turned down.

Durant then proceeded to demonstrate that unsound financing, based on excessive optimism, could make for bad business practices. Within two years General Motors verged on bankruptcy. The company was rescued by two investment banking firms, J. & W. Seligman of New York and Boston's Lee, Higginson & Company. The bankers took control and replaced Durant with Charles Nash, who made Walter Chrysler head of the Buick division. But Durant was far from through. He managed to get financing to buy out Louis Chevrolet, a Swiss-born manufacturer, and to found the Chevrolet Motor Co. Durant kept increasing his own stock holdings in General Motors until he held a commanding position there.

In 1915 Durant became acquainted with some of the Du Ponts through Hamilton Barksdale, a Du Pont son-in-law, and got them interested in General Motors. Barksdale himself was made president of Chevrolet, and the Du Pont Company in 1917 bought $25 million of General Motors stock, an investment which they continued to increase. As they lent more millions to Durant, they were able in time to share control of the company with him and then to take it over completely. These investments, largely at the insistence of Pierre Du Pont and on the advice of financial wizard John Jacob Raskob, were to become the keystone of the Du Pont family wealth.

By the time World War I started, the automobile was an established part of American life, and the United States had taken firm leadership in yet another industry. The 2,000 or more makes of cars that had sought a share of this great new market had already shaken down to a mere handful. The survivors were not only the most efficient producers but the innovators who had a sense of what the public wanted. Thus Vincent Bendix and Charles F. Kettering made places for themselves by devising self-starting mechanisms that could do away with the hand crank and make autos more appealing to women. Cord tires, disc wheels, and all-steel bodies offered greater safety, and twin-six and V-8 engines gave smoother riding. A good-roads movement culminated in the National Good Roads Association, and Congress, after naming a Committee on Roads in 1913, passed a federal assistance act in 1916. President Wilson thought at first that federal aid to highways might be unconstitutional, but he signed the act as an appropriate measure for national defense on the day that a German submarine appeared in Baltimore's harbor.

WINGS

At least as far back as the days of Leonardo da Vinci, men dreamed of devices that would let them fly, but the technology of powered flight did not develop until the late 1800's. The chief American contributor to both the early theory and practice of flight was Samuel Pierpont Langley, a civil engineer, staff assistant at the Harvard Observatory, director of Pittsburgh's Allegheny Observatory, and, after 1887, secretary of the Smithsonian Institution.

Langley started working on model aircraft in Pittsburgh, and at the Smithsonian he built scores of models of flying craft. Finally he constructed a thirty-pound, steam-driven model, sixteen feet long and with a forty-foot wingspan. On May 6, 1896, he launched it over the Potomac, where it stayed aloft for one and a half minutes, flying half a mile before settling on the water; he then repeated the same feat. Six months later another model flew even farther, and Langley felt he was ready to experiment with manned flight.

Provided with government funds, Langley and his assistant, Charles M. Manly, worked on a larger flying machine. It took years, largely because of the difficulty in finding an appropriate engine. On October 8, 1903, they were ready for a test. With Manly at the controls, the spring-driven craft raced down a runway and then pancaked unceremoniously into the Potomac. For his pains, Manly got wet. The same thing happened on the next test, two months later, both failures being attributed to a faulty launching apparatus that somehow caught the rear of the plane. The newspapers snickered over the first failure and jeered so much at the second that Langley gave up his experiments.

But just nine days later, on a sandy beach at Kitty Hawk, North Carolina, Orville Wright flew a powered, heavier-than-air machine for twelve seconds, and his brother Wilbur first repeated the feat and then piloted their primitive airplane 852 feet in fifty-nine seconds, before landing safely. The next morning this accomplishment was mentioned in only three U.S. newspapers, and these did not include the *Journal* in Dayton, Ohio, the brothers' home town.

The Wrights, who were bicycle mechanics, became interested in flying during the 1890's, devouring articles by Otto Lilienthal, Langley, and Octave Chanute and reading everything else they could find on the subject. A sound science of aeronautics was already taking shape. Lilienthal had worked out tables and Langley had stated principles of wind resistance and air pressure. The Wrights began testing these ideas with gliders. Because wind was essential to their experiments, they wrote the Weather Bureau to ask about wind conditions in different localities. One of the windiest spots in the United States, they learned, was the Kitty Hawk region, with an average wind velocity of sixteen miles per hour.

Starting in 1900, the brothers made annual treks to North Carolina to try out their craft, studying lift factors, wind drift, and curved surfaces, and finally determined that wing design was the key factor to flight. After first flying the gliders, they too sought an adequate engine and finally designed their own, as well as their own propeller. Following their first success, they continued to improve their craft, eventually solving the problem of equilibrium in 1905.

Their achievements seemed to attract more attention abroad than in their own country. By the time the U.S. Board of Ordinance and Fortification expressed

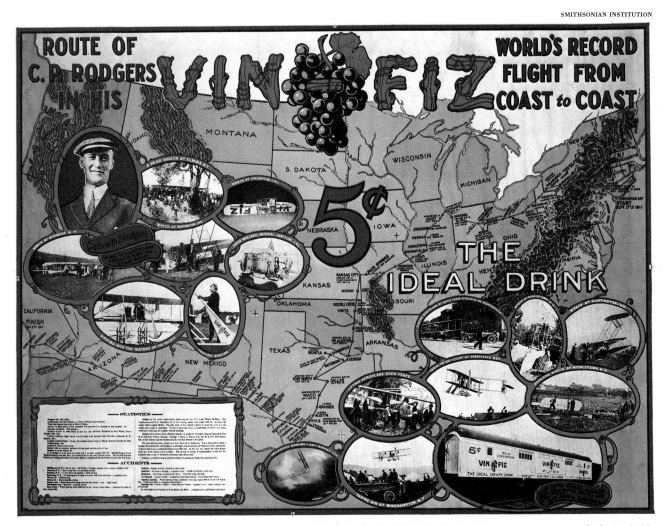

The Armour Company, promoting its nickel grape drink, Vin Fiz, backed Cal Rodgers's daring coast-to-coast flight in 1911.

ON THE JOB FOR VICTORY

UNITED STATES SHIPPING BOARD   EMERGENCY FLEET CORPORATION

Building the merchant marine: a World War I poster, painted by Jonas Lie

interest in their work in May, 1907, England and France had sent representatives to Dayton seeking exclusive rights. That year the brothers went to Europe and organized a company in France. Exhibition flights by Wilbur at Le Mans in 1908 created a sensation in France. In February, 1908, the United States awarded them a $25,000 contract to build a plane that could sustain flight for an hour at a speed of forty miles per hour, landing undamaged, and that could carry two men and adequate fuel to fly 125 miles.

Balloonist Thomas Scott Baldwin was responsible for interesting Glen Curtiss, a daredevil motorcycle rider, in aviation. Curtiss, who had built motors for Baldwin's dirigibles, taught himself the principles of flight and gave New Yorkers their first demonstration of a flying airplane in 1909. Piloting a plane at 47.65 miles per hour, he broke the world's speed record that year and won $40,000 at an international aviation meet in France. In sixty-eight separate hops spaced over forty-nine days, Calbraith Perry Rodgers flew from New York to California in 1911, averaging 51.59 miles per hour. Other barnstormers flew over the Niagara mists and emulated the daring French flyers in "looping the loop." In 1914 Curtiss vindicated Langley by installing a more powerful engine in his old plane and flying it.

By 1913 planes were commonly flying at 100 miles per hour, and Curtiss had designed and flown a hydroplane at San Diego, California. By the time World War I broke out, the United States had several hundred planes, and aircraft manufacture, while hardly an industry, was considerably more than a novelty.

TESTING THE PRODUCTION SINEWS

The fact that America was still largely an economic dependency of Europe was evident from the disquieting effect of the outbreak of European hostilities. When, five minutes before the scheduled opening of trading on August 3, 1914, an official of the New York Stock Exchange announced that all trading would be suspended indefinitely, a cheer of relief arose from the brokers on the floor. What they had feared was the unrestrained dumping of European-held securities, which would certainly have demoralized the market and probably paralyzed the economy.

But underlying changes were taking place. Less than four months later, when the Exchange timorously reopened trading on a restricted basis, the expected dumping took place. But prices, instead of collapsing, actually rose, and a bull market was on its way. Unrestricted trading was resumed in April, 1915.

222

Business itself proved less resilient. Most businessmen cautiously pulled in their horns. Hoarding set in. To ease credit, the Aldrich-Vreeland Currency Act was invoked, permitting banks to issue notes based on commercial paper and corporate securities. The House of Morgan headed a group of New York bankers in forming a gold pool, chiefly to meet foreign demands.

The caution and fears proved largely unfounded. Back of the financial and monetary maneuvering was an extraordinary industrial machine that was about to demonstrate its incredible potential and flexibility. Bernard Baruch was called to Washington to head the War Industries Board, a job for which his Wall Street background gave him precious little experience but which he executed with masterful success. The Morgans located a purchasing genius in Edward R. Stettinius, president of the Diamond Match Company, who organized a group to purchase vital supplies of all kinds at the rate of $10 million a day ("S.O.S." they called themselves, for "Slaves of Stettinius"). Congress in 1916 created a Council of National Defense, which named Walter S. Gifford director of an advisory commission of industry specialists.

All the nation's resources were turned effectively to meeting emergency needs. While the gross national product rose but 15 per cent between 1914 and 1918, there were far more impressive accomplishments in shifting to different and often new types of production. Iron ore output nearly doubled between 1914 and 1917, as did that of copper and zinc, while production of such vital foodstuffs as wheat and corn increased to record levels to help feed large parts of the world.

Much of America's production was destined for shipment abroad, and the export mix was significantly changed. Whereas cotton and foodstuffs had dominated shipments abroad in the previous century, manufactured goods now played a far more important role. Prior to the war years, American exports had exceeded imports by almost $500 million a year, the balance being made up largely by freight payments to foreign shippers and interest and dividends on capital borrowed from abroad. But in the year ended June 30, 1917, the favorable export balance rocketed to $3.6 billion as the nation sent huge quantities of steel, chemicals, and munitions, as well as meats and grains, to other countries. The value of exported explosives alone rose from $6 million in 1914 to $803 million in 1917.

One of the first needs to become evident was for more ships to haul goods. A U.S. Shipping Board was named, both to supervise rates on ocean freight and to help find ways to build up the merchant marine. After the United States entered the war, Congress authorized $4 billion for the work of the Emergency Fleet Corporation, which helped build all manner of ships, even some made of cement. The number of shipyards increased from 61 in 1917 to 341 by the end of the war, and launching ways from 235 to 1,284. During the period of American participation in the war, 875 ships, totaling almost 3 million gross tons, were constructed.

The most notable speedup was in the building of destroyers to combat the menace of submarines. A destroyer, which had taken twenty to twenty-four months to build before the war, was completed just seventeen days after its keel was laid at the Mare Island shipyard in California. Speedy and easily handled destroyers were turned out on the assembly line principle at the new Squantum, Massachusetts, yards, where five keels could be laid in a single day. Ford turned to producing Eagle boats to be used as submarine chasers. And John P. Holland designed an American submarine, the L-boat, whose electric motor permitted it to cruise under water longer than the German U-boats could.

The American automobile industry built the Liberty aircraft engine, which combined the best principles of all engines then being built. The first eight-cylinder, 300-horsepower engine, its parts made in factories across the country and assembled by the Packard Motor Company, was delivered on July 4, 1917. The number of cylinders and horsepower was increased, and production mounted steadily to 1,000 engines a month by June, 1918, and to 150 a day by the end of the war, when 15,000 had been turned out. Auto makers also made trucks and tanks. Trucks had not begun to compete with horse-drawn vans until about 1910, but the war gave their production a tremendous impetus, and about 300,000 were built in 1917. The first tanks were simply armored cars with caterpillar treads. The United States supplied the motors and machine guns, the British built the bodies, and the French provided the assembly.

The nation had already greatly increased its ability to manufacture gunpowder and explosives by the time the United States entered the war, but capacity was then stepped up even more rapidly, mainly by the Du Ponts. With the background of a century in the powder industry, the Du Ponts were firmly established as the nation's leading supplier. But they had not always kept pace with industry's newest technology. When Alfred Nobel in 1866 invented dynamite, an explosive that could be safely controlled, Henry Du Pont, then the patriarch of the family, was skeptical. But young Lammot Du Pont, his nephew and a brilliant chemist, saw the possibilities and talked his uncle into buying the California Powder Company in 1876. When Henry died in 1889, Lammot had been killed in an explosion, and forty-nine-year-old Eugene Du Pont was chosen to head the family business.

In 1899 the firm was incorporated as E. I. Du Pont de Nemours & Co. Eugene died in 1902, and it was

223

decided to sell the company for $12 million to Laflin & Rand, a competitor. But Alfred I. Du Pont, who had already been established as something of a family black sheep, offered to buy the business himself. Instead, the company was given over to a triumvirate of Du Pont cousins—Coleman, Alfred, and Pierre. Looking into the assets, they found that the business was actually worth about twice the sale price that had been proposed. So they made a $4 million offer to buy Laflin & Rand instead, and it was accepted. In 1905 the company was reincorporated in Delaware, with a capital of $60 million.

An antitrust suit was filed against Du Pont by the Roosevelt administration in 1907, and in 1911 the court ordered the company broken up. The Army and Navy Departments, however, asked that the firm be permitted to retain its monopoly in smokeless powder. The Du Pont company was permitted to keep twelve plants making black powder, three for smokeless, and five manufacturing dynamite. A second group, with eight black powder and three dynamite plants, would be known as the Hercules Powder Company, and a third, with six black powder and four dynamite plants, would be organized as the Atlas Powder Company.

When war broke out in Europe, the Du Ponts knew there would be vast new demands for their products and set about expanding. In four months they increased TNT capacity from 330 tons a month to 1,200, and by the end of 1916 they were turning out 100,000 tons of explosives a year, about twenty-five times the rate of two years earlier. But when the United States entered the war, the War Industries Board set a production goal of 45,000 tons a month. Some $85 million of government money went into building the huge Old Hickory plant in Tennessee, along with housing, hospitals, schools, and churches for 30,000 people. Another large plant was built at Nitro, West Virginia, to be operated by Hercules.

With the armistice, $260 million in contracts with Du Pont were cancelled. But the company did not suffer unduly. Profits had leaped from $6 million in 1915 to $57 million in 1915 and $82 million in 1916. With higher wartime taxes, earnings slipped back a little, to $49 million in 1917 and $43 million in 1918. And the company was also moving into new fields. Dyestuffs, made from some of the same raw materials as high explosives, had been a German monopoly before the war, with United States producing less than 3 per cent of its own consumption. Du Pont and others entered this field, and under Pierre's leadership the company bought lacquer and varnish plants, in addition to investing in General Motors. By 1919 the U.S. had taken world leadership in the chemical industry.

An equally significant outcome of the war was the nation's new dominance of world finance. The direct costs of the war were $186 billion, bleeding all the other participants dry. Only the United States could come close to being able to afford—because of its great productive powers—its war costs of $36 billion, including $10 billion in loans to its allies. Europe's gold had drifted to America early in the war. The role of the Lombard Street financiers, ordered in 1915 to confine their efforts solely to war purposes, was easily assumed by Wall Street, which became the world's investment center.

What was perhaps most impressive was how the United States had managed to raise the money needed for war. An income tax, imposed with the passage of the Sixteenth Amendment, was raised in 1916 and again in 1917 to range from 6 per cent on the first $4,000 of taxable income to 63 per cent of all personal income over $1,000,000. With the excess profits and income taxes providing two thirds of the total, government revenues rose from $735 million in the 1914 fiscal year to $1.1 billion in 1917, $4.2 billion in 1919, and $4.6 billion in the year ended June 30, 1919.

But as in the past, most of the money for financing the war came from loans to which American individuals and corporations subscribed. There were five bond issues, the first four known as Liberty Loans and the fifth, after the armistice, as the Victory Loan. Interest rates ranged from 3 per cent to $4\frac{1}{4}$ per cent. In all, the government sought to raise $18.5 billion. The people responded by subscribing $25 billion, of which the government accepted $21.4 billion. An additional $1 billion was raised through the sale of five-dollar savings certificates and twenty-five-cent war savings stamps. Millions of people enjoyed the comfortable, almost godlike, feeling of having the government in their debt.

The word for almost every aspect of American economic life now became "unprecedented," and the differences from the past were not simply those of numbers but of scale. A relatively peace-loving nation had almost instantaneously turned itself into history's greatest arsenal and had brought a mighty enemy to its knees. Now, in almost every industrial and economic area, each advance set a new record. Even the national debt was a superlative: in August, 1919, it hit a high of $26.6 billion, which was close to ten times the post-Civil War peak of $2.8 billion; interest charges alone were now greater than the total prewar costs of running the government.

There was a heady sense of invulnerability in being a world-beating American. But as a nation the United States had barely moved out of adolescence, and it was ill-equipped for world leadership. Its rising prosperity would create gaping imbalances and stark contrasts with want and deprivation elsewhere. Its own arrogance, bombast, and blundering would make it the chief target of world envy and resentment. And it would soon falter and stumble, a victim of its own excesses of confidence.

VI The Rage to Learn

The nation's most valuable asset: an elementary public school class in New York, photographed by Jacob A. Riis in the 1890's

"For the creation of wealth, then,—for the existence of a wealthy people and a wealthy nation,—intelligence is the grand condition. The number of improvers will increase as the intellectual constituency, if I may call it, increases. . . . That political economy, therefore, which . . . leaves out of account the element of a widespread mental development, is nought but stupendous folly. The greatest of all the arts in political economy is to change a consumer into a producer; and the next greatest is to increase the producer's producing power,—an end to be directly attained by increasing his intelligence."

Horace Mann, *Report of the Massachusetts Board of Education*, 1848

The bearer M............... receives this..... as a token of the praise merits. for h.. faithfulness, and good behavior in school; from h.. teacher.

The long-held American conviction that learning will help a person attain success and greatness is evoked by Eastman Johnson's famous painting, opposite, of the young Abraham Lincoln avidly reading by firelight.

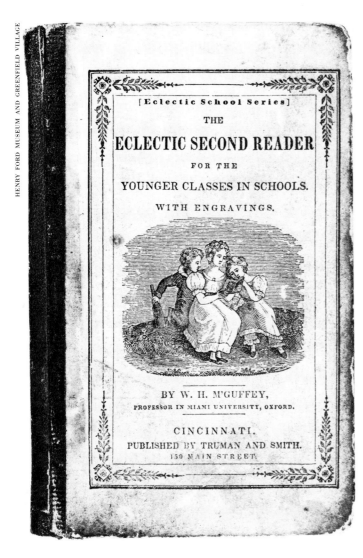

[Eclectic School Series]

THE

ECLECTIC SECOND READER

FOR THE

YOUNGER CLASSES IN SCHOOLS.

WITH ENGRAVINGS.

BY W. H. M'GUFFEY,
PROFESSOR IN MIAMI UNIVERSITY, OXFORD.

CINCINNATI.
PUBLISHED BY TRUMAN AND SMITH.
150 MAIN STREET.

The principal goals of education in the U.S. have been practical: to provide instruction, character, and morals for responsible citizenship and a rise to the top in life. Certificates of merit have rewarded students' good behavior since colonial days (above). Many generations were raised on William Holmes McGuffey's Eclectic Readers (left), which combined moralistic lessons with good literature. Below, a doorknob from one of New York City's public schools, where millions received formative training.

The first underpinnings of many success stories came from dedicated teachers in one-room schoolhouses like the one above, painted by Winslow Homer.

Industrialists like John D. Rockefeller and Andrew Carnegie, shown (left) in a 1914 cartoon, have used their wealth to benefit many educational institutions.

Federal government backing of education was exemplified by the Morrill Act of 1862, which aided the growth of land-grant colleges like Penn State, top right.

Official support of a great black educator: President Theodore Roosevelt visits Booker T. Washington at Tuskegee Institute, Alabama, 1905 (bottom right).

Business schools, with every kind of course to help men and women get jobs, hold them, and rise, have flourished.

Practical business axioms on the walls inspired students at the Rochester Business University, seen in an engraving of 1876.

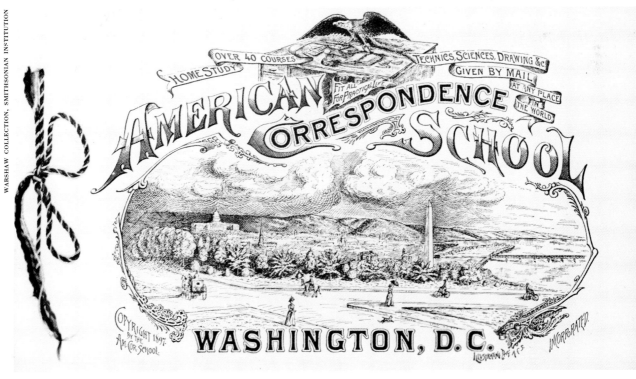

For those unable to leave home, correspondence schools, offering a choice of courses by mail, "fit all for practical life."

A perpetual war on ignorance has been a dominant motif in American life. Prompted by a drive for self-betterment, adults, with and without higher education, have sought easily acquired culture. Lyceum lectures (above), begun in 1826 and dedicated to the "general diffusion of knowledge," were forerunners of modern lecture circuits. The Chautauqua movement, which dates from 1874, grew from religiously oriented gatherings in New York State to nationwide town turnouts (right) to hear speakers on uplifting subjects.

Adult education has ranged from "great books" programs to lectures and courses on bread-and-butter subjects. The 1878 drawing, above, illustrates a John D. Rockefeller address to young men, presumably on how to make money. A more modern class on the same subject, run for investors by the Wall Street firm of Merrill Lynch, Pierce, Fenner & Smith, Inc., is seen below.

7

GIVING THEM
WHAT THEY WANT

1830-1950

The simple needs of the colonial settlers were usually met by itinerant tradesmen—the Yankee peddler with his wagon or his saddle-packs laden with knives and needles and ribbons and kettles. As settlements grew larger they were able to support village shops, and the general store then became the keystone of the nation's system of distributing goods to its people.

But markets in early America, like most of the world's markets up to that time, were mainly local ones, offering the produce and wares of the neighboring community and limited in radius to a horse's-day-long travel. No more was needed, in most cases, because the products of one village or town were largely the same as another's.

What changed all this was the Industrial Revolution, along with technological progress that introduced better and faster means of transport. The gap between factory and retailer was bridged by a fast-growing corps of wholesalers, who served both ends of the chain well. For the manufacturer, the wholesale houses disposed of his production at a predictable price—in the form of a commission geared to his own output. The wholesaler's ranks of "commercial travelers" provided for the manufacturer as much communication with the marketplace as he required. As for the retail merchant, he welcomed the visits of the wholesaler's salesman, because he could restock his depleted shelves without traveling long distances to the sources of supply.

Unlike the traveling peddlers, wholesalers tended to concentrate on groups of products—grocery staples, hardware, textiles—and sometimes they became

brokers, dealing in single products. Such specialization had become so common by the 1860's that it gave rise to the commodity exchanges for large-scale trading in grains, cotton, wool, hides, coffee, and so forth. Patterned after the stock and gold exchanges, these dealt in both "spot" trading, for immediate delivery, and "futures" contracts, for delivery at a specific advance date.

All in all, the system worked very well as long as the economy was fundamentally one of scarcity. But once the means of mass production began to be devised, the seller's market for goods gradually gave way to a buyer's market, bringing with it some new and unfamiliar problems. While people's needs are basically the same, their wants are remarkably diverse. Given enough income so that they may exercise discretion in disposing of part of it, they frequently want so many things that they tend to resist buying until they are "sold," in one way or another.

Producers were among the first to feel this change. As farm and manufacturing output grew, they were faced with periodic gluts of unsold merchandise, so they competed harder for their markets and tried to reach out for new ones. Adam Smith had told them that the market, under the influence of the "guiding hand" of self-interest, would find its own equilibrium of supply and demand. But Smith, although he lived in a time before these remarkable prodigies of supply had taken place, recognized that demand was not fixed but could vary with price. Thomas Malthus went further and saw that the "intensity" of demand could vary with individuals. And Alfred Marshall later developed the concept of the "elasticity" of demand.

It was not the builders and producers, however, who devised means of competing effectively on a national scale. Rather, another breed of businessman, with roots in the merchant community, showed the way to bring to distribution the advantages of the economies of scale that were already being realized in production. Men like John Wanamaker, Marshall Field, Isidor Straus, William Filene, George and John Hartford, Frank W. Woolworth, Richard Sears, and Montgomery Ward were as innovative and pioneering in their own way as had been Samuel Slater, Eli Whitney, Peter Cooper, Cyrus McCormick, Cornelius Vanderbilt, James Hill, and Andrew Carnegie. To envision and build a department store, a mail-order firm, or a chain of grocery or variety stores obviously required an outlook and skills that were different from those needed to set up a factory. But they were equally demanding.

THE DEPARTMENT STORE GROWS UP

The man generally conceded to be the operator of the first department store in the United States was Alexander Turney Stewart, whose Marble Dry-Goods Palace went up at Broadway and Chambers Street in New York City in 1848 and who built the eight-story Stewart's Cast Iron Palace farther uptown in 1862. Stewart came to New York from Lisburn, in northern Ireland, in the early 1820's, taught school for a time, then opened a small dry goods store at 283 Broadway in 1823. His policy of offering goods at a fixed price, with no haggling, was amost unique at the time. A hard, ungenerous man, Stewart traded shrewdly and built his business soundly. In the panic of 1837 he bought at auction the goods of other merchants who had failed. His Cast Iron Palace, covering a whole city block, was the world's largest retail store when it was built. Real-estate investments played a large part in building a fortune of some $50 million, which he left at his death in 1876.

Among other pioneering department stores were Zion's Cooperative Mercantile Institution, which Brigham Young founded in Salt Lake City in 1868; Lord & Taylor, which installed furniture and shoe departments before 1870; and R. H. Macy's, which brought in china, silverware, and book departments at about the same time. But John Wanamaker was perhaps the most innovative and certainly the most flamboyant of the early owners. Almost all the department and large dry goods stores of that era abandoned the practice of haggling with customers and adopted the one-price policy, following this with guarantees of satisfaction or money refunds. But Wanamaker proclaimed these virtues so loudly and persistently that they came to be identified with his store more than with any other.

Faced with an early choice between business and the clergy, Wanamaker said, "I would have become a minister but the idea clung to my mind that I could accomplish more in the same domain if I became a merchant." Announcing that they intended to follow "the Golden Rule of business," he and his brother-in-law, Nathan Brown, opened a men's and boys' clothing store in 1861 in Oak Hall, on the corner of Market and Sixth streets in Philadelphia. Of the $24.67 in receipts from the first day's business, they left the sixty-seven cents in the cash drawer for change, and invested $24 in advertising. The ads never stopped. By 1865 Wanamaker was announcing his money-back guarantee, and he became one of the first merchants to buy a full-page newspaper ad, writing most of the copy himself. Brown died in 1868, and Wanamaker bought his interest from the estate. In the early 1870's, with business booming, he opened branch stores in Pittsburgh, Memphis, St. Louis, Baltimore, Richmond, and Louisville, but eventually sold them to their managers. In 1875 he bought the old Pennsylvania Rail Freight Depot, then on the fringe of Philadelphia, stocked it with $500,000 worth of merchandise, and the following year moved into the refurbished hall, which he called the Wanamaker Grand Depot. So well had the opening been advertised that 70,000 people swarmed into the store on the first day, and the Centennial Exposition in the city helped bring in more crowds. He expanded to New York in 1896, buying the old A. T. Stewart store.

By then Macy's had already established itself as a leading store in New York. Rowland Hussey Macy had got his merchandising start when he opened a thread and needle store in Boston in 1844, followed by a dry goods store at a different Boston location in 1846. He opened another store in Marysville, California (where he had gone with the Gold Rush), in 1850, and the "Haverhill Cheap Store" in Haverhill, Massachusetts, where he advertised a single price and cash purchases and sales, in 1851. In 1858 he opened a fancy dry goods store on New York's Sixth Avenue, well to the north of the main shopping district. In the first year that store did well, showing $85,000 in sales, and Macy started buying one nearby store building after another.

Macy's success was predicated largely on aggressive pricing policies, which meant underselling competitors. The store accepted mail orders as early as 1861, and started annual clearance sales in 1863. Irregular prices ($4.33, $24.47) were first used at Macy's for chinaware and shoes, but these were departments that were leased to outside concessionaires —the glass and china departments to the wholesalers L. Straus & Sons. Free deliveries were offered as far away as Brooklyn, Jersey City, and Hoboken.

After Macy died in 1877, his son, various relatives, friends, and associates had difficulty running the store profitably. Finally, in 1888, Isidor and Nathan Straus, who leased the china department, were sold a 45 per cent interest and taken in as partners. By 1893 they had a 50 per cent interest, and by 1896 they had bought out the last of the partners. The business, then valued at $2,250,000, continued to prosper under the Straus regime, becoming in time the world's largest store, both in business volume and in space occupied under one roof.

Many other stores made their mark on the New York retail scene. Brooks Brothers, the nation's oldest clothing store still in business, began in 1818. Aaron Arnold opened his store, selling mostly imported textiles, in 1825 and later took in a family friend, James

a site rented from the Hudson and Manhattan Railroad. In 1923 Gimbel acquired the Saks Company for some $8 million in stock, and a year later he made a highly successful bid to capture a share of the city's elite trade by opening Saks Fifth Avenue.

Retailing had its offbeat success stories, as well. Lena Himmelstein came to America from Lithuania at the age of sixteen, learned the language and the secrets of the sewing machine, and married a jeweler, David Bryant. When Bryant died of tuberculosis six months after the birth of their son, Lena pawned his wedding gift of diamond earrings to buy a sewing machine and became a dressmaker, specializing in bridal wear.

John Wanamaker (above) pioneered many of the tactics still used in department store merchandising. Right: toy displays in Macy's street windows are one of New York's long-standing Christmas institutions; this example is from the late nineteenth century. The tradition dates from 1858, when Macy's moved "uptown" to Fourteenth Street.

M. Constable, as a partner. By 1843 they had twenty-one employees. Samuel Lord and George Washington Taylor in 1826 started a retail store that was to grow into a substantial department store chain. By 1946 Lord & Taylor became the first major department store to be headed by a woman, Dorothy Shaver.

Another New York landmark, Gimbels, had its start in Vincennes, Indiana, where the Bavarian immigrant Adam Gimbel set up a trading post in 1842 and became a western pioneer of the one-price policy. Gimbel opened department stores in Milwaukee and Philadelphia, and in 1910 his son, Isaac, invaded the New York market, opening a store in Herald Square on

With the ups and downs of the business, the earrings kept going to and from the pawnshop. But real success came when a customer asked her in 1904 to make a maternity garment, something only the Empress Eugénie had worn up to that time. As others heard of it, the comfortable and concealing garment became a specialty of Lane Bryant—the name she had excitedly scribbled when depositing a $300 loan to set up her business. Later the store specialized in clothing for larger women, and many a customer who thought she was a size 42 was pleased to find she could easily wear a Lane Bryant 40.

Nathan M. Ohrbach started his Brooklyn specialty

shop, Bon Marché, Inc., in 1911 and then moved on to Manhattan's 14th Street with his slogan, "A business in millions—A profit in pennies." When Adolph Zukor's neighboring nickelodeon burned in 1923, Ohrbach took over the space for expansion, advertising a grand opening that brought a crush of customers seeking bargains. Sales amounted to $1.5 million in 1924, and Ohrbach expanded as his business grew, opening a modern store in Los Angeles in 1948, and later moving the New York store uptown to Herald Square.

Across the East River in Brooklyn, as the Civil War ended, Abraham Abraham opened a small dry goods store in partnership with Joseph Wechsler. Abraham, just twenty-two at the time, had got his training at the Bettlebeck & Company store in Newark, New Jersey, along with two other young men who were also to start their own department stores one day, Benjamin Altman and Lyman Bloomingdale. Abraham and Wechsler moved their store to the vicinity of the Brooklyn Bridge in 1883, the year the bridge was opened, and at the end of two years were doing $2.5 million a year in sales. After Wechsler sold his half interest to the owners of Macy's in 1893, the store became Abraham & Straus. When Abraham died in 1911, volume had reached $13 million, and the store subsequently expanded until its sales topped $140 million a year.

William Filene, unsuccessful in a manufacturing business in New York during the Civil War, moved back to Boston, where he had started his working career as a tailor. He opened four stores, two at Lynn, Massachusetts, one at Salem, and the other at Bath, Maine. Filene and his sons, Lincoln and Edward, returned to Boston to open a fashion store in 1881. The store prospered, expanded, then moved to larger quarters on Washington Street.

Edward turned out to be the merchandising genius, Lincoln an expert at management, and the two took turns acting as general manager of the store. In 1909 Edward devised one of the most unusual and successful merchandising schemes in department store annals—Filene's Automatic Bargain Basement. Slow-moving merchandise from upstairs would be brought down to the basement, reduced 25 per cent after twelve selling days, another 25 per cent after six more days, a third 25 per cent after another six days, and then given to charity after thirty days. Eventually, special purchase and odd-lot merchandise was brought directly to the bargain basement.

In 1916 Lincoln Filene invited eighteen independent stores to send representatives to a luncheon at New York's Aldine Club, where he proposed the establishment of an organization to study retail store marketing and operations. The Retail Research Association, under his chairmanship, grew out of this meeting. Two years later the Associated Merchandising Corporation was formed as a purchasing affiliate, giving the stores immense central buying power. A.M.C. eventually absorbed the research organization. In 1929 Filene's, Abraham & Straus, and the F. & R. Lazarus & Company of Columbus, Ohio, all members of A.M.C., joined forces in Federated Department Stores, Inc. The individual stores at first retained their corporate identities, but the corporations were eventually dissolved, and these and other stores simply operated as divisions of Federated. The company in time became the largest department store chain, with total sales exceeding $2 billion.

Boston's other major department store, Jordan, Marsh & Company, eventually became a key unit in Allied Stores Corporation, which was to reach an annual sales volume in excess of $1 billion. This store, long Boston's largest, grew out of a wholesale dry goods house opened up by Eben D. Jordan and Benjamin L. Marsh in 1851. By arranging a good line of credit in London in 1853, the firm was able to weather the panic of 1857 and then branch out into retailing through the purchase of George W. Warren & Company on Boston's main shopping street. Much of the store's most spectacular growth came under the leadership of Edward J. Mitton, brought in as a stock boy in 1888.

In the Southeast the major department store grew from a dry goods shop opened on Atlanta's Whitehall Street in 1867 by Morris Rich, with $500 borrowed from his brother. Two of his brothers joined Rich, and the partnership became a corporation in 1901. By 1907 Rich's was the largest store in Atlanta, and it continued to grow, occupying two buildings and doing an annual business of more than $80 million.

The earliest large store development in the West, and one of the earliest in the country, was Marshall Field's in Chicago. It had its beginnings when Potter Palmer, a shrewd young Quaker, opened a retail dry goods store in the center of town in 1852. A few years later Marshall Field came from Massachusetts to work for Cooley, Wadsworth & Company, a wholesale dry goods firm. While Field's employers struggled through the 1857 panic, Palmer was buying up distress stocks. He opened a four-story dry goods store on Lake Street, cut prices, and built up a business that made him known as the "A. T. Stewart of the West."

Field, meanwhile, became first a junior partner of his firm and then managed to scrape up $15,000 to buy a full partnership. Together with Levi Z. Leiter, the firm's chief accountant and a junior partner, Field started looking for greener pastures. Palmer, in poor health from overwork, invited Field and Leiter to run his store, and at the end of the Civil War they joined him in the new firm of Field, Palmer and Leiter. The store's volume was then about $8 million, almost as much as the combined sales of the two leading competitors. When Palmer was bought out by the other partners, he started quietly buying up property on State Street until he owned almost all of it. Field, Leiter & Company in 1868 rented a marble store from him, marking the start of the shift in Chicago's retailing center from Lake Street to State Street.

In 1871 the city was made an official port of entry from abroad, but the first bales of imported goods had hardly cleared the new customs office when Chicago was swept by a devastating fire that virtually wiped out its center. Of the $200 million in property that went up in flames, Field's and Leiter's loss was $2.5 million, although about two thirds was covered by insurance. Everything that could be saved was taken first to the lake front, then to Leiter's house and a nearby school-yard. Within three weeks after the fire, the firm was back in business in an old car barn and plans were under way to put up a new building on Madison Street for the wholesale division.

As differences developed between the partners, stemming mainly from Leiter's desire to concentrate on the profitable wholesale division and Field's to develop the showier retail end, they decided to part company. With a combined fortune of $6 million, most of it from real-estate transactions, either one could have bought out the other. Because he was backed by the junior partners, Field bought out Leiter for more than $2 million in 1881, and the business became Marshall Field & Company.

"Give the lady what she wants" and "The customer is always right" were Field's dicta. Sales grew over the next twenty-five years from $25 million a year to $73 million, and profits rose to $4.8 million. It was in this period that John G. Shedd and Harry G. Selfridge, both of whom Field had hired as stock boys, made their mark in the store's development. Shedd became manager of the wholesale division, building it up substantially, and was then taken in as a partner. Selfridge was mainly responsible for getting the store to branch out from dry goods to a full-line department store. When he felt he was being passed over in his desire to reach the top, Selfridge left Marshall Field in 1904 and opened his own store nearby. His heart did not seem to be in the project, however; he sold the store and, with the proceeds of $1.5 million, left for London to found the impressive English department store that bears his name.

After Field died in 1906, Shedd followed him in the presidency. Shedd had the original store torn down and a new one built, ranking with Macy's and J. L. Hudson's in Detroit as one of the three biggest store buildings in the world. The company continued its growth under Shedd, and the retail end, which had accounted for just a sixth of the company's volume at the start, came to dominate the business. When he retired in 1923, Shedd was succeeded by James Simpson. Under Simpson's leadership, the company spent $28 million

THE HIS AND HER SUBMARINE, THE ULTIMATE IN TOGETHERNESS.

63A Cozy way to get away together for a week-end; take to the high seas, under the sea. Our week-end escape is the MiniSub Mark VII, a freely flooded underwater craft made by Aerojet-General Corporation. Designed to carry two people, it cruises at a speed of 3 to 7.3 miles per hour. The slightly buoyant MiniSub has a hull of plastic impregnated laminated glass cloth. 14' long, 46" high, 90" wide. Weighs 975 lbs. Battery-operated one horsepower motor. 18,700.00. F.O.B. Dallas. Four months delivery. 63B If your mermaid stays home, keep in touch with Sony's Transceiver. It's a very private form of communication. Just press a button to talk, release it to listen. Under optimum conditions, you get clear reception up to 6 miles over land or water (not under). The Sony Transceiver operates on 8 standard penlite batteries. Pair 149.95. Travel Shop. 63C If she comes along, she's all set for life at sea in this John Weitz turtleneck pullover. It's made of a new fabric, developed by General Tire and Rubber Company, called Sea Skin, a plastic with nylon backing. Lined in cotton terry. White, 32-36 sizes. 40.00 (.70). Trophy Room.

The Christmas catalogues of Neiman-Marcus have achieved worldwide celebrity, due in part to unusual offerings like this.

to build the twenty-four-story Merchandise Mart in Chicago for the wholesaling and manufacturing divisions and for rental to agents of manufacturers and jobbers. Completed as the Depression of the 1930's got under way and when the wholesale trade was starting its decline, the Merchandise Mart was never a success. In 1946 it was sold for $13 million to a group headed by Joseph P. Kennedy, whose son was to become President of the United States.

Detroit's great department store, J. L. Hudson Company, was started in 1881 as a men's and boys' clothing shop. Joseph Lothian Hudson had first worked for his father in a clothing store at Ionia, Michigan, where a former partner had been one of the first to take advantage of the boost given to the men's ready-to-wear trade by the Civil War demand for uniforms. But the

"A BUSY BEE-HIVE."
SECTIONAL VIEW OF THE ENORMOUS ESTABLISHMENT OF
MONTGOMERY WARD & CO.
MICHIGAN AVENUE, MADISON AND WASHINGTON STREETS, CHICAGO.

business went under in the 1873 depression. When young Hudson's Detroit store became successful, he searched out the old creditors and repaid them with compound interest. In 1891 he put up an eight-story building and kept adding to it until his store covered a whole block fronting on Woodward Avenue, with forty-nine acres of floor space.

Simon Lazarus was the patriarch of a department store dynasty as numerous and impressive as those begun by Adam Gimbel and Lazarus Straus of Macy's. Arriving in Columbus, Ohio, from Germany in 1850, he opened a men's and boys' clothing store on South High Street the following year. He kept buying other stores and adding new departments. After Simon's death in 1877 his sons Frederick and Ralph took over the business under the name of F. & R. Lazarus & Company, and they continued to add more stores, eventually moving into a five-story building on Town Street.

In 1929 Fred Lazarus, Jr., held a meeting on a yacht in Long Island Sound with Walter Rothschild, president of Abraham & Straus and the owner of the yacht, and Louis Kirstein, general manager of Filene's. They agreed to bring their stores into Federated Department Stores and spread their business risks through an exchange of stock. Bloomingdale's in New York City came into Federated the following year. Lazarus became president of Federated in 1945, when its headquarters were moved to Cincinnati, and since that time Federated Department Stores, Inc. has expanded considerably, bringing in such outstanding stores as Burdine's in Miami, the Boston Store in Milwaukee, and Foley's in Houston.

Not everywhere do department stores give the customer the last word. In Dallas, Herbert Marcus, co-founder of a world-famed store, felt that "not the customer . . . but Neiman-Marcus was always right" and that the customer sometimes needed a little help. Curiously, most Neiman-Marcus customers have gone along with that unorthodox notion. Marcus and his brother-in-law, A. L. Neiman, had left Dallas in 1905 to open an advertising and sales promotion agency in Atlanta, Georgia. They had done very well and after two years had had an attractive offer to sell out. They were offered a choice of Coca-Cola stock plus the Coke distributorship for Missouri, or $25,000 in cash. They took the cash, a decision that Herbert's son, Stanley, later characterized as "bad business judgment." Had they taken the stock, they would have become millionaires in fairly short order without raising a finger, but then Dallas might never have had a department store that offered its customers "his and her" submarines at Christmas.

The store started in 1907 in Dallas on the same note of unrestrained elegance that it has always maintained. Neiman put up $22,000, Marcus $8,000, more was borrowed, and a small building was rented for $9,000 a year. Neiman's wife, Carrie, went to New York to put $17,000 into the most fashionable finery she could buy. Next, the ladies of Dallas, accustomed to buying yard goods and having dressmakers sew their garments for them, had to be educated to wide, sweeping skirts, laced French corsets, and big, beribboned hats.

Other Dallas merchants freely predicted failure, but Neiman-Marcus was a success almost from the day it opened. Good salespeople were found and paid well; a woman fitter, the best in town, was paid $85 a week, even though the partners themselves each drew only $100 a month for living expenses. The store continued to build and to capitalize on its reputation for fine merchandise and good taste, and one investor who put $10,000 into the business when it needed capital after a fire in 1913 eventually saw his stock reach a value of $750,000.

I. Magnin & Company in San Francisco began as a notions store in 1879, prospering first from Mary Ann Magnin's skill with a needle and later from her son John's flair for merchandising. When downtown San Francisco was leveled by the earthquake and fire of 1906, goods were sold from the Magnin home until a new store could be built. In Los Angeles, Arthur Letts opened a small dry goods store in 1893, and when the business went well, he voluntarily settled all the unpaid accounts of an earlier bankruptcy in Seattle. In 1896 he hired John Gillespie Bullock for $12 a week, promoted him rapidly, and ten years later, when Letts took a fifty-year lease on an unfinished seven-floor store building, he suggested that the new store be named for his young protégé. When Letts died in 1927, Bullock's, Inc. was organized to acquire the business from the estate. Subsequently, under the presidency of Percy G. Winnett, Bullock's and I. Magnin joined forces and organized a chain of West Coast department stores from Seattle to Los Angeles.

Another major department store chain had its beginnings when David May gave up an unpromising mining career in Leadville, Colorado, to start a clothing store. Eventually this grew into the May Department Stores, whose coast-to-coast members included Kaufman's in Pittsburgh, the M. O'Neil Co. in Akron, Ohio, and the Famous Barr Co. in St. Louis, whose own history went back to 1849.

THE MAIL-ORDER HOUSES

In the period following the Civil War the rural general store rapidly became for the farmer the source of all the supplies he did not raise or make for himself. But the retail markups were steep — usually 100 per cent — and prices were correspondingly high. Organizations like the Grange were formed to register effectively the farmers' complaints against such things as high prices

Montgomery Ward, with obvious pride, put out this wonderfully detailed print of its new Chicago headquarters in 1899. In Ward's "busy bee-hive" 3,500 workers swarmed.

and excessive middleman profits.

One answer that developed was selling goods by mail. Aaron Montgomery Ward left his job as a $23-a-week salesman for the Marshall Field store in 1872 to start a mail-order business with a friend, George R. Thorne, selling mainly to the grangers. They began with $2,400 in capital, a one-page catalogue, and high hopes. "Our business was looked upon with suspicion by those whom we wished as customers," said Ward later, "ridiculed by retail merchants, doubted by manufacturers and predicted a short life by all." But the enterprise flourished, got one boost from the introduction of rural free delivery in the 1890's, another from the start of the parcel post system in 1913, and eventually became the third largest retail firm in the country in terms of sales.

One of the two larger retailers was Sears, Roebuck & Co., which did not get its start until fourteen years after Ward's. Richard W. Sears began his working career at sixteen to help support his younger sisters and recently widowed mother. He learned telegraphy, became an agent for the Minneapolis and St. Louis Railway at North Redwood, Minnesota, and sold coal and lumber on the side. One day in 1886 a local jeweler refused to accept a consignment of watches shipped by a Chicago jewelry company, so Sears bought the watches himself and, setting his price low enough to make the watches a bargain, sold them to other agents on the line. This worked so well that he set himself up as the R. W. Sears Watch Company, first in Minneapolis and the following year in Chicago, selling his watches by mail. He advertised for a watch-maker in the Chicago *Daily News*, and when Alvah C. Roebuck answered the ad, Sears hired him for $3.50 a week and room and board. Sears sold his watches through express agents, by mail, on the club plan, and by installments, advertising extensively in rural papers. Well off by the age of twenty-five, he retired and moved to Minneapolis in 1889.

Sears did not stay retired long. He was soon back in business with Roebuck under the name of the Warren Company, branching out to sell sewing machines in addition to watches and jewelry. Two years later he sold out to Roebuck and retired again. This period of leisure lasted all of a week before Sears bought back a half interest from Roebuck, and they were soon selling baby carriages, shoes, and other merchandise, and also putting out the famous Sears catalogue, which by 1895 ran to 507 pages.

In 1893 the firm became Sears, Roebuck & Co., and sales reached $388,000. By 1895 volume was over $750,000, but mail orders were being filled as much as thirty or sixty days late, and even then the wrong goods were often sent out. A sales and merchandising genius, Sears proved a dud at administration. But that year Julius Rosenwald came into the firm as vice president,

bringing along his brother-in-law, Aaron Nusbaum, as treasurer and general manager. A clothing merchant, Rosenwald saw the great promise in mail-order selling, and he brought with him an orderly mind and a talent for organization. The "Rosenwald Creed" was made up of many principles of mass selling, each ending with the words "but maintain the quality."

Various special offers were among the company's biggest sellers. Thousands of men's suits were sold at $4.95. Another campaign was for ice cream separators and still another for sewing machines, all underselling the standard makes. Bicycles were offered in 1898 for $13.95 with just $5 down—a price at which Rosenwald's dictum on quality maintenance obviously could not be observed—and 100,000 were sold. Advertising expenditures reached $330,000 that year, or 13 per cent of sales, almost doubled by 1900, and climbed above $5 million by 1907.

By then Sears, Roebuck had gone public, offering both common and preferred shares. As the business continued to expand, a $5 million mail-order plant and office building was constructed in 1906 on Chicago's West Side. Its three million square feet of floor space made it the world's largest business building at the time. A second office was opened in Dallas that year, and this grew into another complete mail-order facility, permitting lower freight rates and faster delivery to the Southwest. Others were opened at Seattle in 1910, Philadelphia in 1920, Kansas City in 1925, and at Los Angeles, Memphis, Atlanta, Greensboro, Boston, and Minneapolis.

The sales curve was a sharply rising hyperbola, from $11 million in 1900 to $40 million in 1910 and $245 million in 1920. But then, in the postwar recession, it turned downward just as sharply. It was not just hard times but new life styles that were encroaching on the mail-order business. A growing number of farmers, who once deemed it an evening's entertainment to pore through the Sears, Roebuck catalogue, now preferred to drive their automobiles to the nearest city department store, even if it were as much as fifty miles away, for the family's Saturday buying spree. Both Sears and Ward's began to think seriously of opening their own retail stores.

The man at Ward's who pushed the idea hardest was General Robert E. Wood, vice president in charge of merchandising. Frustrated at Ward's, he left in 1924 to become vice president of Sears, carrying his special enthusiasm with him. Under his influence, Sears decided to take a first cautious step early in 1925 and opened its initial store—actually just a part of the Chicago mail-order plant. Wood, who became the company's president in 1928, was delighted when the retail outlet turned out to be successful. Seven more stores were opened that year, four of them in mail-order plants. With other store chains concentrating on food,

"THE GOODS WILL BE PROMPTLY SENT"

The Sears, Roebuck catalogue cover girl

To hundreds of thousands of Americans, particularly in rural areas, the annual Sears, Roebuck catalogues were exciting links to an outside world where everything was up to date and dreams came true. From thin sales brochures they grew into "the Great Wish Book," with more than 1,000 pages crammed with illustrations and text, much of it written by Richard W. Sears himself in a manner calculated to bring in money for stoves, saddles, buggies, fishing tackle, and clothing.

Sears, Roebuck's newspaper and magazine advertising was aimed primarily at getting readers to order the catalogue, which then did its best to hook people on the mail-ordering habit. The 1897 catalogue, titled *The Consumers' Guide* and carrying a cover picture of a barefoot Grecian goddess holding a cornucopia from which cascaded pants, upright pianos, rifles, sewing machines, banjos, and bicycles, was almost a textbook on how to order by mail, as well as a tract on the consumer's duty to avoid retail markups.

The store worked hard at convincing its readers that the company really existed in Chicago and would honor mail orders. Catalogues contained pictures of mammoth warehouses, bank testimonials attesting to the vast assets and reliability of the firm, and even offerings for sale of stereopticon views of Sears, Roebuck's headquarters. Instructions for ordering, aimed at immigrants, were run in German and Swedish: "Tell us what you want in your own way, written in any language, no matter whether good or poor writing, and the goods will be promptly sent to you."

Sears imparted economic maxims on almost every other page. "The gold cure for poverty can only be effected with the aid of economy," he wrote. "Take regular doses from this catalogue and be well healed." He promoted a bargain in furniture as a "great anti-trust sale of dressers" and in 1897 claimed that "we are doing more for the farmer and the laborer than all the political demagogues in the country.... Our factory-to-consumer system brings about a revolution in profits, and is in reality a profit-sharing enterprise, as the consumer benefits by the middleman's profits which are cut off by our methods of merchandising."

The catalogues were filled with in-junctions, cautions, and homilies. "We do not exchange new safety razor blades for old ones," the dimwitted were told. "A good many men buy a fine calf or kangaroo shoe and expect it to give the same service as a plow shoe.... A fine shoe is not intended for heavy wear any more than a top carriage is intended to carry a load of wheat."

The company recognized that it sold to the trade as well as to individual consumers, and to protect those who bought for resale it did not put its name and address on any package or piece of merchandise. To get people to order, it used the lure of loss leaders, especially in yellow pages in the back of the catalogue. In 1908 such bargains, at two cents each, included iron quilting-frame clips, a set of cloth-covered elastic sleeve holders, door springs, and brass balls to cover the ends of an oxen's horns. For four cents one could buy a kitchen stove poker, a quart-size tin water dipper, or a box of steel hat pins, and for six cents there were tin cuspidors, wire carpet beaters, or a gross of metal suspender buttons. O.K. gopher traps, cow bells, and pail-sized "Little Daisy" washboards were eight cents each.

Through the years, the catalogue has been an index of changing styles and fads and inventions and conveniences. In 1900 Sears sold mostly derby hats, but by 1915 they had vanished from the catalogue, replaced by soft felts and, in summer, straw skimmers. The 1911 catalogue offered blood purifiers, a host of remedies for liver and kidney ailments, and "pink pills for pale people." By 1913 they were no longer listed. Hand-driven washing machines, cylinder phonographs, and equipment for buggies similarly came and went.

Sears built its business when people could not easily get to central sources of massed consumer products. It was aided by the introduction of rural free delivery in 1896 and by the start of parcel post in 1913. But even with the coming of automobiles, highways, supermarkets, and shopping centers, the Sears catalogues — and mail order — have continued to flourish, accepted and necessary American institutions.

clothing, tobacco, and variety merchandise, Sears moved hardest into the areas they overlooked—hardware, farm implements, and home furnishings. By 1930 there were 338 retail stores and by 1940 there were 595, their sales reaching $515 million, or 69 per cent of the company's total volume.

Montgomery Ward, meanwhile, had been experiencing the same postwar difficulties. But it was not until 1926 that they decided to go into the retail store business. Once the decision was made, however, they moved fast—much faster than Sears had. By the end of 1927 Montgomery Ward had 36 stores; the following year there were 208 more, and in 1929 another 288. By 1931 there were 610 retail stores. But, hit by the Depression, almost three fourths of these stores were operating in the red, and the overall operation showed a loss of $8.7 million that year.

At that point Sewell Avery, who had had no retail experience but who had been chairman of the successful U.S. Gypsum Company, was invited to take charge of Montgomery Ward. Studying the operation, he found that the entry into the store business had been too precipitate, and that retail stores required a different brand of know-how from the mail-order business. Avery recruited Raymond H. Fogler, who had acquired a solid background in the W. T. Grant store chain and who quickly turned around the Montgomery Ward store operation. In 1939 Fogler was made president of Ward's. By then sales had gone up from $176 million in 1932, the year he arrived, to $475 million, and a deficit of almost $6 million was replaced with a $27 million profit. The following year, however, Fogler left Ward's to return to the Grant chain, apparently because of differences with the strong-willed and crusty Avery.

THE CHAIN STORES: A. & P.

Chains of retail trading establishments are not a modern invention, having existed in China more than 2,000 years ago. A drug chain was founded in 1643 in Japan, and in the same century chain mercantile operations were conducted by the Hudson's Bay Company, by Germany's Fugger family, and by others. In the United States a number of local chains and a few that were regional in scope had come into existence before 1850. Even Andrew Jackson had once operated a chain of three retail stores in Tennessee.

The first nationwide chain was the A. & P., the beginnings of which trace back to 1859, and the first variety chain was started by Frank W. Woolworth in 1879. First the trolley, then the automobile, helped the housewife to reach the chain store outlets, but eventually the stores became almost as ubiquitous as the thousands of independent retailers and "corner stores" across the nation.

The great chain store boom took place during the 1920's. By 1929 almost 160,000 stores were operated by more than 7,000 chains, which branched out from the traditional food, drug, and variety fields to clothing, furniture, hardware, and department store outlets. Almost 30 per cent of the national retail volume was being done by chains by the end of the 1920's. Over the next twenty years the number of stores diminished sharply, but the stores tended to grow much larger, and sales of some 107,000 stores in 1948 were over $30 billion, or about a fourth of the national total. In some fields, the chains' share of the national pie was much greater—about 85 per cent for the five-and-tens, almost 50 per cent in shoes, and 39 per cent in groceries. The first national chain, the Great Atlantic & Pacific Tea Company, also became the biggest retailer of all, with sales reaching almost $3.2 billion in 1950.

The genesis of the A. & P. chain goes back to the 1850's, when George Huntington Hartford was hired in St. Louis by George F. Gilman, the son of a wealthy leather merchant and shipowner. The two came to New York, where Gilman asked Hartford to join him in buying clipper ship cargoes, mainly tea, and reselling it at low, or cargo, prices—"cargo pricing" being a term applied to what later became economy selling and is now known as discounting. Tea had always been an expensive product, partly because of its long carrying journey and partly because of the many middlemen who took their cuts; when it was first brought to the colonies, it sold for as high as $30 to $50 a pound.

Gilman and Hartford advertised their tea, first with circulars and then in national media, sold it by mail order, designed strong shipping containers, and offered money-back guarantees. They also developed a club plan, under which people banding together for large purchases would get a third of the price off, and the club organizer would receive a special gift. Their first store was opened on Vesey Street in Manhattan in 1859, and when it was successful they added another. As more stores were opened in the Wall Street and Broadway area, they named their firm the Great American Tea Company. Other grocery items were stocked, also to be sold at cut prices.

In 1869 the mail-order business was separated from the stores, which were incorporated as the Great Atlantic & Pacific Tea Company—a name that reflected the grandeur of the image of the transcontinental railroad, which was completed the same year. In keeping with the name, retail stores were opened in other cities, the chain reaching St. Paul, Minnesota, by 1876. The successful policy of using gifts for the club plan was extended to the stores; various premiums were given to customers; and a brass band in front of the main store on Saturday evenings entertained passers-by with the tune "This Is the Day They Give Babies Away with Half a Pound of Tea."

When Gilman retired in 1878, Hartford, then forty-five years old and the general manager, was made an equal partner in the $1,000,000-a-year enterprise. Two of his sons joined him in the business as soon as they were old enough (around sixteen)—George L. in 1880 and John A. in 1888. In 1880 the company opened its one hundredth store, marking a relatively slow pace of growth that continued over the next three decades. To reach customers who could not get to their stores, A. & P. started using peddlers, selling goods from red, black, and gold wagons, in the 1880's. Under the name of the Great American Tea Company, the wagons by 1910 covered much of the country on their 5,000 routes. Meanwhile, more stores were opened, and sales reached $5.6 million in 1900 and $13 million a decade later.

By then a number of competitors had entered the field, both with store chains and wagon routes. Jones Brothers Tea Co. of Brooklyn, eventually to become the Grand Union Company, got started in 1872. B. H. Kroger, a young Cincinnati grocery clerk, opened a store that he called the Great Western Tea Company and soon followed it with a second and third. His chain was renamed the Kroger Grocery & Baking Company in 1902, when there were thirty-six stores; eventually there were 5,000. The National Tea Company, whose business grew to $315 million by 1950, was begun in 1899, as was the Jewel Tea Company, which started with wagon routes and then bought Chicago's Loblaw chain. The Ginter Company, started in 1895, joined two other Boston concerns, the John T. Connor Company and the O'Keeffe Company, to form First National Stores in 1926.

None of the competition seemed to hurt A. & P., which built up its product lines along with its outlets and sales volume. When Gilman died intestate in 1901, there was no record of his co-ownership agreement with the senior Hartford, and there followed a year of litigation before the Hartfords were given all the company's common stock and the Gilman estate most of the preferred.

In 1912, with government agencies investigating fast-rising living costs (food prices had increased 35 per cent since 1900), as well as banks and trusts, John Hartford began fretting about his company's own costs. These included charges for feeding and stabling horses for deliveries, keeping cash tied up in credit accounts, and the cost of premiums, which in 1900 were worth three times the company's net profits. Hartford watched as some other stores dropped credit sales and deliveries, and noted particularly a small New Jersey chain that had adopted a cash-and-carry policy. With the permission of his father and brother, he opened a small experimental store in Jersey City; he instituted a strictly cash policy, eliminated deliveries, kept inventory low and fixtures to a minimum, cut prices so

that store profits would be reduced from 25 or 30 per cent to 15 or 20 per cent, and put on red paint and a sign saying "A. & P. Economy Store." In the first week business totaled $400. After a few months it reached $800 a week, with satisfactory profits. The company began opening more of the economy units, and its total number of stores rose from 480 in 1912 to more than 2,000 in 1915 and over 4,500 by 1920. Sales over the same period increased tenfold, from $23.6 million to $235 million. When the founding Hartford died in 1917, John became president and George chairman of the board. The brothers continued the rapid expansion, at times opening as many as 200 or 300 stores a week. By 1925 there were 14,000 stores, and sales reached $440 million. Before the 1920's were over, sales had passed the $1 billion mark, and the number of stores peaked at 15,700 in 1930.

With the Depression of the 1930's, A. & P., having already made its operations more flexible by decentralizing and expanding its manufacturing and warehousing facilities, began to look for new ways to conserve cash. Independent stores, often under the lead of wholesalers, had begun to combine into chainlike combinations for mass buying and co-operative management services. John Hartford was able to compete through such policies as buying for current needs only, signing leases for short terms, maintaining the cash-and-carry principle, and holding profits after taxes to less than 2 per cent. Sales slipped to $884 million in 1931, and profits fell off from $30 million to $9 million by 1937. But by 1939 sales rose significantly, and profits reached $18 million.

Instead of opening new stores, A. & P. was now shutting stores down—but still maintaining sales volume. The reason was the advent of supermarkets. They had their genesis in a special type of store opened by the innovative Clarence Saunders in Memphis in 1916. It was no bigger than the ordinary store, but it brought the customer in through a turnstile, led him through a maze of displays, where he could pick up his own selections, and past a cashier on the way out. Not only did Saunders thus originate self-service, but he advertised the idea under the name of Piggly Wiggly and sold franchises for the stores, many of which were taken by Kroger, Safeway, and other major chains. Franchising was copied by others, including the successful Jitney Jungle, of Jackson, Mississippi.

Some of the earliest supermarkets were opened in California by independent merchants in the late 1920's. In the East, Michael Cullen started his sprawling King Kullen markets in such low-rent quarters as vacant repair garages, offering a large number of fast-moving items at cost and grossing $13,000 a week when the average A. & P. store was doing only $70,000 a *year*.

A. & P. had already experimented with somewhat larger stores that carried meats and produce as well as staple groceries. Now John Hartford wanted to take the next step and get into the supermarket business; his brother George first dragged his feet, then gave in. Before 1936 there were no A. & P. supermarkets. By 1937 the company was opening new ones almost as fast as it could find promising locations and closing down three or four of the old stores for each new one opened. By the end of 1950 A. & P. was down to 4,500 stores, the same number it had had thirty years before, but total sales of $3.2 billion were about fourteen times as high as they had been. By 1959 there were 32,000 supermarkets in the nation, or 11 per cent of the total number of food stores, but their sales of $35 billion accounted for 69 per cent of all food store sales.

Through this period of growth, chain stores were not without their special problems, growing mainly out of the bitter opposition of independent merchants. Almost from the start, the chains with their expanded buying capacity posed a threat to the entire retailer-wholesaler system. So well-entrenched was this marketing network that manufacturers generally refused to deal directly with chains in their early days, compelling them to follow the normal buying route through wholesalers in order to protect their own retailer customers from price-cutting competition. The chains did cut prices, nevertheless, and manufacturers brought legal actions.

When the courts, including the U.S. Supreme Court, began to hold all kinds of price maintenance agreements illegal, the antichain movement had to change its strategy. In one state after another, "fair-trade" acts were introduced to legalize these agreements, and after the measures had been passed by forty-two states, Congress in 1937 sanctioned the price maintenance principle in the Miller-Tydings Act.

In 1935 the American Retail Federation was organized by a number of leading department stores and chains, in good part to lobby on behalf of retailers. A congressional investigation was soon called under Representative Wright Patman. Among the first witnesses asked to testify were representatives of A. & P., even though it had not joined the new retailers' organization. But a sensation was created when testimony disclosed a long list of agreements with manufacturers to rebate "advertising allowances," based mainly on volume purchasing. The practice, which was probably predicated on legitimate advertising and sales promotion purposes, had become widely used — and frequently abused — throughout the food business.

The outcome was the Robinson-Patman Act, which became effective in 1936 as an amendment to the Clayton Antitrust Act of 1914. It prohibited discriminatory pricing by manufacturers beyond the amount representing actual savings to the seller, and permitted advertising allowances only if they were offered on a proportionate basis to all customers. In 1938

The Woolworth Building in lower Manhattan, depicted in 1916. Woolworth publicists labeled it the Cathedral of Commerce.

Congressman Patman introduced a bill to tax all chain stores. Various chain store taxes had been proposed by individual states—some of them were defeated, some passed—and courts had sustained the validity of the latter. But Patman's proposed tax was the highest of all, progressing steeply to a levy amounting to $1,000 per store in a chain—multiplied by the number of states in which the chain was operating. For large chains the tax would have been fatal—for A. & P. it would have amounted to more than $500 million, or sixty times its net profit for the preceding year—and the measure became known as the "Death Sentence" bill. The Hartford brothers overcame their traditional reserve to sign ads that ran in 1,300 newspapers, pointing out that they personally were economically secure, but that their 90,000 employees and the farmers and others who supplied their stores were not. Largely under the weight of testimony from farmers, labor leaders, manufacturers, and consumer groups, the bill died in committee.

A. & P. next came under attack in an antitrust indictment. The government brought one action in a Dallas court, dropped that, and brought another in Danville, Illinois. The court found for the government and fined A. & P. $175,000, but the judge said in his ruling, "To buy, sell and distribute to a substantial portion of 130 million people one and three-quarter billion dollars worth of food annually, at a profit of 1.5 cents on each dollar, is an achievement one may be proud of."

WOOLWORTH'S AND THE NOVELTY CHAINS

Frank Winfield Woolworth took a job as general handyman and relief clerk at Augsbury & Moore, the leading store in Watertown, New York, in 1873, just before he turned twenty-one. For his eighty-four-hour work week Woolworth was to receive no pay during a three-month trial period. Passing this test, he then started to earn $3.50 a week, which was raised in stages over more than two years to $6. He left the job to become head clerk at A. Bushnell's carpet and dry goods store, but returned after a year to his old employer, now called Moore & Smith.

The clerk whom Woolworth had replaced at the Bushnell store, and who had left to start his own ninety-nine-cent store, stopped by one spring day in 1878 and suggested to Moore that he offer cut-rate bargains at a special five-cent counter. He related that a New York jobber, Spelman Brothers, had disposed of a heavy overstock of handkerchiefs made to sell at twenty-five cents by getting a retailer to put them on special sale for five cents; he added that he and his partner frequently ran five-cent sales.

Moore thought the idea worth a try. On his New

York buying trip that summer he went to the Spelman firm and ordered $100 worth of five-cent items—crocheting needles, buttonhooks, collar buttons, baby bibs, water dippers, steel pens, harmonicas, and other items. He put young Woolworth in charge of the sale, just a week before the county fair. The goods were laid out on two tables in the middle of the store, under a sign reading, "Any article on this counter—5¢." The table was virtually bare at the end of the day, and Moore wired for a duplicate order.

As other stores copied the sale, Moore & Smith went into the five-cent business enthusiastically, both wholesale and retail. But Woolworth had enough faith in the idea to start an entire store stocking just such items. With $300 worth of merchandise on which Moore had reluctantly extended him credit, Woolworth opened his first store in Utica, New York, in February, 1879. The store made out until the novelty wore off, and Woolworth closed it in June, no longer a debtor but a man worth $225.88. A week later he opened a second store at a better location in Lancaster, Pennsylvania, again with some help from Moore. This store had seven clerks, in place of the two in the first venture. Instead of the barren counters which were traditional in stores at that time, with clerks standing at attention and merchandise stacked on shelves behind them, Woolworth spread his goods out on the counters, invited the customers to handle them, and had his clerks say, "Look around and see what we are selling for five cents." On the first day, sales amounted to $127.65, out of a $140 inventory. Exhausted at the end of the day, Woolworth was already thinking about a branch store.

Four weeks later he opened a "Great 5¢ Store" in Harrisburg, Pennsylvania. It did well, but when the landlord asked for more rent, Woolworth balked and closed the store, opening another one in York, Pennsylvania. This one failed for lack of business, but Woolworth had now built up his net worth to over $2,000. He added a ten-cent line in his Lancaster store, and then opened another five-and-dime in Scranton, Pennsylvania, in 1880. This too was a success. The volume of business in 1881 was $18,000, the next year $24,000. But he sold the Scranton store to his brother, C. Sumner, who had been its manager, and at the start of 1883 Frank Woolworth, now worth $9,000, was back to a single store.

It was not for long. Two stores, one in Philadelphia and a twenty-five-cent store in Lancaster, did not make the grade, but others did. There were seven Woolworth stores, with sales of $100,000, by 1886, and twenty-five, with sales of more than $1,000,000, by 1895. A New York administrative office, where Woolworth worked alone for two years, was opened in 1886, with its "Diamond W" trademark. Sales in 1900 passed $5 million, in fifty-nine stores, and the chain's growth accelerated.

By then there were a number of competitors in the field. John G. McCrory, who had opened his first store in Scottdale, Pennsylvania, in 1881, had twenty stores in 1900. H. Kress & Company, after its beginnings in Memphis in 1896, had built up an eleven-store chain; Sebastian S. Kresge, who had been a partner of McCrory in two stores and had then split off, had only one store, in Detroit; and there were others. In a wild price war with many of his competitors in 1905, Frank Woolworth sold such things as oil stoves, blankets, umbrellas, coffee mills, and nightgowns for a dime apiece. "Don't be afraid to lose a little money," he told his people. "It advertises our stores more than anything else could. . . . We always come out on top."

F. W. Woolworth & Company was formed in 1905 to take in all the stores that Woolworth owned by himself, although he also had partnerships in many others. In 1911, with 318 stores, he invited a number of his present and former associates to join him—S. H. Knox & Co., of Buffalo, with 112 stores; F. M. Kirby & Co., Wilkes-Barre, Pennsylvania, with 96; E. P. Charlton & Co., Fall River, Massachusetts, with 53; his brother, C. S. Woolworth, with 15; and his one-time employer and financier, W. H. Moore, with two—and they merged the stores into one huge company capitalized at $65 million.

Woolworth was president of the company until his death in 1919, six years after he had spent $13 million in cash to put up the skyscraper in New York that was at the time the world's tallest building. F. W. Woolworth & Company by then had more than 1,000 stores, in every state and in Canada, and did an annual business of $119 million. By 1950 the chain had expanded to almost 2,000 stores, with sales of $632 million, and in the next two decades sales approached $2 billion, as Woolworth's diversified into department stores and other retail fields.

Few lines of merchandise escaped the chain store movement. J. C. Penney Co., begun in Kemmerer, Wyoming, in 1902, became one of the biggest dry

---

The Way to Wealth

J. C. PENNEY

"Golden Rule principles are just as necessary for operating a business profitably as are trucks, typewriters, or twine," said James Cash Penney (1875–1971). The seventh of twelve children born to a Missouri farmer who was also a part-time Primitive Baptist preacher, he was highly moralistic and practiced his beliefs in business. When he was twenty-two he let his butcher shop in Colorado (where he had gone to counter tuberculosis) fail, rather than bribe a local hotel man with a weekly bottle of whiskey for his meat orders.

In 1902 he put up $500 of his own and $1,500 borrowed from a bank for a third interest, with two absentee partners, in a dry goods store in the Wyoming mining town of Kemmerer. He named the tiny, 24-by-45-foot store The Golden Rule and kept it open from 7 A.M. until the streets were deserted at night. He conducted his business like a crusader, cutting costs to the bone and using the slogan, which he employed ever afterward, "Live better for less."

Penney did well from the start. In the first year his sales grossed $29,000, and he opened a second store in 1903 and a third one in 1904. In 1907 he bought out his partners for $30,000.

James Cash Penney

Four years later the Penney chain had twenty-two stores, with total sales of more than one million dollars. Penney took in partners in each store, and the chain continued to grow. By 1921, when the number of stores had reached 312, sales were $46 million—the same as Macy's in New York, which had taken sixty-three years to reach that sales mark. The company's stock was listed on the New York Stock Exchange on October 23, 1929, just six days before the market crashed. Penney's sales hit a Depression low of $155 million in 1932, but even in that year the chain showed a $5 million profit, though it passed its dividend. By 1950, with J. C. still active, there were more than 1,600 retail outlets, almost all of them west of the Mississippi River, and annual sales were approaching $1 billion.

The Penney chain operated on the principle of moving its merchandise rapidly, turning over inventory five and six times a year. It was also rigorous in its employee policies, tolerating no smoking or drinking. The pay was low at the start and the hours long, but Penney held out the opportunity of partnership in the individual stores to the best employees.

When he was almost seventy, Penney toured the country, delivering twenty-eight speeches in twenty-three days on "Christian Principles in Business." He could say that they worked. By the time he died at ninety-six, his company had risen to become the nation's fourth largest retailer, and the second (after Sears, Roebuck) in net earnings.

goods chains. What grew into the nation's largest drugstore chain was started by Charles R. Walgreen, a Chicago pharmacist who bought his first small store from his employer, then got a chance to acquire a second one in 1909. A tobacco chain, the United Cigar Stores Company, had its beginning in Syracuse, New York, where George Whelan operated a retail tobacco shop in a singular manner; it had no wooden Indian, no chairs for loungers, and no theatrical posters in the window. In the store was a sign proclaiming, "No loafing—all room needed for business." In 1900 Whelan decided he was doing well enough to open a second store along similar lines. He kept opening stores, first in upstate New York, then in New York City. Following his standard design, his stores were no more than ten feet wide, with no room for loafing. But the little stores did a big volume, and sales totaled $85 million just twenty-five years after Whelan had decided to branch out.

THE ADVERTISING AGENTS

Advertising is as old as the tavern sign, the professional's shingle, and the hawker's cry. But it did not become formalized as a trade until the mid-1800's, and did not blossom into its full modern flower until copywriting genius John E. Kennedy told advertising genius Albert D. Lasker in 1899 that "Advertising is salesmanship in print."

The English had used ads to sell cocoa, and the French employed the device for book sales, but the advertising business seemed to fit best the enterprising and expansive American character. The first ads in America were probably those that appeared in the Boston *News-Letter* of early May, 1704, one seeking information about the strange disappearance of three anvils, each weighing from 120 to 140 pounds, and the other referring inquiries about "a very good fulling mill" for sale or rent on Oyster Bay, Long Island, to William Bradford, public printer in New York.

It was Bradford who got Benjamin Franklin his first job, with his son, Philadelphia printer Andrew Bradford. Franklin was not so grateful that he refrained from criticizing Bradford's *American Weekly Mercury* as a poor excuse for a newspaper. But when he started his own *General Magazine* he was disappointed that advertisers did not believe it could bring better results. Franklin advertised his Pennsylvania Fireplace and wrote some persuasive copy pointing out that ordinary fireplaces caused drafts that made "women . . . get cold in the head, rheums and defluxions which fall into their jaws and gums, and have destroyed early many a fine set of teeth."

There were other proprietary products advertised in early America. But most offerings were for local sales and services—hats, skillets, liquors, Bibles, land, houses, slaves, ship sailings, and, in the case of one enterprising undertaker who used direct mail to those known to be sick, a full line of coffins.

Advertising hardly seemed to be a business in which a young man would seek his fortune—until one young man did. Volney B. Palmer started soliciting ads for a paper edited by his father, the *Mirror*, of Mount Holly, New Jersey. He then switched to the *Miner's Journal*, in Pottsville, Pennsylvania, and around 1841 set himself up in Philadelphia as an advertising agent for country newspapers, with a fuel and real-estate business on the side. But advertising paid, and by 1845 he had a branch office in Boston and soon another one in New York. Palmer was paid by the newspapers, receiving a 25 per cent commission not only on what he sold but also on ads sent directly to the newspapers.

Others soon got into the business, some of them inspired by Palmer's success. When Palmer died, his Philadelphia office was taken over by Joy, Coe & Company, which later became Coe, Wetherill and Company and was absorbed by N. W. Ayer & Son in 1877. The nature of the advertising business took a new turn when George P. Rowell, a New Hampshire farm boy who got a job in 1858 as a bill collector for the Boston *Post*, decided to become an advertising wholesaler. He bought up large blocks of space in country weeklies and retailed it to advertisers in smaller quantities. When this turned out to be a lucrative practice, he moved to New York and soon had a sizable fortune. He began publishing *Rowell's American Newspaper Directory*, which, modeled on a British publication, sought to give for the first time accurate estimates of the circulation of U.S. newspapers.

After the Civil War, retail merchants predominated in the use of advertising to bring in the local trade. But by the 1880's and 90's both local and national media were being fattened with advertising for a great many products and shops. Moving swiftly to take advantage of these developments was N. W. Ayer, for several decades the country's largest agency.

The firm was actually started by Francis Wayland Ayer, who urged his schoolteacher father, Nathan W., to join him in the enterprise. With $250 in capital, Ayer began in 1869 to solicit ads for eleven Philadelphia religious weeklies. By 1871 he was sending ads, many of them for patent medicines, directly to 325 publications in twenty-seven states and placing them in other periodicals through other agents. By 1876 the agency had twenty employees, and its annual volume was $132,000. Around this time Ayer approached one client and proposed a one-year experiment; instead of getting its advertising commission from the media, the agency would seek out the best possible rates and be paid a commission by the advertiser. The commission rate started out at 12.5 per cent, then fluctuated between 10 and 15 per cent for different accounts, and finally was fixed at 15 per cent. The Ayer contract marked a significant transformation in the advertising business. Palmer had started out *selling* ads for the publisher; Rowell had sold ads for himself; and now Ayer was becoming the agent of the advertiser in *buying* space. As the idea spread, it became a major factor in stabilizing the advertising rates charged by media.

Ayer announced in 1885 that almost 75 per cent of the volume of its operations in the preceding year had been done under such contracts with its clients. It became a pretty respectable business, as Ayer received commissions from such large and respectable accounts as Jay Cooke & Co., John Wanamaker, the Singer Sewing Machine Company, Montgomery Ward, Harvard College, Burpee Seeds, Procter & Gamble, Fairy Soap, and Gold Dust cleanser. As another indication of its independence, the Ayer firm in 1880 began to publish the *American Newspaper Annual*, which revealed, as Rowell had earlier, some of the closely held secrets of publishers about their true circulation figures. Until 1914 Ayer made money with the annual

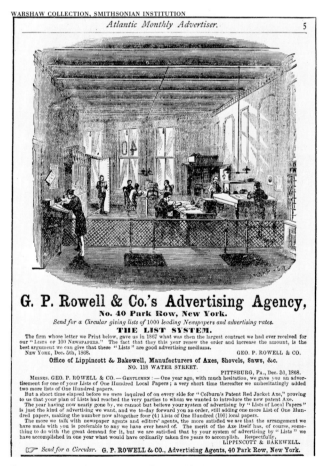

In an 1869 advertisement for itself, George P. Rowell's ad-wholesaling agency made use of a testimonial from a satisfied customer—an advertising device as popular now as it was then.

by selling advertising space in its pages.

Other agencies were also making their marks in the growing industry. A. L. Thomas in 1864 was working for the Boston agency of Evans and Lincoln, which sought ads for *Youth's Companion* and other periodicals. It was not until 1892 that he finally dared to leave the major advertising centers of the East and helped found the Lord & Thomas agency of Chicago. To this firm in 1898 came Albert Lasker, a Texan who had been a sports writer. In six years Lasker moved up from a wage of $10 a week to $25,000 a year, and he eventually estimated that he made between $40 million and $60 million from advertising.

John Hooper, considered the first New York advertising agent, was a former solicitor for Greeley's New York *Tribune* who went out on his own, carrying his office in his hat. J. Walter Thompson was a clerk for Carlton & Smith, which specialized in religious papers. Thompson talked a number of monthly general magazines into selling some of their space, adding them to the agency's list. In 1864 Thompson bought out the agency, which was to become the largest one in the world.

Writing advertising copy had always been left to the advertiser, on the logical assumption that he knew most about his own business. Large advertisers like John Wanamaker had their own writers. But as advertising expanded, competition increased—both among agencies, for the advertiser's business, and among advertisers, for the consumer's eye. Branded and packaged commodities were increasing in number and use, as were trade names and trademarks. Only 121 marks were registered with the U.S. Patent Office in 1870. Four years later there were 1,138, as new trademarks, as well as others long in use, came in for registration. By 1906 there were more than 10,000, and by 1926 almost 70,000. These marks and brands could now develop an identity and a folklore of their own, with inviting ad copy and eye-catching layouts and illustration.

Agencies with the most able writers found they could attract new clients or hold old ones. Enoch Morgan's Sons Company retained Bret Harte to write for their Sapolio soap account as early as the 1870's, and in the wake of his verses there was a wave of advertising in rhyme. Nathaniel C. Fowler, Jr., simply wrote ads to sell goods, choosing one hard sales point and concentrating on it. Elbert Hubbard, perhaps best known as the author of "A Message to Garcia," wrote ads for Wrigley's gum, Heinz products, Gillette razors, and Elgin watches, and advertised himself with the legend, "An advertisement by Elbert Hubbard." At Lord & Thomas, John Kennedy and Claude Hopkins broke new ground in devising copy approaches. Hopkins visited the Schlitz brewery, noted that the bottles were cleaned with steam, and made such a persistent point of this fact in Schlitz advertising that other brewers could not point out they did the same thing without appearing to be following the leader.

John E. Powers went to England as a Willcox and Gibbs sewing machine salesman, and came back to write newspaper ads for Lord & Taylor. His style so impressed John Wanamaker that he hired Powers away. They would have got along famously but for Powers's insistence on the literal truth in his ads. On one tour of the store he was told by the head of the rubber goods department that they had a lot of rotten gossamers—light rainwear—they wanted to get rid of. In the next day's ad Powers wrote, "We have a lot of rotten gossamers and things we want to get rid of." The goods were sold out in a few hours. When Wanamaker bought 600 hats, half with English and half with American labels, Powers announced: "You can take your choice and have an English label or an American label." But when Wanamaker put English labels in all 600, Powers reported that, too, in the ads; when Wanamaker then returned to the original labels, Powers wrote, "Now you can have an American hat with an American label." At that point Wanamaker fired Powers, who turned his talents to free-lancing.

Ayer became the first full-service ad agency in 1899, when, under pressure from a client, the firm added outdoor advertising to its newspaper and magazine departments. That year the agency's Henry Nelson McKinney landed the account of the newly formed National Biscuit Co. and went to work on a major national advertising campaign. This meant not only using all media but also supplying publicity, consulting on marketing problems, and creating the trade names "Uneeda" and "Nabisco" to give the new products a flying start. This first complete campaign also helped bring to a close the homey old era of pickle- and cracker-barrel retailing by substituting the less personal, if more sanitary, packaged product for the familiar old bins of bulk foods.

Advertising slogans became part of the national language. Harley Procter, sales manager of his father's soapmaking company, learned that Ivory Soap was 99.44 per cent pure, and this became the company's proud boast in an era when few people were inclined to cavil about the .56 per cent impurity. The "Milk from contented cows" was Carnation; Schlitz made "The beer that made Milwaukee famous" and Ingersoll, "The watch that made the dollar famous,"; Sweet Caporal cigarettes advised readers to "Ask Dad—he knows," while Packard suggested, "Ask the man who owns one." Blue Moon hosiery introduced cheesecake; the languid Chesterfield girl asked her friend to "Blow some my way."

J. Walter Thompson retired in 1916 at the age of sixty-nine. With his firm's billings at $3 million, he felt advertising had gone about as far as it could, so he sold

out to two of his employees, Stanley Resor and Charles Raymond, the latter in turn selling his interest to James Webb Young and Henry Stanton. The following year Resor married Helen Lansdowne, a brilliant copywriter and advertising woman, and this team quickly demonstrated that advertising could go much further than Thompson had ever dreamed, by bringing in such high-powered accounts as New York Central, Lever Brothers, Scott Paper, Ford, Swift, Shell Oil, Standard Brands, Schlitz, and Eastman Kodak.

As World War I ended, advertising expenditures shot up from the $1.5 billion of 1918 to $2.3 billion the next year. They passed $3 billion in 1925 and peaked at $3.4 billion in 1929, before sagging to a Depression low of $1.3 billion in 1933. After World War II advertising again regained its momentum, and by 1950 total expenditures, exclusive of direct advertising, exceeded $6 billion.

Looking back, Lasker reflected that the three great milestones in the history of the business were the first Ayer contract to represent the advertiser, his own

A famous slogan took on visual reality with a painting by one T. K. Hanna in a 1924 ad that ran in Ladies' Home Journal.

hiring of John Kennedy, and J. Walter Thompson's introduction of unabashed sex appeal ("The skin you love to touch") in Woodbury's soap ads.

ADVERTISING — MEDIA AND ETHICS

Almost from the start, it was the financial support of advertising that made newspapers, and they vied strenuously for this support. In New York, Boston, and Philadelphia, the four-page newspapers carried solid advertising on their front pages and often on the back pages, too.

In New York, James Gordon Bennett took and kept the lead in advertising, largely by virtue of his own determination and industry. Bennett, with a capital of $500, started the *Herald* in 1835 in a dingy basement, using two barrels and a plank for a desk. He wrote his editorials before breakfast, gathered and wrote his news in the morning, and sold advertising in the afternoon. Within a year, circulation was up to 30,000.

Convinced that advertising carried news that people wanted, he concentrated on getting more of it into his paper, but he set down rigid rules for it. All advertisements appeared in solid columns of type, each like the others around it, none ever breaking through the column rule. By 1847, when he could afford it, he announced that no advertisement would be accepted for more than two weeks, because after that it would be stale news. He permitted no large type sizes or ad displays.

One advertiser who managed to break the rules was Robert Bonner, who had purchased the *Merchant's Ledger* in 1851 and converted it into the immensely popular and successful New York *Ledger*. In 1858 he paid Bennett $2,000 for one seven-page ad, and the *Herald* had to expand its size that day from eight to sixteen pages. Bonner's minister called him to task for the extravagance, suggesting that a ten-line, $4 notice would have served the same purpose. Bonner simply asked whether the minister would have noticed such an

OF TRADE AND MARK AND NIPPER

The competition for mass consumer markets demanded the creation of easily identifiable brand names, as well as trademarks that protected products from imitation. They came spilling out, contributing to American life a colorful assortment of symbols, characters, and expressions that became household terms. Among them: the rosy-cheeked Campbell soup kids; Bon Ami's new-hatched chick with the slogan "Hasn't scratched yet"; Morton Salt's girl under the umbrella, proclaiming, "When it rains, it pours" (the salt would not stick in wet weather); and Old Dutch Cleanser's bonneted girl, for which both the product name and the trademark were inspired by a picture in the home of a Cudahy Packing Company executive, showing a Dutch farm girl chasing a goose with a stick.

The Smith Brothers (really William and Andrew) appeared on their cough drop packages in the 1870's and became famous as Trade and Mark. Baker Chocolate's identification was a copy of "La Belle Chocolatier," a painting by Jean Etienne Liotard, commissioned by Austria's Prince Ditrichstein, who had seen a charming waitress (the daughter of an impoverished knight) in a Viennese chocolate shop, and fell in love with and married her. "His Master's Voice" was a painting by artist Francis Barraud, who inherited the dog, Nipper, when his brother died, noted its interest in listening to a recording played on his phonograph, and was inspired to paint the scene, including the brother's casket. He painted out the coffin when he sold the work to the Gramophone Co., Ltd., and Nipper subsequently became the property of the Victor Talking Machine Company and, since 1928, R.C.A.

Both the product and trademark of Twenty Mule Team Borax came from Death Valley, California, where in 1870 borate minerals were discovered in great quantity. Until then they were an expensive import, used mainly in glass-making and gold purification. Trains of

RCA

R.C.A.'s attentive mascot, Nipper, the best-known fox terrier in history

ad, and the reply was that he might well not have.

But the *Ledger* itself, like many other periodicals of its day, did not deign to accept advertising for its own columns. One of the first magazines to do so was the *Atlantic Monthly*, which in 1866 carried a photography ad on the back cover and ads for the Florence sewing machine and Steinway pianofortes on the inside front cover. Within two years the *Atlantic* was carrying many more pages of advertising, including a good deal for patent medicines. *Scribner's Monthly*, started in 1870 by real-estate-rich Roswell Smith, Charles Scribner, and writer Josiah Gilbert Holland, took some advertising from the start. In 1881 Smith bought out Holland, broke with Scribner, and changed the name to the *Century Illustrated Monthly Magazine*, which quickly became the leading monthly in advertising. Fletcher Harper, on the other hand, refused all advertising, other than for the books he published, in *Harper's New Monthly Magazine*, from the time it was founded in 1850 until 1882. But once the bars came down, the publication was wide open, and *Harper's Monthly* led all magazines in advertising volume during the 1890's.

The heyday of the literary magazines, however, was drawing to a close. They were soon to be left far behind in circulation and profits by new publications directed at a much wider segment of the public. Frank A. Munsey and Cyrus H. K. Curtis, both from Portland, Maine, and both intent on making money from publishing, became dominant figures in the magazine field around the turn of the century.

Munsey was a combiner and destroyer of publications. He bought and killed *Godey's Lady's Book* and *Peterson's Magazine*, merged or killed the New York *Morning Sun, Globe, Mail and Express*, and New York *Press*. When the Reid family would not sell him Greeley's old New York *Tribune*, he sold them Bennett's *Herald*, instead. With his own magazine, *Munsey's*, he battled *McClure's, Harper's*, and John Walker's *Cosmopolitan*. When *McClure's* first appeared in 1893, it carried a 15-cent price, and *Cosmopolitan* cut its price to $12\frac{1}{2}$ cents. Munsey then announced: "At 10 cents per copy and $1 a year for subscriptions . . . *Munsey's* will have reached the point . . . below which no good magazine will ever go, but to which all magazines of large circulation in America must eventually come." In 1898 Munsey challenged the advertising fraternity by announcing he would no longer "bribe" them with commissions. But he soon lost so much advertising that he quickly agreed to go back to the commission system.

Unlike Munsey, Curtis was a builder. He began publishing a four-page weekly, the *Tribune and Farmer*, in Philadelphia in 1879. His wife ran a department on items of interest to women, which proved so popular that he decided to issue the *Ladies' Home Journal* as an eight-page monthly supplement. Before long he gave up the *Tribune and Farmer* and borrowed money to advertise and build up the *Journal*. Circulation at the end of 1884, the first year, was 25,000. Five years later he hired Edward Bok away from Scribner's to be his editor. Circulation continued to climb, and by 1900 the *Ladies' Home Journal* became the first magazine to achieve a circulation of 1,000,000.

Partly out of sentiment, Curtis in 1897 paid $1,000 to buy a dying Philadelphia weekly called the *Saturday Evening Post*. He let it scrape along for a year, then decided to build it into a popular magazine as appealing to the American businessman as the *Journal* was to his wife. He began to build up the *Post*, and left a former newspaperman, George Horace Lorimer, in charge while he went to Europe to meet with Arthur Hardy, his choice for editor. He missed Hardy but came back to find Lorimer doing so well that he made him editor. Curtis poured *Journal* profits into the *Post*, which lost $1,000,000 and more a year for a time, before

heavy wagons, drawn by teams of twenty mules, were used to haul the borax out of the desert, and the symbol became a brand name. Twenty Mule Team Borax was marketed to consumers as a cleanser, a digestive aid, a dandruff remover, a complexion improver, a milk preservative, and a cure for bunions and epilepsy.

Some brand names and trademarks became generic terms. After years of experimentation to remove the caffeine from coffee, Dr. Ludwig Roselius, head of a European coffee business, found the answer by accident when a shipment of coffee was soaked in sea water during a storm. It was introduced in France as Sanka (for *sans caffeine*), and General Foods began U.S. distribution in 1928, buying out the patents four years later. Low caffeine coffee has generally been called by that name ever since, no matter what the individual brand names might be. Similarly, candied popcorn is known to most children as Cracker Jack. Sticky tape became Scotch tape through an accident in 1926. To cut the tape's cost, its makers, the Minnesota Mining & Manufacturing Company, reduced the amount of adhesive. A customer complained that the tape was "Scotch" in its stickum and kept falling off. The name, at least, stuck, and is now widely used for all similar products.

it turned the corner. The price was set at a nickel, half that of the going weeklies like *Harper's* and *Collier's*. Circulation climbed from its initial level of 2,000 to 33,000 the next year, 183,000 by 1900 and 1,000,000 by 1909. Advertising gains were just as spectacular, rising from $59,000 in 1899 to $160,000 in 1900, $1,000,000 by 1905, and more than $5 million in 1910. The *Saturday Evening Post* had become the showcase for automobile advertising, beginning with an ad for W. E. Roach's horseless buggy in March, 1900, and running ads for virtually every make of auto and motorcycle being sold from then on.

At the start, radio was not much of an advertising medium, and the stations themselves either forbade or discouraged the use of ads. One of the first to take advertising was New York City's WEAF, and the first advertiser was the Queensboro Corporation, a Long Island City real-estate developer. Others followed with their discreet announcements, but they were not permitted to offer merchandise or describe their products.

Other stations followed similar policies, leading to the use of such programs as the A. & P. Gypsies, the Gold Dust Twins, and the Ipana Troubadors.

These inhibitions did not last very long. Radio advertising soon became persistent, strident, and repetitive, and product names and slogans were endlessly spoken, shouted, and sung. Advertisers were spending more than $10 million on the radio by 1928, much of it for such frequently purchased items as toothpaste, cigarettes, and canned foods, on the one hand, and major purchases like automobiles and household appliances, on the other. Radio audiences reached their peak in 1948, when they began to be lost to television. Network advertising hit a high of $210 million that year, but individual stations took up much of the slack with sales of local time as network revenues slid to about a third of what they had been. Unlike radio, television began accepting advertising as soon as there were audiences large enough to get the message, and the television economy soon became totally dependent

THE SAGA OF 57 VARIETIES

As late as the 1870's, the meal of an average American family could be pretty bland. Everyday fare was likely to be meat, bread, potatoes, and root vegetables. Against this unspiced diet, Henry John Heinz, the son of a German brickmaker in Pittsburgh, took his stand.

While he was still a boy, Heinz raised horseradish in his family's three-quarter-acre garden and sold the surplus to his neighbors. Eventually he began grating it in vinegar and offering it for sale in clear glass bottles to show that it was not falsely diluted with chopped turnips. "To do a common thing uncommonly well brings success," he said, and his life's work, already begun, reflected his words.

Six years after starting his business, Heinz and two partners, brothers named Noble, were prospering. In addition to horseradish they were selling more than 6,000 barrels a year of sauerkraut, celery sauce, vinegar, and pickles. Needing cucumbers in 1875, they contracted with some Illinois farmers to pay sixty cents a bushel for their entire harvest. When there was a bumper crop and prices broke, Heinz's company went bankrupt.

Another business was started shortly with Heinz's brother and cousin, and since Henry was not yet discharged from bankruptcy, it was known as F. & J. Heinz. The struggle to turn the corner continued until 1879, when the new company made a $15,000 profit. Heinz

kept a book of accounts titled "Moral Obligations," in which he charged himself with the debts derived from his three-eighths' share in the old, bankrupt business. Now he started to pay off the debts, turning out more products that added spice and variety to

H. J. HEINZ CO.

H. J. Heinz (foreground) meets with his board of directors, 1909.

on ad revenues.

It was the advertising media that pioneered in marketing research, mainly as a service to their advertisers. Some newspapers are reported to have made questionnaire surveys of their readers as early as 1824. Among the earliest in the field was Stanley Latshaw, Boston advertising representative for the Curtis Publishing Company, who felt that neither the salesmen nor the advertisers knew much about their markets, and that such information was too valuable to be overlooked. His arguments convinced Curtis, who hired Charles Coolidge Parlin, a Wisconsin schoolmaster, to gather information. Parlin started with a study of the agricultural implement industry, questioning manufacturers, jobbers, retailers, and users; all the information gathered went into a 460-page report. More studies followed, including an analysis of department store lines in 1912, and surveys of selling in large cities. Not only did this work bring in more advertising to the Curtis publications, but it led to a more scientific approach to commercial fact-finding.

The U.S. Rubber Company opened a department for such research in 1916, and Swift and Company hired an economist to set up a commercial research department the following year. Advertising agencies were not slow to pick up the cue. Indeed, Henry McKinney of Ayer, trying to take the account of a threshing machine manufacturer from George P. Rowell & Company in 1879, asked for a list of the publications in which the manufacturer planned to advertise. He was told the ads would go anywhere that threshing machines were used. Unhappy with this response, McKinney decided to get the information he wanted. Washington did not have it. So he had the agency's own employees gather the needed data about grain production in the United States and the publications that reached the proper markets, with their rates and estimated circulations. The manufacturer offered to buy the report. McKinney told him it was not for sale but was free to Ayer clients. Ayer won the account.

American meals and brought profits to the new firm. Tomato ketchup had appeared in 1876, pepper sauce in 1879, and apple butter and white and cider vinegar in 1880. As their sales increased, Heinz unveiled new taste tempters: chili sauce, mince meat, mustard, tomato soup, olives, pickled onions and cauliflower, sweet pickles, and the great staple—baked beans in tomato sauce. "The bean is Nature's most nourishing food," read one Heinz advertisement. "They make you strong and require no digestive strength to assimilate them."

The famous "57 Varieties" slogan was dreamed up by Heinz in 1896 while he was riding on the New York City elevated. He saw an advertisement promoting twenty-one styles of shoes. Although he was making more than fifty-seven varieties of products, the poetic cadence of that particular number appealed to him. He adopted it and put it everywhere—on his bottles, jars, and cans, on billboards and signs. It appeared on New York's first electric sign on Broadway, illuminated with 1,200 bulbs that used $90 worth of electricity each night.

In a truly grandiose promotional gesture, Heinz had a 900-foot pier built, jutting out from the Atlantic City boardwalk. On it he exhibited an Egyptian mummy, various paintings, and a chair that had belonged to President Grant. The pier also had a kitchen that dispensed cooking lessons and free samples of Heinz products. In its forty-five years of existence, until a hurricane destroyed it in 1944, Heinz's pier was visited by some 50 million people, who entered it beneath an arch adorned by a brace of giant pickles.

Heinz was ahead of his time in recognizing that a good corporate image was also good business. He bought full control of his firm in 1888, renaming it the H. J. Heinz Company, and near Pittsburgh built a huge brick Romanesque plant that became an attraction for visitors, who got guided tours, free samples, and tiny green plaster pickle pins to wear on their lapels.

The factory reflected Heinz's sense of public image as well as his paternalism. The girls who packed and canned his products were furnished private lockers, clean white uniforms, and weekly manicures. They were given free medical care and homemaking classes, and enjoyed a swimming pool and gymnasium and a 500-seat dining room hung with art works and liberally supplied with fifty-seven condiments. Heinz imported from Germany a musical instrument called an orphenion to provide music during lunch.

The company expanded abroad in 1886, when Heinz called on the Fortnum and Mason store in London; he took seven of his products from his Gladstone bag, made the English purchasing agent taste them, and, to his surprise, received orders for all of them. By 1905 Heinz was bottling in England. In time, the company had numerous plants overseas and was tinning treacle in England and packing jalapeño peppers in Mexico.

Despite the success of Heinz's products, commercially prepared foods were still far from being fully accepted in the United States in the early 1900's. Muckraking literature like Upton Sinclair's *The Jungle* gave the food industry as a whole an unsavory reputation. Heinz wholeheartedly supported the Pure Food Act and even sent his son, Howard, to Washington to lobby for the bill. Though it aroused the ire of many of his competitors, Heinz realized that in the long run the law would instill public confidence in prepared food products, and toward that end he added "Pure Food Products" to his own labels.

In 1919, the year of Heinz's death, his company had more than 6,000 employees in twenty-five U.S. and overseas plants. When the firm finally dropped the "57" from its corporate symbol in 1969, the number of its food products had grown to more than twenty times that figure.

The Cincinnati office of J. Walter Thompson in 1923 made a detailed study of the subscribers to forty-four national magazines in the Cincinnati area, and Curtis Publishing made a similar analysis in Cleveland. In the early days of Young & Rubicam, a former Ayer man was hired to do marketing analysis, and he was paid more than either partner drew. Raymond Rubicam hired George Gallup from Northwestern University in 1932 to be in charge of research for the agency, and Gallup's first undertaking was to analyze the advertising and editorial content of six leading women's magazines. In time, virtually every major agency and publisher had its own staff for conducting research or analyzing the findings.

Although advertising thus became closely allied with the nation's industrial and mercantile interests, and publishers became increasingly dependent on advertisers and their custom, American media have rarely been reluctant to criticize all or parts of the business system in their editorial columns. One reason for this is that business interests themselves are so diverse and widespread that a well-founded editorial assault on one company or industry is usually looked on with interest or indifference by most others. Another, perhaps more cogent, reason is that most advertisers look to media as a means of reaching their own markets, not as editorial voices to be bought and sold, and their concern is mainly with the size and character of the audience.

Muckraking, when there are wrongdoings to be unearthed, is not only good journalism but often good business for a publication. Samuel S. McClure discovered this fact around the turn of the century, and put the brightest writers he could find to the task of disclosing wrongdoing and corruption. He hired Lincoln Steffens and Ray Stannard Baker to look into the conduct of railroads and meat packers. He ran Ida M. Tarbell's soundly researched and brightly written "History of the Standard Oil Company" in 1902. He had Burton J. Hendrick write the revealing "Story of Life Insurance." Other publishers tried to follow suit, but *McClure's* had a long running start on them.

Advertisers, too, came under the magnifying lens of examination. The *Farm Journal* announced in 1880 that it would make good any losses to its subscribers growing out of false advertising. The little *Rural New Yorker* not only made a similar offer but publicly exposed fraudulent advertising in its editorial columns. The *Ladies' Home Journal* announced in 1892 that it would no longer accept patent medicine advertising, and in 1904 it launched an exposé of the patent medicine industry. Lydia E. Pinkham's Vegetable Compound was running newspaper ads asking women to write in to Mrs. Pinkham their questions about feminine problems and physical complaints. The *Journal* reproduced these ads, along with a photo of Mrs.

Pinkham's tombstone, firmly in place for more than twenty years.

New York advertising men joined together in the Sphinx Club, chiefly a social organization, in 1896. In 1903 John Adams Thayer, advertising manager of the *Delineator*, addressed the club and told the ad men to clean their own house of fraud and misrepresentation. The self-reform movement took hold and was adopted in 1905 by the Associated Advertising Clubs of America, which subsequently became the Advertising Federation of America. At a 1911 meeting in Boston, they adopted the slogan of "Truth in advertising" and helped push a model law to penalize misleading advertising, with the result that thirty-seven states adopted the statute or similar ones. The vigilance committees of the clubs became the Better Business Bureau in 1915, and the advertising industry has since undergone recurrent waves of self-examination and criticism.

THE MERCHANDISERS

The transformation of the American market from a local to a national affair, along with the accelerating change from bulk commodities to packaged goods, necessitated a new role for the manufacturers and processors who were producing for the ultimate consumer. The need for identifiable products meant that they could no longer rely on others to take over their entire distribution operation, and that they would have to engage in merchandising and marketing, i.e., moving and selling their wares to the consumer.

It was in the food industries that this trend became most marked. Here, improved farming methods, mass processing, and greater specialization helped bring major efficiencies that changed the nature of the country, as well as its economy. Where nine out of ten persons had once been required to produce and market the food supply, the proportion dropped sharply after the Civil War, and eventually only two out of ten adults were engaged in these activities. Food production and preparation is still the nation's single largest industry, but it has always been one of the most fragmented. Even though large companies like General Foods, Kraft, Borden's, Standard Brands, and Beatrice Foods emerged to become leaders in the industry, most of them resulted from bringing together smaller units, many of which retained their product identities and operating autonomy after the combination took place.

General Foods, made up of many different companies with their own histories and their own well-known brand names, is a case in point. The company grew out of the Postum Cereal Company, Ltd., which was joined by Jell-O at the end of 1925; the present corporate name was adopted in 1929. The consolidations were aimed at effective savings through a number of centralized functions, involving mainly administration and distribution, and at leveling out the seasonal gyrations of individual food industries.

Charles W. Post, suffering from a nervous breakdown, went to a sanatorium in Battle Creek, Michigan. There he became interested in health foods, bought a small farm, and with a helper developed a cereal he called Postum, which he offered to the public in 1895. Next, in 1897, he brought out one of the first ready-to-eat cold cereal products, called Grape-Nuts because of its nutty flavor and the belief that grape sugar was formed during the baking. A corn flake product developed in 1904 was first called Elijah's Manna, then renamed Post Toasties.

Other cereal products were making headway at the same time. In a Nebraska town, a lawyer named Henry D. Perkey watched a man eating what looked like wheat grains and found it was boiled wheat. He tried some, liked it, and was soon making Shredded Wheat Biscuits. In 1900 he built at Niagara Falls a model factory, which he called the "Palace of Light" and pictured on his cereal packages. The American Cereal Company was doing well with its Quaker Oats, dating back to 1878, but very badly with its Wheat Berries and Puff Berries. They sought help from nineteen advertising agencies before coming to Lord & Thomas, where Lasker and Hopkins advised them to stop using pictures of Japanese and Chinese eating rice, and suggested renaming the cereals, which then became Puffed Wheat and Puffed Rice. Hopkins, who always felt that the public wanted to be given a "reason why" for buying a product, visited the plant and decided that being "shot from guns" was what made these cereals extra special.

Peter Cooper, builder of the "Tom Thumb," a pioneer ironmaker, and an early telegraph backer, obtained the first patent on a gelatin dessert. That was in 1845, but neither he nor anyone else did anything about it for another fifty years, when Pearl B. Wait, who manufactured cough medicine, decided to expand into

The Way to Wealth
CLARENCE BIRDSEYE

"Go around asking a lot of damfool questions and taking chances" was the credo of Clarence Birdseye (1886–1956). "Only through curiosity can we discover opportunities, and only by gambling can we take advantage of them." His curiosity about the way Eskimos kept their food fresh—and a gamble that nearly bankrupted him—gave birth to a multibillion-dollar industry that revolutionized the marketing of food in America.

A naturalist and writer of books on wildflowers, western birds, and mammals, Birdseye was educated at Amherst College and worked as a U.S. government purchasing agent and a fur trader in Labrador. In 1912, while among Eskimos in the North, he became interested in the way the natives cared for their food supplies. It was already known that cold storage preserved food, but the methods used seemed to rob it of flavor, and thawed frozen meats and vegetables usually turned to tasteless mush. Slow freezing took up to eighteen hours, but Birdseye had an idea that faster freezing, as occurred in the North, would seal in the freshness.

With $7 worth of brine, ice, and an electric fan, he experimented with quick freezing and achieved his goal. His method was to absorb the heat from the food by exposing it to a circulating mist of brine at 45 degrees below zero Fahrenheit. What took place inside the food was that the tissues and fibers froze rapidly without the formation of ice crystals large enough to burst cell walls. With the cellular contents intact, flavor was retained, and food that was thawed months later tasted as fresh as when it had been processed.

In 1923 he set up Birdseye Seafoods, Inc., gambling all he owned and almost going bankrupt trying to establish a manufacturing and distribution organization. Finally, in 1929, he sold his patents, processes, and plants for $22 million to the Postum Company, which in the same year took on the name General Foods Corporation. By 1934 the Birds Eye–Snider Division of General Foods (which had broken Birdseye's name into two words) was doing 80 per cent of the quick-frozen food business in America.

The Florida citrus fruit industry prospered greatly from the Birdseye process. In 1949 more than 12 million gallons of frozen orange juice concentrate were produced in that state. In general, food industrialists recognized opportunities in eliminating seasonal price swings from yearly sales, bringing crops to market without the perils of spoilage en route, and appealing to time-saving in the kitchen. But there were new risks. The responsibility for uniform quality lay with the packager; initial inventories of food required heavy investments that banks were not always willing to underwrite; and transportation demanded constant attention. Many of those who plunged into the new business during World War II met disaster. In 1947 alone, more than 200 frozen food firms went bankrupt. By 1955, however, frozen foods came in 2,000 different brands produced by 1,551 companies, and American families were consuming more than $2 billion worth of frozen foods a year.

Clarence Birdseye continued to indulge his curiosity. He held more than 250 U.S. and foreign patents in food freezing, spotlighting for store windows, and infrared heating. Among his other inventions were a recoilless harpoon gun for whaling, and a fast, continuous process devised in Peru for converting sugar cane waste into paper pulp.

packaged foods. The name "Jello-O" was coined by his wife, but the business did not do too well. He sold it for $450 to a neighbor, who at one point tried to peddle it for $35. But then the dessert caught on, and sales reached $250,000 in 1902 and just under $1,000,000 in 1906, and it was an established market leader when General Foods acquired it in 1925.

Addison Igleheart's fondness for cakes led him to develop a special flour from the softest parts of winter wheat at his father's little grist mill near Evansville, Indiana. In 1895 a cake pan salesman who needed flour for a demonstration bought some of Igleheart's Swansdown flour. After that, the salesman concentrated on selling the flour, rather than the pans, and orders came from other dealers. General Foods got into bakery product lines with this flour, as well as with the Calumet baking powder developed in a bedroom-office-laboratory by William M. Wright and George C. Rew, and with the packaged coconut business begun by the Franklin Baker Company, which had received a supply of coconuts from Cuba in payment for a shipment of flour. Another product named Baker came into the General Foods organization with the acquisition of Walter Baker and Company, Ltd., a chocolate-making enterprise started in 1780 in Dorchester, Massachusetts.

Young Joel Cheek became a traveling salesman in 1873, working out of Nashville, Tennessee. He sold groceries but was especially interested in coffee, and decided to develop his own blend. When he was satisfied with it, he offered it to one of the South's best-known hotels, the Maxwell House of Nashville. They liked it and began to serve it. It was Theodore Roosevelt who coined its advertising slogan by calling it "good to the last drop," when he was a guest at Andrew Jackson's old homestead in Nashville. Filling out its breakfast menu, General Foods in 1927 bought Log Cabin syrup, named by grocer P. J. Towle for his boyhood hero, Abraham Lincoln; and in 1929 the company added a quick-freezing process developed for juices and other foods by Clarence Birdseye.

Another leader in the packaged product business was the Procter & Gamble Company, formed in Cincinnati in 1837 by William Procter, who molded candles, and his brother-in-law, James Gamble, who boiled soap. Gamble and a helper handled production, while Procter was in charge of the business end, which included peddling candles through the streets and taking them to the wharf for the river trade. Similar roles were assumed by their sons, William Alexander Procter and James Norris Gamble, and the company was making twenty-four kinds of soap by 1878. When too much steam got into one batch, the product turned out to be a hard, white soap that floated, and customers asked for more of it. Harley Procter named it Ivory from a passage from Psalms 45:8, "All thy garments smell of myrrh, and aloes, and cassia, out of the ivory palaces, whereby they have made thee glad." The company's sales reached $200 million in 1930, and eventually climbed as high as $3 billion. Procter & Gamble pio-

The opening in 1883 of the Brooklyn Bridge, "eighth wonder of the world," inspired this highly imaginative trade card. In plugging her concoction for the "female system," Mrs. Pinkham sternly observed, "Only a woman can understand a woman's ills."

neered in having its own products compete with each other, letting each find its own segment of the market. Thus Camay was permitted to fight Ivory, and neither product suffered for it. Other soap makers put in their own bids for dominance—Palmolive, to "keep that schoolgirl complexion," which Lord & Thomas persuaded the B. J. Johnson Soap Company of Milwaukee to push, instead of their Galvanic laundry soap; Woodbury's, which John H. Woodbury decided to promote, in place of his Dermatological Institute; and Lever Brothers' Lifebuoy, which warned in sepulchral tones of the social disasters that awaited those who failed to guard against B.O.

An equally compelling purpose was found for the use of Listerine. Dr. Joseph Joshua Lawrence had developed the antiseptic in 1879 in St. Louis, purchasing the ingredients from a drugstore where Jordan Wheat Lambert was a clerk. Lambert liked the idea of the product, sold it first on a royalty basis, and in time built up a substantial business in its manufacture and sale. Four of Lambert's five sons became vice presidents of Lambert Pharmacal Company, and the fifth, a dark-gray sheep named Gerard, who had managed to go $700,000 into debt, felt he deserved a job in the family business, too. Made general manager in 1922, he decided to push Listerine sales. Working with an advertising agency, he suggested that "bad breath" might provide a worthy theme. They found a clipping from the British medical journal, the *Lancet,* in which the social impediment was termed "halitosis." Halitosis entered the language, Listerine the medicine chests of the nation, Gerard Lambert's debts were paid off, and by 1928 the company was spending $5 million a year in advertising to reveal such homey truths as "Even your best friend won't tell you." Even so, Listerine was a solid cut above most of the patent medicines, nostrums, restorers, and cures for every debility from cancer to fits that made up the hard core of national advertising in its early years. The most active ingredient of many was simply whiskey, and the matronly face of Lydia Estes Pinkham, a devoted member of the Woman's Christian Temperance Union, peered out unself-consciously from the label of her Vegetable Compound over the inscription, "Contains 18% Alcohol."

In the spring of 1886 Dr. John S. Pemberton, a pharmacist, used a brass kettle, a percolator, apothecary scales, and other paraphernalia to get just the syrup he wanted for a soft drink. With three partners— Frank M. Robinson, David Doe, and Edmund W. Holland, an Atlanta banker—he formed the Pemberton Chemical Company, Inc., and a local drugstore agreed to dispense the product. Each partner submitted a name; it was Robinson who suggested both Coca-Cola and the script with which it was to be written. In the first year, twenty-five gallons were sold, $50 taken in,

Advertising was quick to make use of Hollywood's star system (this is Jean Harlow in 1935), and of celebrities in general.

and $46 spent on advertising. The firm changed ownership a number of times, and in 1891 it came under the control of Asa G. Candler, an Atlanta wholesale druggist. A system of independent bottling companies, each given exclusive territorial rights, was developed. This and persistent and extensive advertising, which through the years hung on the single theme of "refreshing," led to booming sales. The familiar Coca-Cola bottle appeared in 1916, three years before Candler sold his interests for $25 million to a group headed by Ernest Woodruff. His son, Robert W. Woodruff, became president in 1923 and made Coca-Cola a world-wide beverage.

An effective method of merchandising national brands was developed by David H. McConnell, who was selling books door to door in 1886 and offering vials of cologne as premiums. When he noticed how popular the fragrances were among housewives, he leased a small loft to make his own and hired women to sell them by canvassing homes. The business was called the California Perfume Company for more than fifty years, but in 1939 it was renamed Avon Products, Inc., after a line of the company's products. The door-to-door selling methods were maintained even after the company became an international organization with sales in excess of $750 million.

Simply producing, branding, packaging, advertising, and marketing products was no guarantee of success. On the contrary, old products died out and new ones emerged constantly. During World War I some old standbys, such as Sapolio, Pears' soap, and Sweet Caporal cigarettes, faded away, while new ones emerged—Pepsodent, Del Monte, Eversharp, and Lucky Strike. The war had popularized the British "fag," and cigarettes, which accounted for only 5 per cent of the tobacco market ten years before the war started, overtook cigar, pipe, and chewing tobacco soon afterward.

In 1911 the U.S. Supreme Court had ordered the American Tobacco Company trust broken up into Liggett & Myers, Lorillard, and American Tobacco, and they were soon engaged in fierce competition for leadership. Another firm, the R. J. Reynolds Tobacco Company, introduced its Camel cigarettes in 1914, and extensive and effective advertising helped make it the leading brand. George Washington Hill, a high-powered salesman and son of the president of American Tobacco, singled out Lucky Strike, a name registered back in 1871, as the brand to challenge the leader. Hill watched the tobacco being "cooked" in the plant and decided on the slogan, "It's toasted," in 1917. By 1925 he had pushed Luckies to third place, with an annual production of 13 billion (about 75 per cent of American Tobacco's total cigarette output), against 34 billion for Camels and 20 billion for Liggett & Myers' Chesterfields. Working with Hill, A. D. Lasker boosted American Tobacco's advertising allotment from $600,000 a year to $20 million a few years afterward. Hill coined the slogan, "Reach for a Lucky instead of a bonbon," and Lasker changed it to "instead of a sweet." Then came "Future events cast their shadows before," "So round, so firm, so fully packed, so free and easy on the draw," and "Sold American." As Lucky Strike moved

AUTOMATIC VENDING MACHINES

Probably the first automatic sales machine was a primitive mechanism for dispensing fixed amounts of holy water, devised about 1,500 years ago by Hero of Alexandria. In the early 1800's machines were used to sell tobacco and snuff in London coffeehouses, but their first use in the United States was most likely in the 1880's, when chewing gum maker Thomas Adams outbid the tobacco tycoon James B. Duke for the rights to a springless scale developed by Percival Everett, an Englishman.

Adams, whose company later became the American Chicle Company, had the device converted to a gum vender, and its success in selling his tutti-frutti gum balls on the platforms of New York City's elevated railway led to the patenting of other machines for dispensing a variety of products, including candy, nuts, tobacco, and perfumes. In 1891 the Automatic Machine Company of Buffalo, New York, came out with a stamp vender that was hailed as honest because it sold a one-cent stamp for one cent. More controversial was an automatic device introduced in Utah which, for $2.50 in silver coins, produced divorce papers ready for witnessing and signing, and bearing the name and address of a local law firm.

The first automatic restaurant, Horn and Hardart Baking Company's Automat, opened on Philadelphia's Chestnut Street in 1902. It was a sensation, but it was not as automatic as it seemed. Customers used nickels to open little glass doors that guarded sandwiches and slices of pie, but employees were kept busy refilling the cubbyholes as they were emptied.

In 1908 the American Water Supply Company of New England used machines to sell penny drinks of water in disposable paper cups. The firm soon envisioned a more profitable future selling the cups rather than the water and, recapitalizing itself as the Public Cup Vendor Company, started a line which it eventually named the Dixie Cup.

Coin-operated locks on public toilet facilities were first installed in 1909 by the Nik-O-Lok Company. Cigarettes went into machines in 1926, and soft drinks the following year, when refrigeration was added to the vending

Charles Grunwald labeled his drawing of an early Automat "Eating by Machinery."

out to take the lead in the battle of the brands, American Tobacco's profits grew from around $12 million in 1926 to $40 million in 1940.

THE MARKETERS

Unlike the producer, the seller of goods has long suffered from a slander that has been built into the fiber of many societies. Trade, wrote Plato, corrupted the trader, and it was therefore a calling that should be forbidden to citizens of Athens. It was "unnatural," said Aristotle, and properly the subject of censure. In the Middle Ages, churchmen felt that traders caused prices to rise above the labor cost of producing goods — the "just price." Even in sales-minded America, the conventional wisdom has generally regarded the salesman as outgoing, intuitive, superficial, and largely untaught. As for the merchant, he has at times been regarded as a profiteer or a parasite who lives off the produce of other men and who adds to the cost of

mechanisms. In 1929 a Chicago automobile parts manufacturer named Nathaniel Leverone was so annoyed at weighing 200 pounds on one coin scale and 70 pounds on another that he decided to go into the business himself. He and eleven friends put up $5,000 apiece and started the Canteen Company. Turning to the automatic vending of candy, they hit on the idea of offering a choice between Hershey and Curtiss products in the same machine, and sales jumped.

In time, there were machines that shined a man's shoes, took his photograph and recorded his voice, checked his suitcase, washed his clothes, changed his bills for more change to put into other machines, even told his fortune and then, if the predictions were dire, sold him life insurance.

During World War II, machines became common in industrial plant canteens. At first, production managers worried that they would encourage dawdling among the workers, but they soon agreed that employees worked more productively if given breaks for refreshments provided by the automatic dispensers.

Throughout the 1920's and 1930's, annual sales made through vending machines never exceeded $25 million. After World War II, however, vending volume skyrocketed, and by 1960 total sales were beyond $2.5 billion a year.

goods but not to their value.

For one period, in the 1920's, the salesman was raised up briefly from this debased state to become the lion of Main Street and the symbol and guardian of national progress and prosperity. Bruce Barton's best-selling book of that time, *The Man Nobody Knows*, went so far as to depict Christ as a great advertising man and salesman. The salesman made things happen; he was the one who, with fixed gaze and all the sincerity his tone could muster, took the reluctant buyer by the lapel, made the sale, and thus kept the wheels of trade turning.

What was wrong with this picture was not so much its inaccuracy and exaggeration as the inefficiency of the system it endorsed. Direct selling *did* work, but for most products it was an appallingly expensive way to move goods. By the late 1920's "profitless prosperity" was a common subject in the business journals; there was a growing feeling that the problem of distributing goods and services was much larger than simply selling, packaging, and advertising. The term "marketing" was coming into more frequent use, and there was a sense that all of a company's operations, from production planning to consumer servicing, were very closely tied together.

The nation's population had risen from 13 million in 1830 to 31 million in 1860, 76 million in 1900, and 106 million by 1920. On the eve of the Civil War, only 21 per cent of the population lived in cities of 2,500 or more; just before World War I there were 51 per cent in such communities. Exerting a major influence on the size of the market was an increase of more than 100 per cent in per capita income in this period, during which prices hardly changed. Although there was substantial inflation over the ensuing fifteen years, average income levels rose even faster, from $285 in 1914 to $680 in 1929.

All these changes had profound economic effects, including the demonstration of some counterintuitive truths about the marketplace. One, for instance, was that distribution *does* add real value to goods and services — in part by putting them where they can be used, and in addition by establishing a mass market to match the capabilities of mass production. Another was that relative increases in distribution costs appear to go hand in hand with higher living standards. Early America, like some underdeveloped parts of today's world, was at its most impoverished when distribution costs were close to zero. In 1869 the costs attributed to the middleman engaged in various marketing roles was 33 per cent of the ultimate sales prices of goods in the United States; in 1948, with living standards markedly higher, middleman costs were 38 per cent. The simultaneous growth of prosperity and the costs of distribution has been succinctly characterized by economist Paul Mazur's oversimplified definition, "Distribution is the delivery of a standard of living."

By themselves, producers and distributors cannot vouchsafe high living standards. At the far end of their pipeline there must be purchasing power—wages that are high enough and widely enough dispersed to permit the purchase and consumption of what has been produced and delivered. And whereas the nation's producers had generally deemed it a professional virtue to pay wages as small as the traffic would bear, marketing people were much more likely to endorse higher wages that might enable the public to buy what they wished to sell.

They also found a way around their customers' immediate inability to pay—the installment plan: a Singer sewing machine was sold to Margaret Hellmuth of 47 Centre Street, New York, on September 30, 1856, when she paid $50 in cash and agreed to pay another $100 in six monthly installments. This transaction introduced a new dimension into the American way of life. The down payment for a Singer got as low as $5, and the idea spread to other manufacturers.

Not too long afterward, specialized institutions for checking credit were formed. Among the earliest were Bradstreet's Improved Mercantile Agency and R. G. Dun and Company. The Lyon Furniture Mercantile Agency was formed in 1876, and the Shoe & Leather Mercantile Agency, Inc. the following year. The first mercantile credit bureau was organized in 1901, and a central bureau for the exchange of credit information took form in 1912. Credit work became a specialized branch of merchandizing and the subject of special courses. With expanding sales of automobiles and other "big ticket" merchandise, most states passed laws based on a Uniform Small Loan Act to regulate the installment sellers and personal loan companies that sprang up.

All these additional complexities in doing business inevitably meant that some people would try to discover what the new forces were and how they worked, in order to help make accurate forecasts and projections. Auguste Comte first used the term "social physics" back in 1820, referring to all the available data on population, wages, prices, rents, and even social behavior. With enough such data, according to modern-day astrophysicist John Q. Stewart, it would be possible to get some average figures on human relationships and behavior that could be quantified and then reduced to laws. The formulation and application of such laws to real situations gradually became a new and more exacting role for the middleman. Yesterday's salesman was turned into one of today's new breed of scientists. The concept of marketing management—of relating distribution to all the other functions of a business and to many other forces in society—slowly took shape.

One of the earliest in this field was Ralph Starr Butler, a professor at the University of Wisconsin who later became an executive of the General Foods Company. "I developed the idea that personal salesmanship and advertising had to do simply with the final expression of the selling idea," he later recalled. "My experience with the Procter & Gamble Company had convinced me that a manufacturer . . . had to consider and solve a large number of problems before he ever gave expression to the selling idea by sending a salesman on the road or inserting an advertisement." After much puzzling over the problem, Butler gave the subject the name of "marketing methods."

The first academic courses in marketing were offered at the Universities of California, Michigan, and Illinois in 1902–3, but it was not until the next decade that marketing was made an important field of study, mainly at Harvard and the University of Wisconsin. In 1924 the National Association of Teachers of Marketing and Advertising was formed as an expansion of the National Association of Teachers of Advertising, and by 1933 it was known simply as the National Association of Marketing Teachers. Those who were on the actual firing line of marketing practice formed the American Marketing Society in 1930. In time, marketing people found a way to distinguish their efforts from those of the students of salesmanship of the past. Where the key objective was once to sell to the consumer what the producer had made, the new emphasis was on getting the producer to turn out what the consumer wanted to buy.

The objective was far easier to state than to achieve. It introduced into business new complexities and perplexities that required a higher order of management skill even to define, much less to solve. So the economy of plenty, long deemed a blissful state that mankind was never meant to achieve, was not an unmixed blessing when it finally came. The easy equilibrium that Adam Smith had said would be attained by the free exercise and interplay of self-interest was turning out to be a precarious balancing act on a very high wire.

VII   Sense of Community

WARSHAW COLLECTION, SMITHSONIAN INSTITUTION

Businessmen have benefited from the good fellowship and pageantry of fraternal bodies like the Veiled Prophets of St. Louis.

"Americans of all ages, all conditions, and all dispositions constantly form associations. They have not only commercial and manufacturing companies, in which all take part, but associations of a thousand other kinds, religious, moral, serious, futile, general or restricted, enormous or diminutive. The Americans make associations to give entertainments, to found seminaries, to build inns, to construct churches, to diffuse books, to send missionaries to the antipodes; in this manner they found hospitals, prisons, and schools. If it is proposed to inculcate some truth or to foster some feeling by the encouragement of a great example, they form a society."

Alexis de Tocqueville, *Democracy in America*, Part II

The frontier need for mutual protection and neighborly assistance, combined with the strong tug of local interests, bred a feeling of hometown "togetherness." Left, top: guarding against sudden Indian attacks on the Oregon Trail, as depicted by pioneer William H. Jackson; bottom: a rural baptism near Richmond, Virginia, about 1896. Right: the old country store, social center of villages, painted by Abbott Graves, 1897. Below: residents of Northbrook, Illinois, give support in Japan in 1972 to Olympic ice skaters from their hometown.

WIDE WORLD

265

The "one for all, all for one" spirit of barn raisings, like this one in Ohio in 1888,

lives on in modern agricultural, business, trade, and professional organizations. 267

The poster at left, idealizing the farmer, was issued by the National Grange, formed in 1867 to provide social, political, and cultural benefits for rural communities.

The county or state fair, pictured below, was—like the camp meeting and market and election day—an exciting social interruption in the lonely routine of farm life.

Grangers who once opposed discriminatory railroad rates have been succeeded by suburban commuters (in pig masks, opposite) banding together to protest poor service.

A peanut sale by businessmen members of a Minnesota Kiwanis Club (lower right) typifies the fund-raising activities of community service clubs for worthwhile causes.

New York Times

KIWANIS INTERNATIONAL

The common business and economic interests of industrialists are represented by the National Association of Manufacturers. Above: its annual banquet.

In World War II diverse businesses cooperated to help each other produce for the war. Left: Buick automakers inspect an aircraft engine they will build.

A 1969 Business Opportunity Fair in Chicago (right) furthered contacts (and contracts) between major firms and minority-owned manufacturing companies.

MONTGOMERY WARD

271

8

---·❦·---

THE
ROLLER COASTER

1918-1941

Europe was exhausted by the years of devastating and bitter conflict, but America had been a combatant only long enough to test its new industrial muscle. Victory was a time for celebration, for indulging in a smug sense of achievement, and for drawing up check lists of what had been learned from "the lessons of the war." For just about every group—labor, progressives, pacifists, suffragists, prohibitionists, utopians of every stripe—these lessons turned out to be no more than a strengthening of the convictions they had already held.

Business was no different. The businessman's panaceas would include such items as fewer government regulations, a return of the railroads to private control, lower taxes, and a quick end to price controls. The fact that they got all these within the relatively short space of a few years made it clear that the immediate postwar period was a businessman's era.

The postwar target was no longer business as usual, because business had grown to unusual proportions during the war. Plants of all kinds had been expanded, and both farm and industrial production were substantially higher than they had ever been before. By the third quarter of 1918, industrial output had risen to 117 per cent of the 1914 level. There was no assurance that the American economy could absorb all this output, but Treasury spending—for continued shipbuilding and military costs, for settling war contracts, for dismissal payments to servicemen, and for reconstruction loans to the Allies—provided a helpful push. Even so, peace was accompanied by a minor business setback, and the production index dropped to 112 per cent of the 1914 level by the second quarter of

1919. But then it moved up sharply to 119 per cent, a plateau at which it remained for about a year. Gains were most marked in auto output and construction.

Released from wartime constraints, prices followed a similar course, dipping early in 1919, then rising even faster than they had during the war. As inventories increased in value, business profits climbed. Anticipating still higher prices, many businessmen ordered more goods than they needed, and some, afraid of getting caught short, double-ordered from different suppliers, giving an exaggerated appearance to demand. Department store inventories rose more than 50 per cent between the spring of 1919 and the spring of 1920. The wholesale price index had climbed to 228 per cent of the 1913 level by 1920.

In the face of this demand for their products, and encouraged by easy lending policies of commercial banks, manufacturers expanded their plant capacity even further. Investment in new plant and equipment during 1920 was around $3 billion, larger than in any other year of the expansive decade of the 1920's.

The first signs of trouble appeared in 1920. Building began to slide early in the year. Then demand for industrial products began to dry up. Industrial production slipped from its 1920 peak of 119 per cent of the 1914 base to 102 per cent in the second quarter of 1921. But prices dropped even faster. The wholesale price index suffered a 33 per cent drop between 1920 and 1921. Farm prices were hit hardest of all. Wheat tumbled from $2.15 a bushel in December, 1919, to $1.44 in December, 1920 (and to less than $1.00 the following year); corn from $1.35 to $.68 a bushel; and cotton from $.36 a pound to $.14.

Governor of New York Franklin D. Roosevelt learns firsthand (left) the problems of a hard-hit man-of-the-Depression.

Labor, understandably reluctant to part with high wartime wages — which had not kept pace with prices — had to give up some of its gains, as unemployment rose from an estimated 3 million early in 1919 to about 4.75 million by 1921. The National Industrial Conference Board reported that average hourly wages rose from 24.3 cents an hour in 1914 to a peak of 62.1 cents in 1920, then dropped to 48.2 cents by December, 1921.

The 1921 setback resulted in 100,000 bankruptcies, but it was the farmers who suffered most. Encouraged by high wartime prices, many had taken their profits, borrowed still more, and invested in the farmer's time-honored capital — livestock, land, and agricultural equipment. With the disastrous price decline, more than 450,000 lost their farms entirely. When the economy finally righted itself by the end of 1922, industry had achieved its adjustment to peacetime needs, prices had stopped dropping, and normal business expansion had resumed. But some industries simply failed to come back. These included shipbuilding, the merchant marine, cotton textile manufacturing, bituminous coal mining, and, worst of all, agriculture.

For all its wartime experiences, or possibly because of it, the United States was inward-looking in the 1920's. This was probably just as well, since the nation showed a singular incapacity to cope with its newly won leadership in world affairs.

The war debts constituted a case in point. America's wartime allies counted on German reparations payments to provide them with the funds they needed to repay their debts to the United States. The reparations bill was not finally fixed until April, 1921, when it was set at $33 billion. But Germany had less than $.6 billion in gold in 1918, and its efforts to make payments in raw materials, finished goods, and labor were largely frustrated by the other nations' resistance to German competition. Germany was all but bankrupted in the effort to pay her bills and went through a wild inflation that made the mark worthless. When Germany defaulted, most of the other nations failed to make payments of either principal or interest on their debts.

In a series of conferences in 1923 and 1924, a committee headed by presidential emissary Charles Gates Dawes developed a plan to scale down the German payments and restore her economy. The war debts of England, France, Finland, and Italy were refunded, in effect reducing them anywhere from 23 to 75 per cent — not unreasonable concessions in view of the fact that they had been incurred largely to buy American goods at inflated wartime prices. With confidence restored in international financial markets by the Dawes Plan,

Low-cost workers, like these G.M. employees in Java, were an added inducement for U.S. plant expansion overseas in the 1920's.

274

American investors were willing to lend to Germany, which then used the gold in reparations payments to England and France, which in turn repaid U.S. debts — the money ending up where it started from. When this system stopped working, principally because Americans began putting most of their available funds into their own stock market, a committee headed by businessman Owen D. Young developed another plan that cut German obligations sharply, but it was doomed by the worsened world economic situation.

It would have made sense for the United States, as a creditor nation, to help redress the balance by importing more than it exported. But the reverse course was followed during the 1920's. Exports remained substantially higher than imports, by as much as $1 billion in 1928. Compounding the problem was the U.S. tariff policy. Partly on the pretext of protecting the market for agricultural products, the Fordney-McCumber tariff was enacted in 1922, replacing the more sensible Underwood Act passed before the war. The new act empowered the President to raise or lower duties as much as 50 per cent in order to equalize foreign and domestic costs of production. But manufacturers were more interested in keeping foreign goods out than in equalizing costs. And the farmers, who gained domestic markets worth perhaps $30 million a year, may have lost overseas markets of $330 million as other nations erected retaliatory trade barriers.

These trade restrictions by other countries, along with Europe's postwar shortage of capital, convinced many American companies, including Standard Oil, General Motors, and International Telephone and Telegraph, to set up subsidiaries, branches, and plants abroad. Between 1919 and 1929, American investments in other countries, aside from government loans, rose from $7 billion to $17 billion, about half of which consisted of security holdings and the other half of direct investments in foreign business enterprises.

THE GREAT PRODUCTION MACHINE

As America emerged from the postwar depression in 1922, the mood quickly became one of confidence and optimism. Factories reopened or stepped up their operating schedules. Industrial production shot up from an index of 58 (based on the 1933–39 average as 100) in 1921 to 73 in 1922, then continued to climb to 110 by 1929. This near doubling of output, accompanied by a mere 12 per cent increase in population, was indicative of the sharp gains in productivity of the working force. National income rose from $59 billion in 1921 to $87 billion by 1929, and real income per person increased from $522 to $716 in the same period — though its distribution among various groups in the population was pretty lopsided.

Improved methods and machinery were turning the

Andrew W. Mellon, Secretary of the Treasury

nation into a vast production machine. The United States, which once had confined its exports almost entirely to foodstuffs and raw materials, was now primarily an exporter of manufactured goods. Its imports were mainly raw commodities that it did not have or that it produced in inadequate supply, such as tin, crude rubber, silk, sugar, and coffee. But to feed the hungry production giant there was also a great outpouring of raw materials from American mines, wells, and farms; by the late 1920's the United States, with 6 per cent of the world's population, was turning out 70 per cent of its oil, almost 50 per cent of its copper, 46 per cent of its iron, 42 per cent of its coal, 54 per cent of its cotton, and 62 per cent of its corn.

The businessmen in charge of these prodigies of production were the heroes of the day, and they had staunch support from the business-minded occupants of the White House — Warren G. Harding, bumbling, easily swayed, intensely loyal; Calvin Coolidge, the "tight-mouthed Puritan" who said, "The business of America is business"; and Herbert Hoover, by instinct humanitarian, by conviction an efficiency engineer.

Harding, seeking to steer the nation in a "return to normalcy," set it on something more closely resembling a confusion course. With no understanding of tariffs (he once told an interviewer, "The United States should adopt a protective tariff [to] help the struggling industries of Europe"), he was given power under the Fordney-McCumber Act to raise or lower duties. His chief fiscal adviser was Andrew Mellon, his Secretary of the Treasury; as one of the nation's wealthiest — and most conservative—men, Mellon often behaved as though the preservation of the country's bastions of wealth were his primary duty.

Still, the pulse of events in the 1920's was determined more by what businessmen were doing in a largely laissez-faire state than what government did or failed to do. And nowhere did the actions of businessmen have more impact on the country than in the automobile industry.

In 1914 a respectable total of 469,000 cars and trucks were produced in the United States. By 1929 almost twice that number of trucks alone came off the assembly lines. The total number of motor vehicles registered in the country climbed from 1.3 million in 1914 to 10.5 million in 1921 and 26.5 million—or more than one for every five people—in 1929.

Employing almost 500,000 people directly, the automobile industry accounted for more than 7 per cent of all manufacturing workers and almost 9 per cent of manufacturing wages. But indirectly hundreds of thousands more—one estimate placed it at 4 million—drew their livelihood from motor vehicle production. The industry was also chiefly responsible for a tremendous expansion of petroleum production.

Gasoline, which had once been discarded as an undesirable by-product in the manufacture of kerosene and lubricating oils from crude petroleum, had passed kerosene in consumption by 1915. Researchers set to work finding improved methods of "cracking" crude oil, or reducing it to its lighter components. In 1914 only about 16 per cent was converted into gasoline; better refining methods boosted the proportion to 35 per cent by 1926, and eventually to 45 per cent. The early motorist filled his tank with a can and funnel, but soon there were roadside pumps. The first filling stations were built before the war; by 1929 there were some 120,000 of them, and by 1940, 425,000.

Oil companies looked for new sources for their production—starting offshore drilling off the California and Gulf coasts, and seeking out drilling in-

The Way to Wealth
CHARLES F. KETTERING

Before he was nine years old, Charles Franklin Kettering (1876–1958) dismantled his mother's sewing machine to study its construction. A few years later, with the first money he earned—cutting a neighbor's wheat—he purchased a telephone instrument by mail order (even though his part of rural Ohio did not have a phone system), simply to take it apart to see how it worked. A born tinkerer and Mr. Fix-it, Kettering became an important developer of the modern automobile and one of the nation's wealthiest men.

Hampered by poor eyesight, he took six years to work his way through Ohio State University to get a bachelor's degree in electrical engineering. In 1904 he began doing research for National Cash Register Company, developing business machine innovations and the company's first electrically operated cash register. In his spare time he worked on the problem of devising an efficient electrical ignition system for automobiles; he set up a shop in a barn near his home in Dayton and recruited colleagues at N.C.R. to work with him.

In those early days of automobile manufacturing, ignition was unreliable and frustrating. Cars were equipped

Charles F. Kettering

with a dual system that was far from satisfactory: the dry batteries that were used lasted only about 200 miles, and the magneto sparking would often fail in slow traffic. Kettering's "Barn Gang," as it was known, developed an improved system, good enough for Cadillac to use it in its 1909 models. Kettering and his associates that same year formed the Dayton Engineering Laboratories Company, later called Delco, with a capital stock of $150,000.

Cadillac continued to draw on Kettering's inventiveness. In 1912 he developed the first self-starter, which eliminated the balky hand crank and made automobile driving easier for women. His company invented reliable headlights, perfected the V-8 engine, and created numerous other improvements for cars. When United Motors offered to buy Delco for $9 million, Kettering sold, receiving stock as well as cash. Eventually United Motors became General Motors Corporation, with "Boss Ket" as vice president.

Up to his time, inventors had usually worked in secret, protecting what they discovered in the hope of personal gain. Kettering believed in working cooperatively with other engineers, and as head of General Motors Research Corporation he pioneered the principle of the research team. "Research," he explained, "is simply trying to find out what we are going to do when we can't keep doing what we are now doing." What he was trying to do, he once said, was "make G.M. some money, fill a new human want, and put some men to work."

One problem that plagued auto-

terests and concessions abroad. Standard Oil Company of New Jersey's president, Walter Teagle, announced that his company was interested in every oil producing area in the world, and his company joined others in developing the Turkish Petroleum Company, later known as Iraq Petroleum. In the 1920's The Texas Company acquired prospective oil lands in Colombia and Venezuela, as well as interests in the Arabian American Oil Co. and in Bahrein in the Middle East and on the Indonesian island of Sumatra.

The automobile itself was steadily being improved upon, from the standpoints of mechanical performance, comfort, and ease of operation. The closed car became standard in the 1920's, and the introduction of heaters made winter driving more pleasant. Balloon tires, for a softer ride, came in during the early 1920's. As cars grew more powerful, partly through the introduction of high-compression leaded gasoline, such safety features as four-wheel brakes and safety glass began to be used.

Henry Ford, the industry's long-time leader, con-

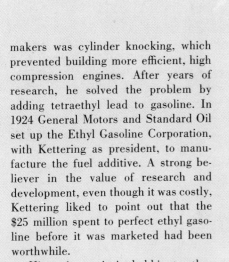

makers was cylinder knocking, which prevented building more efficient, high compression engines. After years of research, he solved the problem by adding tetraethyl lead to gasoline. In 1924 General Motors and Standard Oil set up the Ethyl Gasoline Corporation, with Kettering as president, to manufacture the fuel additive. A strong believer in the value of research and development, even though it was costly, Kettering liked to point out that the $25 million spent to perfect ethyl gasoline before it was marketed had been worthwhile.

His native curiosity led him to other fields. In 1927 he established a research foundation to "find out why the grass was green," hoping that the secrets of photosynthesis would reveal how to manufacture food from the air. In 1945, with G.M. President Alfred P. Sloan, he set up the Sloan-Kettering Institute for Cancer Research in New York, giving $4 million to it. He never took a personal interest in accumulating wealth, but when he died at eighty-two he was worth more than $100 million and ranked among the fifty richest people in the United States. Much of his money he left to fund further research.

tinued to go his singular way. In 1919, a year in which his company earned over $69 million, he paid out more than $100 million to buy out the other stockholders, after threatening them with starting a competing firm. Still chary of eastern financiers, he nevertheless borrowed $75 million from bankers in Boston and New York to expand his River Rouge plant. Then he used every means he could to repay the loans. In spite of a slumping auto market in 1920, he dumped cars on his dealers, demanding payment in cash; those whose local credit was inadequate either lost their franchise or went broke. Ford cashed in his Liberty Bonds, cancelled contracts with suppliers, and closed down his plants, putting 60,000 out of work the day before Christmas, 1920. But Ford paid up his debts and remained master of his own house.

In 1924 Ford production reached 1,600,000 units, capturing 51 per cent of the U.S. market. But the times were beginning to pass Ford by. While he still insisted on turning out his one-model, one-color (black), low-priced car, more affluent American automobile buyers were beginning to look less for utility and more for variety, style, and convenience. They got what they wanted from General Motors and Chrysler. "Why did I buy my first 'Chevvie'?" asked historian James Truslow Adams rhetorically. "Because Ford . . . would not put a self-starter in the 'tin Lizzie,' of which I had bought three in annual succession."

General Motors, meanwhile, was coming under a leadership far more suited to modern big business operations. After William Durant had finally been forced out of G.M. in 1920, Pierre Du Pont had sought to rationalize the hodgepodge of automakers, parts makers, financing firm, refrigerator manufacturer, and other subsidiaries Durant had accumulated and pasted together. The company had less than 20 per cent of the nation's automobile business in the early 1920's, but the Du Pont name proved a powerful influence in getting leading bankers, including J. P. Morgan & Co., to distribute more G.M. stock when cash was needed.

As the auto industry became the national leader in value of manufactured products during the 1920's, a new breed of managers—rational, orderly, and dedicated to efficiency—began to take charge. One of these was Walter Chrysler, who had left General Motors to go into retirement, then came back to rejuvenate the struggling Maxwell Motor Car Company and, in 1923, to start his own company. Another was Alfred P. Sloan, picked by Du Pont to head General Motors in 1923. Sloan put into effect a reorganization plan that Durant had once sloughed off.

By 1926 G.M. had 30 per cent of the U.S. auto market and had surpassed Ford in sales, a leadership it was to widen steadily. That same year the new Chrysler Corporation moved from twenty-seventh place in the industry to fifth. By 1928 Chrysler had bought

Dodge Brothers, Inc. and had launched two cars, the Plymouth and the De Soto, and in 1929 Chrysler Corporation became one of the Big Three in automaking.

Ford finally decided on what had become inevitable: a restyling of his automobile. In 1927, having produced 10 million Model T's, he shut down production in all his plants while his engineers and designers worked in closely guarded secrecy on tooling for a new model. His Model A, introduced in 1928 with a massive advertising campaign built around planned suspense, showed that Ford had finally given in on the matters of color, style, and convenience. The car was a success, but it came too late to play much of a role in the booming auto market of the twenties.

THE HIGH CONSUMPTION ECONOMY

The development of the family car as a national institution was one of the earliest signs—and certainly the most prominent—that the world's first mass consumption economy was taking shape in the United States. Not only were there greater quantities of consumer goods being produced, but there was also a mounting variety of things from which to choose. The economies of mass production had made possible this new dimension in economic life, although there were other forces at work as well. One of these was the growth of mass marketing techniques that were bringing new efficiencies into the selling and distribution processes. Another was the expansion of the economic middle class, whose income—or expectation of earnings—was great enough to permit such "discretionary" purchases as autos, household appliances, fine clothing, travel, and education. Finally, the automobile was knitting together city and country, and modern suburbia was taking shape.

This process was accompanied by more subtle changes in the life style of a great many Americans. Their deep-seated egalitarianism motivated them to try to become not immensely wealthy but one degree wealthier than they already were. Socioeconomic

THE MOVIE INDUSTRY

To all the world Hollywood is synonymous with dreams. But behind the stars and make-believe, the production, distribution, and exhibition of moving pictures grew to become, in the twentieth century, one of America's top-gross industries, surpassed only by agriculture, steel, and transportation.

Before World War I, the center of motion picture production was moved from the New York City area to Hollywood, a quiet little village near Los Angeles, where sunshine, needed for moviemaking, was more abundant and reliable than in the East. The product captivated millions, and movie magnates became rich overnight. Marcus Loew, a onetime furrier, moved from a loft in Covington, Kentucky, where he showed episodic snatches of film, to an association with Adolph Zukor in New York's Union Square. Within a decade, Loew owned a chain of lavishly fitted theaters across the country, while Zukor was forming the production company that eventually became Paramount Pictures. Loew took over the old Metro Company when it ran into financial difficulties with the costly *Four Horsemen of the Apocalypse*, and in 1924 he bought out producer Samuel Goldwyn, and then merged with Louis B. Mayer Productions to form Metro-Goldwyn-Mayer the following year, ushering in an era when producers like Goldwyn and Cecil B. De Mille spent as much as $1,000,000 on a single picture. M-G-M became the industry's producing and distributing giant, with Loew and Nicholas M. Schenck running the New York end and Mayer and Irving Thalberg in charge of production in California.

World War I helped to make the production of films almost an American monopoly. The cellulose nitrate necessary to manufacture film was used by European nations for explosives, and by the end of hostilities, the leadership of America's movie industry was firmly established at home and abroad. But the showmanship of the Americans had also contributed to Hollywood's leadership. Epic-sized productions, beginning with David Wark Griffith's $110,000

Cecil B. De Mille (seated) and cast members of his film The Squaw Man, *in 1913*

gradations narrowed, as people thought of themselves as part of the upper lower, lower middle, or upper middle classes. As sociologist Daniel Bell has pointed out, the older Protestant ethic of frugality and work for work's sake was giving way before new standards of abundance, prodigality, and immediate rewards. With parsimony no longer a virtue, there was a bit of a stigma attached to the inability to keep up with the neighbors in the matter of washing machines, floor lamps, and porcelain plumbing fixtures.

Novelty began to have immense appeal. No sooner was a toaster purchased and installed than payments began on a new vacuum cleaner. The use of leisure time became a preoccupation of many. The number of golf courses tripled during the decade to reach almost 6,000. Annual spending on hunting and fishing equipment reached an estimated $750 million. College football gate receipts climbed to $21 million a year. Total spending on sports, travel, recreation, and amusements reached an estimated $10 billion by 1929. The movies

Birth of a Nation in 1915, were cast with stars whose glamorous publicity increased their attraction at the box office.

It was an expensive business, but returns were high. From 1921 to 1930 the total capital invested in the industry rose from about $78 million to almost $850 million. In one of those years, 1925, there were some 20,000 movie houses in the United States, selling 130 million admission tickets a week and grossing a total of $550 million. Almost 700 feature films were produced, and 300,000 persons were employed in the production, distribution, and exhibition phases of the industry.

The first practical device for recording sound on film was developed by the General Electric Laboratories in 1926. Warner Brothers was first to use the medium that year with *Don Juan*, and Will Hays, the industry's czar, spoke from the screen at the opening of the program. The following year came Warner's big "talkie" hit, *The Jazz Singer*, and theaters all over the country rushed to reconvert their equipment to provide for sound. Western Electric Company, a subsidiary of American Telephone & Telegraph, became a leading producer of sound recording and reproducing equipment for motion pictures in 1927, and was responsible for continued technical advances in the field.

became the most popular indulgence of great masses of people. Movie theaters evolved in short order from the austere nickelodeons, ranged with camp chairs rented from undertaking parlors, to great gilded palaces that were the showplaces of their times.

Radio entered American life even more precipitately than the movies. During the war the government had taken over the stations of the largely British-owned Marconi Wireless Telegraph Company of America, the only firm in the country able to handle transatlantic radio communication. General Electric Company, owner of the Alexanderson high-frequency alternator, then the best means of transmitting over long distances, had been negotiating a transfer of patent rights to American Marconi before the war, and resumed the talks in 1919.

But then the U.S. government stepped in, halting the negotiations. Reluctant to see the new communications medium fall under foreign control, government authorities acted to create what could have amounted to an American radio trust. It was Franklin D. Roosevelt, then Acting Secretary of the Navy, who wrote to General Electric requesting that the talks with Marconi be suspended. The outcome was the formation of a new company, the Radio Corporation of America, set up by General Electric's Owen D. Young. The fledgling R.C.A. took over American Marconi's entire business and assets. Because key radio patents were scattered among a number of large companies, cross-licensing agreements were worked out with General Electric and A.T.&T., both of which obtained substantial stock interests in R.C.A., as did Westinghouse in a later patent pool arrangement. By 1930 the government had had second thoughts and brought suit over these agreements, and General Electric and Westinghouse entered into a consent decree to divest themselves of R.C.A. stock—something A.T.&T. had done on its own a number of years before.

Among the many early radio hobbyists was Dr. Frank Conrad of Pittsburgh, who aired his own programs regularly and who talked Westinghouse into building a powerful transmitter in East Pittsburgh. The first operating license was granted to this station, designated KDKA, by the Department of Commerce on October 27, 1920, and the station broadcast the Warren Harding–James Cox election returns the following week. R.C.A. soon got into the field, broadcasting the Jack Dempsey–Georges Carpentier prize fight from a temporary station at Hoboken, New Jersey, in July, 1921. In New York City, A.T.&T. opened Station WEAF in 1922. By the end of 1922 there were thirty stations licensed, and by 1924 there were 500.

R.C.A.'s 1922 catalogue of radio equipment was entitled *Radio Enters the Home*, and it listed crystal radio sets for as little as $25.50. Westinghouse offered the lowest-priced set using a vacuum tube, the Aeriola

U.S. radio broadcasting—a $412 million industry by 1929—began at Pittsburgh station KDKA (above), November 2, 1920.

Senior, which sold for $75.90 with batteries and antenna. More elaborate receivers were built by General Electric, which offered a three-tube set in two steel boxes for $250, and by Westinghouse, which had a similar set in a wooden box selling at $261.75 and an eight-tube Aeriola Grand at $401.

In 1926, David Sarnoff, general manager of R.C.A., formed the National Broadcasting Co. by setting up wire links among the R.C.A. stations and WEAF, acquired from A.T.&T. Competition came in 1927 from a loosely organized group called the Columbia Phonograph Broadcasting System, which a Philadelphia cigar manufacturer, William S. Paley, helped organize into the Columbia Broadcasting System early in 1929.

To an increasingly entertainment-minded public, radio quickly came to represent a major medium of amusement rather than communication. Early programming tended to pattern itself on the content of phonograph records and vaudeville acts. People congregated around the first sets purchased in a neighborhood, or bought their own as soon as they could afford them. Not one home in 10,000 had a radio in 1920. By 1922 there were 60,000 in use, and by 1928 there were 7.5 million. The value of the radio industry's product rose from $11 million in 1921 to $412 million in 1929.

Such visible evidence of prosperity as the growth of radio, movies, and motor cars led many an American to feel he had arrived at the state of affluence, or was

about to. It was not a mood in which labor unions figured to do well, and organized labor indeed did badly in the 1920's.

President Wilson tried to extend the wartime truce between capital and labor at an industrial conference in 1919, but employers insisted on their right to hire and fire as they saw fit. The courts added their bit in giving industrial firms the upper hand over their workers. A state law forbidding employers from forcing their workers to sign yellow-dog contracts, in which they would agree not to join a union, had been overthrown by the Supreme Court in 1915. In 1918 and 1922 the Court declared federal child labor laws unconstitutional, and in 1923 it ruled against a minimum wage law for women.

The American Federation of Labor lost almost a third of its 4.1 million members between 1920 and 1929. Employer influence had corresponding gains. Company unions grew from a handful in 1917 to hundreds, with a total membership of more than 1.4 million, ten years later.

Various welfare plans were instituted by some employers, partly to stave off union initiatives and partly because of a growing humanitarian tendency on the part of management. A number of employees got free medical services, subsidized sports and recreational activities, paid vacations, and low-cost lunches. Group insurance by 1927 covered 4.7 million workers, with total coverage estimated at $5.6 billion. A 1926

280

WESTINGHOUSE, INC.

survey showed that more than 400 firms, employing 4 million, had pension plans, almost all of them started since 1911.

Some of the most antilabor activities of the decade were undertaken in a movement euphemized as the "American plan." This was a program in which employer associations, chambers of commerce, and such organizations as the National Association of Manufacturers and the American Bankers Association sought to weaken organized labor and to promote open-shop practices by means of publicity and propaganda. It enrolled thousands of employers in various open-shop associations and generally drew the support of farmers. These efforts fell on fertile soil and flourished in the climate of the 1920's.

BUILDING THE PYRAMIDS

Like other prosperous periods, the 1920's were years of consolidation for many businesses. The iron, steel, and machinery industries led the trend, but there were major consolidations as well in food processing, automobile manufacturing, movie making, banking, and public utilities. During the decade more than 8,000 manufacturing and mining companies and almost 5,000 public utilities disappeared through mergers or acquisitions.

These constituted a relatively small proportion of all businesses, since there were more than 300,000 nonfinancial corporations in the country in 1929. But many of the combinations took place among the larger business entities. The assets of the nation's 200 biggest business enterprises swelled from $43.7 billion in 1919 to $81 billion in 1929, a growth rate from two to three times as high as that of smaller concerns. At the end of the period these 200 corporations, controlled by approximately 2,000 individuals, held an estimated half of the nation's corporate wealth and 38 per cent of all the business wealth, and they received 43 per cent of the net income of all nonbanking corporations.

In addition to outright combination, there were a number of other devices to bring business organizations under more closely unified control—voting trusts, holding companies, patent pools, and trade agreements. Cartels—agreements to divide up markets according to specified formulas—were illegal as far as domestic law was concerned, although American concerns could and did take part in international cartels, which multiplied after the war. Among the U.S. firms that entered into agreements with foreign firms to exchange patents and divide world markets were Diamond Match, Bendix Aviation, U.S. Steel, General Electric, Westinghouse, and Standard Oil of New Jersey. Cartels covered such products as radio tubes, electric lamps, copper, lead, steel rails, magnesia, and titanium.

The holding company, whereby one company was created merely to hold stock—often controlling interests—in others, became a more and more popular device. Such states as Delaware and New Jersey, with the most permissive corporation laws, were able to derive a considerable portion of their revenues from corporate fees and taxes. Of 573 corporations whose stock was traded actively on the New York Stock Exchange in 1928, only 86 were not holding companies, while 395 were both holding companies and operating companies, and 92, or almost one in six, did nothing more than hold the securities of other companies.

Once the idea of the holding company became established, it was but a short step to form one holding company to hold the stock of others, and to pile still others on top of that, like the building blocks of a pyramid. En route to the top, the securities of the various companies would be offered to the public, although enough voting stock to maintain control would be held by the original organizers. The result would often be what President Franklin D. Roosevelt was to describe as "a ninety-six-inch dog wagged by a four-inch tail." Among the leading pyramid builders of the era were the Van Sweringen brothers in railroads, Samuel Insull in utilities, and A. P. Giannini in banking.

At their peak, the Van Sweringens, who had started in real estate in the Cleveland area, controlled an empire made up of coal mines, suburban developments, trucking companies, office buildings, a hotel, a department store, and 23,000 miles of railroads, all of it valued at more than $3 billion. Their own wealth reached almost $130 million before they finally lost control of their holdings in the 1930's. A major figure whose financial manipulations probably outdid those of the Van Sweringens was Insull. But rather than choose an old and troubled industry like the railroads, Insull went into the new and rapidly expanding electric utility business.

Largely because of the increased use of electric power by industry, but also because housewives were demanding, and getting, electric vacuum cleaners, refrigerators, washing machines, and smaller appliances, electric power consumption rose rapidly during the decade. The value of electrical products manufactured rose from $800 million in 1921 to $2.3 billion in 1930. The increased efficiency resulting from the use of electrical power and from the flexibility of being able to place an electrical motor anywhere in a plant was reflected in a great many industries. Labor time was reduced almost 100 per cent in making glass light bulbs, over 50 per cent in cigar manufacture, and output per man quadrupled in making inner tubes for tires. Greater efficiency also went into the production of electricity itself, so that the amount of fuel used increased only about 20 per cent between 1920 and 1929, while output more than doubled.

THE VAN SWERINGEN PYRAMID

Railroad monarchs of the 1920s—Otis P. (left) and Mantis J. Van Sweringen

In the boom days of the twentieth century, two brothers from Ohio were among the most spectacular, and successful, pyramid builders. When the bust came, their skill at financial manipulation could not save them, and everything they had built tumbled down.

Oris Paxton and Mantis James Van Sweringen were born in the hills overlooking Wooster, Ohio, and were brought to Cleveland by their widowed father in the 1880's. When their father died in 1893, O. P. was fourteen and M. J. was twelve. They left school, and O. P. got a job as an office boy, turning the job over to his brother when he was promoted to clerk. Both worked hard and saved money. In 1900 they decided to go into the real-estate business, contracting for an acre of land that had once been part of a swampy tract owned by the Shaker sect. Although the plot was three miles from the nearest street railway, the brothers managed to sell it by offering subdivision lots at $25 a front foot and agreeing to carry the buyers until it could be resold for $30 a front foot.

They took more options, sold more land, then borrowed enough to buy 4,000 acres. As the scale of their operations grew, they laid plans to build a rapid transit line from their Shaker Heights development, and bought four acres in the heart of Cleveland for a terminal. In proceeding to acquire their right of way, however, they ran into the Nickel Plate Railroad.

Owned by the New York Central, the Nickel Plate paralleled much of the Central's trackage—and indeed had originally been built as a blackmail scheme against the Lake Shore & Michigan Southern, which became part of the Central system. The Interstate Commerce Commission had ordered the Central to divest itself of the Nickel Plate, so when the Van Sweringens came along to bargain for a right of way, they found a railroad for sale.

In 1916 they made a deal to buy the railroad for $8.5 million, of which $2 million was in cash and the remainder in notes, payable annually over a ten-year period. They borrowed the cash from a bank, on the strength of their contract to buy the railroad. Then they organized under a Delaware charter the Nickel Plate Securities Co., to hold their railroad, their downtown property, and their debts. A sale of stock in the holding company provided enough to pay off the bank loan. They purchased about $500,000 worth of the stock themselves but ended up owning $10.5 million worth, most of it in payment for their land and their trouble.

Their pyramid building was partially interrupted by the wartime takeover of the railroads by the government. When the Transportation Act of 1920 returned the railroads to private ownership, the Nickel Plate prospered. Under the able management of J. J. Bernet, who had formerly been with the New York Central, the line increased its earnings on common from something over 6 per cent in 1916 to more than 10 per cent in 1920 and 25 per cent in 1921. By 1923 the ten notes to the Central had been fully repaid.

The Van Sweringens set about buying more railroads almost as early as they could. Borrowing against the Nickel Plate, they bought the Lake Erie & Western from the Central, then picked up the Toledo, St. Louis & Western much as they had bought the Nickel Plate—on the installment plan. The three lines were consolidated in 1923 as the New York, Chicago & St. Louis Railway Co., with 1,600 miles of track and some $200 million in assets. With the blessing of the House of Morgan, the brothers bought the controlling interest in the coal-rich Chesapeake & Ohio, using Nickel Plate mortgage bond proceeds for the purchase, early in 1923. The Vans also fell under the approving gaze of George F. Baker, president of the First National Bank in New York, who sold them enough stock in the Erie to control that railroad. In 1924 they started to buy into the Pere Marquette Railroad. Meanwhile, in 1923, ground had been broken for their $60 million Cleveland terminal, including a fifty-two-story office tower.

By the fall of 1925 their holdings included control of 9,245 miles of railroad and assets of about $1.5 billion. Refused I.C.C. permission to combine their holdings into a single system, they did the next best thing. By means of the Alleghany Corporation, a holding company organized early in 1929, they were able to bring all their rail interests into a single pool of control, and at the same time to sell almost $160 million in preferred stock and bonds, while maintaining a majority of the voting common stock. Looking westward, they began buying control of the Missouri Pacific Railroad, using bank loans and the proceeds from the sale of more Alleghany bonds. By May, 1930, their objective achieved, the Van Sweringen brothers took their first vacation, a two-week inspection tour of the property for which they had just paid $100 million.

Through the Denver, Rio Grande & Western, Van Sweringen roads now extended from New York City to Salt Lake City. And the brothers were already dealing with Arthur Curtiss James, of the Western Pacific, to acquire the final link and to become the first to control a coast-to-coast railroad system.

The Vaness Company, the Van Sweringens' personal basket, stood at the apex of their pyramid. Vaness owned most of the General Securities Corporation, which in turn controlled

Alleghany. All of these were holding companies, as was the Chesapeake Corporation, on the next step down. Although each company had a controlling interest in the one just below it, the actual percentage of ownership by the top company grew smaller and smaller on the way down, and was actually as little as a twenty-fifth of one per cent for some of the operating companies at the bottom.

In October, 1930, a year after the market crash, the prices of Van Sweringen securities began a disastrous slide. Since most of their holdings were pledged against a variety of bank and other loans, and with earnings fast disappearing from their operating properties (Missouri Pacific revenues dropped from $504 million in 1929 to $293 million in 1932), the Van Sweringens retained control of their empire only through the forbearance of the Morgans.

Finally, in September, 1935, various shares pledged against loans from Morgan and others went up for sale in a dingy little auction room at 18 Vesey Street, in the Wall Street area. There were only two bidders—J. P. Morgan & Co., with its upset bid of just over $3 million, and Midamerica Corp., offering $3,121,000. Midamerica was the creature of George A. Ball, a Muncie, Indiana, fruit-jar manufacturer and a Nickel Plate director. Ball gained control of the Van Sweringen holdings but promptly gave the brothers a ten-year option to buy a controlling interest in Midamerica for just $8,250, as well as the right to vote that interest for the life of the option.

So the Vans were back in charge, but there were more debts overhanging Alleghany—three bond issues totaling $85 million—that gave the real voting power to the Guaranty Trust Co., as trustee, whenever they wished to exercise it. M. J. Van Sweringen died a few months after the sale, leaving an estate of $3,068, and his brother died less than a year later, leaving a net indebtedness of $80 million, more than half of it owed to the Morgans. In 1937 control of Alleghany's common stock was purchased from Ball for $6.3 million by Robert R. Young and Frank P. Kolbe, partners in a New York brokerage firm, along with Woolworth heir Allan P. Kirby, who put up most of the cash. The Van Sweringens' pyramid was history.

The pattern for the public utility holding company was first laid down by the Electric Bond & Share Company, formed by General Electric in the early 1900's to hold the utility company shares it had acquired in exchange for expensive power generating equipment. But when G.E. dropped out of the utility business in 1924, under threat of an antitrust action, the field was left wide open for more logical contenders, like the Edison companies.

Samuel Insull, son of a poor London clergyman, was a great admirer of Thomas Edison. When young Insull answered a newspaper ad seeking a stenographer, he was happy to get the job but thrilled to learn that it was with an Edison enterprise. So assiduously did he apply himself that Edison sent for him when he needed a secretary.

He moved up rapidly in the Edison organization and was made president of the Edison power company in Chicago when he was still in his thirties. Under his deft management, his firm was able to take over other companies until he had monopolized electric power production in Chicago. Insull learned everything there was to know about the management of utility companies, and gradually he acquired interests in power firms on his own account. To raise more money for such acquisitions, he formed the Middle West Utilities Company in 1912, selling stock to the public but keeping enough voting shares to retain control. He went on acquiring more power companies, mostly in the South and Midwest, and forming more holding companies to raise money for still more purchases.

At the top of his pyramid was Insull Utility Investments, Inc., controlled by his family and his investment bankers, Halsey, Stuart & Co. of Chicago. Next came the Corporation Securities Company of Chicago, known as Corps to the insiders. Under these two top holding companies—each of which had an interest in the other—were four major utility systems: Middle West Utilities, with 111 subsidiaries; People's Gas, Light & Coke, with eight; Commonwealth Edison Company, with six; and the Public Service Company of Northern Illinois. A fifth system, Midland United Company, with thirty subsidiaries, was controlled by the other four. These systems served 4.5 million customers and produced more than 10 per cent of the nation's electric power in 1930, when their combined assets were valued at $2.5 billion.

Although Insull had studiously avoided involvement with New York bankers, he was unable to create his huge utility empire without incurring vast amounts of debt. And when stock prices began to erode in 1929, the collateral behind these loans weakened, and so did his credit. The gravest threat to his corporate edifice, however, came not from the banks, but from Cyrus Eaton, a Cleveland financier—who, curiously enough, was to team up a few years later with Halsey, Stuart,

Insull's investment bankers, in a running battle with New York financial interests over competitive bidding for new security issues of utility companies. Eaton had accumulated a sizable block of Insull stock. In order to keep these shares from being dumped on the market, Insull bought them up, at Eaton's price. To get the funds, Insull went to the New York banks for the first time in 1930.

But stock prices continued to drop, and the security that Insull had put up could no longer cover his loans. The banks took over the collateral and got control of the Insull companies, forcing him to resign. In April, 1932, the Lincoln Printing Company of Chicago filed a petition asking that Insull's top holding companies be put into receivership, triggering one of the biggest business failures in U.S. history. Losses to investors, by conservative estimate, ran more than $700 million.

As the tangled web of holding and operating companies began to be unraveled, Owen D. Young, who represented the New York interests, admitted that he could not fathom the corporate maze, and it was likely that Insull did not fully understand it either. Under criminal indictment, Insull fled the country, but he was brought back from Turkey to face his accusers. Not only was he acquitted, but the proceedings brought out facts that should have helped raise him in the public esteem. As power output had increased and as costs had been brought down, he had followed a consistent policy of lowering rates. He had long advocated that corporations be held accountable to the public. And while his own financial empire had collapsed, he had run his operating companies well, and not one of them had failed in the debacle. In his own defense, Insull might have used the words of Supreme Court Justice Louis Brandeis: "There is no such thing to my mind . . . as an innocent stockholder."

Insull was far from alone in creating public utility holding companies, and his downfall did not mark their end. The Federal Trade Commission reported that the sixteen largest utility groups in 1915 controlled 22.8 per cent of generating capacity; in 1925, the sixteen largest interests controlled 53 per cent of the total. Even as late as 1936, the dozen largest groups controlled 49.7 per cent of power generating capacity, and one holding company alone, Electric Bond & Share, controlled 11.5 per cent.

Combination fever spread even to banking in the 1920's, in the form of mergers and chains as well as holding companies. Although the volume of business being done kept increasing, the total number of banks kept diminishing, dropping from 31,000 in 1921 to 22,000 ten years later.

Three New York banks got to the $2 billion area in resources when the Guaranty Trust Company took over the Bank of Commerce, the National City merged with

Samuel Insull leaves a Chicago jail after his acquittal, 1934.

the Farmers' Loan & Trust Company, and the Chase National Bank became the biggest of all by joining forces with the Equitable Trust Company. Two holding companies, the Guardian Detroit Union Group, Inc. and the Detroit Bankers Company, took over most of Detroit's larger banks. Banking chains formed across the country, so that by late 1929 there were 273 such groups, with 18 per cent of the nation's banking resources.

The biggest of the chain bankers was California's Amadeo Peter Giannini, the son of an Italian immigrant. At the age of twelve Giannini was getting up around 2 A.M. to work in his stepfather's produce firm until it was time to go to school. He became a partner in the firm at nineteen and was well enough off to retire at thirty-one, when he started to dabble in real estate and became a director of a bank. In 1904 he headed a group that scraped up $150,000 in capital, in part through door-to-door solicitation, to start business in a remodeled tavern as the Bank of Italy, primarily to serve small businesses and working men in San Francisco's Italian district.

Giannini began opening other branches in California, and by 1918 had a chain of twenty-four banks from Santa Rosa to Los Angeles, with total resources of $94 million. As the movie, oil, and real-estate businesses boomed in the state, his chain began to expand even more rapidly in the 1920's. He would sell stock in holding companies, then use the capital to buy stock in local banks until he had enough to convert them into branches of either his Bank of Italy or his main Los Angeles institution, the Bank of America. By 1929 he had 453 branch banks in California, with resources of more than $1 billion, and Transamerica Corporation, his Delaware-chartered top holding company, was operating in other states as well. His banking empire reached into New York, where he had the Bank of America, with thirty-two branches. Giannini's interests also expanded into utilities and insurance and mortgage companies.

When stock prices plunged after 1929, Transamerica fell from a 1929 peak of $67\frac{3}{8}$ to a low of $2\frac{1}{2}$ in 1932. Giannini lost his New York bank, but his basic banking organization held firm, and his Bank of America was eventually to become the world's largest. Not given to speculation himself, he once pointed out that his Bancitaly Corporation stock was priced at more than it was worth. His basic belief was in branch banking, and this was a service that apparently filled a real economic need.

RIPPLES IN THE RISING TIDE

World War I, like most major wars, produced a pent-up demand for construction, particularly housing, that fueled a rush of building activity for a decade afterward. Building in 120 cities, which probably represented something more than half of the national total, reached $919 million in 1916, and fell off to $373 million in 1919. The following year it touched a new high of $1.2 billion and kept climbing until it peaked for the decade in 1925 at $3.4 billion.

The old American penchant for land speculation took shape early in the decade. There was a flurry of buying in the neighborhood of major government power and munitions plants at Muscle Shoals, Alabama, when it was thought the government would turn these facilities over to private industry. This died down, but it was soon replaced by a much larger boom in Florida land. Long a favorite playground of the rich, Florida now seemed far more accessible to the middle class because of the automobile and rising prosperity. First the more attractive parcels were sold and resold, at constantly increasing prices. The boom then broadened from cities to unimproved land, to swampland, and even to land under water. Then, with prices totally out of line with any foreseeable real value, the bubble burst in 1926, and mortgage payments were defaulted by the hundreds. Miami bank clearings, which hit a peak of more than $1 billion in 1925, were less than a seventh of that amount by 1928.

The collapse brought hardly a ripple to the rising tide of speculation. The stock market was still a place where almost anyone could get rich. Even a small

amount of money, invested in stocks on a margin as small as 10 per cent, could multiply quickly in the bull market—which had already lasted so long that few believed there was any direction but up for stock prices to go.

During the early and middle 1920's, prices on the stock market retained a reasonable relationship to the general level of business activity and reflected the extraordinary expansion of the automobile, oil, entertainment, and electric power industries. About 1927, however, stock prices began shooting up faster than business expansion, a phenomenon that created its own momentum and kept lifting prices even more rapidly in 1928 and much of 1929.

The volume of trading on the New York Stock Exchange increased spectacularly, from 143 million shares in 1918 to 318 million in 1920, 460 million in 1925, 920 million in 1928, and 1,125 million in 1929. The Dow-Jones average of blue-chip industrial stocks rose from 100 in the fall of 1924 to 381.17 five years later, while the Dow-Jones railroad stock average climbed more modestly, from 100 in September, 1925, to a high of 189.11 four years afterward.

As word of this bonanza spread, barbers, cab drivers, hatcheck girls, and shoeshine boys caught the contagion and pursued the latest hot tips. Many Americans had first learned about investing when they bought their Liberty Loan Bonds in 1918. Others had been offered an opportunity to buy the stock of their employers, as one of the worker welfare plans. But the vast majority of Americans shied away from such investments, in part because of residual Puritanism and mainly because they simply did not know how to buy stocks.

How many actually owned stocks is difficult to say. Corporations had 18 million stockholders on their books in 1928, and 20 million in 1929. But since many owned shares in different companies, it was estimated on the basis of income tax returns that there were not over 9 million stockholders in all. Certainly the number was growing rapidly. Holders of American Telephone & Telegraph increased from 139,000 in 1920 to 567,000 in 1930, and of the Pennsylvania Railroad from 117,000 to 207,000 in the same period. Only a small proportion of these had active trading accounts. New York Stock Exchange member firms had 1.4 million accounts on their books in 1929, of which an estimated 600,000 were margin—thus speculative—accounts. The substantial growth in trading on margin was indicated by the increase in loans to brokers—funds which were in turn loaned to traders—from $2.5 billion in early 1926 to $3.5 billion in mid-1927 and then to $6.6 billion in October, 1929.

There was money to be made as the market soared; some took their profits, but most went back for more. Wright Aeronautics shot up from 69 to 289 in 1928 alone. Radio Corporation of America went from 85 that year to a high of 549 in 1929. One syndicate of insiders (including Mrs. David Sarnoff, the wife of R.C.A.'s president) turned in a trading profit of $4.9 million on Radio Corporation stock in just over a week in March, 1929.

As the stock market frenzy increased in 1928 and 1929, the little man in the market was more likely to put his money into investment trusts, which offered the supposedly expert guidance of their organizers and managers, and which mushroomed in that period. A new investment trust appeared every two days in 1928, and the rate accelerated in the early months of 1929, when some $3 billion in their securities were sold. Their sponsors ranged all the way from the reputable House of Morgan, which offered the United Corporation, to the American Founders Group, which kited a $500 initial capital into a family of trusts holding securities valued at more than $1 billion. The value of investment trust assets rose from less than $1 billion in early 1927 to $8 billion in late 1929, as some 4.5 million Americans poured their savings into the trusts.

Perhaps the outstanding stock salesman of the era was Charles E. Mitchell, who had risen from humble beginnings in Boston's unfashionable suburb of Chelsea to the presidency of the National City Bank of New York, after having headed the bank's investment affiliate, the National City Company. The investment firm had at first dealt mainly in bonds, including those of foreign governments. Later, it sold stock as well, and by 1929 it had 350 salesmen working out of fifty-eight different cities and selling, among other issues, stock of the National City Bank itself.

Some voices of warning were raised, most notably that of Herbert Hoover. While Secretary of Commerce he had cautioned against both the Florida land bubble, as early as 1925, and speculation in stocks. As loans and investments climbed, rising for Federal Reserve member banks from $24 billion in 1922 to $35.5 billion in 1929, Hoover warned the Federal Reserve against creating excessive credit, but his protestations went unheeded by officials and unheard by the public.

Money flowed readily, and Wall Street was the sea into which it settled. Commercial banks used fewer dollars for short-term business loans, their traditional and most prudent investments, and put more into the long-term financing of securities and real estate. As the yield on call loans to brokers grew higher and more attractive, funds drained from all over the country to the big capital reservoirs in New York. The Federal Reserve finally tried to close off the flow early in 1929 by ordering member banks to stop lending for speculative purposes. But the banks, perhaps using their own definitions of what constituted speculation, continued to lubricate the market with money, as did the wealthier corporations. Indeed, corporate treasurers

were eager to get interest that climbed to 12 per cent or more for their temporarily unneeded funds, and for a time in 1929 they supplied to the call loan market as much as, or more than, the banks — $49 million by Cities Service Company, $69 million by Standard Oil of New Jersey, and $100 million by Electric Bond & Share and its subsidiaries.

There were plenty of soft spots in the boom, and the softest one of all may have been in agriculture. The farmer who sold the same amount of produce in 1921 as he had sold in the years before the war could buy only three fourths as much with his proceeds. This situation improved somewhat as farm prices recovered over the next few years, but at no time during the 1920's was the prewar price parity achieved between the things the farmer bought and those he sold.

Many a farmer watched his capital dwindle away. The total value of agricultural land dropped from $79 billion in 1920 to $58 billion in 1927, a period during which farm mortgage debt increased by nearly $2 billion. The bankruptcy rate rose from 21 per 100,000 farms in 1920 to 120 in the 1924–26 period. Things were not quite as bad as some of the statistics made them sound. The prewar parity base period, for one thing, had been one of the most prosperous in the history of American agriculture. Now farm efficiency was growing rapidly. The Farm-all tractor, which could be used not only to pull, but to push, haul, sow, cultivate, and harvest, came into use by the hundreds of thousands. It sent many farm workers to the cities, so that the remaining income was divided among fewer people. The chief sufferers were the marginal farm operators, who were forced to abandon farming; an estimated 13 million acres of farm land went back to woodland and brush between 1919 and 1924.

Closely related to the plight of the farmer was a steady stream of bank failures during the 1920's — mostly among small town banks. Banks failed at the rate of one a day in 1922, and almost two a day over the next seven years. The collapse of land booms in Florida and elsewhere contributed to the high-water mark of 976 bank failures in 1926, more than 3 per cent of the total number of banks in the nation.

Unemployment was small but chronic during the decade. It dropped from the relatively high postwar recession levels to as low as 1.5 million in 1926, then climbed back to around 1.8 million in 1929. Much of the unemployment was technological, as the labor required per unit of output dropped 38 per cent between 1920 and 1929. Fewer than this proportion were let go, of course, since higher production took up much of the slack, and the displaced workers, along with additions to the labor force, found new and growing opportunities in service industries and trade. What aggravated the overall problem was that the unemployed were left to shift largely for themselves. The United States, with

Have you placed a Sentimental Value on your Horses out of proportion to the work they are able to perform?

BAILOR MOTOR CULTIVATORS

This 1920 ad reflects the move toward farm mechanization, a trend accompanied by the shift of "excess" farmers to the cities.

its traditions of self-reliance and mutual help, was slowest among the industrial nations in providing any measure of security against such hazards as unemployment or superannuation.

Even in the more prosperous industries, larger proportions of the total income went to profits, and a smaller percentage went toward wages and salaries. Industrial wages remained at a virtual standstill after 1922. As a result, increasing quantities of goods were bought on credit, with at least some of these purchases relying on unrealized paper profits from stock market speculation. The invisible problems did not provide much fodder for Alfred E. Smith in his unsuccessful campaign for the Presidency in 1928.

THE MARKET CRASH

The election of Herbert Hoover set off a "victory boom" in the stock market. Stocks rose sharply the day after the election on a near record volume of 4.9 million shares. Scarcely a week later there was another good rise, as a turnover of 6.6 million shares shattered all records, and this was followed in a few days with a 6.5-million-share day.

In the following month the market suffered a bad break, but then stock prices steadied and had a strong recovery, often on heavy volume, in the first month of 1929. Loans to brokers increased by $260 million, and the *Commercial and Financial Chronicle* declared that there was "a public duty for anyone in authority . . . to speak in unsparing terms in denunciation of what is going on." The Federal Reserve banks had raised the discount rate three times in 1928, and in February the board pressured member banks to stop speculative loans, but hardly "in unsparing terms."

In March the Federal Reserve Board began meeting daily but issued no orders and made no statements about its deliberations. The silence made traders uneasy. Following a Saturday meeting of the board, the market had a bad sell-off on Monday. The rate on call loans, which had risen to 12 per cent at the close of 1928, now went up to 14 per cent, as some banks grew more cautious about lending. On the following day, March 26, there was an even sharper break, some stocks losing 30 points or more, as 8.2 million shares changed hands. Call money went up to 20 per cent.

There was still no word from the Federal Reserve Board, but the National City's Charles Mitchell was heard from. His bank would loan money to halt the liquidation of stocks, he announced, and would borrow from the Federal Reserve Bank of New York (of which Mitchell was a director) to do so. The market rallied after this announcement, and money rates dropped. On March 27 the National City said it would make $25 million available for call loans, $5 million when the rate got up to 16 per cent, and another $5 million for each additional point it rose up to 20 per cent. No word of objection came from the Federal Reserve Board.

The great upward march of stocks got under way. Prices kept climbing. From June through August, usually a period of light volume but of higher prices, stocks increased in value by about a third, a sharper rise than they had had for the entire year of 1928.

Stock traders came back from their Labor Day holiday in an ebullient mood and sent the market still higher on a turnover of 4.4 million shares. The Federal Reserve discount rate had gone up to 6 per cent during the summer, and call money had settled down to a rate of around 9 per cent. But such key business indicators as steel output and industrial production had been on the downgrade since June. And there were many who thought the market too high, and said so publicly. Among them were the financier Paul Warburg, Alexander Dana Noyes of *The New York Times*, and Colonel Leonard P. Ayres, economist for the Cleveland Trust Company, who predicted a "creeping bear market." Roger W. Babson, whose investment counseling service was widely followed, said in a September 5 talk that a crash was en route that would probably

bring the Dow-Jones averages down 60 points or more, and that this would be followed by "a serious business depression."

The market had a sharp setback that day, in what came to be known as the Babson Break. The market turned up the next two days, then became irregular for a month or more. In Britain the disclosure of a stock promotion fraud occasioned a sharp break on the London Stock Exchange, and the Bank of England raised its rediscount rate to 6.5 per cent. There was a sympathetic reaction on the New York market, and funds moved toward England.

Starting around mid-October, the New York stock market turned very weak, on increasing volume. More than 6 million shares were traded on October 23, including 2.6 million in the final hour, with many blue chips losing 15 to 25 points and speculative issues even more. The ticker ran 104 minutes late.

On the following day, Thursday, October 24, trading grew hysterical. After the previous day's break, brokers had begun to call on some of their accounts for more margin. When this was not forthcoming, the accounts were sold out. This added to the general air of panic, and tickers fell so far behind that almost no one knew the current price of any issue. Wild rumors swept the financial district, of suicides, of stocks falling to zero. Trading for the day totaled 12.9 million shares.

But Black Thursday turned out to be not all that somber. Possibly mindful of the Morgan rescue pool in the 1907 panic, Morgan partner Thomas Lamont called a noon meeting of the Street's leading bankers—the

Humor in the midst of national despair: the market crash as reported by Variety, *the bible of U.S. show business*

STAGE   BROADWAY   SCREEN

VARIETY

PRICE 25¢.

Published Weekly at 154 West 46th St., New York, N. Y., by Variety, Inc. Annual subscription, $10. Single copies, 25 cents. Entered as second-class matter December 22, 1905, at the Post Office at New York, N. Y., under the act of March 3, 1879.

VOL. XCVII. No. 3   NEW YORK, WEDNESDAY, OCTOBER 30, 1929   88 PAGES

WALL ST. LAYS AN EGG

Going Dumb Is Deadly to Hostess In Her Serious Dance Hall Profesh

DROP IN STOCKS ROPES SHOWMEN

Kidding Kissers in Talkers Burns Up Fans of Screen's Best Lovers

A hostess at Roseland has her problems. The paid steppers consider their work a definite profession calling for specialized technique and high-power salesmanship.

"You see, you gotta sell your personality," said one. "Each one of we girls has our own clientele to cater to. It's just like selling dresses in a store—you have to know what

Hunk on Winchell

When the Walter Winchells moved into 204 West 55th street, late last week, June, that's Mrs. Winchell, selected a special room as Walter's exclusive sleep den for his late hour nights. She shushed the

Many Weep and Call Off Christmas Orders — Legit Shows Hit

MERGERS HALTED

Talker Crashes Olympus

Paris, Oct. 29.
Fox "Follies" and the Fox Movietone newsreel are running this week in Athens, Greece, the first sound pictures heard in the birthplace of world culture, and in all

Boys who used to whistle and girls who used to giggle when love scenes were flashed on the screen are in action again. A couple of years ago they began to take the love stuff seriously and desisted, but the talkers are reviving the ha ha for film osculators.

Heavy loving lovers of silent picture days accustomed to charming audiences into spasms of silent

National City's Mitchell, the Guaranty Trust's William C. Potter, the Chase National's Albert H. Wiggin, and Seward Prosser of the Bankers Trust. Along with the First National's George F. Baker, they raised a pool on the order of $200 million to shore up the market. As word of the meeting got out, prices began to rally. Then at 1:30 Richard Whitney, acting president of the Exchange and a Morgan floor trader, strode over to the trading post for U.S. Steel and put in an order for 10,000 shares at 205, the price of the previous sale. Then he went on, placing orders for some twenty bellwether stocks. The market came back, Steel closing at 206, up two points for the day.

Stock prices held their own the next day, then fell off on Saturday. On Monday there was a severe break, on volume of 9.3 million shares. Then came Black Tuesday, October 29, when a record 16.4 million shares were traded, although a closing rally kept losses below those of the previous day. U.S. Steel closed at 174. The governors of the Exchange, meeting secretly that day, decided against closing down the Big Board but agreed to put the Exchange on shorter hours as soon as the market showed signs of getting stronger. When stocks rose the following day, they announced a short session on Thursday, and a closing on Friday and Saturday.

There was another recovery during the short day's trading, but the downslide resumed the following Monday and continued through November 13, by which time paper losses amounted to $30 billion. Many could not believe or fathom the extent of the disaster. Assistant Secretary of Commerce Julius Klein announced that the market collapse had affected only 4 per cent of the people; the *Saturday Evening Post* proclaimed that "Main Street is buying goods"; and New York's mayor, Jimmy Walker, called on movies to show only cheerful pictures.

Not everyone was caught in the collapse. For years afterward there would be stories of those who had got out just in time, either miraculously or with rare insight. Bernard Baruch began liquidating stocks and buying bonds and gold as early as 1928, and was advising others to do the same. Joseph P. Kennedy, whose son was to be elected President of the United States in 1960, reportedly sold out his extensive holdings when his shoeshine boy began to advise him about the market.

Stocks recovered smartly in the early months of 1930, when U.S. Steel again climbed toward 200, but the market suffered another sharp drop in June. After that there was a dismal and nearly uninterrupted slide until the middle of 1932. U.S. Steel could be bought for 22, American Telephone for 72, General Motors for less than 8, Radio Corporation for 2½, and Montgomery Ward for 4. The Dow-Jones industrial stock average had slumped to 62.7 by the start of 1933, while the rail average was down to 28.1. At the bottom in July, 1933, stocks had dropped more than 80 per cent, and about $74 billion in values had been wiped out.

WHY?

Looking back, Herbert Hoover said: "When we fully understand the economic history of the twenties, we shall find that the debacle which terminated another apparently high prosperous period was largely . . . a failure of industry to pass its improvement . . . on to the consumer."

That was certainly part of the answer. In a larger view it would appear that, in a time of rapid and major change, the economic tools of one era were inadequate to deal with the problems of the next. The postwar period was such a time of change in the United States and, indeed, in much of the world.

Industrialization was closing in on people, narrowing the areas of individual choice. The frontiers had long been closed. Centuries of population increase had wiped out the gains of discovery, so that in the Western world there was now less land per person than there had been in the Europe of 1500. Mechanization of agriculture in the United States was making the small farm an anachronism. More and more people in the swelling cities had to rely on the jobs they could find in the production and the service industries.

Overall, the 1920's were undoubtedly, if unevenly, prosperous. From 1923 through 1929, population increased 9 per cent, while individual income grew by 21 per cent, with virtually no change in the cost of living. While manufacturing output increased at the rate of 4.5 per cent a year, employment increased at the rate of only 1 per cent and the average earnings of workers in manufacturing industries went up only 1.6 per cent a year. Obviously, these workers could not buy all they were producing, since most of the larger income went into corporate profits, growing at the rate of 7.3 per cent a year. A substantial part of these profits found its way into new plants and equipment, and thus into still more production of goods that the workers could not afford to buy.

In a subsistence economy such an imbalance would have led to starvation, homelessness, and exposure to the elements. But the United States was far from a subsistence economy, although a great many people were not far above that level. A 1929 study by the Brookings Institution showed that 2.4 per cent of the American population were wealthy or well-to-do, with family incomes of more than $10,000 or individual incomes of more than $5,000 a year; another 19.6 per cent were comfortable, with family incomes of over $3,000 and individual incomes above $1,500; of the remaining 78 per cent, more than half could be considered impoverished, with family incomes of less than

$1,500 a year or individual incomes of less than $750.

Thus, almost four fifths of all Americans could be considered as having little or no discretionary income, at a time when the great wave of prosperity relied chiefly on discretionary purchases of such consumer durables as autos, housing, and home appliances and furnishings. While the consumption of food and other necessities, as well as services, increased notably during the decade, the boom was essentially built on sales of durable goods. Their production grew almost 65 per cent between 1922 and 1929, while nondurables expanded less than 40 per cent.

When consumers did not have the cash to buy all the cars, refrigerators, and other products being produced, credit purchases helped take up the slack. Installment selling was the legitimate child of an era of rising expectations, and this relatively new marketing technique caught on quickly among both buyers and sellers. From little better than a standing start at the end of World War I, sales on installments rose to an estimated $7 billion by 1929, creating a very significant addition to current purchasing power.

But even the magic of credit needs a sounder basis than simple hope. With the housing shortage ended, home building turned down after 1926. Automobile sales fell 22 per cent in 1927. Well before the stock market break, softness had been noted in sales of appliances and auto accessories. As unsold goods began to pile up, there was increasing talk about overproduction. But the real problem was underconsumption—or at least improper income distribution for making a mass consumption society work.

It is true that the corporations were responsible for the creation of a large part of the wealth they were gathering in. But the economic system was not geared to large accumulations of capital by the producers. For one thing, it betokened inadequate price competition and, as Hoover had noted, prices had remained too high. For another, it undermined the principle by which the Federal Reserve System was supposed to match

The Way to Wealth
JOSEPH P. KENNEDY

In 1908 the editors of the yearbook at Boston Latin School predicted that Joseph Patrick Kennedy (1888–1969) would make his fortune "in a very roundabout way." By the 1960's Kennedy's fortune was close to $500 million, his sons had become enshrined in American history, and he had indeed gained wealth in a roundabout fashion.

The son of a Boston politician, Kennedy was twenty when he graduated from high school. He went on to Harvard and then, with some string-pulling in his behalf, got a job as a state bank examiner, where he learned the fundamentals of finance. When the Columbia Trust Company, a small bank in which his father had an interest, was threatened by a take-over, young Kennedy was enlisted in the fight. By wheeling and dealing, he managed to save the bank and at twenty-five was elected to its presidency.

In 1914 he married the daughter of Boston's colorful mayor, John F. ("Honey Fitz") Fitzgerald. Then, using various sources of influence, he succeeded in getting himself named a trustee of the Massachusetts Electric Company. Asked why he wanted to join the utility's board, he replied: "Do you know a better way to meet people like the Saltonstalls?"

World War I was imminent when Kennedy was hired by Charles M. Schwab to help manage Bethlehem Steel Company's Fore River shipyard at Quincy, Massachusetts. At the end of the war he tried to get shipbuilding orders from Wall Street broker Galen Stone, who was also the chairman of a shipping company. Instead, Stone hired him to manage the Boston office of his firm, Hayden, Stone & Co. The salary, $10,000, was half of what Bethlehem had paid him, but Kennedy sensed he had moved to a field with a bigger potential.

And so it turned out. He rapidly picked up the workings of stock pools. Their principle was simple: a group of insiders traded an idle issue back and forth, using the ticker-tape record of their transactions as an advertising medium to lure outsiders, whose purchases pushed the price up. The pool members would sell near the peak, and even sell short as the stock slid back to its real market value. Another broker said Kennedy was the perfect speculator because he had "a passion for facts, a complete lack of sentiment, and a marvelous sense of timing."

Intrigued by the motion picture industry, Kennedy piloted a venture that bought up a chain of movie houses, and in 1927 he sold to the Radio Corporation of America, which wanted outlets for its talking picture equipment, an interest in the theaters for $500,000. Kennedy reportedly consummated the deal with David Sarnoff while the two men consumed shellfish in an oyster bar. The theater company, known as the Film Booking Office, then bought 200,000 shares in the Keith-Albee Vaudeville Circuit for $4.2 million.

In 1928 Kennedy merged all his entertainment interests to create Radio-Keith-Orpheum. R.C.A. swapped its Film Booking Office stock for 20 per cent of R.K.O., gaining 200 more theaters for its Photophone equipment, and Kennedy sold out all of his stock for more than $5 million. Independently he had made two films—one a $950,000 flop, and the other a moneymaker starring his protégée, Gloria Swanson. But his fling with Hollywood was over.

So, too, were his speculations in the stock market. In 1928 he started selling off his shares. "Only a fool holds out for the top dollar," he said, demonstrating again his remarkable sense of timing. As the repeal of Prohibition approached, he was right once more. Going to London, he secured the Ameri-

the flow of money and credit to the pace of business activity. The machinery called for this to be done through loosening or tightening the supply of short-term funds for business activities. But as business piled up so much surplus cash that much of it was kept in interest-bearing deposits, the banks had to look elsewhere to invest their funds. Between 1921 and 1929 member banks of the Federal Reserve System doubled their loans on securities and more than tripled those on city real estate, while the amount of short-term commercial loans was almost unchanged. With business virtually independent of the banks, there was not much the Federal Reserve could do to exercise control. Raising the discount rate or selling government securities had little effect; there was just too much investment money around.

Whatever the causes of the 1929 debacle were, cures proved even harder to find. Businessmen who had appeared able to supply all the answers during most of the 1920's were as much at a loss as anyone.

Wrote Utah businessman Marriner Eccles, who was later to become chairman of the Federal Reserve Board: "Night after night . . . I would return home exhausted by the pretensions of knowledge I was forced to wear in a daytime masquerade." No longer heroes, some business leaders—Mitchell, Insull, the Van Sweringens—were being marked as the villains of the day.

If businessmen were at a loss, government leaders were not much better. But the imperative for action fell on them. Hoover summoned industrialists, bankers, and labor leaders to the White House for a series of meetings. He called on them to carry on business as usual, to keep employment and wages up, and to continue construction programs or start new ones. Publicly he made cheerful statements, but privately he told one group of top business leaders that he expected a major economic depression.

He called on the elements of the Federal Reserve to lower the discount rate and to buy government bonds

UPI

can agency for Haig & Haig, Ltd., John Dewar & Sons, Ltd., and Gordon's Dry Gin Co., Ltd. When he sold his Somerset Importers operation in 1946, he received $8 million for his original investment of $100,000.

The Irish in Kennedy could not resist politics. He plumped soundly for Franklin D. Roosevelt, and in 1934 was named chairman of the Securities and Exchange Commission, the new federal regulator of Wall Street's activities. After a year and a half in the job, he resigned to become a consultant to corporations. His first client was R.C.A., whose different classes of stock were the object of disputes between shareholders. Kennedy reorganized the outstanding issues, then repeated his magic with the issues of Paramount Pictures and the Hearst newspapers. Sarnoff paid him a fee of $150,000 for his efforts at R.C.A.; Paramount's payment was $50,000; and Hearst paid him $10,000 a week.

Kennedy still longed for something else. His eye was again on a government appointment, and he told friends that he deserved something for the $600,000 a year he paid in taxes. In 1937 he was given the job of running the U.S. Maritime Commission. But the reward he really sought came in the form of the ambassadorship to the Court of St. James's. His tenure in London ended

Ambassador Joseph P. Kennedy in 1940

badly, for he urged an accommodation with the Nazis—mainly because he hoped that war could be avoided.

In December, 1941, he returned to the United States and entered real estate in New York, making more millions. But his biggest deal was for Chicago's Merchandise Mart, the world's largest commercial building. Constructed in 1930 by Marshall Field, the twenty-four-story structure had ninety-three acres of rentable floor space. In 1945 Marshall Field carried it on their books as worth more than $21 million, but the firm needed cash and sold it to Kennedy for just $12,956,516. Of that amount, Equitable Life Assurance Society put up a $12.5 million mortgage loan. In 1949 Kennedy wrote a new mortgage with the Prudential Insurance Company of America for $17 million, increasing his equity by $4 million. By 1963 the Mart's value was $75 million, and it generated an annual rental revenue of $13 million, more than the original purchase price.

In his waning years, beset by illness and eventually a stroke, Kennedy moved his fortune into tax-exempt securities and an oil venture that enjoyed depletion allowances. It formed the sizable financial base that helped to back three of his sons in their successful rise to the U.S. Senate and to presidential potential.

and commercial paper, which they promptly did. He asked Congress to reduce income taxes, and he urged governors and mayors to expand their public works programs. Few promised anything concrete. In New York, Franklin Roosevelt replied that he was asking for a construction program "limited only by estimated receipts from revenues without increasing taxes."

Perhaps the most ill-considered move was a new and higher tariff. Tariff revision had been in the congressional hopper through much of 1929. Finally, in June, 1930, the Smoot-Hawley Tariff Act was passed. Though there had been no special demand for a highly protective tariff, either within or outside his party, Hoover signed it, against the advice of hundreds of economists.

None of the emergency measures seemed to be producing the desired results, and after the middle of 1930 Hoover appeared to have decided to let matters work themselves out. Throughout his government career Hoover had demonstrated that he was not one to let deficiencies go uncorrected if he could find ways to remedy them, and he had made notable contributions in such areas as traffic safety, government organization, and greater co-operation between industry and labor. But now he felt that the disease went to the very heart of the system, and that the system itself would have to throw it off.

Two of Hoover's last two emergency moves were probably the most significant of any he made. As Europe's credit structure was threatened in the backwash of America's economic problems, he proposed in 1931 a year's moratorium on all government war debt and reparations payments. The affected nations accepted the proposal, and Congress added its stamp of approval. But well-conceived though the action was, it came too late to head off the looming troubles. A crisis in Austria, resulting from the problems of its most powerful bank, the Credit Anstalt, was communicated to Germany, where private bankers asked for a moratorium on their short-term debts as well. Next came a British crisis, and England left the gold standard in September. Foreign bonds fell on the New York market, and other bonds moved down in sympathy.

These liquidation pressures cut sharply into the amount of money in circulation in the United States, and banks began to feel the pinch, with 305 suspended in September, and 522 in October. Then Hoover made his second good move. He called a meeting of financiers in Washington to set up a special lending agency to be known as the Reconstruction Finance Corporation.

The R.F.C. became a reality in February, 1932, with an initial capital of $500 million subscribed by the government. Charles Dawes was made its chief. The capitalization was increased to $2 billion before long. Although relief and public works were included in its charter, it operated primarily as a reservoir of capital for distressed financial institutions and agricultural credit agencies.

Eventually the R.F.C., under the energetic management of Texas banker Jesse Jones, a Roosevelt appointee, proved itself one of the most effective agencies for recovery and became something of a monument to Hoover. In making loans of more than $10 billion to help fight the Depression, it managed to turn in a substantial profit to the Treasury.

ENTER THE NEW DEAL

During his four-year term of office, Herbert Hoover presided over three and a half years of depression, including many of its dreariest days. Between 1929 and 1932 the general level of American business activity slowed to about half of what it had been. Gross national product dropped from $104 billion in 1929 to $58 billion in 1932, while national income fell from $81 billion to $41 billion, and the index of industrial production, based on the 1923–25 average as 100, tumbled from 119 to 64. There were 85,000 business failures in the three-year period, with total liabilities of $4.5 billion.

Unemployment statistics reflected the measurement of human suffering. At the nadir in 1933, an estimated 13 million people, or 25 per cent of the work force, were out of work. Some estimates were lower, some as high as 16 million. The precise figure was all but impossible to determine, because many were seeking jobs who might otherwise not have been deemed part of the labor force—wives and children of unemployed or partially employed men, and the aged whose savings had been wiped out.

Virtually everyone and every business fell victim to the vicious cycle of unsold merchandise, lower production, wage cuts and layoffs, lower purchasing power, and still more unsold goods. Machinery was left to rust in place, and residents of every city and town in industrial America looked at the silent factory chimneys and longed for the sight of rich, black smoke. Pay cuts were almost universal. Store clerks received as little as $5 or $10 a week, and servants worked for $10 a month plus room and board.

By early 1930 the unemployed, often under the goading of aroused Communists, were demonstrating in a number of cities; other unfortunates queued up in long bread lines or at soup kitchens. In autumn, 1930, a special promotion was put on by the International Apple Shippers Association, in which apples were sold to the unemployed on credit, to be retailed on the streets at five cents each until the public finally felt surfeited with apples—and five cents became too high a price. President Hoover bore the brunt of criticism; old newspapers were called "Hoover blankets" and

"Hoovervilles," tarpaper-shack shantytowns named derisively for the President, were common Depression sights in U.S. cities.

makeshift shantytowns that sprang up in and around cities became known as "Hoovervilles."

Things could hardly have got worse for the U.S. farmer, but they did. The 1930 wheat crop was slightly above average, but prices sank to $.71 a bushel for the first four months of the marketing season, against $1.09 in the previous year. Between 1929 and 1933, production of farm commodities dropped 6 per cent, while prices slid 63 per cent. The production of nonfarm goods fell much more, but their prices dropped much less.

Nature added to the problems with the worst drought on record in the 1930 growing season, followed by a milder drought the following year, and a rainless summer in 1932 that raised clouds of dust and despair over the Great Plains. Wheat and cotton output dropped sharply that year, but even this did not forestall the price slide.

But bank failures provided the major crisis of the early Depression years. During 1932 more than 1,400 banks failed, and the rate was accelerating early in 1933. The governor of Nevada had declared a bank holiday back in October, 1932. In Detroit the Union Guardian Trust Company had already received $12.5 million in help from the R.F.C., and was seeking more in early February, 1933. Henry Ford turned a deaf ear to R.F.C. requests that he leave his funds in the Detroit banks. When loan negotiations failed, Michigan Governor William A. Comstock declared an eight-day

closing for all banks in his state. President Hoover tried to prevent the closing, then decided that the problem belonged logically to President-elect Franklin D. Roosevelt, who would take office the following month. By March 3, the day before Roosevelt took office, seventeen more states had closed their banks, and Treasury Department officials in both administrations tried to persuade the remaining states to declare bank holidays. In the early morning hours of March 4, Governor Herbert H. Lehman of New York and Governor Henry Horner of Illinois issued proclamations that closed their banks.

Roosevelt took his oath of office under gray, rainy skies, then immediately called Congress into special session. On March 6 he made the bank holiday nationwide and at the same time embargoed the transportation or withdrawal of gold. Three days later Congress passed an Emergency Banking Act, giving the Secretary of the Treasury the power to call in all gold and gold certificates. In his first radio "fireside chat," on Sunday evening, March 12, the President explained that all the banks except those that were basically unsound would be permitted to reopen; this news alone inspired a wave of public confidence.

Completely sound banks were allowed to reopen and make unrestricted payments to depositors, and in a few days half the nation's banks, with 90 per cent of all bank resources, were permitted to open in this manner. A fourth of all the banks were allowed to pay out only part of their deposits. A third group were put under the charge of "conservators," and about 1,000 banks, or 5 per cent of those in the country, were simply shut down. Money began to flow back to the banks and into the economy. By the end of 1933, losses to depositors amounted to just over $1 billion.

Throughout the 1932 election campaign and in the early days of his term, Roosevelt had sensed in the mood of the people a powerful desire for change and for action. Not especially wedded to any economic theory or dogma, he was completely willing to experiment, to try out new things, and to shake off the mantle of traditional thought that had immobilized Hoover. While traditionalists and conservatives were bitterly opposed to this boat-rocking, Roosevelt was essentially not unlike the average businessman—pragmatic, willing to test ideas and procedures, and perfectly satisfied to retain what worked and to throw out what did not.

In this spirit, the New Deal entered its first phase —that of pushing recovery—and was soon simultaneously carrying out the second, that of promoting permanent reform. These actions ushered in a period in which the government was to become the nation's largest employer, chief initiator of major new projects, and most important financial manager. Government built on a grand scale and also destroyed on a scale that was probably unprecedented in peacetime, on the simplistic logic that this was the way to cure overproduction and to rectify price imbalances.

English economist John Maynard Keynes published his major work, *The General Theory of Employment, Interest and Money*, in 1936, but the New Deal had by then already begun to put some of its doctrine into practice. The government had engaged in heavy deficit spending to provide employment, to create purchasing power, and to "prime the pump" of the nation's economy. Such countercyclical efforts would have a "multiplier" effect, Keynes said, in the private sector of the economy—which could then

KEYNESIAN ECONOMICS

To traditional economists, the Depression of the 1930's was as puzzling as it was dismaying. The hard times ground on, with no signs of improvement, and the usual business cycle of decline and recovery no longer seemed to be working. According to an old axiom, as money became cheaper, business would begin to borrow again, investing in expansion and creating new jobs; gradually, the economy would move up. But this time it was not happening. By 1933 an army of 14 million American workers were unemployed, without the means to produce or purchase. In the absence of markets, businessmen failed to borrow, and the grim stalemate continued.

Because of the political necessity to relieve unemployment, the New Deal stumbled on a solution. It created work and "primed the pump" of the nation's economy with government funds. In actuality, what it did was put into practice the doctrine of a British economist, John Maynard Keynes, who soon became the guiding philosopher of the Roosevelt administration's economic policies.

As a Cambridge University don, Keynes had made a $2 million fortune

John M. Keynes, flanked by Bertrand Russell (left) and Lytton Strachey (right), 1914

of his own by skillful operations in the international currency and commodity markets. He had married a Russian ballerina, was a darling of the Bloomsbury group of poets and artists, and during World War I had purchased $100,000 worth of French paintings for London's National Gallery to help the Anglo-French balance of payments. As a commission, he had got a Cézanne for himself in the deal. He had a dry wit and a tart tongue: once, when asked about the long-run effects of an economic theory, he replied, "In the long run we are all dead."

Keynes had watched the worldwide depression and had abandoned the orthodox view that low interest rates

move on its own and eventually proceed to get into trouble again by overinvesting and overexpanding.

So while businessmen frothed and fulminated over the new powers of government, they also participated, as much as any group, in trying to help make those policies work, if not in setting their original directions. About 80 per cent of the nation's businessmen opposed the New Deal, many bitterly, according to the *Kiplinger Washington Letter* in the spring of 1935. Nevertheless, many business leaders supported Roosevelt, and others seemed at least to sense that his deepest motivation was, like theirs, to make the American business system work.

THE EARLY EMERGENCY ACTS

The famous Hundred Days that started the New Deal saw a rush of legislation that changed the nation's course in almost a dozen different ways. Congress passed measures aimed at currency inflation, abandon-

ment of the gold standard, banking reforms, regulation of security sales, establishment of the Tennessee Valley Authority, assistance to farmers in obtaining credit and making mortgage payments, creation of the Civilian Conservation Corps, reduction of farm surpluses, and the enlistment of industry in a massive effort to create new jobs.

As in every major depression, there was great pressure for inflation coming from the debtor classes, which included a large part of the population, especially the farmers. So it was not surprising that the government's new inflationary powers were embodied in the Agricultural Adjustment Act. After much pulling and hauling between an inflation-minded Congress and the conservatives in and out of government who dreaded the end of the gold standard, the administration got what it wanted: broad powers to bring about inflation through a managed currency.

By the time this law was enacted in May, 1933, the President had taken the country off the gold standard

would attract business into pouring money into expansion. He saw that as the economy dried up, income contracted and savings disappeared, squeezing large numbers of people entirely out of the money economy. That was what had happened in the United States. In 1929 Americans had saved $3.7 billion of their income. In 1932 and 1933 they saved nothing. Business corporations, which had banked $2.6 billion after taxes and dividend payments during the boom period, lost $6 billion in 1933.

In 1934 Keynes, then fifty-one years old, visited President Franklin D. Roosevelt and urged even greater government spending as the means to end the economic stagnation. Business growth, he pointed out, had put $15 billion into circulation through wages and profits in 1929, but less than $1 billion in 1932. The decline, he argued, was irreversible without meaningful government intervention.

Keynes's economics applied to good times as well as bad. If an economy could no longer recover from a severe depression without the government's "priming the pump," it was equally true, he contended, that business on its own could not maintain a boom period indefinitely. Investment in expansion would eventually lead to the saturation of the marketplace, and

economic contraction would begin again. Thus, in both prosperity and depression the government would have to take measures to counteract the normal workings of the business cycle.

Keynes's beliefs were shared and illuminated by the American social commentator Walter Lippmann. "In substance," Lippmann explained in early 1934, "the state undertakes to counteract the mass errors of the individualist crowd by doing the opposite of what the crowd is doing. It saves when the crowd is spending too much, it borrows when the crowd is saving too much; it economizes when the crowd is extravagant, and it spends when the crowd is afraid to spend. . . . it taxes when the crowd is borrowing, and borrows when the crowd is hoarding; it becomes an employer when there is private unemployment, and it shuts down when there is work for all."

In sum, government, in the Keynesian view, could no longer keep its hands off business. Its actions, though they might be misconstrued—as they often were during the deficit spending period of the New Deal—were not to stifle business, but to assist its revival. Keynes himself did not believe in a complete abandonment of laissez faire. In 1934 he wrote *The New York Times:* "I see the problem of recovery in the following light: How soon will normal business

enterprise come to the rescue? On what scale, by which expedients, and for how long is abnormal expenditure advisable in the meantime?" Nonetheless, he and his disciples had postulated the necessity for business and government to push and pull against each other.

In 1944 Keynes played a major role at the Bretton Woods Monetary and Financial Conference, which, in an attempt to stabilize international economies, set up the International Monetary Fund and the institution that became the World Bank. But he lost a battle to prevent the world's currencies from being defined in terms of the U.S. dollar and voiced the opinion that the treaty was "written in Cherokee." Keynes's objection was that the dollar was pegged to gold—a standard that he considered nothing more than a fetish—and he correctly forecast that there would not be enough gold in the world to fuel the international economic needs. He wanted to retire gold from its monetary use in exchange for a new reserve money whose name he suggested be *bancors*.

Keynes died in 1946, a knight and a director of the Bank of London. The economic principles he expounded did not die, but have continued to influence the federal government's economic policies since World War II, through good times and bad.

by administrative decree. The tests of a true gold-standard currency require that it have a fixed gold content, that there be gold coins in circulation, that paper money be convertible into gold on demand, and that the flow of gold in and out of the country be unrestricted. When gold hoarding and gold export were forbidden and member banks were required to turn in their gold and gold certificates to the Federal Reserve, the United States was effectively off the gold standard.

The stock market, sensing inflation to come, began to turn up, and trading during the early summer months of 1933 was heavier than the average for 1929. In the near certainty that Prohibition would be repealed, alcohol stocks were manipulated to unrealistically high levels. Crop prices turned up but then broke again late in the summer. In October the President announced that the Treasury would buy gold at $31.36 an ounce, compared to the legal price of $20.67 and the current world market price of just under $30. By mid-January, 1934, the price was raised to $34.64, and, under the authority of the Gold Reserve Act, later that month to $35 an ounce, which cut the dollar to 59.06 per cent of its former value.

When the official price of gold was still $20.67, the President adopted the politically popular 16:1 ratio, which made coined silver worth $1.29 an ounce. Late in 1933 he ordered the Treasury to buy all the silver mined in the United States at 64½ cents an ounce, or 21½ cents above the going price. Although silver had no real monetary significance, it had dropped from a level of $1.12 an ounce in 1919, and legislators from the silver-mining states were simply looking for a boost to their economies.

Some of the earliest New Deal reforms involved regulation of the banking and securities businesses. The Glass-Steagall Banking Act of June, 1933, required the separation of investment affiliates from banks that were members of the Federal Reserve System—a divorcement that the National City and Chase National had already hastily effected. Conversely, the act forbade investment bankers from engaging in commercial banking or even being directors of commercial banks. It also created the Federal Deposit Insurance Corporation to guarantee bank deposits up to $5,000 and thus forestall runs on banks in times of stress.

In his campaign for greater control over stock exchanges, the President enlisted the help of New York Stock Exchange member firms that were disenchanted with the leadership of Richard Whitney, who had become president of the Exchange. New federal

In 1934 violent dust storms forced thousands of families, like this one in Oklahoma, to flee the drought-stricken Dust Bowl.

296

powers were embodied in the National Securities and Exchange Act of 1934, which added to the disclosures that publicly held corporations were required to make and created a Securities and Exchange Commission to administer both acts. Named as its first chairman was the seasoned Wall Street operator Joseph P. Kennedy. The need for such government controls was subsequently underscored by revelations of extremely questionable practices by the National City's Mitchell and the Chase National's Wiggin, as well as the arrest and imprisonment of Whitney for embezzlement.

The farmer's share of the New Deal pie came in the Agricultural Adjustment Act, whose purpose was to give the farmer greater purchasing power through crop restrictions, marketing agreements, and crop loans. Possibly the most badly conceived aspect of the agricultural program was the wanton destruction of foodstuffs in the midst of widespread hunger through the land. To keep production down, fruit was permitted to rot in the orchards; many crops were turned under by plows; and because of the large surplus of both hogs and feed corn, more than 6 million swine were slaughtered, with most of the pork becoming fertilizer and less than 10 per cent distributed as food for the needy. The fertilizer, in turn, could only serve to make for higher farm production.

Much of the surplus problem was taken care of when the worst drought in seventy-five years cut across the great heartland of the nation in 1934, reducing crops by as much as a third. Another, lesser drought followed in 1936. By that time, however, the Supreme Court had ruled in the Hoosac Mills case that the production controls in the Agricultural Adjustment Act constituted an illegal invasion of the rights of the states, although the loan and marketing features of the law were held valid.

When 1937 crops turned out to be the largest in a number of years, including an all-time record cotton production, the Department of Agriculture concluded that "in years of normal weather the farmers can produce more than the market can be depended on to take at reasonable prices." Secretary of Agriculture Henry A. Wallace pushed his plan for an "ever-normal granary," which involved crop storage in good years and an effort to provide a relatively even flow of exports. Appropriate legislation was passed late in 1937.

Farm mechanization proceeded almost without pause. The number of tractors approximately doubled, to 1.6 million, between 1930 and 1939. Texas engineers John and Mack Rust invented an automatic cotton picker in 1927, but its superiority was not conclusively demonstrated until 1936, when it was shown that it could pick about 100 times as fast as a field hand. Other machines were developed for mowing and chopping hay, so that it could be stored for winter feed in less space. But the most solid technological advance

A cartoonist's view of the New Deal's many alphabet agencies

was in rural electrification, as the number of farms supplied with electrical power grew from around 100,000 in 1919 to 2 million, or 29 per cent of all farm homes, in 1940.

The agency that was as responsible as any for this development was the Tennessee Valley Authority, created by an act passed in May, 1933. For many years public and private power advocates had engaged in a running controversy centering on Muscle Shoals, a fast-dropping section of the Tennessee River in northwestern Alabama. During the war, Congress had appropriated money for the Wilson Dam, which was to supply power for one of two nitrate plants in the area. The dam, which cost $145 million, was not completed until 1925, when the power it produced was sold to private companies for distribution. But Nebraska Senator George Norris successfully fought off all efforts to sell the power plant to private interests and was able instead to push through measures to have the government sell power directly to rural communities. His bills were twice vetoed, by Coolidge in 1928 and then by Hoover in 1931, and the matter rested at a stalemate.

But then the New Deal formed the T.V.A., consisting of a board of three members with broad powers to operate the Muscle Shoals properties, to develop the Tennessee River with flood control, improved navigation, new dams, and hydroelectric plants, and to engage in the production and sale of explosives, fertilizer, and electric power. As perhaps the most uniformly successful New Deal undertaking, the T.V.A. accomplished all its objectives. Power output increased slowly while dams were being constructed and generating plants built, but then it increased spectacularly, with power revenues rising from about $800,000 in 1934 to more than $20 million in 1941. A substantial part of the sales were made to private utility companies, especially in the earlier years, and Wendell Willkie, as president of the Commonwealth and Southern Power Company, attracted the attention of other business leaders when he managed to arrange a particularly favorable deal with the T.V.A.

Resentful as the power companies were over these developments, they were even more bitterly opposed to the passage of the Public Utilities Holding Company Act in 1935. President Roosevelt had demanded this legislation, and both houses of Congress had launched investigations into the industry. The act as passed forbade extreme pyramiding of holding companies and gave the S.E.C. jurisdiction over the acquisition of new properties and the issuance of securities. In a provision that some called the "death sentence" to public utility holding companies, it required that all such companies trim down to single integrated systems within three years. The death sentence appears to have been commuted. By 1937 the gross revenues of the utility industry were the highest in its history.

MAKING JOBS

Late in March, 1933, the President asked Congress to pass three measures designed to alleviate human distress. The first would provide employment to a corps of young men who would be paid subsistence wages to work in national forests and in various conservation projects. The second was to provide grants to the states for giving direct relief. And the third would seek to mobilize labor and industry in putting more of the unemployed back to work.

The Civilian Conservation Corps was created quickly; it put 300,000 to work in the first year and remained a fixture of the New Deal until 1942, when able young men were more urgently needed in the armed services. The second request was met with the creation in May of the Federal Emergency Relief Administration, which was designed to distribute $500 million in relief to the states through the Reconstruction Finance Corporation. The third was filled in June, when the National Industrial Recovery Act was passed.

The N.I.R.A. appropriated $3.3 billion to finance public works through a newly formed Public Works Administration, designed to make a frontal attack on some of the more obvious symptoms of the Depression —unemployment and closed factories. Using a co-operative approach, the National Recovery Administration (N.R.A.) sought to bring together labor, capital, and government under the N.I.R.A. in a concerted and determined effort to achieve economic recovery.

To labor, the act promised a guarantee of collective bargaining rights, minimum wages, maximum hours, and a ban on child labor. To employers, it promised virtual cartelization of industries, with limitation of production, higher prices, and exemption from antitrust laws. Government, of course, would reap the general benefits of increased industrial activity, including larger tax collections and lower costs of providing for the needy, as well as good marks from the electorate.

Named administrator of the N.R.A. was bluff, craggy-featured General Hugh S. Johnson, who had been an executive of the Moline Plow Company of Moline, Illinois. His staff drafted industry codes for fair competition, invited industry and labor to public hearings, and submitted revised codes for the President's signature. Codes were drawn for the ten largest industries by September. To assure the co-operation of employers there was a steady drumbeat of publicity designed to create public pressure to sign the codes. The N.R.A.'s Blue Eagle, derived from the American Indian thunderbird symbol, began to appear in public prints and on store windows, and was emblazoned on every kind of package, including the costumes of Broadway chorus girls.

From June to October, employment rose by 2.5 million, or 6.8 per cent, mostly in industries covered by the N.R.A. The average number of hours worked dropped 12.7 per cent in the same period. But gradually the disparate aims of industry and labor began to make themselves felt, violations of the act became more and more common, and the administrative machinery for enforcing compliance became clogged. Finally, in 1935, the Supreme Court found in the Schechter case that the act called for an unconstitutional delegation of legislative authority to the administrative branch, and that in any event it could not apply to companies not in interstate commerce. Almost at once, unemployment increased, wages were cut, and working hours lengthened. But like a phoenix rising from the ashes, the concepts of the N.I.R.A. were to return in other, more enforceable legislation.

Harry L. Hopkins, a New York social worker, was named to head the Federal Emergency Relief Administration, and he set out to distribute the funds to the poor as rapidly as he could. But in the moral climate of the times a stigma was still attached to direct public relief, and some of the needy simply would not apply for nor accept the surplus commodities that were available. To get around this difficulty, the Civil Works Administration was created in November, 1933, and during the following eight months jobs were given to 4.3 million people who worked on 180,000 different projects. A minimum of the $950 million spent was for materials and most of the money went into wages, which averaged almost $15 a week.

Still larger appropriations for public works were made by Congress early in 1935, when the President

In late 1936, during one of the nation's first sit-down strikes, union leaders head a parade of Detroit G.M. workers.

created the Works Progress Administration—later to be known as the Works Projects Administration, also under Harry Hopkins. This program continued into 1942, spending a total of more than $13 billion, including $2.7 billion contributed by local sponsors, and giving jobs to 3.8 million, or about a third of the unemployed.

Until the Social Security Act was passed in 1935, such matters as unemployment insurance and old age pensions had been left to the states, which were slow to adopt these measures and penurious in their grants. The new law created a contributory plan for old-age insurance that was to be progressively widened in its application, and it also encouraged the states to develop systems of unemployment insurance.

Although the Supreme Court had cut the heart out of the National Industrial Recovery Act, its labor provisions remained intact. Congress fortified these further in 1935 with Senator Robert Wagner's National Labor Relations Act, which guaranteed the right of collective bargaining and forbade certain acts by employers that might be construed as intimidation of union members.

But labor still had to organize on its own. This they did with an enthusiasm that contrasted sharply with their lethargy of the 1920's. The seeds were laid in the early Depression years, when the number of workers involved in strikes rose from 158,000 in 1930 to 812,000 in 1933. Union membership then grew from 3 million in 1933 to 3.9 million in 1935.

Still, labor had its growing pains. The A.F.L. departed reluctantly from its basic craft unionism when it issued charters to some "federal unions" in shops that could be organized more effectively by industry than by craft. The 1934 convention of the A.F.L. voted overwhelmingly to step up the organization of industrial unions in the steel, automobile, aluminum, oil, radio, and rubber industries, but the union's executive committee dragged its feet. There was a heated showdown between opposing factions at the 1935 convention. Three weeks later John L. Lewis of the United Mine Workers led a group of eight industrial unions in the formation of a Committee for Industrial Organization. President William Green warned that "dual unionism" would split and weaken labor. The executive council ordered the new committee to dissolve; when it refused, all the C.I.O. unions were suspended from the A.F.L. early in 1937.

The C.I.O., which had already appropriated $500,000 for an organizing campaign among the steelworkers, changed its name to the Congress of Industrial Organizations and set to work in earnest to organize steel. But the autoworkers, under the militant leadership of an ex-preacher, Homer Martin, beat steel to the punch. At the end of 1936, members of the

299

Lindbergh refueling before his transatlantic flight, 1927

United Automobile Workers occupied the Flint, Michigan, plant of General Motors' Fisher Body Company in the nation's first major "sit-down" strike. Similar strikes spread through other plants, and within weeks G.M. recognized the new union and signed a contract.

Less than a month after the union victory at G.M., U.S. Steel's biggest subsidiary, the Carnegie-Illinois Steel Company, surprised almost everyone by settling with the steelworkers without a strike. Most other steel companies fell right into line, but four important companies—Bethlehem Steel, Youngstown Sheet and Tube, Republic Steel, and Inland Steel, collectively known as "Little Steel"—successfully resisted unionization until 1941.

INDUSTRY MOVES AHEAD

While the major initiatives of the 1930's were those of the government, and although business remained largely on the defensive, there were plenty of bold forward moves by industry. The increasing use of electrical power kept the utilities industry growing.

The end of Prohibition meant that Canadian companies like Samuel Bronfman's Distillers Corporation-Seagrams Limited could expand into the United States. Massive construction projects helped the rapid growth of such builders as Morrison-Knudsen Company, Inc., which started with a capital of $600 in 1912 and by the 1930's was sending its bulldozers to help build the Bonneville, Grand Coulee, and Hoover dams, and participating in the construction of the San Francisco–Oakland Bay Bridge.

But the industry that advanced as fast as any was aviation—both in airframe building and commercial transport. When World War I ended, there was no real place in the economy for all the planes that had been built, or the talents of the thousands of young men who had learned how to fly. An early initiative was taken in 1918 by the Post Office Department and the Army, which started an experimental airmail service between New York and Washington, soon abandoned. The following year the Post Office alone started a New York-to-Chicago airmail run, and by 1924 had expanded it to a transcontinental service. It was not long after this that Congress passed the Kelly Act, which required that the jobs be turned over to private air transport concerns.

The private flying companies at the time were tenuous little operations that sorely needed some reliable source of revenues. In the early 1920's, recent Yale graduate Juan Terry Trippe had bought a few well-used surplus war planes and started the Long Island Airways System to carry passengers from New York City to the Hamptons on the island. The business did not take hold, and Trippe then lost out on a bid for the New York–Boston mail route. But he had good connections, and with financing help from Cornelius Vanderbilt Whitney, Percy Rockefeller, and William Vanderbilt he managed to stay in the commercial airlines business. His group was one of three that bid in 1926 for the contract to fly mail from Key West to Havana. The second was Florida Airways, organized by war aces Eddie Rickenbacker and Reed Chambers to fly between Atlanta and Miami. The third was Pan American Airways, run by Captain J. K. Montgomery. Pan American was awarded the contract in July, 1927. But Trippe had had the foresight to get operating rights from the Cuban government. This made the mail contract useless to any line but his own. The following year all three groups merged as the Aviation Corporation of the Americas, operating the Pan American line, with Trippe as president.

Charles A. Lindbergh's nonstop flight across the Atlantic in 1927, for which a $25,000 prize had been offered, helped fire the imagination of Wall Street investors, and the fledgling industry drew strong financial support. A Seattle-to-Los Angeles line founded by Vern Gorst, later sold to timber heir William Boeing, became a key link in one major air transport company, United Air Lines. Eastern Airlines formed to serve the East Coast; Transcontinental & Western, the Middle and Far West; and Cyrus R. Smith's American Airlines to span the continent along with United. To provide these growing lines with planes, new airframe companies developed, with Boeing, Glenn L. Martin, and Donald Douglas among the important names in this field.

Douglas, a brilliant young aeronautical engineering instructor at Massachusetts Institute of Technology, was hired by Glenn L. Martin in 1915, but he branched off on his own in 1920. Financed by David R. Davis, he built the Cloudster, the first airplane that could lift a useful load equal to its own weight. He then got contracts to build Navy torpedo planes and for transport craft to fly the mails. The plane that won a worldwide reputation for virtual indestructibility was the Douglas DC-3, first flown in 1935, which could carry twenty-one passengers a distance of 1,480 miles at 195 miles per hour, and boasted a 95-foot wingspan, 1,000-horsepower Pratt & Whitney engines, retractable landing gear, and a variable pitch propeller.

With the advent of these Douglas planes and the later Boeing four-engined Stratoliners, airlines could make money just carrying passengers and were freed of their dependence on mail contracts. Air passenger traffic increased from 50,000 in 1928 to more than 400,000 in 1930 and more than 3 million in 1940. Airline miles flown swelled from 11 million in 1928 to 120 million in 1940, including 94 million passenger miles. Except for the fact that most of the cost of the nation's 2,600 airports and landing fields had been borne by the taxpayers, the air transport industry was managing on its own.

More important than the growth of any single industry, however, were the strides made in industrial research during the 1920's and especially in the 1930's. Much of the early work was carried on by industry associations, and the U.S. Chamber of Commerce reported that sixty-eight groups had more than 500 research projects under way in 1925.

World War I had demonstrated that U.S. technology was far behind that of Europe in many fields, and it was here that some of the most important new advances were made. The chemical industry became especially active in finding new products and improving old ones. Union Carbide concentrated on petrochemicals and was joined in that field by Monsanto Chemical, which had got its start before the war by challenging the German monopoly in saccharin. The American chemical industry by 1929 was turning out products valued at $3.75 billion.

The development of plastics first grew out of a search for substitutes for scarce materials. Plastics research branched out in many directions after the

Inventor Wallace Carothers, developer of nylon for Du Pont.

expiration in 1920 of Dr. Leo Baekeland's patents on his Bakelite phenolic plastics. The slow-burning cellulose acetates were developed for use in clear wrapping materials, molded products, and photographic film. Styrene, used in synthetic rubber, was brought out by Dow Chemical Company. Vinyl resins, for coating and packaging, came into use by 1930. And Dr. Wallace Carothers was hired away from Harvard in 1928 by the Du Ponts, who put him in charge of a laboratory where he could explore polymerization—the synthesis of long-chain molecules that resemble those of living tissues. By 1934 he had produced a synthetic filament that was to revolutionize the textile industry—nylon, which went into pilot plant production in 1938. Before the United States entered World War II, Du Pont was supplying 400 textile mills with the fiber, mostly to be used in ladies' hosiery.

The metal and metalworking industries sought to catch up to European technology through research. New alloys were developed for steel to give it the desired properties of hardness, ductility, strength, and corrosion resistance for its various uses. As the use of aluminum increased in the 1930's, first in motor parts, auto trailers, and railroad cars, and later in aircraft, aluminum alloys were improved by heat treatment, and new methods of fabricating the metal were devised.

Universities were slower in getting into industrial

research. But at the University of Kansas, Dr. Robert Kennedy Duncan, a chemistry professor, got business concerns to sponsor fellowships to help them solve their industrial problems. The Mellons became interested and brought Duncan to the University of Pittsburgh in 1913 to form the Mellon Institute of Industrial Research, specializing in chemistry.

Gordon Battelle, the son of an Ohio industrialist, saw a growing need for research laboratories that could be used by industry. His death in 1923 cut short his plans, but his will provided for the establishment of an independent research organization. Starting operation with a $3 million endowment in 1929, the Battelle Memorial Institute quickly established a major franchise in metallurgy, branched into other fields, and increased its resources by doing contract research for a wide variety of industrial clients. Before World War II, Battelle had developed capabilities in a number of scientific fields that were of growing importance to industry and to the nation's defense effort.

THE DEPRESSION ENDS

In retrospect, observers divide the great Depression of the 1930's into three parts—the long, nearly uninterrupted decline for three and a half years to the low point of March, 1933, the gradual upturn for another three and a half years until August, 1937, and the final roller coaster plunge and ascent leading to the war production period.

By 1936 industrial activity had come back almost two thirds of the way from its low point, and in 1937 the physical volume of production reached 1929 levels, although the dollar volume was substantially lower. But it was at this point that President Roosevelt decided that business could take the reins again in driving toward economic recovery. As government revenues rose from $4.1 billion in 1936 to $5.3 billion in 1937, he cut spending and reduced the deficit by $1.75 billion.

Then came the relapse. Business activity began to turn lower in August, and the stock market broke sharply in September. The familiar but unwelcome signs of depression returned—mass industrial layoffs, swelling relief rolls, the filling up of W.P.A. job quotas, and new requests for more public works appropriations.

For two years the recession continued on its course, perhaps now more discouraging than ever, after recovery had seemed so near. For all the social changes it fashioned, the New Deal never really succeeded in bringing back prosperity or ending unemployment. Gross income from manufacturing fell from $68 billion in 1929 to $28 billion in 1932, then recovered to $61 billion by 1937. Net income showed a similar trend. Total retail sales dropped from $49 billion in 1929 to $25 billion in 1933, and had recovered only to $42 billion by 1939. Not until 1937 did the total number of unemployed dip below 8 million, but as late as 1939 the jobless rolls were still around the 10 million mark. Although government spending had raised the national debt from $16 million (after a drop from the 1919 peak of $36 billion) to $56 billion by 1941, these repeated deficits produced little of the "multiplier effect" that Keynes had declared they would bring.

Perhaps no one was more disappointed at this unhappy turn than Roosevelt himself. In a seeming fit of pique he turned on the businessmen, for whose co-operation he had long appealed, and called for an investigation of economic concentration, declaring that "private enterprise is ceasing to be free enterprise." Congress met his request by forming the Temporary National Economic Committee, its membership divided equally among administration officials and congressmen. One member was Thurman Arnold, whom Roosevelt named Assistant Attorney General and who promptly began enforcing the antitrust laws more vigorously than ever before.

Just as the T.N.E.C. was finishing its work, war broke out in Europe. Prices rose, with basic commodities spurting 25 per cent higher in September, 1939, alone, and hoarding began to set in. The Federal Reserve index of industrial production rose from 106 per cent of the 1935–39 average to 125 per cent by the end of the year. In the same period manufacturing employment rose almost 10 per cent and payrolls 16 per cent.

Economic depression, however, like prosperity, has a momentum of its own. In spite of massive new demands for the products of industry and agriculture, sizable sums were still being spent in 1940 and 1941 for farm aid and work relief. But by July, 1940, Congress had authorized more than $12 billion in defense spending; by the following spring the total reached $35 billion, or more than World War I had cost the United States. Dozens of new plants were being built, mostly financed by the government. Furnaces were stoked, assembly lines set in motion, and men and women found a warm welcome at employment offices. The Federal Reserve index of industrial production climbed from 130 in the fall of 1940 to 168 at the end of 1941 and 174 in April, 1942.

Almost every able-bodied man not in military service, as well as millions of women, were at work, many spending long overtime hours at the job. The long, despairing Depression was over. The nation, its business system, and its industrial machine were confronted with serious new threats. But this was a challenge that businessmen and industrialists knew they could deal with. Back in their own element once more, they felt a renascent confidence in their own capabilities.

VIII Innovative Knack

A big United Aircraft Corporation Sikorsky helicopter demonstrates the feasibility of the high-speed delivery of heavy loads.

"The difficult we do immediately; the impossible takes a little longer."

Anonymous, World War II period

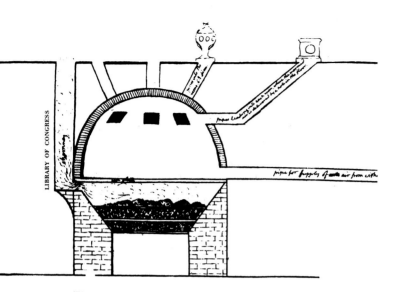

The central heating of buildings was an American innovation conceived by the inventive Thomas Jefferson, among others. His drawing (above) shows a horizontal shaft carrying air to a fire, and upward shafts to a chimney and heating pipes.

The skyscrapers of New York and other U.S. cities have been top attractions for foreign visitors. One of the first of these architectural wonders was the triangular, twenty-two-story Flatiron Building, seen at right rising in New York in 1901.

Samuel F. B. Morse's ingenious devising of a dot-dash code, shown below in his 1837 memorandum, was first used on slugs in a crude, mechanical forerunner of his telegraph. Later, a simpler code to be tapped out by key was given to operators.

HAROLD W. RAMBUSCH ASSOCIATES

Elegant theaters billed as "cathedrals of the motion picture," like New York's Roxy (above), finished in 1927, provided an atmosphere of escape from the realities of the world and helped build the fortunes of the film industry. The rugged and versatile jeep (right), designed by Delmar G. Roos and Willys, became an international legend in World War II.

U.S. ARMY

NO CASH

Now you can drive any brand new car of your choice <u>without putting a penny down</u>. All it takes is an American Express Money Card and a lease from Avis. And even if you aren't a cardmember, give us a call. We'll quote you an unbeatable rate on any car you want to drive.

Avis rents and leases all makes ... features Plymouth

Three ideas that have become familiar characteristics of modern-day life: on the opposite page is a limited-access superhighway, a fisheye-lens view of a cloverleaf intersection in Los Angeles; above, John Dessauer, Chester Carlson, and Joseph C. Wilson of Haloid (later Xerox) demonstrate an early dry-copying machine in Rochester, New York, 1948; at left is an advertisement for the use of a credit card, the key to a new system of personal finance that spread from America to the rest of the world during the 1960's.

307

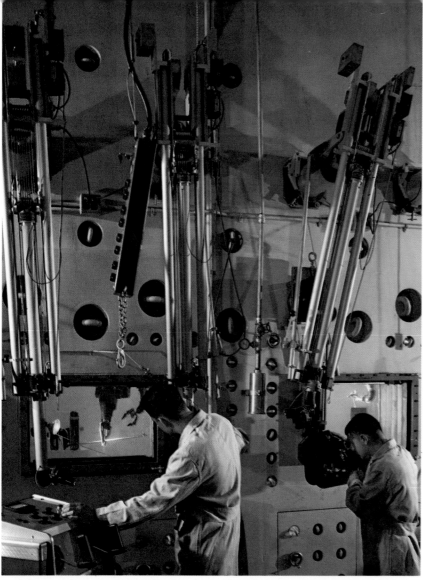

Despite the fact that between 1940 and 1960 the number of farms and farm workers was cut by half, innovative agricultural practices like aerial crop spraying and round-the-clock harvesting by itinerant contractors (opposite page, top and bottom) more than doubled the productivity per farmer. Left: working with radioactive materials, by-products of the atom bomb that have many peaceful uses for industry and science, technicians in California manipulate "hot" substances with robot arms through radiation-proof walls. Below: one of the United States Lines' automated container ships, capable of transporting more than 1,000 prepacked containers.

Above: computers make possible the use of automatic welding equipment on the Vega assembly line of General Motors. Left: I.B.M.'s computerizing of equations helps solve many industrial, engineering, and scientific problems at a saving of time and cost to computer users. Opposite: engineers monitor the details of a moonshot on 450 computer-driven consoles in the launch firing room at Kennedy Space Center, Florida.

9

THE AGE OF ORGANIZATION

1940-1960

Through the long Depression decade, government had been repeatedly frustrated in its efforts to reverse the economic tide; business and industry had felt throttled and chastised; and much of the work force despaired that it might never be called on to make maximum use of mind and muscle. And yet America remained a coiled spring, ready to release its great energies as soon as the right combination of circumstances presented itself.

It was war that uncoiled the spring, slowly at first, more swiftly as additional countries in Europe and Asia were drawn into the hostilities, and with explosive force when the United States itself became a participant. Shortly after war broke out in Europe in September, 1939, the United States revised the neutrality acts to permit sales of arms to combatants, and again early in 1941 to permit greater aid through a "Lend-Lease" program to nations whose defense was deemed vital to U.S. interests.

A War Resources Board was named in 1939 to survey defense needs. The following year the President appointed a Council of National Defense, made up of members of his Cabinet, along with a National Defense Advisory Commission. The N.D.A.C. met with Bernard Baruch, who had been head of the War Industries Board in World War I. Baruch described defense and war mobilization as essentially a job of organizing resources that already existed. He urged the formation of industry committees, the establishment of priorities, the imposition of price controls, and the centralization of authority in a single agency. None of his recommendations was implemented immediately, but gradually he was found to be right on all counts.

All of Baruch's policies were eventually followed, except for the single superagency; by the time it became clear that this was needed, the mobilization program had grown too big and become too dispersed to be brought under such centralized control.

The many war agencies that sprang up were, however, placed under the administrative direction of the Office of Emergency Management, which was part of the Executive Office of the President. The job of overseeing production, first for defense and then for war, fell to a series of agencies given successively broader powers and larger responsibilities: the National Defense Advisory Commission; the Office of Production Management, under former General Motors President William S. Knudsen; the Supply, Priorities, and Allocations Board; and finally, on January 7, 1942, just a month after Pearl Harbor was attacked, the War Production Board, under former Sears, Roebuck executive Donald Nelson.

With the nation at war, the government and its agencies could count on co-operation from almost every quarter. But the needs were gargantuan and the problems formidable. How could industries, large and small, be assigned critical roles most swiftly? How should manpower and materials be allocated to keep power plants, trains, motor trucks, and elevators running and in repair? At what point would military requests have to yield to civilian needs? How much of this year's resources could be used to help meet next year's larger production goals?

Fortunately, some experience had been gained and some momentum built up during two years of defense effort and of helping to supply friendly nations. At the

With mass-production methods learned in World War II, William J. Levitt built his first 17,000-home Levittown on Long Island (left), accelerating suburban sprawl.

start of 1940 the United States had a powerful Navy, virtually no munitions industry, and an Army that was smaller than that of the Netherlands or of Greece. Its potentials could be measured in vast supplies of many key raw materials, the world's best manufacturing facilities, superlative abilities in science and engineering (including a group of brilliant refugee scientists), and manpower of exceptional quality, including large numbers with mechanical and manual skills. But the newly recruited citizen army trained with wooden guns and went into maneuvers with farm wagons and trucks meant to represent tanks. By the summer of 1940 the nation had only 500 tanks, 5,000 military planes, less than 100 million pounds of powder (of which about half was left from World War I), and barely 2 million rifles, almost half of them 1903 model Springfields.

Even in peacetime, however, some companies had been learning lessons that would serve them well in supplying the needs of modern warfare. Light planes had been built that could fly faster than 300 miles an hour as far back as 1935, and up to 375 miles an hour by 1937. In 1938 Britain bought 400 trainers from North American Aviation and 200 bombers from Lockheed. France that year ordered 100 fighters from Curtiss-Wright and 100 fighters and bombers from Martin Aircraft. The following year the two countries came back for more than 3,000 planes, and in the first half of 1940, while the U.S. Army and Navy ordered some 4,500 planes, the British and French placed orders with U.S. firms for 8,000 planes and 13,000 engines.

Ever since World War I America had boasted, sometimes to the point of ennui, of its productive genius. The United States produced more pig iron and steel than Germany and Russia combined, and about twice as much petroleum as all the rest of the world. But now the nation's problem was one of scarcity, rather than plenty. Its sources of supply for many vital materials were threatened. It needed rubber, tin, silk, chromium, tungsten, magnesium, manganese for steelmaking, and mercury. It needed more than it had of aluminum, hides, tool steel, graphite, copper, wool, and optical glass. From the standpoint of waging a war, rubber and aluminum were the most critical items.

Some of the shortages were quickly overcome. The government built new aluminum plants for private companies to operate, and the supply was adequate for essential needs by 1942. A small Cleveland company, Basic Refractories, Inc., was joined by British interests in a new magnesium mining and processing venture, into which the government's Defense Plant Corp. poured more than $90 million. The new facility proved to be too large for the small company to handle, and Anaconda Copper took over its management. Production got up to 120 million pounds a year, more than was needed, and the lightweight metal, most of which

The 1,254-mile Big Inch pipeline (above, in Pennsylvania) was rushed to completion to carry oil more safely than by tanker.

had gone into incendiary bombs and tracers, began to be used in alloy form for airframe construction.

The steel industry had its own special kinds of shortages. Whereas its dominant product had always been strips, which were no more than three eighths of an inch thick, wartime demands called for plates for shipbuilding and armor, which had to be five eighths of an inch or more in thickness. This meant more steel, new cutting machinery, and larger cooling yards. More electric furnaces were needed for added quantities of tool and die steel.

Rubber presented a special problem. Virtually the entire world supply of 1.3 million tons, almost half of which was consumed by the United States, came from the Far East, mainly the Indonesian islands. The United States had only 126,000 tons in reserve at the end of 1939, when it was estimated that annual needs would be 755,000 tons, or much more if the country were to be drawn into the war. Although the urgency of the need was clear, the nation did not move as rapidly as it might have done in filling this need. Synthetic rubber products were developed in the 1930's by the Du Ponts and others. The B. F. Goodrich Company in 1940 produced a synthetic rubber tire from a product called "Ameripol," made from petroleum, coal tar, molasses, and potatoes. Approximately $1 billion was invested in the development of synthetic rubber as the nation's output moved up rapidly from 1,000 tons in 1939 to 400,000 tons in 1942 and then to 836,000 tons by 1944.

Tires were rationed in the first month after U.S. entry into the war and, partly to conserve rubber, gasoline was rationed in the East in May and throughout the country before the end of 1942. Gasoline supplies had also been threatened, however, by German submarines that operated freely off the East Coast, leaving in their wake hulks of tankers and ribbons of black oil.

Oil industry representatives met in Tulsa, Oklahoma, in March, 1942, and recommended the construction of a twenty-four-inch oil pipeline from the Southwest to the East Coast. The idea was accepted, steel was allocated by the War Production Board, and the first 531-mile section was completed to Norris City, Illinois, by the following January. Another 723 miles completed the "Big Inch" line, and crude oil was arriving in Philadelphia through the line by August, 1943. The "Little Big Inch" line, a twenty-inch pipeline for carrying refined petroleum products from Beaumont, Texas, to Linden, New Jersey, was started in April, 1943, and was transporting gasoline the following January. The government paid more than $140 million to build the two lines, which carried about 40 per cent of the crude oil and petroleum by-products that went to the East, much of it for transshipment abroad.

THE IMPOSSIBLE TAKES LONGER

When Britain told the United States, shortly after her disastrous rout at Dunkirk, that America would have to increase military plane production from 200 a month to 3,000 a month within a year and a half, the idea had seemed ludicrous. Then, when America entered the war, President Roosevelt outlined even more ambitious two-year production goals—60,000 planes, 45,000 tanks, and 8 million deadweight tons of new merchant shipping in 1942, and 125,000 planes and 75,000 tanks in 1943. To many, including some hard-bitten production men, these targets sounded like unattainable dreams. Not only was the sheer volume of output staggering, but bomber and fighter aircraft were among the most complicated and difficult items to manufacture.

But not everyone sneered. Indeed, industry's best production people simply decided that the way to get the job done was to start doing it. Government agencies, labor, and the public joined in the let's-do-it attitude. Labor asked for, and frequently got, a meaningful role on plant production committees. Businessmen wanting to advise government were named to industry committees. And military and other government procurement officers sent their inspectors into plants and their accountants to pore over company books. A great many contracts called for payment on the basis of "cost plus a reasonable profit," and the customer wanted to make sure he was getting his money's worth.

Yet all of them knew that industry's know-how was of paramount importance. The War Production Board could establish quotas, set priorities, and help guide the flow of men and materials, but it had to rely on industry for what came off the end of the production line.

Machine-gun production provided a good case in point. As far back as 1937 the Army's tiny Detroit ordnance office had surveyed local plants as potential manufacturers of the Browning .30-caliber machine gun. One likely candidate, they found, was G.M.'s Saginaw Steering Gear Division. When contracts were eventually signed, the Saginaw division was required to produce its first acceptable machine gun by December, 1941, a total of 40 guns by January, 1942, 80 in February, 160 in March, and still more thereafter. As it worked out, the plant site was chosen in November, 1940, construction was rushed to completion, and the first gun was turned out in an old storage building late in March, 1941, months ahead of schedule. The assembly lines began to move in April, when the new plant was dedicated; by March, 1942, when 280 machine guns were to have been produced, Saginaw had delivered more than 100 times that number. And the average price per gun had dropped from $667 to $144.

It was experiences like this that led one production

THE INFINITE BENEFIT

By 1940 most of American industry had learned to measure its efficiency by the cost-benefit test — that is, balancing the cost of an operation against the benefits derived. But there were some goals, such as winning a war or bringing it to an end more quickly, or reducing sharply the number of casualties and deaths, that could not be measured in terms of costs.

During World War II American government and industry invested enormous sums in the mobilization of scientific and technological brainpower. In June, 1940, Dr. Vannevar Bush, president of the Carnegie Institution, was named head of a new National Defense Research Committee, which later became the Office of Scientific Research and Development. Some 6,000 scientists were enlisted in various research projects across the nation, and a punch-card system was developed to locate the scientific and technical qualifications of more than 500,000 individuals.

The most spectacular wartime achievements of American science came in the laboratories, particularly in the fields of electronics and nuclear physics. The proximity fuse was a case in point. A fuse — the triggering element for an explosive charge — could be made to act with a timing device or on contact with another object. But in such uses as antiaircraft fire, it was estimated that these fuses could bring down no more than one plane for every 2,800 rounds. What had long been sought was a fuse that would detonate its charge when it came within striking range of its target.

Radio equipment could be made to serve this purpose. But the problem was fitting the radio device into a shell. To solve it meant condensing a radio receiving set, a transmitting station, and a power plant into a unit the size of an ice cream cone, in the pre-transistor days when even a small radio was about the size of a loaf of bread. Furthermore, this mechanism had to be built to withstand the shock of firing, a force about 20,000 times that of gravity. The basic problem was solved when Raytheon Company, Western Electric, and Hytron Corporation were able to produce

Ernest O. Lawrence

tiny tubes rugged enough to take the jolt, and early models were tested successfully in the summer of 1942.

Vastly more complex and far more decisive in bringing the war to an end was the development of the atom bomb. The scientific roots of nuclear weapons lay in Albert Einstein's theory of the interchangeability of matter and energy, according to his famous formula, $E = mc^2$. This indicated that small amounts of matter might be transformed into vast amounts of energy, since the energy produced would be equal to the mass of the matter multiplied by the *square* of 300 million meters

J. Robert Oppenheimer

per second, which is the speed of light.

The fundamental problem was one of making such a reaction take place when and where it was wanted. Scientists conjectured that if a sufficient quantity of a highly radioactive substance, such as the form of uranium known as U-235, was brought together, it would start, sustain, and build up a reaction culminating in a massive release of energy. The remaining problems were to determine just how much U-235 was needed (the "critical mass"); to find adequate supplies of uranium (which makes up only four parts per million of the earth's crust); and, most difficult of all, to find ways to separate out the scarce U-235 (less than one per cent of the total amount of uranium) from the much more common U-238.

Enrico Fermi, an Italian refugee who had joined the staff of Columbia University, brought some of these questions to the attention of the Navy. In the summer of 1939 three other foreign-born scientists — Albert Einstein, Leo Szilard, and Eugene P. Wigner — urged a Lehman Brothers consultant, Alexander Sachs, to alert higher authorities to this matter. Sachs got President Roosevelt to name an Advisory Committee on Uranium, under Dr. Lyman J. Briggs, director of the National Bureau of Standards. After the uranium question was reviewed by a committee of distinguished physicists named by Frank Jewett, president of the National Academy of Sciences and of the Bell Telephone Laboratories, large funds were made available for research.

Work went on in many places. Using the University of California cyclotron, Professor E. O. Lawrence transmuted uranium into two previously unknown elements, neptunium and plutonium, the last of which seemed to be another candidate for sustaining an atomic chain reaction. Dr. Arthur H. Compton was put in charge of producing a controlled chain reaction with unseparated uranium, in order to produce plutonium. His group, directed by Fermi, succeeded in doing this in December, 1942, in a squash court under the grandstands of Stagg Field at the University of Chicago.

The Army was placed in charge of most of the construction of plants to produce fissionable materials beginning in the summer of 1942, and it took over the entire atomic bomb project by May, 1943. Colonel James Marshall formed the Manhattan District in the Corps of Engineers, and Brigadier General Leslie R. Groves took command of the vast enterprise in September, 1942. With advice from the Stone and Webster Engineering Corporation, Marshall selected a site west of Knoxville, Tennessee, for the erection in three adjoining valleys of a large gaseous diffusion plant, an electromagnetic separation plant, and a plutonium pilot plant. Here the new city of Oak Ridge sprang up, growing to a population of 78,000. The M. W. Kellogg Company designed the gaseous diffusion plant, the J. A. Jones Construction Company built it, and the Carbide and Carbon Chemicals Corporation was given the operating contract. Westinghouse, General Electric, Allis-Chalmers, and Stone and Webster all had roles in equipping or building the electromagnetic plant, which was operated by the Tennessee Eastman Company. The Du-Pont Company built and operated the plutonium facilities, including a large plant for plutonium production at Hanford, Washington.

In 1943 and 1944, the government poured hundreds of millions of dollars into the project. On a mesa at Los Alamos, New Mexico, once the site of a small ranch school, the world's best-equipped physics laboratory was established and staffed by a group of scientists under J. Robert Oppenheimer, including Niels Bohr, who had fled from Denmark, and Nobel prize winner I. I. Rabi. Here the first atomic bomb was constructed, placed on a steel tower in the remote countryside at Alamogordo Air Force Base, 120 miles southeast of Albuquerque, and set off on July 16, 1945. The single most expensive weapon in history, it represented an investment of $2 billion. Perhaps more important, it reflected an unprecedented mobilization of the resources of government, business, and the scientific community in a common purpose.

man to describe his company's approach to some of the seemingly unreasonable requests made by government. "The difficult we do immediately," he said. "The impossible takes a little longer."

Beset by a sense of great urgency, procurement officials both in and out of the military followed the quickest and simplest route by giving most war contracts to the biggest suppliers, and the automobile industry was unquestionably the nation's major industrial resource. It used more than half of the nation's malleable iron, 75 per cent of its glass, 80 per cent of its rubber, and large quantities of other materials. When the war began, it employed 500,000 people directly; another 7 million relied on it indirectly. During the first two years of the war its $3 billion in manufacturing facilities was augmented by another $1.1 billion in government-built plants.

About a third of all war orders went to just ten firms, General Motors alone accounting for $14 billion. Scarcely more than 100 of the nation's 184,000 manufacturing plants had received defense orders in 1940 and 1941. Tens of thousands of businesses in non-essential lines had to fold up during the war, although others found ways to convert to war work, and still others started up and grew from tiny beginnings in machine shops and garages.

It was the automobile industry, familiar with the capabilities of many other firms, that showed how to spread the work by farming out war orders or parts of war orders. While the public thought of it as made up almost wholly of the Big Three, the industry actually consisted of some 850 automakers and parts companies, many of them big businesses in their own right, along with many thousands of subcontractors and suppliers in almost every state in the union.

Military procurement officers soon learned some of the tricks of subcontracting. One manufacturer, given a large contract to build Hispano-Suiza cannon, asked the government to finance a $5 million plant expansion. But army and production agency officials found that almost all of the 121 parts could be made by smaller neighboring firms as subcontractors, and no expansion was needed.

Industry's production men brought some of their know-how directly into government agencies. Early in the defense period Ford, Willys, and Bantam all submitted bids on a rugged, personnel-carrying vehicle for the Army. Willys was low bidder, but the Army decided to give the contract to Ford, with its great mass-production capacity. Knudsen, however, refused to approve the contract. Ford could make dozens of other products needed for defense, he argued, while Willys should concentrate its efforts on what it knew best—making motor vehicles. It was Willys that got the contract to build 16,000 "jeeps" and then turned out thousands upon thousands more during the war.

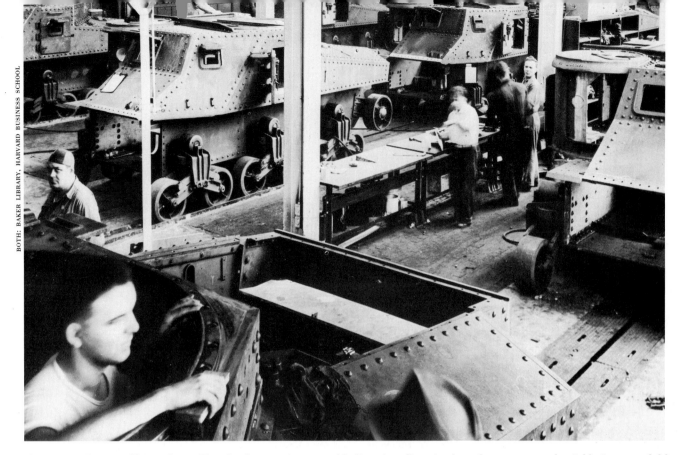

Conversion for war: M-3 tanks on Chrysler Corporation assembly lines in a Detroit plant that was erected quickly in a cornfield

The first major tank contract went to Chrysler Corporation, which got its order and blueprints in early summer, 1940, began building its plant in the fall, and had pilot models out the following spring. After Pearl Harbor, when the great munitions speedup began, Chrysler let other manufacturers in to study its methods, and some 250 came in a five-month period. Subsequently, some of the smaller firms were the first to switch over from the M-3 tank to the newer M-4 model. They in turn were able to teach Chrysler, which then managed to convert to the new models without losing a day's production.

It was in the aircraft industry, however, that former competitors showed the most generous spirit of co-operation. Concentrated substantially in the West, the industry began a voluntary exchange of information on its own. When, under government urging, an Aircraft War Production Council was formed, North American head J. H. ("Dutch") Kindelberger was named its first president. His initial act was to call on all department heads in his own company to give competitors anything they needed—"processes, methods, even tools and materials that we are not planning to use immediately." When the production manager of Bell Aircraft at Buffalo reported a critical need for 90,000 cable terminals, the supplies were on their way from four other aircraft companies the following day. Such sharing became increasingly important as the aircraft industry grew from fewer than 50,000 workers

in 1939 to more than 2 million, or about an eighth of the nation's manufacturing work force, at its peak late in 1943. By early 1944 an estimated 1,000,000 engineering man-hours had been saved through pooling of information and research.

The sharing of production secrets was not confined to the industry itself. Late in 1940 Knudsen called a meeting of the motor industry in Detroit, showed aircraft parts to the carmakers, and asked whether they could turn them out. Auto men were soon swarming through the aircraft plants. Briggs and Fisher Body began making parts for North American, and Chrysler, De Soto, Hudson, and Goodyear Tire were subcontracting for Martin.

The dissenter was Ford's Charles E. Sorenson, who felt that his company should be making not parts for others, but the whole plane—airframe, engines, and all. It was not long before Ford was doing just that. Sorenson visited the Consolidated plant to watch B-24's being assembled and observed what seemed to him total disorganization, with workers clambering over fuselages all over the plant. He began laying out in his mind an aircraft assembly plant to his own standards of mass production and efficiency. At Willow Run the government built for Ford the world's biggest aircraft plant—a mile long, a quarter of a mile wide, with 975 acres of buildings, 1,600 machine tools, 7,500 jigs and fixtures, and a gigantic overhead conveyer system. Construction started in April, 1941, and the first B-24

The woman worker, celebrated as "Rosie, the Riveter," was vital to the war effort. Above: a Curtiss Helldiver assembly line

Liberator bombers were coming off the line eleven months later, although full production was not reached for more than a year after that. Willow Run epitomized one side of America's mass-production genius and showed it could be applied to highly complex products. The other side was demonstrated by some of the smaller and less efficient aircraft plants, whose informal flexibility helped them adapt more readily to the changes and modifications the Air Corps was endlessly demanding as a result of combat experience.

Another notable prodigy of production occurred in the shipbuilding industry. Possibly the major maritime development of the war was in landing craft. Where once only rubber boats might have been considered for beach landings, Dunkirk had taught the usefulness of almost every type of vessel. President Roosevelt called a White House conference of shipbuilders in April, 1942, to launch a program for building hundreds of craft to land troops, supplies, tanks, and even railroad locomotives on beaches. The program for building these vessels was stepped up sharply for the North African invasion that November.

In one phase of the program, in order to be sure of getting 600 tank lighters, the Navy ordered 1,100. When the design was criticized, one of the new craft was tested against another boat designed by Andrew Jackson Higgins, whose New Orleans yard had built boats impartially for rumrunners and federal agents during Prohibition days. The Higgins boat won out,

but it was the end of May before it was decided to build 1,000 lighters to that design, and the original deadline was September 1. Even so, more than half were delivered on time, and the rest were completed before the end of November.

The miracle man of wartime merchant shipbuilding, however, was Henry J. Kaiser. As an audacious paving and construction contractor, he had submitted lower bids than much larger firms on government contracts in the 1930's, and he had helped build the Bonneville and Grand Coulee dams. Once, when members of a West Coast cement combine showed reluctance to deal with him, Kaiser nevertheless bid on 5 million barrels of cement for the Shasta Dam, even with no cement company. Turned down for a loan by his friend, A. P. Giannini, Kaiser went to Jesse Jones at the R.F.C. and was offered $3 million at 5 per cent interest. Giannini then decided the risk was good enough to offer the money at 4 per cent, and Kaiser founded his Permanente Cement Co. Kaiser also got into steelmaking and magnesium processing during the war, but his great triumph was in building almost 1,500 ships in two shipyards at Richmond, California. Introducing prefabrication and assembly line techniques, along with welding, he produced British-designed Liberty ships in an average of forty-one days, turning one out in a record eight days.

The final production record of World War II shows that industry not only achieved the seemingly fantastic goals that had been set, somewhat incredulously, back in 1941 and 1942, but usually exceeded them. In its entire history up to World War II, the American aircraft industry had not managed to build 30,000 planes; wartime output was 300,000. American industry produced 2.6 million army trucks, 86,000 tanks, more than 100,000 gun carriages, and almost 20 million machine guns and rifles. With only a slight increase in cars and just about the same number of locomotives, American railroads in 1944 moved four and a half times the passenger traffic and two and a half times the freight ton-miles of 1939. The merchant fleet was expanded from 10.5 million tons in September, 1939, to 54 million tons in May, 1945, even while the Navy was undergoing a tenfold increase in fire power and some 65,000 landing craft were being built.

In some ways the triumphs were as much those of the spirit as of material prowess. For most Americans the war was in every sense a common enterprise. Although the unemployed had numbered some 9 million before the war, far more than that number of men and women went into the armed forces, and employment still expanded from 47.5 million to 54 million between 1940 and 1945. "Moonlighting" became a common practice, as workers held one job by day and another by night. Millions of women, many with husbands in service, took jobs and maintained their homes. At one point women made up 37 per cent of the work force in industries handling prime contracts. Aided by such co-operation, American industry was outproducing all the Axis powers combined within a year after Pearl Harbor. And toward the end of 1944 the War Production Board felt secure enough to order cutbacks in some war materials and to permit increases in civilian production.

Federal expenditures, which had totaled $12.8 billion in the 1941 fiscal year, rose to $100 billion four years later. The cost of running the government for the 1941–45 period was $318 billion, of which $282 billion, or almost 90 per cent, went for war purposes.

The Way to Wealth

CLINTON W. MURCHISON

"I've never been without some cattle, and I hope to die with more cattle than anyone in the world," said Clinton Williams Murchison (1895–1969). Known more familiarly in business as Clint, he was the personification of the twentieth-century self-confident Texan, as earthy as the soil of that state, as expansive as the Texas horizons. He made money in cattle, but more in oil and other enterprises.

With Sid Richardson, a lifelong friend from his hometown of Athens, Texas, he switched early in his life from trading cattle to trading oil leases. It was a speculative game played with paper, buying and selling leases on parcels of potentially oil-rich land. The two men's shrewd wheeling and dealing made them money, and Murchison turned to the production of oil, wildcatting his way to an income of $30,000 a month. In the late 1920's he sold his interests for $5 million and retired— briefly. "What else is a fellow going to do but work?" he asked. "I can't play the piano."

In the 1930's he built the Southern Union Gas Company to sell the natural gas that other oilmen thought was unmarketable. The utility experienced lean years but eventually spun off its oil and gas leasing and producing subsidiaries; stockholders, receiving the new companies' shares, enjoyed a 500 per cent return within ten years. Another bonanza was Delhi Oil, which was formed by Southern Union and whose stock was offered for sale to the utility's shareholders. It has been figured, in sum, that if a Southern Union investor had bought 10,000 shares in the utility at $1 per share in 1942, bided his time and exercised his options, he would, by 1952, have made a profit of $2.8 million.

Murchison went into debt to pyramid his own holdings. "Cash makes a man careless," he said. "So long as you add value, debt is sound." He prospered by pioneering the so-called reversionary interest in the oil business. He would sell oil properties at a moderate price in return for a buyer's agreement that when production paid back his investment plus interest, half of all future production would revert to Murchison. Drillers were attracted by the deal, believing that because of government prorations (limitations placed on oil production to prevent price slumps), Murchison would have a long wait. But Murchison sensed that with the approach of World War II the demand for U.S. oil would skyrocket. Proved right, he sold his regained 50 per cent interests for cash, again attaching a reversionary interest clause to the new deals.

By 1943 he had expanded into other fields. He became something of a one-man conglomerate, owning cattle ranches, chemical companies, Dallas's only taxicab service, a life insurance

Clint Murchison, Sr.

This was more than ten times the direct cost to the U.S. of World War I, and far higher than the entire cost of running the government since its founding, including all the earlier wars.

Because the government had done a creditable job of paying the costs out of current revenues, the national debt rose just over $200 billion, from $49 billion in 1941 to $259 billion in 1945. Taxes and other government income paid for 43 per cent of all federal expenses during the five and a half years that ended December 31, 1945, compared to less than a third of government expenses paid out of current revenues in World War I. Most of the remaining money was raised through the sale of bonds and notes by the U.S. Treasury.

THE POSTWAR MOOD

Most of the fighting nations, weary and dispirited, were simply relieved to know the long war had come to an end. But the United States, far from having its

company, the Martha Washington candy makers, a fishing tackle plant in Michigan, and a 75,000-acre ranch in Mexico. In addition, he acquired controlling interests in the American Mail Line, the Henry Holt publishing company, a chain of theaters, a Mexican silverware factory, the Diebold office equipment firm, *Field & Stream* magazine, public utilities, banks, and Colorado's Royal Gorge Bridge with its associated amusement facilities. It was a magpie's nest of acquisitions but reflected Murchison's lusty philosophy: "Money is like manure. If you spread it around, it does a lot of good. But if you pile it up in one place, it stinks like hell."

His sons continued in their father's tradition. John Dabney and Clint, Jr., bought 32,000 acres of marshland within the city limits of New Orleans for $300 an acre, drained the property, and made a killing. In 1961, the two men—then in their thirties—wrested control of the Van Sweringens' old Alleghany Corporation (the New York holding company with $122 million in assets) away from Woolworth heir Allan P. Kirby.

When Clint, Sr., died, he did not own more cattle than anyone in the world. But he had created a financial maze of more than 100 enterprises worth in excess of $300 million.

energy sapped, seemed invigorated. In spite of a widespread expectation of an economic downturn that would come with the cancellation of war contracts and the return of millions of servicemen to the labor force, the consciousness of great achievement created a mood of buoyant confidence. And there were even some, like the businessmen's Committee for Economic Development, who forecast a postwar upturn in business and in employment.

When this actually took place, the nation simply turned to the most pressing business at hand—helping rebuild the war-shattered countries and restoring a viable world economy. The first measures toward these ends had been taken even before the war ended, with the plans for the formation of the United Nations and an economic conference in 1944 at Bretton Woods, New Hampshire. There it was proposed to establish an $8.8 billion International Monetary Fund, primarily to stabilize world currencies, and an International Bank for Reconstruction and Development (World Bank), capitalized at $8 billion, mainly to help the war-ravaged countries rebuild and to finance projects in underdeveloped areas.

Both of these agencies came into being, with the United States supplying a substantial part of the initial capital. To encourage more world trade, the United States renewed the reciprocal trade agreements immediately after the war, and it joined some forty other nations two years later in a broad agreement to reduce tariffs on major commodities. But none of this seemed to be helping enough or working fast enough. Although American imports rose rapidly to more than $7 billion, exports increased even faster, and a wide "dollar gap" was created, as other countries found themselves short of gold or dollars with which to buy American goods. Their industries simply could not manage to produce for their own needs, let alone provide goods for export.

Then, at the Harvard commencement exercises in June, 1947, Secretary of State George C. Marshall proposed that the United States join other nations in providing help to their laggard industries. The non-Communist European nations, led by France and England, responded with alacrity. They outlined recovery plans, set production goals, and put a price tag of $22 billion on the entire program. The United States passed the Marshall Plan Act, creating a new Economic Co-operation Administration, in April, 1948, the same month that the participants abroad set up a permanent Organization for European Economic Co-operation. U.S. appropriations for the first year of the plan were $6.1 billion, and they eventually totaled $12 billion, almost all of it for economic aid, divided about evenly between food and agricultural commodities and industrial products. The Marshall Plan succeeded on all counts. By 1951 Western Germany and

France passed their prewar levels of industrial production. It alleviated the problem of the dollar shortage, so that other nations were able to buy more in the United States. And politically, by helping private industry spearhead industrial recovery, it blunted the sharp advances that socialism had been making in Western Europe.

The postwar reconversion of American industry went even more smoothly. Although government expenditures were cut by more than 50 per cent within two years after the war, employment climbed steadily, from 54 million in 1945 to 61 million by 1952. Wartime and postwar inflation was a vexatious problem, particularly when most price controls were lifted. But per capita income was rising even faster, moving from $1,082 in 1939 to $1,566 in 1953, expressed in constant (1953) dollars. And even though average weekly working hours had dropped from forty-eight in 1929 to forty in 1952, the output of all goods and services doubled in the same period, to a record high of $345 billion.

Plagued by a housing shortage and starved by the wartime disappearance of automobiles and appliances, consumers went on a postwar buying spree for durable goods of all kinds. Their scramble for these products continued for a number of years, but with diminishing intensity, as the sellers' market almost imperceptibly turned into a buyers' market, and the nearly lost art of salesmanship had to be revived.

Automobiles, refrigerators, automatic home laundries, and homes in the suburbs became more and more commonplace as personal income rose and the American middle class expanded. Organized labor had grown in numbers since the Depression years but had declined in militancy and to a degree in public esteem. Federal labor legislation was aimed mainly at curbing union power, starting with the War Labor Disputes Act of 1943, continuing through the antifeatherbedding Lea Act of 1946, and culminating in the Taft-Hartley Act of 1947.

Labor itself sought to assume an air of middle-class respectability. In 1949–50 the C.I.O. threw out eleven unions suspected of Communist domination, including the United Electrical Workers and the West Coast longshoremen under Harry Bridges. The long-time presidents of the A.F.L. and C.I.O., William Green and Philip Murray, both died in 1952, and they were succeeded by Walter Reuther in the C.I.O. and George Meany in the larger A.F.L. U.S. labor leadership was being passed along to a new breed who did not feel uncomfortable in the board rooms of their antagonists and who, indeed, felt that good management practices were required to serve their members properly. The A.F.L. and C.I.O. entered into a nonraiding pact and finally, in 1955, moved to reaffiliate.

America had long thought of itself as a boundless storehouse of raw materials. An occasional Cassandra would predict that the end was in sight for iron or copper or petroleum, but these warnings would be forgotten as new and larger supplies were found, or new technologies made some old products obsolete. But so rapidly had materials been used during the war and so fresh was the memory of supply shortages that official concern was reflected by the naming of a President's Materials Policy Commission, under the chairmanship of William S. Paley, chairman of the Columbia Broadcasting System.

Reporting in 1952, the commission found that vital raw materials were indeed being used up at an alarming rate in America. In 1900 the United States produced about 15 per cent more raw materials than it consumed; by 1950, in spite of vast new discoveries, the nation was consuming 10 per cent more than it produced, and importing the rest. The United States had become the world's major importer of copper, lead, and zinc, which it had once exported. Even in iron ore, petroleum, and lumber, American resources that had once seemed all but limitless, the United States had become a net importer.

Wartime science had helped point the way toward the use of numerous substitute materials, and many of these, such as plastics and synthetic rubber, had proved superior in many ways to the materials they had replaced. In industry a number of new metals and new uses for old metals were turning up. When supplies of tungsten from China were cut off during the war, molybdenum was substituted and was found to be a highly useful alloy metal, along with manganese, chromium, and vanadium. Titanium and zirconium, both widespread in the crust of the earth, became highly important metals after a German refugee, Dr. William Kroll, turned over discoveries on their extraction to the U.S. Bureau of Mines. Beryllium, a lightweight metal with great tensile strength and resistance to corrosion, became an important alloying material.

There were even more significant shifts in the materials used as sources for energy, as well as in the efficiency with which these materials were used. In the postwar period the value of energy delivered increased at the high rate of 6 per cent a year, which made for a doubling in about twelve years. Coal, which was the source of almost half of all the fuel energy used in 1946, declined to scarcely a fourth by 1957, as more convenient forms of energy were found. Gas and oil, for example, could provide much more energy in relation to weight. Petroleum, which furnished less than 5 per cent of the nation's power and heat in 1900, had become the source of more than 40 per cent by 1953. Natural gas became more popular as a heating fuel, tripling in use in the postwar decade.

The changes in fuel use offered new opportunities

to business. A gas engineer, E. Holley Poe, headed a group of businessmen that bid on the Big Inch and Little Big Inch pipelines in 1947. Their offer of $143 million, which was slightly more than the government had paid to build the lines, was the highest of thirteen bids, and the new Texas Eastern Transmission Corporation took over the 3,182 miles of pipeline and 1,993 miles of right of way from Texas to the East Coast. They converted the lines to handle natural gas rather than oil and refined petroleum products, and within three months after its incorporation in May, 1947, Texas Eastern was one of the largest natural gas carriers in the nation.

Oil became a popular fuel worldwide, and the oil business grew more international in nature. In 1946 the United States consumed 70 per cent of the free world's oil, but this share dropped to just 41 per cent within twenty years. Standard Oil Company of New Jersey, which grew in the postwar years much larger than the original Standard Oil trust had been, extended its operations through much of the world. It controlled Creole Petroleum Corp., holder of one of the world's largest oil-producing properties in Venezuela; it acquired a 30 per cent interest in Aramco in 1948; it participated in an Iranian oil consortium in 1954; through an affiliate it discovered oil in Libya

The top plug of a Phillips Petroleum plutonium-fueled reactor at the A.E.C.'s experimental reactor testing site in Idaho

in 1959; and it developed supply and marketing organizations throughout Western Europe.

Businessmen showed some reluctance in moving into atomic energy as a source of power. The Atomic Energy Act of 1946 took the entire nuclear enterprise out of the hands of the Army and turned it over to a new Atomic Energy Commission, chaired by David Lilienthal. The A.E.C. became a huge monopoly, which in 1948 spent $463 million at Oak Ridge alone, had a larger investment in real estate than General Motors, and ran more buses than the city of Philadelphia. It worked on a wide range of projects, including the production of radioactive materials for medical and scientific research, the use of atomic power to propel submarines, and the building of nuclear reactors as sources of electrical power. The A.E.C. also offered generous bounties to successful uranium prospectors; one impoverished young Texas geologist, Charles Steen, inspired a western uranium rush when he discovered an ore body in Utah valued at more than $100 million.

The A.E.C. carried on much of its work through contracts with private business, and the largest of the contracting firms, General Electric, subcontracted more than half to smaller firms. But most companies shied away from atomic work, for a variety of reasons: the research was expensive, the materials were both dangerous and difficult to work with, commercial prospects seemed remote or nonexistent, and the whole business was tainted with the smell of warfare and destruction. Du Pont, which had operated the Hanford Works for a total profit of $1 and which was eager to rid itself of the "merchants of death" image that had grown up around it, got out of the business even before the A.E.C. was created and let the Army turn the Hanford operation over to General Electric.

In the early postwar years, the atom did not look very promising as a general source of energy, and the A.E.C. felt that its important commercial possibilities were at least twenty years away. But as energy needs mounted, as the costs of atomic installations came down, and as the consciousness of the pollution created by burning fossil fuels increased, the first atomic power plants were being built and operated by a number of utility companies long before that time.

RENEWING THE OLD INDUSTRIES

American industry, long under the constraints of depression and war, was impatient to test its new technical knowledge and greater productive skills on the product-hungry postwar market. The very first cars turned out were much like the prewar models, but automakers were soon adding horsepower, increasing streamlining, and experimenting with molded plastic bodies. Tubeless tires became standard equipment,

American Motors President George Romney with 1959 models of the compact Rambler, one of the auto industry's big successes

and power steering, power brakes, and then even powered windows, were introduced. Air conditioning became the premium luxury in cars.

The sellers' market was especially helpful to the smaller manufacturers, who needed merely to produce automobiles, since they virtually sold themselves. Henry Kaiser joined the independent carmakers when he bought the huge Willow Run plant where Ford had been building planes and went into business with Joseph W. Frazer. With no prewar production, they were unaffected by pricing restraints for the early Kaiser and Frazer models. The independent automakers' share of the market, including sales by Kaiser-Frazer Corp., moved up from about 10 per cent prewar to 18.5 per cent in 1946.

The auto independents, which would have been regarded as big business in almost any other industry, had sales of $9.5 billion from 1947 to 1953, and earnings before taxes of $648 million. Then in mid-1953, after these firms had increased their capital assets by an average of about 200 per cent, the sellers' market came to an end suddenly. As their share of the auto market skidded to a mere 5 per cent within a year, the independents sought to strengthen themselves through merger. Kaiser bought up the assets of Willys Motors in 1953, and the following year Nash and Hudson joined forces under the name of American Motors and two other car builders merged to form Studebaker-Packard Corp.

The independents seemed to be hanging on by their teeth; Kaiser Motors gave up carmaking and had its $91 million in debts assumed by Henry Kaiser's more profitable enterprises. But at least one of the smaller auto manufacturers was slated for one more joy ride when American Motors president George Romney made an accurate reading of changing American tastes and produced the compact Rambler in

1958, turning his company's long string of deficits into a healthy profit. He had virtually this entire market to himself for two or three years until the Big Three were able to produce their own compact cars.

The steel industry, too, had no problem in selling all it could produce after the war, but it was under the cloud of obsolescing equipment and a long-standing lethargy about improving its production techniques and technology. Of the major producers, only Republic Steel had done much about better and cheaper pig iron production through blast furnace improvements.

It was U.S. Steel, however, that took the postwar lead in rejuvenating its facilities. One important lesson had been learned from the use of low-grade ores, which had been "beneficiated" by heating and forming into pellets of uniform size and shape. So effective was this in increasing blast furnace production that the same thing was done to high-grade ores. The ingot capacity of "Big Steel's" Tennessee Coal & Iron plant was nearly tripled through the beneficiation of both coal and ore, along with some blast furnace improvements, with only a small upturn in man-hours. An 80-inch hot-strip mill at Gary, Indiana, with a rated capacity of 600,000 tons when it was built in 1936, was rolling 3 million tons in 1953, with the addition of a reheating furnace, automatic controls, and no additional manpower. At Lorain, Ohio, a new automatic seamless-pipe mill at the National Tube Division turned out four times the product of an older mill, with far fewer employees.

Even so, the steel industry went into a moderate decline after 1955, with total production dropping about 13 per cent by 1960. One reason was a gradual increase in imports, as foreign makers managed to cut costs with cheaper labor and the use of efficient new plants. A second reason was the greater competition from such other materials as prestressed concrete in construction, plastics, and aluminum. And finally there was some displacement of steel "by air," as design and engineering changes, such as unitized construction of cars, made possible the use of less material.

Aluminum came of age as a major industry during and immediately after the war, when the government poured millions into new aluminum plants and when a strong element of competition entered the industry. In 1940 the Aluminum Co. of America had 90 per cent of the ingot aluminum market, but a federal court found in favor of the company when the government sought to end the monopoly. Federal Judge Learned Hand again found in 1945 that Alcoa had done nothing illegal, but he urged the government to dispose of its plants to other integrated firms to prevent a monopoly.

Thus others came into the picture, among them Reynolds Metals and, once more, Henry Kaiser. Starting with a base of his wartime magnesium plant, Kaiser expanded into aluminum right after the war on a scale that produced $150 million in sales for his Kaiser Aluminum & Chemical Corp. within five years. Originally he thought of this venture as a means of assuring metal for his auto bodies, but it grew into a major source of profit in his industrial empire. By 1956 its sales had risen to $330 million and its net profit to $40 million, or more than the total net earnings from his wartime shipbuilding operations. In 1953 Anaconda joined the industry, investing $65 million in the new Anaconda Aluminum Company. And although Alcoa's share of the market had slipped to just 40 per cent by 1955, the company's sales that year reached $825 million, almost four times the $219 million of 1940 when it was in complete control, and its profits before taxes climbed to a record of $143 million.

Chemicals became another giant among the postwar industries. Sales totaled about $3 billion by 1950, more than four times what they had been a dozen years earlier. The industry's role had been largely managerial and advisory for the wartime synthetic rubber, explosives, and atomic plants built by the government. After the war, the chemical companies moved off on their own into expanding basic chemicals, dyes, plastics, fibers, resins, coatings, drugs, and scores of other products used by other industries and individual consumers. The most dramatic gain was in plastics output, up 600 per cent in a decade to 750,000 tons, valued at $500 million, by 1950. By 1954 the leading chemical companies had invested some $250 million in the development of just one plastic substance, polyethylene.

Du Pont remained in the forefront of the industry, its sales rising from $299 million in 1939 to $978 million in 1948. Union Carbide & Carbon, however, showed an even faster rate of gain, from $170 million to $632 million. Dow Chemical, with $171 million in sales, had passed Monsanto's $162 million. And well behind these were the two companies that the court had ordered spun off from Du Pont before World War I—Hercules Powder, with 1948 sales of $129 million, and Atlas Powder, with $43 million.

The nation's 100,000 or more merchant builders got a slow start in trying to fill the wide gap of housing needs. But one of them, William Levitt, effected a minor revolution in home building techniques, managing to cut costs and speed construction by means of mass production methods. Near its home base of Manhasset, Long Island, Levitt & Sons, Inc. put up more than 17,000 homes in five years, creating the new community of Levittown where there once had been potato fields. Through the 1947–52 period of rising prices, Levitt kept his costs down to $10 a square foot, compared with $12 to $15 for other builders of small houses. He then turned to building another Levittown in Pennsylvania, a $200 million project for the housing, shopping, and recreational needs of 70,000 people.

A postwar boom in high-rise buildings began around 1947 in a selective group of cities, such as New York, Washington, Chicago, Houston, and Dallas, and continued almost without interruption. By 1960 some $2 billion had been invested in construction in Manhattan, one third of it in apartments, the rest in office buildings. Leading a group of enterprising builders who had put up 132 buildings by 1959 to increase available office space by 50 per cent were the Uris brothers, Harold and Percy, followed by the Tishman Realty & Construction Co., Inc. and Erwin Wolfson's Diesel Construction Company.

Major innovations in new construction were the metal and glass curtain walls, hung without exterior scaffolding, and the prevalence of air conditioning. Virtually every major new office building had central air conditioning, and Du Pont's development of a non-poisonous, nonexplosive coolant gas, Freon, made the new luxury appliance practical for housing. Retail sales of air conditioning systems and units climbed from 48,000 in 1946 to ten times that number in 1952.

Shorter working hours and higher incomes meant expanding uses of leisure time. The total "leisure" market by the mid-1950's amounted to more than $20 billion in spectator and participant sports, a wide variety of amusements, recreational and pleasure travel, boating, hunting and fishing, and a host of similarly enjoyable activities, including dining out. The Diners' Club started around 1950 with an idea and a $75 mailing list of sales managers, and by 1960 it had developed into an organization whose members charged $149 million in credit purchases at restaurants and stores around the world.

As buyers began to seek more for their dollars, new selling and marketing techniques were developed. Starting with a $4,000 investment in a retail store,

A suburban outlet of Korvettes, one of the first chains of discount-priced stores that revolutionized merchandising methods

a young man named Eugene Ferkauf brought discount pricing into department-type stores in the East. By following the great migration of the middle class to the suburbs, seeking high traffic locations, and minimizing markups, he built his Korvette store chain to a gross of $55 million in 1956, then launched a major expansion program and sold 1,000,000 shares of stock to the public.

A great many of the older industries seemed to need only a touch of imagination or daring to achieve unprecedented success. Perhaps symptomatic was what happened to the *Wall Street Journal*, which had been published for the financial community since 1899. Under president and former editor Bernard Kilgore it moved to become the daily publication of the entire business community, and its circulation ballooned from less than 33,000 in 1941 to about 725,000 at the end of 1960, making it the sixth largest newspaper in the country and the largest national newspaper. Magazine publishing, meanwhile, attained the stature of big business, as Time, Inc., created with a starting capital of $86,000 in 1923 by Henry R. Luce and Briton Hadden, and McGraw-Hill, Inc. moved into the ranks of the nation's leading industrial corporations. But the all-time leadership in magazine sales went to DeWitt Wallace's *Reader's Digest*, with a worldwide circulation of 21 million in 1960 and 30 million by 1971.

UPPER AIR TURBULENCE

While government expenditures, and military outlays in particular, dropped sharply after the war, they rose again during the Korean War period and remained high throughout the 1950's. Although this spending gave some support to the entire economy, it was a special boon to the aircraft industry, which in hardly more than the span of a generation had become the nation's largest employer.

America's air carriers, however, were among the very few major airlines in the world not directly subsidized by their government but left to make the grade largely on their own. It was no easy task. Their planes obsolesced every few years, often before they could be written off, and they were invariably replaced by more costly new equipment. Some of these costs could be paid for out of earnings, in years when there were earnings; almost always they required outside sources of financing. Even so, the airlines managed to grow into a major industry, with revenues totaling more than $1 billion by 1951, with passengers reaching about 40 million a few years later, and with an employment of close to 1,000,000.

The biggest U.S. flag line was Pan American, and the largest domestic line was American Airlines. American grew out of a 1934 reorganization of the struggling little American Airways, and Cyrus R. Smith was named its first president. Smith ran the company well enough to move it ahead of its competitors in 1939. Right after the war he took an $80 million gamble to replace his entire fleet of smaller craft with new fifty-two-passenger DC-6's and forty-passenger Convair 240's for shorter hauls. Shortages of equipment, a series of accidents, and poor service combined to make the early postwar years unprofitable for all airlines, American included. But by the final quarter of 1948, American turned the corner, cutting its loss for the year to $2.9 million. The next year the gamble had paid off and American earned $7 million, following this with a profit in 1950 of $10.4 million on total revenues of $119 million.

The airline which grew to the fourth largest in domestic and second largest in international rank was Trans World, which came under the domination of Howard Hughes, an eccentric Croesus who clung to the shadowy background while his lucrative enterprises piled up millions in the foreground. The spring that fed this and most other Hughes enterprises was the Hughes Tool Co., founded by his father in 1908. Not long after the great Spindletop oil strike in 1901, the senior Hughes had developed and patented a line of superior oil well drilling equipment, including more than 400 types of bits for cutting through rock. The company was earning about $1,000,000 a year when the son inherited it in 1924. It lost money in the early Depression years, then went back into the black in 1935. Profits rose to more than $3 million in 1937, stayed near that level through the war and then, with oil exploration stepped up, climbed sharply to $14 million in 1950, $24 million in 1954, and to $29 million —on a gross of just $120 million—in 1956.

Hughes first bought about 20 per cent of the airline's stock for $1.5 million in 1939, when it was still solely a domestic carrier named Transcontinental and Western Air. He continued buying until he had paid around $65 million for 5.2 million shares, or almost 80 per cent of the total outstanding. In taking control, Hughes brought to T.W.A. the advantage of a barrel of available cash, along with the disadvantage of his penchant for not letting managers manage and for procrastinating on key decisions.

In June, 1944, T.W.A. became the first airline to seek Civil Aeronautics Board authority to fly around the world, and the following year it won approval for flights across the Atlantic and thence to the Middle and Far East. Hit by postwar problems, including a pilots' strike and the grounding of all its Lockheed Constellations for modification, T.W.A. lost a staggering $18.9 million from 1946 through 1948. The Hughes Tool Co. buoyed up the line with a $10 million loan, in exchange for convertible notes and the right to name the majority of directors.

In an ensuing management shakeup, both President Jack Frye and Chairman T. B. Wilson resigned. Thereafter the line, while its operations were profitable in most years, underwent frequent management changes. One president, Carter L. Burgess, served out his term in office and left the company without ever meeting Hughes. At times T.W.A. was run by an operating committee when it had no president.

Such turbulations made it difficult to get financing for the large sums the airlines needed in the late 1950's to convert to jet-powered fleets. T.W.A. decided to skip the intermediate turbo-prop stage, in which a turbine was able to increase greatly the engine's power in driving a propeller, and to go right to jets, which used a concentrated jet of exhaust gas to give the plane its forward thrust, making for faster, higher, and smoother flight. Early in 1956 Hughes used his tool company to order for the airline about $500 million worth of jets and related equipment (an amount that was somewhat smaller than conservative estimates of his personal wealth at the time). By the end of 1958 these commitments had been reduced to around $280 million through bank loans, a sale of stock, and use of some Hughes Tool Co. cash reserves. To borrow the rest, Hughes had to put all his T.W.A. stock into a voting trust that the lenders controlled.

But the problems of the airlines were hardly more than a microcosm of the troubles that came to plague the plane builders. Having built immense plants to meet wartime needs, they sought to keep the plants going and the thousands of workers employed after the war. To a large extent, this was made possible by continuing large military orders for planes, but the airframe builders remained in the shadow of two major threats: sudden cutbacks of government orders, and displacement by new technologies.

Working in their favor politically was the fact that the economy of the increasingly populous western states was tied closely to the industry. Of the six big companies in the business, four were in California— Douglas at Santa Monica, Lockheed at Burbank, Convair at San Diego, and North American at Inglewood —and Boeing was at Seattle; Martin was at Baltimore in the East. All these firms were eager to increase their production for civilian purposes, but only two, Boeing and Douglas, were big enough, experienced enough, and willing to lay out the immense sums in development work to take the leadership in the stakes for the big new jet passenger aircraft.

Lockheed had built the first American jet, the F-80 Shooting Star, just before the war ended. Boeing then decided to gamble heavily on jets, and by 1948 was building jet bombers for the Air Force. Helped by Korean War orders, Boeing put its own funds into the development of a prototype all-jet tanker, which could easily be modified for air transport use. Although the company was unsuccessful in its efforts to land a government order for the tanker, it managed to get permission in 1955 to rent unused military facilities to build commercial planes. Douglas, meanwhile, had announced plans to proceed from only a preliminary design and build a commercial jet.

In the race to dominate the market for the big transports, Boeing had the advantage of long lead time in design; Douglas, on the other hand, had been selling commercial craft continuously since 1934, except for the war years, and its late arrival gave it greater flexibility in making changes the customers might want. Both began selling hard in 1955, when Pan American placed one of the first orders—for twenty Boeing 707's and twenty-five Douglas DC-8's. United Air Lines and National went to Douglas, but American placed a large order with Boeing. Douglas landed the Canadair order, but Boeing won out with B.O.A.C., largely because Boeing had a prototype in flight, while the Douglas plane was still on paper. A T.W.A. order for thirty-three planes went to Boeing, predictably, since Hughes had never got along well with Douglas officials. By 1956 Boeing announced it had passed the break-even point, and succeeded in establishing itself solidly as a supplier of commercial aircraft.

On the record, the decade of the 1950's was a spectacular one for the plane builders. Sales of the twelve top companies rose from $1.2 billion in 1950 to

mass-production genius was needed to build a Titan, or even one or two dozen.

To assure their own survival, most of the aircraft makers shifted part of their resources into the new fields of high technology. By 1960 Martin was 80 per cent in missiles and electronics, North American and Lockheed were 40 per cent in these areas, and even Douglas was only about 50 per cent committed to airframes. Convair had become a part of General Dynamics Corporation, a giant that had grown out of a tiny Groton, Connecticut, firm called the Electric Boat Company, which Navy Captain Hyman Rickover had persuaded to build the first atomic-powered submarines.

Among the companies most successful in changing over to sophisticated science was the once relatively insignificant Hughes Aircraft Company, which Howard Hughes had started almost as a hobby in 1934. Until

Prime and sub-contractors joined to produce new military weapons like the intercontinental ballistic missile Titan II.

$7 billion in 1959, a gain of 500 per cent, compared with a 90 per cent increase for all manufactures. But there were danger signs ahead. The backlog of unfilled orders for the twelve firms had risen from $3.5 billion in 1950 to $11 billion in 1956, then slipped back to under $8 billion. The emphasis of government orders was shifting away from large fleets of aircraft and toward more technically sophisticated equipment; the investments in air flight were leveling off or declining, while those in missiles and space flight were on the increase.

These new areas of government work did not require the traditional expertise of the airframe builders, such as the intricate scheduling of the work of thousands of men in an aircraft plant. Instead, they called for the precise fashioning and assembling of many delicate parts. An entire Titan intercontinental missile weighed only about 110 tons, most of it being fuel and only 15,000 pounds being hardware. No

1948 Hughes Aircraft was never much more than an unsuccessful builder of airframes, losing $750,000 on sales of $2 million that year. Then Hughes decided to turn the company into a kind of advanced electronics laboratory. He hired two brilliant electronics researchers, Dean Wooldridge, who had worked for Bell Labs, and Simon Ramo, who had been with General Electric. They gathered around them a topnotch technical staff. An electronic guidance system that they worked out won a development contract for the Falcon air-to-air guided missile. They went on in 1950 to win an Air Force competition for the design of a fire- and navigational-control system for the F-102 interceptor—a keystone in the nation's air defense strategy. The value of the products delivered by the company to the military rose from $8.6 million in 1949 to close to $200 million in 1953, and its profits in the same period went up from $400,000 to about twenty times that figure.

But after a series of disagreements with Hughes,

Ramo and Wooldridge resigned in September, 1953, followed by a group of the company's key executives. The two scientists joined Thompson Products, Inc. in a new venture called the Ramo-Wooldridge Corp. Ramo-Wooldridge then proceeded to develop capabilities in working out management systems, and became the top manager for such missile and space projects as the Titan, the Thor, the Minuteman, and the Atlas programs.

Hughes Aircraft did not stand still, however. It remained the chief supplier of Falcon missiles and fire-control systems in the Air Force's interceptor programs, building its sales by 1958 to $500 million and its after-tax profits to around $15 million. But by then Hughes had turned over his interest in the company to a new Howard Hughes Medical Institute, and was therefore unable to use its earnings to help bail out his heavy commitments for T.W.A.

one-man rule, outside administrators were hired, and a gradual separation took place between ownership and management. And as this division grew more marked, it became the rule for the top-men in corporations to work for salaries, rather than for the profits of the business.

Management became a proficiency apart from the traditional skills required by a business. Corporations still needed executives who were familiar with sales, marketing, and finance, but what they needed even more were people who were capable simply in the arts of management. As Du Pont President Crawford Greenewalt noted, "Specific skill in any given field becomes less and less important as the executive advances through successive levels of responsibility." The professional manager was no longer noted for making all the important decisions by himself, as the guiding geniuses and autocrats of business had once

The sequence shots above show it being fired from an underground storage silo at Vandenberg Air Force Base, California.

So important did government work become to many American companies and industries that the ability to win contracts was raised to the level of a high business art, often involving entire corporate departments. A number of former military leaders, including Douglas MacArthur, Brehon Somervell, Lucius Clay, and Leslie Groves, were named to high corporate offices. A "contract society" developed, largely around Washington, D.C. In his farewell address before leaving office President Dwight D. Eisenhower felt constrained to warn "against the acquisition of unwarranted influence, whether sought or unsought, by the military-industrial complex."

THE MANAGEMENT REVOLUTION

Up until about 1900 or 1910 American business was run primarily by entrepreneurs: the owners of a business were also its managers. As businesses grew too big for

done. Instead, it was up to him to organize his company's resources, including its best brainpower, for making and executing decisions, often collectively. The manager held his job because he was good at it, not because he owned the company.

One consequence of this new pattern—and of the increasing dispersion of stock holdings—was that the managers were effectively in control of their companies. What Adolf Berle and Gardiner Means called the "active property" of a business, its facilities and organization, had become more important than its "passive property," or stocks and other securities. By the same token, it was these large corporations, rather than Wall Street or the banks, that had the most profound effect on the national economy. Whereas the House of Morgan in 1950 had resources of $667 million, General Motors had working capital of $1.6 billion, more than twice as much.

One of the important problems in running a huge

corporation was inherent in size itself: how to obtain the advantages and economies of scale and at the same time maintain the flexibility and responsiveness of a smaller business. The breakthrough in achieving this result, according to former General Motors Chairman Frederic Donner, made the large modern business organization possible. But the roots of this change lay back in the 1920's, rather than in the 1940's and 1950's, when most of the business colossi grew up.

One of the first major reorganizations in American business took place in 1919, when the highly centralized Du Pont Company decided that its divisions could operate better if given greater autonomy. The plan was worked out by Donaldson Brown, the company treasurer, who set up a system of planning, evaluation, and financial controls in which the basic objective became a return of approximately 10 per cent on invested capital. Each division or department manager was charged with a certain amount of investment and held accountable for the desired return, based on a system of financial controls that included detailed forecasts of sales, cash needs, working capital, major expenditures, and profits.

An executive committee, made up of the president and the company's top officers, took on the function of setting overall policies, working closely with a high-level finance committee. A number of other centralized departments were given such company-wide functions as long-range research, purchasing, and traffic, and as such could be considered service departments for the divisions. But the day-to-day operating decisions were left solely to the officers and managers of the divisions and plants. The pattern was not unlike the staff-and-line organization of the military, except that the operating chiefs—the managers on the line—had considerably more leeway and decision-making power. The plan proved eminently workable, and it was given credit for the ease with which Du Pont almost doubled its plant and passed the $1 billion mark in sales in five years after World War II.

Unlike Du Pont, General Motors had not been over-centralized but rather was almost totally lacking in central control. With the resignation from G.M.'s presidency late in 1920 of William Durant, who "could create but not administer," in the words of Alfred Sloan, the organization plan that had been drawn up earlier by Sloan began to be put in effect. It started with the formation of a new executive committee, made up of President Pierre S. Du Pont and the top staff officers; the division managers who had previously been members of the top executive group became an advisory operations committee. Donaldson Brown came over from Du Pont and, as vice president for finance, set up his system of financial controls, forecasts, and equations for measuring return on investment. These gave the executives the kind of overview of operations

Master organizer Charles E. Wilson overhauled General Electric and, later, directed industry's role in the Korean War.

that diminished their need to administer the operations of the divisions.

When Sloan became president in 1923, he moved even closer to the Du Pont pattern. The executive committee took firmer control of such policies as pricing and product lines, in part to forestall the kind of chaos that might result if each of the divisions felt free to compete with the others. Brown was made head of the general sales committee, since his system of controls had such an important bearing on problems of production and sales. And some of the functional committees were revamped to fit real experience. Central purchasing, for example, which had seemed such a natural development, proved to be oversimplified; so a new general purchasing committee was organized, its members coming mainly from the divisions.

The Depression years, with the contraction in sales and the need to economize, required even greater coordination of G.M.'s activities, in order to react more readily to changing conditions. A single policy committee replaced the finance and executive committees in 1937, and the operating executives became an administration committee. This facilitated a wartime shift to a war administration committee, which virtually ran the company during the years when the great need was for production.

G.M.'s war production capabilities were enhanced

by its investments in aviation, some of them going back to 1929, when it bought out the Allison Engineering Company and invested in the Bendix Aviation Corporation and in the Fokker Aircraft Corporation of America. The Fokker stock was eventually turned into what amounted to a controlling interest in North American Aviation, which in turn held controlling blocks of Eastern Airlines and T.W.A., until divestment of airline shares was required by the Air Mail Act of 1934. G.M. sold its North American and Bendix interests in 1948.

The G.M. organization plan appeared to serve the corporation well. In the forty-five years after General Motors Corporation was organized in 1917, car and truck sales expanded from 205,000 a year to 5.2 million, employment from 25,000 to more than 600,000, shareholders from 3,000 to over 1,000,000, and sales from $270 million to $14.6 billion. A combination of motivation and opportunity, provided by policies of incentive compensation and decentralized operations, led to a continuing flow of able management personnel. The company's leadership also extended to such matters as rationalization of wage scales, exemplified by the introduction of Charles E. Wilson's productivity wage increase formula in 1948. And, longer than any other American company, G.M. has been recognized as holding the No. 1 position in the nation, without any sign of top-heaviness or suggestion of organizational breakdown.

What preceded the reorganization of General Electric was not a management that was deficient but one that had been too good at its job. When Gerard Swope retired from the company's presidency in 1939, its sales had reached $342 million, far too great an operation to be kept in one man's mind, unless the mind were as incredibly agile and retentive as that of a Swope. But he also possessed the acumen to recognize that, with more growth in sight, a major corporate overhaul was going to be necessary, and he groomed Charles E. Wilson ("Electric Charlie," to distinguish him from G.M.'s "Engine Charlie") for the post.

War orders sent G.E. sales up to $1.4 billion by 1943. Four years later the company was doing almost this amount of business in peacetime output—but in scores of scattered plants and a bewildering array of products and services, ranging from electric fans to atomic power. By then, however, Wilson had the reorganization quietly under way, bringing in Ralph Cordiner to take charge of the planning. They restructured the company into a corporate pyramid, with departments (e.g., home laundry equipment) making up divisions (e.g., major appliances), and divisions joined in groups (e.g., appliances and electronics), with an executive vice president in charge of each. Management personnel were divided into three groups—executive, operating, and service, the latter made up of

specialists in marketing, research, and other fields, including one group that concentrated only on problems of business organization. By the time the reorganization was complete enough to be submitted to public scrutiny in 1951, Cordiner was president of G.E. and sales were up to $2.3 billion.

The Ford Motor Co. at the end of World War II was sadly in need of reorganization. It was a poor third in the auto industry to G.M. and Chrysler, and losses were running at the rate of more than $100 million a year. Henry Ford II, who had become president at the age of twenty-eight in 1945, after the death of his father, decided something needed to be done. He threw out a number of the old guard, including Harry Bennett, who had used strong-arm tactics as an employee relations tool, and brought in Ernest R. Breech as executive vice president. Breech had spent some twenty years in and around the General Motors organization, holding posts that included assistant treasurer, chairman of North American Aviation, and president of Bendix. Young Ford let him write his own ticket in reshaping the auto company.

Much of what Breech brought to Ford was the G.M. management system, with financial analysis and controls, profit targets, and clear responsibility given to division heads. What he had to contend with, however, were outmoded practices and the foot-dragging of old-line executives. Nevertheless, he did turn Ford Motor around, and in 1954, after the buyers' market had returned, the company had record sales of more than 1,000,000 vehicles in the first six months, with Ford actually beating out Chevrolet during two quarters for the first time in eighteen years.

From 1940 to the mid-1950's a number of other large corporations were reorganized for a variety of reasons and in a variety of different ways, but most of them settled into the centralized-policy, decentralized-operations mold that had been pioneered by Du Pont. Standard Oil of New Jersey accomplished virtually the same result, although it was made up of subsidiaries, rather than divisions, in the early war years. William White in 1952 gave greater authority to district general managers of the New York Central, which was in essence a corporation stretching out over 10,000 miles. U.S. Steel was put together, as G.M. had been, too loosely, and Myron Taylor began pulling together the operating companies in the 1930's. But it was not until the 1950's that Chairman Irving S. Olds and President Benjamin F. Fairless turned Big Steel into an operating company, as its profitable predecessor, the Carnegie Steel Company, had been. Westinghouse underwent two major changes, the first in the 1930's from a headquarters-dominated company to a group of highly autonomous divisions, and the second in the 1940's and 1950's, under banker-lawyer Gwilym A. Price and management consultant Mark Cresap, to a staff-and-line organization. Minnesota Mining & Manufacturing set up management committees and decentralized individual authority simply because the owner-managers realized that the company would outlive them.

Of all the policies that management can control, it was clear to the new breed of executives that those involving price were of paramount importance. Charging what the traffic would bear was viable enough for the days when making as much money as possible as fast as possible was considered a legitimate business objective. But in the postwar era a large number of professional managers turned toward other corporate objectives, such as stability of earnings, flexibility, and long-term survival. By increasing efficiency and lowering prices, even in the absence of intense competition, many an executive felt he was performing a service more worthy of his abilities than simply making money.

THE GREAT VIDEO SWEEPSTAKES

Few products have ever moved as rapidly from the stage of scientific innovation to that of big business as television did in the postwar period. The basic discoveries, made initially in Europe, stemmed from the 1920's, but it was not until the late 1930's that they were translated into usable products. A pioneer in set manufacture was Allen Du Mont, who set up shop in an old pickle plant in New Jersey and started a small television network in the East to promote the sale of sets.

But Radio Corporation of America actually put the largest resources into early television development. After David Sarnoff persuaded his big shareholders to let R.C.A. run the patent pool for radio and license other manufacturers, the company naturally came to dominate research in both radio and television. But the war interrupted the company's fairly extensive television development work, which did not then resume on a large scale until 1946, when the National Broadcasting Company's facilities in New York and Washington were linked by coaxial cable with Philadelphia and Schenectady to create the first major network.

The postwar climate for technology was profoundly affected by what had happened during the war: it had grown more versatile, more sophisticated, and far more competitive. So it was unsurprising that a great many companies were prepared to enter the television market. But the early investments generally outran income, even though the public had put close to $1 billion into sets by 1948. In that year there were four networks—N.B.C., C.B.S., A.B.C., and Dumont—and fifty stations, whose total revenues of $8.7 million were hardly a third of their expenditures of $23.6 million. The New York *News*, for example, had figured on losses of $500,000 a year at the start when it opened its station, WPIX, in June, 1948, but the first year's actual deficit was more than $1.5 million. Undeterred,

hundreds of others sought broadcast licenses from the Federal Communications Commission.

Many doomsayers, including former N.B.C. head Merlin Aylesworth, were quick to forecast the demise of radio. While network radio did suffer from television competition, most radio advertising had always been local, and total radio advertising revenues rose from $617 million in 1948 to $723 million in 1952, even while television time sales climbed from almost nothing to $580 million.

Movies were hit harder. At a time of rapid population growth, fast-rising personal incomes, and price inflation, their revenues failed to keep pace. Box-office income increased 34 per cent between 1941 and 1948, while average admission prices advanced 60 per cent, and personal income was up more than 150 per cent. Between 1946 and 1948 there was an actual drop of 13 per cent in box-office dollar gross, to just under $1.4 billion, according to the Audience Research Institute. Within a few years, however, filmmakers' fortunes revived as they began to sell their old releases to television and to use their facilities for TV production.

Television set sales began to climb more rapidly than ever, totaling $2.25 billion in retail value in 1950, when the number of manufacturers had increased to eighty, from just fourteen in 1947. By 1953 almost half of all American homes wired for electricity had sets. Broadcasters and advertisers became aware that they were vying for an even greater prize—the long hours for which people sat with eyes glued to the screen. For television had an obsessive quality that kept its audience staring at some of the same scenes in two-dimensional miniature that they might see in three-dimensional life size by merely looking around them.

The fight for color domination took over the next act. In this field C.B.S. had had the audacity to challenge R.C.A. on the technological front. Back in 1936, C.B.S. chief William S. Paley had hired Peter Goldmark, a young Hungarian with a brilliant record of innovation in television engineering. Goldmark developed a mechanical system of color TV, which C.B.S. proposed for immediate adoption as far back as 1940, when the F.C.C. held hearings on television standards. It was much too early for a color ruling, however; F.C.C. hearings were resumed after the war, and C.B.S. finally got its system approved in 1950.

The rub was that there were already millions of black and white sets in use and the C.B.S. system was not compatible—that is, its color broadcasts could not be viewed on a black and white receiver. Set manufacturers, feeling that they wanted first to saturate the market for black and white sets, were unwilling to provide the color adapters the system required. In 1951 C.B.S. merged with Hytron Radio & Electronics Corp., the fourth largest manufacturer of radio and television tubes, thereby getting a color television manufacturing capability, but not one important enough to affect the entire market. The F.C.C. eventually reversed its decision and approved R.C.A.'s electronic, compatible color system.

By 1955 N.B.C. and C.B.S. were each scheduling fifteen hours of color programming a week, including major sports events and a variety of such glittering shows as *Our Town* and the Sadler's Wells Ballet company. But it was N.B.C. and its parent, R.C.A., that had the major investment in color technology—some $65 million up to that point—and were therefore pushing it hardest.

Color television was caught in a kind of vicious spiral, the more vicious because of the massive infusions of money that were required. Advertisers would not come in until enough sets were in use; the sets could not be sold until there was more programming; and large amounts of expensive color programming could not be undertaken until there was advertising to pay for it. R.C.A. launched, not very successfully,

a major promotion ("Big Color Is Here") for color television, but the $795 and $895 price tags were too high to develop a mass market. Sales in 1956 totaled about 120,000 color-television sets, most of them by R.C.A., but this was still too slow a pace, since it was felt that it would take about 1,000,000 sets in use to attract advertising in significant volume.

R.C.A.'s sales in 1956 reached an all-time record $1.1 billion, but before-tax profits were only $80 million. In good part because of a loss of some $14 million in its drive for color TV, the profit margin was down to 7.1 per cent of sales, the lowest since the reconversion year of 1946, which in turn had been the lowest since 1933. The company's investment in color eventually surpassed $100 million, more than double the $50 million it had spent in developing black and white TV, before it turned its first profit on color television in 1960. But the real payoff was to start in the next few years, with a breakthrough in 1961 and a fivefold increase in color TV profits the following year.

The Way to Wealth
WILLIAM S. PALEY

Starting as a Philadelphia cigar maker, William S. Paley became the builder of the Columbia Broadcasting System and one of the leading figures in the radio and television industries. It was the power of radio as an advertising medium that led him to change businesses.

Born in 1901, Paley received a B.S. degree from the University of Pennsylvania and joined his father's firm, the Congress Cigar Company, as vice president and secretary. There he became intrigued by the fact that a $6,500-a-week outlay to advertise his father's cigars on a radio program called the "La Palina Smoker" had in a short time resulted in more than doubling their sales.

The cigar-promoting program was aired on the Columbia Phonograph Broadcasting System, a fledgling network begun in 1927, about a year after the National Broadcasting Company had introduced its Red and Blue networks. The Columbia system was a joint operation of two new companies, United Independent Broadcasters and the Columbia Phonograph Company. Paley's interest in the medium soon induced him to spend $450,000 to buy

into the arrangement. He left the cigar business to become president of United Independent Broadcasters, and the network was renamed the Columbia Broadcasting System. At twenty-eight Paley was presiding over a radio chain of sixteen stations that stretched from Philadelphia to Council Bluffs, Iowa. In 1929, his first year at the helm, he amassed gross billings of $4,785,981, compared with $72,500 in sales two years before, when the network had started. By 1935 C.B.S. had ninety-seven stations and claimed to be the world's largest radio network. Its gross in 1937 was $34.2 million.

Almost from the start, Paley had decided to use talent as a weapon with which to draw audiences away from the competing N.B.C. network. He launched the Columbia Artists Bureau as a subsidiary and helped to build radio stars like Kate Smith, Bing Crosby, and Morton Downey. The bureau booked its contract artists into off-the-air entertainment spots and in 1935 grossed more than $2 million on its own.

That same year two men joined C.B.S. who, perhaps as much as Paley, were to shape the network's future: an

education expert named Edward R. Murrow and Frank Stanton, an industrial psychologist. They created two distinct characteristics in the network, one a devotion to intensive news coverage, the other a passion for appealing to mass popularity. Paley, for his part, concentrated on having the network do its own programming, rather than act merely as the carrier signal for what advertising agencies, sponsors, and independent producers packaged. His policies and astute leadership paid off when C.B.S. passed N.B.C. in time sales for both radio and television in April, 1953.

In the new television medium, C.B.S. profits rose from $25 million to $49 million between 1959 and 1964. By the latter date, Paley and Stanton, who had become president, were reorganizing the company to reflect its growing interests as a conglomerate. Broadcasting came to represent only one of four divisions of C.B.S., which also owned record and book clubs, two publishing houses, toy and musical instrument manufacturing firms, and even the New York Yankees baseball team. In 1969 the company that Paley had built became a billion-dollar grosser.

SEARCH AND RESEARCH

Wartime experience transformed research from un-pampered stepchild to industry's bright hope for the future. Between 1940 and 1958 research and development expenditures rose from $900 million a year to more than $10 billion, most of that amount administered by business corporations.

The great bulk of this effort was directed toward applications—preferably profitable applications—of what was already known. But the two companies long noted for their activities in this field, the Bell Telephone System and General Electric, also devoted a considerable amount of their research energies to expanding the frontiers of knowledge. So, on occasion, did Du Pont, Eastman Kodak, and some of the larger drug companies. Almost as a direct outgrowth of its war work, Douglas Aircraft spun off its research and development department as a separate entity called Rand (for R and D) Corporation, which became known as the first "think tank" because of its concentration on abstract and theoretical problems, chiefly for the government. By the mid-1950's General Dynamics, General Motors, and Avco Manufacturing had top-ranking physicists on their payrolls, and Glenn L. Martin formed a new subsidiary, RIAS, Inc., solely to explore new scientific knowledge.

The most substantial research investment by private business was that made by American Telephone & Telegraph and Western Electric, its manufacturing subsidiary, which between them poured well over $1 billion into the Bell Telephone Laboratories in the first sixty years of the century. In 1942 Bell Labs opened the nation's largest industrial research center at Murray Hill, New Jersey, where in the single year of 1958 the budget ran to $180 million, half of these funds provided by the government to carry out Western Electric contracts.

The telephone system itself was Bell's first major problem, since it involved the ability to tie every phone to every other phone across miles of wire, exchanges,

TEXAS INSTRUMENTS

On October 1, 1953, Texas Instruments, Inc., was listed for the first time on the "Big Board" of the New York Stock Exchange. Its price: $5.25. By 1960, each share was worth $256. The spectacular rise in value mirrored a business success that resulted largely from the combination of the rapid exploitation of scientific advances and a boom in government spending. The principal product accounting for Texas Instrument's growth was the transistor, but the company's origins were in oil.

In 1917 an Oklahoma-trained physicist named John Clarence ("Doc") Karcher thought it might be possible to use reflected sound waves to map underground oil and gas deposits. He started a firm called the Geological Engineering Company, which failed, although the basic concept of reflective seismology proved more durable. Backed by Everette Lee De Golyer, an eminent geologist and executive of Amerada Petroleum Company, Karcher joined with other scientists in a subsidiary of Amerada, the Geophysical Research Corporation. The company did well during the late 1920's exploring for oil, and in 1930 Karcher and his associates struck off on their own,

TEXAS INSTRUMENTS

J. Erik Jonsson

founding Geophysical Services, Incorporated.

G.S.I. offered an Aluminum Corporation of America sales engineer, John Erik Jonsson, from whom it had purchased some aluminum, a job running its manufacturing of instruments.

Jonsson proved to be the financial genius of G.S.I., a devotee of electronic products, and a prophet who saw their application for military purposes.

On December 6, 1941, G.S.I. reorganized, splitting away from an oil producing partner, Coronado Corporation. The war led it into making magnetic airborne detection devices for locating submerged submarines. Sales to the armed services amounted to only $1.1 million during World War II, but Jonsson pushed for closer ties with military procurement officers as a stabilizing factor to the company's chancy ventures at searching for oil.

The Cold War helped business. Former military and civilian government officials joined the company. In 1947 G.S.I. received a contract for a low-altitude bombsight. Other government orders followed for sophisticated instruments, and by 1948 the company showed sales of $5 million. In 1949 G.S.I. had 792 employees and annual sales of $6.4 million. The figure rose to $15.4 million in 1951, during the Korean War, and the company's name was changed (because the Navy complained of confusion between two of its suppliers) to Texas Instruments.

The transistor had first been demonstrated by Bell Laboratories in 1948. Jonsson was interested, and the day after Western Electric offered to license

and relay stations, a job that grew more complex with each new phone that was installed. When the enormous potential of the problem first occurred to the forethinking engineers around 1910, they began to design automatic equipment, including dial phones, and these were being installed within ten years. By the mid-1950's, when the company was having difficulty maintaining its staff of 250,000 telephone operators, it would have needed six times that number under the old manual system. The immensely complex switching problem was dealt with by something called "logic circuit design," and the difficult matter of transmitting signals from the weak, voice-generated electric currents became known as "information handling." These terms, later to become much more familiar in computer technology, were indicative that the telephone system itself was simply a giant computer, and it was being "programmed" to produce the desired results every time an individual dialed a number.

The need to design large and complicated systems gave rise to the concept of "systems engineering," which Bell engineers introduced to the military early in World War II. They in turn passed the idea on to defense contractors, among whom it became an extremely useful—and fashionable—method of planning their webs of interdependent and interrelated activities.

Largely to meet the needs of Western Electric, the Bell Labs also remained in the forefront of electronics research, a wartime prodigy that grew into a postwar colossus. One of the innovations developed by the National Bureau of Standards to compress the proximity fuse into its tiny space, for example, was the printed circuit, which radio makers quickly adopted in their postwar manufacture. Factory sales of electronics equipment rose from around $500 million in 1940, when it was largely confined to radio, to $10 billion by 1960.

A sizable part of the prewar electronics industry was in vacuum tubes, output of which rose from 52 million in 1930 to 115 million in 1940 and then to more than 400 million, made by about forty different companies, in 1950. The vacuum tube grew out of experiments in incandescent lighting by Thomas Edison, who noted that electrons would traverse the open space from a heated filament to a cold plate. The English physicist John A. Fleming first used this to build a rectifying tube, and the addition of a wire grid for control by Lee De Forest in 1906 made it the triode tube which was to become such an integral and lucrative element of radio.

But the tube makers were about to be rudely surprised. Bell Lab researchers John Bardeen and Walter H. Brattain, following the theoretical formulations of William B. Shockley, found they could amplify a small electric current by placing two tiny wires on a small block of germanium. This device, which they called a transistor, could thus produce much the same effect as a vacuum tube, but much more quickly and with no breakable glass tube, no vacuum, and no filament to heat.

The tube makers looked into the new discovery worriedly but decided there was no imminent threat to their business because much more development was needed. But Bell Labs solved the problems quickly, and by 1951 some germanium diodes were going into the better television sets. Then Western Electric let everyone in by offering licenses for transistor manufacture to all comers, with the mere payment of a $25,000 advance on royalties. Bell Labs held an eight-day symposium to teach transistor technology to the licensees, and thirty-nine companies attended, among them many that had not even been in the vacuum tube business.

Some of the new names moved ahead fast. Transitron Electronic Corp. of Wakefield, Massachusetts, not even founded until 1952, within five years had passed

transistor makers, Texas Instruments sent in its $25,000 check, the required advance against royalties. The company hired a Bell Laboratories scientist, Gordon Teal, to handle research and invested some $2 million in efforts that brought the price of the germanium transistor down from the $10–$16 range to $2.50. At that level, its use could be expanded from miniaturized equipment, mainly hearing aids, to portable radios. Profits from this new market were not large, but Texas Instruments was initiated into some of the mysteries of mass manufacturing techniques.

The next challenge was to build transistors from another semiconducting material, silicon, which could withstand extremely high temperatures. Texas Instruments scientists accomplished this goal by 1954 and gave the company a lead that left it without effective competition for the next four years. Sales climbed rapidly, from $28.7 million in 1955 to $193 million in 1959, an estimated $80 million of which was in the semiconductor field. Although the days of incredible stock price performance ended in the late 1960's, the company continued its dramatic growth. By the 1970's it had moved into the list of the top 200 industrial firms in the United States and had sales of well over $800 million.

Sylvania and was on even terms with G.E. in transistor manufacture. Ahead of them all was Texas Instruments, a company that up to that time had been known chiefly for its use of sophisticated instrumentation in exploring for oil deposits.

The spectacular growth of the electronics industry came not only in components but in end products as well, television and missile guidance systems being two cases in point. One of the small companies that grew big rapidly was Ampex Corp., of Redwood City, California, whose sales mounted from $388,000 in 1950 to around $65 million in 1960, when net profit was $4 million. Part of its secret was that its founder, Alexander M. Poniatoff, who started the business with six employees in a furniture loft, was adept at keeping his engineers alert and inventive.

Among the company's earliest products were taped sound recorders for radio stations and for phonograph transcriptions. In a race with R.C.A., among others, to develop a television recorder, the company in 1951 put Charles Ginsburg, a brilliant young radio engineer, in charge of this project. In 1956, after a series of interruptions and setbacks, Ampex introduced its video tape recorder, which became its biggest moneymaker. The machine scored an international coup when the Ampex representative at a Moscow trade fair in 1959 maneuvered Russian Premier Nikita Khrushchev and U.S. Vice President Richard Nixon within range and recorded their famous "kitchen debate." The tape was brought back to the U.S., and the debate was on U.S. television two days later. Not seen in this country, however, was the instant replay demonstrated to Khrushchev, who conceded, "This we do not have."

OF CAMERAS AND COPIERS

Not all of the more startling and significant inventions of the postwar period were the work of the teams of scientists and technicians working in well-equipped laboratories. Some were brought forth by inspired individuals whose careers more closely resembled those of Eli Whitney and Charles Goodyear, except that they came to be more widely appreciated and more handsomely rewarded in their own time.

Edwin H. Land was a seventeen-year-old Harvard freshman when he took a leave of absence to study, chiefly at the New York Public Library, the effect of light polarizing filters in eliminating automobile headlight glare. He perfected sheets of polarizing material, applied for a patent, and returned to Harvard in 1929, but he soon joined a young physics instructor to form Land-Wheelwright Laboratories and to continue re-

An Ampex video-tape instant replay of the famous "kitchen debate" at the 1959 Moscow trade fair amuses its participants.

search on polarizers.

In 1937 Land organized the Polaroid Corp. and so impressed such influential backers as James P. Warburg, Averell Harriman, and Lewis Strauss that they provided $375,000 in capital and gave him voting control and a free hand. Sales, mainly of Polaroid sunglasses and a glare-free study lamp, climbed from $142,000 in 1937 to $1,000,000 in 1941, when the company began to work on military optics and increased sales almost to $17 million by 1945. But the end of the war brought a sharp drop in business to $5 million in 1946 and $1.5 million—with an operating loss of $2 million—in 1947.

But by then Land had developed something new: a camera that could take a picture and produce a print within sixty seconds. With no sales organization and with almost no advertising budget, the company hired a Bell & Howell vice president, J. Harold Booth, as its executive vice president and turned the problem over to him. Booth and his sales manager offered exclusive rights to sell the camera for thirty days to one department store in each major city, provided they did the advertising. Sales started at Boston's Jordan Marsh store in November, 1948, and were spectacularly successful. The promotion then moved from one city to another, with similar results. A decade later, with sales of $59 million, Polaroid had overtaken Bell & Howell and General Aniline & Film in photographic sales and was second, if a very laggard second, to giant Eastman Kodak. Land, with some 240 patents to his credit, then proceeded to develop a color process for his camera and signed an agreement with Eastman to provide materials.

Another lone inventor, and one whose career was long dogged with hardship and misfortune, was Chester Carlson. As a boy in California, young Carlson had had to provide a large measure of support for his ailing parents. He made his own way through the California Institute of Technology, then came east to work at the Bell Labs but lost his job as a Depression casualty in 1933. He next worked for a law firm, studying law at night, and then specialized in patent work for P. R. Mallory & Company.

Carlson decided there should be a better way to make copies of legal documents and technical drawings than the slow and costly methods in use. Like Land, he used the New York Public Library as a source of research into photoelectrical—and thus dry—means of copying. He developed and patented a crude mechanism for his product in 1937 but was unsuccessful in his efforts to get backing from any of the major companies in related fields of work.

Not until 1944 was he able to interest anyone in his new process. That year he mentioned his patents casually to a research engineer from Battelle Memorial Institute, Russell Dayton, who was enthusiastic about

M.I.T.'s Norbert Wiener, pioneer in the field of cybernetics

the possibilities. Battelle took it on as a self-sponsored research project, adding a number of significant improvements and developments to the copying process.

As the war drew to an end, Battelle was looking about, with little success, for a commercial firm that was willing to underwrite further research and development. At the same time, a small Rochester, New York, firm, the Haloid Company, was looking for new products that might be related to its own field of photocopying but would not run into the crunching competition of Eastman. Its research director, John Dessauer, learned of Carlson's invention through a technical journal, and Haloid was soon having serious talks with Battelle. By the beginning of 1947 they had a contract, with Haloid underwriting research in exchange for a license to manufacture an as yet undeveloped machine.

It was 1950 before the first installation of a machine was made for the process known by that time as xerography. The equipment was cumbersome and difficult to use, requiring a large number of steps. But because it was useful in producing paper lithographic plates for a new office lithography machine being sold by Addressograph-Multigraph Corp., the machine was able to pay its own way while further development was undertaken.

The machines were greatly improved by 1955, when Haloid's sales rose to $21 million, three times as high as they had been in the first year of the agreement with Battelle. That year the contract was revised, Battelle giving up its 8 per cent royalty for a block of stock, thus giving the company more funds for product and market development. The company by then had changed its name to Haloid Xerox, and in 1961 it was again changed simply to Xerox Corporation.

The company's desk-sized, automatic 914 office copying machine was brought out early in 1960, after a total investment of $40 million. It could produce one copy in thirty seconds and additional copies of the same item at the rate of eight seconds each, and could copy from single sheets or pages in a book. Xerox Corporation's gross revenues hit $100 million by 1962 and rose far above $1 billion by the end of the decade. Carlson became a multimillionaire, spending his last years seeking out worthy causes for his largesse; Battelle Memorial Institute's total endowment rose to about ten times what it might otherwise have been; and Xerox grew in size and stature to where it could nearly match the dimensions of Eastman, its Rochester neighbor.

TAKING CHARGE BY MACHINE

Control mechanisms on machinery go back at least as far as the fly-ball "governor" by which James Watt in 1788 was able to control the speed of his steam engine. The Jacquard loom, perfected in 1804 by Joseph M. Jacquard, was made to weave to specific designs by means of cards with holes punched in them, and similar devices were used to produce music in Victorian parlors by means of player pianos.

It was not until fairly recent times, however, that scientists and logicians showed that all such processes followed common principles in their operation, and that these could be formulated into a system for controlling all kinds of discrete mechanical activities. Such a system would have sensors to detect what was happening, a communications link to carry the message from the sensors to the control unit, a logic unit to assemble and analyze the information and to determine what, if any, changes needed to be made, another communications line carrying orders back to the scene of action, and motor devices to make the necessary changes. In describing this control theory, which he termed "cybernetics," M.I.T's Norbert Wiener showed

THE BACKGROUND OF I.B.M.

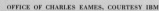

Ancestor of the computer: Hollerith's tabulator, employed in the 1890 census

The lineal forebear of the modern computer—and of the International Business Machines Co.—was a nineteenth-century mechanical counter devised by a man named Herman Hollerith. After receiving an engineering degree at Columbia University, Hollerith went to Washington, D.C., to help one of his professors work on the 1880 national census, which took seven years to compile and tabulate. One day Hollerith heard someone suggest that there should be a machine able to do such painstaking work. Drawing inspiration from a railroad ticket in which a conductor punched holes to show his height and weight, Hollerith fashioned a pantographic punch that could record an individual's vital statistics by means of holes in a card, which could be read with the help of electromagnets. In the 1890 census the device saved an estimated $5 million and permitted the census tabulation to be made in three years.

Hollerith formed the Tabulating Machines Company and opened a plant in Washington, but his business sense and sales talents fell short of his inventive abilities. The firm was consolidated in 1911 into a group of computing-scale and time-recording companies by Charles R. Flint, an active promoter of business combinations. The new association, known as the Computing-Tabulating-Recording Company, drifted along, badly in need of capable management. To overcome the deficiency, Flint in 1914 hired as president forty-year-old Thomas J. Watson, who had been a crackerjack salesman and sales manager for the National Cash Register Co., but who had fallen out with its top management.

Watson moved vigorously to reshape the firm. Apparently more on the strength of his own personality than on C-T-R's meager promise, he managed to borrow $25,000—later increased to $40,000—from the Guaranty Trust Company. Over Hollerith's glum objection, he started a laboratory modeled after one set up by his friend Charles Kettering at National Cash Register, and put researchers to work improving on Hollerith's machine.

By 1920 Watson had tripled C-T-R's gross, and he announced that it would double to $30 million in the following year. This was not to be, in the depression year of 1921, however. The tabulating machine business held up fairly well, because it was on a lease basis, but the computing-scale and time-recording businesses all but collapsed. The scale business did not recover until after it was sold to the Hobart Manufacturing Company in 1933.

basic similarities in the performance of these functions by human beings and by machines. Thus, when an individual essays to walk a straight line, the eye and the inner ear sense deviations and send their messages to the brain, which sorts out the information, makes a decision, and then sends its messages back to the appropriate muscles, which then obey the commands sent to them. In the case of a projectile, an inertial sensor might determine any deviation from its course and send this message back by radio to a control unit, which would then make the proper calculations and radio the course-correcting orders back to motor mechanisms on the projectile. The advantages possessed by the machine are that it responds more quickly and is less prone to error in carrying out fixed routines that respond to physical laws.

Much earlier, a number of people had become aware that mathematical computation also lent itself readily to the kind of cold logic of which machines were capable. French mathematician Blaise Pascal

C-T-R, meanwhile, having extended its activities to Canada, Europe, Latin America, and the Far East, changed its name to the International Business Machines Co.

The New Deal legislation of the Depression served I.B.M.'s interests well. The company won the contract to do the bookkeeping under the Social Security Act, which amounted to 120 million postings a year. Passage of the Wages and Hours Law gave new life to its time-recording business. Watson finally achieved his 1921 target of $30 million in sales in 1937, and by 1940 his company, with almost $50 million in sales, was the largest in the office machines industry. The war brought orders for many more accounting machines, which I.B.M. produced, along with automatic rifles, fire control instruments, and other military hardware, and sales rose to $140 million by 1945. Watson's company was then twice the size of National Cash Register, but I.B.M. had not yet put its brand on the newly emerging electronic computer business. Over the next quarter century its activities in that field would catapult it to the position of one of the nation's half-dozen biggest industrial companies.

devised a calculating machine in 1642 that worked by means of a series of wheels and ratchets. A multiplying and dividing machine designed by Gottfried Leibniz was built in 1694. Charles Babbage, Lucasian professor of mathematics at Cambridge, built a "difference engine" for making tabulations in 1822, and received large grants from the British government for an "analytical engine" that would run on steam power and could be operated from a set of programmed instructions on punched cards. But the engineering ability of the times was not up to the task, and machines like those he envisioned were not built until about a century later.

It had long been felt that information, as diverse and multifarious as the whole gamut of human activity, could not be reduced to a form by which it could be handled by machines. But in 1948 a Bell Labs mathematician named Claude Shannon wrote a paper entitled "A Mathematical Theory of Communication," showing that information too could be reduced to quantified terms. Information was already being represented by means of letters, numbers, and other symbols, so it could also be reduced to numerical terms, including the binary notation that lent itself to representation by an electrical current being turned either on or off.

The means for performing all these functions — control of mechanical devices, mathematical computation, and information handling — came together in the device known as the computer. The use of electrical equipment made it faster than the human brain, electronics added another order of magnitude to its speed, and human ingenuity contributed still more, enabling computers to function in millionths and billionths of a second.

The company whose name became virtually synonymous with computers was International Business Machines. I.B.M. sales climbed after the war, reaching $156 million in 1948. But it was not truly keeping abreast of the newly emerging computer industry. At the University of Pennsylvania, J. Presper Eckert, Jr., and John W. Mauchly had built their giant Eniac and, forming the Eckert-Mauchly Computer Corp., sold their computer to Army Ordnance in 1946. Relay-type computers were being constructed by Bell Labs. But I.B.M. still looked at the electronic brains as hardly more than academic playthings.

President Thomas J. Watson, however, had a firm belief in the advancement of education and science, and this helped him take a small role in computer development. Dr. W. J. Eckert of Columbia was using two coupled I.B.M. business machines to calculate astronomical tables as early as 1933, and this led to the establishment of the Watson Scientific Computing Laboratory at the university. Before World War II a Harvard mathematician, Howard H. Aiken, sought help for a project in which several I.B.M. machines would be interconnected to solve complex problems; I.B.M. contributed $500,000 and some of its best engineering talent. Aiken completed his five-ton, fifty-foot Automatic Sequence Controlled Calculator, or Mark I, in 1944 and announced it to the press, but hardly mentioned I.B.M.'s role. This so angered Watson that he ordered his engineers to do better, thus moving I.B.M. into computer development out of little more than pique. By 1948 the company was displaying its new Selective Sequence Electronic Calculator.

To Tom Watson, Jr., this new technology had the smell of the future about it, and he pushed hard for more development. By early 1949 Aiken had produced his Mark II and was working on a Mark III model. An advanced machine called the Ednac was being built by the University of Pennsylvania for the Army. Raytheon was working on a high-speed computer under government contract, and Eckert-Mauchly was testing a small machine called the Binac. And by 1951 Remington Rand, which had bought out Eckert-Mauchly and modified the Eniac, sold its first Univac I to the Census Bureau.

I.B.M. stepped up its computer development after Tom Watson, Jr., took over the presidency in 1952. It brought out a scientific model designated the 701, then one with greater data-handling ability, the 702, to compete with Univac for the business market. Even before the 702 was available, I.B.M. announced that it was working on more advanced series, the 704 and 705. It was with the latter two that the company managed to assume industry leadership. The first computer sale to a private company was a Univac delivered in 1954 to General Electric by Sperry Rand, which had absorbed Remington Rand. By mid-1955 Sperry Rand installations still had a slim lead over the I.B.M. 700 series, but a year later I.B.M. had installed 76 of its machines, with 193 more on order, while Univac had 46 installed and 65 on order.

I.B.M. pioneered in a number of important computer improvements, such as magnetic core storage, which made for larger computer memories, and random access, which permitted rapid retrieval of individual records stored on discs. But its real edge came in one of the company's oldest strengths: customer sales and service. While other companies concentrated on hard selling, I.B.M. was carefully grooming its buyers on the proper use of the machines, even before they were delivered, and sending out service crews to make repairs whenever bugs appeared.

I.B.M. sales passed the $1 billion mark in 1957. By the end of the decade I.B.M. was far out in front of an industry whose sales were nearing $2 billion a year, with a far greater potential ahead. Other firms, contenting themselves with the race for second place, lined up behind: Sperry Rand, Burroughs, Minneapolis-Honeywell, R.C.A., Philco, National Cash Register, General Electric, and Control Data. Many were losing money in their electronic data processing divisions, some as much as $100 million a year.

But there was no longer any question about the market. Computers were firmly entrenched in industry, government, and education. Most firms, after some early fumbling, were learning how to use their data processing installations profitably. For those businesses too small to have computers, or that wished to take advantage of the lower unit costs of large computers, there were service bureaus that offered the use of their data processing facilities.

About a third of the computers in use were put to work primarily on scientific and engineering calculations. A few were beginning to be used as the brains of process control systems in electric power, steel, petroleum, and chemical plants. But most were given the jobs of simplifying record-keeping and paper work and of solving business problems. The computer was at its best when there were vast amounts of data and a bewildering array of choices—finding the most efficient ways to operate oil refineries, scheduling shipments to cut transportation costs, predicting needs for labor and materials months in advance, and eliminating experimental models of planes or space vehicles by simulating designs on the drawing board. To cut down the handling of billions of bank checks, the most tedious chore in banking, "mark-sense" machines that could read certain types of characters were being installed in computer systems. And, at least experimentally, computers were being taught to learn from experience, to correct their own errors, to program other computers, and to behave "heuristically"—that is, to find, as human beings do, not necessarily the best answer, but a good one, in matters calling for judgment.

Although some were inclined to decry the inroads that the new machines were making on some of the more thoughtful work of people, they might well have considered what could have happened without the computer. The nation was continuing to grow bigger, busier, and more suffused with paper. With business enterprises and government activities growing, service occupations swelling, and production, consumption, and markets expanding, the United States was bidding fair to make itself a nation of clerks—typists, bookkeepers, filers, and paper handlers. The number of people in these occupations had increased 58 per cent in the 1940's, and another 33 per cent by 1960, when they numbered 9.1 million, as against, for example, only 5.8 million farmers. If this was to be a continuing trend, then computers had arrived just in time. Like other labor-saving devices, they were assuming the kind of drudgery that could only serve ultimately to stifle the human spirit; in that way they were freeing people to move on to more difficult and demanding challenges.

IX Organizational Genius

A wonder of the auto age: bodies drop on chassis at Henry Ford's first moving assembly line, Highland Park, Michigan, 1913.

" The American challenge is not ruthless, like so many Europe has known in her history, but it may be more dramatic. . . . Its weapons are the use and systematic perfection of all the instruments of reason. Not simply in the field of science, where it is the only tool, but also in organization and management. . . ."

Jean-Jacques Servan-Schreiber, *The American Challenge,* 1967

The laying of the Atlantic cable, which began in 1857, was organized by Cyrus W. Field and financiers and inventors, seen at left in one of their meetings.

J. P. Morgan's organizational talents created U.S. Steel, the first billion-dollar corporation. At right is the notice of its formation, March 3, 1901.

The schematic view below, issued about 1880, shows the organization of activities (though not the contemporary uncleanliness) in a pork packing plant.

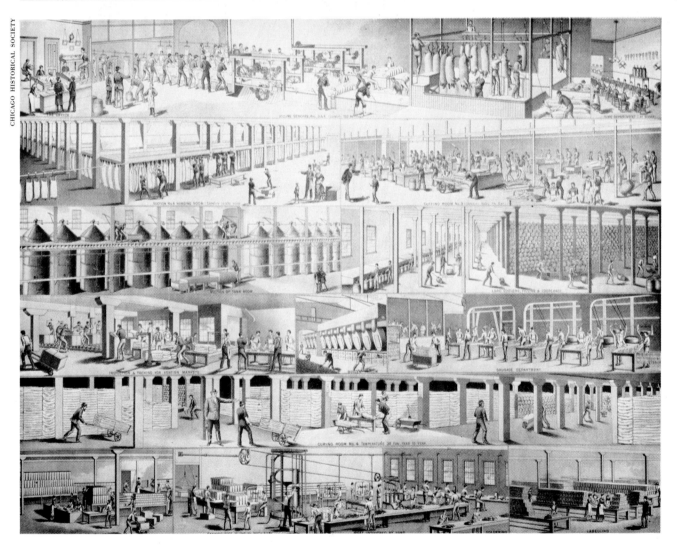

FINANCIAL.   FINANCIAL.   FINANCIAL.   FIN

Office of J. P. MORGAN & CO.,
23 Wall Street, New York.

To the Stockholders of   March 2, 1901.

Federal Steel Company,
National Steel Company,
National Tube Company,
American Steel and Wire Company of New Jersey,
American Tin Plate Company,
American Steel Hoop Company,
American Sheet Steel Company.

The UNITED STATES STEEL CORPORATION has been organized under the laws of the State of New Jersey, with power, among other things, to acquire the outstanding preferred stocks and common stocks of the Companies above named, and the outstanding bonds and stock of the Carnegie Company.

A SYNDICATE, comprising leading financial interests throughout the United States and Europe, of which the undersigned are Managers, has been formed by subscribers to the amount of $200,000,000, (including among such subscribers the undersigned and many large stockholders of the several Companies,) to carry out the arrangement hereinafter stated, and to provide the sum in cash and the financial support required for that purpose. Such Syndicate, through the undersigned, has made a contract with the United States Steel Corporation, under which the latter is to issue and deliver its Preferred Stock and its Common Stock and its Five Per Cent. Gold Bonds in consideration for stocks of the above named Companies and bonds and stock of the Carnegie Company and the sum of $25,000,000 in cash.

The Syndicate has already arranged for the acquisition of substantially all the bonds and stock of the Carnegie Company, including Mr. Carnegie's holdings. The bonds of the United States Steel Corporation are to be used only to acquire bonds and 60 per cent. of the stock of the Carnegie Company.

The undersigned, in behalf of the Syndicate, and on the terms and conditions hereinafter stated, offer, in exchange for the preferred stocks and common stocks of the Companies above named, respectively, certificates for Preferred Stock and Common Stock of the United States Steel Corporation, upon the basis stated in the following table, viz.:

For each $100 par value of stock of the class mentioned below, the amount set opposite thereto in Preferred Stock or Common Stock of United States Steel Corporation at par:

NAME OF COMPANY AND CLASS OF STOCK.	Preferred Stock.	Common Stock.
Federal Steel Co., Preferred stock	$110	
Common stock	4	$107.50
American Steel and Wire Co. of N. J., Preferred stock	117.50	
Common stock		102.50
National Tube Co., Preferred stock	125	
Common stock	8.80	125
National Steel Co., Preferred stock	125	
Common stock		125
American Tin Plate Co., Preferred stock	125	
Common stock	20	125
American Steel Hoop Co., Preferred stock	100	
Common stock		100
American Sheet Steel Co., Preferred stock	100	
Common stock		100

(Header: Amount of New Stock to be delivered in par value.)

With reference to the last four Companies the aggregate amount of stocks so to be offered was arranged with the principal stockholders of those Companies, who have requested the distribution of such amount among the four Companies to be made in the percentages above stated.

Proper adjustment will be made in respect of dividends upon all the deposited preferred stocks, so that the registered holders of receipts for such preferred stocks will receive the equivalent of dividends thereon, at the rates therein provided, from the last dividend period up to APRIL 1, 1901, from which date dividends on the Preferred Stock of the United States Steel Corporation are to begin to accrue. Deposited common stocks must carry all dividends or rights to dividends declared or payable on or after MARCH 1, 1901, and no adjustment or allowance will be made in respect thereof.

For the purpose of avoiding the necessity of interruption in the declaration and payment of dividends, when earned, upon the common stock, concurrently with the payment of dividends upon the preferred stock, there has been inserted in the charter of the United States Steel Corporation a provision to the effect that whenever all quarterly dividends accrued upon the preferred stock for previous quarters shall have been paid, the Board of Directors may declare dividends on the common stock out of any remaining surplus or net profits.

Statements furnished to us by officers of the several companies above named, and of the Carnegie Company, show that the aggregate of the net earnings of all the companies for the calendar year 1900 was amply sufficient to pay dividends on both classes of the new stocks, besides making provision for sinking funds and maintenance of properties. It is expected that by the consummation of the proposed arrangement the necessity of large deductions heretofore made on account of expenditures for improvements will be avoided, the amount of earnings applicable to dividends will be substantially increased and greater stability of investment will be assured, without necessarily increasing the prices of manufactured products.

The certificates for stocks of the Companies above named must be deposited as stated below, in exchange for TRANSFERABLE RECEIPTS issued by the respective depositaries, for which application will be made for listing on the New York Stock Exchange. The deposited certificates must be accompanied by suitable assignments and powers of attorney in blank, duly executed and having attached thereto the proper War Revenue stamps, and also, if required, suitable assignments or transfers of all dividends or rights to dividends upon deposited common stocks declared or payable on or after MARCH 1, 1901. Every deposit shall be upon the following further terms and conditions:

1. The undersigned, acting in behalf of the Syndicate, shall have full control over the deposited certificates, including power to deliver the same under said contract to the United States Steel Corporation in consideration of the issue of Preferred Stock and Common Stock of said Corporation.

2. The certificates for shares of the United States Steel Corporation, deliverable to depositors, shall be delivered at an office or at offices in the City of New York to be designated by the undersigned by advertisement in at least two newspapers in the City of New York. Such certificates may be issued in the names of the respective holders of the receipts entitled thereto or may be issued in such other names as the undersigned may select, in which event they shall be indorsed for transfer in blank at the time of delivery. The undersigned at their option may deliver temporary certificates for such shares pending the preparation and delivery of engraved certificates.

3. At any time prior to the deposit hereunder of two-thirds in amount of all outstanding shares of the capital stock of any one or more of the above-named Companies, (which two-thirds in each instance shall include two-thirds of the outstanding preferred stock of such Company,) the undersigned in their discretion may withdraw the offer herein made to depositors of shares of any such Company of whose capital stock two-thirds shall not have been deposited; and, in such case, no act or notice of withdrawal shall be required other than advertisement thereof at least once in each of two daily newspapers in the City of New York. Upon any such withdrawal, the deposited shares of such Company shall be returned without charge, upon surrender of the respective receipts issued therefor. The Undersigned, in their discretion, may consummate the proposed transaction as to the stocks of any Companies herein named, irrespective of the deposit of the stocks of any other Company or of any withdrawal as to any other Company.

4. The Undersigned are authorized to proceed with the proposed transaction whenever in their sole judgment a sufficient amount of the stocks of said companies, or of any of them, shall have been deposited. They reserve the right, at any time, in their discretion, to wholly abandon the transaction and to withdraw their offer herein contained, as to all the depositors, by publication of notice of such withdrawal in two daily newspapers in the City of New York; and in that event all the deposited shares shall be returned without charge upon surrender of the

344   *With others under construction, a vessel is launched at Henry Kaiser's Portland,*

Oregon, shipyard, one of seven in which he produced a ship a day for World War II.

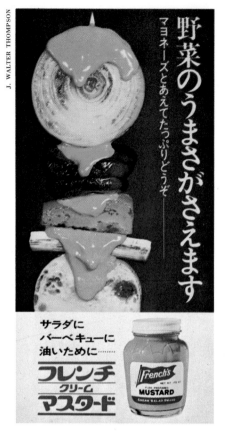

Left: fifty families a day filled out title closings for William Levitt's mass-produced homes at Levittown, Long Island, in 1947. Above and below: ads by J. Walter Thompson's worldwide organization, appearing in overseas publications, help sell U.S. products abroad.

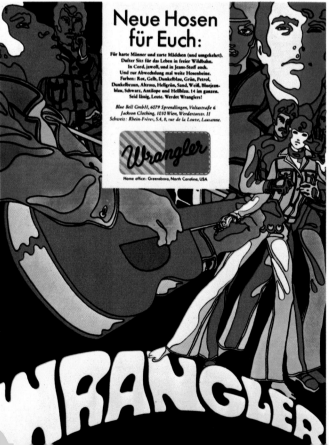

346

Two of history's largest enterprises, requiring the combined organizational efforts of industry and government, were the building of the atom bomb and the Marshall Plan's task of helping reconstruct the economies of Europe shattered by World War II. At top is a view of the front face of a production reactor operated by General Electric at the Hanford Atomic Energy Center, Washington. At right is the loading of a shipment of Marshall Plan wheat, bound for Greece.

New York Times — D. GORTON

Agribusiness, public utility consortiums, and multinational corporations are products of America's modern age of organization. Left: California broccoli is harvested for Freshpict, a subsidiary of the Purex Corporation. Below: New Mexico's Four Corners power plant, criticized for its pollution, is run by Arizona Public Service but feeds electricity to six of twenty-three members of a combine of power suppliers spread across the Southwest. Right: directors and senior management of Citicorp and Citibank meet in Tokyo for Asia-Pacific operations reports.

KARL KERNBERGER

10

─────◦─◦‹ ❦ ›◦─◦─────

THE NEW AGE
OF RESPONSIBILITY

1960-1972

"Nobody can understand a billion dollars," wrote Louis D. Brandeis in a pre-World War I attack on giant corporations, almost none of which even approached one billion dollars in assets, capitalization, or annual sales at that time. Scarcely more than a half century later the sum, if still incomprehensible, was certainly more in evidence. The corporation with sales or assets of one billion dollars or more was becoming a commonplace and there were even some individuals—Howard Hughes and J. Paul Getty—whose personal fortunes were apparently greater than that figure. Federal budgets rose to hundreds of billions, and the total U.S. production of goods and services climbed inexorably toward one trillion dollars—which is 1,000 billion dollars—and beyond.

From 1960 to 1970 U.S. population increased from 181 million to 205 million, a gain of something more than 13 per cent. In the same period the gross national product rose around 48 per cent, from $658 billion (in constant 1970 dollars) to $977 billion, while personal income was up 59 per cent, from $504 billion to $801 billion.

Providing the backdrop for rising living standards were the millions of enterprises that made up the nation's business community, but most visible were the hundreds of giant corporations at the core of the economy. For these companies, the Brandeis billion-dollar barrier was no more than a passing grade. Some 200 concerns, led by American Telephone & Telegraph with $50 billion, had assets of at least one billion dollars. More than 150, including 120 industrial corporations, had sales or revenues ranging from one

billion dollars to $19 billion in 1970, and five—A.T.&T., Prudential Insurance, Metropolitan Life Insurance Company, Standard Oil Company of New Jersey, and International Business Machines Corp.—had a net income from sales or investments of more than $1 billion each. General Motors, long the sales leader among industrial companies, was knocked out of this select group in 1970 by a two-month strike and a general economic slowdown, but it had reported sales of $24 billion and a net income of $1.7 billion in the previous year.

With such record-shattering profits, it was almost predictable that losses, when they came, would be unprecedented too. General Dynamics, hit by huge jet plane write-offs at its Convair division, lost $143 million in 1961, the largest annual deficit reported by any company up to that time. Studebaker Corp. lost $81 million in 1963, American Motors lost $76 million in 1967, and Brunswick, writing off losses on its automatic bowling equipment, slipped $77 million into the red in 1965. Toward the end of the decade conglomerate corporations took over these doubtful honors, when Ling-Temco-Vought showed losses of $38 million in 1969 and $70 million in 1970, while Northwest Industries in 1970 wrote down its railroad assets to a realistic level and reported a deficit of $227 million for that year. The grand champion loser, however, turned out to be the Penn Central Railroad, which slipped into bankruptcy in 1970 with a loss of $500 million, a debacle that would have spun the entire economy into a catastrophic nose-dive in any other country or any other era.

Such resounding deficits by once prospering enterprises symbolized the great fluidity of American business. There was much shifting and churning among the 500 largest industrial corporations. Companies moved up and down the list constantly, and as many as 10 per cent or more might be displaced by newcomers in any one year.

Perhaps the most descriptive statistics of the post-war decade were those that disclosed the upward economic mobility of American families. In 1950 more than one family out of four had an income of less than $3,000 a year (expressed in 1969 dollars); by 1960 only about one family in six remained in this group, and by 1969 it included fewer than one family in ten—although this meant that there were still 4.8 million such impoverished families. At the other end of the scale, one family in nine had an income of $10,000 or more in 1950; by 1960 this top group included every fourth family, and by 1969 it took in 46 per cent of all families, and almost one family in five had an annual income of $15,000 or more.

Two factors contributed to this spread of affluence. The first was that the economy had somehow managed—mainly by pulling and hauling between labor and management—to distribute purchasing power well enough so that all the goods that were produced could be bought, with enough money left over as savings to generate the capital flows needed for new investment in plant and equipment. The second was rising productivity—that is, greater output of goods and services per man-hour worked. This measure of productive potential increased at an accelerating rate in the private sector: from 1850 to 1889, output per man-hour rose at an average rate of 1.3 per cent a year; from 1889 to 1919, it advanced 2 per cent a year; the annual gain from 1919 to World War II was 2.5 per cent; from 1947 to 1960 it was 3.1 per cent; from 1960 to 1965 the output for each hour worked increased by 3.6 per cent annually; it slipped to 2.1 per cent from 1965 to 1970, before rebounding to around the 4 per cent level in 1971–72.

But in the late 1960's and early 1970's prosperity seemed to be creating at least as many problems as it solved. Internationally, the United States was losing ground. Some of the losses were charted by Peter G. Peterson, President Richard Nixon's assistant for economic affairs and a former chairman of Bell & Howell Co. Between 1950 and 1970 the U. S. share of world steel production had dropped from 46 per cent to 20 per cent, of auto production from 76 per cent to 31 per cent, of total industrial output from 39 per cent to 30 per cent. The trade balance had been slipping year by year, until by 1971 U.S. exports were $2 billion less than imports.

Moreover, an increasing number of Americans made no secret of their disenchantment with the values of a society that set such great store on ma-

terial well-being. Much of the criticism came from the young, who tended to pay scant regard to the direction in which society was moving, but found much to criticize instead in its shortcomings and in what the nation had achieved—or failed to achieve. To the orthodox boast that the United States was able to keep its economy at a high level even while fighting a war abroad, their response was bitter, sometimes violent, disapproval of the Indochina war. It was oddly the best and worst of times; what another age might have regarded as utopian, the disaffected now described as being more akin to purgatory.

NEW DIRECTIONS FOR BUSINESS

By the 1960's business was caught up in a cycle of rapid change. Now wedded to technology, industry continually explored new applications for scientific discoveries; habituated to change, the public responded readily to the new and ever newer; and business needed to be endlessly alert and adaptable to the changes in people's moods, preferences, and styles of living. Any business that was slow to detect the new directions placed itself in jeopardy.

Following the lead of Korvette, discount stores sprang up around every major city, catering largely to the needs of the mixed white- and blue-collar families that had moved to the suburbs and were struggling to hold house and car and barbecue pit together. In the early 1960's there was a flurry of new discount houses, and about 2,000 were in business by 1962. In some sizable communities the discounters were responsible for as much as 25 per cent of the general merchandise business; no fewer than eight large discount stores served the 100,000 people of the Los Angeles suburb of Covina. Seeking to keep pace with changing tastes, the Korvette chain added grocery, furniture, and auto servicing units, and even had a fling with fashion clothing lines. Its sales volume moved up from $180 million in 1961 to $800 million in 1966, making Korvette one of the nation's leaders in the general merchandise field.

Another major new trend in retail sales was franchising, by which a company would give individual dealers the right to sell a widely advertised product or service, usually in exchange for an initial fee and a percentage of gross profit. Franchising was not a new method of doing business in some fields, notably the automobile business and such hotel and restaurant chains as Howard Johnson's. But companies in many other lines were becoming aware of its advantages. The franchiser could develop wide distribution without a huge investment in outlets, and his dealers had built-in incentives to succeed. The franchise holder, for his part, got advice in site selection and construction planning, training in his new business, and a known product that would give the enterprise a running start. By 1970 some 1,200 companies, of which about 90 per cent had begun in the preceding fifteen years, had around 500,000 franchised outlets.

Among the fastest-growing franchise operations were such food dispensers as the McDonald chain of short-order food stands, and the International House of Pancakes restaurants, which opened 185 units in seven years. McDonald's was able to charge $100,000 or more for a franchise, offering in return an intensive training course, a fat operating manual, monthly visits by field service managers, and such day-to-day reminders as "lubricate and adjust potato-peeler belt." Some franchisers operated a number of their own units, on occasion buying them back from dealers. Others branched out. International House of Pancakes expanded into tool and equipment rentals and business colleges. Minnie Pearl's Chicken System became Performance Systems, Inc., moving into such fields as day-care centers and transmission repairs.

Franchising operations also developed their unique troubles. Closing of unsuccessful outlets could mean a narrowing of distribution to the point at which big advertising outlays could not be supported. And differences developed between companies and franchisees. Chicken Delight dealers brought an antitrust action, claiming they were overcharged for food products and equipment, and franchisees for Shakey's Pizza claimed in a court action that they were overcharged as much as six times for some ingredients. Even a group of Ford dealers banded together to complain about such company practices as inadequate reimbursement for repairs under warranties. But franchising appeared to be a firmly established business by 1970, accounting for better than 25 per cent of all retail sales.

Such established and mature industries as textiles were given a strong push by major changes in apparel styles. Except for a few important firms like Burlington Industries, the company that James Spencer Love

---

The Way to Wealth
CHARLES REVSON

Few businesses have required as much flexibility and sensitivity to changes in consumer tastes as cosmetics. These qualities, along with a shrewd marketing sense and a driving perfectionism, were possessed in abundance by Charles Haskell Revson, born in 1906, the son of a Russian immigrant.

Until he was twenty-six Revson worked as a textile buyer and as the local manager for a nail polish manufacturer in New York City. In the 1920's and early 30's, women could adorn their fingernails in a choice of three shades: light, medium, or dark—or, when the makers waxed more poetic, Old Rose, Pink, or Red. Revson speculated that women would like something more striking, such as an opaque enamel that could be offered in a variety of tones and hues. With a borrowed $300, he and his brother Joseph and a chemist named Charles R. Lachman cooked up their first batch of nail enamel over a Bunsen burner in a Manhattan loft. Within two years the Revlon Nail Enamel Corp.—which used Lachman's initial letter and demonstrated Revson's flair for mellifluous names— had sold $60,000 worth of its new prod-

Charles Revson

ucts. In 1939 Revson introduced matching lipstick and fingernail enamel and launched color-coordinated cosmetics that changed the face of the make-up trade.

Originally his products were sold only through beauty salons, and therefore mainly to well-heeled ladies. But Revson expanded his outlets, leasing beauty shops in department stores and selling his dramatically named cosmetics (e.g., *Fire & Ice, Cherries in the Snow*, and *Love Pat*) over the counter.

Driving his subordinates as hard as he did himself, he developed a reputation, not wholly deserved, for clashing with his executives and advertising agencies. Yet his enterprise became the industry's chief training school, and former officials of his firm were peppered through the top posts of other companies.

In 1955 Revlon stock went public at $12 a share. Seventeen years later that share was worth $420, and Revson's own holdings were valued at more than $100 million. He lives accordingly. His 275-foot yacht, *Ultima II*, is second in size only to that of the Greek shipping magnate Aristotle Onassis.

Revson's special pride is his company's research center, which employs 100 chemists and has $2 million worth of equipment. He has a keen appreciation of the role of technology in developing new products and in testing old ones to assure their quality, safety, and uniformity. This concern has also led him into new fields. While other cosmetics firms were increasingly being acquired by pharmaceutical houses, Revlon moved toward the ownership of companies that manufactured ethical and proprietary drugs. Gradually, from his $300 of borrowed money and his Bunsen burner, he built a conglomerate with annual sales of $400 million in more than eighty countries.

REVLON

The modern textile industry: a circular knitting machine of Burlington Industries, Inc. knits yarn into a tube of fabric.

had built from a small cotton mill in 1923 to a giant with sales of over one billion dollars at his death in 1962, the American textile industry was largely fragmented into hundreds of small, mainly family-owned, concerns. In some fields, notably low-priced apparel, they found it difficult to compete with imports from Japan, where just five chemical-textile companies controlled 80 per cent of that country's fiber and textile industry. While the U.S. industry sought governmental action in helping it to compete with goods from abroad, it probably benefited much more from a fashion revolution that got under way in the mid-1960's, when synthetic yarns helped boost the sales of knits and the new technique of double-knitting. With new styling coming into men's and children's, as well as women's, wear, total sales of fashion goods — including toiletries, shoes, and hairpieces — climbed to $50 billion by 1967.

Tax laws and accounting methods contributed to the growth of the business of renting and leasing such diverse items as evening wraps, automobiles, jet aircraft, and heavy industrial machinery. It even became profitable, in some cases, for the owner-operator of an office building or hotel to sell it and then lease it back. The lessor could usually get a good return on his investment, could deduct depreciation charges before determining taxes, and at times could get a tax credit for his investment. The lessee could avoid a large capital outlay and could charge the entire rental cost to current operations. A number of companies sprang up to lease such industrial items as printing presses, machine tools, large computers, and boxcar-sized freight containers. The most prominent of all the leasing companies was Hertz Corp., founded in Chicago by automobile salesman Walter Jacobs in 1918 with twelve Model T Fords, and controlled at various times by John Hertz, by the Yellow Cab Manufacturing Co., by General Motors, and by Omnibus Corp. Shifting its emphasis in the 1950's from truck rentals to car rentals, Hertz began buying out rivals in high-traffic areas throughout the country, until it was stopped by an antitrust consent decree in 1960. In a sharp-pencil business where a month's delay in the sale of its used autos could make the difference between profit and loss, Hertz managed to maintain a consistently wide lead over its two chief competitors, Avis, Inc., whose aggressive advertising made a special virtue of being No. 2 in the field, and National Car Rental Systems, Inc. In 1966 Hertz Corp. was purchased by R.C.A.

Characteristic of the decade of the 1960's was the emergence of the concept of the "knowledge industry," which Princeton economist Fritz Machlup pointed out was growing much faster than the rest of the economy. The knowledge industry was an uneven mixture of education, printed and electronic communication, computers, and various management and executive functions, but it shared the common focus of disseminating information and ideas rather than the production and distribution of goods and services. These activities, Machlup pointed out, were responsible for a quarter of the gross national product in 1955. Ten years later they were shown to account for fully a third of a much larger G.N.P. Machlup's findings were fortified by another study by Edward F. Denison, which indicated that education had been the principal factor in productivity increases since 1929.

The computer industry, perhaps more than any other, placed heavy reliance on knowledge—obviously in the development of hardware and software, but almost as importantly in the use of its products. Customer-minded I.B.M. retained its dominance of this industry, in spite of highly sophisticated and hard-hitting competition. At the start of 1961 fully 71 per cent of the general-purpose computers in use, valued at $1.8 billion, were I.B.M.'s; three years later I.B.M. had built 76 per cent of the $5.8 billion worth of computers in use.

But I.B.M. had already decided that its product line was too diverse and that its engineering groups were expanding their energies in too many different directions. Late in 1961 the company determined that a single family of computers was needed, all using the same peripheral equipment, speaking the same language, built for the same software, and appropriate for both business and scientific applications. Development of such a system would be tremendously expensive. Programming alone, on which the company was then spending about $10 million a year, would cost an estimated $125 million.

The decision was to go ahead with what was called the System 360 (so named because it would encompass 360 degrees of the world of computers). Over the next four years the company's investment was something on the order of $5 billion in the project that Bob O. Evans, manager of the 360 line, called "You bet your company." As one gauge of the system's complexity, the hardware averaged 30,000 components per cubic foot, compared with 5,000 per cubic foot in the transistorized second generation of computer equipment and just 2,000 in the first generation of vacuum-tube machines. The new line, which was intended to make obsolete most existing computers, including I.B.M.'s, was announced by Chairman Thomas Watson, Jr., in April, 1964. A month later more than one billion dollars of the equipment was ordered.

As the U.S. computer market climbed to $6 billion and $7 billion a year, I.B.M. in 1971 accounted for about three quarters of the nation's computer sales and two thirds of the world's. Two major contenders, first G.E. and then R.C.A., dropped out of the race entirely. The company that emerged, somewhat sur-

prisingly, as No. 2 in the industry was Honeywell, a Minneapolis firm that had started out in the business of manufacturing electrical controls. For $500 million in stock and notes, Honeywell acquired G.E.'s computer business in the U.S. and abroad, thereby lifting its own revenues to $2 billion in 1971, double what they had been. The explanation given for the purchase was that it provided Honeywell with a "critical mass"—that is, a large enough business base to enable it to compete with I.B.M. in research and marketing.

The computer industry's business curve stayed on the upgrade. Even though a number of computer users felt uncertain whether their investments in the machines had paid off, others found more sophisticated and valuable uses for their equipment. A computer analysis enabled Anheuser-Busch to cut its advertising budget for Budweiser beer by 20 to 30 per cent without affecting sales. Litton Industries' Ingalls Shipbuilding Division used a computer to predict what its competitors would bid on new business, and then underbid them. And Johnson & Johnson was so successful in an inventory-control system that would keep stores from running out of their products that the move backfired when customers changed their purchasing patterns.

New technologies continued to point to more directions for business to follow. In computer development, tiny silicon chips with circuits inscribed on them could carry hundreds and thousands of times as much information as the magnetic cores they replaced. The microcircuits increased the speed of the computer's memory enough to keep pace with its logic system, but both remained many times faster than most data input and output devices.

Science moved ahead on many fronts. As the world's supplies of fossil fuels—coal, oil, and gas—continued to be used up, the cost of nuclear energy came down to a competitive range, and breeder reactors were developed to produce their own fuel. Scientists sought practical ways to use the energy from within the earth and the sun. The nation's successful space effort had enabled it to put men on the moon a year ahead of schedule, and less spectacularly to place weather and communications satellites in orbit around the earth and to learn much of scientific value. Then there were devices like the maser, for amplifying weak microwaves, developed in 1951 by Charles Hard Townes, and its much more prolific offspring, the laser, first produced in 1960 by Theodore H. Maiman at Hughes Aircraft. Glass, liquid, and gaseous lasers were developed and dozens of uses found, ranging from cancer surgery to cutting metal or making extremely fine measurements. In various experimental and developmental stages were dozens of new products and processes—supersonic trains to travel in tubes, the high-speed electrostatic spinning of yarn, and the making of steel and steel products directly from ores. All these could be turned to the benefit of mankind, usually the faster if business could see its way to doing so at a profit.

THE EXPENSIVE AIRCRAFT

While the coming of the jet age may have proved a boon to air travelers, it spelled repeated and continuing troubles for most of the aircraft manufacturers. Development costs of new planes were so astronomical, and competition so keen, that immense losses were suffered whenever a new plane or a new generation of aircraft was developed. General Dynamics wrote off $425 million in losses, for example, when the Convair 880 and 990 jets came too late and with too little to compete with the Boeing and Douglas models.

The least painful way to absorb these costs, of course, was to have the government underwrite the development of military aircraft and then to transfer some of the know-how to civilian plane building. This consideration, along with actual orders for military planes, kept much of the aircraft industry squarely in the middle of the military-industrial complex, with its necessary politicking and the establishment of special relationships so important to the government contract business.

Expenditures of the U.S. Department of Defense rose from about $50 billion a year to $80 billion during the 1960's, and something over half of these amounts went into procurement contracts. Although the department had more than 20,000 prime contractors, it was not unusual for the 100 largest contractors to get about two thirds of this business—or contracts totaling some $25 billion or more. Military business consistently accounted for a large part of the aircraft industry sales, which rose during the decade from about $8 billion to a record $17.4 billion in 1968, before tapering off.

Competition was naturally intense for the awards to design and build any new type of aircraft. When the government decided early in 1960 on a $2.2 billion program to develop the TFX (Tactical Fighter Experimental) plane, three engine manufacturers and nine airframe companies or combinations of companies got into the bidding. The rules of the game were made stiffer than ever by the new Secretary of Defense, Robert Strange McNamara. Intent on greater unification of the services, he insisted on a single plane design that would meet the separate requirements of both the Air Force and the Navy. And noting that cost overruns had raised the initial estimates on some military contracts by as much as three to ten times, he also demanded realistic pricing by the competing bidders.

After the first bids were submitted late in 1961, the field was quickly narrowed to two contestants—Boeing and a combination of General Dynamics and Grumman Aircraft. They were asked to submit revised bids to a special selection board made up of representatives of the services. On four separate occasions during 1962 the two competitors went before selection boards, and each time Boeing got the preference. But the Defense Department overruled the boards and awarded the TFX contract to General Dynamics-Grumman, on the grounds that its basic design would require fewer changes in being adapted to the different services and that its price estimates, although obviously too low, were more realistic than Boeing's.

The next major military aircraft plum was the C-5A, a cargo carrier that could haul payloads about two and a half times as large as any then being flown. The C-5A would be able to end the reliance on slow and vulnerable sea transport for all but the most bulky military cargo, such as fuel supplies. After the plane was given the go-ahead late in 1964, Boeing, Lockheed, and Douglas competed for the airframe, and General Electric and Pratt & Whitney for the engine. General Electric and Lockheed were selected in 1965, but not until the various competitors had spent some $60 million on engineering and other costs in an effort to win the contract.

After three years of competition among plane builders, the Federal Aviation Administration selected Boeing late in 1966 to build a supersonic transport plane (SST), deemed the richest prize in aviation history. Boeing's design was for a plane with variable-sweep wings that could be swiveled out for the relatively slow speeds of take-off and landing and then drawn back toward the fuselage for supersonic flight. But in 1968 the company announced that the swiveling mechanism and other structural requirements added more weight than had been expected, and that this would mean a full year's delay in bringing out the SST. The new design called for a fixed wing, like that of the Concorde, a competing supersonic transport being developed jointly by the British and the French, but unlike the Concorde the SST would have a large horizontal tail. However, within a few years the design became academic, as opposition to the plane developed on the grounds of high costs and the environmental affront of a sonic boom, and the project was killed in Congress. Although its costs were reimbursable by the government, Boeing had dissipated its major efforts for seven years in what turned out to be a blind alley, while its competitors had moved ahead on more productive fronts.

One of the places where Boeing had lost out was in developing the airbus, a new airliner concept with a market estimated at $15 billion. Using a new high-thrust engine first developed by G.E. for the C-5A, the wide-bodied plane would be able to carry 250 to 300 passengers on medium and short hops, at much lower costs per seat-mile than existing craft. Such a plane would be ideal for trips within the continental United States or Europe. When American Airlines asked the industry to build the aircraft, Lockheed and Douglas set right to work on designs. But Boeing, which had decided to use the new engines on its long-range 747's, was too heavily committed to that plane and the SST to take on the costs of still another new model. Douglas moved ahead with work on the DC-10, using the G.E. engine, and Lockheed on its TriStar L-1011, for which it contracted to use a new Rolls-Royce engine.

It was in this period that some of the major airframe makers began running into new problems, in part because of the natural perils of the high stakes game they were playing, in part because of a severe tightening in the U.S. money market, and in part simply because of bad management. Douglas was the first to feel the pinch, when the company lost $27.6 million on sales of more than one billion dollars in 1966, after they had earlier informed their bankers that they were expecting to show a $20 million profit for the year. The bankers immediately cut off a $100 million line of credit, spoon-feeding the company's needs while they took a closer look at its condition.

The verdict was that Douglas was indeed in bad shape, lagging in such modern management techniques as careful long-term planning and tight operating con-

trols. Its sales per employee were only about half that of comparable companies, and it had overloaded the payroll with workers before it had any use for them. The prescription was for a merger with some strong company that could bring in large amounts of cash and better management capabilities. Likely candidates were invited to submit their proposals, and there was a prompt response from North American Aviation, General Dynamics, and McDonnell Aircraft. Others that asked to be considered were Martin-Marietta; Signal Oil & Gas Co. of Los Angeles, which had a subsidiary, Garrett Corp., in the aerospace business; and Sherman Fairchild, a key figure in Fairchild Camera and Fairchild Hiller and the largest identified stockholder in I.B.M.

All the merger candidates presented their proposals to a special negotiating committee, which reviewed them in detail early in 1967. One by one, the various offers were turned down for failing to meet all the criteria the Douglas board had established. The choice was finally narrowed to McDonnell and North American, and McDonnell was picked because it was willing to pay more cash for working control of Douglas stock. Not long afterward the two companies combined as McDonnell Douglas.

The newly merged giant moved vigorously toward increased efficiency and profitable operations. In February, 1968, it announced the first sale of the new

T.W.A. directors hold the first board meeting aloft in a 747 in December, 1969, just before the plane began commercial runs.

airbuses, a $400 million order for twenty-five DC-10's from American Airlines. But the next month Lockheed scored a greater coup, announcing the sale of 144 of its TriStar airbuses to Eastern, T.W.A., and a British firm, Air Holdings, Ltd. Orders for 28 more from Delta and Northeast brought the sales total for Lockheed to $2.58 billion, but its price tag of around $15 million per plane undercut Douglas by $1,000,000.

Then troubles began to overtake Lockheed. Because of cost overruns on four separate programs for the government, including the C-5A, the company faced losses that might have run as high as one billion dollars. The disputed contracts were eventually settled at a loss to Lockheed of $480 million, of which $290 million had already been written off. An equally serious problem loomed with the bankruptcy of Rolls-Royce in 1971, raising the prospect that the British manufacturer would be unable to deliver the engines for the TriStar airbus, on which Lockheed was relying to get back, after a nine-year hiatus, into the business of supplying commercial aircraft. But the nationalized Rolls-Royce firm agreed to pay further development costs and to supply the engines to Lockheed for $1,020,000 each, a price increase of $180,000. This would cut more from profits on the TriStar, already trimmed down by the competition with Douglas.

Back of all the problems of the aircraft manufacturers was the fact that demand was not great enough to support an industry as large as this one had grown, particularly since defense requirements placed less and less emphasis on large numbers of manned aircraft. Military orders in the early 1970's were the smallest since 1946 for navy planes and the lowest since 1935 for the Air Force. And the gap could not be filled by commercial airlines, themselves on a feast-or-famine basis and wary of making huge capital commitments for ever more expensive equipment.

U.S. airlines had ordered about $6 billion in new jets, mainly Boeing 747's, Douglas DC-10's, and Lockheed TriStar L-1011's, for delivery from 1970 through 1973. But 1970 turned out to be one of the worst years in their history, with the eleven domestic trunk lines showing a combined net loss of $85 million. With such results, the airlines would be hard pressed to pay for even the planes they had ordered, but rigorous cost-cutting helped turn the 1970 loss into a small profit in 1971, and the Civil Aeronautics Board expected the eleven lines to show combined earnings of $350 million in 1972.

MERGER AND CONGLOMERATION

Business prosperity brings growth, and growth begets combination. During the years following World War II, mergers were consummated at the rate of 700 or 800 a year. A congressional committee inquiry showed that the nation's 500 leading industrial companies alone reported 3,404 mergers and acquisitions between 1951 and 1961, an average of almost seven per company. Business marriages increased steadily in the 1960's, climbing to close to 3,000 in 1967 and to an estimated 4,000 in 1968, which was about four times the rate of a decade earlier. Finding willing merger candidates became a thriving business for corporation brokers, investment dealers, and even banks and accounting firms.

Yet even as big businesses grew, small businesses proliferated. At the turn of the century there were 1.25 million firms in the United States, or one for every sixty people; in the mid-1960's, there were 11.4 million businesses, or about one for every eighteen.

Over the same period, the forces of antimerger and antitrust also gathered force and momentum in surges of renewed activity. The first wave came under Theodore Roosevelt, William Howard Taft, and Woodrow Wilson's Progressive movement; the second was sparked by Franklin D. Roosevelt's denunciation of "economic royalists" and the trustbusting by Thurman Arnold in the 1930's and 1940's; and in the 1960's Richard W. McLaren, chief of the government's Antitrust Division, led an attack on business combinations on the ground that they caused "human dislocations" and led to a "radical restructuring" of the economy.

In the constant interplay of their powers, both business and government tested the limits of what the law might allow—and sometimes of how far they could get away with transcending the boundaries of the law. In early 1961 a federal court in Philadelphia found twenty-nine corporations, including General Electric and Westinghouse, guilty of a price-fixing conspiracy that involved about $650 million in sales of electrical equipment, and the court levied almost $42 million in fines, sent seven executives to jail, and suspended twenty-four other jail sentences. The government had other weapons too, not only to fight price agreements but also to combat industrial price increases. In 1962, stung by a sharp attack by President John F. Kennedy, U.S. Steel and other steelmakers rescinded an announced price increase, and in 1966 President Lyndon B. Johnson forced the rollback of an aluminum price rise by threatening to release large quantities of the metal from the nation's stockpile.

Yet even those companies that sought conscientiously to stay within the law and hew to national policy felt a sense of uneasiness and uncertainty about antitrust policy. There was no consensus definition of monopoly, and enforcement authorities showed a tendency simply to use size as a measure of concentration, just as Brandeis had flayed "the curse of bigness" fifty years earlier. And indeed the business system itself appeared to foster a tendency toward growing concentration within industries. As far back as the 1930's Adolf A. Berle and Gardiner C. Means showed in a monumental study that the share of the nation's nonfinancial corporate wealth controlled by the 200 largest corporations rose even during the Depression, from 49 per cent in 1929 to 55 per cent in 1932.

The main question at issue was whether this was good or bad for national economic well-being. Berle himself pointed out in the 1960's that "bigness is here to stay because it is needed." And the American public obviously had much greater tolerance for bigness than it had for unregulated monopoly and price-fixing, particularly in the European cartelization form that the electrical conspirators had adopted. Popular opinion was reflected in the Celler-Kefauver Act of 1950, in which Congress prohibited corporate acquisitions whose effect would be "substantially to lessen competition or tend to create a monopoly."

The drive toward merger was nevertheless irresistible. Virtually forbidden to expand greatly in their own industries, many companies used mergers to diversify, for a number of reasons—to counteract cyclical or seasonal swings, to supplement a mature and declining market with a new and growing one, to combine the advantages of tax credits in a losing business with the earnings of a profitable one, or simply to try to build an enterprise that could make money out of two that could not.

A nondiversifying merger of the last type was the biggest of the decade, joining the New York Central and Pennsylvania railroads into the Penn Central. With the operating income of both lines well below that of even the depressed 1930's, a merger was first proposed in 1957 by Central Chairman Robert R. Young, a few months before he died a suicide. The merger itself did not take place until 1968, having run the long obstacle course of hearings, approvals, and negotiations. It turned out to be a case of total incompatibility, with mismatched management and conflicting personalities, and in the space of two years

---

The Way to Wealth

H. ROSS PEROT

The rise of a service economy, regarded by many as a natural development in a nation moving beyond industrialization, has offered unforeseen business opportunities. The computer industry, for example, became big enough for fortunes to be made on its fringes as well as at its center. H. (for Henry) Ross Perot, a thirty-two-year-old I.B.M. salesman in Dallas, had already sold his annual quota of computers by the middle of January, 1962. When the company then assigned him to office duties, the young Texan felt thwarted and left to start his own business in computer services.

A Naval Academy-educated son of a horse and cattle trader, Perot had always enjoyed selling, even newspapers and magazines as a youngster. He foresaw that corporations that bought expensive computer hardware might have a difficult time putting it to its fullest use. He decided that the time was ripe to sell software by contract to computer-using clients. Struck by the words of Henry David Thoreau in *Walden,* "The mass of men lead lives of quiet desperation," he determined not to be counted with the masses. From his own savings he bought some computer time from Southwestern Life

H. Ross Perot

Insurance Co.'s data processing equipment and started selling his services to sizable companies.

His first customer enabled him to build a staff made up of two other I.B.M. salesmen and a systems engineer. As his business grew, he continued to hire the best people he could find, pirating most of them from I.B.M. "Eagles don't flock," was his motto. "You have to find them one at a time."

By 1968, his Electronic Data Systems Corp. showed a net profit of $1.6 million on $7.7 million in sales. Perot

decided to go public. In a market in which stock buyers were irrationally optimistic about new issues, particularly of computer companies, 650,000 shares of E.D.S. were offered at $16.50 a share, more than 100 times earnings. The stock rose to $23 a share that same day and to $33 a month later. Perot, who had kept more than 9 million shares for himself, was worth more than $300 million on paper. "At any price per share," he said, "I'm worth more than I dreamed I'd be."

Three years later, with his net worth estimated at $600 million, he headed a group that put up some $50 million to save the failing New York Stock Exchange firm of duPont Glore Forgan, Inc., the third largest brokerage house in America. A man of many energies, he instituted efficiencies—mostly by speeding up paperwork—at duPont Glore Forgan that introduced a new degree of discipline on Wall Street. "I feel strongly that every one ought to make every contribution he can to the country," said Perot. "I'm best able to make my contribution in the area of business."

A more dramatic contribution that he tried to make to the country in 1969 —chartering a jet plane to carry relief supplies to American prisoners in North Vietnam during the Indochina war— made him nationally known, but proved unsuccessful.

the railroad had plunged into the largest bankruptcy in the nation's history.

Most mergers, particularly those of the diversifying type, fared better. Rockwell Manufacturing spread out from meter manufacturing to a great many industrial products and increased its sales from $9 million in 1940 to $76 million in 1955. Minnesota Mining & Manufacturing grew even faster, increasing sales in the same period from $4 million to $230 million as it diversified from sandpaper manufacturing to more than 1,000 products.

One of the most spectacularly diversifying companies was the General Tire & Rubber Co., run by William F. O'Neil and three of his sons, Michael, John, and Thomas. Before World War II the company's business was confined almost wholly to tire manufacture, and its sales in the first year after the war totaled $106 million, still mostly in tires. But by then the company had helped finance the start, and bought a major interest in, Aerojet-General, a subsidiary that became a leading manufacturer of rocket engines. In the 1940's and 1950's General Tire also bought into radio and television broadcasting, and in 1955 made a deal with Howard Hughes to purchase R.K.O.'s 750-picture film library for $25 million, a sum that was quickly recovered in sales of television rights. By 1963 General Tire, having expanded in chemicals, plastics, and space ventures, crossed the one billion dollar mark in sales.

More than simply a diversifier, General Tire was one of the first of the conglomerates. These were groups of merged companies brought together primarily on the premises that good management practices were much the same in all types of business and that the larger size of the parent could be a distinct advantage in such areas as financing. These benefits did not come as a sudden revelation to business. Companies like General Electric, Armour, and Ford had long been active in a variety of fields, with G.E. in as many as fourteen separate industry categories. But in the 1960's conglomeration was becoming the basic growth method for a number of companies. More than half of the mergers reported by the Federal Trade Commission in 1966 were considered to be of the conglomerate type, since they crossed broad industry lines.

One of the earliest diversifier-conglomerators, and also one of the first to use tax laws for turning one company's losses into another's higher profit, was Textron American, Inc., renamed simply Textron in 1944. Started as a textile firm by Royal Little in 1923, the company began to make acquisitions in its own field after World War II, then began to spread out to other industries in the 1950's. By 1968 Textron had acquired or combined with sixty-one other companies; it was out of the textile business but had total sales of $1.7

billion in chain saws, fountain pens, helicopters, and a host of other products.

Another fast-growing conglomerate was Gulf & Western Industries, which came into the 1960's as an auto bumper manufacturer with $8 million in sales and a small net loss. By 1967 it had acquired more than eighty other companies, including Paramount Pictures, South Puerto Rico Sugar, and New Jersey Zinc, and earned $70 million on sales of $1.3 billion.

International Telephone & Telegraph moved into the ranks of the top ten industrial companies largely by way of the merger route. The company had been created by Colonel Sosthenes Behn, who brought together a number of telephone, telegraph, and communications equipment manufacturers around the world. Sales had already reached $766 million and earnings were $29 million in 1959, the year Harold Sydney Geneen became president. Geneen expanded the company's communications interests, but also spread into other areas—general manufacturing, insurance, small loans—and acquired such sizable companies as Bell & Gosset, Avis, Sheraton Corp., and Levitt & Sons. After a long delay in getting Federal Communications Commission approval in its bid to take over the American Broadcasting Company, the company called off the acquisition. In 1971 the court ordered I.T.&T. to dispose of Avis, Levitt, and some other interests, in order to retain the Hartford Fire Insurance Company. I.T.&T. sales in 1970 reached $6.4 billion, almost nine times what they had been when Geneen took the helm.

Two of the more spectacular conglomerates of the 1960's, Litton Industries and Ling-Temco-Vought, were largely the creatures of two men who were almost opposites in background and training. Charles B. Thornton at the age of twenty-eight was a full colonel in charge of installing business planning and control systems in the Air Force. When he left the service, he brought along nine of his brighter young officers, and they joined Ford Motor Co. in a group known as the Whiz Kids. Among the nine were Robert McNamara, who became U.S. Secretary of Defense, and Arjay Miller, who became president of Ford.

Thornton left Ford in 1948 to become a vice president of Hughes Aircraft, where he helped pioneer that company's work in advanced electronics. He was one of those who broke away from Hughes in the summer of 1953, along with Roy L. Ash and Hugh Jamieson, and the three of them were able to get Lehman Brothers to raise $1.5 million for the purchase of a small manufacturer of microwave tubes in California. Founder Charles Litton, who was retiring, took his $1,000,000 share in cash, rather than in stock of the new Litton Industries. The company earned $154,000 on sales of $3 million in the first nine months. Four years later sales had reached nearly $100 million,

Charles B. "Tex" Thornton at a Litton Industries meeting

and net profits were nearly $4 million. By then Litton had undertaken seventeen mergers and acquisitions, including the purchase for $18 million of the Monroe Calculating Machine Co. of Orange, New Jersey, whose sales were more than $40 million a year.

Litton continued to grow, acquiring Ingalls Shipbuilding Corp., the third largest private shipbuilding yard in the country, in 1961. In the company's first ten years thirty-seven companies were acquired, mostly for stock, and sales reached $540 million and earnings $22 million. Using a system of careful controls and measurement of monthly performance against plans and forecasts, Litton for more than fourteen years continued to show quarterly profits that were higher than those of the corresponding profits a year earlier. The system finally showed weaknesses when some problems turned out to be more serious than anticipated, and there was a drop in quarterly earnings early in 1968. But by then the company's sales were running at the rate of $1.8 billion a year and even the reduced quarterly profits amounted to $7.2 million. In 1970 Litton reported earnings of $69 million on sales of $2.4 billion.

James Joseph Ling started in business as a small Dallas electrical contractor with $3,000 obtained from the sale of his house in 1946. Predictably, under the guidance of its energetic founder, Ling Electric

did well, grossing almost $70,000 in its first year and increasing sales steadily until they reached $1.5 million in 1955. That year Ling decided to go public. But when underwriters showed little enthusiasm, he studied financial reports and prospectuses and haunted brokerage houses. Ling Electric issued 800,000 shares; Ling kept 400,000 and got permission from the State Securities Commission to sell the other 400,000 at $2.25 a share. Ling sold more than 100,000 shares on his own, and he got friends to hand out prospectuses at a booth at the Texas State Fair and to peddle some stock door-to-door. The issue was sold out within three months.

Ling was soon buying more companies, first a West Coast electrical contracting firm, then a sagging electronics company that made vibration-testing equipment. Sales in 1958 hit $6.9 million and in the following year, with the purchase of electronics and sound-equipment manufacturing companies, they increased sevenfold to $48 million.

The company was on its way. Ling next merged with Temco Electronics & Missiles Co. of Dallas to form Ling-Temco Electronics. With his eye on the sophisticated scientific and engineering staff of Chance Vought Corporation, he started to buy that company's stock in 1960, acquiring control the following year, and the company became Ling-Temco-Vought. Sales in 1962 reached $325 million.

Ling then devised Project Redeployment, a unique method of increasing the market value of the company's holdings and thus of its own stock. Eleven divisions were consolidated into three subsidiaries, LTV Aerospace Corp., LTV Electrosystems, Inc., and LTV Ling Altec, Inc. For each share of L-T-V stock turned in, the company offered one share of stock in each of the subsidiaries plus $9 in cash. By this means, a market value was created for the subsidiaries, most of whose stock the company held. The market value of its holdings in LTV Aerospace, for example, was $117 million, compared to a book value of just $18 million for its assets. This, along with a $60 million sale of debentures in Europe, provided sources of cash for more purchases.

L-T-V acquired the Okonite Company, an electrical cable manufacturer, in 1965, Wilson & Co. in 1967, and in 1968 the Jones & Laughlin Steel Co. and the Greatamerica Corporation, a holding company which in turn owned a bank, insurance companies, the National Car Rental System, and Braniff International Airways. Most of the latter group were spun off, but Braniff was retained. Wilson & Co. was "redeployed" in three parts—the meat-packing and food operations, Wilson Sporting Goods Co., and Wilson Pharmaceutical & Chemical Corporation, creating separate market values for each of the units. The acquisitions helped boost L-T-V sales to $1.8 billion by 1967 and

The largest assembled "family" of stockholders: owners of shares in A.T.&T. at the corporation's annual meeting in 1970

$3.8 billion by 1970, but difficulties encountered in some of the divisions resulted in net losses of $38 million in 1969 and $70 million in 1970.

THE INSTITUTIONAL INVESTORS

For the growing number of American families with discretionary income, stock ownership became increasingly common. A New York Stock Exchange survey showed almost 31 million individuals owning stock in 1970, as against 20 million five years earlier and only 6.5 million in 1952. More than two thirds of these stockholders had incomes of $10,000 or more, but the largest single group—some 9 million—were in the $10,000 to $15,000 income bracket.

It was likely that the great bulk of these holdings were for investment purposes, but periodically there were surges of stock trading that were obviously speculative. In the early 1960's many people, mesmerized by tales of the rapid climb in some stock prices, were gripped by a passion for new issues. To be sure, there were plenty of shining examples: $100 invested in Litton Industries multiplied in value to more than $5,000 in seven years; Korvette came out at $10, then climbed to $111; Texas American Oil moved quickly from $.50 a share to $5.63; and Dynatronics, which was brought out at $7.50, was worth $25 the next

day. Between 1951 and 1961 there was an increase of more than 700 per cent in new issues of $300,000 or more. But most of these new ventures, as their stock prospectuses duly warned, had little more to go on than hope; a great many purchasers watched prices dwindle to the vanishing point as these hopes faded.

Total security trading increased enormously during the decade. The number of shares of stock traded on registered exchanges in the United States more than tripled, from 958 million shares to 3.2 billion shares, while the value of these shares had a slightly smaller increase, from $38 billion to $103 billion. Bond trading on the New York Stock Exchange rose in the same period from $1.3 billion to $4.5 billion. Perhaps an even more important trend was the increasing role of institutions in the market. In 1960 individuals accounted for 69 per cent of all public stock trading on the New York Stock Exchange, while such institutions as banks, mutual funds, and insurance companies were responsible for the remaining 31 per cent. By 1969 these proportions were virtually reversed, with individuals making only 38 per cent of the trades and institutions 62 per cent.

It was through these institutions that most Americans had at least some stake, if once removed, in the nation's security markets. Almost 140 million people, or close to 70 per cent of the population, were covered

362

by life insurance policies in 1970 and thus had some interest in the $207 billion in assets of the life insurance companies. Making up the bulk of their investments were $74 billion in mortgages and $73 billion in corporate bonds, with just $15 billion put into stocks and $11 billion into government securities. Other millions of Americans had investment interests through trusts and pension funds, many of which were administered by trust departments of banks, and through mutual funds.

A good deal of public attention was focused on the mutual funds, although they could not be counted among the largest repositories of investment funds. Their total assets at the end of 1970 were $50.7 billion, less than the combined asset total of the two largest banks — Bank of America, with almost $30 billion, and First National City Corp., with $26 billion — or the two largest insurance companies — Prudential's $30 billion and Metropolitan's $28 billion. Yet the mutual funds were perhaps the fastest-growing of all investment institutions.

In their new popularity the mutual funds were in a sense the successors to the fast-selling investment trusts of the 1920's, which were so disastrously caught up in the stock market crash of 1929 and which became both contributors to and victims of collapsing stock prices. Almost all of the investment trusts of that period were closed-end trusts, with a fixed number of shares and in many cases with bonds or preferred shares senior to the common. Mutual funds, on the other hand, were open-end investment trusts, which had only one class of securities participating in earnings and which could continue to issue additional shares as long as they found buyers for them. These open-end funds weathered the Depression relatively well, and in 1940 their total asset value was $450 million, as against $614 million for the closed-end trusts. Then, over the next thirty years, the mutual funds had more than a hundredfold increase in total assets, while the closed-end trusts grew in value only about seven times.

Part of the rapid growth of open-end trusts could be attributed to the safeguards written into the Investment Company Act of 1940, which some mutual fund executives helped draft. That act of Congress and various state laws effectively limited the acquisition of any one company's stock by an investment trust to 10 per cent of the company's outstanding shares or 5 per cent of the assets of the trust. The funds were permitted to retain their holdings, however, if rising prices sent the value of the stocks in their portfolios above the 5 per cent level. Thus the Dreyfus Fund, which began buying Polaroid stock in 1953, eventually owned close to 1,000,000 shares, which at one time represented 9 per cent of the fund's assets. Spurred by the record of such successful investments, a number of

old and new funds in the 1960's made asset growth their major objective, and the more spectacular of these performance-minded trusts came to be known as the "go-go" funds; as many of their higher-flying glamor stocks came in for a landing in the bear market of the late 1960's, some of these funds found that a considerable slice of their assets had "gone-gone."

With the kind of money that came into the mutual funds in the 1950's and 1960's, it was not remarkable that they attracted a variety of dreamers and schemers. One of these was Bernard Cornfeld, a fund salesman for Investors Planning Corp. who vacationed in Europe in 1955 and stayed to sell mutual fund shares to American servicemen and expatriates. He switched to the Dreyfus Fund, and his Investors Overseas Services, headquartered in Geneva, soon became their largest sales agency, specializing in selling long-term automatic reinvestment programs, a pet idea of Cornfeld's. He expanded his operations and started funds of his own; the largest, the Fund of Funds, got its investment expertise simply through buying the shares of other mutual funds. Because it deemed some of the practices of I.O.S. questionable, the Securities and Exchange Commission forbade it to sell to Americans, but Cornfeld thrived on sales of shares and programs to nationals of other countries. By the end of 1969 I.O.S. was managing more than $2 billion invested in seventeen different funds. It had offered its own stock publicly at $10 a share and the price quickly rose to $19, making paper millionaires even out of some of Cornfeld's regional sales managers.

But by the spring of 1970 the whole structure was tottering. Most of the big cash balance had been dissipated, much of it in loans to insiders and friends. The bear market and redemptions of shares dropped I.O.S. asset values to $1.7 billion. Operating losses were running at the rate of $1,000,000 a month, and I.O.S. stock slipped to $1.50 a share, contributing to the demoralization of no-longer-rich branch managers. Cornfeld lost control, and the I.O.S. board, under Sir Eric Wyndham White, formerly a high-ranking British civil servant, undertook the painstaking task of rebuilding the company and its reputation.

TOWARD A WORLD ECONOMY

World War II and its aftermath made the United States the principal focus of the world's economy. Not only was this country the great productive machine that supplied itself and others with goods, but other nations sent their valuables, including 60 per cent of the world's gold supply, to U.S. havens for safekeeping during the war.

Largely on U.S. insistence, the Bretton Woods Conference had overridden Lord Keynes's objection that gold was "a barbarous relic" and had put the free world on a limited gold standard—or a gold exchange standard, by which a nation's currencies would be backed by gold or reserves of "key" currencies, such as the dollar and the pound. The dollar was the only currency mentioned in the Articles of Agreement of the International Monetary Fund, and it was the United States that stood ready to redeem its own currency for gold, at the rate of $35 an ounce, for any foreign government or central bank that accumulated too many dollars.

For a long period there were no such dollar accumulations, and indeed the "dollar gap" reflected the hunger of other nations for dollars with which to buy American goods and build up their own industries. The Marshall Plan was devised to speed up the process, and a General Agreement on Tariffs and Trade was put into effect at Geneva in 1947 to facilitate the flow of international commerce. The central role of U.S. currency was evident from the fact that about two thirds of the world's trade came to be conducted in dollars as the "transaction currency."

Gradually, as the United States loaned and gave away dollars and increased its imports and investments abroad, the dollar gap disappeared. From 1950 on, for every year but one, there was a deficit in the U.S. international account. By the time the European Economic Community—the "Common Market"—came into being in 1958, the first sizable deficits had appeared in the U.S. balance of payments.

The important point was that these deficits were cumulative and built up a stock of dollars abroad that hung over U.S. gold reserves like the dirk, if not the sword, of Damocles. At any time they could create a run on the U.S. Treasury, and this actually took place in the fall of 1960, when the price of gold on the London free market moved above $40 an ounce. In the backwash of these events came some overdue realignments of currencies—the German mark and Dutch guilder were revalued upward 5 per cent—but speculators, looking for still more action, were busy trading weak currencies for strong. At this point the "Basel Club," a group of the world's leading central bankers who met regularly at the Bank for International Settlements in Basel, Switzerland, stepped into the picture. The German Bundesbank and the Federal Reserve Bank of New York announced they were prepared to buy all dollars offered against marks, even for future delivery, and actually bought $350 million forward. The Swiss National Bank offered a deposit of $200 million to the Bank of England. As a result, speculative ardor quickly cooled. The central banks also formed a pool to stabilize gold prices on the London market. This consortium proved highly effective during major world disturbances, such as the Cuban missile crisis of 1962 and the assassination of President John F. Kennedy in 1963.

Imbalances of international payments continued through the 1960's and, while they never amounted to more than one-half of one per cent of the nation's output of goods and services, their effect was aggravated by fiscal and monetary problems on the domestic scene. One of these was inflation, which the government did almost nothing to abate and which gained impetus from a sharp economic upturn in 1964–65. Businessmen raced to borrow funds to build inventories and expand plants.

The United States had not yet learned, as many other nations had, that inflation, continued over long periods of time, builds up expectations of more inflation and thus becomes a self-fulfilling prophecy. The Federal Reserve System seemed incapable of filling one of the roles of a central bank—that is, to create and maintain uncertainty about the future course of prices. The Fed finally applied the brakes to easy money in mid-1966 by raising reserve requirements. Interest rates rose steeply, but businessmen continued their heavy demand for loans, certain that they could make the money earn more than it was costing them. As deposits dropped and loans increased, commercial banks were caught in the "credit crunch," and many took large losses in selling bonds and other securities from their portfolios at depressed prices. Then, as loan demand tapered off, the Fed resumed its expansionary credit policies.

Gold continued to drain from the U.S. Treasury, and from 1957 to 1967 the nation's gold stock dropped by $10 billion, to $13 billion, with some $28 billion in dollars still held abroad. Under a classical gold standard, such a gold loss would tighten credit at home, slow economic expansion, reduce prices, and raise exports while holding down the demand for imports. But the effects of the gold losses were more than counteracted by purchases of U.S. government securities—some by the holders of dollars abroad and $23 billion by the Federal Reserve in its open market operations. So the underlying problem, instead of correcting itself, grew progressively more threatening.

Back of the U.S. dilemma was the larger world problem. International trade—which, like all trade, needs to be lubricated with an adequate supply of money and credit—had grown much faster than the gold supply. As official reserve currencies, the dollar and the pound took up some of the slack, but the pound had been subject to repeated attacks and devaluations and the dollar was beginning to look shaky in relation to some other currencies. What was needed, many said, was a mechanism for creating international credit similar to the way that commercial and central banks could increase credit within a growing national economy. After much international haggling, the International Monetary Fund was made the vehicle for issuing a limited amount of "paper gold"—special rights by which nations could draw against their reserves in the fund.

The special drawing rights proved a temporary palliative, but pressure on the dollar continued. Finally, in 1971 the U.S. government decided to take a number of drastic measures—stopping all redemption of dollars in gold, imposing a 10 per cent import surtax, and putting a freeze on domestic prices and wages for ninety days. Implementation of the program was accelerated when banks, corporations, and speculators shifted their holdings of almost $4 billion in dollars to other currencies and assets in the second week of August. On August 13 the White House received a note from the Bank of England asking that its $3 billion in dollar holdings be guaranteed against devaluation. The U.S. Treasury, which had helped rescue sterling numerous times during the 1960's, turned down the request coldly. And on August 15 President Nixon announced the first phase of his new economic program.

Phase I, considering its heavy emphasis on voluntary compliance, was remarkably successful. The consumer price index increased by only .3 per cent and wholesale prices actually dropped between August and October. Nations that were heavy exporters to the United States, notably Japan and Germany, were forced to take a hard look at their trade policies, and some revalued their currencies upward. Phase II of the program, aimed at a rate of inflation no higher than 2 to 3 per cent, was already under way when the import surtax was removed and the dollar was devalued about 8 per cent—a kind of *mea culpa* gesture made mainly at French insistence.

While a number of the governmental measures of the 1960's and early 1970's were dramatic and unprecedented, the business community was perhaps responsible for even more significant changes in the world economy. Exporting American products was already an old story. More than a century before, Singer was selling more sewing machines abroad than at home. A book published in England around 1900, *The American Invasion*, described the threat to British enterprise presented by companies like Singer, Mc-Cormick, and H. J. Heinz.

But in the years immediately after World War II it required a combination of daring and great faith to seek overseas markets, and even more so to establish branches and build plants abroad. A handful of companies showed the requisite courage or imprudence to set up such beachheads in the face of currency restrictions, tight government regulation, high taxes, and resolute competition. For most, the gamble paid off. I.B.M. was one of the first to expand its overseas operations, which it changed from the status of a division to that of a subsidiary, I.B.M. World Trade Corp., in 1950.

The major movement abroad by American business firms, however, did not take place until the formation of the Common Market, with its accompanying relaxation of trade restrictions and special inducements offered by the member governments. U.S. companies opened large new machinery and chemical plants to serve the expanding European market, and these were followed by a variety of other enterprises, mainly in the food, pharmaceutical, rubber, automobile, and petroleum industries. Existing European plants were acquired, and European companies were both bought into and bought out. U.S. direct investment abroad grew from $12 billion in 1950 to $49 billion in 1965 and $78 billion in 1970.

While most Europeans were well aware of the benefits that flowed to them from these infusions of capital and management, there were some who resented this American "take-over" of their industry. The French seemed particularly nettled by what was termed the "colonization" of France by U.S. business. In his book *The American Challenge*, Jean-Jacques Servan-Schreiber raised the alarm by warning: "In fifteen years the world's third industrial power, after the U.S. and the U.S.S.R., could well be not Europe, but *American industry in Europe*." But French economist Pierre Uri made a cooler assessment. Noting that American capital represented only about one per cent of the total invested in Europe, whereas Europeans had owned about 15 per cent of the capital invested in the United States in the preceding century, he commented dryly, "One will acknowledge no doubt that America came out pretty well from the colonization."

High growth and profit potentials were clearly a key inducement to investment overseas. In 1959 Eastman Kodak's foreign sales rose just 9 per cent, but its profits on those sales were up 51 per cent. I.B.M. World Trade Corp. showed a 13.5 per cent return on gross revenues, compared to earnings of only 10.4 per cent on sales in domestic operations. Armstrong Cork had a 65 per cent profit increase on a 12 per cent gain in overseas sales. But more than just being a route to higher profits, direct investments abroad gave rise to a wholly new business concept: multinationalism.

The evolution was gradual and nearly imperceptible. American business abroad first moved in the traditional patterns of the exploiter of resources, such as copper and oil, in undeveloped areas, contributing capital, equipment, and know-how. Then branches and sales offices were opened, staffed largely by local workers, and in time local branch managers and executives were appointed. The companies shifted their production of components and assemblies to the plants where operations were most efficient, sometimes because of larger or better labor supplies, at other times because they were close to supply sources or markets. And before long, as economies grew more stable, companies were basing a great variety of decisions—on financing, staffing, deployment of plants—on simple cost-benefit equations rather than political considerations or the convenience of the parent firm.

By the late 1960's a number of American firms were conducting a considerable part of their business abroad. Those with more than half of either their assets or sales overseas included Colgate-Palmolive, Standard Oil of New Jersey, Singer, Heinz, and Chas. Pfizer. Ford Motor had 40 per cent of its assets and 36 per cent of its sales in twenty-seven foreign countries. I.T.&T. was in sixty different countries and PepsiCo operated in 114.

Ownership of some companies became increasingly multinational as their stock became widely distributed around the world, the result of investment by foreigners, the purchase of overseas businesses for equity, and stock options and awards to executives abroad. In 1965 General Motors distributed shares to 850 executives outside the United States and Canada, and the stock of such blue-chip companies as G.E., G.M., and Eastman Kodak were actively traded on European exchanges.

In effect, by adopting a world approach and outlook, business was succeeding where nation-states had long failed. While diplomats and statesmen talked loftily of their hopes of building an international commonwealth, the multinational companies were quietly creating one.

THE CORPORATION AND ITS RESPONSIBILITIES

In the late 1960's there were demands from many quarters, and some suggestions from business itself, that corporations should serve other masters besides their owners. Such a concept of the corporation as a vehicle for the public good was not the newest, but in fact the oldest, of the corporation's distinguishing features. In the earliest days of the corporation,

A TWENTIETH-CENTURY MALTHUS

While computers made possible the solution of a host of problems that men once dared not even attempt to solve, those who knew computers best made them the tools of a totally new approach to problem-solving. One of these pioneers was Jay W. Forrester, a diffident M.I.T. professor who had been the chief architect of Whirlwind, perhaps the most sophisticated computer of the late 1940's.

During the 1950's Forrester was director of M.I.T.'s Digital Computer Laboratory, where he was an early worker with models and simulation—that is, using computers to determine future behavior of highly intricate systems. In 1957 a Ford Foundation grant enabled the M.I.T. group to explore business systems, and out of this grew the methods of what Forrester called "industrial dynamics"—the constant interaction of the many factors and forces affecting a business or manufacturing enterprise.

Forrester discovered some principles of system behavior that would emerge again and again in his later work. For one thing, he found that the behavior of complex systems—such as a large corporation, a city, or a human society—was fundamentally different from that of simple systems, like those involved in warming one's hands at a fire, adding numbers, or steering a car. The problems arising in simple systems could be dealt with intuitively, whereas intuitive solutions usually aggravated the difficulties of extremely complex systems, where the best answers were often *counterintuitive.*

So Forrester's computer models were designed to seek out fundamental, rather than apparent, sources of trouble. In his 1961 book, *Industrial Dynamics,* for example, he warned young industries of the perils of building up sales to the point where production facilities could not keep up with orders—and in that way losing sales in the long run. Corporate policies believed to be safeguards against difficulties, he advised, could well be the major causes of problems.

When John F. Collins, mayor of Boston from 1960 to 1967, was invited to M.I.T. as a visiting professor early in 1968, Forrester became involved with him and a series of politicians and urban authorities in an exploration of city problems. Forrester saw that a city is a relatively closed system, with a number of key forces constantly interacting. He decided that the important variables were housing, population, and industry, and that changes in these three were the central processes involved in either growth or stagnation.

Forrester developed a model of a city, let his computer find the outcome of the dynamic forces at work, and kept changing his model until it behaved like real cities do. The natural metamorphosis of an aging city, he found, tends toward too much housing and too few jobs for the underemployed. In this condition, the city does not work very well; it attracts the unskilled but offers them little opportunity, thus trapping them in poverty. At the same time, it shifts taxes toward those with the greatest mobility, encouraging the departure of the people and industries that it needs the most and setting up a spiral of urban decline.

In his 1969 book, *Urban Dynamics,* Forrester again pointed out that simple, "obvious" prescriptions can be bad medicine for cities, too. Building subsidized housing for low-income families may seem like the reasonable, human solution to overcrowded slums. But the unfeeling computers showed that such programs would bring the underemployed to the city, raise tax levels, discourage industry, and in-

366

English charters had been granted on the mercantilist premise that the companies would serve the national interest as well as their own. So the corporation appeared to have come full circle in its development.

In the intervening centuries, the United States far outstripped England in using the corporate form, and businessmen found it a natural vehicle with which to organize capital and manpower. J. P. Morgan made it a useful instrument for controlling large accumulations of capital as the more affluent members of a growing middle class sought profitable ways to deploy their savings. In the 1880's the corporation was strengthened by court rulings that declared it a legal "person," entitled to the protection of the due process clause of the Fourteenth Amendment.

The corporation was very unlike a person, however, in its limited freedom of action, since the law held it strictly to those powers expressly authorized in its charter. In 1881, for example, a Massachusetts court prohibited a railroad from guaranteeing the expenses of a music festival along its route. The Illinois Supreme Court in 1898 ruled that it was *ultra vires*—i.e., beyond the legal powers of a corporation and its officers—for a company to build a town of 10,000 to house its workers and their families.

But as public attitudes changed, new laws and court rulings reflected these shifts. Courts upheld contributions by railroads to attract plants, by hotels to support conventions, and by land companies to pay for a bridge and improved railroad service. A Missouri court in the late 1920's approved the construction of a large company town. Tax laws endorsed corporate giving in a 1936 amendment to the Internal Revenue Code that permitted a deduction of up to 5 per cent of taxable income for contributions. But the landmark decision was handed down in 1953, when stockholders of the A. P. Smith Manufacturing Company, a maker of valves and hydrants, challenged the corporation's unrestricted gift of $1,500 to Princeton University. In approving the gift the New Jersey court said, "Just as

crease joblessness. Said Forrester: "The belief that more money will solve urban problems has taken attention away from correcting the underlying causes and has instead allowed the problems to grow to the limit of the available money, whatever that amount might be."

Spurred by a grant from the Independence Foundation, Forrester moved on to an even more ambitious study of global dynamics. Because industrial growth had long been deemed the key to a better, happier world society, Forrester built his new model around those factors that had been growing exponentially for centuries—population, capital investment, pollution, food consumption, and standard of living—to see how their further growth rates might affect the quality of life.

The computer again showed that the obvious measures for the betterment of mankind's lot—such as producing more food or increasing capital investment—would eventually result in greater and more unbearable pressures in such things as population, pollution, and depletion of resources. But the one overwhelming fact that emerged from his 1971 book, *World Dynamics*, was obvious: exponential growth of population or industrialization, starting from any level, must sooner or later make them more a detriment than a boon. Malthus had been right, after all, Forrester decided, and said, "His assertion is not erroneous; it is merely incomplete."

Somehow, Forrester concluded, mankind must abandon its millennia-old commitment to growth and seek some level of equilibrium instead. Because the quality of life on the planet may already have passed its peak, the ideal balance might be reached only by going backward, not forward. The computer data indicated that the rate of using natural resources should be cut by 75 per cent, capital investment by 40 per cent, the birth rate by 30 per cent, generation of pollution by 50 per cent, and even food output by 20 per cent. The "green revolution" begun by introducing high-yield grains to less-developed countries in the late 1960's could conceivably boomerang, since increased food production has traditionally stimulated population growth and industrialization.

A further study was underwritten by the Club of Rome, a prestigious group of some seventy-five industrialists, educators, scientists, and thought leaders, founded by Aurelio Peccei, economist and consultant who formerly headed Olivetti. Dennis Meadows, a Forrester disciple, took charge of the project, which consisted in good part of testing and refining the original world model. The basic computer forecasts of coming world crisis remained undisturbed. Population, which 200 years ago was doubling at the rate of once every 1,500 years, was now doubling every thirty-two years, Meadows found. There was no foreseeable possibility, he said, that the earth could support 14 billion people—the number that would be reached after two more doublings. The Club of Rome distributed a preliminary report of the Meadows study, published early in 1972 as *The Limits to Growth: A Global Challenge*.

Forrester's more thoughtful critics did not argue with his inexorable arithmetic, but they pointed out that he had reckoned without one virtually limitless element: man's ingenuity. Yet Forrester and Meadows may have brought the world a step closer to demonstrating that men, motivated by conscience, enterprise, and creativity, can change their ways of thinking and doing to find solutions to problems that none thought were problems the day before.

the conditions prevailing when corporations were originally created required that they serve public as well as private interests, modern conditions require that corporations acknowledge and discharge social as well as private responsibilities."

As is often the case with the law, the decision reflected an evolution that had already taken place. General Electric's first president, Charles A. Coffin, had placed service to the public ahead of business success. In the mid-1920's, one of his successors, Owen D. Young, described the role of corporate managers as "trustees of an institution," rather than just as representatives of the stockholders. The beneficiaries of that trust were more than 100,000 employees (entitled to a "cultural wage," he felt, rather than just a "living wage"), the stockholders, and the company's millions of customers.

Some of the more thoughtful leaders of large corporations continued to grapple with the problem of maintaining a balance of the interests of stockholders, customers, employees, and the public. "Business must account for its stewardship not only on the balance sheet but also in matters of social responsibility," said Sears, Roebuck chief Robert E. Wood. And Frank Abrams, head of Standard Oil of New Jersey, stated, "We have equal responsibilities to . . . stockholders, customers, and the public generally, including government."

Abrams saw this concern for society as a whole as a sign of growing professionalism among managers. As the operation of the business system had tended to separate management from ownership, the new class of hired managers had acquired enormous economic power and in most cases a deep sense of responsibility about the exercise of that power. Where management decisions did not appear to create a conflict between the interests of the public and those of the owners of a business—as in producing more goods at lower cost and thereby increasing profits through volume sales at low prices—there was no problem. But running a business was never that simple. Managers were confronted with increasingly difficult choices: between high profits, for example, and the company's best long-term interests, or between maximizing profits and meeting social obligations.

One danger lay in a dilution of management's sense of responsibility. A manager who acted as a trustee for society might find he was less a trustee for the owners of a business or its employees. In one instance, in 1971, Nat Sherman, the founder and chairman of the automobile muffler firm Midas International Corp., wrested the operating control of the company away from his son, Gordon, who he thought was dissipating the corporation's assets for social purposes.

Most businessmen, however, were cast in a more traditional mold. Under the goad of competition, they sought to maximize profits simply to assure survival, which was still regarded as the first responsibility of any business. Although the corporation was undergoing a kind of evolution toward greater social concern, even one of the leaders in engineering this change, Henry Ford II, pointed out, "No business can survive if it neglects the axioms of sound management. . . . Business cannot hire more people than it needs, or . . . for more than their work is worth."

Nevertheless the pressures on business mounted. They came first in the form of government encouragement through loans and programs for low-income housing, job training, and helping minority group members start private enterprises. Some stockholders added their weight, mainly by seeking to be heard at annual meetings on behalf of consumerism, minority hiring, and protection of the environment. A suit was pressed to make Dow Chemical Co. submit to stockholders a proxy proposal banning the production of napalm—even after the company had stopped producing napalm in 1969.

Some of the pressures came from within the corporations themselves—from those who feared that government would force business to assume responsibilities it did not take on voluntarily, from businessmen who were personally disturbed about past failures in social areas, and from the ranks of younger managers who felt business should be deeply engaged in solving social problems. But perhaps the strongest influence was that of the public and its expectations of business. Studies in 1970 showed that 60 per cent of the adult population believed that business was obligated to fight environmental pollution; smaller, but substantial, percentages felt that business should support public education, hire and train the disadvantaged, and help rebuild city slums. While business responded to these popular sentiments, it was often with the cosmetic of public relations rather than with any more fundamental effort to cure social ills.

But there were also conscientious attempts to cope with the problems of the times. Indeed, a good many businessmen and corporations had been active in these areas long before the general public was much aware of them. Businessmen inspired the stockholder suit in the A. P. Smith case, and they then started the Council for Financial Aid to Education to promote fund-raising for colleges. At the instigation of President James Conant of Harvard in the late 1940's, Time Inc. President Roy E. Larsen helped to start and then headed the National Citizens Commission for the Public Schools. Ford initiated safety engineering of its automobiles in the early 1950's, but car buyers were not interested. In 1955 the International Paper Company launched a program of supporting schools in cities where it had plants, budgeting $172,500 initially and doubling that after ten years. For years electric utilities sought permission to use cleaner fuel, but regulatory agencies, conscious that higher costs would mean larger power bills, turned them down.

Industry generally was far ahead of the public in its consciousness of environmental pollution. In one 1965 survey only 17 per cent of adult Americans rated pollution as a major problem, but long before that time many devices for controlling industrial emissions, especially the solid particles known as "particulate matter," had been developed and were in widespread use. The air in such cities as Chicago, Pittsburgh, and St. Louis had been considerably cleaned up since the 1940's. Industry was spending some $300 million a year on the abatement of air pollution in 1965, almost ten times as much as government spent for research and enforcement. These expenditures then rose dramatically, reaching an estimated $1.5 billion to control air and water pollution in 1971. The Interior Department estimated that industy would have to invest $3 billion between 1970 and 1974 to treat effluents from its plants, while municipalities would have to spend $10 billion for water treatment. Industries were on target in 1971, but the municipalities were spending only about half of what was required.

Measuring costs against benefits could be relatively simple in some cases, exceedingly complex in others. Automobiles, thought to be responsible for about half the nation's estimated 200 million tons of air pollutants in 1968, had about 60 per cent less hydrocarbons and carbon monoxide in 1970, at a cost of about $80 per car; the cost of meeting federal standards for 1975 was estimated at $300 per car, plus about a 10 per cent reduction in gasoline mileage. The Environmental Protection Administration placed the social cost of industrial emissions of sulphur and nitrogen oxides, more than half of which were generated by power plants burning coal and oil, at $8.3 billion a year. Yet the public, which resisted the erection of nuclear power installations, became more incensed over power shortages and failures than over pollution.

No simpler was the situation regarding minorities, particularly blacks, with the interlinked problems of inferior education, low-paying jobs, poor housing, and cultural lag. There had long been a tacit assumption in American society that the black's social and economic status was the consequence of natural forces—an assumption in which a large part of industry and even most blacks acquiesced. As blacks became more aware of the economic gap between themselves and whites in the 1960's, many also became more resentful. When this problem began to erupt into violence in the late 1960's, the national response was a mixture of guilt and alarm, both of which seemed to stimulate overreaction.

Some sought comfort in agreeing with Alexis de Tocqueville that the danger of violence and revolt was greatest when conditions were improving, not when they were at their worst. Others pointed out that New York's Harlem was the world's wealthiest black community, or that the U.S. poverty line of $3,500 for a family of four would be deemed affluence in most of the world. But the hard fact was that the problem was one of people living in the United States, not in the rest of the world, and that their expectations were those of the prosperous 1960's, not of the 1830's or 1930's. Almost half the difference in income between whites and blacks could not be ascribed to differences in education or ability, M.I.T. Professor Lester Thurow found, but was simply part of the cost of being black.

To some extent, industry had displayed early leadership in correcting some of these injustices. As far back as 1946, "nonwhites" working for Chrysler numbered 12,000, or 17 per cent of its employees. But under union seniority rules, many of these were the first to be laid off when production lines shut down. In time, as black workers gained seniority, large numbers worked steadily in the auto plants, and 33,000 nonwhites made up 23 per cent of the Chrysler work force by 1968. The company signed up its first black dealer

Workers at an I.B.M. computer components plant in Brooklyn's Bedford-Stuyvesant, a center of chronic unemployment

in 1963, and hundreds of black workers were promoted to foreman, to salaried jobs, and to supervisory management and executive positions.

When business was finally aroused to the extent and gravity of minority problems, it undertook initiatives on dozens of fronts. In 1961 Lockheed became one of the first large corporations to enlist in a voluntary program for providing jobs to unemployed minority workers. Ford and General Motors recruited actively in slum areas, and kept workers on even when they failed to measure up to employment standards. General Electric plant managers were required to report regularly their percentage of nonwhite employees, compared to the percentage of nonwhites in their localities. Standard Oil of Indiana insisted on jobs for minority workers in the construction of its new $100 million office building. A number of companies offered help in the form of loans, guarantees, training, and counsel to aspiring minority group enterprisers.

A good many of these programs, by ordinary standards, were failures. Xerox Corporation found that the cost of hiring and training hard-core unemployed was four times that for other workers. Aerojet-General invested $1.3 million in 1966 in a plant in the Watts district of Los Angeles, where 440 people, more than half with police records, were soon working on a $2.5 million government contract. But after a hopeful start the Watts Manufacturing Co. continued to show losses and have high labor turnover. The Boise Cascade Corp. joined a black-owned construction firm to form Boise-Burnett Corp. in 1967, but in 1971 had to write off almost $40 million in pretax losses stemming from the subsidiary's operations.

The most successful ventures appeared to be the most businesslike. Archie Williams, a twenty-eight-year old black, bought two supermarkets in Boston's Roxbury ghetto from the Purity Supreme chain, got sound operating advice as well as financing and purchasing help, and was soon running his stores at a profit. I.B.M. applied its normal business standards to a plant it opened in Brooklyn's Bedford-Stuyvesant district, and was able to turn out computer components at a cost lower than that charged by outside suppliers.

With its pragmatic outlook, American business had always learned to live with the mood and climate of the times. The mood that was emerging in the 1970's was one of greater expectations in the contributions that business would make in matters affecting the environment, urban decay, race, and consumerism. The question that remained was: who would pay the costs?

At least part of those costs, it appeared, would come from profits. The case could be made from the experience of General Motors, not only the biggest business of all but the classic example of good corporate management. Under fire from many quarters,

G.M. deliberately decided to emphasize social responsibility. The consequences soon showed up. In 1965 its earnings amounted to 26 per cent of net worth and in 1966 to 21 per cent. For the next five years profits averaged only 15 per cent of net worth and never rose as high as 20 per cent, in good years or bad. Obviously the company was absorbing some of its higher costs, notably higher labor costs not compensated for by productivity gains. Similar results throughout industry could mean a lower rate of capital formation, less investment, and slower industrial growth, an outcome that some perceptive observers earnestly approved.

But others were equally convinced that only more growth could provide the answers, and business was moving to solve some of society's problems in its traditional manner. Private companies experimentally took over some of the more difficult problem areas in public education, accepting compensation on the basis of performance. As hospitals staggered under the burdens of serving a growing and more demanding population, new proprietary hospital chains came into being— American Medicorp, Inc., Hospital Corporation of America, and others—demonstrating that good management practices could help provide quality health care at lower cost.

Companies with large staffs of systems analysts and engineers—Litton, T.R.W., Aerojet-General, I.B.M., North American Aviation, Lockheed—were developing new ways to attack social problems. When the state of California sought bids for research studies on crime, pollution, transportation, and a centralized state information system, the awards were won by Aerojet-General, Space-General ,Corporation, North American Aviation, and Lockheed.

The scope of society's problems was also being expressed in traditional business terms—that is, in the size of the markets they represented. Thus the market for providing decent housing for all Americans amounted to trillions of dollars, for improving education to hundreds of billions, and for cleaning the environment to $300 billion.

Essentially, what was taking shape was America's commitment to the future. In a great many ways, the new American dream bore a striking resemblance to its predecessor. To be sure, the old one was often a short-range dream based on hard realities, one of getting and providing, of increasing amounts of hardware that was ever slicker and shinier and more automatic. But in the shadow of that dream there was always another one—of greater ease and mobility, of lifting ancient burdens from men's shoulders, of learning and knowing and growing. It was part of an even more pervasive dream of a free and open society, and that was the last one that Americans were likely to abandon.

X   *Social Conscience*

Consumer advocate Ralph Nader pursues a U.S. tradition of subjecting business and government to public scrutiny and reform.

66 The institutions established for self-government have been founded with intent to secure justice and independence for all. The social relations among the whole body of the people are humane and simple. The general spirit of the people is liberal, is kindly, is considerate. . . . Every genuine American holds to the ideal of justice for all men, of independence . . . of material well-being for all the well-behaving and industrious, of peace and goodwill among men."

Charles Eliot Norton, *True Patriotism*, 1898

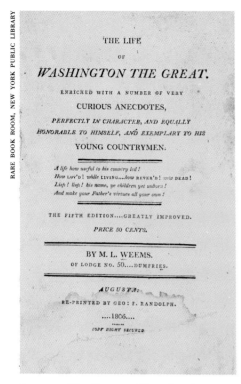

Lessons like Parson Weems's cherry tree story furthered respect for ethical conduct.

New York City's Howard Mission and Home for Little Wanderers, pictured in 1868, typified institutions reflecting Americans' inherent charitableness.

Concern for fellow men and belief in justice for all runs deep. The current has produced reformers like abolitionist William Lloyd Garrison, who fought slavery.

A social-justice landmark was the first U.S. pension plan, instigated by A.T.&T. President Theodore Newton Vail (above) in 1913.

Humane sentiment in U.S. was exemplified by Henry Ford's "peace ship" mission of 1915 (right), a vain try at ending World War I.

Though not political activists or social reformers, businessmen usually respond to pressure for change, not only to survive but to employ their talent in solving problems. Opposite page: water pollution is combated by International Paper Company's environmental management specialists, shown testing the quality of waste water being clarified at their Ticonderoga, New York, plant. Left: an I.B.M. physicist, one of eighteen professionals on leave with full pay to teach at black colleges, instructs students at North Carolina's Shaw University. Below, left: Xerox's Joseph C. Wilson involved himself and his company in social and educational enterprises for public betterment; right: sociologist Saul Alinsky helped organize powerless community and labor groups to win a share in the decision-making process and a voice in affairs that affect them.

Business and culture find a community of interests: commissioned art, including an Alexander Calder mobile (above) graces the offices of New York's Chase Manhattan Bank. Right: the interior garden of the Ford Foundation building in New York. Its large funds, derived from the fortune begun by Henry Ford, benefit many spheres of American life, including the cultural.

RECOMMENDED READING

Allen, Frederick Lewis, *The Lords of Creation*, Harper & Brothers Publishers, 1935.

Bailyn, Bernard, *The New England Merchants in the Seventeenth Century*, Harper & Row, 1964.

Bartels, Robert, *The Development of Marketing Thought*, R. D. Irwin, 1962.

Baxter, James Phinney, *Scientists Against Time*, Little, Brown & Company, 1946.

Blumberg, Phillip I., "Corporate Responsibility and the Social Crisis," Boston University *Law Review*, Spring, 1970.

Boorstin, Daniel J., *The Americans. The Colonial Experience*, Random House, 1958.

Brandeis, Louis, *Other People's Money*, Stokes, 1940.

Bruchey, Stuart, *The Roots of American Economic Growth*, Harper & Row, 1965.

Burlingame, Roger, *Engines of Democracy*, Charles Scribner's Sons, 1940.

Chamberlain, John, *The Enterprising Americans*, Harper & Row, 1963.

Clough, Wilson, *Intellectual Origins of American National Thought*, Corinth Books, 1961.

Cochran, Thomas C., and Miller, William, *The Age of Enterprise*, Harper & Row, 1942.

Committee for Economic Development, *Social Responsibilities of Business Corporations*, June, 1961.

Faulkner, Harold, *American Economic History*, Harper & Brothers Publishers, 1954.

Ferry, John William, *A History of the Department Store*, Macmillan, 1960.

Friedman, Milton, *Capitalism and Freedom*, University of Chicago Press, 1962.

Gras, N. S. B., and Larson, Henrietta M., *Casebook in American Business*, Appleton-Crofts, Inc., 1939.

Hacker, Louis M., *The Triumph of American Capitalism*, Simon & Schuster, 1940.

Hendrick, Burton, *The Age of Big Business*, Yale University Press, 1919–21.

Hoyt, Edwin P., *The Vanderbilts and Their Fortunes*, Doubleday, 1962.

Josephson, Matthew, *The Robber Barons*, Harcourt Brace, 1934.

Lebhar, Godfrey M., *Chain Stores in America*, Chain Store Publishing Corporation, 1952.

Locke, John, *An Essay Concerning Human Understanding*, Oxford University Press, 1924.

Mahoney, Tom, *The Great Merchants*, Harper & Brothers Publishing, 1955.

Mitchell, Broadus, *Depression Decade*, Rinehart, 1947.

Moody, John, *The Masters of Capital*, Yale University Press, 1921.

Morison, Samuel E., and Commager, Henry S., *Growth of the American Republic*, 2 vols., Oxford University Press, 1937.

Nelson, Donald, *Arsenal of Democracy*, Harcourt Brace and Company, 1946.

Nettels, Curtis P., *The Roots of American Civilization*, Appleton-Century-Crofts, 1963.

Nevins, Allan, *Ordeal of the Union*, Charles Scribner's Sons, 1947.

Oliver, John W., *History of American Technology*, The Ronald Press Company, 1956.

Samuelson, Paul A., *Economics*, 8th ed. McGraw-Hill, 1970.

Schachner, Nathan, *Alexander Hamilton*, A. S. Barnes, 1946.

Schlesinger, Arthur, Jr., *The Age of Jackson*, Little, Brown, 1946.

Sloan, Alfred P., *My Years With General Motors*, Doubleday, 1963.

Soule, George, *Prosperity Decade, 1917–1929*, Rinehart, 1951.

Taylor, George R., *The Transportation Revolution, 1815–1860*, Rinehart, 1951.

Thompson, Holland, *The Age of Invention*, Yale University Press, 1921.

Turner, Frederick Jackson, *The Frontier in American History*, Henry Holt and Company, 1947.

Wood, James Playsted, *The Story of Advertising*, The Ronald Press, 1958.

PERMISSIONS

INDEX

Page numbers in **boldface** refer to illustrations.

Abraham & Straus, 238, 241
Acme Oil Co., 177
Acts of Trade, 28-33
Adams Express Co., 126
Addressograph-Multigraph Corp., 337
advertising, 142, **188-89**, **219**, 236, 242, **243**, 243, 246, 249-56, **250**, **259**, 261, 279, **346**; patent medicines, 243, 249, 253, 256, 259; soaps, cosmetics, and toiletries, 104, **188**, 250, **251**, 251, 252, 254, 259; tobacco industry, **66**, 66-67, **189**, **195**, 195, **234**, 251, 260-61
Aerojet-General Corp., 360, 370
A.F.L.-C.I.O., 322; see also American Federation of Labor; Congress of Industrial Organizations
agricultural implements and machinery, 98, 99, 117, 120, 156, 169, 170, 198, 199, **287**, 289, 297, **308**; cotton gin, 52, 62-63; combine, **148**, 169; plow, 52, 62, 98, 117, **120**, 120, **148-49**; reaper and mower, 98-99, 133, 134, 135, 169, 219; seed drill, 53, 99; tractor, **38-39**, **75**, 286, 297
Aircraft War Production Council, 318
Air Force, 319, 327, 328, 329, 358
Air Mail Act, 331
alcoholic beverages, 14, 15, 20-21, 24, 26-30 passim, **29**, 51, 68; Prohibition and Prohibitionists, 171, 296, 300
Aldrich-Vreeland Act, 194, 223
Alleghany Corp., 282, 283, 321
Allied Stores Corp., 238
Allis-Chalmers, 317
Allison Engineering Co., 331
Almy, Wm., 27, 64, 65
Altman, Benjamin, 238
Aluminum Co. of America, 209, 325
aluminum industry, 209, 301, 314-15, 324, 325, 358
Amalgamated Copper Co., 210, 213
Amerada Petroleum Co., 334
American Airlines, 301, 326-27, 328, 357, 358
American Bankers Association, 281
American Bell Telephone Company, 181-82, 197, 206
American Bridge Co., 204
American Broadcasting Co., 332, 360
American Car and Foundry Co., 197
American Cereal Co., 257
American Chicle Co., 260
American Cigar, 195
American colonies: agriculture, 13, 16, 17, 20, 24, 26, 27, 28, **29**, 30, 31, 34; business and industry, 19-34 passim; class system, 15-16, 17, 22-26 passim, 28, 31, 33, 34, 119; Dutch, 13-19 passim, 21, 26, 31, 34; exchange mediums of, **8**, 9, 14, 20, 24, 26, 27, 30, 31, 34, 47, 56; French, 14; immigration, 13, 14-15, 16, 21; and Indians, 9, 13, 14, 16, 29; and Indians, trade, 10, 14, 18, 20, 21, 24; labor, 13, 16, 25; land, 15-16, 17, 19, 25, 28, 31, 119; population, 14; religion, 12, 18-19, 22-23, 23-24; shipping, 17, **19**, 24, 25-27, **29**, 31, 33, 34, 54; slavery, 13, **14**, 14-15, 17, 20, 24, 25, 27, 29; trade and tariffs, 10-34 passim, **29**, **31**
American Cyanamid Co., **350**
American Express Co., **307**
American Federation of Labor, **173**, 173, 217, 218, 280, 299, 322
American Mail Line, 321
American Medicorp, Inc., 370
American Motors Corp., **324**, 324, 351
American Retail Federation, 246
American Revolution, 33, 34, 47-48, 50
American Sheet Steel Co., 204, 205, **343**
American Smelting and Refining Co., 197, 210, 213
American Steel and Wire Co., 170, 204,

205, **343**
American Steel Hoop Company, 204, 205, **343**
American Stock Exchange, 137
American Sugar Refining Co., 197, 198, 199
American Telegraph Co., 133, 134, 135
American Telephone and Telegraph Co., 182, 206-7, 216, 279, 280, 285, 289, 334-35, 339, 351, **362**, **372**
American Tin Plate Co., 204, 205, **343**
American Tobacco Co., 67, 182, 195, 197, **234**, 260-61
American Water Supply Co., 260
Ampex Corp., **336**, 336
Anaconda Aluminum Co., 325
Anaconda Co., 209, 210, 211, 314, 325
Anheuser-Busch, Inc., 355
antitrust action see monopolies and trusts, federal action and legislation
A. & P. see Great Atlantic & Pacific Tea Co.
Appleton, Nathan, 95-96, 101
Arabian American Oil Co. (Aramco), 277, 323
Armour Co., 170, **221**, 360
arms manufacture, 34, 60, 62, **63**, 63-64, 69, **72-73**, **74**, 98, 101-2, 131, 133, 134, **140**, 141, 314
Armstrong Cork Co., 365
Arnold, Thurman, 302, 358
Arnold Constable Corp., 237
Articles of Confederation, 48, 49
Ash, Roy L., 360
Associated Advertising Clubs of America, 256
Associated Merchandising Corp., 238
Associated Press, 135
Astor, John Jacob, 57, 67-68, **112**, 121, 136, 180
Astor, John Jacob, II, 158
Astoria (Washington Irving), 68
Atchison, Topeka, and Santa Fe Railway, 182
Atlantic and Great Western Railroad, 129
Atlantic & Pacific (telegraph co.), 163, 164
Atlantic Cable Co., 134
Atlas Powder Co., 224, 325
atomic energy see nuclear energy
Atomic Energy Commission, 323
Automatic Telegraph Co., 179
automatic vending machines, **260**, 260-61
automobile industry, 200, 209, 218-20, **219**, 262, 273, **274**, 275, 276-78, 280, 281, 290, **310**, 322, 323-24, 324-25, 330-31, **341**, 352, 365, 369; advertising, **219**, 251, 254, 278; labor, 219, **299**, 299-300; leasing companies, 354; pollution, 369; World War I, 223; World War II, **270**, **305**, 314, 315, 317, **318**, 318, 320
Avco Manufacturing Co., 334
Avery, Sewell, 244
aviation and aviation industry, **42**, 175, 220-23, **221**, **300**, 300-301, **303**, 314, 320, 326-29, 356-58, **357**; Civil Aeronautics Board, 327, 358; Federal Aviation Administration, 356; World War II, **270**, 314, 315, 316, 318-19, **319**, 320
Avis, Inc., **307**, 354, 360
Avon Products, Inc., 259-60
Ayer & Son, N. W., 249-50, 251, 255

Babson, Roger W., 288
Baekeland, Dr. Leo, 301
Baker, George F., 193, 211, 213-14, 215, 282, 289
Baker and Co., Ltd., Walter, 252, 258
Baldwin Locomotive Works, 89, **90**, 90, 127
Baltimore & Ohio Railroad, 88-89, 90, 128, **129**, 157, 173, 182
Bancitaly Corp., 285
Bankers Trust Co. (N.Y.), 213, 289
Bank for International Settlements, 364
banking, 11, 50, 51, 55-57, **57**, 67, 85, 91, 94-100 passim, **94**, **95**, **97**, 136, 141, 165, 194, 211-13, 215, 281, 286, 287, 293-94, 295, 296, 340; Aldrich-Vreeland Act, 194, 223; bonds issued by, 94, 364; commercial paper, 56, 96,

292; deposits, 96, 137, 291, 364; failures and suspensions, 286, 292, 293; Federal Deposit Insurance Corp., 296; Federal Reserve Act, 194, 215, 216; Glass-Steagall Banking Act, 296; investment by, 135, 362, 363; loans, 56, 95, 96, 137, 138, 157, 273, 285, 286, 287, 288, 291, 364; mergers and chains, 284-85; mortgages, 56, 363; National Banking System opposed, 56, 96, 136, 156, 171, 172; notes issued by, 56, 94, 96, 97, 98, 136, 137, 194, 223; savings banks, 135, 136
Bank of America (Calif.), 285, 363
Bank of Commerce (N.Y.), 284
Bank of England, 288, 364, 365
Bank of Italy (Calif.), 284, 285
Bank of Massachusetts, 56, 96
Bank of New York, 56
Bank of the United States, First, 56, **57**, 57, 67, 85
Bank of the United States, Second, 57, 94-96, **95**, 99
Baruch, Benard, 223, 289, 313
Basic Refractories, Inc., 314
Battelle Memorial Institute, 302, 337, 338
Beatrice Foods, 256
Behn, Col. Sosthenes, 360
Bell, Alexander Graham, 177, 179, 180-81
Bell, Daniel, 279
Bell Aircraft, 318
Bell & Gosset, 360
Bell & Howell Co., 337
Bell Telephone Laboratories, 334-35, 339
Belmont, August, 195-96, 197, 201
Bendix Aviation Co., 281, 331
Berle, Adolf A., 329, 359
Bessemer, Henry, 132, 167
Bethlehem Iron Co., 167
Bethlehem Steel Corp., 167, 205, 300
Better Business Bureau, 256
Biddle, Nicholas, 94-95, **95**, 98
Birdseye, Clarence, 257, 258
Birdseye Seafoods, Inc., **77**, 257
Black Ball Line, 121
blacks, 369; and business, 218, 368, 369-70, **375**; see also slavery
Bland-Allison Act, 172
Bloomingdale's (dept. store), 238, 241
boats and ships, **18**, **73**, 87-88, **88**, **100**, 121-22, 122-23, **124**, 223, 323, 328
Boeing Co., 300, 301, 327, 328, 356, 357, 358
Boise Cascade Corp., 370
bonds, 362; bank, 94, 364; Confederate, 142, 155; corporate, 181, 194, 363; federal, 68, 85, 99, 142, 156, 161, 162, 164, 171, 194, 195, 196, 197, 217, 224, 285, 291; foreign, 181; state, 121; Treasury, 195, 321
Borden, Gail, 132, 133
Borden, Inc., **188**, 256
Boston, 17, 18, 21, 104, 119, 128, 130, 252; commerce, 24, 25, 27, 31, 61, 238; shipping and shipbuilding, 19, 25, 31, 33, 34, 54, 90, 121
Boston and Albany Railroad, 90
Boston and Worcester Railroad, 130
Boston Stock Exchange, 137
Brandeis, Louis D., 284, 351, 358
Braniff International Airways, 361
brand names, **188-89**, 250, 252-53
Breech, Ernest R., 331
Bretton Woods Conference, 295, 321, 363-64
brokers and brokerage, 85, 91, 98, 136, **233**, 285, 286, 287; see also investment and stock market
Bronfman, Samuel, 300
Brooks Brothers (store), 237
Brotherhood of Locomotive Engineers, 173; Firemen, 173
Brown, Moses, **27**, 27, 62, 64
Brown Brothers & Co., 137, 180
Brunswick Corp., 351
Bryan, William Jennings, **108**, **196**, 197
Budge, Schiff & Co., 181
Buick (auto. co.), 220, **270**
building and construction, 21, 70, **77**, 83, 105, 136, 162, 174, 191, **266-67**, 273, 285, 290, 300, **304**, **312**, 322,

324, 325, **346**, 366-67, 368, 370
Bullock's, Inc., 241
Bulova Watch Co., **114**
Burdine's (dept. store), 241
Burlington Industries, Inc., 353-54, **354**
Burroughs Corp., 340
Byrd, William, II, **28**, 28

Cadillac Automobile Co., 219, 220, 276
Calhoun, John, 91, 92, 140
California, **40**, 118, 124, 162, 169, 208; discovery of gold, **38**, 99, 122, 124, 125, 160, 171
Cambria Iron Works, 167, 168
Camden and Amboy Railroad, 127
Campbell Soup Co., 252
Canada, 14, 27, 28, 29, 68, 137, 179, 194
canals, 61, 85, **86**, 86-87, 88, 91, 93, 94, 96, 127, 128, 138
Canteen Co., 261
Canton Iron Co., 89
Carbide and Carbon Chemicals Corp., 317
Carey, Mathew, 92
Carlson, Chester, **307**, 337, 338
Carnation Co., 251
Carnegie, Andrew, **113**, 119, 156, 166-69, 193, 204-5, **206**, 206-7, 228, 236; Autobiography, 168; "The Gospel of Wealth," 206, 207
Carnegie-Illinois Steel Co., 300
Carnegie Steel Co., 204, 205, 207, 331
Carothers, Dr. Wallace, **301**, 301
carriages, wagons, and stagecoaches, 68, 84, 86, **126-27**, 126-27, 129, 130, 218
Carver, George Washington, **112**
cattle and livestock, 16, 17, 26, **29**, 54, 64-65, **152**, 169-70; dairy industry, 27, 54, 117-18, 132; meat packing and preservation, 54, 55, 118, 132, **152**, 170, 198, 223, **342**
Central Pacific Railroad Co., 160-61, 161-62
chain stores, 236, 237, 238, 241, 244-49; see also discount stores
Champion, Albert, 220
chartered companies, 9, 10, 14, 15, 366-67
Chase, Salmon P., 142
Chase Manhattan Bank (N.Y.), **376**
Chase National Bank (N.Y.), 284, 289, 296
Chemical Bank (N.Y.), **45**
chemical industry, 69, 223, 224, 301, 325; see also explosives and munitions
Chesapeake & Ohio Canal, 127, **129**
Chesapeake & Ohio Railroad, 162, 282
Chesapeake Corp., 283
Chevrolet Motor Co., 220, 331
Chicago, 90, 128, 173, 209, 239, 369; business and commerce, **118**, 118, 170, 238-39, **240**, 242-44, **271**; Merchandise Mart, 239, 291
Chicago and North Western Railroad, 181
Chicago Board of Trade, 137
Chicago, Burlington & Quincy Railroad, 162, 201, 202
Chicago, Milwaukee & St. Paul Railroad, 181, 213
Chrysler, Walter, 220, 277
Chrysler Corp., 277, 278, **318**, 318, 331, 369-70
Citicorp and Citibank, **349**
Cities Service Co., 363
City Bank (N.Y.), 201, 213
Civil Aeronautics Board, 327, 358
Civil War, 92, 117, 120, 132, 137, 141-42, 155, 158-59, 170, 171
Clay, Lucius, 329
Clayton Antitrust Act, 215, 216, 246
Cleveland, Grover, 158-59, 172, 194, 195, 196
Clinton, DeWitt, 87
clock- and watchmaking, 64, 101, 102-3, **114**, 131, 250, 251
clothing and fashion, 18, 21, 28, **68**, 70, **72**, 106, 123, 130, 133, 141, 174, 175, 353, 354; see also sewing machine; textiles and textile industry
Club of Rome, 367
Cluett, Peabody & Co., Inc., **189**

379

coal, 87, 100, 125, **146**, 156, 193, 202, 203, 275, 322; anthracite, 70, 90, 101, 105, 123, 182; bituminous, 68, 70, 100, 101, 169, 182, 274; and labor, **115**, 169, **172**, **217**, 218, 299
Coca-Cola Co., **259**, 259
Coe, Wetherill and Co., 249
coffee and coffee trade, 12, 30, 235, 253, 275
Colgate, William, 103, **104**, 104
Colgate-Palmolive Co., 366
Colorado Fuel and Iron Co., 204, 213, 218
Colt, Samuel, 60, **74**, 98, 101-2, 133, 134, **140**, 141
Columbia Broadcasting System, 280, 332-33
Committee for Economic Development, 321
commodity market and exchanges, **4**, 137, 235
Common Market, 364, 365
Commonwealth and Southern Power Co., 298
Commonwealth Edison Co., 283
Communications Satellite Corp., **80**
computer industry, **310**, **311**, 335, 338-40, **350**, 354, 355, 359, 366-67, **369**
conglomerates see mergers and conglomerates
Congress of Industrial Organizations, 299, 322
Consolidated Edison Co., 179, 213
Consolidated Gas Co., 213
Constitutional Convention, 49, 51
construction industry see building and construction
Continental & Commercial National Bank (Chicago), 214
Continental Congress, 33, 48, 51
Continental Tobacco, 195
Control Data Corp., 340
Convair, 327, 328, 351, 356
Cooke, Jay, 142, 164-65, 180, 217
Cooke & Co., Jay, 137, 142, 164, 165, 182, 250
Coolidge, Calvin, 23, 275, 297
Cooper, Peter, **89**, 89, 101, 119, 127, 133, 167, 236, 257
Cooper & Hewitt Works, 167
copper, 68, 69, 118, 125, **146**, 180, 206-7, 209-10, 223, 275, 281, 314, 322, 365
Cordiner, Ralph, 331
Corliss, George Henry, 131, 156, **174**, 174
corn, **4**, 17, 20, 26, 31, 99, 117, 155, 170, 197, 223, 273, 275; see also grain
Cornell, Ezra, 89, 106
Cornfeld, Bernard, 363
Coronado Corp., 334
Corp. Securities Co. of Chicago, 283
Cortelyou, George B., 212
Coster, Charles, 198, 204
cotton, 16, 21, 27, 52, 60, 62, 63, 64, 65, 92, 96, 99-100, 117, 130, 138, 139, 140, 141, 155, 156, 273, 274, 275, 293, 297; cotton gin, 52, 62-63; trade, 52, 55, 59, 62, 63, 64, 91, 92, 99, **100**, 100, 121, 138, **139**, 142, 180, 223, 235
Council of National Defense, 223, 313
Coxe, Tench, 68-69
credit and installment purchasing, 262, 287, 290, **307**
Crédit Mobilier, 162
Creole Petroleum Corp., 323
Cresap, Mark, 331
Crocker, Charles, 161, 162, 163, 211
Cullinan, Joseph S., 202-3
Cunard Line, 121, 123
currency see gold; monetary system and exchange; silver
Curtis, William E., 195, 196
Curtis Publishing Co., 253-54, 255, 256
Curtiss, Glen, 222
Curtiss-Wright Corp., 314, **319**
Cushing, John Perkins, 119, 121

D aly, Marcus, 209-10
dams, **145**, **190**, 297, 300, 319
Danbury Hatters case, 198
Dawes, Charles Gates, 274, 292
Dayton Engineering Laboratories Co.,

276
Debs, Eugene V., 217
debt: federal, 34, 50-51, 56, 57, 85, 118-19, 142, 195, 224, 274-75, 292; personal, 22, 23, 26, 27, 34, 47-48, 51, 96, 171, 274, 286; state, 50, 51, 84, 90, 96, 121
Deere, John (and Deere & Co.), 98, 117, **120**, 120, 198
Deering (co.), 169
De Forest, Lee, 208, 335
De Golyer, Everette Lee, 334
Deisel Construction Co., 325
Delaware and Delaware River, 19, 52, 58, 84, 88, 197, 281
Delaware and Hudson Canal Co., 85
Delaware and Hudson Railroad, 88
Delaware, Lackawanna & Western Railroad, 125
Delco, 276
Delhi Oil Corp., 320
Del Monte Corp., 260
Delta Air Lines, Inc., 358
Denison, Edward F., 355
Denver, Rio Grande & Western Railroad, 282
department stores, 236-39, **237**, **239**, **240**, 241, **243**, 244, 246, 273; see also chain stores; discount stores
De Peyster, Abraham, 25
depressions: (ca. 1820), 83; (ca. 1839-45), 96, 98; (1873-78), 165, 177; (1893-96), 200; (post World War I), 273, 274, 275; (1930's), 290-99 passim, **293**, 302, 313
De Soto (auto. co.), 318
Detroit Bankers Co., 284
Detroit Edison Co., 198
Diamond Match Co., 182, 281
Dick Co., A. B., 178-79
Diebold, Inc., 321
Diners' Club, Inc., 325
Dingley Act, 194
discount stores, 325-26, **326**, 352, 362
Disston Co., 102
Distillers Corp.-Seagrams Ltd., 300
Dodge, Gen. Grenville, 162
Dodge Brothers, Inc., 278
Donner, Frederic, 330
Douglas Aircraft, 301, 327-28, 334, 356, 357
Dow Chemical Co., 301, 325, 368
Drake, Edwin L., 125-26
Draper, John William, 103
Drew, Daniel, 120, 128-29, 137, 159-60
Drexel, Anthony J., 182
Drexel & Co., 137
Drexel, Morgan and Co., 158, 182
Dreyfus Fund, 363
drug manufacture, 325, 334, 353, 365
drug store, 244, 249
Duke, James Buchanan, 182, 195, 197, 260
Dumont (television), 332
Dun and Co., R. G., 262
Dun reports, 141
Du Pont, Alfred I., 224
Du Pont, Coleman, 224
Du Pont, Eleuthère Irénée, 67, 69, 92, 103
Du Pont, Eugene, 223
Du Pont, Henry, 223
Du Pont, Lammot, 141, 223
Du Pont, Pierre S., 220, 224, 277, 330
Du Pont de Nemours & Co., E. I., 223-24, 301, 315, 317, 323, 325, 330, 331, 334; in early days, 67, 69, 103, 141, 216, 223; General Motors investment in, 220, 224, 277
Durant, William Crapo, 218, 219, 277, 330
Duryea, Charles E., 218
Dutch West India Company, 14, 15-16, 19, 21

E astern Airlines, 301, 331, 358
East India companies, 9, 31-32
Eastman, George, 174, 208
Eastman Kodak Co., **76**, 174, 251, 334, 337, 338, 365, 366
Eaton, Cyrus, 283-84
Eccles, Marriner, 291
Eckert, D. W. J., 339
Eckert, Gen. Thomas, 164

Eckert-Mauchly Computer Corp., 339, 340
Economic Co-operation Administration, 321
Edison, Thomas Alva, 78, 177-80, 208, 283, 335
Edison Illuminating Co., 179, 210, 213
education, **22**, 106, 156-57, 225, **225-32**, 354-55, 368, 370, **375**; Morrill Act, 141, 142, **229**
Electric Boat Co., 328
Electric Bond & Share Co., 209, 283, 284, 286
electricity, 174, 177-82, 207-9, 218, 255, 281, 283-84, 297, 300, 322, 323; see also nuclear energy; telegraph; utilities; water systems and hydroelectric power
Electronic Data Systems Corp., 359
electronics industry, 316, 328, 334-36, 354-55; see also computer industry
Elgin, Joliet and Eastern Railway, 204
Environmental Protection Administration, 369
Equitable Life Assurance Soc., 203, 209, 214, 217, 291
Equitable Trust Co., 284
Erie Canal, **86**, 87, 93, 104, 127
Erie Railroad, 128, 129, 138, 157, 158-59, 160, 163, 182, 200, 201
Ethyl Gasoline Corp., 277
European Economic Community see Common Market
Evans, Oliver, **60**, 60, 61-62, 99, 131
explosives and munitions, 67, 68, 69, 141, 216, 223, 224, 278, 297, 314, 325

F airchild, Sherman, 357
Fairless, Benjamin F., 331
Famous Barr Co., 241
Faneuil, Andrew, 25, 27
Faneuil, Benjamin, 25
farmers, 16, 25, 54, 56, 83, 91-92, 96, 98, 105, 117, 137, 140, 155, 157, 171, 235, 274, 281, 286; National Grange of the Patrons of Husbandry, 171, 172, 241-42, **268**
Federal Aviation Administration, 356
Federal Communications Commission, 332, 333, 360
Federal Deposit Insurance Corp., 296
Federal Emergency Relief Administration, 298
federal government securities, 291, 363, 364; notes, 50, 51, 59, 142; see also bonds, federal; Treasury Department, bonds and notes
Federal Reserve Act, 194, 215, 216
Federal Reserve System/Federal Reserve Board, 97, 99, 216, 286, 287, 288, 290-91, 296, 364
Federal Steel Co., 198, 204, 205, **343**
Federal Trade Commission, 216, 284, 360
Federated Department Stores, Inc., 238, 241
Ferkauf, Eugene, 326
Field, Cyrus, 133-34, **343**
Field, Marshall, 236, 238-39, 291
Field, Matthew, 133
Filene, Edward A., 217, 238
Filene's Sons Co., Wm., 236, 238, 241
First National Bank (Chicago), 214
First National Bank (N.Y.), 211, 212, 213, 215, 282, 289
First National Bank of Boston, 214
First National City Corp., 363
First National Stores, 245
Fish, Stuyvesant, 201
Fisher, George, 132-33
Fisher Body (auto. ind.), 318
fishing and trade, 9, 17-18, 24, 26, **29**, 29, **77**, 123, 257; see also whaling
Fisk, Jim, **155**, 159, 160, 163, **164**
Flagler, Henry M., 176
Fleischmann & Co., **44**
Flint, Charles R., Jr., 182, 338
flour, 59, 60, 61, 130, 139, 170, 258; see also grain
Foley's (dept. store), 241
food processing and food industry, 118, 169, 255, 256-58, 281, 365; canning, vacuum, 131, 132, 170, 204; frozen foods, **77**, 257; marketing, 235, 244-46, 325, 352, 353; meat packing and

preservation, 54, 55, 118, 132, **152**, 170, 198, 223, **342**; packaging, 251, 256, 257
Ford, Henry, **38-39**, **78**, 193, 218-20, 277, 278, 293, **373**, **377**
Ford, Henry, II, 331, 368
Ford Foundation, 366, **377**
Ford Motor Co., **219**, 219-20, 223, 251, 277, 278, 317, 318-19, 324, 331, **341**, 353, 360, 366, 368, 370
Forney-McCumber Act, 275
Forrester, Jay W., 366-67
France, 22, 34, 50, 179, 321; and Austria, 55; business and commerce, 9, 14, 18, 27, 29, 34, 58-59, 157, 204, 321-22, 356; colonies and land in New World, 14, 18, 20, 27, 29, 34, 52; Franco-Prussian War, 165; Louisiana Territory, 57; Napoleonic wars, 58; World War I, 223, 274-75; World War II, 314
franchising, 84, 245, 252-53
Franklin, Benjamin, 20, 23, 32, 33, 61, **71**, 105, 136, 249
Frazer, Joseph W., 324
Frey, Jack, 168
Frick, Henry Clay, **146**, **169**, 169, 204, 212
Frye, Jack, 327
Fugger family, 11, 244
Fuller, R. Buckminster, **191**
Fulton, Robert, 87-88, **88**
furs and fur trade, 9, 14, 17-21 passim, 26, **29**, 31, 55, 67, 68, 121, **152**

G allatin, Albert, 57, 65, 69
Gallup, George, 256
Gamble, James, 103, 258
Garrett Corp., 357
gas, natural, 104, 137, 174, 322-23
Gary, Elbert H., 204, 205, 212
Gates, John W., 170, 203, 204, 205, 217
Geneen, Harold Sydney, **43**, 360
General Agreement on Tariffs and Trade, 364
General Aniline & Film, 337
General Dynamics Corp., 328, 334, 351, 356, 357
General Electric Co., 179, 180, 198, 199, 209, 213, 279, 280, 281, 283, 317, 323, 331, 334, 336, 340, **347**, 355, 356, 358, 360, 368, 370
General Foods Corp., 253, 256-57, 258
General Motors Corp., 220, **274**, 275, 276, 277, 289, **299**, 300, **310**, 315, 317, 329, 330-31, 334, 351, 354, 366, 370; Du Pont, investment in, 220, 224, 277
General Securities Corp., 283
General Tire & Rubber Co., 360
Geophysical Services, Inc., 334
Gerry, Elbridge, 31
Getty, J. Paul, 351
Giannini, Amadeo Peter, 281, 284-85, 319
Gifford, Walter S., 223
Gillette Co., **189**, 250
Gilman, George F., 244, 245
Gimbel, Adam, 237, 241
Girard, Stephen, 57, 67, 180
Gisborne, Frederick N., 133
glassmaking and glass industry, 21, 31, **58**, 61, 68, 69-70, 104, 132, 209, 314, 317, 325
Glass-Steagall Banking Act, 296
Goelet, Peter, 67
gold (currency and exchange), 9, 11-12, 23, 26, 31, 56, 57, 94, 96, 98, 99, 121, 125, 137, 138, 141, **155**, 163, 171-72, 194-97, 209, 210, 211, 223, 292, 293, 295-96, 363-64, 365; Gold Reserve Act, 296; as political issue, 195, **196**, 197; sent to U.S. for safekeeping, 224, 363; and silver, coinage ratio fixed, 171-72; see also monetary system and exchange
gold, prospecting for, 12, 13, 38, 99, 122, 124, 125, 160, 171
Gold and Stock Telegraph Co., 157
Gold Reserve Act, 296
Gompers, Samuel, **173**, 173, 218
Goodrich Co., B. F., 315
Goodyear, Charles, 98, 103, 131-32, 133, 336
Goodyear Tire & Rubber Co., 318

Gorges, Sir Ferdinando, 15
Gould, Jay, **155**, 159, 160, 163-64, **164**, 165, 173, 179, 200, 201, 210
Grace, William Russell, **175**, 175
grain, 20, 26, 53, **60**, 60, 61, 99, 117, 118, 130, 137, 139, 170, 235, 257, 367; grain elevator, 60, 99, **149**; trade, 17, 27, **29**, 31, 34, 55, 68, 99, **118**, 118, 141, 142, 223, 235
Grand Union Co., 245
Grange *see* National Grange of the Patrons of Husbandry
Grant Co., W. T., 244
Greatamerica Corp., 261
Great Atlantic & Pacific Tea Co. (A. & P.), 244-46, 247, 254
Great Britain, 47-48, 51, 124, 134, 140, 160, 321; banking and finance, 84, 96, 99, 194, 288, 292, 364, 365; business and industry, 47, 50, 60, 61, 64, 83, 97, 98, 101, 117, 120, 131, 157, 195, 235, 356; mining, 132, 167, 168, 193, 204; railroads, 88, 89, 90, 127, 132, 179; Revolution of 1688, 33; trade and shipping, 9, 15, 17-18, 19, 22-33 *passim*, 47, 48, 58, 59, 61, 83, 120, 121, 122-23; War of 1812, 57, 59, 68; West Indies colonies, 14, 15, 21, 28, 29, 47, 62; World War I, 223, 274-75; World War II, 314, 315
Great Northern Railroad, 166, 200-201, 202, 203
Greeley, Horace, 135, **136**, 136, 209, 253
Green, William, 299, 322
Greenback party, 171
Greenewalt, Crawford, 329
Grenville, George, 20, 29, **30**, 30, 31
Grumman Corp., 356
Guaranty Trust Co. (N.Y.), 203, 204, 213, 214, 215, 283, 284, 289
Guardian Detroit Union Group, Inc., 284
Guffey Petroleum Co., J. M., 199
Guggenheim, Meyer, 193, 210
Gulf & Western Industries, Inc., 360
Gulf Oil Corp., 199, 209

Haloid Co., **307**, 337
Halsey, Stuart & Co., 283-84
Hamilton, Alexander, **49**, 49-52, 68, 91, 194; *The Federalist*, 50; Report on a National Bank, 50, 51, 56; Report on Manufactures, 50-51, 51-52, 59, 68; Report on the Public Credit, First, 50; Report on the Public Credit, Second, 51
Hamilton Manufacturing Co., 70
Hanford Atomic Energy Center, 323, **347**
Hanna, Mark, 209
Hannibal & St. Joseph Railroad, 210
Hanover Bank (N.Y.), 213
Harkness, S. V., 176
Harlem Railroad, 128, 137
Harriman, Edward H., 181, 193, 200-204 *passim*, 210
Harrison Land Act, 52
Hartford, George Huntington, 244, 245
Hartford, George L., 236, 245, 246, 247
Hartford, John A., 236, 245, 246, 247
Hartford Fire Insurance Co., 360
Hartford Rubber Works, 218
hatmaking, 21, 28, **68**, 70
Hayden, Stone & Co., 290
Haynes, Elwood, 218
health care and medical research, 323, 370; drug manufacture, 325, 334, 353, 365; patent medicines, 243, 249, 253, 256, **258**, 259
Hearst, George, 161, 210, **211**, 211
Hearst, William Randolph, 198, 211
Hearst Corp., 211, 291
Heath & Co., 163
heating, 101, 104-5, 304, 322-23; *see also* coal; electricity; gas, natural; nuclear energy; petroleum and petroleum industry
Hefner, Hugh, **191**
Heinz Co., H. J., **189**, 250, 255, 365, 366
Heinze, Frederick A., 210-11
Henry, Joseph, 106, 207
Hercules Powder Co., 224, 325
Hertz Corp., 354

hides and skins, 21, 68, 69, 235, 314
Higgins, Andrew Jackson, 319
Higginson, Henry Lee, 206
Hill, George Washington, 260
Hill, James J., 165-66, 193, 200-201, 202, 203, 236
Hobart Manufacturing Co., 338
Hoe & Co., R., 106, 135, 175
Hogg, James Stephen, 203
holding companies, 177, 197, 281, 282-83, 298
Hollerith, Herman, 338
Holley, Alexander, 132, 167
Holliday, Cyrus K., 162
Homestake mine (S.Dak.), 210, 211
Homestead Act, 141
Honeywell, Inc., 355
Hope & Co., 181, 287
Hopkins, Claude, 250-51, 257
Hopkins, Harry L., 298, 299
Hopkins, Mark, 161, 162-63, 211
Hormel, Jay, 217
Horn and Hardart Baking Co., **260**, 260
Howard Johnson Co., 352
Howe, Elias, 76, 98, **132**, 132-33
Howe Co., 102
Hubbard, Gardiner G., 180-81
Hudson (auto. co.), 318, 324
Hudson, J. L., 239, 241
Hudson River Railroad, 129, 158
Hughes, Howard, **42**, 327, 328, 329, 351, 360
Hughes Tool Co., 327
Hunt, Walter, 132, 133
Huntington, Collis P., 161, 162, 163, 201, 211
Hytron Radio & Electronics Corp., 316, 332

Igleheart, Addison, 258
Illinois Central Railroad, 128, 138, 201
Illinois Steel Co., 167, 204
Illinois Trust and Savings Bank, 214
immigration, 13, 14-15, 16, 21, 47, 93, 103-4, 105, **110**, 117, 118, 162, 166, 169, 171, 173, 218
indigo trade, 17, 26, **29**, 30
Industrial Revolution, 50, 64, 83, 120, 235
Industrial Workers of the World, 218
Ingalls Shipbuilding Corp., 355, 361
Inland Steel, 300
Insull, Samuel, 209, 281, 283-84, **284**, 291
insurance (for workers), 175-76, 217, 280, 299
insurance companies, 61, 85, 91, 135-36, 142, 175-76, 214, 217, 256, 362-63
International Bank for Reconstruction and Development, 295, 321
International Business Machines Corp., **310**, 338-40, 351, 355, 365, **369**, 370, **375**
International Harvester Co., 198, 199
International Monetary Fund, 295, 321, 364
International Paper Co., 368, 374
International Telephone and Telegraph Corp., **43**, 275, 360, 366
Interstate Commerce Commission, 161, 172, 214, 282
inventions, 52, 60-64, 97-99, 103, 106, 130-35 *passim*, 178-79; *see also* research, industrial and scientific
investment and stock market, **41**, 84, 85, 91, 96, 98, 119, 128, 135-38, 157, 159, 180-81, 217, 224, **233**, 275, 281, 285, 286, 287, 296, 362-63; Dow-Jones averages, 285, 288, 289; exchanges, 137, 235; foreign investment (by U.S.), 181, 194, 275, 277, 364, 365-66; foreign investment (in U.S.), 51, 52, 84, 85, 90, 96, 99, 117, 118, 119, 121, 128, 157, 158, 165, 180, 182, 194, 196, 197, 222, 223, 365, 366; government regulation and reform, 291, 295, 296-97, 298, 363; margin trading, 137, 285, 287; speculation, 128, 137, 157, 165, 285-86, 287, 362; stock tickers, 157, 178
investment banking, 136-37, 164, 180-81, 286, 296
investment trusts, 286, 363
Investors Overseas Services, 363

iron and iron industry, 20, 21-23, 28, **29**, 34, 59, 61, 68, 69, 87, 91, 92, 101, 102, 105, 118, 122, 123, 125, 127, 130-31, 432, 141, **147**, 156, 167, 168, 173, 181, 193, 205, 213, 217, 223, 275, 281, 314, 317, 322, 324; *see also* steel and steel industry

Jackson, Andrew, 66, 90, 91, 92, 94-96, **95**, **97**, 98, 214, 244
James, Arthur Curtiss, 282
Jamestown Colony, 9, 10, 13, 17, 21
Jefferson, Thomas, 32, 48, 49, 51, 56, 57-58, 59, 63, 68, 69, 85, 91, 194, 214, **304**; as landowner, 17, 31, 52, 53
Jewel Tea Co., 245
Jewett, Frank, 316
Johnson, Gen. Hugh S., 298
Johnson, William T., 139-40
Johnson & Johnson, 355
joint-stock companies, 9, 11, 12, 21, 24, 61
Jones, Jesse, 292, 319
Jones & Laughlin Steel Co., 167, 361
Jones Brothers Tea Co., 245
Jonsson, John Erik, **334**, 334
Jordan Marsh Co., 238, 337
Judah, Theodore, 161, 162
Juniata Iron Works, 101

Kaiser, Henry J., **190**, 319, 324, 325, **344-45**
Karcher, John Clarence, 334
Kaufman's (dept. store), 241
Kellogg Co., M. W., 317
Kelly Act, 300
Kendall, Amos, 133, 134
Kennecott Copper Corp., **146**, 210
Kennedy, John E., 249, 250, 251-52
Kennedy, Joseph C., 117, 118
Kennedy, Joseph Patrick, 239, 289, 290-91, **291**, 297
Kettering, Charles F., **276**, 276-77, 338
Keynes, John Maynard, **294**, 294-95, 302, 363
Kidder, Peabody & Co., 214
Kilgore, Bernard, 326
Kindelberger, J. H., 318
King Kullen Grocery Co., 245
Kirby, Allan P., 283, 321
Kirby & Co., F. M., 248
Kirstein, Louis, 241
Knights of Labor, Noble and Holy Order of the, 173
Knox, Philander, 198
Knox & Co., S. H., 248
Knudsen, William S., 313, 317, 318
Kolbe, Frank P., 283
Korean War, 326, 327
Korvettes, 325-26, **326**, 352, 362
Kraft Foods, 256
Kresge, Sebastian S., 247
Kress & Co., S. H., 248
Kroger Grocery & Baking Co., 245
Kuhn, Abraham, 180
Kuhn, Loeb & Co., 180-81, 201, 214

Labor, 54, 59, 60, 70, 83, 99, 100, 101, 102-3, 105, 117, 119, 135, 136, 162, 171, 172-73, 216, 217-18, 280-81, 299-300, 321, 322, 340; "American plan," 281; American Working Men's party, 105; automobile industry, 219, **299**, 299-300; blacks and minority groups, 218, 368, 369-70; boycott ruled illegal, 198; children, 52, 102-3, 105, 280, 298; collective bargaining, 298, 299; colonies, 13, 16, 25; government legislation, 194, 198, 214, 322, 339; Greenback party, 171; hours and wages, 57, 70, 83, 102, 105, 135, 162, 173, 174, 216, 219, 262, 274, 287, 289, 291, 292, 298, 322, 331, 339, 365; mining and metals, **115**, 168, 169, **172**, **217**, 217, 218, 299, 300; overseas, 365; railroads, 162, **172**, 173, 198, 217; Socialist Labor party, 218; strikes, 70, 105, 135, 142, 156, 171, **172**, 173, 198, 218, **299**, 300; unemployment, 138, 274, 286-87, 292-93, 294, 298, 302; Union Labor party, 171; welfare, insurance, and pension plans, 175-76, 216-17, 261, 280-81,

285, 299, 363, **372**; women, 105, 135, 174, 280, **319**, 320; World War II, 314, 315, 318, **319**, 320; yellow-dog contracts, 280
Lake Erie & Western Railroad, 282
Lake Shore & Michigan Southern Railroad, 282
Lake Shore Railroad, 160
Lambert Co., 103
Lambert Pharmacal Co., 259
Lamont, Thomas, 288-89
Land, Edwin H., 336-37
land: (1607-1783), 15-16, 17, 19, 25, 28, 31, 119; (1783-1820), 52-53, 57, 59, 63; (1815-50), 91, **92**, 93, 96-97, 99; (1840-65), 117, 118, 120, 124, 128, 129, 138, 140, 141, 143, 155; (1865-90), 160, 161, 162, 165, 166, 171; (1890-1941), 193, 285, 286
Lane Bryant, Inc., 237
Lapham, Lewis H., 203
Lasker, Albert D., 249, 250, 251-52, 257, 260
Lazarus & Co., F. & R., 238, 241
Lea Act, 322
lead, 68, 69, 118, 125, 182, 210, 281, 322
leather products and shoe manufacturing, 20, 21, 55, 59, 61, 68, 70, 103, 133, 173, 197; *see also* hides and skins
Lee, Higginson & Co., 214, 220
Lehigh Railroad, 129, 200
Lehman Brothers, 360
"Lend-Lease" program, 313
Lever Brothers Co., 251, 259
Levittown (N.Y., Pa.), **312**, 325, **346**
Lewis, John L., 299
Liggett & Myers, Inc., 67, 251, 260
lighting and illumination: candles, whale and sperm oil, 18, 27, 103, 104, 118, 123, 258; carbon arc lamps, 179; gaslight, 104, 137, 174; kerosene, 176, 199, 276; *see also* electricity; petroleum and petroleum industry
Lincoln, Abraham, 161, 196-97, **226**
Ling-Temco-Vought, 351, 360, 361-62
Little, Jacob, 120, 137
Little, Royal, 360
Litton Industries, 355, 360-61, 362, 370
Lockheed Aircraft Corp., 314, 327, 328, 356, 357, 358, 370
Loeb, Solomon, 180
Loew, Marcus, 278
London: Crystal Palace Exhibition, 133, **134**, 134-35
London Company of Feltmakers, 28
London Stock Exchange, 288
Lorain Steel Co., 204
Lord & Taylor, 236, 237
Lord & Thomas, 250, 257, 259
Lorillard (co.), **66**, 66-67, 260
Love, James Spencer, 353
Lowell, Francis Cabot, 65, 70, 101
LTV, 361
Lucas, Anthony Francis, 199, 202
lumber, timber, and wood products, 19, 20, 21, 24, 26, **29**, 30, 61, 68, 118, 122, 130, 139, **150**, 155, 322

McClure, Samuel S., 256
McCormick, Cyrus (and McCormick Harvester), 98-99, 117, 119, 133, **134**, 135, 169, 173, 198, 219, 236, 365
McCoy, J. G., 169-70
McCrory, John G., 248
McDonnell Douglas Corp., 357-58
McGraw-Hill, Inc., 326
machine tools industry, 131, 193, 314, 315, 354
Machlup, Fritz, 354-55
McKay, Donald, **122**, 122
McKinley, William, 194, 197, 198, 204, 207, 216
McKinney, Henry Nelson, 251, 255
McLaren, Richard W., 358
McNamara, Robert S., 356, 360
Macy & Co., Inc., R. H., 236-37, **237**, 238, 239, 248
Magnetic Telegraph Co., 133, 134
Magnin & Co., I., 241
mail-order houses, **240**, 241-44, **243**
Maiman, Theodore H., 355
Marconi Wireless Telegraph Co. of America, 208, 279
marketing and merchandising, 219,

235-62, 278; brand names and trademarks, **188-89**, 250, 252-53; chain stores, 236, 237, 238, 241, 244-49; credit and installment purchasing, 262, 287, 290, **307**; department stores, 236-39, **237, 239, 240,** 241, **243,** 244, 246, 273; discount stores, 325-26, **326,** 352, 362; door to door, 259-60; franchising, 84, 245, 252-53; leasing, 354; mail-order houses, **240,** 241-44, **243**; management studies, 262; pricing, 244, 245, 246, 290; supermarkets, 245, 246; wholesalers, 235; *see also* advertising
Marsh, Benjamin L., 238
Marshall, John, 88, 91
Marshall Field & Co., 239
Marshall Plan, 321-22, **347,** 364
Martin Aircraft, 301, 314, 318, 327, 328
Martin-Marietta, 357
Marxism and communism, 135, 171, 218, 292, 322
Mason, George, 31
Massachusetts (colony), **8,** 10, 15-28 *passim*, 30, 32, 34, **35**
Massachusetts (state), 52; banking and finance, 56, **94,** 96, 136; business and commerce, 61, 64, 65, 101, 102, 102-3, 105, 123, 131, 223; Shays's Rebellion, 48, 171
Massachusetts Bay Colony, 18-19, 20; *see also* Puritans
Mauchly, John W., 339
Maury, Matthew, 122, 133
Maury & Ward, 102
Maxwell, James Clerk, 207
Maxwell Motor Car Co., 220, 277
May Department Stores, 241
Mazur, Paul, 261-62
Means, Gardiner, C., 329, 359
Mellon, Andrew W., **275,** 275-76
Mellon & Sons Bank, T. (Pittsburgh), 169, 209
Mellon Institute of Industrial Research, 302
Mercantile National Bank (N.Y.), 210, 211, 213
mercantilism, 23-33 *passim*
Mergenthaler, Ottmar, 175
mergers and conglomerates, 281-85, 351, 358-62
Merrill Lynch, Pierce, Fenner & Smith, Inc., **233**
Mesabi Range (Minn.), **147,** 181, 205, 213
metalworking, 101-3, 130, 131, 141, 301
Metro-Goldwyn-Mayer, Inc., 278
Metropolitan Life Insurance Co., 176, 351, 363
Michigan Central Railroad, 138, 160
Michigan Southern Railroad, 160
Michilimackinac Co., 68
Midamerica Corp., 283
Midas International Corp., 368
Middlesex Mills, 131
Middle West Utilities Co., 283
Midland United Co., 283
Midvale Steel Co., 217
military equipment and supplies, 52, 69, 141, 167, 170, **305,** 315, 317, 320, 356, 358; atomic bomb, 316-17; missiles and guidance systems, **328,** 328, 329, 336; submarines, 87, 223, 323, 328; tanks, 223, 314, 315, **318,** 318, 320
military-industrial complex, 329, 334, 335, 356
Miller, Arjay, 360
Miller-Tydings Act, 246
minerals and mining, **39,** 68, 69, 102, 124-26, 137, 138, 146, **147,** 167-69, 180, 209-11, 275, 281, 314-15, 316, 317, 322, 324-25; labor and unions, **217,** 217, 218, 299
Minneapolis-Honeywell, 340
Minnesota Iron Co., 204
Minnesota Mining & Manufacturing Co., 253, 332, 360
Missouri Pacific Railroad, 163, 170, 173, 282, 283
Mitchell, Charles E., 286, 287-88, 288-89, 291, 297
Mohawk & Hudson Railroad, 89
molasses trade, 12, 15, 21, 24, 28-29, 29-30; *see also* rum and rum trade

monetary system and exchange, 47, 49-52 *passim*, 56, 85, 94-99 *passim*, 118-19, 125, 136-38, 141, 142, 163, 171-72, 194-97, 215, 216, 223, 289-96 *passim*, 321, 364-65; colonies, **8,** 9, 14, 20, 24, 26, 27, 30, 31, 34, 47, 56; commodity money, 20, 26; Confederate, 142; "greenbacks," 142, 156, 163, 171; International Monetary Fund, 295, 321, 364; "paper gold," 365; "shinplasters," 96; wampum, 18, 26; *see also* banking; barter system; debt; depressions; Federal Reserve System/Federal Reserve Board; gold; notes; panics, financial; silver
monopolies and trusts, 19, 22, 23, 32, 67, 84, 91, 156, 172, 177, 182, 194, 197-200, **199,** 214-16, 281; cartels, 281; Celler-Kefauver Act, 359; Clayton Antitrust Act, 215, 216, 246; federal action and legislation, 67, 177, 194, 198-99, 205-6, 214, 215, 216, 246, 302, 358, 359; holding companies, 177, 197, 281, 282-83, 298; Sherman Antitrust Act, 194, 198, 214, 215; *see also* mergers and conglomerates
Monroe Calculating Machine Co., 361
Monsanto Chemical Co., 81, 301, 325
Montgomery Ward & Co., Inc., 217, **240,** 242, 244, 250, 289
Moore, W. H., 182, 247, 248
Morgan, John Pierpont, 137, 179, 180, 181, 182, **192,** 193, 196-97, 200-205 *passim*, 211-15 *passim*, **212,** 217, 367
Morgan, Junius S., 180, 182
Morgan & Co., J. P., 196, 198, 200, 206, 207, 210-15 *passim*, 220, 223, 277, 282, 283, 286, 288, 289, 329, **343**
Morrill Act, 141, 142, **229**
Morris, Gouverneur, 31, 59
Morris, Robert, 31, 34, 48-49, 50, 56
Morrison-Knudsen Co., Inc., 300
Morse, Samuel F. B., **62,** 98, **105,** 106, 133-34, 177, **304**
Morton, Levi P., 137, 182
Mott, Charles, 220
movie industry, 208-09, **259,** 278, 278-79, 280, 281, **304,** 332
Munsey, Frank A., 198, 253
Murchison, Clinton Williams, 159, **320,** 320-21
mutual funds, 362, 363
Mutual Life Insurance Co., 203, 204, 214

Nader, Ralph, **371**
Nash (auto. co.), 324
National Airlines, Inc., 328
National Association of Manufacturers, 217, **270-71,** 281
National Banking Act, 136
National Biscuit Co., 251
National Broadcasting Co., 280, 332, 333
National Bureau of Standards, 335
National Car Rental System, Inc., 354, 361
National Cash Register Co., 199, 276, 338, 339, 340
National City Bank (N.Y.), 181, 201, 211-12, 213, 215, 284, 286, 287-88, 289, 296
National Grange of the Patrons of Husbandry, 171, 172, 241-42, **268**
National Industrial Recovery Act, 298, 299
National Labor Relations Act, 299
National Securities and Exchange Act, 296-97
National Shawmut Bank (Boston), 214
National Steel Co., 204, 205, **343**
National Tea Co., 245
National Tube Co., **168,** 204, 205, 324, **343**
National Watch Co. (Elgin), 131, 250
Navigation Acts, 17, 26-27, 33, 47
Neiman-Marcus Co., **239,** 241
Nelson, Donald, 313
Netherlands, 13, 50, 165, 364; colonies and exploration, 13-19 *passim*; trade, 9, 14-19 *passim*, 21, 26, 31, 34
New Amsterdam, 14, 16, 17, 19, 21
Newcomen, Thomas, 60, 61, 87
New Deal, 156, 294-99, 302

New England: banking and commerce, 54, 55, 57, 59, 91; textiles and manufacturing, 61, **65,** 70, 83, 84, 90, 91, 100, 101-2, **102,** 119, **139**
New Haven Railroad, 137
New Jersey, 48, 52, 197, 281; as colony, 16, 21, 32; iron and steel, 20-21, 69, 101, 105
New Jersey Zinc, 360
newspapers, 106, 134-35, 198, 249, 250, 252-53, 255; *see also* advertising
New York (British colony), 16, 19, 25, 26, 27, 31, 32, 34
New York (state), 52, 90; banking and finance, 136, 137, 138, 156, 293; business and commerce, 48, 54, 61, 69, 89, 101; transportation, 87, 127, 128
New York and Erie Railroad, 89, 90
New York Central Railroad, 89, 128, 157, 158, 159, 160, 182, 200, 201, 251, 282, 331, 359
New York Curb Exchange, 137
New York *Journal of Commerce,* 141
New York, Newfoundland & London Electric Telegraph Co., 133-34
New York Stock Exchange, 85, 137, 157, 163, 165, 181, 212, 215, 222, 285, 288, 289, 296, 362; beginnings of, **2,** 51, 85, 137
New York Times, The, 135, 288, 295
New York *Tribune,* 135, 136, 175, 253
Nickel Plate Securities Co., 282
Norfolk & Western Railroad, 200
Norris, George, 297
Norris Co., 90, 127
North American Aviation, 314, 318, 327, 328, 331, 357, 370
North American Co., 198
Northeast Airlines, Inc., 358
Northern Pacific Railroad, 164, 165, **166,** 166, 182, 201, 202, 203
Northern Securities Co., 198, 202-3
Northwest Industries, Inc., 351
notes: bank, 56, 94, 96, 97, 98, 136, 137, 194, 223; Confederate, 142, 155; federal, 50, 51, 59, 142; Federal Reserve, 216; personal, 56, 57; Treasury, 57, 194-95, 321
Noyes, Alexander Dana, 288
nuclear energy, **309, 323,** 323, 325, 328, **347,** 355, 369; atom bomb, 316-17

Oak Ridge (Tenn.), 317, 323
office machines and equipment, 174, 178-79, **307,** 337-40
Office of Production Management, 313
Ogdensburg and Lake Champlain Railroad, 201
Ohio Life Insurance and Trust Co., 138
Ohrbach, Nathan M., 237-38
oil *see* petroleum and petroleum industry
Okonite Co., 361
Old Colony Trust Co. (Boston), 214
Olds, Irving S., 331
Olds, Ransom E., 218
Oldsmobile (auto. co.), 220
Organization for European Economic Cooperation, 321
Otis, Elisha Graves, 174

Pacific Associates, 161, 162
Pacific Fur Co., 68
Pacific Mail Steamship Co., 124
Packard Motor Co., 223, 251
Paley, William S., 280, 322, 332, 333ʼ
Palmer, Potter, 238-39
Palmer, Volney B., 249, 250
Palmolive-Peet Co., 104
Pan American World Airways, Inc., 175, 300, 326, 328
panics, financial: (1792), 51, 59; (1819), 53, 57, 83; (1830s), 86; (1837), 96, 98; (1854), 137; (1857), 135, **138,** 139, 141; (1869), **154,** 163, 201; (1873), 165, 169, 170; (1884), 182; (1893), 194; (1907), 211-13, **212;** (1929), 285-89 *passim*, **288,** 363
paper industry, 28, 30, 31, 34, 68, 106
Paramount Pictures Corp., 278, 291, 360
Patent Arms Manufacturing Co., 102, **140,** 141

patent medicines, 243, 249, 253, 256, **258,** 259
patent pools, 279, 281, 332
patents, 63, 97, 131
Patman, Wright, 246-47
Patterson, W. A., 218
Peabody, George, 180, 182, 206
Peabody, Joseph, 54
Pemberton Chemical Co., Inc., 259
Pencroyd Iron Works, 167
Penn, William, 15
Penn family, 34, 52
Penn Central Railroad, 351, 359-60
Penney, James Cash, **248,** 248
Pennsylvania, 48, 52, 69, 92-93, 94, 96; as colony, 13, 15, 16, 22-23, 24, 34; minerals and mining, 89, 92, 101, 105, 125-26, **146,** 167-68, 169, 177, 182, 202
Pennsylvania Canal System, 87
Pennsylvania Co., 197
Pennsylvania Railroad, 89, 125, 128, 129, 157, 158, 173, 177, 181, **200,** 200, 201, 209, 285, 359
Pennsylvania Rock Oil Co., 125
Pepperrell family, 24, 34, 52
PepsiCo, Inc., 366
Pere Marquette Railroad, 282
Performance Systems, Inc., 353
Perkins, George W., 198, 199, 220
Permanente Cement Co., 319
Perot, H. Ross, 359
petroleum and petroleum industry, **40,** 124, 125-26, 137, **153,** 174, 176-77, 197-98, 199-200, 202-3, **203,** 275, 276-77, 314, 315, 320, 322-23, 365; Big Inch and Little Big Inch pipelines, **314,** 315, 323; gasoline, 200, 276, 277, 315; kerosene, 176, 199, 276
Pfizer, Inc., 366
pharmaceutical industry, 325, 334, 353, 365
Philadelphia and Reading Railroad, 194
Philco, 340
Philipse family, 16, 34, 52
Phillips Petroleum Co., **323**
Phipps, Henry, 169, 204
Piggly Wiggly Corp., 245
Pilgrims, 18-19, **35;** *see also* Plymouth Colony
Pillsbury Co., 170
Pinkham, Lydia Estes, 256, **258,** 259
Pittsburgh, Fort Wayne & Chicago Railroad, 129
Pittsburgh Glass (co.), 209
Pittsburgh Reduction Co., 209
plastics, 301, 322, 324, 325
Plymouth Colony, 10, 15, 17, 18, 21, **35;** *see also* Massachusetts Bay Colony
Polaroid Corp., 337
pollution, 350, 367, 368-69, 370, 374
Poniatoff, Alexander M., 336
Pony Express, 126-27
population and census, 53, 54, 117, 367; (Revolutionary period), 14; (1790-1800), 53; (1820-50), 54, 84, 93, 261; (1850s), 118, 130; (1860), 117, 118, 134, 140, 157, 261; (1880), 338; (1890), 157, 338; (1900), 193, 218, 261; (1920s), 261, 289; (1960-70), **351;** tabulators and computers used, **338,** 338, 340
Populist party, 171, 197
Post Office, 50, 123, 126, 242, 300, 331
Postum Cereal Co., Ltd., 256, 257
Pratt & Whitney, Inc., 131, 301, 356
Price, Gwilym A., 331
price control, 273, 313, 322, 365
Principio Iron Works, 20-21, 101
printing industry, 62, 70, 106, 175
Procter & Gamble Co., 103, **188,** 217, 250, 251, 258-59
Prudential Friendly Society, 175-76
Prudential Insurance Co. of America, 291, 351, 363
Public Service Co. of Northern Illinois, 283
Public Utilities Holding Company Act, 298
public works programs, 292, 295, 298-99, 302
Pujo, Arsène, 214-15
Pullman Palace Car Co., 174, **186,** 197; strike, 198, 214
Pure Food Act, 255

Pure Oil Co., 199
Purex Corp., **348**
Puritans, 18, 22-23, 23-24, 26, 105, 171; *see also* Massachusetts Bay Colony; Pilgrims

Radio Corp. of America (R.C.A.), 208, **252**, 252, 279, 280, 286, 289, 290, 291, 332, 333, 336, 340, 354, 355
radio equipment and industry, 254, 279-80, 280, 281, 316, 332, 335, 336
Radio-Keith-Orpheum (R.K.O.), 290, 360
railroads, 88-90, **90**, 93, 94, 100, 101, 105, 117, 118, 126-27, 127-30, 129, 138, 141, 155-68 *passim*, **162**, **166**, 172, 174, 176, 178, 179, 182, 193, 194, 197, 198, **200**, 200-203, 213, **269**, 273, 355; and the government, 161, 162, 165, 194, 199, 214, 273, 282, 320; investment in, 85, 90, 96, 127, 128, 129, 135, 137, 138, 157, 158, 159, 160, 163, 164-65, 180, 181, 201, 210, 215-16, 285, 289; and labor, 162, **172**, 173, 198, 217; sleeping and dining cars, 167, 174, **186**, 197; transcontinental, 38, 160-61, 161-62; *see also* Interstate Commerce Act; Interstate Commerce Commission
railways, street, 128, 129-30, 180, 209
Raleigh, Sir Walter, 9, 10, 13
Ramo, Simon, 328-29
Rand Corp., 334
Raskob, John Jacob, 220
Raytheon Co., 316, 340
Reading Railroad, 138
Reconstruction Finance Corp., 292, 293, 298, 319
Red Star Line, 198
Remington and Sons, Eliphalet, 174
Remington Rand, 340
Republic Steel Corp., 300, 324
research, industrial and scientific, 301-2, 316-17, 323-25, 334-37, 339-40, 355-56
research, marketing, 255-56
Resor, Stanley, 251
Revlon, Inc., 353
Reynolds Metals Co., 325
Reynolds Tobacco Co., R. J., **189**, 260
RIAS, Inc., 334
rice and rice trade, 17, **29**, 34, 52, 155
Richardson, Sid, 159, 320
Rich's (dept. store), 238
Rickenbacker, Eddie, 300
roads and highways, 61, 84, 86, 88, 91, 94, 96, 126, 220, **306**
Robinson-Patman Act, 246
Rockefeller, John Davidson, **42**, 119, 176-77, **183**, 197-98, 202, 204, 205, 206, 213, 214, 228, **233**
Rockefeller, Percy, 300
Rockefeller, William, 176, 213
Rockefeller, Andrews & Flagler, 176
Rockefeller family, 193, 201, 202, 210, 213, 215, 218
Rock Island Railroad, 200
Rockwell Manufacturing Co., 360
Roebling, John A., 101, 128, 174, **187**
Rolfe, John, 17
Rolls-Royce, 357, 358
Romney, George, **324**, 324
Roosevelt, Franklin D., 214, **272**, 279, 281, 292, 358; Depression and New Deal, 293-99 *passim*, **297**, 302; World War II, 313, 315, 316, 319
Roosevelt, Nicholas, 88
Roosevelt, Theodore, 211, 216, **229**, 258; and business, 193, 198-99, 203, 205, 206, 213, 224, 358
Rosenwald, Julius, 242
Rothschild, Walter, 241
Rothschild family, 181, 195, 196
Rowell & Co., G. P., 249, **250**, 255
rubber and rubber industry, 98, 103, 131-32, 133, 275, 277, 314, 315, 317, 365; synthetic, 301, 315, 322, 325
Rubicam, Raymond, 256
rum and rum trade, 14, 15, **20**, 20-21, 27, 28, **29**; *see also* molasses trade
Russell, Majors and Waddell, 126
Russian American Co., 68
Rust, Mack, 297
Ryan, Thomas Fortune, 209

Safeway Stores, Inc., 245
Sage, Russell, 163, 164
St. Paul, Minneapolis & Manitoba Railroad, 165, 166
Saks Fifth Avenue, 237
salt, 18, 26, 125, 182
Sanders, Thomas, 180, 181
Santa Fe Railroad, 162
Sarnoff, David, **112-13**, 208, 280, 290, 291, 332
Saunders, Clarence, 245
Savage Iron Works, 127
Schiff, Jacob H., 137, **180**, 180-81, 201, 202, 214
Schlitz Brewing Co., Joseph, 250-51
Schwab, Charles M., **113**, 168, 169, 193, 204, 205, 210, 290
Scott Paper Co., 251
Scovill Manufacturing Co., 103
Scribner, Charles, 253
Scripps newspapers, 198
Sears, Roebuck & Co., 217, 242-44, **243**, 248
Sears Watch Co., R. W., 242
Securities and Exchange Commission, 291, 297, 298, 363
Selden, George B., 218
Selfridge, Harry G., 239
Seligman, J. & W., 180, 220
sewing machine, 60, **76**, 98, 131, **132**, 132-33, 174, 219
Shannon, Claude, 339
Shaver, Dorothy, 237
Shays's Rebellion, 48, 171
Shell Oil Co., 199, **251**
Sheraton Corp., 360
Sherman, Gordon, 368
Sherman, Nat, 368
Sherman Antitrust Act, 194, 198, 214, 215
Sherman Silver Purchase Act, 172, 195
shipbuilding, 19, 24, **29**, 55, 59, 121, 122-23, 274; World War I, 223, 273; World War II, 315, 319, 320, **344-45**
shipping: (1607-1783), 17, **19**, 24, 25-27, **29**, 31, 33, 34, 54; (1783-1820), 47, 54-55, 56, 58-59, 61; (1815-50), 84, 86-87, 88, 90, 93, 99-100, 119; (1840-65), 117, **118**, 119-27 *passim*, 136, 138, 139; (1865-90), 155, 156, 158, 160, 162, 166, 170, 175, 176, 177; (1890-1918), 198, 208, **222**, 223; (1918-70), 274, **309**, 315, 319, 320, 322; piracy and privateering, 26, 34, 54, 58, 59; *see also* canals; railroads
Shockley, William B., 335
shoe manufacturing, 21, 61, 70, 103, 130, 133, 173, 197
Sholes, Christopher Latham, **76**, 174
Sibley, Hiram, 133, 134, 135
Signal Oil & Gas Co., 357
silk and silk trade, 21, 27, 30, 121, 275, 314
Silliman, Benjamin, Jr., 125
silver (currency and exchange), 9, 11-12, 23, 26, 31, 56, 57, 94, 96, 125, 137, 138, 141, 163, 171-72, 194, 210, 211, 296; Bland-Allison Act, 172; and gold, coinage ratio fixed, 171-72; as political issue, **196**, 197; Sherman Silver Purchase Act, 172, 195; Subsidiary Coinage Act, 125; *see also* monetary system and exchange
silver mining, 12, 13, 125, 162, 171, 211
Singer Sewing Machine Co., 133, 135, 219, 250, 262, 365, 366
Slater, Samuel, 27, 64, **65**, 65, 66, 100, 236
slavery, 63, 99, 100, 138, 139, 140, 142, 155, 171; Abolitionists, 27, 63, 140, 171, **372**; in colonies, 13, **14**, 14-15, 17, 20, 24, 25, 27, 29; Fugitive Slave Act, 141
Sloan, Alfred P., 277, 330
Smith, Adam, 32, 33, 91, 156, 235, 262
Smith, Cyrus R., 301, 326
Smith, Capt. John, **8**, 13, 17, 19
Smith, Roswell, 253
Smith Manufacturing Co., A. P., 367, 368
Smoot-Hawley Tariff Act, 292
snuff, **66**, 66, 195
soap, cosmetics, and toiletries, 27, 103, 104, 118, 258-59, 259-60, 353; advertising, 104, 188, 250, **251**, 251, 252, 254, 259

Sorenson, Charles E., 318
South, 138-41, 155-61; banking and finance, 140, 142, 155; land, agriculture, and trade, 13, 15, 17, 25, 31, 52, 63, 91, 92, 99, 138-42 *passim*, 155, 156; railroads, 138, 155, 156, 160, 162, 182, 200
Southern Pacific Railroad, 161, 162, 201, 202
Southern Union Gas Co., 320
space exploration and industry, 79, 80, **328**, 328, 329, 336, 355; moon landings, **39**, **311**, 355
Space-General Corp., 370
Spain, 34, 50, 63; colonies, 9, 11-12, 13, 27; trade, 11, 24, 27, 28, 34
Spencer, Herbert, 156, 157, 206, 214
Sperry Rand Corp., 340
Stamp Act, **30**, 30-31
Standard Brands, Inc., 251, 256
Standard Oil Co. of Indiana, 370
Standard Oil Co. of New Jersey, 177, 197-98, 199, 200, 202, 203, 213, 214, 275, 277, 281, 286, 323, 331, 351, 366
Standard Oil Co. of Ohio, 176-77, 197
Standard Oil Trust, 177, 197, 323
Stanford, Leland, **161**, 161, 162, 163, 211
Stanley Electric Co., 198
steam engines, 60, 61-62, 64, 87-88, **88**, 89, 90, **100**, 100, 102, 122-23, 131, 156, 169, **174**, 174, 209, 338
steel and steel industry, 20-21, 69, 98, 120, 124, 156, 160, 167-69, **168**, 174, 193, 204-6, 223, 278, 281, 301, 314, 315, 324-25, 352, 355-56, 358; Kelly-Bessemer process, 131, 132, 167, 204; labor and unions, 168, 217, 299, 300; open hearth process, 167
Steen, Charles, 323
Steffens, Lincoln, 256
Stephens, Uriah, 173
Stettinius, Edward R., 223
Stevens, Col. John, 87
Stewart, Alexander Turney, 236
Stillman, James, 181, 193, 201, 211-12, 213, 215
stock exchanges, 137, 235; *see also* New York Stock Exchange
stock market *see* investment and stock market
Stone and Webster Engineering Corp., 317
Straus & Sons, L., 236
Strauss, Lewis, 337
Studebaker Co., 86, 218
Studebaker Corp., 351
Studebaker-Garford, 218
Studebaker-Packard Corp., 324
sugar and sugar refining, 12, 26, 29, 52, 59, 68, 155, 182, 197, 198, 199, 275
Supreme Court, 94, 214; American Sugar Refining Co. case, 198; American Tobacco Co. case, 67, 195, 260; Charles River Bridge case, 91; child labor, 280; Dartmouth College case, 91; Gibbons v. Ogden, 88; "Granger laws," 172; Great Northern Railroad case, 201; Hoosac Mills case, 297; Interstate Commerce Commission cases, 172, 214; minimum wage for women, 280; Northern Securities Co. case, 203; price maintenance cases, 246; Schechter case, 298, 299; Standard Oil Co. of New Jersey case, 199, 214; United States Steel Corp. case, 206; yellow-dog contracts, 280
Sutter, Johann Augustus, 124
Swansdown, 258
Swift and Co., 251, 255
Swope, Gerard, 331
Sylvania, 336
systems behavior, 366-67

Taft-Hartley Act, 322
tanks and trucks, 223, 314, 315, **318**, 318, 320
tariffs and duties, 10-11, 20, 23, 24, 26, 29-33, 48, 51, 52, 55, 59, 68, 69, 91-93, **92**, 99, 141, 156, 171, 194, 216, 275, 292, 321; Dingley Act, 194; General Agreement on Tariffs and Trade, 364; Fordney-McCumber tariff, 275; McKinley tariff, 194, 204; Morrill Act, 141, 142, **229**; Smoot-Hawley Tariff Act, 292; Tariff of Abominations, 92; Underwood-Simmons Tariff Act, 216, 275; Walker tariff, 93, 141; Wilson-Gorman Act, 194; *see also* taxation
taxation, **30**, 30-31, 49, 51, 84, 292, 354, 359, 365, 367; income tax, 142, 156, 194, 216, 224; *see also* tariffs and duties
Taylor, George Washington, 237
Taylor, Myron, 331
tea trade, **31**, 31-32, 121, 244
Teagle, Walter, 277
Teal, Gordon, 335
telegraph, 98, 106, 118, 119, 133-35, 138, 163-64, 178, 180, 207, 208, **304**; transatlantic cable, 133-34, 157, **342**
telephone, 180-82, 206-7, **208**, 219, 334-35
television industry, 254-55, 332-33, 336
Temco Electronics & Missiles Co., 361
Tennessee Coal, Iron and Railway Co., 204, 212-13, 324
Tennessee Eastman Co., 317
Tennessee Valley Authority, **145**, 295, 297-98
Tevis, Lloyd, 210, 211
Texaco, Inc. (Texas Co.), 199, 203, 277
Texas American Oil Corp., 362
Texas Eastern Transmission Corp., 323
Texas Instruments, Inc., 334-35, 336
Texas Pacific Railroad, 162
textiles and textile industry, 16-17, 19, 21, 27, **46**, 60, 64-66, **65**, **81**, 100-101, **102**, 104, 105, 119, 130, 131, 135, **139**, 139, 156, 235, 274, 301, 338, 353-54, **354**, 355; trade, 17, 28, 30, 68, **100**, 121, **139**, 180, 354; *see also* clothing and fashion; cotton; silk and silk trade; wool
Textron, Inc., 360
Textron American, Inc., 360
Thompson Co., J. Walter, 250, 251, 252, 256, **346**
Thompson Products, Inc. 329
Thornton, Charles B., 360, **361**
Thurow, Lester, 369
Tidewater Pipe Co., 177
Time, Inc., 326
tin, 68, 69, 102, 204, 217, 275, 314
Tishman Realty & Construction Co., Inc., 325
tobacco and tobacco industry, 13, 17, 26, 28, **66**, 66-67, 99, 117, 139, 155, 195, 249, 260-61; advertising, **66**, 66-67, **189**, **195**, 195, **234**, 251, 260-61; trade, **1**, 13, 17, 24, 26, **29**, 34, 52, 59, 260; trusts, 67, 182, 195, 197, 260
Toledo, St. Louis & Western Railroad, 282
Townshend Acts, 31, 32
trade: (1607-1783), 10-34 *passim*, **29**, **31**; (1783-1820), 47, 48, 51, 52, 54, 55, 58-59, 68; (1815-50), 83, 87, 91, 92, 96, 99, 100, 120; (1830-1950), 235-62; (1840-65), 117, 119, 120-21, 123, 138, 141, 142; (1865-90), 155, 157, 160, 180; (1890-1918), 193-94, 198, 214, 223; (1918-41), 246, 275, 281; (1940-60), 321, 322; (1960-72), 352, 364, 365; Acts of Trade, 28-33; balance of payments, 23, 28, 30, 31, 96, 121, 223, 364-65; Common Market, 364, 365; Embargo Act, 58; Federal Trade Commission, 216, 284, 360; General Agreement on Tariffs and Trade, 364; Nonintercourse Act, 58; triangular trading, 14-15, 20, 24, 27, 29, 55, 121; *see also* Interstate Commerce Act; Interstate Commerce Commission; tariffs and duties
trademarks, 250, 252-53
Transamerica Corp., 285
Transcontinental and Western Air, 301, 327
Transitron Electronic Corp., 335
transportation, 84-92 *passim*, 94, 121-30 *passim*, 157-66 *passim*, 235, 278; bicycle, 174, 218; bus, 129, 209; carriage, 68, 129, 130; jeep, **305**, 317; stagecoach, 84, **126-27**, 126-27; street railway, 128, 129-30, 180, 209;

subway, 209; trolley car, 174, 209; wagon, 86, 130, 218
Trans World Airlines, Inc., 327, 328, 329, 331, 357, 358
Treasury Department, 50, 99, 163, 171, 172, 194, 195, 196, 197, 211, 212; bonds and notes, 57, 194-95, 321
treasury system and subtreasury system, 97, 98-99
Trenton Iron Co., 101, 119
Trippe, Juan, 300
trusts *see* monopolies and trusts
TRW, Inc., 370

Underwood-Simmons Tariff Act, 216, 275
Uniform Small Loan Act, 262
Union Carbide Corp., 301, 325
Union Guardian Trust Co. (Detroit), 293
Union Pacific Railroad Co., 160-61, 161-62, **162**, 163, 181, 202
United Aircraft Corp., **303**
United Air Lines, Inc., 301, 328
United Automobile Workers, 299-300
United Cigar Stores Co., 195, 249
United Copper Co., 210-11
United Mine Workers, **217**, 299
United Pipe Line Co., 177
U. S. Bureau of Mines, 322
United States Lines, **309**
United States Mail Steamship Co., 123
United States Rubber Co., 217, 218, 255
U. S. Shipping Board, 223
United States Steel Corp., 85, **147**, **168**, 181, 199, 205-6, 207, 212-13, 217, 281, 289, 300, 324, 331, **343**, 358
United States Telegraph Co., 135
uranium, **39**, 316, 323
Uris Buildings Corp., 325
utilities, public and private, 60, 91, 180,

197, 209, 283-84, 298, 300, 323, **348**, 368-69; *see also* electricity; gas, natural; nuclear energy

Vacuum Oil Co., 177
Vail, Theodore Newton, 181, 219, **372**
Vanderbilt, Cornelius, 88, **116**, 119, 123, 124-25, 128, 129, 136, 158-60, 165, 236
Vanderbilt, Cornelius, II, 158, 159
Vanderbilt, William Henry, **158**, 158, 160, 164, 176, 182, 200
Vanderbilt, William Kissam, 158, 159
Vaness Co., 282-83
Van Sweringen, Mantis James, 281, **282**, 282-83, 291
Van Sweringen, Otis Paxton, 281, **282**, 282-83, 291
Victor Talking Machine Co., 252
Villard, Henry, **166**, 166, 180, 198
Virginia (colony), 9, 10-11, 13, 15, 17, 25, 28, 33; business and commerce, 1, 13, 17, 21, 22, 23, 26, 28
Virginia Company of London, 9-11, 13, 22
Vought Corp., Chance, 361

Wages and Hours Law, 339
Walgreen, Charles R., 249
Walker tariff, 93, 141
Wallace, DeWitt, 326
Wall Street Journal, 326
Waltham Watch Co., 131
Wanamaker Co., John, 179, 208, 236, 250, 251
Warburg, James P., 337
Warburg, M. M., 181
Warburg, Paul, 288
Ward, Aaron Montgomery, 236
War Industries Board, 223, 224
Warner Brothers, 279
War Production Board, 313, 315, 320

War Resources Board, 313
water systems and hydroelectric power, 60, 61, 64, **65**, 100, 104, 105, **144-45**, **150**, 170, 174, **190**, 209, 297-98, 300, 319, 369, **374**
Watson, Thomas J., 338, 339
Watson, Thomas J., Jr., 340, 355
Watt, James, 61, 87, 338
Wechsler, Joseph, 238
Wells, Fargo & Co., **126-27**, 127
Western Electric Co., 279, 316, 334-35
Western Electric Manufacturing Co., 181
Western Federation of Miners, 218
Western Union Telegraph Co., 133, 134, 136, 164, 179, 180, 181, 207
West Indies: British colonies, 14, 15, 21, 28, 29, 47, 62; business and commerce, 12, 15, 19, 20, 21, 24, 27, 28-29, 47, 52, 120-21; French colonies, 20, 29; Spanish colonies, 27
West India Company *see* Dutch West India Company
Westinghouse Electric Co., 179, 198, 209, 213, 279-80, 281, 317, 331-32, 358
whaling (and whale oil), **18**, 18, 24, 27, 104, 123-24, **124**
wheat, 59, 98-99, 117, 137, 142, **148**, 197, 223, 273, 293; *see also* flour; grain
Whelan, George, 249
Whiskey Rebellion, 51, 171
White Star Line, 123, 198
Whitney, Asa, 160
Whitney, Cornelius Vanderbilt, 300
Whitney, Eli, **62**, 62-64, **63**, 97, 102, 131, 236, 336
Whitney, Richard, 289, 296, 297
Wiener, Norbert, **337**, 338-39
Wiggin, Albert H., 289
Willys Motors, **305**, 317, 324
Wilson, Charles E. (General Electric), **330**, 331

Wilson, Charles E. (General Motors), 331
Wilson, Joseph C., **307**, **375**
Wilson & Co., 361
Wilson-Gorman Act, 194
Wilson Pharmaceutical & Chemical Corp., 361
Winnett, Percy G., 241
Wood, Jethro, 52, 62, 98
Wood, Robert E., 242, 368
Woodbury's (soap), **251**, 251, 252, 259
Woodruff, Ernest, 259
Woodruff, Robert W., 259
wool, 16, 19, 60, 64-65, 92, 101, 130, 139, 314; trade, 16, 28, 55, 59, 65, 69, 91, 235
Wooldridge, Dean, 328-29
Woolworth & Co., F. W., 244, **246**, 247, 248
Works Progress Administration (Works Projects Administration) 299, 302
World Bank, 295, 321
World War I, 216, **222**, 222-24, 273, 274-75, 285, 292, **373**
World War II, 270, 302, 313-21, 335
Worthington Co., 174
Wright Aeronautics, 285-86

Xerox Corp., 337-38, 370, **375**

Yellow Cab Manufacturing Co., 354
Young, James Webb, 251
Young, Owen D., 275, 279, 284, 368
Young, Robert R., 159, 283, 359
Young & Rubicam, Inc., 256
Youngstown Sheet and Tube Co., 300

Zinc, 210, 223, 322
Zion's Cooperative Mercantile Institution, 236
Zukor, Adolph, 238, 278